P.H.M

SYMPOSIUM ON J. L. AUSTIN

International Library of Philosophy and Scientific Method

J. L. AUSTIN

Photograph: by Ramsey and Muspratt, 1951

Symposium on
J. L. AUSTIN

edited by

K. T. Fann

LONDON
ROUTLEDGE & KEGAN PAUL
NEW YORK: HUMANITIES PRESS

First published 1969
by Routledge & Kegan Paul Ltd
Broadway House, 68-74 Carter Lane
London, E.C.4
Printed in Great Britain
by W & J Mackay & Co Ltd, Chatham
© *K. T. Fann* 1969
SBN 7100 6486 1

CONTENTS

CONTENTS

We want to replace wild conjectures and
speculations by quiet weighing of linguistic facts.

LUDWIG WITTGENSTEIN

PREFACE

UNTIL his premature death in 1960, J. L. Austin exercised in post-war Oxford an intellectual authority similar to that of Wittgenstein in Cambridge. He completed no books of his own and published only seven papers, which he was obliged to publish as a condition of their being delivered. However, through lectures and talks, Austin became one of the acknowledged leaders in what is called 'Oxford philosophy' or 'ordinary language philosophy'. Soon after his death, the published papers, together with three previously unpublished, were collected as *Philosophical Papers* by J. O. Urmson and G. J. Warnock (see the bibliography). In addition, Warnock has skilfully reconstructed from Austin's lecture notes the course of lectures on the theory of perception which constitutes *Sense and Sensibilia,* and the William James Lectures which Austin delivered at Harvard in 1955 has been edited by Urmson as *How to Do Things with Words.* All three volumes have become classics in analytical philosophy and few would dispute that among analytic philosophers Austin stands out as a great and original philosophical genius.

Collected here are critical essays on Austin's philosophy written by well-known philosophers, many of whom knew Austin personally. A number of essays included were especially written for this volume, but the majority have appeared previously in various journals or books, not all easy to obtain. Some of these have been revised by the authors for republication and others are reprinted here in their original forms. Editor's notes are indicated by asterisks and page references to other selections in this book are added in brackets.

I wish to thank the authors, the editors, and the publishers for their kind permission to reprint these essays. I am most grateful to the authors who have made special contributions to this volume. To Irving Thalberg and Ted Honderich I am indebted for assistance in various ways. For assisting in the preparation of the bibliography, I thank Marilyn Anderson. Special thanks are due to L. W.

Forguson not only for his important contributions, but also for his many valuable suggestions and kind help throughout the course of preparing this volume.

The sources of the papers included in this volume are as follows:

'John Langshaw Austin: A Biographical Sketch', by G. J. Warnock. Reprinted from the *Proceedings of the British Academy* (1963), by permission of the author and the Oxford University Press.

'Austin's Philosophy', by J. O. Urmson. Reprinted from Paul Edwards (ed.): *The Encyclopedia of Philosophy* (New York: Random House, Inc., 1967), by permission of the author and Random House.

'J. L. Austin, 1911–1960', by Stuart Hampshire. Reprinted from the *Proceedings of the Aristotelian Society* (1959–60), by permission of the author and the secretary of the Society. Comments by Urmson and Warnock were published in *Mind* (1961), and reprinted here by permission of the authors and the editor.

'An Original Philosopher', by David Pears. Reprinted from *The Times Literary Supplement* (9 February 1962), by permission of the author and the publisher.

'Austin at Criticism', by Stanley Cavell. Reprinted from the *Philosophical Review* (1965), by permission of the author and the editors.

'A Symposium on Austin's Method', by J. O. Urmson, W. V. O. Quine, and Stuart Hampshire. Urmson's contribution and abstracts of Quine and Hampshire's contributions were published in the *Journal of Philosophy* (1965), and reprinted here by permission of the editor and the authors. The original versions of Quine and Hampshire's contributions are published here for the first time.

'Austin's *Philosophical Papers*', by Roderick Chisholm. Reprinted from *Mind* (1963), by permission of the editor and the author.

'Austin's Philosophy of Action', by L. W. Forguson. The French version of this paper appeared in *Archives de Philosophie* (1967). The English version is printed here by permission of the author and the editor of *Archives de Philosophie*.

'A Plea for Linguistics', by C. G. New. Reprinted from *Mind* (1966), by permission of the editor and the author.

'Ifs and Cans', by P. H. Nowell-Smith. Reprinted from *Theoria* (1960), by permission of the editor and the author.

'Austin on Abilities', by Irving Thalberg. An original contribution to this volume.

'Assertions and Aberrations', by John R. Searle. Reprinted from B. Williams and A. Montefiore (eds.): *British Analytical Philosophy* (London: Routledge & Kegan Paul, 1966), by permission of the author and the publisher.

'Mentioning the Unmentionable', by Alan R. White. Reprinted from *Analysis* (1967), by permission of the author and Basil Blackwell, Ltd.

'Austin on Truth', by Jon Wheatley. An original contribution to this volume.

'A Critical Study of *Sense and Sensibilia*', by R. J. Hirst. Reprinted from the *Philosophical Quarterly* (1963), by permission of the editor and the author.

'Austin's Argument from Illusion', by Roderick Firth. Reprinted with revisions from the *Philosophical Review* (1964), by permission of the editors and the author.

'Real', by Jonathan Bennett. Reprinted with revisions from *Mind* (1966), by permission of the editor and the author.

'Has Austin Refuted Sense-data?' by A. J. Ayer. Reprinted from *Synthese* (1967), by permission of the author, the editor, and the publisher.

'Has Ayer Vindicated the Sense-datum Theory?' by L. W. Forguson. An original contribution to this volume.

'Rejoinder to Professor Forguson', by A. J. Ayer. An original contribution to this volume.

'Critical Review of *How to Do Things with Words*', by Walter Cerf. Reprinted with revisions from *Mind* (1966), by permission of the editor and the author.

'Intention and Convention in Speech Acts', by P. F. Strawson. Reprinted from the *Philosophical Review* (1964), by permission of the editors and the author.

'Austin on Performatives', by Max Black. Reprinted from *Philosophy* (1963), by permission of the editor and the author.

'In Pursuit of Performatives', by L. W. Forguson. Reprinted from *Philosophy* (1966), by permission of the editor and the author.

'Do Illocutionary Forces Exist?' by L. Jonathan Cohen. Reprinted with a new note from the *Philosophical Quarterly* (1964), by permission of the editor and the author.

'Meaning and Illocutionary Force', by Mats Furberg. An original contribution to this volume.

Part I

General Introduction

JOHN LANGSHAW AUSTIN, A BIOGRAPHICAL SKETCH

G. J. Warnock

JOHN LANGSHAW AUSTIN was born in Lancaster on 26 March 1911. His father, G. L. Austin, was at that time practising as an architect; but, after serving in the Army during the First World War, he did not return to that profession, and shortly after being demobilized he moved with his family—there were five children—to Scotland, where he became Secretary of St. Leonard's School, in St. Andrews. This was Austin's home until, from 1933 onwards, he came to live more or less permanently in Oxford.

In 1924 Austin went, with a scholarship in classics, to Shrewsbury, a school with which, in a phrase he used later, he soon established a *modus vivendi*. This phrase implies, perhaps, a not particularly warm affection for the place and time, and indeed he was emphatically not one of those for whom their old school and schooldays bulk large in reminiscence. But he thought well enough of Shrewsbury to raise the question, in 1955, of sending his own two sons there (though in the end he did not do so); and his own time in the school was in fact conspicuously successful. He was moderately fond of games, and was in due course captain of his House at fives; but chiefly, and even among those of his contemporaries who were more single-mindedly athletic in their interests, he was respected as something of an intellectual prodigy. In the opinion of Mr. D. S. Colman (later a Fellow of Queen's but at that time teaching at Shrewsbury) in his later years in the school Austin was already an accurate and sensitive scholar, particularly in Greek—'far above the usual level even of an able Sixth Form'; and if in character and temperament he was then (as indeed he was always) quite without eccentricity, appearing even to be 'a

3

reasonably typical Salopian of the period', it could already be foreseen that he would achieve real academic distinction. As a House
Monitor his authority, which he did not hesitate to exercise, was
unquestioned, as was also the strict sense of justice by which it was
directed; his juniors found him a little remote, but by no means
ineffectual; and in any case they were (Mr. Paul Dehn reports)
'proud of him'. In 1929 he duly justified their pride and his own
high promise by his election to a scholarship in classics at Balliol.

As an undergraduate at Oxford he was again predictably successful—academically, that is, for he neither made nor attempted
to make any other sort of mark on the university's life at that time.
He played some games, and greatly enjoyed acting with the Balliol
Players; but his ambitions, and his distinction, were intellectual.
In 1930 he was *prox. acc.* in the Ireland and Craven; and in 1931
he won the Gaisford Prize for Greek Prose, and was placed in the
First Class in Classical Mods. It was at this time, when he began to
read Greats, that he made his first serious acquaintance with
philosophy; and it is important to notice that, like so many other
English philosophers, he came to that subject already highly accomplished as a classical scholar and linguist. It cannot be doubted
that the study of Aristotle, to which his training naturally attracted
him, was an important particular influence on his later work, nor
that, more generally, he owed in large measure to his classical
education both his intense concern for linguistic accuracy and his
perennial, even passionate, interest in the phenomenon of language
itself. That this was his own training was, as he knew, significant
for him; but he was very far from assuming, for that reason, that
it was the best sort of training to have. It is possible that he himself would have preferred to be a scientist, and certain that he
would have wished to know a great deal more about the sciences.
Though his education was cast entirely in a traditional mould, his
own views on education were not in the least traditional; his
exacting habits of thought led him to question the value of the
educational method by which he had acquired them, and he was
sometimes inclined to think that he had wasted a great deal of
time.

Among his tutors at Balliol, Austin was most deeply impressed
by the most eccentric—C. G. Stone, the author of *The Social
Contract of the Universe*. His affection and admiration for Stone were
real and lasting; but it is surely impossible to find in this personal

4

attachment any trace of philosophical influence. It seems to be the case that Austin as an undergraduate absorbed from the surrounding atmosphere—that he did not, at any rate, immediately and unthinkingly repudiate—some respect for the current orthodoxies of Idealism; but the teacher by whom, then and later, he was most sharply stimulated in philosophy—often, indeed, to disagreement —was Prichard, who was at that time (as Austin was to be later) White's Professor of Moral Philosophy. There was here an undoubted temperamental affinity. In reading Prichard's writings one may often feel him to have been at sea in a subject of whose nature he had no clear conception; he was capable both of holding fast to some remarkable prejudices, and also of boldly espousing some most extraordinary and implausible doctrines. On the other hand (like Moore) he had no truck with rhetoric; he never hid difficulties beneath a smooth literary surface; in his lectures and classes, as in his writings, it was evident that work was going on. He stayed down to earth; and if he had no general conception of the nature of philosophical problems, exactly the same could have been said at any time of Austin himself.[1] If in Prichard's case and not in Austin's this strikes one as a disability, this is perhaps because Prichard was, in practice, much less critical and open-minded than he was in intention. Not everyone whose policy it is to do without dogma succeeds in doing so. On at least two occasions Austin argued with Prichard in an exchange of letters—in 1937 on the meaning of ἀγαθόν and εὐδαιμονία in Aristotle's *Ethics*, and just ten years later on the analysis of 'promising'. This last had long been a particular preoccupation of Prichard's; and his concern may well have contributed to the genesis of Austin's long and patient investigation of 'performative utterances', which dated (as Austin has recorded himself) from 1939.

In 1933, a few months after being placed in the First Class in Greats, Austin was elected, after examination, to a Fellowship at All Souls.

His philosophical interests and activities in these years before the second war were, in some ways, very different from those of

---

[1] I mean by this that, though Austin did have a general view as to how a problem comes to be dubbed 'philosophical', it was a central point in this view that philosophical problems cannot and must not be presumed to be of any single, well-defined kind: their general character must not be prejudged. This is further discussed below.

the post-war years. His undergraduate essays, of which a few survive among his papers (and in which the marvellously neat and elegant handwriting is evidence of the immense pains he took), seem mostly to have been concerned not with the contemporary state of philosophical argument, but with the detailed and scholarly investigation of its history. This was a line which Austin followed for some years. He wrote out very fully, and must have delivered almost verbatim, richly detailed and learned lectures on certain books of the *Nicomachean Ethics*. He worked for some years—writing out, here again, immensely neat and copious notes—on the philosophy of Leibniz, about whom he also read a paper to the Philosophical Society. He wrestled from time to time with the philosophy of Kant, and also of Plato, particularly in the *Theaetetus*. He lectured again after the war on Plato and Aristotle, but, I think, with a difference: in the later lectures scholarship was in the background; their primary aim was not to impart detailed knowledge about a text, but straightforwardly to expound its philosophical argument in the hope of extracting illumination from it. Though he remained, of course, deeply versed in the history of philosophy, and always valued the study of 'classical' texts as an educational discipline he did not continue after the war the kind of scholarly work of which he did so much in the thirties. (His editing of H. W. B. Joseph's lectures on Leibniz (1949), and his translation of Frege's *Grundlagen* (1950), belong in a rather different category.) His first published paper, which appeared in 1939, though it does not deal directly with an historical question, contains about twenty explicit historical references. Such references, in his later writings, are rare.

It was during the thirties that, in this country, the philosophical scene was first enlivened by the dismissive *brusqueries* of Logical Positivism. What did Austin make of this? He was sympathetic to the general intention. He disliked and distrusted (in this following Prichard and Moore) the rhetoric, pretension, and obscurity that are apt to accompany metaphysical ambitions, and correspondingly approved the workshop, no-nonsense atmosphere of the Vienna Circle and its adherents. But he distrusted equally the positivistic addiction to quasi-scientific technical jargon; and though he believed that philosophical problems could in principle be definitively solved, he reacted instinctively (as well as for excellent reasons) against the production of alleged solutions with such staggering rapidity. Logical Positivism was itself, after all, just another ambitious philosophical theory, marked scarcely less, in Austin's view, for all its down-to-earth intentions, by mythology and obscurity than the theories it purported so confidently to demolish. It shared, as he thought, far too many of the defects of its intended victims.

He had not at this time—indeed, as was remarked above, he never had—any doctrine of his own as to the nature of philosophical problems in general. Nor had he, as perhaps he had later, any general views about philosophical method. His general belief, then as always—and this scarcely amounts to a doctrine—was that both the statements and alleged solutions of philosophical problems were characteristically *unclear*, and that this was owing partly of course to human frailty but chiefly to the ambition to settle far too much far too quickly. He believed (like Moore) that, if progress was to be made, *many* questions would have to be raised, *many* facts surveyed, *many* arguments deployed step by step and narrowly criticized: questions ought to be distinguished and considered strictly one at a time, and no effort spared to make it *wholly* clear what question was being asked and *exactly* what answer was proposed to it. The effect, in discussion in the thirties, of this dogged resistance to haste has been described as 'powerfully negative', and so no doubt it was (if one remembers how philosophers are prone to go on); but conspicuously it was not dull, and, above all, not negligible. Austin spoke early with the unmistakable tone of natural authority.

In 1935 Austin left his research appointment at All Souls to become a Fellow and tutor at Magdalen. Though he was, as a tutor, exceedingly effective and skilful, I doubt whether it would be correct to say that he positively enjoyed teaching, at any rate within the limits imposed by the Greats curriculum. But he thought it an immensely important part of a philosopher's business, indeed a large part of the justification for his existence as such. It was not that he thought it mattered whether people in general held correct, or even any, philosophical opinions; what *was* vitally important was that as many as possible should acquire the habit of, and some skill in, clear and methodical thinking, and should be, as it were, immunized against the wilder kinds of confusion, myth-mongering, and intellectual trickery. This had with him the force of a moral and political conviction; like Dr. Johnson, he valued truthfulness almost with fanaticism; and he believed, with good reason, that even a brief acquaintance with the conscientious practice of his style of philosophy could have a lasting and salutary intellectual effect. But though his teaching was, deliberately, sharply astringent, he was always strikingly kind to and considerate of his pupils themselves—some of whom, to my knowledge, have found it hard to believe in the trepidation which Austin could arouse on occasion in his colleagues. He would temper the wind to the shorn (and unpretentious) lamb.

Austin married Jean Coutts in 1941. There were four children of the marriage, two daughters and two sons. For the rest of his life he found in his home and family a satisfaction and happiness which he found nowhere else, and I have no doubt that this devotion explains in large measure the impression of detachment, of remoteness even, which he sometimes made in other settings. Sometimes, not always: he was naturally well mannered, could entertain delightfully if the occasion required it, and besides had too many live interests to be easily bored. But in general the affabilities of club and college meant little to him; he did not need, or want, the distraction of many acquaintances.

By this time Austin was already in the Army; after a spell of preliminary training at Aldershot and Matlock in the summer of 1940, he had been commissioned in the Intelligence Corps and posted to the War Office in London. His first important employment was on the German Order of Battle, work which demanded exactly the kind of detailed accuracy which was, of course, immensely congenial to him. But in 1942 he took over the direction, at G.H.Q. Home Forces, of a small section which had recently been formed, to do the preliminary intelligence work for an invasion of Western Europe; and this was the field in which he became an unrivalled authority. His section, whose earlier days had been rather haphazard, was soon operating with method, rapidity, and a clear purpose. Though his standards were exacting, those under his command were enlivened by the confident sense of solid work getting done, of real progress being made. Professor A. J. Beattie, who served with Austin at this time, records that 'his superiors in rank very quickly learned that he was an outstanding authority on all branches of intelligence work, and they soon depended on his advice far more than would normally have been considered proper in any headquarters'.

In the following year Austin's section was vastly enlarged and transferred, under the name of the Theatre Intelligence Section, to 21st Army Group. Of this larger affair Austin as a major—and later, when S.H.A.E.F. was formed, a lieut.-col.—was of course not formally in command; but by this time his knowledge was so voluminous, his expertise so great, and his judgement so highly valued, that in practice he continued in charge of all the work. Before D-Day he had accumulated a vast quantity of information on the coast defences of northern France, on the base areas, supplies, formations, and transport system behind them, and indeed on every aspect of the German defence forces and civilian administration in that 'theatre'. Weekly, and later daily, reports were issued recording changes in the German dispositions; and a kind of guidebook was compiled for the use of the invading troops, in whose title—*Invade Mecum*—those who know Austin's writings will recognize his style. It has been said of him that he directed this huge volume of work 'without ever getting into serious difficulty of any kind' and, more impressively, that 'he more than anybody was responsible for the life-saving accuracy of the D-Day Intelligence.'

Over the same period Austin was frequently called on for advice and help with the problem of the German V-weapons. This lay rather outside his sphere, and formally was the responsibility of the Air Ministry; but he was able to contribute to the identification of launching-sites and to the solution of the problem of their intended use.

In the summer of 1944 he moved with his section, first to Granville in Normandy, and afterwards to Versailles. At this time he was not dealing, as he had been, with day-to-day developments, but with strategic intelligence directed to operations some months ahead. This work was done with his accustomed meticulous thoroughness, but he seems to have found it, in the last stages of the war, increasingly uninteresting. At the very end of the war he took part in, and was fascinated by, the interrogation of prominent enemy prisoners; but he told Professor Beattie later that, 'if he were to become involved in another war', he would like to be employed on problems of supply. No doubt the unlimited intricacies of the logistics of warfare tempted him as a new field to conquer, a new maze to be mastered.

He left the Army in September 1945 with the rank of lieut.-col., and the O.B.E. His work before D-Day was acknowledged by the French with the Croix de Guerre, and by the Americans with appointment as an Officer of the Legion of Merit. There is no doubt that he had rendered service of the highest value.

The university to which he returned was, at any rate in the field of philosophy, in a remarkable condition at that time—and, one may well feel, looking back, an enviable one. As the war went on it had been, of course, progressively depopulated: afterwards, as it seemed in a moment, it was crammed and overflowing. Undergraduates, of whom now several generations were pressing into residence simultaneously, were anything up to ten years above the usual age; most had been in the services; and one had the impression that a large proportion knew, with more maturity and independence of judgement than is usually to be looked for among undergraduates, that after the war years work was what they wanted. Politics were prevailingly left-wing, optimistic, progressive; there was a general, confident sense of many things to be done. Senior members also wore something of a new look. Many had returned, like Austin, from distinguished war service; but also posts falling vacant in the previous six years had seldom been filled, so that there followed a sudden rush of new appointments. In philosophy there had not yet quite vanished the stimulating sense of an Old Guard opposition; but such pre-war 'radicals' as, conspicuously, Ryle and Ayer could now be regarded as advancing on what looked like a large and unmistakably 'winning' side, with such names—perhaps somewhat heterogeneously assembled—as Waismann, Berlin, Paul, Hampshire, Hart, Urmson, and soon many others, on its muster-roll. No doubt such quasi-belligerent categories look, retrospectively, slightly absurd, even undesirable; no doubt the sharp sense of philosophical black-and-white was naïve, the optimism unfounded; but the sense of new things going on, of new starts being made towards what seemed quite attainable goals, was strongly invigorating, and by no means confined to, though common among, undergraduates of the period.

This sense of philosophical vitality was not wholly due to the mere release of energies pent up by the war: it was in large part a matter of the state of the subject itself. Ryle, who had succeeded Collingwood as Waynflete Professor, was already making, in the work which led up to *The Concept of Mind*, what was perhaps the first systematic and really large-scale application of the new philosophical style to large traditional problems; and it was at this time also that the later work of Wittgenstein, long cloistrally prosecuted in Cambridge, came to be known in wider circles—and was, some may think, none the worse for a breath of fresh air. There really was, in the subject at that time, a good deal to be excited about.

Austin's place in this animated scene was one of high authority, and his presence there contributed substantially to its animation. He produced in the summer of 1946, in his contribution to the symposium 'Other Minds', perhaps still the most frequently cited of all his papers, and the first which bears unmistakably his characteristic imprint; henceforward it was certain that any paper of his would be an 'occasion', and his was an opinion that any of his colleagues was most anxious to have.[1] But Austin himself was little capable of zeal, and his critical powers were too sharp to permit of any easy optimism. In 1947 he began, in his lectures, that demolition of currently fashionable doctrines on perception which came to be known under the title *Sense and Sensibilia*; and he did not join at any time in the general deference to Wittgenstein. The personal atmosphere surrounding Wittgenstein's work in philosophy strongly repelled him; and it is of course crucial also that Wittgenstein rejected, deliberately and on principle, exactly that ideal of finality, of definite, clearly and fully stated solutions, which Austin regarded as alone worth seriously striving for. That Wittgenstein influenced his views has been sometimes suggested, but is certainly untrue.

Austin's very general opinions about philosophy had not changed since before the war, nor did they change thereafter. He believed that what had descended to our time under the name of philosophy was the tangled residue of a formerly even vaster tangle; there had been, as it were, an original gaseous mass of undifferentiated problems from which, as certain kinds of questions and methods gradually became clear, planets broke away in the form of independent disciplines—mathematics, the physical

---

[1] Professor Berlin had at one time, on his mantelpiece in New College, a large card, roughly two feet by six inches, obtained presumably from some car-dealer and bearing the legend AUSTIN; he kept it 'as a reminder that there are acute critics at work': and shrewd undergraduates from other colleges who attended Austin's lectures could often bring their tutors to an anxious standstill with the simple formula 'But Mr. Austin says . . . '.

sciences, formal logic, psychology, and so on.[1] If so, what remained in the domain and under the title of philosophy was at least highly unlikely to consist of any one kind of problem, and no single method was likely to be, quite generally, the key to progress. Problems, then, ought simply to be approached with no preconceptions, set out in the clearest possible light, and discussed in any way that might seem to be relevant and effective; the needed virtues were truthfulness, and above all industry and patience; the typically fatal philosophical failings were inaccuracy and oversimplification, and above all the impetuous proliferation of bogus 'solutions'.

This Austin had long believed, and always did believe; but he had formed, I think, since before the war two new views about philosophical procedure. The first and most notorious of these was that 'ordinary language' should not only, in the interests of clarity and common understanding, usually be employed by philosophers; it should also be, thoroughly and in detail, studied by them. This view, which has aroused strong passions and been fantastically misinterpreted, cannot here be discussed at length, though I shall return to it briefly in a moment. (It is really quite simple.)

The other view, which has been rarely discussed largely because, I believe, it has never been taken seriously, may be guessed to have arisen directly from his war experience: it was that philosophy could be, and should be, a co-operative pursuit. It may be thought perhaps, that it always has been; at any rate where, as in Oxford, many philosophers are gathered together, there has always been discussion, in every degree of formality. But Austin meant, and meant very seriously, much more than that. He had been faced in the war, we must remember, by vast and complicated problems, problems which might well, at first glance, have looked simply insoluble. However, they had been solved; and they had been solved by the patient, minutely detailed labour of scores, even hundreds, of trained investigators, and by the persistent, system-

---

[1] At Royaumont in 1958, a French questioner put to Austin the figurative inquiry 'Is philosophy an island, or a promontory?' Austin said in his answer: 'If I were looking for an image of this kind, I think I should say that it's more like the surface of the sun—a pretty fair mess.' See his 'Performative-Constative', and the ensuing discussion, in *Philosophy and Ordinary Language,* ed. C. E. Caton, University of Illinois Press, 1963.

atic co-ordination of their inquiries and their findings. The problems of philosophy are comparably vast and complicated; why then should they not be similarly attacked? If (as Austin had long believed) the road to large truths runs through the patient accumulation of incalculably many small truths, does it not seem that here—as, after all, with most research in the sciences—is work for many independent but co-ordinated brains? It is clear that Austin would have liked to have in philosophy an organized 'section', a disciplined team of investigators, very much on the model of his Theatre Intelligence Section of a few years before.

I believe I have never heard this notion discussed except as a mildly amusing private quirk of Austin's; but I wonder how many of those who saw it in this light could have properly explained why it should not be taken seriously. No doubt Austin saw himself as such a section's director; but was this mere vanity? Can it be doubted that he would have done such work extraordinarily well? No doubt in Oxford, where the demands of teaching are unusually heavy and there is (outside the scientific departments) no structure of authority, to form and keep such a team in being would be practically very difficult; but it would be absurdly conservative to take for granted that such practical difficulties could not be overcome. No doubt, again, it can be held that there are grave dangers to academic freedom in empowering any one individual to direct the work of others; but such power is often rightly given, and not always abused. The only valid objection, plainly, to Austin's idea would be the contention that philosophy is not a subject of that kind; that it is, one might say, an art rather than a science; that there are no sufficiently definite, objective, impersonal problems to which many workers could usefully make their impersonal, partial, cumulative contributions. This may be so; but do we all know it to be so? Austin's idea (as Chesterton once said about Christianity) has not been tried and found wanting; it has been found difficult and not tried: and many (he would have thought) who regarded his idea as merely quirkish themselves believed that philosophical problems were objectively soluble, but were unwilling to take seriously the implications of that opinion.

It is relevant to mention here Austin's 'Saturday mornings'—weekly meetings during term, held from time to time in various colleges, and normally lasting from two to three hours.[1] For I believe it could be said that, in the first years after the war, these meetings were a kind of pilot project for, or perhaps merely the closest practicable approximation to, the kind of systematic collaboration that Austin had in mind. Certainly they were, at first, quite strictly organized. Attendance (by invitation) was formally restricted to persons both junior to Austin and employed as whole-time tutorial Fellows, and informally (naturally enough) to persons judged likely to be in sympathy with the matters in hand. A field of inquiry—for example, in one term the concept of a *rule*—was systematically divided into areas, and each area assigned to some one of those present for investigation (there were about ten in all). Results were to be fairly formally reported, and records kept in writing. It is a high tribute to Austin's unique personal authority that, among colleagues of strong individuality, perhaps temperamentally individualistic, and certainly extremely hard-worked in other ways, such a project ever got started at all. The sense of purpose, of method, of work, was certainly invigorating; but the supererogatory labour involved was perhaps excessive; and it is not surprising that, before very long, certain rigours were relaxed. Though the meetings continued, they became progressively more informal, attendance at them more heterogeneous, their aim less sharply defined.[2]

Very often the topic for a term's discussion would be the critical examination of some currently fashionable semi-technical term—the term 'disposition', for example, or 'symbol', or 'class'; for a time mathematical logic[3] came under scrutiny; sometimes a text would be discussed—Frege's *Grundlagen*, Aristotle's *Ethics*,

---

[1] These were, for many people and for many years, the best of all philosophical occasions; they deserve both fuller discussion than they can be given here, and discussion also by someone whose experience of them goes further back than mine. I first attended, I believe, in the autumn of 1951.

[2] In discussion with Arne Naess at Berkeley in 1958, Austin appears to have spoken as if he still regarded some kind of systematic co-operation in philosophy as not only desirable, but also practicable. However, the record of this discussion is neither perfectly clear nor certainly reliable. (It goes without saying that Austin was careful to distinguish the programme he had in mind from the kind of Gallup-poll, empirical team-work which Naess believed in, and which Austin regarded as, in principle, misguided.)

[3] A curious by-product of Austin's interest in logic was his card-game CASE, which he devised during 1951 and discussed (and played) with, among others, Mr. and Mrs. Burton Dreben. His idea, pursued with characteristic

Wittgenstein's *Philosophical Investigations*, and (in the term before Austin's death) Chomsky's *Syntactic Structures*. There was always evident in detail—and in fact on this the vitality of the meetings entirely depended—the extraordinary fertility and force of Austin's mind; but he had always in addition, I believe, one general aim—to get the topic, whatever it might be, pulled out of the rut. No one could well have been more free than Austin from the domination of *idées reçues*; but he rightly saw the routine repetition of current doctrines, the uncritical employment of fashionable jargon, as *the* major obstacle to progress in philosophy. Some critics have complained that in his writings he appears at times to be dealing directly with no standard, identifiable problem of philosophy; this is so, and was even more so in his philosophical talk; but it is by no means attributable to inadvertence. His point was that standard problems are approached by deeply rutted tracks; there are orthodox manoeuvres which lead into accustomed morasses; there are familiar, well sign-posted highroads to well-populated dead ends. Hope lies in considering what has *not* yet been considered, in trying what has *not* yet been thought to be the right road—above all, in examining the small, neglected, preliminary details which, *because* they have been neglected, seem unfamiliar. It was for this sort of reason that, at his 'Saturday mornings', Austin characteristically sought to discuss what his colleagues had *not* spent the rest of the week discussing, and what sometimes might seem so far off the beaten track as scarcely to be recognizable as philosophy.[1] That this policy could be, in his hands, uniquely stimulating is known to many from long personal experience.

Austin's practical abilities, already well proved in his war service, soon came to be employed also in university administration. He was Junior Proctor in the year 1949–50, and, in his field of special responsibility as such, initiated and carried through a major rationalization of the Statutes governing the conduct of

[1] It was for this good reason, and not from cantankerousness, that Austin once turned down a suggested topic on the ground that 'we would enjoy it too much'.

literalness and pertinacity, was primarily to test the merits of the frequently made suggestion that operations in formal logic are 'like moves in a game'; but he plainly took great pleasure also, for their own sakes, in the sheer ingenuities of his invention, and in the technical problem of drafting clear and comprehensive rules. The rules of games had been studied in detail at some of his earliest 'Saturday mornings'.

examinations. As a member of the innumerable committees and Boards which Proctors must attend he is characteristically remembered for 'great care over detail', and the then Secretary of Faculties has said that 'once we got a proposal past Austin we could be pretty certain that it was watertight'. He was chairman of the Sub-faculty of Philosophy for two years from 1953, an active member also of the Faculty Board, and, later, of the Hebdomadal Council and the General Board of the Faculties. His standards in this often dreary work were exceptionally high; it seemed never to occur to him, as, alas, it does to many, to economize effort by giving formal approval to half-understood matters regarded as other people's business; he always knew what was going on, and had formed views about it. He could never have attended any meeting as a mere 'brute voter'. This of course meant hard work, even though, as was clear enough, he could grasp a case and weigh arguments with extraordinary speed.

But his hardest practical work of all—and also the most congenial to him—was done as one of the Delegates of the Press, the body with whom rests final responsibility for the conduct of the vast business of the University Press. In this capacity the present Secretary has said of him simply that he was 'the best Delegate I ever knew'; and he certainly interested himself in the business of the Press not only very ably, but far more extensively than is normally to be expected. As a Delegate from 1952—in which year he also became White's Professor—he was particularly interested on the publication side, in school books and children's books; more expectedly perhaps, in the field of language and linguistics particularly in the supplements to the *New English Dictionary*; and of course in philosophy, in which field he himself initiated the Press's new series of translations of Aristotle. But besides this he was a frequent and valued visitor to the printing works and the mill, to the Press's London offices, and in due course also to the offices in New York. From 1957 he held the most important office of Chairman of the Delegates' Finance Committee, and in this capacity his practical judgement, clarity of mind, and endless readiness to take pains over details were conspicuously valuable.

It would be unprofitable, even if it were possible, here to attempt any kind of summary of Austin's contribution to philosophy. Some of his works now in print are unhappily, owing to his early death, not in the form that he would finally have given them; what more he might have done it is useless to conjecture; but what was already done forms a body of work of the highest quality and, one must expect, of lasting significance. That work speaks for itself; but one or two general comments may properly be made here, partly in the hope of counteracting what appear to be prevalent tendencies to misunderstanding.

There is, first of all, a question of emphasis. In much discussion of Austin's work that I have seen and heard there has been, I think, a certain implication that very general views about the nature of philosophy, very general doctrines of philosophical tactics and strategy, were what Austin chiefly wished to convey, his particular views on this problem or that being almost incidental. But this in fact is wholly the wrong way round. Austin's own view was that nothing but particular problems was seriously worth discussing at all. Generalities about philosophy, large questions of method—what he once called 'the cackle'—were interesting enough in their way, but were little more really than gossipy distractions from the serious business. The question he would himself have asked of any piece of philosophy is not 'What theory of the nature of philosophy is implicit in this?', or 'What principles of method are here applied?', but simply 'Does this advance discussion of the problem dealt with?' And this is the question he would wish his own readers to ask. It is true that he had, and occasionally (always with some reluctance) discussed, general policies and precepts which are at once characteristic, original, and highly intriguing; but he valued these only so far as they seemed to serve him well; and the pertinent question is not whether those general policies are, or are likely to prove, uniquely and universally effective (two claims which Austin would never have made), but whether, in the particular cases in which he pursued them, discussion of those cases was advanced thereby. It is of course possible that discussion of Austin's highly individual methods of work, or of his very general opinions about philosophy, not merely gratifies the philosophical hankering for generality, but is actually more rewarding than discussion of his views on particular topics: this may be so: but let it at least be remembered that Austin did not himself think that it was so, and above all that he made for his methods no more ambitious claim than that, in his hands, they seemed to lead to certain definite advances in the treatment of the particular problems he chose to deal with.

Next, a word on that well-worn topic, 'ordinary language'; for here too there seems a danger of Austin's position being misunderstood. Two views in particular are often wrongly attributed to him: first, the view that philosophical problems in general are generated wholly by, or wholly consist in, confusion and misuse of language; and second, the view that 'ordinary language' is sacrosanct, immune from criticism and insusceptible of supplementation or amendment. It is certain that Austin held neither of these views. He did not believe that there was any one answer at all to the question how philosophical problems arise, or to the question what *kind* of problems they are; he believed rather, as has been mentioned above, that philosophy was characteristically a mixed bag, some of whose contents were there precisely because their nature was as yet quite obscure. Again, thinking of 'ordinary language' as he did—as an instrument unselfconsciously evolved by speakers confronted with an immense and ever-changing variety of practical contingencies—he naturally recognized that it might in certain ways be confused or incoherent and even, for certain purposes, totally inadequate.

Those, then, are two doctrines about language which he did not hold, and in fact quite clearly repudiated more than once in his writings. But he was, of course, intensely and persistently interested in language. This was for two entirely different reasons.

The first was this. At least one of the principal tasks of the philosopher, in any field, is discrimination: at least one important element in clear understanding is consciousness of, and ability to make, distinctions. But we all learn to mark, as soon as we begin to learn anything, enormously many distinctions; in learning to speak our native language, we learn to mark both gross differences and some very fine *nuances* in learning when, and when not, to use its words and phrases. But it is, at the very least, highly unlikely that a natural language should be as it is, should have evolved as it has, for no particular reasons; though of course there will be indefinitely many distinctions, some perhaps crucially important for special purposes, which in ordinary speech there has been no occasion to mark, yet where ordinary speech *does* make a verbal distinction it is at least highly probable that there is a distinction to be made, that the difference of expression corresponds to some difference in the cases. We need not assert dogmatically that this is always so or that, even when it is so, that fact is necessarily of interest; we need claim no special merit for our own native tongue; but at any rate we have in our language, as it were ready-made, an enormous stock of discriminations, and to take this stock seriously —to examine what it contains—seems, as a precept of method, to be merely good sense. If we want to know, as in philosophy we often do, whether some two cases are to be discriminated, we should at least begin by considering whether we speak of them in the same way, for if we do not, then *probably* they can be distinguished, and *probably* the distinction is of not negligible significance. Austin never claimed more than that this was, in philosophy, *one* good way to *begin*: and I do not see how this modest (though original) claim can be seriously disputed, once it has been correctly understood.

But language is of importance in philosophy not merely as a pointer to distinctions; very often it is itself the topic under investigation. Austin's argument here was that recent philosophical discussions of language, or of particular departments of language, have tended to be unsatisfactory and amateurish for the reason that they have usually been undertaken in an excessively piecemeal, provisional, hand-to-mouth style. There is a lot more to a language than 'the meaning' of its words and phrases; nor is it clear *what* more is meant to be comprised in the popular but over-accommodating notion of its 'use' or 'uses.' Philosophical talk about language urgently needed, Austin thought, a firmer theoretical foundation; and so, from (as it appears) an initial interest in promising, and the idea (soon judged to be inadequate) of the 'performative' utterance, he was led to embark (and he scarcely claimed to have done more) on a really *general* theory of what he called 'speech-acts'—of what kinds of things are done in speaking, of how they are done, and how they may go right or wrong. This was, of course, the programme of his William James Lectures of 1955, on which at the date of his death he was still at work; this programme brought him, as he knew, to the ill-defined frontier between philosophy and linguistics; and it is probably on, or even across, this frontier that, if he had lived, he would most have wanted to go on working.

Austin's death in February 1960 left a terrible gap, all the more keenly felt for being quite unforeseen. His fine-drawn features—his face, as Shaw said of Voltaire's, was 'all intelligence'—had for some months looked rather worn and tired; but in the end he was scarcely known to be ill before it was clear that he was dying. No one, I believe, outside his family could have claimed to know him well; but of those who knew him even a little I know of no one in whom respect and admiration were not accompanied by affection also. Except in impersonal matters he was, one may guess, a shy man, wary of self-revelation and more than uninviting of self-revelation by others. He could not treat people irresponsibly, casually, with frivolity, and could not but prefer no personal relationship at all to the confusion and falsity of a personal involvement not taken seriously; the facile genialities which come so naturally to many must have repelled him, I believe, as basically untruthful. Thus he appeared to some as a remote and even a cold personality. His manifest integrity and sharp-edged intelligence could be very daunting, and he was surely without the dull and comfortable desire that the surface of life should at all times look smooth and easy. It was not only in philosophy that he was unable to practise, and little able to tolerate, evasions and pretences. That he was, and could not help being, a formidable person is true; but that he was cold is not. It is because his kindness, his affections, and for that matter his aversions, were so real they could not, without falsity, have been indiscriminately displayed; and he was not capable of falsity.

Above all it should be remembered that, formidable though he often was, there was in him no stiffness or stuffiness, no pedantic rigour. In conversation he was capable of, one might almost say addicted to, the rashest flights of speculation and fantastic extravagence; he was always utterly without pomposity; his lectures and discussions, even when he was philosophically in deadly earnest, were continuously entertaining, and sometimes wildly funny. His way of speaking—rather dry and slow, very clear and with all edges, as it were, very sharply defined—was splendidly expressive of both the characteristic merits of his matter, and the characteristic wit of his style. It was also, on occasion, an effective polemical instrument; for he could, and sometimes did, reduce philosophical propositions to helpless absurdity by simply reading them aloud.[1] He was very far from thinking that philosophy was

---

[1] His voice is recorded, most fortunately though not, alas, very well, on a tape made when he lectured at Gothenberg in October 1959, while he was visiting universities in Norway and Sweden. This tape is now in the possession of Mr. J. O. Urmson.

a form of entertainment; but he believed that its practice was all the better for being agreeable, and he accepted with relish the ample targets which it offered him for ridicule. It seemed to him a short step from solemnity to pretentiousness and fraud, and he used his natural wit deliberately as a weapon against bogus profundities. In his hands philosophy seemed at once more serious, and more fun.

Austin visited Harvard as William James Lecturer in the spring term of 1955, and the University of California in the autumn of 1958. In both cases he made a most powerful impact on those who heard him; and in Berkeley, even before the semester he spent there, he was strongly solicited to take a permanent appointment. By this invitation he was certainly greatly tempted (though it is not true, as has been stated, that he had finally resolved to accept it). He was fascinated, I believe, by the whole phenomenon of America—by its size, by its populousness and resources, by the sense there of endless possibilities and a wide-open future. His temperament, as Professor Hampshire has said, was that of a radical reformer; there were many new things that he would have liked to do in new ways, and to secure the co-operation of others in doing; and it is clear that he felt that in America such things might be done—much more easily than in Oxford, where the system might be unkindly regarded as one of ossification tempered by anarchy. It seems too that he was personally in some ways more at ease in America—that he found in that atmosphere of uncomplicated, undesigning friendliness a greater clarity and freedom, and in himself (one may guess) less inclination to be on his guard. He was, though, very English; and perhaps it is not surprising that he found a final decision to leave England impossible to make.

In considering, finally and perhaps parochially, what philosophy in Oxford lost by his early death, what comes most to mind, I believe, is his authority. His abilities were outstanding; his work was important and continuously interesting; but above all his presence there had provided, so to speak, a centre of gravity. His was the initiative that one naturally hoped for. It was his opinion that one instinctively waited to hear. His, one might almost say, were the standards that had to be satisfied. His death deprived philosophy in Oxford of one, perhaps the most conspicuous, of its most able practitioners; but in his death the subject lost also, and far more than proportionately, something of its own life.

AUSTIN'S PHILOSOPHY

J. O. Urmson

IN the years before the Second World War Austin devoted a great deal of his time and energy to philosophical scholarship. He made himself an expert in the philosophy of Leibniz and also did much work on Greek philosophy, especially Aristotle's ethical works. At this period his own thought, although notably acute and already distinctive in style, was largely critical and altogether lacked the positive approach that distinguished his postwar work. His one published paper belonging to this early period, 'Are There *A Priori* Concepts?' very fairly represents the astringent style and outlook that gave him the reputation of being a rather terrifying person. According to Austin's own statements, it was not until the beginning of the war that he began to develop the outlook on philosophy and method of philosophizing that marked his mature work, and it is of this work alone that an account will be given.

AIMS AND METHODS

The practical exigencies of lecturing and the traditions of paper reading (especially in symposia, to which some of his important papers were contributions) prevented some of the most characteristic features of Austin's preferred methods and aims from being clearly and fully exemplified in his written work. Lecturing is essentially a solo effort, whereas Austin believed that the best way of doing philosophy was in a group, and papers, especially in symposia, are almost inevitably on topics of traditional philosophical interest, whereas Austin preferred to keep the traditional problems of philosophy in the background. We shall therefore start by giving some account of the method and aims that Austin always advocated and practiced, most notably in meetings held regularly on Saturday mornings in the Oxford term with a group of like-minded Oxford philosophers.

Language. Austin did not present his aims and methods as the only proper ones for a philosopher; whatever one or two uncautious remarks in his British Academy lecture 'Ifs and Cans' may suggest to the contrary, he did not claim more than that his procedures led to definite results and were a necessary preliminary for anyone who wished to undertake other kinds of philosophical investigation. But he certainly considered them so valuable and interesting in their results and so suited to his own linguistically trained capabilities and tastes, that he never felt it necessary to investigate for himself what else a philosopher might usefully do. What he conceived of as the central task, the careful elucidation of the forms and concepts of ordinary language (as opposed to the language of philosophers, not to that of poets, scientists, or preachers) was, as Austin himself was well aware, not new but characteristic of countless philosophers from Socrates to G. E. Moore. Nor were the grounds for this activity especially novel. First, he claimed, it was only common prudence for anyone embarking on any kind of philosophical investigation, even one that might eventually involve the creation of a special technical vocabulary, to begin with an examination of the resources of the terminology already at his disposal; clarification of ordinary language was thus the 'begin-all,' if not the 'end-all', of any philosophical investigation. Second, he thought that the institution of language was in itself of sufficient interest to make it worthy of the closest study. Third, he believed that in general a clear insight into the many subtle distinctions that are enshrined in ordinary language and have survived in a lengthy struggle for existence with competing distinctions could hardly fail to be also an insight into important distinctions to be observed in the world around us—distinctions of an interest unlikely to be shared by any we might think up on our own unaided initiative in our professional armchairs.

It is not too soon to remove at this stage some common misconceptions about Austin's aims and methods. First, although he was not concerned with studying the technical terminology of philosophers, he had no objection in principle to such terms; he thought that many such technical terms had been introduced inappropriately and uncritically, as is clear from his discussion, in *Sense and Sensibilia,* of the sense-datum terminology, but he used much of the traditional technical vocabulary of philosophy and added many technical terms of his own invention—as almost any page of *How to Do Things With Words* will bear witness. Second, Austin did not think that ordinary language was sacrosanct; he certainly thought it unlikely that hopelessly muddled uses of languages would survive very long and felt that they were more likely to occur in rather specialized and infrequently used areas of our vocabulary, but there was never any suggestion that language as we found it was incapable of improvement; all he asked was that we be clear about what it is like before we try to improve it.

Technique. We have seen that there was nothing essentially novel in Austin's philosophical aims; what was new was the skill, the rigor, and the patience with which he pursued these aims. Here we are dealing with Austin's own personal gifts, which cannot be philosophically dissected. Nor did Austin have any theory of philosophical method; what he had was a systematic way of setting to work, something on a par with a laboratory technique rather than with a scientific methodology. This technique, unlike the skill with which he followed it, was quite public and one that he was willing and eager to employ in joint investigations with others, so we can easily give an account of it.

A philosopher or, preferably, a group of philosophers using this technique begins by choosing an area of discourse in which it is interested, often one germane to some great philosophical issue. The vocabulary of this area of discourse is then collected, first by thinking of and listing all the words belonging to it that one can—not just the most discussed words or those that at first sight seem most important—then by looking up synonyms and synonyms of synonyms in dictionaries, by reading the nonphilosophical literature of the field, and so on. Alongside the activity of collecting the vocabulary one notes expressions within which the vocabulary can legitimately occur and, still more important, expressions including the vocabulary that seem to be *a priori* plausible but that can nonetheless be recognized as unusable. The next stage is to make up 'stories' in which the legitimate words and phrases occur; in particular, one makes up stories in which it is clear that one can appropriately use one dictionary 'synonym' but not another; such stories can also be found ready made in documents. In the light of these data one can then proceed to attempt to give some account of the meaning of the terms and their interrelationships that will explain the data. A particularly crucial point, which is a touchstone of success, is whether one's account of the matter will adequately explain why we cannot say the things that we have noted as 'plausible' yet that in fact we would not say. At this stage, but not earlier, it becomes profitable to examine what other philosophers and grammarians have said about the same region of discourse. Throughout (and this is why Austin so much preferred to work in a group) the test to be employed of what can and what cannot be said is a reasonable consensus among the participants that this is so. Such a consensus, Austin found, could be obtained in an open-minded group most of the time; where such agreement cannot be obtained the fact should be noted as of possible significance. Austin regarded this method as empirical and scientific, one that could lead to definitely established results, but he admitted that 'like most sciences, it is an art', and that a suitably fertile imagination was all important for success.

It was the lack of thoroughness, of sufficient research before generalization, in previous investigations of language, whether by those who called themselves grammarians or by those who called themselves philosophers, that Austin most deplored. He seriously hoped that a new science might emerge from the kind of investigations he undertook, a new kind of linguistics incorporating workers from both the existing linguistic and the philosophical fields. He pointed to other 'new' sciences, such as logic and psychology, both formerly parts of philosophy, as analogues and was indifferent about whether what he was doing 'was really philosophy'.

So much must suffice as an account of the method of work that Austin advocated. It has been based on a set of notes for an informal talk, characteristically entitled 'Something About One Way of Possibly Doing One Part of Philosophy'. As Austin admitted in those notes, he had said most of this in his papers 'A Plea for Excuses' and 'Ifs and Cans', and to all who worked with him it was familiar from his practice. Although inevitably, as we have noted, this method could not be followed in writings (it is in any case a method of discovery and not of presentation), its use underlies and can be discerned in his published work. Thus before writing 'Words and Deeds' or *How to Do Things With Words* he went right through the dictionary making a list, which still survives, of all verbs that might be classed as 'performative' in his terminology. The art of telling 'your story' is amusingly illustrated over and over again in his paper 'Pretending' and, indeed, in all his other published writings. His insistence that it is a mistake to dwell only on a few well-examined notions in a field of discourse is illustrated by his concentration on such notions as 'mistake', 'accident', and 'inadvertence' (in 'A Plea for Excuses') and on the use of 'I can if I choose' (in 'Ifs and Cans'), rather than on 'responsibility' and 'freedom', in his papers that have a bearing on the free-will problem. Similarly, when his Saturday morning group turned its attention to aesthetics Austin betrayed far more interest in the notions of dainty and dumpy milk jugs than in that of a beautiful picture.

WORK

It is not possible to give a systematic account of Austin's 'philosophy', for he had none. His technique lent itself rather to a set of quite independent inquiries, the conclusions of none of which could serve as premises for a further inquiry; his discussions of the language of perception (in *Sense and Sensibilia*), the concept of pretending, the notion of truth, and the terminology of excuses were all based on the study of speech in those fields and not on any general principles or theories. Nor would it serve any useful purpose to attempt to summarize his various investigations one by one, since they depend so much for their interest and force on the detailed observations about language that they contain. It will be more useful to discuss, first, what he thought of as his main constructive work—the doctrine of illocutionary forces that arose out of his earlier distinction of performative and constative utterances, contained in *How to Do Things With Words*—and, second, the application of his technique to the criticism of some traditional theories about perception as found in his *Sense and Sensibilia*.

Theory of illocutionary forces. Austin's theory of illocutionary forces arose from his observation that a considerable number of utterances, even those in the indicative mood, were such that in at least some contexts it would be impossible to characterize them as being true or false. Examples are 'I name this ship the *Saucy Sue*' (which is part of the christening of a ship, and not a statement about the christening of a ship), 'I promise to meet you at two o'clock' (which is the making of a promise and not the report of a promise or a statement about what will happen), and 'I guarantee these eggs to be new-laid' (which is the giving of a guarantee and not a report of a guarantee). These utterances Austin called 'performative', to indicate that they are the performance of some act and not the report of its performance; he did not speak as some do who purport to discuss his views, of 'performative *verbs*', for the verb 'promise' can well occur in reports—for example, 'I promised to meet him'. To provide the necessary contrast, Austin coined the technical term 'constative' to apply to all those utterances that are naturally called true or false; he thought that 'statement' and similar words often used by philosophers roughly as he used 'constative' had in ordinary use too narrow a meaning to serve the purpose.

For a time Austin appears to have been fairly satisfied with this distinction, which he gave in print in his 'Other Minds' article in 1946, using it to illuminate some features of utterances beginning 'I know . . .'. But although the distinction is clearly useful at a certain level, Austin began to doubt whether it was ultimately satisfactory. He found it impossible to give satisfactory criteria for distinguishing the performative from other utterances. The first person of the present indicative, which occurs in the three examples given above, is clearly not a necessary feature; 'Passengers are warned to cross the tracks only by the bridge' is an act of warning as much as 'I warn you to cross . . .'. Further, in a suitable context 'Don't cross the tracks except by the bridge' may also be an act of warning (as in another context it might be an act of commanding); this makes it necessary to distinguish the *primative* performative from the *explicit* performative, the latter, but not the former, making clear what act was being performed in its formulation.

Still more important, the constative seemed to collapse into the performative. Let us consider the four utterances 'I warn you that a train is coming', 'I guess that a train is coming', 'I state that a train is coming', and 'A train is coming'. The first of these is an act of warning, the second is surely one of guessing, the third apparently one of stating, while the fourth may be any of these as determined by context. Thus, the various forms of constatives— stating, reporting, asserting, and the rest—seem to be merely a subgroup of performatives. It might seem that still one crucial difference remains, that while performative utterances may be in various ways unhappy (I may say 'I promise to give you my watch' when I have not got a watch, or am speaking to an animal, or have no intention of handing the watch over), the characteristic and distinctive happiness or unhappiness of constatives is truth and falsehood, to which the other performatives are not liable.

In a brilliant, if not always immediately convincing, discussion (Lecture XI of *How to Do Things With Words*) Austin tried to break down even this distinction. First, we cannot contrast doing with saying, since (in addition to the trivial point that in stating one is performing the act of uttering words or the like) in constative utterances one is stating, describing, affirming, etc., and these acts are on a par with warning, promising, etc. Second, all constatives are liable to all those kinds of infelicity that have been taken to be characteristic of performatives. Just as I should not promise to do something if I do not intend to do it, so I should not state that something is the case unless I believe it to be so; just as my act of selling an object is null and void if I do not possess it, so my act of stating that the king of France is bald is null and void if there is no king of France; just as I cannot order you to do something unless I am in a position to do so, so I cannot state what I am not in a position to state (I cannot *state*, though I can hazard a guess about, what you will do next year). Further, even if we grant that 'true' and 'false' are assessments specific to constatives, is not their truth and falsity closely parallel to the rightness and wrongness of estimates, the correctness and incorrectness of findings, etc.? Is the rightness of a verdict very different from the truth of a statement? Further, to speak of inferring *validly*, arguing *soundly*, or judging *fairly*, is to make an assessment belonging to the same class as truth and falsehood. Moreover, it is only a legend that 'true' and 'false' can always be appropriately predicated of constatives; 'France is hexagonal' is a rough description of France, not a true or false one, and 'Lord Raglan won the battle of Alma' (since Alma was a soldiers' battle in which Lord Raglan's orders were not properly transmitted) is exaggerated—it is pointless to ask whether it is true or false. It was on the basis of such considerations as these that Austin felt himself obliged to abandon the distinction between the performative and the constative.

To replace the unsatisfactory distinction of performatives and constatives Austin introduced the theory of illocutionary forces. Whenever someone says anything he performs a number of distinguishable acts, for example, the *phonetic* act of making certain noises and the *phatic* act of uttering words in conformity with grammar. Austin went on to distinguish three other kinds of acts that we may perform when we say something: first, the *locutionary* act of using an utterance with a more or less definite sense and reference, for example, saying 'The door is open' as an English sentence with reference to a particular door; second, the *illocutionary* act, which is the act I may perform *in* performing the locutionary act; third, the *perlocutionary* act, which is the act I may succeed in performing by means of my illocutionary act. Thus, in performing the locutionary act of saying that a door is open I may be performing an illocutionary act of stating, or hinting, or exclaiming; by performing the illocutionary act of hinting I may succeed in performing the perlocutionary act of getting you to shut it. In the same way, by performing the locutionary act of saying 'Down with the monarchy' I may succeed in the perlocutionary act of bringing about a revolution, whereas in performing the locutionary act I would be inciting to revolution (successfully or unsuccessfully).

We now see that the constatives, along with performatives, can be construed as members of one particular subclass of illocutionary forces. Thus, in his provisional classification of illocutionary forces Austin had a subclass of *expositives*, which included the 'constative' acts. In performing a locutionary act we may be affirming, denying, stating, describing, reporting, agreeing, testifying, rejoining, etc., but in performing a locutionary act we may also perform an act with *commissive* force, as when we promise, bet, vow, adopt, or consent; with *verdictive* force, as when we acquit, assess, or diagnose; with *exercitive* force, as when we appoint, demote, sentence, or veto; or with *behabitive* force, as when we apologize, thank, or curse.

Such is the crude outline of Austin's theory of illocutionary forces. Though his own exposition is of course much more full and rewarding, he said of it (*How to Do Things With Words*, p. 163): 'I have purposely not embroiled the general theory with philosophical problems (some of which are complex enough almost to merit their celebrity); this should not be taken to mean that I am unaware of them.' We may be permitted to illustrate the philosophical importance of bearing in mind the distinctions Austin made with one example of our own. Very often in recent years philosophers have set out to explain the meaning of the word 'good' or of sentences containing the word 'good'. Some of them have done so by saying that in such sentences the speaker expresses his own feelings (attitudes) and evokes similar feelings (attitudes in others). It might well seem that here they have set out to give an account relevant to locutionary force and that they have instead given one possible illocutionary force ('In saying that it was good I was expressing my favourable attitude toward it') and, alongside it, one possible perlocutionary force ('By saying that it was good I evoked in him a favourable attitude'). It should be clear in the light of Austin's work that such an account will not do. But Austin said very little about locutionary force in detail, and one of the most pressing general questions that arise from his work is that of the relationship between illocutionary force and locutionary force; while recognizing that they are different, and that locutionary force is in some way prior, can we, for example, conclude that the locutionary force of utterances containing the word 'promise' can be explained without reference to the typical illocutionary force of 'I promise'? This is far from clear.

Criticism of traditional philosophy. We have examined in outline an example of Austin's work on a piece of clarification of language without any reference, save incidental, to the traditional problems of philosophy. We shall now turn to *Sense and Sensibilia*, which is emphatically a polemical discussion of one of the central problems of epistemology. But we shall find the essential features of Austin's method still present, the presentation only being different. Austin had recommended that when the method is used as one of inquiry the vocabulary and phrases, natural and odd, that occur to us should be studied and conclusions drawn *before* the conclusions of traditional philosophy are compared with them. Here, however, when he presents results he at each stage presents first the traditional philosophical theses and then shows their errors by confronting them with the actual facts, linguistic and otherwise.

In *Sense and Sensibilia*, Austin examines the doctrine that we never directly perceive material things but only sense data (or ideas, or sense contents, etc.), in so far as that doctrine is based upon the so-called argument from illusion. He maintains that it is largely based on an obsession with a few words 'the uses of which are oversimplified, not really understood or carefully studied or correctly described' (*Sense and Sensibilia*, p. 3). With special reference to Ayer and Price, he shows how illusions are traditionally confused with delusions, are defined in terms of belief that one sees a material thing when in fact one does not (whereas some illusions, such as one hatched line appearing to be longer than another of equal length, involve nothing of the sort), and are taken to include such phenomena as sticks looking bent in water, which are not illusions at all. A portion of the argument that clearly exhibits his method at work is where he contrasts the actual complexities and differences in our use of 'looks', 'appears', and 'seems' with the traditional confusion of these terms in traditional philosophy. Especially interesting is the discussion of the traditional accounts of 'reality'; these he contrasts with the multifarious uses of the word 'real', which takes its significance only from the implied contrast in context with 'artificial', 'fake', 'bogus', 'toy', 'synthetic', etc., as well as with 'illusory' and 'apparent'.

But it is perhaps more important now for us to notice another element in the argument that is very characteristic but that we have as yet given little notice, which is Austin's care to avoid over-simplification and hasty generalization of nonlinguistic, as well as linguistic, fact. The ordinary man does not, as is so often stated or implied in accounts of the argument from illusion, believe that he always sees material things; he knows perfectly well that he sees shadows, mirror images, rainbows, and the like. The number of kinds of things that we see is large and to be settled by scientific investigation, not by philosophy; the question whether the invariable object of perception is a material thing or a sense datum is thus absurd. Again, it is not true that a straight stick in water normally looks like a bent stick out of water, for we can see the water; an after-image does not look like a coloured patch on a wall; a dream is distinguished by the dreamlike quality that occasionally, but only occasionally, we attribute to some waking experience. Again, he points out that situations in which our perception is queer may arise because of defects in sense organs or peculiarities of the medium or because we put a wrong construction on what we (quite normally) see, and it is a mistake to attempt to give a single account of all perceptual error. None of these are linguistic points, and Austin had no purist, theoretical notion that he was prohibited as a philosopher from any attention to nonconceptual issues; he thought that philosophical error did arise from empirical error.

Once again, it would be pointless to attempt to reconstruct the whole argument of *Sense and Sensibilia* here; we must be content with noticing the few points made that perhaps have some bearing on a general understanding of his general position. But it should perhaps be stressed that Austin in these lectures discussed only one theory of perception as based on one particular kind of argument; although one may expect to get help from it in study of other problems in the field of perception, it would be a mistake to suppose that the book contains a full study of all problems of perception or to criticize it because it leaves many difficult problems unanswered.

It is hardly imaginable that anyone would ever deny that Austin displayed a very great talent in the kind of work he chose to do. Some have criticized him on the ground that there are more important things for philosophers to do than this; on that point Austin always refused to argue, simply saying that those who preferred to work otherwise should do so and asking only that they not do what he did in the traditional slipshod way. To those who said that philosophers should work with an improved scientific language he replied flatly that the distinctions of ordinary language were of interest in their own right and that one should not modify what one does not fully understand, but he offered no theoretical objections to such projects. He was content to work in a way which he felt he understood and found rewarding. As for the assertion sometimes made, that Austin's kind of work is private to his own peculiar gifts and that it was therefore a mistake for him to recommend the method to others, time alone can decide.

A final word should be said about Austin's relation to other philosophers. He greatly admired G. E. Moore, but it is a mistake to view his work as an offshoot of Cambridge philosophy. Moore, like Austin and unlike most Cambridge philosophers, had a linguistic and classical background rather than a scientific one. Austin owed no special debt to Russell and was far more unlike Wittgenstein than is sometimes recognized. For Wittgenstein an understanding of ordinary language was important because he believed that the traditional problems of philosophy arose from misunderstandings of it, but Wittgenstein had in mind gross category mistakes, and he wished to study ordinary language only so far as was essential for eliminating these. Austin was interested in fine distinctions for their own sake and saw the application of his results to the traditional problems of philosophy as only a by-product. He was uninterested in the party conflicts of philosophy, following always his individual bent.

J. L. AUSTIN, 1911–1960

Stuart Hampshire

PHILOSOPHY is more than any other inquiry burdened with the knowledge of its own past. Like the descendants of an ancient family who still live in a small apartment, equipped with every modern device, in a corner of their ancestral home, philosophers at this time are apt to be at once proud of the great ambitions of their ancestors, and of the monuments that they have left, and at the same time half-ashamed of their heritage, as of something now embarrassingly over-ambitious, from which they must hasten to dissociate themselves. Consequently an anxious and defensive tone has crept into much of the philosophical writing and discussion of the last thirty years, the tone of men who are anxious to show that in spite of their conspicuous origins, they are no less productive, unpretentious, unassuming, and modern in outlook, than workers in other fields. They may still live in the great house, but only in a corner of it, in which they lead very ordinary useful lives. As for the rest of the building, they are always available to show the public round with the proper historical explanations. This uncertainty about the relation of the present to the past has produced a certain strain and ambiguity of intention, also an undue sensitiveness to public opinion.

Of all the philosophers whom I have known as contemporaries, or as near-contemporaries, Austin was the least embarrassed, and the least uncertain, about philosophy itself and its role. He had made up his mind for himself, independently of the current slogans, and he knew exactly what he was doing. As G. E. Moore in an earlier generation, so Austin in his generation had an authority that was immediately recognized by his colleagues, and in both cases the authority was founded, not only on unequalled intellectual powers, but also on a startling directness and sureness of purpose.

Austin stood aside from all the indirections and uncertainties of method, to which philosophers are now liable, for a simple reason: that he was constitutionally unable to refrain from applying the same standards of truthfulness and accuracy to a philosophical argument, sentence by sentence, as he would have applied to any other serious subject-matter. He could not have adopted a special tone of voice, or attitude of mind, for philosophical questions. He was by training a classical scholar and he thought as a classical scholar thinks. Clause by clause, sentence by sentence, a sequence of thought is constructed, until no rough approximations are left. If it is accurate in each one of its parts, it is accurate as a whole. This is the only way in which truthful prose can be written or spoken, and it is the only way in which anything already written can be truthfully interpreted and assessed. He had no need of a theory of philosophical method and therefore no need of a theory of philosophy itself. From the earliest date of which I can speak from personal knowledge, the year 1936, his 'method', which is better described as a style of habit or thought, was unvarying, in spite of at least one conversion in his philosophical interests. Before the war he was already characteristically suspicious of traditional formulations of the traditional problems of metaphysics, and to this extent he agreed with the logical positivists of that time. But he had not yet found his own way with dictionaries and grammars and the exact observation of usage. This was a gradual conversion. But from the beginning he refused to adopt any special and elevated tone for the discussion of philosophy, and he refused to accept from others any peculiar inherited canons of argument. Particularly during the 1930s, when technical pretensions were rife, these refusals had the effect of fair, and devastating, comment on the Emperor's New Clothes. He continued in this vein of patient literalness, through changing fashions, until the end. He could not have brought himself to approach philosophical problems in any other way. Any other way would simply have seemed to him untruthful.

As with Moore, so also with Austin there was a tendency among those who felt his authority to turn his individual style of thought into a general method of solving problems. There is always this desire to make any outstanding individual a type. The distinction and individuality are then comfortably reduced to manageable and imitable proportions. But the results of such a reduction of an individual style to a general method are often trivialities. History may, or may not, show that this has happened again; it is still too early to judge. But we are concerned at this time with Austin's own philosophical conclusions and achievements, as they appeared in discussion and in his publications.

There is a central problem of interpretation. Did he propose a general theory of language, as a structure that, accurately interpreted, 'is in order as it is' (Wittgenstein's phrase)? Did he believe, and believe for good reasons, that a careful, systematic plotting of the distinctions already marked in standard usage would undermine the foundations of all, or of most, philosophical problems? After recalling his programmatic remarks in the Presidential Address 'A Plea for Excuses', the symposium on 'Other Minds' and many oral discussions, it seems to me that the evidence is not clear. He distrusted programmatic discussions for two reasons, each in itself a sufficient reason for him: first, that from their nature they must involve vague and sweeping generalizations which cannot be altogether accurate: secondly, that they are a diversion from the detailed inquiries that are needed at the present time. But in the assessment of his own work, particularly on knowledge ('Other Minds', *Proc. Arist. Soc.*, Symposium, *Supplementary Volume XX*, 1946) and on problems connected with free-will ('Ifs and Cans', *Proc. British Academy*, 1956 and 'A Plea for Excuses', *Proc. Arist. Soc.*, 1956/7), the issue cannot now be avoided. Did he try to show, and did he succeed in showing, that the kind of considerations that he here adduced would by themselves lead to adequate solutions, if they were pressed further with equal care and subtlety?

I shall distinguish two slightly different theses that can plausibly be attributed to him: a strong and a weak theses.

II

The strong thesis may be seen as something like an application of Leibniz's Principle of Sufficient Reason to established forms of speech. For every distinction of word and idiom that we find in common speech, there is a reason to be found, if we look far enough, to explain why this distinction exists. The investigation will always show that the greatest possible number of distinctions have been obtained by the most economical linguistic means. If, as philosophers, we try to introduce an altogether new distinction, we shall find that we are disturbing the economy of the language by blurring elsewhere some useful distinctions that are already recognized. This, as a corollary of the Principle of Sufficient Reason, is a Principle of Continuity in language: every possible position (sense) is occupied (signified). Conversely, there is a presumption that to every verbal difference there corresponds a difference of sense which has its indispensable place. In very detailed lectures on perception, famous in Oxford under the title *Sense and Sensibilia*, Austin tried to show that each of the great variety of idioms clustering round the apparently simple verbs 'look' and 'seem' plays a necessary part, and that the clumsy and naïve dichotomy of sense-datum and material object blurs every necessary distinction and is inadequate to the complexity of experience. He delighted to show that this dichotomy, which was in recent times supposed to rest on distinctions already marked in language, in fact rests on pure invention. In general he considered philosophers' inclination towards dramatic dichotomies as essentially primitive, as a mark of the pre-history of the subject, from which we could now at last escape by attention to the complex facts of language. In regular discussions with colleagues at Oxford, he methodically pursued the facts connected with the notion of a rule, examining the rules of many different kinds of game, and of course finding that there are many different kinds of rule. With this range of subtly varying examples in mind, a philosopher will be less confident that the rules of language are like the rules of a game, as if this were a triumphantly clear conclusion: which kind of rules in which kind of game? All that is philosophically interesting will disappear in the vagueness of the comparison at this level of generality. The comparison only comes alive when we descend to the details and set one kind of rule against another. Similarly in the article 'A Plea for Excuses', and in seminars and discussions, he explored the variety of significant ways in which our language allows us to modify the bald statement 'He did so-and-so', strengthening or diminishing its force and its implications. Each of the adverbial qualifications—'deliberately', 'intentionally', 'on purpose', 'by mistake' and so on—has its own place in a system of graduated differences, and in each case we shall grasp the peculiar point by assembling typical examples. It would be a mistake to neglect any distinction as trivial, because it has played no familiar part in any philosophical problem. Only accuracy and completeness over the whole range of distinctions will locate disputed distinctions in their proper position. Austin had begun this kind of investigation in a class with Professor Hart in 1948, concentrating on legal concepts associated with action and responsibility. He had found a rich vein of 'facts' in the legal cases.

If we methodically investigate the whole spectrum of qualifications of the bald statement 'He did it', we may hope that, by this method of approximation, we shall have finally marked the boundaries of the central concept of action. A frontal assault on the typical philosopher's question 'What is an action?' will lead nowhere, because it is an invitation to smother the facts with an invented formula. 'What is an action?' Compare 'What is real?' and 'What is Truth?' It is the mark of the primitive, of the prehistory of philosophy, to pose questions in this linguistically abstract, and utterly general, form. I recall a lecture to a surprised summer-school audience not long after the war in which he listed some of the many different contrasts that may be implied in the various uses of the phrase '[a] real so-and-so': real [flowers] versus artificial, a real [character in a story] versus an imaginary one, real [courage] versus imperfect, and so on, with more and more subtly varying examples. What then is the use and basis of any generalized contrast between Reality and some supposed antithetical term, e.g., Appearance? The conclusion was that 'real' is an 'adjuster-word' which has to be watched in its role. It is a vulgarity to insist that anything less than a frontal assault on the 'great' problems is a retreat into triviality. If we are to arrive at a clear notion of Truth, we need a detailed review of the various ways in which a statement may go wrong, of the various dimensions of failure in statement-making. And we must not from the beginning assume a simple, ungraduated notion of a statement, or of a descriptive utterance, as of something uniform and unmistakable. Here again we shall find, if we will only pause to look at the facts, a continuous spectrum of kinds of utterance, each with its peculiar liabilities to mistake. The most famous of his discoveries in this field was of the element of performativeness that enters into many kinds of utterance ordinarily classified as statements, and particularly into utterances that are claims to knowledge. This was certainly a substantial discovery, which no one can henceforth neglect in giving an account of knowledge ('Other Minds', *Proc. Arist. Soc., Supplementary Volume XX*, 1946).

Behind this policy of looking for graduated differences, and shades of qualification, around the hypnotizing central concept (Action, Knowledge, Real, True, Rule), was the conviction that every difference of idiom has its justification in the subtle economy of language as a whole. On occasion, both in discussion and in publications ('Excuses', *Proc. Arist. Soc.*, 1956/7), Austin would suggest that the implied Principle of Sufficient Linguistic Reason is to be justified as Burke justified some other established institutions of England—social and political institutions. These are the distinctions that have stood the test of time and that embody the wisdom of long experience. They must represent a gradual effort of adaptation to 'the human predicament', and they cannot easily be bettered by any projecting reformer (Russell, Quine, Goodman), who sits down in an armchair to determine how we should speak clearly in the light of reason. No workable alternative will be found by *a priori* legislation and by brisk projects of logical reform. The distinctions are organically connected, and the amputation of an offending part will destroy the mutual adjustment, and therefore the life, of the whole.

The weaker thesis is a negative one, and claims no single and exclusive programme for advance in philosophy. It is a fact that we introduce and explain the distinctions that are required for the special purposes of philosophical analysis by reference to some existing distinctions marked in common speech. The philosophical distinctions, and the technical terms in which they are stated, may be refinements of established usage, refinements needed only in answering unusual questions. But they cannot be clear and intelligible, and the philosophical answers cannot be clear and intelligible, unless the distinctions from which they have been refined are themselves accurately recorded. In talking about sense-data, we shall be talking about we-know-not-what, if we have introduced these entities by reference to such phrases as 'the penny looks elliptical', and if we have in fact misreported, and over-simplified, the conditions under which such phrases are used, and the implications that they in fact carry with them. The weaker, or negative, thesis is that we must first have the facts, and all the facts, accurately stated before we erect a theory upon the basis of them. And this is much more difficult, and demands more patient and co-operative labour, than has ever been recognized by philosophers up till the present time. They have been content to seize on a few favourite examples, constantly recurring in the literature, and have then built their theories on this thin and biased foundation. We cannot be sure of the place, and therefore of the representative value, of any particular specimen of the use of an idiom, unless we have once traversed the whole range of its possible uses, and of the uses of other adjacent idioms that belong to the same range. Philosophers are apt, unconsciously, to choose the very example from current usage that constitutes plausible evidence for the particular rational reconstruction that they wish to advocate. A rival school of philosophers concentrates attention on another range of well established uses of the philosophically interesting word or phrase, and, on this selected basis, suggests a quite different rational reconstruction of the essential purpose and meaning that lie behind the various uses of the word or phrase. The effect of this casualness and impatience is the notorious and scandalous inconclusiveness of philosophical argument.

It is the most important of all the facts that now need to be recorded about Austin, as a philosopher, that he certainly did himself consider this alleged scandal of inconclusiveness to be a scandal. Since it was a constant point of difference between us, he often, and over many years, had occasion to tell me that he had never found any good reason to believe that philosophical inquiries are essentially, and of their very nature, inconclusive. On the contrary he believed that this was a remediable fault of philosophers, due to premature system-building and impatient ambition, which left them neither the inclination nor the time to assemble the facts, impartially and co-operatively, and then to build their unifying theories, cautiously and slowly, on a comprehensive, and therefore secure, basis. To stop the endless pendulum motion of rival theories, each as plausible and partially founded as the other, is the serious work of philosophy at this time. During a sabbatical year, free from teaching and lecturing, he tried by himself to accumulate a vast range of examples of different types of predication with a view to building, on this unbiased foundation, a general theory of naming and describing. He did not succeed in this enterprise, and he did not believe that he had succeeded. The article 'How to Talk' (*Proc. Arist. Soc.*, 1952–3), with which he was altogether dissatisfied, emerged from this work. But he still believed that a group of philosophers, working together for some considerable time, could collect a sufficient range of graded examples to permit, for the first time, some really well-founded generalizations. If this were not done, and if philosophers remained content with their hasty improvisations, we should continue on the old round of rival theories, each resting on its selected examples, and each and all of them exposed by evident counter-examples.

Austin believed at this time that the accepted grammatical-logical classifications of terms, and of types of statement (the classifications of non-formal logic) could be made far more precise and specific. A new set of technical terms was needed for a new philosophical grammar. The grammar books—and he read them carefully—were full of the ghosts of a primitive logic and of a primitive ontology. Here was constructive work that needs to be done, and only philosophers are sufficiently disrespectful of old theories to do it with undeceived attention to the facts. But, clinging to their ancient amateur status, as Platonic gentlemen who do not handle mere facts, they continue to discuss (for example) hypothetical statements in terms of the utmost generality, without distinguishing among the great variety of forms, syntactically or pragmatically different, of 'If . . . then' sentences. Austin had a scholar's feeling for grammar and for the shades of meaning to which a translator attends. Both as a teacher and in discussion among his colleagues, he was an enemy of the easy amateur tradition of linguistic analysis in all its surviving forms. His idea of organized and co-operative work in the philosophical study of language was the belief that amateurs must become artisans. On the one side mathematical logic, which has substituted disciplined work and established results for casual speculation in one large area of philosophy: on the other side, as the other heir of speculative, post-Russell philosophy, a real, in the place of a pretended, study of language. At a time when American foundations were considering means of promoting philosophical research, Austin privately expressed the belief that a large, co-operative, centrally directed project of linguistic analysis might indeed lead to solidly based results, and that uncontrolled private enterprise could accomplish very little. The sceptical arguments of his friends left him quite unmoved.

I may seem to have established no clear difference between Austin's stronger and weaker theses about the existing forms of language. The difference can perhaps be best summarized in a few sentences. The weaker thesis was that an exhaustive and methodical, and, ideally, a co-operative, study of the full facts of common usage in all traditionally disputed areas, is an indispensable *preliminary* to any philosophical advance. The stronger thesis was that the multiplicity of fine distinctions, which such a study would disclose, would by itself answer philosophical questions about free-will, perception, naming and describing, conditional statements. The crude distinctions, which are presupposed in every statement of these questions, will be seen to be intolerably remote from the facts. Thereafter we should move forward from the artificial questions, posed in these inaccurate and intolerably general terms, to the precise and various distinctions that in fact concern us in the conduct of life or in science. Almost all the semi-informed discussions of the linguistic method in philosophy have centred on this second thesis, because it can be much more easily and satisfactorily confused with Wittgenstein's theory of language in *Philosophical Investigations*. Even those who want to overlook significant differences in order to create a man of straw, called 'linguistic philosophy', as a target, cannot plausibly assimilate the weaker thesis to Wittgenstein's later teaching.

Plainly there was no immediate need for Austin to decide between these alternatives. Whatever the ultimate issue, the work immediately to be done, in teaching and in criticism, was the same. For Austin philosophy as an inquiry, and the teaching of philosophy, were so intimately connected that it often seemed impossible to distinguish the ends that he prescribed for philosophy from those that he prescribed for the teaching of philosophy. He very strongly believed in the educational value of philosophy, rightly taught, and believed in it in a way that is traditionally associated with Greats at Oxford: namely, that it is an irreplaceable training in habits of exact argument, and that it is a prophylactic against intellectual pretentiousness and muddle. In this, and in several other respects, he had been influenced by the example of Prichard, who, as the scourge of pretentiousness and muddle, was the dominant figure among Oxford philosophers when Austin was an undergraduate. Of Prichard it was often said that, a strict and unworldly philosopher, he had in effect, and without explicit intention, trained several generations of civil servants in exact drafting, and that he had only reinforced habits of mind that had first been formed by Latin and Greek proses. This is the effect of the peculiar position of philosophy at Oxford as an accepted educational instrument. It has its continuing effects also on the quality and direction of Oxford philosophy, considered as an independent inquiry. In Austin's generation, the social and political implications of the teaching of philosophy, and of the forming of habits of thought in a ruling class, were certainly not unnoticed, and he was acutely conscious of them. He seriously wanted to 'make people sensible' and clear-headed, and immune to ill-founded and doctrinaire enthusiasms. He believed that philosophy, if it inculcated respect for 'the facts' and for accuracy, was one of the best instruments for this purpose. He had a great respect for practical activities of reform, and, as was shown during the war and within the university, immense and devoted ability in them. It is necessary to mention these facts, because the general tendency of the kind of linguistic analysis with which Austin is associated is constantly misjudged, at least as far as he is concerned. He was always responsibly interested in public affairs. As a young Fellow of All Souls, he began to learn Russian and visited the Soviet Union. At that time he would argue fiercely about politics from an uncommitted, but characteristic, point of view, which was half authoritarian and yet never conservative. So far from being neutral, detached, and therefore conservative, in relating philosophy to wider interests, he sometimes seemed to subordinate philosophy itself to education. He thought that a training in the true, patient method of philosophical analysis was having, and would continue to have, an effect that was the reverse of conservative. He certainly was not surprised by the hostility of the various established orders, whether Christian or secular, and of the merely conventional, *bien pensant* publicists. He was consciously a radical reformer, who had suggested a specific, and largely original, interpretation of that which constitutes clear thinking on abstract topics. He knew that this was an achievement that would rightly be regarded as subversive. He knew that he was (in his own words) 'tampering with the beliefs' of his audience, merely by insinuating unusual standards of verbal accuracy into the dissection of hallowed arguments. The true conservatives, in philosophy as in politics, are those who accept discussion of traditional problems within the traditional terms. However heterodox the conclusions on which the supposed rebels congratulate themselves, no Church or ruling party feels itself seriously threatened by this re-shuffling of the officially approved cards. But there are signs of official fear, and therefore of righteous anger, when the whole game of established argument and counter-argument is held up to ridicule. Austin did, with intention and responsibly, use the weapon of ridicule as a natural side-effect of analysing philosophical pomposity: for example, in examining the arguments for the existence of sense-data and many other traditional arguments. If you considered this style of detailed analysis ill-adapted to the material and ineffective, you would reasonably consider the ridicule to be misplaced also. But it is dishonest to pretend that linguistic analysis of a minute, literal, word-by-word kind is not revolutionary, both in intention and in effect, in philosophy, or to pretend that it confirms the plain man in his uncriticized opinions. One of the strongest of the plain man's uncriticized opinions is that philosophical issues are too profound and peculiar to be discussed in any such pedestrian, literal terms. Those of us who, as philosophers, are not convinced of the final effectiveness of linguistic analysis know only too well that we are never without these, and other, embarrassing allies.

If one advances step by step, from one particular truth, accurately stated, to another, and if one never rushes forward to a premature generalization, until the ground has been fully surveyed, one may indeed find oneself arriving at revolutionary conclusions, at least in philosophy. For no one had ever followed this path before, and it is therefore impossible to tell in advance where it may lead. In at least one case, the theory of knowledge (*Proc. Arist. Soc., Supplementary Volume XX*, 1946, 'Other Minds') it did in fact lead to results, which are everywhere acknowledged as relevant, as new, and as of permanent significance.

III

In conclusion there are more scattered, personal and particular features of Austin's philosophical development between the 1930s and 1960 which ought to be recorded. In virtue of his authority and his innovations in the years after the war, the personal history is of some general significance for philosophers.

He arrived at his own distinctive position in philosophy slowly in the five years before the war. As an undergraduate at Balliol, he had been influenced by Prichard, whose lectures and classes he attended and whom he bombarded with questions and objections.

I think that his interest in performative utterances was in part traceable to Prichard, who used to ask 'What do we mean when we say "I agree" ', and then add 'I am blowed if I know'. Secondly, he read essays to the famous and eccentric Balliol tutor, half Roman historian and half philosopher, Stone, the author of *The Social Contract of the Universe*. Austin was deeply impressed by him as a person and as a tutor. In 1936 he and Professor Berlin held an unconventional and unforgettable class on C. I. Lewis' *Mind and the World Order*. He was already challenging the validity of any technical term for which no clear rule of use could be derived from within ordinary language. But he had not yet made this habit a principle. From 1936 to 1939, Austin attended informal weekly discussions in Berlin's rooms, with Ayer, Woozley, MacNabb, and myself. On these occasions he challenged every technical term in the discussion, as part of a philosophical mythology, unless a plain example, or set of examples, had first been made the focus of the discussion. As the philosophical atmosphere was at that time full of the technical terms of the Vienna Circle, the effect was powerfully negative. In these years we discussed principally sense-data and phenomenalism, hypothetical propositions, and necessary truth. Austin was at that time interested also in Leibniz, and read a rather formal paper to the Philosophical Society, within a Leibnizian framework, which questioned the grounds for believing that every proposition has a contradictory. He was at this time still uncommitted to any general programme in philosophy, but he was strongly influenced by Moore. In common with others of his generation at Oxford, he knew very little of Wittgenstein's later work. Although he shared their hostility to the pretensions of tradition metaphysics, he always attacked both the methods of argument, and the summary conclusions, of the philosophers of the Vienna Circle. Above all, he disliked the rapidity with which they arrived at their conclusions. A philosophical argument with Austin, which was always concentrated on one, or perhaps two, definitely stated examples, commonly lasted for about three hours, until the various plausible interpretations had been exhausted: and he would often return to the topic later in the week, and these arguments would prolong themselves over a term. From 1937 onwards, and increasingly as the war approached, we discussed politics, and he regularly attended the electoral meetings of one of our colleagues, Lord Hailsham, as a heckler. During the war, and during his service as an intelligence officer, there were few opportunities for discussing philosophy. I think that it is certain, from the evidence of a particular conversation, that his natural love of concrete and detailed investigations, and of discoveries that gradually emerge from careful accumulations of fact, had already during the war led to fixed intentions in philosophy. Must philosophy always be unscholarly, vague, inconclusive, tentative? How can we know what would emerge from a planned and patient assault on the facts of the conceptual scheme, as it actually exists? Should there not be a moratorium on all theories until the facts that might form intelligent grammars and dictionaries are reasonably well ordered? Is it not laziness and dishonesty to continue to exchange one hasty theory for another, and to prolong indefinitely that pattern of plausible pretence which we call the history of philosophy? The plausibility of Descartes and, worst of all, of Hume were particular examples that he would quote. He distrusted their literary skill, the smoothness of the surface, and their light attitude towards recalcitrant facts, which made the total scheme brilliant and convincing. Aristotle stood for virtue and on the other side, because his conclusions were not unearned, and because he was more interested in making true statements, however dull, than in being interesting and dramatic. If due allowance is made for the great difference of scale, Austin's strong reaction against the sweeping generalizations about language, which were the legacy of logical positivism, was not unlike Aristotle's patient pruning of the Platonic philosophy. Many, perhaps most, of the great philosophers have survived in memory by the force of their exaggerations. Austin was always suspicious of the dramatic rhetoric of philosophers, and of that further exploitation of personality which has been such a comical, and perhaps harmful, feature of contemporary philosophy. He tried, in lecturing and in teaching and in writing, to reduce the tone of discussion to a plain, under-labourer's style, and to make philosophical argument as unassuming and relaxed as a botanist's argument. He was disgusted by those (and there have been many) who find in philosophy an excuse for re-making the world in their own image, and who realize their fantasies and wishes in an intellectual construction that pretends to be truth. The first virtue, in any inquiry, is respect for existence and for its variety. If this modesty is not taught in universities, and by philosophers, concern for truth will nowhere survive.

I think that there was more to be learnt from him than from any other philosopher of his generation. He had an entirely original and unprejudiced mind, a very strong instrument of natural scholarship, and serious and generous purposes. He was certainly the cleverest man that I have known among teachers of philosophy. He made a contribution, which was entirely his own, to one particular strand in English thought, and the consequences of his work will remain a living issue.

COMMENTS

J. O. Urmson and G. J. Warnock

Professor Hampshire's account of the late J. L. Austin is felicitous, perceptive, and valuable. However, it seems to us at certain points liable to disseminate just the kind of misunderstanding of Austin's position which Hampshire himself deplores, and it is not, we think, over-officious to say so at once.

Hampshire distinguishes and discusses at length two theses, 'strong' and 'weak', which can, he thinks, 'plausibly be attributed' to Austin. The 'strong' thesis he states as follows: 'For every distinction of word and idiom that we find in common speech, there is a reason to be found, if we look far enough, to explain why this distinction exists. The investigation will always show that the greatest possible number of distinctions have been obtained by the most economical linguistic means. If, as philosophers, we try to introduce an altogether new distinction, we shall find that we are disturbing the economy of the language by blurring elsewhere some useful distinctions that are already recognized.'

It is, however, quite certain that Austin did not accept this thesis—or at least that he did not accept all of its several parts. No doubt he believed that there was always a reason why the distinctions of word and idiom in common speech should have come to be drawn; but he did not take for granted that such reasons must be good and sufficient. No doubt he believed also that linguistic innovation, the introduction of new kinds of terms into a body of existing usage, was more dangerous and difficult than philosophers by habit have been ready to recognize. But in *A Plea for Excuses* he wrote: 'Certainly, then, ordinary language is *not* the last word: in principle it can everywhere be supplemented and improved upon and superseded.' In that same article he recognized that systematic investigation of human behaviour might give grounds for modifying, or for supplementing, our existing linguistic resources for commenting upon it. We recollect his saying in conversation that certain areas of 'common speech'—those, namely, in which common speakers for common purposes had no strong interest in, no occasion for, nicety and clarity of distinction—were most unlikely to prove fruitful subjects for investigation. Finally, in his own philosophical practice, particularly in his lectures on 'Words and Deeds', he had no hesitation in marking new distinctions with his own new technical terms, of which 'performative' and 'constative' are only the best-known examples. Such terminological invention he regarded not only as admissible, but as sometimes necessary.

Austin would certainly have regarded the notion of 'the greatest possible number of distinctions' as incoherent, but this perhaps is a minor matter.

Later Hampshire re-states this 'strong' thesis in words which seem actually to express a rather different thesis, as the proposition that 'the multiplicity of fine distinctions which such a study [sc. of common speech] would disclose, would by itself answer philosophical questions about free-will, perception, naming and describing, conditional statements'. There is some risk of ambiguity here. Is the expression 'philosophical questions' to be understood as prefixed by 'some', or by 'all'? If the former, then the thesis is scarcely a 'strong' one and scarcely controversial; *some* questions, surely, could be answered by attention to 'fine distinctions'. But if the thesis is intended to express a claim about *all* philosophical questions, then it is quite certain that Austin did not subscribe to it. In the last sentence of *Ifs and Cans* he wrote that, if some parts of present day philosophy should be taken up into a new and comprehensive 'science of language', there would still be plenty left. In his lectures called 'Sense and Sensibilia' he undertook to deal only with a certain *kind* of philosophical worry. In general, as Hampshire himself quite rightly says, Austin 'had no need of a theory of philosophical method and therefore no need of a theory of philosophy itself.' His regard for 'truthfulness and accuracy' in the use, and in description of the use, of words and phrases stands in no need of a specially philosophical justification; and he regarded it as merely premature to make general claims for the efficacy of this 'method'. What its limitations might be, and what, if it should prove at some point inefficacious, should then be tried instead—

these were questions which only time and hard work could answer.

To Hampshire's 'weak' thesis, that 'we must first have the facts, and all the facts, accurately stated before we erect a theory upon the basis of them', Austin might well have agreed—with reservations as to the significance of the phrase *all* the facts'. But this unambitious statement cannot properly, or even plausibly, be magnified into a guiding *doctrine* for his own, or into a recipe for anyone else's, philosophical practice.

Austin defended his own way of doing philosophy—which he sometimes called 'one fashion' of philosophy—as congenial to one who had, as he had, predominantly linguistic interests and training; and he claimed that, when applied to fairly definite and limited problems, it was capable of producing definite results. Large assertions such as those 'strong' theses tentatively attributed to him by Hampshire he would certainly have regarded, besides repudiating them, as worthless. Such theses are not propounded in his writings published or unpublished; and we at least do not recollect, from many years of philosophical discussion with Austin, any hint that he accepted them. The notion that, all the same, they are somehow implied by his philosophical practice could be substantiated only if, as is plainly not the case, that practice could be made intelligible in no other way. But Austin sometimes gave, in much less ambitious terms, his own explanations. Why should these not be taken as meaning just what they say?

AN ORIGINAL PHILOSOPHER

David Pears

THE late J. L. Austin published seven papers in his lifetime. They are all included in *Philosophical Papers*, which is the first of his posthumously published works. The earliest of them, '*A Priori* Concepts', appeared in 1939, and the latest, 'Pretending', in 1958, two years before his death. There are also three papers that he did not publish, one of which, 'Performative Utterances', was given as a broadcast talk in 1956. They are written in various styles to suit the different occasions for which they were intended, but all with absolute lucidity. However, they are not all equally easy reading. For three of them continue discussions to which other people had already contributed at the annual meetings organized by the Mind Association and the Aristotelian Society, and, though he always makes it perfectly clear what thesis it is that he is taking up or criticizing, the background is naturally missing in such cases.

Sense and Sensibilia is a set of lectures on perception, which were first given in Oxford in 1947 and revised many times in the next twelve years. The notes for them were highly condensed, because he was able to give a perfectly formed lecture from very little written material. The version that is now published was reconstructed by Mr. G. J. Warnock with marvellous skill and sympathy. It is written in an easy, informal style, and is a better record of Austin's characteristic way of doing philosophy than the papers that he contributed to set debates.

In the earliest of the papers his mistrust of the terminology of philosophers is already conspicuous. He thought that one of the reasons why so many philosophical controversies are protracted and indecisive is that both sides have accepted an unrealistic terminology. If two people invented a game and then discovered in

49

the course of play that the rules did not cover certain contingencies that inevitably arose, or that they were contradictory, neither of them could hope for victory, and the only reasonable thing for them to do would be to go back and make the rules more realistic. Similarly in philosophy a lot of co-operative work has to be done before the competitive stage, which most people find more enjoyable, can begin. Suppose, for instance, that two philosophers accepted the technical term 'T', and, when one of them put forward the thesis that all T's are X, the other produced an example of something that certainly was not X, and yet did seem to be a T: then it would be lamentable if neither of them knew whether it was a T or not, so that they were unable to determine whether the original thesis was true or false.

This is, of course, a very simple way in which technical terminology can lose contact with reality. It would be absurd if it happened often in science. But in philosophy new terms are introduced at moments of great but ill-defined need, so that even this simple kind of lack of realism is frequent. And there are other, more complex kinds. For instance, two technical terms can live a life of official incompatibility for centuries, although all the time there were perfectly familiar examples to which they both apply, if only someone had noticed them. Alternatively, the official view may be that together they cover everything, although there are examples to which neither of them applies. Or a technical term may be ambiguous, or it may combine two ideas that are sufficiently important to be kept apart, or it may introduce confusion into the principles of classification.

Austin has been credited with the view, or at least with an inclination towards the view, that in philosophy technical terminology is necessarily unrealistic because the maximum number of valid distinctions has already been drawn and marked in non-technical language. But there probably never has been a philosopher less likely to generalize so wildly, and the view is explicitly repudiated in the early paper, 'The Meaning of a Word', and in Section VII of the lectures on perception, and implicitly rejected in two later papers in which he himself introduces some new technical terminology into philosophy, 'How to Talk', and 'Performative Utterances'. What he believed was that technical terminology is unrealistic if it is introduced hastily, and that in philosophy its introduction nearly always is hasty. That cannot be represented even as an inclination towards the view that it is necessarily unrealistic.

However, there are several things that explain why this misunderstanding occurred. First, though his philosophy never changed direction, it was more critical at the beginning and more constructive at the end; and the relentless way in which he undermines traditional terminology in some of his early work might suggest that he believed that no such apparatus could be well founded.

But the misunderstanding also has another, more important source. Many philosophical problems first arose at a time when the areas of human experience with which they are concerned had not been touched by science or by any other exact discipline (many have remained in this state, and perhaps some will continue in it). However, that did not mean that the philosopher was confronted by completely unclassified material. On the contrary, the ordinary, non-technical ways in which people thought about a particular area of their experience, like sense-perception, and in which they described it, would provide him with many well-founded distinctions from which he could start (Aristotle's work often begins in this way). Now even if technical distinctions are added later—Wittgenstein compared them to suburbs built around the old city—the central mass of ordinary distinctions still remains important, and it is reasonable to require, as Austin did, that, when a philosopher introduces some new technical terms of his own, they should at least be founded on these ordinary distinctions. But that requirement is easily misconstrued. For the emphasis on the non-technical foundation of the technical terminology of philosophy creates the illusion that all the technical terminology of scientists is being rejected, and this illusion, in its turn, reinforces the illusion that all technical terminology is being eliminated from philosophy.

The idea that Austin regarded terminological innovations in science as inadmissible is, of course, the more bizarre of the two. Linguistic conservatism, carried to that point, would be so mad that it is surprising to find it even considered in these books (it is dismissed explicitly in 'A Plea for Excuses', and implicitly in Section X of the lectures on perception). But there is something about Austin's method that explains even this misunderstanding.

He made two assumptions, neither of them new: the first was that language reveals the structure of thought; and the second was that, if a system of thought has been functioning successfully for a long time, the distinctions underlying its classifications of its objects will be well founded. Given these two assumptions, it was natural to concentrate on non-scientific language. But though this reason for concentrating on non-scientific language might seem to imply mistrust of scientific language, all that it really implies is that the former possesses a credential that guarantees realism—its long service—whereas the latter often lacks that credential. But recent enrolment does not necessarily mean lack of realism, and if a scientific term is introduced carefully to meet a definite need it will last. This kind of introduction will also ensure a long life for a philosophical term. But it is, of course, the cause of longevity that is important, rather than the longevity itself. A long life of what Wittgenstein called 'running idle' would be worthless.

These misinterpretations of Austin's philosophy deserve to be mentioned, because a good way of presenting the truth is to start from the falsehoods beyond it, and because anyway they have won some acceptance. But it is particularly necessary to understand the nature of Austin's critique of the technical terminology of philosophy, not only because it is important in itself but also because of the way in which his constructive work grew out of it. For his critical work and his positive contributions to philosophy were closely connected.

The connexion between them is complex, but it is not difficult to trace one main line of development. Suppose that Austin wished to get rid of a piece of unrealistic technical terminology. Then it was sometimes enough merely to cite familiar examples, described in non-technical language, which philosophers had simply overlooked. But there were also many cases where it was necessary to penetrate below the level of non-technical language and thought, and to try to discover what lies beneath it. For the structure of the non-technical system often needs to be explored thoroughly before it is possible to say whether or not the technical philosophical system fits on to it properly.

However, there were other reasons why he undertook this exploration, which, in fact, occupied most of his time. One was that he wanted to correct another fault which, according to him, often vitiated philosophical writing, the unrealistic use of non-technical terminology (the lectures on perception contain good examples of this kind of criticism, which is as important as his criticism of technical terminology). But the most important result of the exploration was his own constructive work. The transition was a natural one, since the facts that he used in criticizing others deserved to be investigated for their own sake. In general, what he wanted to stop was philosophical thinking without understanding. If that aim were realized the negative consequence would be that unrealistic technical terminology and the unrealistic use of non-technical terminology would both be eliminated from philosophy, and the positive result would be an understanding of the realities with which philosophy ought to be concerned.

His constructive procedure was usually to take a familiar word or group of words and to describe those features of their use that reveal their meaning. Given the first of his two assumptions, the result would be an account of the conceptual scheme that underlies the part of language that was being examined. The simplest example of this kind of work is the paper 'Pretending'. But even here one learns a lot, and that might be found surprising because the concept is so familiar. Yet this phenomenon was noted long ago by Socrates: the analysis of a familiar concept only has to go a little deeper than usual and it produces a result about which people do not feel able to say whether they are learning it for the first time or are merely being reminded of it.

There are more complicated pieces of work of this kind in the lectures on perception. Here Austin attacks the traditional theory that there are only two kinds of objects of perception, material objects and sense-data (sense-data, of course, have been given various names in different periods, and the distinction between the two kinds of thing has been presented in this century as a distinction between two languages). So the general plan of these lectures is polemical, the most frequently criticized text being Professor A. J. Ayer's *Foundations of Empirical Knowledge* (1940). But at many points Austin abandons criticism, in order to develop his own ideas independently. Whether he is working in a constructive or a critical way, his procedure in these lectures is always the same; patiently to try to understand the complex system of non-technical language and thought whose evolution has been conditioned by the complex facts of sense perception. This book is a classic, and the subject is permanently altered by it.

In the other book the best examples of this kind of work are to be found in the paper 'Other Minds' and in the presidential address to the Aristotelian Society, 'A Plea for Excuses'. In the latter he examines the various ways in which what at first sight seems to be a person's action can fail to be his action in the full sense of those words. Each of these ways is marked by an appropriate adverb or qualifying phrase, and some of them are held to diminish responsibility. Incidentally, the discussion is a good example of his readiness to start from technical language: for some of the distinctions are taken from legal terminology.

The paper 'Other Minds' contains an original and important discussion of knowledge and belief, and here too the same analytic procedure is employed. But technical terminology is used too: for it is here that he first introduced his distinction between performative and descriptive utterances. This distinction is also discussed in an informal way in the broadcast talk, but its full elaboration is to be found in the lectures on 'Words and Deeds', which have yet to be published.* In fact, the collection contains only one paper in which he systematically develops technical distinctions of his own, 'How to Talk', which is about different kinds of predication. It is often said that a philosopher who engages in thorough analysis of non-philosophical terminology runs the risk of losing himself in details: but Austin was always more impressed by the opposite danger, that, if he introduced new philosophical terminology of his own, he would lose himself in generalities. However, he used the second procedure increasingly towards the end of his life.

In all his work, critical and constructive, his paramount purpose was to keep philosophy in close contact with human experience. The result is that his positive achievements have a firmness and solidity that are rare in the history of the subject. Some find this exciting, others unnerving. It is as if the way to represent the third dimension on a plane surface had just been discovered—or, rather, rediscovered, because Austin's realism was not entirely new. The particular way in which it relied on language was new, and so too were the meticulousness and devotion with which he practised it. But other philosophers in other periods have preached a return to

* This is published as: *How to Do Things with Words*.

realism and practised it. The practice is exceedingly hard, but those who follow it win their intellectual freedom by using only what they understand of the apparatus offered to them by tradition, and then, if they do not see things as they are, at least they gave themselves a chance of doing so. Their work always has a distinctive freshness and strength. These qualities are conspicuous in Austin's books. One feels, as one reads them, that philosophy, or at least parts of it, might become rather more like science, and that philosophers might confront their subject more and one another less.

Philosophy done by Austin looks so different from philosophy done by others that its novelty has been exaggerated by both admirers and detractors. It is true that he made use of the evidence of language in a new way, but what he was trying to win from it was the kind of understanding that other philosophers had sought in other ways. So the goal was the same even if the method was different. But people have also exaggerated the extent to which he used a new method in philosophy. For it ought to be possible to put a method into precepts, but his only precept was that certain linguistic facts, hitherto largely neglected by philosophers, ought to be studied more carefully. His own success in following this precept should be attributed to his extreme sensitivity to language, which was, of course, essential for doing philosophy in his particular way, and to the extraordinary sharpness of his mind, which would have made itself felt whatever way he had chosen. No doubt it looks as if there must be more than this behind his work, some undivulged set of methodological precepts or theoretical assumptions, and that is perhaps the reason why he has been credited with the bizarre views about language that were mentioned earlier. But the true explanation leaves no room for such things.

It has been said that in philosophical discussion Austin, like Socrates, had a paralysing effect on others. This has an obvious application to his criticism, but it also applies to the way in which he developed his own ideas. For when he thought about something he kept very close to it and used every detail as a foothold, so that movement was, by philosophical standards, slow. But that is not the same thing as immobility, and what he inhibited in others was speed. Did he exaggerate the dangers of covering great distances in a few sentences? Or was his sure-footed style necessary?

There really is an analogy with Socrates. When Socrates was asked whether virtue could be taught, he said that he was unable to answer the question because he did not know what virtue was. He meant, of course, that he did not know exactly what it was. It is understandable that many people found his way of doing philosophy maddening. For consecutive thought is such a difficult achievement that it is natural to feel resentment when someone takes up the first word and questions its exact application. He is not playing the game. But of course he is not. That is his whole point.

However, Austin's way of making thought more realistic differed from Socrate's way. When Socrates tried to find out what virtue was, or what anything else was, he always looked for a definition which would tie the term down to its object in a straightforward way. But when Austin analysed a term, he did not look for such a simple connexion with reality. He believed that it would often turn out to be applicable to a variety of different cases, which could not be brought under any general formula. This was why he always collected such a wide range of examples and paid such close attention to detail. He never had the feeling that Wittgenstein stigmatized as 'the craving for generality' or 'the contemptuous attitude towards the particular case'. It is curious that some people have thought that when Austin made philosophy more empirical he made it easier. If anything, he made it more difficult. But, of course, what he really did was to show how difficult it is.

It would be a lengthy task to place him in relation to other philosophers in this century. But since two points of similarity with Wittgenstein have been mentioned—insistence on the detailed study of language, and of language in use—it would be as well to say how very unlike they were in other ways. Austin was less interested than Wittgenstein in the aetiology of unrealistic philosophical theories and in the part which is played by imagination in producing them. Wittgenstein would try to discover what pictures had come between thought and reality, and he would describe them with intuitive sympathy and understanding; whereas Austin would simply set to work to bring the discussion down to earth. Another, more important difference between them was that Austin believed in the possibility of systematic philosophy, whereas Wittgenstein, in his later period, did not.

His true precursor was G. E. Moore (though this would need to be qualified in many ways). He and Bertrand Russell were divided on a question that has always divided philosophers, the question whether non-technical language and thought need to be reformed. The reformers' case is that non-technical language cannot cover the new facts of science, and that there are philosophical arguments which show that it cannot even deal coherently with the old facts. Austin conceded the first of these two points, but maintained that it showed only that supplementation was needed, not correction: the second point he rejected, because he held that a careful examination of the part of language that was being condemned would nearly always show that it was the philosophical arguments that needed correction.

Whether or not non-technical language needs reform, is it as rich a vein as Austin believed it to be? He has been criticized for working it too assiduously, and there is some truth in this. Admittedly, it is, in general, a good policy to continue a search even beyond the point where returns begin to diminish, but there are, as he was well aware, other levels of language to be worked. For instance, even the primitive science of the British Empiricists of the seventeenth and eighteenth centuries is relevant to their account of perception. But in his lectures he does not examine the causal argument for the existence of sense-data (and says that he does not), and this leaves an important gap in his treatment of the traditional dualistic theory.

His critics are mostly preoccupied with the general question, to what extent he was working in the same field as earlier philosophers. This is partly a question of historical fact and partly a question of value. Even the historical question is hard to answer, because the originality of Austin's philosophy and the novelty of its form make it hard to see the underlying continuities. The question of value, which is difficult to answer for other reasons, arises in two ways: some believe that the perennial problems of philosophy are the important ones, so that neglect of them is a fault; and other believe that much of traditional philosophy is ill founded, so that its elimination is a virtue. Both beliefs are debatable, and it is obvious that neither of them is likely to be wholly true or wholly false. It would also be necessary to determine how much can be achieved in Austin's way (and how much he thought could be achieved). Is his kind of work a necessary element in all parts of philosophy? Is it, perhaps, the whole of some parts of philosophy? Or more than this, or less?

Fortunately he was only an original philosopher, so that we do not have to choose between following him in everything and totally rejecting the example that he set. He himself found such pretentious dilemmas ridiculous, and it is ironical that his particular intellectual qualities should sometimes have led others to make him into that kind of figure. But the scope and potentiality of his kind of work are difficult enough to assess without such nonsense. The first thing to be done is to try to see it for what it was.

AUSTIN AT CRITICISM

Stanley Cavell

EXCEPT for the notable translation of Frege's *Foundations of Arithmetic* and whatever reviews there are, *Philosophical Papers* collects all the work Austin published during his lifetime.[1] In addition, this modest volume includes two papers which will have been heard about, but not heard, outside Oxford and Cambridge. The first is one of the two pieces written before the war ('Meaning', 1940) and shows more clearly than the one published a year earlier ('Are There *A Priori* Concepts?', 1939) that the characteristic philosophical turns for which Austin became famous were deep in preparation.[2] The second previously unpublished paper ('Unfair to Facts', 1954) is Austin's rejoinder to P. F. Strawson's part in their symposium on truth, a debate which, I believe, Austin is widely thought to have lost initially, and to lose finally with this rejoinder. Austin clearly did not concur in this opinion, repeating the brunt of his countercharge at the end of the course of lectures he gave at Berkeley in 1958–59.[3] The remaining five papers have

---

[1] J. L. Austin, *Philosophical Papers*, ed. by J. O. Urmson and G. J. Warnock (Oxford, 1961).

[2] Curiously, the 1940 paper is the most Wittgensteinian of Austin's writings, in presenting an explicit theory of what causes philosophical disability and in the particular theory it offers ('We are using a working-model which fails to fit the facts that we really wish to talk about').

[3] These lectures, which he gave for many years at Oxford, were published posthumously under their Oxford title, *Sense and Sensibilia*, ed. by G. J. Warnock. Austin's original paper on 'Truth' (1950) is, of course, reprinted in the book under review. The remaining previously published papers are: 'Other Minds' (1946), 'A Plea for Excuses' (1956), 'Ifs and Cans' (1956), 'How to Talk—Some Simple Ways' (1953), and 'Pretending' (1958). All page references to these papers are cited according to their occurrence in *Philosophical Papers*. The concluding paper—'Performative Utterances'—is the transcript of a talk Austin gave for the B.B.C. in 1956; it is now superseded by the

all become part of the canon of the philosophy produced in English during the past generation, yielding the purest version of what is called 'Oxford philosophy' or 'ordinary language philosophy'. I will assume that anyone sharing anything like his direction from the English tradition of philosophy, and forced into his impatience with philosophy as it stands (or patience with the subject as it could become), will have found Austin's accomplishment and example inescapable.

As with any inheritance, it is often ambiguous and obscure in its effects. Two of these provide the subjects of my remarks here: the first concerns Austin's methods or purposes in philosophy; the second, related effect concerns the attitudes toward traditional philosophy which he inspires and sanctions.

I

I wish not so much to try to characterize Austin's procedures as to warn against too hasty or simple a description of them: their characterization is itself, or ought to be, as outstanding a philosophical problem as any to be ventured from within those procedures.

To go on saying that Austin attends to ordinary or everyday language is to go on saying, roughly, nothing—most simply because this fails to distinguish Austin's work from anything with which it could be confused. It does not, in the first place, distinguish his work from ordinary empirical investigations of language, a matter which has come to seem of growing importance since Austin's visits to the United States in 1955 and 1958. I do not say there is *no* relation between Austin's address to natural language and that of the descriptive linguist; he himself seems to have thought there was, or could be, a firmer intimacy than I find between them. The differences which, intuitively, seem to me critical, however, are these. In proceeding from ordinary language, so far as that is philosophically pertinent, one is in a frame of mind in which it seems (1) that one can as appropriately or truly be said to be looking at the world as looking at language; (2) that one is seeking necessary truths 'about' the world (or 'about' language) and therefore cannot be satisfied with anything I, at least, would

publication of the full set of lectures he used to give on this topic, and gave as the William James Lectures at Harvard in 1955, under the title *How to Do Things with Words*, ed. by J. O. Urmson.

recognize as a description of how people in fact talk—one might say one is seeking one kind of explanation of *why* people speak as they do; and even (3) that one is not finally interested *at all* in how 'other' people talk, but in determining where and why one wishes, or hesitates, to use a particular expression oneself. What investigations pursued in such frames of mind are supposed to show, I cannot say—perhaps whatever philosophy is supposed to show. My assumption is that there is something special that philosophy is about, and that Austin's procedures, far from avoiding this oldest question of philosophy, plunge us newly into it. I emphasize therefore that Austin himself was, so far as I know, never anxious to underscore philosophy's uniqueness, in particular not its difference from science; he seemed, indeed, so far as I could tell, to like denying any such difference (except that there is as yet no *established* science—of linguistics or grammar perhaps—to which philosophy may aspire to be assimilated).

The qualification 'ordinary language', secondly, does not distinguish this mode of philosophizing from any other of its modes—or, I should like to say, does not distinguish it philosophically. It does tell us enough to distinguish hawks from handsaws—Austin from Carnap, say—but not enough to start a hint about *how* ordinary language is appealed to, how one produces and uses its critical and characteristic forms of example, and why; nor about how and just where and how far this interest conflicts with that of any other temper of philosophy. The phrase 'ordinary language' is, of course, of no special interest; the problem is that its use has so often quickly suggested that the answers to the fundamental questions it raises, or ought to raise, are known, whereas they are barely imagined. Austin's only positive suggestion for a title to his methods was, I believe, 'linguistic phenomenology' ('Excuses', p. 130), and although he apologizes that 'that is rather a mouthful' (what he was shy about, I cannot help feeling, was that it sounds rather pretentious, or anyway philosophical) he does not retract it. This title has never caught on, partly, surely, because Austin himself invests no effort in formulating the significance of the phenomenological impulses and data in his work—data, perhaps, of the sort suggested above in distinguishing his work from the work of linguistic science.

Another characterization of Austin's procedures has impressive authority behind it. Professor Stuart Hampshire, in the memorial written for the *Proceedings of the Aristotelian Society* (1959–60)* on the occasion of Austin's death, provides various kinds of consideration—personal, social, historical, philosophical—for assessing Austin's achievement in philosophy. The device he adopts in his own assessment is to 'distinguish two slightly different theses that can plausibly be attributed to him: a strong and weak thesis' [p. 35]. The strong thesis is this: 'For every distinction of word and idiom that we find in common speech, there is a reason to be found, if we look far enough, to explain why this distinction exists. The investigation will always show that the greatest possible number of distinctions have been obtained by the most economical linguistic means' (ibid.). 'The weaker, or negative, thesis is that we must first have the facts, and all the facts, accurately stated before we erect a theory upon the basis of them' [p. 38]. The weaker thesis is 'negative', presumably, because it counsels study of ordinary language as a preliminary to philosophical advance, whereas the stronger claims 'that the multiplicity of fine distinctions, which such a study would disclose, would by itself answer philosophical questions about free-will, perception, naming and describing, conditional statements' [p. 41].

Hampshire's characterizations were quickly repudiated by Austin's literary executors (J. O. Urmson and G. J. Warnock, *Mind* [1961], 256–7),† the weaker thesis on the ground that it is an 'unambitious statement which cannot properly, or even plausibly, be magnified into a guiding *doctrine* . . . or recipe', the stronger on various grounds according to its various parts or formulations, but primarily on two: that Austin did sanction at least *some* new distinctions, and that he certainly did not claim that *all* philosophical questions could be answered by attention to fine distinctions. Urmson and Warnock are concerned, it emerges, to repudiate the idea that any such 'large assertions' are contained or implied in Austin's writings (or conversations). They conclude by saying: 'Austin sometimes gave . . . his own explanations. Why should they not be taken as meaning just what they say?'

I want in Section II to take up that challenge explicitly, if briefly. Immediately, it seems clear to me that Urmson and Warnock have trivialized Hampshire's formulations, whatever their several shortcomings. His weak thesis is hardly affected by being called an 'un-

* Reprinted in this volume.
† Reprinted here following Hampshire's paper.

ambitious statement' rather than a doctrine or a recipe, partly because it is not unambitious in Austin's practice, and partly because of Austin's conviction, and suggestion, that most philosophers have not merely proceeded in the absence of 'all the facts', but in the presence of practically *no facts at all*, or facts so poorly formulated and randomly collected as to defy comprehension. The issue raised is nothing less, I suggest, than the question: what is a philosophical fact? What are the data from which philosophy may, and must, proceed? It would be presumptuous to praise Austin for having pressed such questions to attention, but it is just the plain truth that nothing he says in 'his own explanations' begins to answer them.[1]

The strong thesis, in turn, is unaffected by switching its quantification from 'all' to 'some', for the issue raised is whether attention to fine distinctions can 'by itself' answer *any* philosophical question. At the place where Urmson and Warnock confidently assert that *some* questions can be answered in this way—a matter they take as 'scarcely controversial'—they omit the qualification 'philosophical', and offer no suggestion as to the particular way in which such answers are effected.[2] Finally, were we to let Urmson and Warnock's deflations distract us from philosophical curiosity

---

[1] If such questions strike a philosopher as fundamental to his subject, or even as relevant, then I do not see how it can be denied that their answer is going to entail 'large assertions' for which, moreover, so far as they concern Austin's practice, all the facts are directly at hand, sc., in Austin's practice. To accept Austin's explanations as full and accurate guides to his practice would be not only to confuse advice (which is about all he gave in this line) with philosophical analysis and literary-critical description (which is what is needed), but to confer upon Austin an unrivaled power of self-discernment. It is a mystery to me that what a philosopher says about his methods is so commonly taken at face value. Austin ought to be the last philosopher whose reflexive remarks are treated with this complacency, partly because there are so many of them, and partly because they suffer not merely the usual hazards of self-description but the further deflections of polemical animus. I return to this in the following section.

[2] Part of Hampshire's suggestion is that accepted philosophical theses and comparisons are drained, set against Austin's distinctions, of philosophical interest. This is a familiar enough fact of contemporary philosophizing, and it suggests to me that one requirement of new philosophical answers is that they elicit a new source of philosophical interest, or elicit this old interest i n a new way. Which is, perhaps, only a way of affirming that a change of *style* in philosophy is a profound change, and itself a subject of philosophical investigation.

about Austin's procedures, that could only inflame our psychological curiosity past composure; for the gap between Austin's unruffled advice to philosophical modesty and his obsession, to say the least, with the fineness of ordinary language and his claims to its revelation would then widen to dream-like proportions. His repeated disclaimer that ordinary language is certainly not the last word, 'only it *is* the *first* word' (alluded to by Urmson and Warnock), is reassuring only during polemical enthusiasm. For the issue is why the first, or *any*, word can have the kind of power Austin attributes to it. I share his sense that it has, but I cannot see that he has anywhere tried to describe the sources or domain of that power.

My excuse for butting into this controversy is that both sides seem to me to sanction a description of Austin's concerns which is just made to misdirect a further understanding of it and which is the more harmful because of its obvious plausibility, or rather its partial truth. I have in mind simply the suggestion that Austin's fundamental philosophical interest lay in drawing distinctions. Given this description of the method, and asked to justify it, what *can* one answer except: these are all the distinctions there are, or all that are real or important or necessary, and so forth, against which, it cannot be denied, Austin's own words can be levelled. Too obviously, Austin *is* continuously concerned to draw distinctions, and the finer the merrier, just as he often explains and justifies what he is doing by praising the virtues of natural distinctions over homemade ones. What I mean by saying that this interest is not philosophically fundamental is that his drawing of distinctions is always in the service of further purposes, and in particular two. (1) *Part* of the effort of any philosopher will consist in showing up differences, and one of Austin's most furious perceptions is of the slovenliness, the grotesque crudity and fatuousness, of the usual distinctions philosophers have traditionally thrown up. Consequently, one form his investigations take is that of repudiating the distinctions lying around philosophy—dispossessing them, as it were, by drawing better ones. And better not merely because finer, but because more solid, having, so to speak, a greater natural weight; appearing normal, even inevitable, when the others are luridly arbitrary; useful where the others seem twisted; real where the others are academic; fruitful where the others stop cold. This is, if you like, a negative purpose. (2) The positive purpose in

Austin's distinctions resembles the art critic's purpose in comparing and distinguishing works of art, namely, that in this crosslight the capacities and salience of an individual object in question are brought to attention and focus. Why comparison and distinction serve such purposes is, doubtless, not easy to say.[1] But it is, I take it, amply clear that their unique value is not accidentally joined to a particular task of criticism. They will not do everything, but nothing else evidently so surely defines areas of importance, suggests terms of description, or locates foci of purpose and stresses of composition: other works tell what the given work is about. In Austin's hands, I am suggesting, other words, compared and distinguished, tell what a given word is about. To know why they do, to trace how these procedures function, would be to see something of what it is he wishes words to teach, and hints at an explanation for our feeling, expressed earlier, that what we learn will not be new empirical facts about the world, and yet illuminating facts about the world. It is true that he asks for the difference between doing something by mistake and doing it by accident, but what transpires is a characterization of *what a mistake is* and (as contrasted, or so far as contrasted with this) what an accident is. He asks for the difference between being sure and being certain,

[1] That it is as much a matter of *comparing* as of distinguishing is clear—and takes its importance—from the way in which examples and, most characteristically, stories set the stage for Austin's distinctions. This is plainly different from their entrance in, say, philosophers like Russell or Broad or even Moore, whose distinctions do not serve to compare and (as it were) to elicit differences but rather, one could say, to provide labels for differences previously, somehow, noticed. One sometimes has the feeling that Austin's differences penetrate the phenomena they record—a feeling from within which the traditional philosopher will be the one who seems to be talking about mere words. The differing role of examples in these philosophical procedures is a topic of inexaggeratable importance, and no amount of words about 'ordinary language' or 'make all the distinctions' will convey to anyone who does not have the hang of it how to produce or test such examples. Anyone who has tried to teach from such materials and methods will appreciate this lack, which makes it the more surprising that no one, to my knowledge, has tried to compose a useful set of directions or, rather, to investigate exactly the ways one wishes to describe the procedure and notice their varying effectiveness for others, or faithfulness to one's sense of one's own procedures. Perhaps what is wanted really is a matter of conveying 'the hang' of something, and that is a very particular dimension of a subject to teach—familiar, for example, in conservatories of music, but also, I should guess, in learning a new game or entering any new territory or technique or apprenticing in a trade.

but what is uncovered is an initial survey of the complex and mutual alignments between mind and world that are necessary to successful knowledge. He asks for the difference between expressing belief and expressing knowledge (or between saying 'I believe' and saying 'I know') and what comes up is a new sense and assessment of the human limitations, or human responsibilities, of human knowledge; and so on.

As important as any of these topics or results within his investigations is the opportunity his purity of example affords for the investigation of philosophical method generally. Here we have, or could have—appearing before our eyes in terms and steps of deliberate, circumstantial obviousness—conclusions arrived at whose generality and convincingness depend, at least intuitively, upon a play of the mind characteristically philosophical, furnished with the usual armchairs and examples and distinctions and wonder. But how can such results have appeared? How can we learn something (about how we—how I—use words) which we cannot have failed to know? How can asking when we would *say* 'by mistake' (or what we call 'doing something by mistake') tell us what in the world a mistake *is*? How, given such obvious data, have philosophers (apparently) so long ignored it, forgetting that successful knowledge is a human affair, of human complexity, meeting human need and exacting human responsibility, bypassing it in theories of certainty which compare knowledge (unfavourably) with an inhuman ideal; or elaborated moral philosophies so abstracted from life as to leave, for example, no room for so homely, but altogether a central, moral activity as the entering of an excuse? What is philosophy that it can appear periodically so profound and so trivial, sometimes so close and sometimes so laughably remote, so wise and so stone stupid? What is philosophy that it causes those characteristic hatreds, yet mysterious intimacies, among its rivals? What kind of phenomenon is it whose past cannot be absorbed or escaped (as in the case of science) or parts of it freely admired and envied while other parts are despised and banished (as in art), but remains in standing competition, behind every closed argument waiting to haunt its living heirs?

II

One pass to these questions is opened by picking at the particular charges Austin brings against his competitors, past and present. His terms of criticism are often radical and pervasive, but this should not blunt an awareness that they are quite particular, characteristic, and finite. And each of them, as is true of any charge, implies a specific view taken of a situation. This is, indeed, one of Austin's best discoveries, and nothing is of more value in the example of his original investigations than his perfect faithfulness to that perception: it is what his 'phenomenology' turns on. That it fails him in criticizing other philosophers will have had various causes, but the productive possibility for us is that he has shown us the value of the procedure and that we are free to apply it for our better judgement.

I must limit myself to just one example of what I have in mind. Take Austin's accusing philosophers of 'mistakes'. It is worth noticing that the man who could inspire revelation by telling us a pair of donkey stories which lead us to take in the difference between doing something 'by mistake' and doing it 'by accident' ('Excuses', p. 133, n. 1) uses the term 'mistake' in describing what happens when, for example, Moore is discussing the question whether someone could have done something other than what in fact he did ('Ifs and Cans'). Now in the case of shooting your donkey when I meant to shoot mine, the correctness of the term 'mistake' is bound to the fact that questions like the following have definite answers. What mistake was made? (I shot your donkey.) What was mistaken for what? (Your donkey was mistaken for mine.) How can the mistake have occurred? (The donkeys look alike.) (How) could it have been prevented? (By walking closer and making sure, which a responsible man might or might not have been expected to do.) But there are no such answers to these questions asked about Moore's discussion—or perhaps we should say that the answers we would have to give would seem forced and more or less empty, a fact that ought to impress a philosopher like Austin.

What has Moore mistaken for what? Should we, for example, say that he mistakes the expression 'could have' for 'could have if I had chosen'? Then how and why and when can such a mistake have occurred? Was it because Moore has been hasty, thoughtless, sloppy, prejudiced . . .? But though these are the sorts of answers we are now forced to give (explanations which certainly account for mistakes, and which Austin is free with in accounting for the disasters of other philosophers), they are fantastic in this context; because there is no plausibility to the suggestion, taken seriously, that, whatever Moore has done, he has made a mistake: these charges are thus, so far, left completely in the air. Such charges can equally account for someone's having been involved in an accident or an inadvertence or the like. But, as Austin is fond of saying, each of these requires its own story; and does either of them fit the conduct of Moore's argument any better than the term 'mistake'? Then perhaps the mistake lies in Moore's thinking that 'could have' *means* 'could have if I had chosen'. But now this suggests not that Moore *took one thing for another* but that he took a tack he should not or need not have taken. This might be better expressed, as Austin does sometimes express it, by saying that Moore *was mistaken* in this, or perhaps by saying that *it was a mistake for him to*. But to say someone is mistaken requires again its own kind of story, different from the case of doing something by mistake or from making a mistake. In particular it suggests a context in which it is obvious, not that one thing looks like another, but why one would be led to do the mistaken, unhappy thing in question. The clearest case I think of is one of poor strategy: 'It is a mistake to castle at this stage.' This charge depends upon there being definite answers to questions like the following. Why does it seem to be a good thing to do? Why is it nevertheless not a good thing to do? What would be a better (safer, less costly, more subtle, stronger) thing to do instead? Such questions do fit certain procedures of certain intellectual enterprises, for example, the wisdom of taking a certain term as undefined, the dangers of appealing to the natural rights or the cult emotions of a certain section of the voting population, the difficulties of employing a rhyme scheme of a particular sort. What is Moore trying to do to which such a consideration of pluses and minuses would be relevant?

One may feel: 'Of course it is not a matter of better or worse. If Moore (or any philosopher) is wrong he is just wrong. What is absurd about the suggestion that he may have reasons for doing things his way is the idea that he may wish to tally up the advantages of being right over those of being wrong, where being right (that is, arriving at the truth) is the whole point. Cannot to say he has made a mistake—or, rather, to say he is mistaken—just mean that he is just wrong?' But it seems, rather, that 'mistaken' requires the idea of a wrong alternative (either taking one thing for another, or taking one tack rather than another). Is such an alternative, perhaps, provided by Austin's account of 'could have' (as sometimes indicative rather than subjunctive), and is Moore to be considered mistaken because he did not adopt or see Austin's line? But of course the problem of alternatives is a problem of what alternatives are open to a particular person at a particular moment: and what is 'open to' a particular person at a particular moment is a matter of some delicacy to determine—nothing less than determining whether someone could have done or seen something. However this may be, we still need, if we are to say 'mistaken', an account of why he took the 'alternative' he did. There seem to be just two main sorts of answers to such a question: either you admit that it is an attractive or plausible or seemingly inevitable one, *and account for such facts*, or you will find nothing of attraction or plausibility or seeming inevitability in it and assign its choice to ignorance, stupidity, incompetence, prejudice, and so forth. When Austin is discussing Moore, his respect pushes him to suggest the former sort of explanation, but he is clearly impatient with the effort to arrive at one and drops it as soon as possible (see, for example, pp. 154, 157).

Calling philosophers prejudiced or thoughtless or childish is a common enough salute among classical philosophers: one thinks of Bacon's or Descartes's or Hume's attitudes to other, especially to past, philosophers. It is time, perhaps, to start wondering why such charges should be characteristic of the way a philosophy responds to a past from which it has grown different or to a position with which it is incommensurable.

Other terms of criticism are implied in Austin's occasional recommendations of his own procedures. For example, one reason for following out the branches of Excuses thoroughly and separately is that 'Here at last we should be able to unfreeze, to loosen up and get going on agreeing about discoveries, however small, and on agreeing about how to reach agreement.' It is hard to convey to anyone who has not experienced it the rightness and relief words like these can have for students who have gone over the same distinctions, rehearsed the same fallacies, trotted out the same topics seminar after term paper, teaching assistant after lecturer, book after article. And the rightness and relief were completed in his confession that the subject of Excuses 'has long afforded me what philosophy is so often thought, and made, barren of—the fun of discovery, the pleasure of co-operation, and the satisfaction of reaching agreements'. These are real satisfactions, and I can testify that they were present throughout the hours of his seminar on this topic. It would hardly have occurred to anyone, in the initial grip of such satisfactions, to question whether they are appropriate to philosophy (as they obviously are to logic or physics or historical scholarship) any more than they are, in those ways or proportions, to politics or religion or art; to wonder whether their striking presence in our work now did not suggest that we had changed our subject.

The implied terms of criticism in this recommendation are, of course, that we are frozen, tied up, stopped. Granted a shared sense that this describes our position, one wants to know how we arrived at it. Sometimes Austin attributes this to our distended respect for the great figures of the past (see, for example, 'Excuses', p. 131), sometimes to general and apparently congenital weaknesses of philosophy itself: 'over-simplification, schematization, and constant obsessive repetition of the same small range of jejune "examples" are . . . far too common to be dismissed as an occasional weakness of philosophers'. And this characteristic weakness— something he refers to as 'scholastic', following the call of the major line of British Empiricists—he attributes 'first, to an obsession with a few particular words, the uses of which are over-simplified, not really understood or carefully studied or correctly described; and second, to an obsession with a few (and nearly always the same) half-studied "facts" ' (*Sense and Sensibilia*, p. 3). So far the criticisms proceed on familiar Baconian or Cartesian ground; the philosopher of good will and the man of common sense will work together to see through philosophy and prejudice to the world as it is.

At some point Austin strikes into criticisms which go beyond the impatience and doubt which begin modern philosophy, new ones necessary perhaps just because philosophy seems to have survived that impatience and doubt (or emasculated them, in turn, into academic subjects). I find three main lines here. (1) Most notably in *Sense and Sensibilia*, he enters charges against philosophers which make it seem not merely that their weakness is somehow natural to the enterprise, imposed on men of ordinary decency by an ill-governed subject, but that their work is still more deeply corrupt: we hear of philosophers having glibly 'trotted out' new uses of phrases (p. 19); of subtle 'insinuation' which is 'well calculated' to get us 'where the sense-datum theorist wants to have us' (p. 25); of bogus dichotomies, grotesque exaggeration, gratuitous ideas (p. 54)—phrases which, at this point, carry the suggestion that they are deliberate or wilful exaggerations and the like, and pursued with an absence of obvious motivation matched only by an Iago. (2) On more than one occasion he suggests that philosophical delinquency arises from a tendency to Dionysian abandon: we are warned of the blindness created in the *'ivresse des grandes profondeurs'* (p. 127) and instructed in the size of problems philosophers should aim at—*'In vino*, possibly, *"veritas"*, but in a sober symposium *"verum"* ' ('Truth', p. 85). (3) Finally, and quite generally, he conveys the impression that the philosophers he is attacking are not really serious, that, one may say, they have written unauthentically (cf. *Sense and Sensibilia*, p. 29).

I cannot attempt here to complete the list of Austin's terms of criticism, any more than I can now attempt to trace the particular target each of them has; and I have left open all assessment of their relative seriousness and all delineation of the particular points of view from which they are launched. I hope, however, that the bare suggestion that Austin's work raises, and helps to settle, such topics will have served my purposes here, which, in summary, are these: (1) To argue that, without such tracing and assessment and delineation, we cannot know the extent to which these criticisms are valid and the extent to which they project Austin's own temper. (2) To point out that Austin often gives no reasons whatever for thinking one or other of them true, never making out the application to a philosopher of a term like 'mistaken' or 'imprecise' or 'bogus' or the like according to anything like the standards he imposes in his own constructions. This discrepancy is not, I believe, peculiar to Austin, however clearer in him than in other philosophers; my feeling is that if it could be understood here, one would understand something about the real limitations, or liabilities, of the exercise of philosophy. (3) To register the fact that his characteristic terms of criticism are new terms, new for our time at least, though not in all cases his alone; and that these new modes of criticism are deeply characteristic of modern philosophy. (4) To suggest that if such terms do not seem formidable directions of criticism, and perhaps not philosophical at all (as compared, say, with terms such as 'meaningless', 'contradiction', 'circular', and so forth), that may be because philosophy is only just learning, for all its history of self-criticism and self-consciousness, to become conscious of itself in a new way, at further ranges of its activity. One could say that attention is being shifted from the character of a philosopher's argument to the character of the philosopher arguing. Such a shift can, and perhaps in the Anglo-American tradition of philosophy it generally does, serve the purest political or personal motive: such criticism would therefore rightly seem philosophically irrelevant, if sometimes academically charming or wicked. The shift could also, one feels, open a new literary-philosophical criticism, in a tradition which knows how to claim, for example, the best of Kierkegaard and Nietzsche. Whatever the outcome, however, what I am confident of is that the relevance of the shift should itself become a philosophical problem. (5) To urge, therefore, a certain caution or discrimination in following Austin's procedures, using his attempts to define in new and freer and more accurate terms the various failings—and hence the various powers —of philosophy, without imitating his complacency, and even prejudice, in attaching them where he sees (but has not proven) fit. It suggests itself that a sound procedure would be this: to enter all criticisms which seem right, but to treat them phenomenologically, as temptations or feelings; in a word, as data, not as answers.

These purposes are meant to leave us, or put us, quite in the dark about the sources of philosophical failure, and about the relation between the tradition of philosophy and the new critics of that tradition, and indeed about the relation between any conflicting philosophies. For quite in the dark is where we ought to know we are. If, for example, that failure of Moore's which we discussed earlier is not to be understood as a mistake, then what is it? No doubt it would be pleasanter were we able not to ask such a question —except that philosophy seems unable to proceed far without criticizing its past, any more than art can proceed without imitating it, or science without summarizing it. And anything would be pleasanter than the continuing rehearsals—performable on cue by any graduate student in good standing—of how Descartes was mistaken about dreams, or Locke about truth, or Berkeley about God, or Kant about things-in-themselves or about moral worth, or Hegel about 'logic', or Mill about 'desirable', and so forth; or about how Berkeley mistook Locke, or Kant Hume, or Mill Kant, or everybody Mill, and so forth. Such 'explanations' are no doubt essential, and they may account for everything we need to know, except why any man of intelligence and vision has ever been attracted to the subject of philosophy. Austin's criticisms, where they stand, are perhaps as external and snap as any others, but he has done more than any philosopher (excepting Wittgenstein) in the Anglo-American tradition to make clear that there is a coherent tradition to be dealt with. If he has held it at arm's length, and falsely assessed it, that is just a fault which must bear its own assessment; it remains true that he has given us hands for assessing it in subtler ways than we had known. The first step would be to grant to philosophers the ordinary rights of language and vision Austin grants all other men: to ask of them, in his spirit, why they should say what they say where and when they say it, and to give the *full story* before claiming satisfaction. That Austin pretends to know the story, to have heard it all before, is no better than his usual antagonist's assumption that there is no story necessary to tell, that everything is fine and unproblematic in the tradition, that philosophers may use words as they please, possessing the right or power—denied to other mortals—of knowing, without investigating, the full source and significance of their words and deeds.

It is characteristic of work like Austin's—and this perhaps carries a certain justice—that criticism of it will often take the form of repudiating it as philosophy altogether. Let me conclude by attempting to make one such line of criticism less attractive than it has seemed to some philosophers to be.

A serviceable instance is provided by a sensational book, published a few years ago by Mr. Ernest Gellner (*Words and Things*, London, 1959) in which this author congratulates himself for daring to unmask the sterility and mystique of contemporary English philosophy by exposing it to sociology. First of all, unmasking is a well-turned modern art, perhaps *the* modern intellectual art, and its practitioners must learn not to be misled themselves by masks, and to see their own. I mean both that unmasking is itself a phenomenon whose sociology needs drawing, and also that the philosophy Gellner 'criticizes' is itself devoted to unmasking. If, as one supposes, this modern art develops with the weakening or growing irrelevance of given conventions and institutions, then the position of the unmasker is by its nature socially unhinged, and his responsibility for his position becomes progressively rooted in his single existence. This is the occasion for finding a mask or pose of one's own (sage, prophet, saint, and so forth). Austin was an Englishman, an English professor. If I say he *used* this as a mask, I mean to register my feeling that he must, somewhere, have known his criticisms to be as unjustified as they were radical, but felt them to be necessary in order that his work get free, and heard. It would have served him perfectly, because its Englishness made it unnoticeable as a pose, because what he wanted from his audience required patience and co-operation, not depth and upheaval, and because it served as a counterpoise to Wittgenstein's strategies of the sage and the ascetic (which Nietzsche isolated as the traditional mask of the Knower; that is, as the only form in which it could carry authority).

Far from a condemnation, this is said from a sense that in a modern age to speak the truth may require the protection of a pose, and even that the necessity to posture may be an authentic mark of the possession of truth. It may not, too; that goes without saying. And it always is dangerous, and perhaps self-destructive. But to the extent it is necessary, it is not the adoption of pose which is to be condemned, but the age which makes it necessary. (Kierkegaard and Nietzsche, with terrible consciousness, condemned both themselves and the age for their necessities; and both maintained, at great cost, the doubt that their poses were really necessary—which is what it must feel like to know your pose.)

The relation of unmasking to evaluation is always delicate to trace. Gellner imagines that his sociological reduction in itself proves the intellectual inconsequence and social irrelevance or political conservatism of English philosophy. (His feeling is common enough; why such psychological or sociological analyses appear to their performers—and to some of their audience—as reductive in this way is itself a promising subject of psychological and sociological investigation.) Grant for the argument that his analysis of this philosophy as a function of the Oxford and Cambridge tutorial system, the conventions of Oxford conversation, the distrust of ideology, the training in classics and its companion ignorance of science, and so forth, is accurate and relevant enough. Such an analysis would at most show the conditions or outline the limitations—one could say it makes explicit the conventions—within which this work was produced or initiated. To touch the question of its value, the value of those conventions themselves, as they enter the texture of the work, would have to

74

be established. This is something that Marx and Nietzsche and Freud, our teachers of unmasking, knew better than their progeny.

Still, it can seem surprising that radical and permanent philosophy can be cast in a mode which merges comfortably in the proprieties of the common room—in the way it can seem surprising that an old man, sick and out of fortune, constructing sayings (in consort with others) polite enough for the game in a lady's drawing-room, and entertaining enough to get him invited back, should have been saying the maxims of La Rochefoucauld.

Seven published papers are not many, and those who care about Austin's work will have felt an unfairness in his early death, a sense that he should have had more time. But I think it would be wrong to say that his work remains incomplete. He once said to me, and doubtless to others: 'I had to decide early on whether I was going to write books or to teach people how to do philosophy usefully.' Why he found this choice necessary may not be clear. But it is as clear as a clear Berkeley day that he was above all a teacher, as is shown not merely in any such choice, but in everything he wrote and (in my hearing) spoke, with its didactic directions for profitable study, its lists of exercises, its liking for sound preparation and its disapproval of sloppy work and lazy efforts. In example and precept, his work is complete, in a measure hard to imagine matched. I do not see that it is anywhere being followed with the completeness it describes and exemplifies. There must be, if this is so, various reasons for it. And it would be something of an irony if it turned out that Wittgenstein's manner were easier to imitate than Austin's; in its way, something of a triumph for the implacable professor.

A SYMPOSIUM ON AUSTIN'S METHOD*

I. J. O. Urmson

AUSTIN, though he admired the methods and objectives of some philosophers more than others, held no views whatever about *the* proper objective or *the* proper method of philosophy. One reason for this is that he thought that the term 'philosophy', without any stretching, covered, and always had covered, a quite heterogeneous set of inquiries which clearly had no single objective and which were unlikely to share a single method. Another reason is that he thought that those inquiries which had continued to be called philosophical and had not hived off under some special name (as have, for example, physics, biology, psychology, and mathematics) were precisely those for the solution of whose problems no standard methods had yet been found. No one knows what a satisfactory solution to such problems as those of free-will, truth, and human personality would look like, and it would be baseless dogmatism to lay down in advance any principles for the proper method of solving them.

All philosophers, therefore, are entitled to pursue those problems which most urgently claim their attention and to which their ability and training are best suited; and they are entitled to use any technique that seems hopeful to them, though we cannot expect that every technique will be equally successful. Austin, for his part, thought that he had developed a technique for tackling certain problems that particularly interested him, problems about the nature of language. He did not imagine that he had first formulated the problems and he did not imagine that he had dis-

* Presented in a symposium on 'The Philosophy of John Austin' at the sixty-second annual meeting of the American Philosophical Association, Eastern Division, December 29, 1965.

covered the only possible method of tackling them; but he thought that he had devised a sort of 'laboratory technique' which could be fruitfully used for finding solutions to them very much fuller, more systematic, and more accurate than any hitherto. The justification for the use of the technique was its success in practice; if another technique proved more successful it would be better. In deserting Austin's technique for this we would not be abandoning one theory of the nature of philosophy for another, but doing something more like substituting the camera for the human eye in determining the winners of horse races. This technique, like other research techniques, could not be fully exhibited in action in the conventional book, article, or lecture. Though Austin gave some general indications about it in his writings, particularly in 'A Plea for Excuses' and 'Ifs and Cans', its details are inevitably less widely known than his more conventional work, though this clearly drew heavily on the results obtained by the use of the technique. Yet Austin himself thought it his most important contribution, and hoped that a systematic use of it might lead to the foundation of a new science of language, transcending and superseding the work of traditional philosophers, grammarians, and linguisticians in that field. So a fairly full account of it by someone (myself) who frequently observed Austin employing it may well be of more value than any critical comments I might make on his published writings. Moreover, I think that a knowledge of it does help in the understanding of the general character of the published writings. In giving my account of this technique of Austin's I shall make use of some notes by Austin, too fragmentary, brief, and disordered for publication, characteristically entitled 'Something about one way of possibly doing one part of philosophy'.

It will be best to start with as factual as possible an account of the actual employment of the technique, not searching as yet for a philosophically helpful account of what it is being used for. Let it suffice at present to say that the aim is to give as full, clear, and accurate account as possible of the expression (words, idioms, sentences, grammatical forms) of some language, or variety of language, common to those who are engaged in using the technique. In practice the language will usually be the mother tongue of the investigators, since one can employ the technique only for a language of which one is a master.

We cannot investigate a whole natural language at a sitting, or

77

series of sittings; so we must first choose some area of discourse[1] for investigation—discourse about responsibility, or perception, or memory, or discourse including conditional clauses, to mention first areas traditionally of interest to philosophers; or discourse about artifacts, or discourse in the present perfect tense, to add less traditional fields of investigation. Austin always recommended that beginners on the technique should choose areas that were not already philosophical stamping grounds. Having chosen our area of discourse, we must then collect as completely as possible all the resources of the language, both idiom and vocabulary, in that area. If we have chosen the field of responsibility, for example, we must not start by offering generalizations about voluntary and involuntary actions, but must collect the whole range of terms and idioms adumbrated in 'A Plea for Excuses'—words like 'willingly', 'inadvertently', 'negligently', 'clumsily', and 'accidentally', idioms like 'he negligently did X' and 'he did X negligently'. In the field of artifacts we must collect all such terms as 'tool', 'instrument', 'implement', 'furniture', 'equipment', and 'apparatus'. In this task common sense is needed; a useful collection of terms and idioms require art and judgment; thus it probably would be a mistake to omit the term 'furniture' when examining discourse about artifacts, but it is unlikely to be necessary to include all names for all kinds of furniture—'table', 'chair', 'stool', etc. Moreover, the notion of a field of discourse is imprecise, and we may initially be unclear whether a given term should or should not be included in it. Austin's precept was that, when in doubt whether a term was necessary or really belonged to the field in question, we should start by including it, since it is easier to strike out later terms that turn out to be intruders than it is to repair omissions. The most obvious devices for getting a fairly complete list are: (*a*) free association, where the investigators add any terms to the initial few that occur to them as being related; (*b*) the reading of relevant documents—not the works of philosophers but, in the field of responsibility, such things as law reports, in the field of artifacts

---

[1] I write 'area of discourse'; Austin's notes speak merely of an 'area'. There is little point in searching for a precise definition of an 'area of discourse'; terms are part of a single area of discourse if it is of interest to compare and contrast their employment, and if not, not. Some expressions may usefully be studied as falling into two different areas. There is no certain test of whether a term falls into a given area or not, prior to our investigation.

such things as mail-order catalogues; (c) use of the dictionary, less ambitiously by looking up terms already noted and adding those used in the definitions until the circle is complete, or, more ambitiously, by reading right through the dictionary—Austin, who must have read through the *Little Oxford Dictionary* very many times, frequently insisted that this did not take so long as one would expect.

At the stage of preliminary collection of terms and idioms the work is more quickly and more exhaustively done by a team. Austin always insisted that the technique was at all stages best employed by a team of a dozen or so working together; the members supplemented each other and corrected each other's oversights and errors. Having collected its terms and idioms, the group must then proceed to the second stage in which, by telling circumstantial stories and conducting dialogues, they give as clear and detailed examples as possible of circumstances under which this idiom is to be preferred to that, and that to this, and of where we should (do) use this term and where that. Austin's two stories of the shooting of the donkey to illustrate the circumstances in which we should, when speaking carefully, prefer to say 'accidentally' or 'by mistake' will indicate the sort of thing to be done at this stage ('A Plea for Excuses', *Philosophical Papers*, p. 133). It is also important to tell stories and make dialogues as like as possible to those in which we should employ a certain term or idiom in which it would not be possible, or would strike us as inappropriate, to use that term or idiom. We should also note things which it is not possible to say in any circumstances, though not manifestly ungrammatical or otherwise absurd (Aristotle's observation that one cannot be pleased quickly or slowly is the sort of thing that is meant here). This second stage will occupy several sessions; it is not a matter to be completed in a few minutes.

We have now got our lists of terms and idioms (first stage), and a list of circumstantial stories illustrating how these expressions can and cannot occur, according to context. Experience shows that a group, not just a group of Oxford philosophers but, say, a mixed American and British group, can reach virtual unanimity on these matters. Maybe something that seems perfectly in order to all the rest will sound odd to one member, or vice versa. When this happens it can be noted down and it may be of interest. But getting things right up to this stage is a group activity, and it is easy for a single individual to make mistakes initially that he can be brought to see. The device of a statistical survey of 'what people would say' by means of a questionnaire is no substitute for the group, (1) because there cannot be the necessary detail in the questionnaire, (2) because the untrained answerers can so easily make mistakes, (3) because we are raising questions where unanimity is both desirable and obtainable. The group is its own sample, and its members can always ask their friends and relations 'What would you say if . . .?' as required.[1]

Austin always insisted that during the work so far described all theorizing should be rigidly exlcuded. We must make up detailed stories embodying the felicitous and the infelicitous, but carefully abstain from too early an attempt to explain why. Premature theorizing can blind us to the linguistic facts; premature theorizers bend their idiom to suit the theory, as is shown all too often by the barbarous idiom found in the writings of philosophers who outside of philosophy speak with complete felicity. But eventually the stage must come at which we seek to formulate our results. At this stage we attempt to give general accounts of the various expressions (words, sentences, grammatical forms) under consideration; they will be correct and adequate if they make it clear why what is said in our various stories is or is not felicitous, is possible or impossible. Thus it is an empirical question whether the accounts given are correct and adequate, for they can be checked against the data collected. Of course, if we have rushed the earlier stages new linguistic facts may be later adduced that invalidate the accounts, this is the universal predicament of empirical accounts. But though the accounts are empirical, the discovery and formulation of adequate ones is a matter requiring great skill and some luck; there is no rule of thumb available.

We may now, if we wish, go on to compare the accounts that we have thus arrived at with what philosophers have commonly said about the expressions in question (or with what grammarians

[1] An illustration: so shrewd an operator as Noam Chomsky says on p. 15 of his admirable *Syntactic Structures* that 'Read you a book on modern music?' is not a grammatical sentence of English. Consider the dialogue: A. 'Please read me a book on modern music. B. 'Read you a book on modern music? Not for all the gold in Fort Knox!' Chomsky should have been working in a group. The statistical datum that Urmson allows, Chomsky disallows, this sentence is of no interest. Chomsky has made one of his few errors, as a group of us discovered while reading him.

have said). If one does so one may go on to a further project, the examination of traditional philosophical arguments in the light of the results of the technique. This type of project is illustrated by Austin's *Sense and Sensibilia;* here a thumbnail sketch only is given of the use of the technique on various groups of terms: 'illusion', 'delusion', and 'hallucination'; 'looks', 'appears', 'seems', etc.; 'real', 'apparent', 'imaginary', etc.; Austin then tries to show that various traditional arguments depend for their apparent plausibility on the systematic misconstruction and interchange of these and similar key terms. The book illustrates this stage of the inquiry; I do not now ask whether it is a successful illustration.

So much for the actual technique which Austin recommended. Briefly, a group of interested people collects the terms and idioms specially connected with an area of discourse; produces examples in context of the healthy use of these expressions and morbid examples of their misapplication; finally, gives accounts of these expressions which will explain the observed facts about what we do and what we do not say when employing them.

Why did Austin want to do this?

1. He thought that by the use of this technique one could make explicit a surprisingly and excitingly rich and subtle set of distinctions, of sufficient practical importance to have been incorporated into the structure of the language under investigation. In making them explicit one simultaneously gains a richer understanding of a language in which one is interested and of the non-linguistic world the language is used to talk about (in distinguishing mistakes from accidents, etc., one sees more clearly the ways in which actions can be defective). The distinctions made in one language need not be the same as those made in another; one does not discover distinctions that must be made, but ones which can be, and are, made. No doubt for special technical purposes or when we are faced with new situations, the distinctions we can thus find ready-made are inadequate, and we need to invent new ones. But Austin thought that the distinctions which *philosophers* thought up in their studies and employed instead of those in ordinary language were very jejune and poverty-stricken by comparison with those already made in ordinary[1] language. Certainly

---

[1] Here, as commonly among Austin and his associates, 'ordinary' is a technical term, meaning 'nonphilosophical'; thus the terms of modern physics are for present purposes part of ordinary language. The term is unfortunate

many of the philosophers who so act do so because they maintain that the distinctions of the natural languages are unworthy of serious interest and must make way for those of a specially constructed 'scientific' language; Austin thought that this could be explained only by the unawareness of these philosophers of the subtlety of ordinary language. Austin did not want to deny that in various places and ways a natural language could embody conceptual muddles; he had no *a priori* certainty that language must always be 'perfectly in order as it stands'; he merely thought that a far closer examination of the resources of language than has been traditionally made yields surprisingly rich dividends.

This first aim, as Austin well knew, is no novelty; but he thought that it had been pursued in too piecemeal and too unsystematic a manner, with insufficient effort to collect data, to yield a full reward.

2. Austin hoped that this work might be the beginning of a new science of language, which would incorporate the work of philosophers, grammarians, and linguisticians. A close look at the actual facts of language quickly invalidated, he maintained, most of the prevalent schemata, theories, and generalizations. A new terminology was needed for the accurate study of language, which would emerge in its study; the distinction of locutionary, illocutionary, and perlocutionary acts, made in *How to Do Things with Words*, was intended as a contribution to this new terminology.

3. Austin also believed that the careful examination of the ways in which we talk in a given field would save us from some of the muddles into which philosophers fall in discussing the traditional problems of philosophy. These problems at least arise in ordinary language; so a close examination of this language will be at least a 'begin-all' if not an 'end-all' in the prudent examination of them.

---

because it is also true that Austin investigated mainly the resources of ordinary (= 'everyday', 'non-technical') as opposed to technical language. Austin was not opposed to the coining by scientists and other technical people of useful terms, nor to the investigation of them by philosophers; he himself did not investigate them partly because he thought that he had not the necessary background knowledge, partly because the philosophical problems that most interested him did not arise in such areas. Also Austin was not opposed to philosophers' inventing technical terms for their own use, which he constantly did himself; the point made in the text is that in studying the expressions of a natural language we shall find matter of greater interest than in studying the proposed alternatives of philosophers.

If a philosopher wishes to use words in 'special' senses, no doubt he may, and is not necessarily mistaken in principle; but a conceptual revision will prudently be based on a thorough understanding of what is being revised. Too often philosophers do not use words in new carefully thought-out ways, but rather use ordinary language in a rather deviant manner, while at the same time relying on the entailments and implications of non-deviant use. I have already mentioned Austin's attempt to illustrate this unhappy feature of philosophical practice in *Sense and Sensibilia*.

4. Austin hoped that both the detailed examinations of areas of speech and the new concepts about language therein evolved would be of help to such other disciplines as jurisprudence and economics. I imagine that Hart would not object to my pointing to his work on jurisprudence as a case where this has happened.

Finally, the question may be raised: why do this sort of thing rather than something else? Let me quote quite literally Austin's own note on this point, which is intelligible enough as it stands:

> Shan't learn everything, so why not do something else? Well; not whole even of philosophy but firstly always has *been* philosophy, since Socrates. And some slow successes. Advantages of slowness and cooperation. Be your size. Small men. Foolproof × geniusproof. Anyone with patience can do something. Leads to discoveries and agreement. Is amusing. Part of *personal* motive of my colleagues to avoid interminable bickering or boring points of our predecessors: also remember all brought up on classics: no quarrel with maths etc., just ignorant.

This sketch of Austin's techniques is now complete. As is clear, and as he knew, neither his aims nor his methods were wholly new in outline. What is new is the insistence on a technique designed to produce something much more precise and systematic than had hitherto been achieved, and the belief that the technique, patiently and systematically followed, could be the beginning of a new science of language, capable of standing alone with its own procedures and secure results.

But, though the sketch is complete, I should like to add some remarks of my own about Austin's claim that it was possible for a group to attain virtual unanimity about what can and cannot be said in various contexts and on the accounts of the various expressions based on these data. It is on this point that he has been most often criticized and misunderstood.

First let us consider the status of this claim. It is well known to everybody else, and need not be presumed to have escaped Austin's attention, that natural languages are not unchanging and monolithic; in fact they evolve continuously through time, and at any given time dialects and idiolects of geographically and socially separated groups and persons can be distinguished. If Austin had therefore claimed that any group of, say, English speakers, however collected, would give unanimous reports on what they would say in various circumstances, his claim would obviously be false. But though not an unchanging monolith, language is not a Heraclitean river either, certainly not a set of private Heraclitean rivers. Though I do have to guess, divine, speculate, in trying to follow a sports report in an American newspaper, my interpretation of American writings on law, music, history, and the like is no more speculative than that of British writings, though one has to be aware of a few special idioms. What Austin essentially wished to claim was that it was not as a matter of fact difficult to collect a group together in which speech differences were of marginal importance, and that where initially there was disagreement it should not be too readily ascribed to divergent speech habits; nearly always these initial disagreements would disappear after careful discrimination and presentation of cases. The claim is, therefore, the empirical one that groups are readily to be formed the members of which would all make the same linguistic discriminations. It is no doubt true that groups could be contrived of which this would be false, and Austin did not need to deny it.

Secondly, let us consider on what questions unanimity is to be achieved; critics who misunderstand Austin on this point often think that he is obviously wrong and that nothing better than unrevealing statistics can ever be available. Let us suppose that a vocabulary including the words 'fleshy', 'chubby', 'fat', 'portly', and 'obese' is under consideration and we embark on the difficult task of trying to discriminate among them. Now it is easy to imagine a human figure such that, if asked to choose one of these words to describe it, members of a group would give widely different answers; it is absurd to imagine that Austin intended to deny this. He would rather have claimed that if this happened the group could arrive at unanimity that all the different answers were possible answers. This would be ground for the conclusion that the words in question were not mutually exclusive. But to pose questions where such an array of answers is possible is a clumsy use of the technique. More valuable questions would be such as: 'Consider Winston Churchill; would you call him (*a*) chubby, (*b*) portly?' Would we not give a virtuously unanimous answer to each of those questions. We could go on to ask such a question as 'Can you envisage a figure which we should describe as chubby but not fleshy or as fleshy but not chubby?' Austin thought that unanimity could be obtained on whether such figures could be envisaged, and, if so, which. In sufficiently imprecise situations it will always be possible to say different things; it is essential to ask questions in so sufficiently detailed and precise circumstances that one thing will be seen to be more appropriate to say than another. Austin's claim was that it was easy to gather groups such that there would be agreement on what was most appropriate. In making this claim Austin was certainly not wholly wrong; I have been a member of such a group under Austin's guidance more than once where his claim was abundantly fulfilled; I have also joined in groups, with and without Austin, where little headway was made. In these latter cases were we inefficient or was Austin's claim falsified in them? I do not know how to answer that question. Certainly Austin, more than anybody, has enabled many of us to find a richness in language greater than we had ever expected to find.

But what of those, and there are such, who, when confronted with the data and results of what seems to the group to be a successful exercise of the Austinian technique, reply that the refinements and the subtle distinctions claimed to be discovered in language are the products of the imagination of the group, that they themselves do not find these riches in language? Or what of those who use a quite different language, such as ancient Greek, of which the conceptual framework is importantly different? Some of the former objectors may just have dirty ears; but to neither group need the results, provided that they are clear and definite, be devoid of interest. For while part of the interest of them is claimed to lie in their illumination of actual language, of our own ways of talking, none the less any set of fine discriminations may be of interest. Clarification of, say, the ancient Greek distinction between *arete* ('virtue') and *enkrateia* ('continence') does not cease to be of interest to us because we do not employ it ourselves; similarly, such distinctions as Austin indicates in 'A Plea for

Excuses' would not cease to be of interest even if we did not recognize them, as I largely do, as giving us a better understanding of our own way of talking.

II. W. V. O. Quine

ONCE there were but a handful of therapeutic positivists and a multitude of chronic metaphysicians. Now there are therapists in every college. The epidemic has been stemmed and the therapy is routine. How are the veteran therapists hereafter to occupy their minds? One way is by directing their efforts against a continuing but less virulent form of the infection, namely, against philosophical perplexity in the lay mind. Ryle in his *Dilemmas* had a successful go at this. Another way is by continuing the kind of language study that went into the therapy, but continuing it now as a line of pure research. Characteristic writings of Austin's seem to fit in here.

Austin's technique as Urmson has described it is a mode of introspective inquiry into semantics, conducted by native speakers in groups. It is an inquiry that is continuous with portions of linguistics, and probably capable both of benefiting from professional work in that field and of supplementing it. Despite its philosophical antecedents, it is an inquiry whose affinities in linguistics are not in theoretical linguistics; they are in lexicography. It is an inquiry into subtle differences in the semantics, or circumstances of use, of selected English phrases.

Semantic theory is plagued by the lack of an acceptable general definition of meaning. A definition of meaning simply as circumstances of use is inadequate because of vagueness as to how much may relevantly be included under 'circumstances'. However, that general problem of demarcating the circumstances is a problem that plagues semantic theory and not lexicographic practice, nor, in particular, Austin's kind of inquiry. As long as one limits oneself to volunteering specific circumstances of use of expressions, the problem of meaning does not arise. There is a certain immunity in the concrete case.

The nature of this immunity may be clarified by an analogy from proof theory. Consider the notion of a mechanical method. In order to prove or even clearly state Godel's theorem of the incompletability of number theory, or Church's theorem of the undecidability of quantification theory, we have to define the notion of a mechanical method; and recursiveness was the answer. But in showing the decidability of a theory we need no definition of mechanical method; we just present a method which everyone would call mechanical. Similarly Austin was able to present specific circumstances of use without broaching the problem of meaning.

For that matter, the same can be said of what Carnap calls explication—the sort of conceptual reduction that figures prominently in the philosophy of mathematics and elsewhere. Each explication stands on its own merits, without broaching the general problem of synonymy or meaning. But I digress.

Austin's manner of semantic inquiry contrasts with main trends in linguistics in being avowedly introspective. Any linguist certainly introspects his language much of the time, but Austin was unusual in adhering to introspective data exclusively. Such data are said to be untrustworthy because of their subjectivity, but, as Mr. Urmson explained, Austin had an ingenious remedy for that: he gained objectivity by group introspection.

This remedy is an instance of a perhaps more widely useful strategy. In its general form the strategy consists in exploiting the subjective and then objectifying it afterward by a social summation over individual subjects. The strategy has uses also apart from the introspective situation. Thus suppose some exotic field linguist from overseas were here testing us to see what things we apply various terms to. He would find, by induction from sample tests, that each of us will apply the term 'pup' on sight to just the things to which each of us will apply 'young dog'. In this way he will discover that our terms 'pup' and 'young dog' are coextensive. But he could not, by that method, equate 'bachelor' with 'unmarried man'; for no two of us will even apply 'bachelor' on sight to all and only the same persons, let alone 'unmarried man', given our differences in acquaintance and information. However, our visiting linguist can still equate 'bachelor' with 'unmarried man' after all if he resorts to the strategy of first studying each subject in isolation and only afterward objectifying by a social summation. He will find that each of us will apply 'bachelor' just when *he* will apply 'unmarried man'.

Let me broach next the utterly boring question, as Urmson called it, of how to classify Austin's introspective semantics. Is it to be called philosophy? To call it that does not, from Austin's point of view as described by Urmson, say much about it; philosophy is 'a heterogeneous set of enquiries'. I applaud this casual attitude toward the demarcation of disciplines. Names of disciplines should be seen only as technical aids in the organization of curricula and libraries; a scholar is better known by the individuality of his problems than by the name of his discipline. If deans and librarians class some of his problems as philosophical, that is no reason for him to be concerned with other problems that they class as philosophical: his further concerns might just as well be problems that are classed as linguistic or mathematical. For that matter, naming disciplines even fosters philosophical error. To take the most glaring case, why do people insist on viewing all parts of physics, however theoretical, as in some degree empirical, and all parts of mathematics, however practical, as purely formal? No such contrast would emerge sentence by sentence, or problem by problem, without reference to the nominal demarcation of disciplines. But again I digress.

Does calling Austin's distinctive activity philosophical say *any-thing* about it? The one salient trait of philosophical inquiries, according to Austin as represented by Urmson, is that for want of standard methods they have not yet hived off under some special name. This criterion is not helpful. The want of standard methods in Austin's work is surely not so dire as to prevent its hiving off under the special name of linguistics.

Actually Austin's work has a genuine tie to philosophy, in a more substantial sense than just what hasn't hived off. It comes in his choice of idioms for analysis. He was no Baconian inductivist, amassing random samples of the world or of the dictionary and scanning them with untendentious eye for unpreconceived uniformities. The *arrière pensée* of *How to Do Things with Words* emerges toward the end of that book: it is 'an inclination to play Old Harry with . . . (1) the true/false fetish, (2) the value/fact fetish' (p. 150).

That book would have been different, in respect of one of its avowed motives at any rate, if Austin had appreciated Tarski's work on truth. Ironically, I think it was over-attention to a demarcation of disciplines that deprived him of Tarski's insights. It was over-attention to the demarcation of the study of English usage. But this in turn was due, I think, to a basic impatience with philosophical perplexity.

There are two ways of rising to problems. Thus take the perturbations of Mercury. I suppose that before Einstein some astronomers pondered these with an eager curiosity, hoping that they might be a key to important traits of nature hitherto undetected, while other astronomers saw in them a vexatious anomaly and longed to see how to explain them away in terms of instrumental error. Attitudes toward philosophical problems vary similarly, and Austin's was of the negative kind. Hence his tendency to limit a philosophical venture to the study of word usage; for language criticism was the method of therapeutic positivism, the method of the *Ueberwindung der Metaphysik*.

What counts as true even for Tarski's theory of truth is language, granted. But the value of Tarski's theory stands forth only if at the second level, talking *of* truth, we look beyond language to logic.

In his scintillating essay 'Truth', Austin himself went part way down Tarski's path. In a footnote he even cited Tarski's paradigm, ' "It is raining" is true if and only if it is raining', and commented: 'So far so good.' Then he looked into usage to add to the story. Tarski, in contrast, concentrated on the mathematical significance of his paradigm. For all its surface triviality, the paradigm is quickly shown to have extraordinary powers. For one thing, it suffices, of itself, to determine truth uniquely. If there are two truth predicates 'True₁' and 'True₂', both fulfilling the paradigm, then the two are coextensive. More remarkable still, as Tarski showed, not even one truth predicate can quite fulfil the paradigm, on pain of contradiction. Yet, as he went on to show in the more laborious stretches of his 'Wahrheitsbegriff', a predicate fulfilling the paradigm can after all be constructed suitable to any preassigned language that is fixed in vocabulary and formal in its logical structure, provided that we bring to the construction certain set-theoretic aids from beyond the bounds of the preassigned language itself. A conclusion that follows from all this is the openness of set theory: for each consistent set theory there is a stronger. This follows also from Gödel's work; and Tarski's work strikingly illuminates Gödel's.

The problem of the perturbations of Mercury turned out to be one of the keys to the relativity of space and time, and the problem of truth turned out to be one of the keys to the relativity of set theories.

I quoted Austin as saying that *How to Do Things with Words* was prompted in part by an animus against the true/false fetish. Yet the relevance of the book to the fetish is not clear, if we think of truth in terms of Tarski's paradigm. The paradigm works for evaluations, after all, as Smart has noticed,[1] as well as for statements of fact. And it works equally for performatives. 'Slander is evil' is true if and only if slander is evil, and 'I bid you good morning' is true of us on a given occasion if and only if, on that occasion, I bid you good morning. A performative is a notable sort of utterance, I grant; it makes itself true; but then it is true. There are good reasons for contrasting and comparing performatives and statements of fact, but an animus against the true/false fetish is not one of them.

Developments in *How to Do Things with Words* that were prompted directly or indirectly by Austin's animus against the true/false fetish are best understood rather as explorations of the gulf between sentence and statement. His work on this will doubtless be continued by others. As for 'the value/fact fetish', his work seems rather to depict the intertwining of value and fact than to discredit the distinction—though someone may discredit it. Anyway his inclination to play Old Harry with those two fetishes has issued in perceptive work that should be relevant to the philosophy of law and other domains.

Historians of science tell us that science forges ahead not by an indiscriminate Baconian inductivism but by pursuing preconceptions, even mistaken ones. I see in Austin's work this kind of progress.

III. Stuart Hampshire

IN order to follow the philosopher whom we are commemorating as far as I can, I will descend immediately to cases, forgetting the abstractness of my abstract. Some years ago (1953), I published a short essay under the title 'Self Knowledge and the Will'; the article contained a brutally short, and inadequately argued, suggestion that the word 'try' might be used in explicating the sense of the sentence 'He could have acted otherwise', in contexts of moral censure and evaluation.

[1] J. of Phil., 1965, p. 346.

Austin, interested in the word 'can', wanted to discuss this thesis with me, both formally in his class for graduate students, and privately elsewhere: and we did discuss it. I had known that the suggestion, as I had made it, was over-simple, open to many objections by counter-example, some of which I thought *could* be answered, but I did not yet know how. After my discussions with Austin the situation was very different in two respects, one obvious, the other less so; I had learnt that my original suggestion was much more crude and over-simple, and open to more damaging counter-examples, than I had thought; secondly, he had, by express design, gradually led me to wonder whether *any* suggestion of this degree of generality on this kind of topic *could* possibly be other than over-simple, and open to a great variety of counter-examples. He wanted to suggest, by the way in which he produced his counter-examples—some apparently far-fetched or trivial, some obviously, and on any view, serious and not eccentric—that the very enterprise of trying to determine the use of 'can' and 'could' in such sentences in such very general contexts is a hopeless and misconceived enterprise; hopeless, at least, if one is looking for some general formula, or an equivalence, or for some weaker form of analysis. He thought, at that time, that, if the search for possible counter-examples was pushed far enough, with sufficient patience, with complete honesty, and freedom from prejudice, any sensible philosopher, who had liberated himself from the inherited habits of philosophers, would no longer hope to determine the use of 'can' in any general formula, within the context of moral censure, advice and evaluation. Such a scepticism about philosophical analysis had not been anticipated by Moore, who, with H. A. Prichard, had been the strongest influence on him.

What were the grounds, stated and implied, of this scepticism? This is the question that I am suggesting for discussion, because I am now, as I was then, altogether uncertain about the truth of the matter. What is the status, or proper use, of counter-examples in philosophy? This will be my principal question for discussion.

On this occasion Austin brought forward a number of counter-examples to show that there are many situations in which it is altogether natural to say 'He can't try to do X now'; for there is a very common use of the word 'try', in which 'try' is replaceable by 'make an attempt'. It evidently makes sense to say of a person that he is just not at the moment in a position to, and that therefore he cannot, make an attempt, and try, to do some specific thing.

In trying to meet this objection, it might occur to one to distinguish two senses, or two uses, of 'try', and to restrict the claim that 'He can try to do X' is always a truism to one of these senses, or uses, of 'try': this would be a sense, or use, of 'try' in which to try is to take the steps known to the agent as likely to lead to the required result. But this suggestion provoked a more fundamental objection, supported again by counter-examples: how do you establish that there really are two, or just so many, distinct senses, or uses, of 'try'? Is it not possible, if one looks carefully, to mention examples which do not fall easily and definitely under one heading rather than another; with sufficient patience can I not produce a great mass of intermediate cases; are you not just stipulating that there are these distinct uses? And this makes your formula totally uninformative: Why not finally just look at the cases in their different contexts? Do not assume in advance that they form an easily recognized pattern, even what is now sometimes called a spectrum of cases. If you have a very large array of different cases of 'try' and 'can' with different verbs laid out before you, will you not have the information which you were originally seeking—what may be called 'the facts'? 'At least you can always *try* to do better'. Imagine many hours on this one sentence, with a group of people in a seminar inventing contexts as a background for it; one will gradually arrive at an immense, untidy range of cases, with small differences to be noticed on several different scales. Time, patience, and co-operation make the difference: the previously selected examples, which seemed to one mind to illustrate a definite difference, are swept away in a flood of intermediate and unclassifiable cases. And it is the contexts, the plausibly imagined, or remembered, dialogues and situations, that gradually destroy the impression of clear distinctions of use. For one soon sees that one is multiplying uses to correspond with variations of context: the different uses become different language games, and the different language games become different social situations. After many hours with this one sentence, one may be left without even the *desire* to maintain a distinction between 'try' as 'attempt' or 'begin', 'try' as 'test', et cetera. The conclusion, forced by the weight of an indefinite number of examples, is that one finally understands the two or three allegedly distinct uses, with which one began, only when one has inserted all the other uses which different contexts of dialogue and situation suggest. One is finally left with the impression that it is the point of the English word 'try' to cover this vast variety of cases, carrying slightly different implications in slightly different verbal contexts and social situations. This method of exhaustiveness and patience with counter-examples was both recommended, and used, by Austin on the word 'see', and would (he thought) usefully be extended to 'touch', 'hear', 'feel' and to other words in this family, such as 'look', 'seems', 'appears', 'sounds' and many others. Then we would be clarifying the cluster of problems that fall under the misleading title of *the* problem of perception. This problem may originally have been provoked by an over-simple theory of knowledge, which had first recklessly divided perceptual statements into two types, and then recklessly invented two corresponding senses of 'see'. Similarly, I had been interested in the problem of the will, and, less immediately, in the definition of freedom, and had chosen the word 'try' as a possible starting-point. But one needs to start again, from the beginning: forget the wholly inaccurate dichotomies which theory-laden anxieties have suggested in the past.

It seemed to me ten and more years ago, when we were discussing the will, and it still seems to me now, that one has to distinguish among problems. There are some philosophical problems, as there are some historical problems, which present themselves as essentially general and which cannot be broken down into their more specific elements: they cannot be broken down, because they are intended to be generalizations of specific problems; and just this legitimate demand for a missing general principle creates the problem. To stay with the same example: one might say to someone who asks for a general principle governing the use of 'can' with verbs of action in the context of moral evaluation, censure and advice: 'Surely you realize that there is an immense variety of different types of evaluation and censure, all of which can be called moral, and which are associated with interestingly different assessments of skills, abilities, opportunities, powers, legal, physical and other kinds; and that, over and above these differences, there are differences, which depend upon the verb of action involved: also the differences between a long-standing ability and an ability that exists at one moment and not at the next: and similarly for opportunities. Surely you see that the language that we use every day in serious human transactions does not register some sharp opposition between failures of will and failures of other kinds; it registers a range of gradations'. There is a philosopher's reply to this—'In your insistence on accuracy, and faithfulness to the facts of language, you may be saying one of two things, one acceptable, the other disputable. The first is simply a warning against unqualified generalization, and is a demand that exceptions and qualifications should be noted, in the interests of accuracy, when a statement of general principle marking the relation of a man's will to his powers is attempted. The second, stronger and unacceptable thesis is that *any* general formula will be to some extent inaccurate, to some extent unfaithful to the complexity and openness of the concepts, and *therefore* will be untrue, and therefore should not be asserted. If this is intended, your argument rests on an unacceptable notion of truth and of the relation between truth and accuracy. A historian, or an economist, may set himself to answer a general, in the sense of a summary, question about economic change in a certain period: perhaps the specific facts are complex, and perhaps any summary statement will be open to some qualifications and counter-examples. But it does not follow that the only true statements that can be made are specific statements of fact e.g. that such-and-such transactions occurred during the period; it may also be true to say, in summary of the specific facts, something like 'There was a definite tendency, throughout this period, for the smaller landowners to sell out to the larger landowners'. This is a summary statement; but it may be true. There is a sense of 'accurate' that is associated with 'specific' and 'exact'. But there is no requirement that all true statements should be specific. In the discussions with Austin, I might have succeeded in showing, by a range of examples, that statements to the effect that someone ought to have acted differently are *generally* rebutted by statements to the effect that he could not have acted differently if he had tried: I might have shown that many of the exceptions to this general tendency in our speech can be explained by some subsidiary principles, which are exemplified in other regions of language; but it might still have been left with a number of recalcitrant examples, drawn from familiar speech, which I could not explain in this way, and where no general principle is discernible. I would not have been prevented from asserting the discernible principles, provided that I did not claim a greater accuracy than the subject-matter allows.

The actual discussions with Austin did not follow this course. I was convinced, by his evidence, that there are objections of *principle* to the thesis that I had proposed. To see an objection of principle behind the counter-examples is to see what purposes in thought or speech would be frustrated if one changed one's linguistic habits in the way suggested by the original thesis. The counter-examples from familiar speech have then shown one that there is a price to pay, and an option, which one had not previously recognized; and to contemplate an option is not the same as merely to contemplate the collapse of the original thesis into an unorganized array of facts.

After all, I am not helpless in the matter: I can *decide* how I will assess a man's will to do something in certain types of context, and I can try to persuade others that there are reasons for adopting the same methods of assessment. It is finally misleading to speak always of 'the facts'; for there is also the element of personal decision; and this is particularly evident, when one is determining an appropriate use of language in the context of moral judgments. For he who puts a general question about the will, and who feels this to be a problem and who has a real desire for an answer, will want to make a decision of principle about how he should in future apply a certain range of words in a certain type of context: of course he will make this decision on the basis of a careful account of his present habits, as they have existed up to now. But the search for a general principle is a search, not so much for an accurate general *description* of existing habits, his own and that of others in his environment, but rather for a principle of guidance to be adopted for the future. Therefore a suggested counter-example, accurately drawn from established habits, does not *by itself* rebut the principle proposed: the counter-example does not bear to the proposed general principle exactly the same relation that a negative instance bears to a factual generalization. The counter-example is rather a challenge, which leaves an alternative: I can decide that this counter-example is a loose way of speaking, which I am now, in the light of the principle, ready to abandon. This in fact happened in the discussions with Austin at his seminar: some of the counter-examples were dismissed by those present as socially acceptable, but loose, unserious, ways of thinking. They admitted that they might talk in this way, for social convenience or from habit, but claimed that they did not want to be committed, in any strict context, to the normal implications of these forms of words. 'Meaning what one says', or 'intending one's words to be taken seriously', are certainly notions which admit of degree. The philosophical question is, not only whether certain forms of words used in certain described contexts would sound odd, unusual and socially deviant, but also a quite different question: whether I, in the contexts described and supposing them to be serious contexts of strict speech, would choose to be committed to this form of words with all their normal implications.

The facts of language are social facts: the doubts, and the problems, sometimes arise on the far side of the social. As Friedrich Waismann said, he who genuinely feels a philosophical problem, when he reflects on a range of claims that he habitually makes on certain evidence and in certain contexts, is like a social or religious protestant, a radical reformer, who is prepared to condemn the loose practices in which he participates. It will often be of no service to say to him—'Observe the subtle variations in their common practices, their adaptation to common needs'. The Socratic and Cartesian impulses to start again—'I know this is what I, in common with others, am in the habit of saying: but do I really have the knowledge which, strictly speaking, justifies me in speaking (and thinking) like this?'

This is the main, but not the only, reason why I think it is a mistake to mention science in connexion with Austin's practice (of systematically and co-operatively assembling examples), even if he occasionally mentioned it himself. His arguments, as one would expect of a philosopher who was not making a contribution to logic, were almost always *ad hominem* arguments: they were short, simple arguments, and they were not compelling, but they were persuasive. The examples and counter-examples, many more drops than are usually selected from the ocean, illustrated but did not prove: they illustrated some principles which, he would suggest, guided our linguistic habits in some critical area, principles that we usually could abandon only at too great a sacrifice of our purposes in communication or in thought, purposes that are more complex than most philosophers had previously led us to believe. He was not unlike any other philosopher in wanting to see, all at once, and therefore from some superior vantage point, the interconnexions between different areas of discourse ('know', 'true', 'see' and 'seems', 'real', 'if', 'can', 'mean'). But he did think that it had proved a mistake to choose too high a vantage point, from which the confusion of things on the ground could not be seen at all.

Three of his discoveries of principle behind seeming anomalies of use have altered whole areas of philosophical discussion: first, the principle that we need to assess utterances as correct or incorrect, successful or unsuccessful, along several different axes: second, the principle that we need performative uses of sentences, which are not trivial and marginal and easily isolated uses of sentences, with its corollary that claims to knowledge should be compared with claim-making in general. Thirdly, he noticed features of the grammar of 'can' and 'could', and of the conditional sentences in which they occur, and thereby reopened lines of inquiry into free-will that had been previously blocked. He came quite near, but certainly not all the way, to a fourth achievement: to uncovering the principle that is violated by attempts to define, without circularity, the phenomenal object of vision.

I talked to him often enough about philosophy, from 1936 onwards, to know with certainty that he had no *constant* philosophical method. He was experimental and he relied on cleverness and on having an idea, and then working it out. He failed, after some years work, to find plausible principles behind the various features of the uses of 'true'; his simplification, a suggestion of principle, here was not persuasive. But he still thought it wrong in principle to try to answer questions about truth by reference to comparatively superficial features of the use of language in dialogue, as some of his critics did. He did not use what might wrongly be called 'Austin's method' at this point. He spent a year of leave from teaching in search of some outline of an informal system of semantic predicates: but he did not get as far as he had hoped. In many years of regular discussion I never knew him to give the expected reply to a philosophical question. He merely looked for the centre of the problem; sometimes he missed, but on at least three occasions he found it.

Part II

Philosophical Papers

AUSTIN'S PHILOSOPHICAL PAPERS

Roderick M. Chisholm

AUSTIN'S way of doing philosophy seems to have involved two quite different stages. The first 'proceeds from "ordinary language"' and consists in 'examining *what we should say when*, and so why and what we should mean by it'; the second consists in the application of this 'field work' to traditional problems of philosophy. Austin was without equal in carrying out the first stage of this type of procedure and it is here that the major significance of the present book is to be found. Some of these papers—certainly 'Other Minds' and also, I think, 'A Plea for Excuses', 'How to Talk', and 'Ifs and Cans'—are among the most important contributions that have been made to philosophy since the end of the Second World War. But when Austin came to apply his findings to problems of philosophy—when he used his information about 'what we should say when' to criticize philosophical statements which, very often, were not intended to carry any implication whatever about what anyone would say when—then, I think, he was less successful.

I shall summarize these papers, with one exception, only to the extent needed to justify my remark about the second stage of Austin's procedure. So far as the first stage is concerned, I cannot offer any serious criticisms. And it was doubtless this stage that seemed most important to Austin.

2. 'How to Talk—some simple ways' (1953) is inappropriately titled, not only because it is about something other than what the title suggests it is about, but also because it is very difficult and might even be cited as an illustration of how philosophers ought not to talk. What Austin says in the paper is very important indeed—and also relevant to what he says in a number of the other papers. I shall try to formulate the essential points in a terminology

which is somewhat more orthodox philosophically than that which Austin uses.

Consider a man who points to a dog and says 'That's a mastiff'. Here we seem to have as simple and straightforward a 'speech-act' as anyone could wish. But Austin would tell us that, in all probability, the man is doing one or another of four quite different things—either 'calling', 'exemplifying', 'describing', or 'classing'. To understand these four concepts we must realize that, even though the word 'mastiff' may be the best one available, it is likely to have one or the other of two limitations. Dogs being what they are, either the word will fail to 'do justice to the multiformity' of the concept of being a mastiff, or else it will 'neglect the full specificity' of the particular dog. There is something about the fur, say, that leads one to question the man's statement. The question could be put in any one of the four following ways, depending upon whether the issue is a matter of 'calling', 'exemplifying', 'describing', or 'classing'.

'That dog's a *mastiff*—with wiry fur like that?'
'*That* dog's a mastiff—with wiry fur like that?'
'That dog's a *mastiff*? You forget his wiry fur.'
'*That* dog's a mastiff? You forget his wiry fur.'

The first two formulations suggest that our man has the wrong idea of what it is to be a mastiff; the last two, that he is not paying sufficient attention to the particular dog; the first and third suggest that what is in question is the nature of the particular dog; and the second and fourth, that what is in question is what it is to be a mastiff. I suggest, then, that Austin's four concepts may be distinguished in the following way.

Suppose that we utter the sentence '*s* is a P', where '*s*' is being used to denote a certain particular thing and 'P' to connote a certain set of properties or characteristics. And suppose, further, that in uttering the sentence we know we are doing some injustice to the concept of what it is to be a P or we know that we are neglecting some property or characteristic of the particular thing *s*. Then:

(1) If we have been examining *s* in order to answer the question 'What kind of a thing is *s*?' and if we indicate the results by saying '*s* is a P', we are *calling s* a P.

(2) If we have been examining *s* in order to answer the question 'What would be an example of a P?' and if we indicate the results by saying '*s* is a P', we are *exemplifying* what P is by means of *s*.

(3) If we have been reflecting upon just what it is to be a P, in order to answer the question 'What kind of a thing is *s*?' and if we express our conclusions by saying '*s* is a P', we are *describing s* as a P.

(4) If we have been reflecting upon just what it is to be a P, in order to answer the question 'What would be an example of a P?' and if we express our conclusion by saying '*s* is a P', we are *classing s* as a P.

Thus *calling* and *describing*—(1) and (3)—are alike in that each is intended to answer the question, 'What kind of a thing is *s*?' *Exemplifying* and *classing*—(2) and (4)—are alike in that each is intended to answer the question, 'What would be an example of a P?' *Calling* and *exemplifying*—(1) and (2)—are alike in that, the results of examining *s* having been decided upon, we are saying that the results warrant application of 'P' to *s*; hence, if the examination has been properly carried out and there has been no 'misperception', and if our statement '*s* is a P' is false, we can be accused of not knowing what it is to be a P (or of not knowing what 'P' means). And *describing* and *classing*—(3) and (4)—are alike in that, the criteria of what it is to be a P having been decided upon, we are saying that they are more or less, or pretty much, satisfied by *s*; hence if we have not 'misperceived' *s* and if our statement '*s* is a P' is false, we can be accused of not taking into account certain relevant characteristics of *s*.

Is there also something common to *calling* and *classing*—(1) and (4)—and to *exemplifying* and *describing*—(2) and (3)? Here we have an interesting result with respect to *negation*.

The negative utterance, '*s* is not a P', made in the kind of context we have been considering, indicates that we are either *exemplifying* or *describing*. For if we are *calling* and not *exemplifying* (i.e. if we are answering 'What kind of a thing is *s*?' and have *not* been reflecting upon what it is to be a P), there would be no point in our saying '*s* is not a P'. Or if we are *classing* and not *describing* (i.e. if we are answering 'What would be an example of a P?' and have not been examining *s*), then again there would be no point in saying '*s* is not a P'. The negative utterance, therefore, indicates either that we have been looking *s* over in order to find an instance of a

P, or that we have been reflecting upon what it is to be a P in order to decide what kind of a thing *s* is. Hence negation is appropriate to *exemplifying* and *describing*—(2) and (3)—and inappropriate to *calling* and *classing*—(1) and (4).

Austin introduces the subject by considering a 'model' of the following sort: our world is one in which there are simple things, each having a single property ('individual items, each of one and only one definite type'); the world is a black and white one—that is to say, for each thing and each type, the thing either clearly is of that type or it is not; and our language is one in which certain words denote things ('refer to items') and other connote properties (have certain 'item-types' as their 'sense'). In this model world, we do not have the problem we encountered with the dog and the concept of being a mastiff; if the 'names' and the 'items' fit at all they fit exactly. Where there is thus no problem of fit, the four concepts just distinguished may be replaced by simpler ones. Corresponding to *calling, describing, exemplifying, and classing*, respectively, there are: *placing* (also called 'cap-fitting' and thus '*c*-identifying'), *stating, instancing*, and *casting* (also called 'filling-the-bill' and thus '*b*-identifying').

Austin began the paper by asking: 'Can to describe X as Y really be the same as to call X Y? Or again the same as to state that X is Y?' If I have interpreted him correctly, the distinction between calling and describing is as I have put it above; and *stating* is like describing except that when we state that X is Y there is no problem of fit. Where we might *describe* Spengler as a philosopher, we would *state* that Plato was a philosopher.

The paper contains, or seems to contain, dozens of new technical terms. Austin took care, apparently, never to use a technical term that any other philosopher had ever used. For instance, he summarizes the point about negation, above, by saying 'the sentence form SN is in order when we are matching *the* (given) sense/type to *a* (produced) type/sense, but not in order when we are matching *a* (produced) sense/type to *the* (given) type/sense'. But I think that the essential points of the paper are what I have reproduced. I would say that the paper is of very first importance to philosophy, despite the way in which it is expressed.

The distinctions which Austin makes here are also relevant to a number of the other papers.

3. The presuppositions of 'How to Talk' are at odds—or seem

to me to be at odds—with some of the conclusions of Austin's first two published papers: 'Are There *A Priori* Concepts?' (1939) and 'The Meaning of a Word' (1940).

In the first of the early papers, he said that 'it cannot be sense to say that sensible circles are more or less "like" the universal "circularity" ' and he ridiculed the thought that a sensible figure might be 'an approximation to' a geometrical figure. But the problem of 'How to Talk' was precisely this problem of 'approximation' and 'more or less like' as a relation between 'the type of the item' and 'the sense'—the problem that arises when 'the sense does not exactly match to the type' or 'the type does not exactly match to the sense'.

In 'The Meaning of a Word', he sets forth, with considerable care, ways in which philosophers *could* go wrong in using such expressions as 'the meaning of a word', and he concludes, with somewhat less care, that philosophers who have talked about 'meanings', 'universals', or 'concepts' *have* gone wrong in the ways that he describes. He says of C. W. Morris, for example, that Morris 'makes some of the crudest possible remarks about "the designatum" of a word: every sign has a designatum, which is not a particular thing but a *kind* of object or *class* of objects. Now this is quite fictitious an entity as any "Platonic idea": and is due to precisely the same fallacy of looking for "the meaning (or designatum) of a word".' But surely Austin's 'item-type' ('sense-giving . . . consists in allotting a certain item-type to a certain vocable as its "sense" ') is intended to name exactly what Morris's 'designatum' was intended to name.

There are indications that Austin did not feel entirely comfortable with his term ' "sense" '. He said, in 'How to Talk,' that he would not 'go into the "metaphysical statu。" of types and senses (nor of items)'; and he added, uncharacteristically, that the term ' "sense" ' is 'not ultimate in speech theory' and that 'if we went back to the rudiments' of this science, types and senses 'might appear as constructions'. The fact remains, however, that when he comes to consider his four types of 'speech-act' and their variants, he is led to the concepts of *sense* and *type*, and he gives no indication at all of how his various distinctions could be made without them. Had he tried to justify his remark that ' "sense" might appear as a construction', then, I think, he would have found himself dealing with 'the so-called problem of universals'.

4. 'Other Minds' (1946) remains the most impressive of Austin's writings. Here we have an exhaustive, if not definitive, treatment of 'what sort of thing does actually happen when ordinary people are asked "How do you know?" '; an application of this treatment to questions that philosophers have raised about 'other minds'; Austin's view about 'performative utterances', a view which, needlessly and unfortunately, is obscured in the later 'Performative Utterances' (1956); and a statement, not entirely clear, about the relation of performative utterances to knowing.

The question 'How do you know?', Austin points out, could mean the same as 'How do you come to be in a position to know?' and the latter question may be understood in different ways, depending upon whether—in the terminology of 'How to Talk'—the issue concerns calling, exemplifying, describing, or classing. Or one could be asking 'How do you tell?' which may also be understood in these different ways. It could also be that one is challenging the speaker's credentials, or possibly 'disputing his facts'. In the course of his discussion, Austin calls attention to several very important distinctions, which I will not attempt to summarize, and he then turns to the problem which Professor Wisdom had taken up in a paper entitled 'Other Minds'.[1] Wisdom had made such statements as 'A person, B, cannot learn the correctness of a prediction about a person, A's, sensations in the way in which A himself does'—expressing a familiar view which, according to Austin, may well be 'the original sin' by which 'the philosopher casts himself out from the garden of the world we live in'. I wonder, though, whether Austin has done justice to the view.

Philosophers have traditionally drawn a distinction between what they have labelled as 'direct' and 'indirect' knowledge, or 'immediate' and 'mediate' knowledge, both sets of labels being quite obviously incorrect, at least in English (for when we ordinarily use these labels we do not use them to make the distinction which philosophers have had in mind); and what is worse, so far as correctness is concerned, the philosophers have gone on to say, of that knowledge which they incorrectly call 'indirect' of 'mediate', that it is knowledge by means of 'signs', 'clues', or 'symptoms'. Austin makes it perfectly clear that these terms *are* incorrect in this

[1] Which, with Austin's paper, constituted a symposium. Wisdom's paper appears in the *Proceedings of the Aristotelian Society*, Supplementary vol. xx (1946), and in Wisdom's book, *Other Minds* (Oxford, 1952).

use. But when we have learned this, we do not learn, necessarily, that the philosophers were confused in drawing the distinction they did draw, or that the distinction is not of importance to philosophy or to the problem of 'other minds'.

The questions which lead to the distinction are not 'How do you know?', in any of the senses which Austin distinguishes, or 'Why do you believe?' They are the Socratic questions which a philosopher may put to himself—for example, 'What is my justification for thinking I know this?'—where his concern is *not* to question anyone's facts or credentials or to learn in what respect the type of the item matches the pattern of the sense.[1] Knowing that he does know, the philosopher asks himself 'What is my justification for thinking I know this?' in order to make explicit and to generalize the criteria of justification, or evidence, which he and other rational men can find themselves employing. And when he does ask himself such questions, and does not give up, he learns this. Some of the things he knows (say, that that bird is a goldfinch) are such that, when he asks himself 'What is my justification for thinking I know this?', he will answer by citing *something else* that he knows (the bird has a patch of yellow on his wings). But if he continues his Socratic questioning long enough, he will find that there are some things which are such that, if he were to ask himself 'What is my justification for thinking I know this?', he will *not* then go on and appeal to anything else. Many philosophers would say, technically and incorrectly, that these are things 'he knows directly, or immediately'. The point may also be put by using a technical phrase of Mr. Strawson's. We could say that there are statements which are such that (i) the question concerning our justification for thinking we know them to be true is 'a question which does not arise', and which are also such that (ii) we may relevantly cite them when, concerning certain *other* statements, the question of our justification for thinking we know them to be true *does* arise. Once the distinction is grasped, however, it is easier to say, incorrectly, that these are statements or propositions which we know 'directly' or 'immediately' (just as Austin finds it easier to speak, incorrectly, of 'linguistic legislation' than to spell out the perfectly clear concept which his technical term abbreviates).

[1] According to Xenophon, Charicles said this to Socrates: 'You generally ask questions when you know quite well how the matter stands; these are the questions you are not to ask', *Memorabilia*, I, 2, 36.

Once we have the distinction between what is known 'directly' and what is known 'indirectly' (i.e. what is known, but not known directly, in the technical sense of 'directly' just described), then it is obvious that the statement or proposition that *I* do not feel quite well, if it is true, belongs in the first group, and the statement or proposition that *he* does not feel quite well, if it is known, belongs in the second. And this is one of the things that Wisdom was saying.

But Austin does point out—and this is important and relevant —that many of the statements (e.g. the statement that I am angry) which philosophers have tended to put in the first group do not belong there at all.

5. What is a performative utterance? As Austin notes in 'Performative Utterances' (1956), almost every utterance may be said to be performative in that it has effects, and is intended to have effects, other than carrying out the act of describing (or of calling, classing, exemplifying, etc.). The philosophically interesting sense of 'performative utterance', as Austin uses the expression, is that in which it applies to utterances in which 'the little word "hereby" either actually occurs or might naturally be inserted'—hence, many of the utterances beginning with 'I promise', 'I baptize', 'I ask', 'You are commanded', 'Trespassers are warned', 'Passengers are requested', and the like.

Austin found it difficult to define this strict sense of 'performative utterance'. As the examples indicate, a performative utterance may be put in the first, second, or third person; none of the grammatical criteria which come readily to mind are adequate to all of the examples we could think of. We might consider saying that performative utterances are 'neither true nor false'—but this would give us, at best, a necessary and not a sufficient condition. And it is not at all clear that being neither true nor false is even a necessary condition. A performative utterance—at least the sentence uttered —may satisfy the criteria of truth which Austin lays down in his paper entitled 'Truth'. And Austin seemed to feel that an utterance beginning with 'I state that . . .' might be performative; he said of such utterances that they 'do have to be true or false, that they *are* statements'.[1] In the paper entitled 'Performative Utterances'

[1] Cf. C. S. Peirce: 'What is the nature of assertion? We have no magnifying-glass that can enlarge its features, and render them more discernible; but in default of such an instrument we can select for examination a very formal

Austin seems to despair of being able to draw any clearcut distinction:

> We see then that stating something is performing an act just as much as is giving an order or giving a warning; and we see, on the other hand, that when we give an order or a warning or a piece of advice, there is a question about how this is related to fact which is not perhaps so very different from the kind of question which arises when we discuss how a statement is related to fact. Well, this seems to mean that in its original form our distinction between the performative and the statement is considerably weakened, and indeed breaks down.

I wonder whether Austin did not despair too readily. He had sought to describe those characteristics of *utterances* which would make them merely performative. Suppose instead we try to describe those characteristics of *performances* which would make them merely utterable.

There are acts (e.g. requesting) which have the following characteristic: when circumstances are right, then to perform the act it is enough to make a certain utterance (e.g. 'I request . . .') containing an expression which the speaker commonly uses to designate such an act. This is not to say that when the utterance is made the expression is being used to designate *that* particular performance of the act. (There are reasons for adding that it is not then being used to designate any other performance of the act.) The 'standard way' of making a request, among English-speaking people, is to say 'I request . . .'; analogously for promising, ordering, guaranteeing, baptizing. Let us say, then, of anyone who

---

assertion, the features of which have purposely been rendered very prominent in order to emphasize its solemnity. If a man desires to assert something very solemnly, he takes such steps as will enable him to go before a magistrate or notary and take a binding oath to it. Taking an oath is not mainly an event of the nature of a setting forth, *Vorstellung*, or representing. It is not merely saying, but is *doing*. The law, I believe, calls it an "act". At any rate, it would be followed by very real effects, in case the substance of what is asserted should prove untrue. This ingredient, the assuming of responsibility, which is so prominent in solemn assertion, must be present in every genuine assertion. For clearly, every assertion involves an effort to make the intended interpreter believe what is asserted, to which end a reason for believing it must be furnished.' *Collected Papers*, v. 386; cf. also pp. 383-5, and ii. 178. These passages, incidentally, are relevant to Austin's remark, in a footnote to 'Truth', that 'Peirce does not, I believe, distinguish between a sentence and a statement'.

performs an act in this way, that his utterance is a performative utterance—in a *strict* sense of this term. (If this type of definition is adequate, it has the advantage of being applicable to utterances made in languages other than English.)

An utterance of 'I want' is *not* performative in the strict sense, for it cannot be said to constitute an 'act' of wanting. But it is often used to accomplish what one might accomplish by means of the strict performative 'I request'. We may say, therefore, that an utterance of 'I want' may be performative, in an *extended* sense of the term 'performative'.

I suggest that the utterance of an expression (e.g. 'I want') is performative, in an *extended* sense of the term, if it is made in order to accomplish that act in virtue of which the utterance of some other expression (e.g. 'I request') can be performative in the strict sense defined. Sometimes, when I say 'I want', I may be describing my psychological state in order to tell someone what I would like him to do—in order to get him to do something which I might also get him to do by saying 'I request'.

What is the relation of all this to 'I know'? It is clear that utterances of 'I know' are not performative in the strict sense of the term, for knowing is not an 'act' which can be performed by saying 'I know'. (To say 'I promise that *p*', at least under certain circumstances, *is* to promise that *p*, but to say 'I know that *p*' is never itself to know that *p*.) But 'I know' is related to 'I guarantee', and to other such performatives, in the way in which 'I want' is related to 'I request'. And thus an utterance of 'I know' may be performative in the extended sense of the term.

'I want' is not always a substitute for 'I request'. I may tell you what I would like even when I know there is no possibility of your helping to get it for me. And 'I know' is not always a substitute for 'I guarantee'. I may tell you—confess or boast—that I know some of the things that you also know and on an occasion in which you neither need nor want my guarantee.

But Austin said, in 'Other Minds': 'To suppose that "I know" is a descriptive phrase is only one example of the *descriptive fallacy*, so common in philosophy. . . . Utterance of obvious ritual phrases, in the appropriate circumstances, is not *describing* the action we are doing, but *doing* it ('I do'). . . .' Here it looks very much as though Austin was assuming, mistakenly, that 'I know' is performative in the strict sense and not merely in the extended sense.

An utterance of 'I want' may serve both to say something about me and to get you to do something; an utterance of 'I know', similarly, may serve both to say something about me and to provide you with guarantees. To suppose that the performance of the latter non-descriptive function is inconsistent with a simultaneous performance of the former, descriptive function, might be called an example of the *performative fallacy*, which has also become very common in philosophy. (Austin, in effect, calls attention to the latter fallacy at the end of the paper on truth, where he criticizes Strawson for supposing that, since 'It is true' performs the function of expressing agreement, etc., it therefore does not perform the function of stating anything. 'It is true', incidentally, would be performative only in the extended sense.)

Austin seems to have felt, and others have certainly felt, that his remarks about 'I know' have helped to clear up some of the muddles of the theory of knowledge. After noting how the utterance of 'I believe' is a way of playing it safe, he writes: '. . . saying "I know" is taking a new plunge. But it is *not* saying "I have performed a specially striking feat of cognition, superior, in the same scale as believing and being sure, even to being merely quite sure"': for there *is* nothing in that scale superior to being quite sure. Just as promising is not something superior, in the same scale as hoping and intending, even to merely fully intending; for there is nothing in that scale superior to fully intending. When I say "I know", I *give others my word: I give others my authority for saying* that "S is P".' This passage *suggests* that epistemologists, from the time of the *Theaetetus* on, have been looking in the wrong place for the way to draw the distinction between knowledge and true opinion, and that if only they would examine the distinction between performative and non-performative utterances they would find what they have been looking for.

When we consider 'I know', we realize, as Austin says, that the phrase is not to be said lightly and, if we are philosophers, we may ask what the conditions are that entitle us to say it. 'If you say you *know* something, the most immediate challenge takes the form of asking "Are you in a position to know?": that is, you must undertake to show, not merely that you are sure of it, but that it is within your cognizance.' If a man is entitled to say 'I know that p', it may well be, then, that he has performed no striking feat of cognition, superior in the same scale as believing and being sure, but *p* does 'fall within his *cognizance*'. And if *p* is thus within his cognizance, then, surely, whether or not he *says* 'I know', he *does* know. ('He knows, but he isn't saying.')

If it is true that 'I know' is performative only in what I have called the extended sense of the term, and if this performative function must be described in such phrases as 'falling within one's cognizance', then to suppose that 'I know' is performative and not descriptive would also be to commit the 'fallacy of accident'.

The talk about performative utterances does not answer the question of the *Theaetetus*; for the question was, in effect, 'What is the difference between saying, of a man, that he has true opinion that *p*, and saying of him that *p* falls within his cognizance?' But Austin's remarks do suggest an important clue. it seems to me. Suppose we consider his statement 'When I say "I know", I give others my word: I give others my authority for saying that "S is P"' and revise it to read: 'If a man knows that S is P, then he has the *right* to give others his word—to give others his authority for believing that S is P.' (And this, incidentally, shows that there may be point in saying of a man that he *knows* that he seems to have a headache. We are not saying that there is an inner light which reveals this fact to him, or that he has performed a striking feat of cognition; we are saying that he has the right to give others his word for this fact and to assure them that they may safely rely upon his authority.)

6. 'Truth' (1950) seems to me one of the least satisfactory of Austin's papers. The principal topics of the paper are: (1) Austin's defence of the view that the 'primary' use of 'true' is its application to *statements*; (2) his answer to the question 'When is a statement true?' and (3) his criticism of the view that 'true' is 'logically superfluous'. Let us begin with the second of these topics.

Austin describes some of the conditions which must be satisfied in order for there to *be* a language in which statements may be made. These include, among other things, the existence of two sets of conventions: '*Descriptive* conventions correlating the words (= sentences) with the *types* of situation, thing, event, etc., to be found in the world' and '*Demonstrative* conventions correlating the words (= statements) with the *historic* situations, etc., to be found in the world.' Using these concepts, he answers the question 'When is a statement true?' in the following way: 'A statement is said to be true when the historic state of affairs to which it is correlated by the demonstrative conventions (the one to which it "refers") is of a type with which the sentence used in making it is correlated by the descriptive conventions.' Austin does not object to saying, for short, that a true statement is one which 'corresponds to the facts'.

In proposing his definition, Austin must have been thinking of the simplified world and language which he was to envisage in 'How to Talk', for the definition seems to apply only to simple affirmative sentences. As Brentano had pointed out, in his lecture 'On the Concept of Truth',[1] there are many types of statement to which a definition of this sort does not apply: negative statements, mathematical statements, statements about possibility and impossibility, statements about what Austin prefers to call 'types' ('Violet is more like blue than green'), subjunctive conditionals, compound statements, quantified statements, not to mention that strange class of statements which, in 'The Meaning of a Word', Austin cites as being neither analytic nor synthetic (' "This x exists", where x is a sensum, e.g. "This noise exists" '). But if the definition is adequate in application to simple affirmative statements, perhaps there is no theoretical difficulty involved in extending it to other types of statement.

The more interesting question is the first one: 'whether there is not some use of "is true" that is primary, or some generic name for that which at bottom we are always saying "is true".' Austin says that there is such a 'primary' use and that it is the application of 'true' to *statements;* Brentano, who raised the same question, said that there is such a use and that it is the application of 'true' to *iudgements.* Austin dismisses the latter view in the following way:

> Some say that 'truth is primarily a property of beliefs'. But it may be doubted whether the expression 'a true belief' is at all common outside philosophy and theology: and it seems clear that a man is said to hold a true belief when and in the sense that he believes (in) *something which* is true, or believes that *something which* is true is true. Moreover if, as some also say, a belief is 'of the nature of a picture', then it is of the nature of what cannot be true, though it may be, for example, faithful.

Here we have three different objections. The third is not to be taken seriously, since there is no good reason at all for supposing

[1] Delivered in Vienna in 1889 and published as the first essay in the posthumous *Wahrheit und Evidenz* (Leipzig, 1930). Brentano raises many of the questions that Austin does, and answers them differently.

that a belief is 'of the nature of a picture'. The second holds, *mutatis mutandis*, of the view that 'truth is primarily a property of statements' ('It seems clear that a man is said to make a true statement when and in the sense that he states *something which* is true, or states that *something which* is true is true'). But the first point—that the expression 'a true belief' is not common outside philosophy and theology—is well taken, so far at least as contemporary English is concerned. (But it would also be to the point to make 'field studies' of other languages and to note such facts as that the German word for 'true' is a part of the German word for 'perceive'.) Ordinary people say that beliefs or judgements are 'correct' or 'mistaken', and philosophers, wishing to say the same thing, say that they are 'true' or 'false'. But I think that those who have held that the 'primary' use of 'true' is its application to beliefs or judgements may well grant this point about the ordinary use of 'true' in contemporary English. What they wish to say might also be put in this way: 'The concept of a *correct belief* is primary and that of a *true statement* is not primary.' What could this mean?

The issue is not one of definitional priority; for either concept may be defined in terms of the other. We may define 'correct belief' by reference to 'true statement' (e.g. a belief is correct if the statements which express it are true, etc.), or we may define 'true statement' by means of 'correct belief' (e.g. a statement is true if it expresses a correct belief, etc.). Those who would say that 'correct belief' is 'primary' have something further in mind:

Since the term 'correct', in our present use, refers to beliefs, let us say that it refers to what is *psychological*, and since 'true', in this use, refers to statements, let us say that it refers to what is *linguistic*. Now there is at least one clear sense in which the psychological term 'correct' may be said to be primary and in which the linguistic term 'true' may be said not to be primary: in order to say what the linguistic term means (in its application to statements in natural languages) it is necessary to refer to what is psychological, but in order to say what the psychological term means it is *not* necessary to refer to what is linguistic. For when we say what the linguistic term 'true' means (if Austin is right), we must refer to 'a stock of symbols of some kind which a communicator ("the speaker") can produce "at will" and which a communicatee ("the audience") can *observe*'; we must be able to 'observe' similarities; and there must be '*conventions*' in which we '*appoint*' certain symbols to describe certain types and in which we *correlate* certain symbols with historic states of affairs 'to be *found* in the world'. Moreover, some of the psychological terms which I have italicized are to be taken in what Professor Ryle has called their 'achievement' sense: when it is said that the communicatee must be able to *observe* the symbols, what is meant is, not merely that these symbols must 'fall within his field of vision' or 'serve as source of sensible stimulation', *but also* that the communicatee must *observe that* they are the symbols which in fact they are. And when we try to define this achievement sense of 'observe', then, if I am not mistaken, we must use the type of definition we might also use to define 'correct belief'. 'A man observes that a certain historic state of affairs is of a certain type, provided (at least) he takes the state of affairs to be of that type and the state of affairs is of that type' (I say 'at least' because presumably we should add another qualification to indicate that the man *knows* and does not merely *believe*). And the *taking* to which we are thus led looks very much like correct belief.

When, on the other hand, we start with the concept of *correct belief*, we are *not* led, similarly, to the linguistic concepts which that of *true statement* involves. And this fact—that we can explicate *correct belief* without falling back upon *true statement*, and that we cannot explicate *true statement* without falling back upon *correct belief*—gives us one clear sense in which the correctness of beliefs may be said to be 'primary' and the truth of statements not.

The doctrine that 'true' is not 'logically superfluous'—the third major point of Austin's essay—is an essential part of the case for 'facts'.

7. In 'Unfair to Facts' (1954) we find Austin in considerable agitation about the strange statement, 'Facts are things in the world', or, as he also put it, ' "Facts" are "things-in-the-world" ', a statement which he believed to be true. Austin and P. F. Strawson had taken sides in a perennial controversy, which might be said to go back to Aristotle's remarks about 'being in the sense of the true'. (Another notable occurrence of the same controversy, in the present century, was that between Meinong, who put the case for facts, and Brentano and his followers, who put the case against them.)

In the first of two papers entitled 'Truth' (1949), Strawson had defended a set of theses about the use of 'true'; Austin's paper entitled 'Truth' (1950) criticized some of the theses of Strawson's first paper; Strawson replied to these criticisms in his second paper (1950) and criticized what Austin had said; 'Unfair to Facts' (1954) is Austin's rejoinder.[1] The discussion is very difficult to follow because one cannot always be sure what is being used as a premise and what as a conclusion.

Strawson, then, defended the following theses about 'true' in his first paper—theses which were intended also to apply, *mutatis mutandis* to 'false' (he notes that ordinary people usually say 'not true' and not 'false') and to 'truth' and 'falsehood': 'To say of a statement that it is true is not to make a further statement' and thus not to ascribe a property or relation to the statement said to be true. 'S is true' does not ascribe a property or relation to S; if it says anything about the subject-matter of S, it says the same thing about it that S does; 'S is true' is a statement within, and not about, the frame of discourse in which S occurs. But to say that a statement is true is to do something different from, or additional to, just making the statement; 'true' has a 'job of its own to do', e.g. that of giving our assent, backing, or admission to the statement said to be true (and 'not true' and 'false' serve to indicate dissent and denial).

These theses seem most plausible when we consider the use of 'true' in such statements as 'It's true that all men are mortal' and 'Yes, that's true'. In the second example, and in other types of case, 'true' also performs a useful abbreviatory function—a function which Strawson emphasizes in his second paper.

But Austin contended, in *his* paper on truth, that to say of a statement that it is true *is* to say that the statement bears a certain relation to something else—the something else being a fact, or the facts. Strawson turns to facts in his second paper and tries to show that they are 'pseudo-objects' and that Austin's kind of talk about them involves a fundamental mistake. Strawson's case against facts, as I understand it, involves five different points. One of these seems to be acceptable to many metaphysicians; another—I shall list it last—seems to be inconsistent with what he says about 'true'; and three of them presuppose what he says about 'true'. And what he says about 'true', moreover, seems to me to be false.

Here, then, is the case against 'Facts are things in the world':

[1] P. F. Strawson, 'Truth', *Analysis*, vol. ix (1949), reprinted in Margaret Macdonald's *Philosophy and Analysis* (Oxford, 1954); and 'Truth', *Proceedings of the Aristotelian Society*, vol. xxiv (1950). The latter paper is part of the symposium in which Austin's paper on truth appeared.

(i) Facts, unlike particular things, cannot be dated or located (Strawson adds that you cannot spill coffee on them). But this first point, which is hardly conclusive by itself, has led some metaphysicians to say, not that facts are 'pseudo-objects', but that they are 'ideal' or 'eternal' objects, 'timelessly ingredient in the actual'. (ii) 'Fact', like 'true', has an abbreviatory use, enabling us to express in a convenient and economical way what otherwise might require a long chain of *that*-clauses and assertive sentences. But this point, too, is inconclusive. As Strawson notes, the word 'object' has a similar abbreviatory use—but it is not true that all objects are 'pseudo-objects'. And the metaphysician will say that the *that*-clauses and assertive sentences which the word 'fact' abbreviates are all related to facts: they correspond with them if they are true and fail to correspond if they are false. Strawson's next two points are aimed at *this* contention. (iii) The metaphysician argues: 'There are true statements; to say that a statement is true is to say that it corresponds with a fact; therefore there are facts.' But if the theses of Strawson's *first* paper are true, the second premise of this argument is false; hence the metaphysician's rejoinder to Strawson's second point is inconclusive. (iv) The theses which were applied to 'true' in the first paper may *also* be applied to 'fact', in at least one of its uses. What Strawson says of 'true', in 'It's true that all men are mortal' and 'Yes, that's true', may also be said of 'fact' when 'true' in these statements is replaced by 'a fact'. And finally (v) Strawson attempts to show that those who speak of 'the correspondence between statement and fact' have been misled by the following mistake. They 'think of a statement as "describing that which makes it true" (fact, situation, state of affairs) in the way a descriptive predicate may be used to describe, or a referring expression to refer to, a thing'; but actually there is no reason for supposing that statements bear any such relation to any thing or group of things. It would be a mistake, evidently, to suppose that 'The monarch is deceased' is related to anything in the way in which 'the monarch' is related to the monarch.

The last of these points, if I am not mistaken, conflicts with what Strawson had said in his first paper about 'true'. He had admitted in the first paper that his theses do not hold of 'true' as it is used in such 'semantical' statements as:

(T) 'The monarch is deceased' is true if and only if the monarch is deceased.

But he argued that the phrase 'is true if and only if' which appears in such statements is only a misleading synonym for 'means that'. If this argument is sound, then his theses about 'true' are readily accommodated to statements such as T. But the argument replaces T by the following relational statement:

(R) 'The monarch is deceased' means that the monarch is deceased.

And R, contrary to the final point about 'facts' above, seems to affirm a relation between a statement (or sentence) and something else, a relation comparable to that which holds between 'the monarch' and the monarch. The metaphysician is now in a position to suggest that *fact*—or, more likely, *situation* or *state of affairs*—is exemplified by the second term of this relation. If we try to talk him out of this by telling him that R is really only another way of expressing what T expresses, then we seem to be left with a use of 'true'—the one in T—which does not fit Strawson's original theses.

If I were making a case for facts, in reply to Strawson, I would consider more carefully his theses about the use of 'true'. Austin does this in the paper on truth, suggesting, among other things, that Strawson has committed what we referred to above as the 'performative fallacy', and noting (implausibly, it seems to me) that when we say 'it is true' we are asserting something about purely conventional relations. His case against the 'no truth' view is not as strong as it might be.

There is one class of statements using 'true' to which Strawson's theses do not obviously apply. I am referring to those statements in which the subject-matter of the statement said to be true is in no way indicated or suggested. For example: 'If *he* testifies, what he says will be true', 'Every statement is either true or false', and (from Strawson's second paper) 'In any language in which statements can be made at all, it must be possible to make true and false statements'. In these examples 'true' is not used to give assent, backing, or admission. If we recall the fate of 'psychologism' in logic, we are not likely to say that they are statements which assert, or express, what someone under some condition or other *would* assent to, back up, or admit. (If we say, instead, that they are concerned with what people *ought* to admit, etc., we will be going considerably beyond Strawson's theory.) To accommodate Strawson's theses to these statements, I think it would be necessary to show that 'true' here performs an abbreviatory function. And the only way to show this, I think, would be to replace 'true' in these statements by some other 'semantical', or 'intentional', term, just as Strawson had done in the case of the 'is-true-if-and-only-if' statements. Can we do this?

If we could assume that the witness will speak only in affirmative non-compound, subject-predicate sentences, we might construe 'What the witness says will be true' as abbreviating 'The witness will make a statement in which he will apply to a thing a term designating a property which the thing does have'. Since the witness may also use relational sentences, however, we should add: '*or* he will apply to a set of objects a term designating a relation which holds among the members of that set'. Since he may also use sentences which are conjunctions, we should add: '*or* he will make a statement, in which he . . . or in which he . . ., *and* in which he . . . or in which he . . .'. And, if we know how, we must add still more clauses to take care of the possibility that he may use sentences of still other forms—subjunctive conditionals, for example—taking care, all the while, that none of our new statements has the appearance of formulating a relation between a statement and the object of a *that*-clause. If we succeed, the statements which would replace 'What the witness says will be true'—and, *a fortiori*, those replacing 'Every statement is either true or false' and 'In any language in which statements can be made at all, it must be possible to make true and false statements'— will be very long indeed; hence it may seem proper to say that the old statements are 'abbreviations' of the new ones. But the trouble is, or one trouble is, that most of us do not know what these longer statements would be. And to say that a man uses A as an abbreviation for X, when he does not have the slightest idea what X might be, is, at the very least, an 'incorrect' use of the word 'abbreviation'.

The thesis that facts are 'pseudo-objects' is not unlike the 'phenomenalism' of Mach and other nineteenth-century philosophers. Mach contended, it will be recalled, that 'body, ego, matter, and mind' are 'intellectual abridgements', and from this thesis he inferred that 'the world does not consist of mysterious entities, which by their interaction with another, equally mysterious entity, the ego, produce sensations, which alone are accessible'.[1] But neither Mach nor subsequent phenomenalists succeeded in spelling

[1] From 'Introductory Remarks' to *The Analysis of Sensations* (1890).

out just what it is, on any particular occasion, that is supposed to abridge what. The 'abbreviatory statement-devices' are in a better position, for there are *some* clear examples of how these devices are supposed to work. But there are other cases where the status of these devices is much more problematic. An essential part of being fair to facts, I should think, would be to indicate that Strawson's case against them rests upon this problematic theory of abbreviations.

Appealing to etymology, Austin notes that 'fact' was originally used as 'a name for "something in the world" ' (cf. 'feat') and that its subsequent connection with *that*-clauses arose out of this earlier use. (Meinong appealed to etymology, in behalf of the same cause, to show that the 'that' of our *that*-clauses is nothing more than a demonstrative pronoun. 'I believe that Socrates is mortal', he said, comes from: 'I believe *this*: Socrates is mortal.' The 'this', he argued, is not here used to designate a linguistic entity. And Brentano tried to show—what the case *against* facts seems to require—that such psychological statements can be paraphrased without the use of any propositional clauses at all.[1]) To suppose that 'fact' is a name for a pseudo-entity, Austin says, is 'to treat a wholesome English expression as though it were a philosopher's invented expression'. He cites examples of sentences containing 'fact' and in which (he says) 'fact' has no obvious connection with *that*-clauses. These include: 'The collapse of the Germans is a fact', 'He has had no personal experience of the facts he reports', 'What are the facts?' and also (perhaps less fair to facts) 'Fevers are facts' and 'The condition of the cat is a fact'. And he makes several interesting points about the 'grammar' of 'fact' and uses these to critize some of the things which Strawson said in his second paper. But *his* case for facts, I think, is not enough to dissuade anyone who had been persuaded by what Strawson said.

8. At the beginning of 'Ifs and Cans' (1956), Austin states that he intends to discuss two large questions:

(1) 'Whenever . . . we say that we can do something, or could do something, or could have done something, is there an *if* in the offing—suppressed, it may be but due nevertheless to appear when we set out our sentence in full or when we give an explanation of its meaning?'

---

[1] See Meinong's *Über Annahmen*, 2nd edn. (Leipzig, 1910), p. 48; and Brentano's *Psychologie vom empirischen Standpunkt*, ii (Leipzig, 1925), pp. 158–72.

And (2) 'if and when there *is* an *if*-clause appended to a main clause which contains a *can* or *could* or *could have*, what sort of an *if* is it? What is the meaning of the *if*, or what is the effect or the point of combining this *if*-clause with the main clause?'

With respect to the first of these questions, he notes that it is one thing to say (*a*) that categorical sentences beginning with 'I can', 'He could have', etc., carry with them an implicit *if*-clause which is always understood and capable of being supplied, and that it is quite another thing to say (*b*) that such sentences may be paraphrased or explicated by means of other sentences which contain *if*-clauses. If, for example, we said that 'I can' means the same as 'I can if I try' we would be affirming (*a*), and if we said that 'I can' means the same as 'I will succeed if I try', we would be affirming (*b*).

What Austin says about *ifs* in connection with (2) is very important, it seems to me. He points out that the *ifs* of such sentences as 'I can if I choose', 'There are biscuits on the sideboard if you want them', 'I paid you back yesterday if you remember', and 'You may exercise your rights if you want to', are not the *ifs* of casual (or other) conditions. For sentences of the form 'if *p* then *q*', in which the *if* is the *if* of condition may be contraposed to 'if not-*q* then not-*p*'; but none of the sentences just cited may be so contraposed. It is relevant to note that these non-conditional *if* sentences are not *if-then* sentences; even if we put the *if*-clause first, it would be unnatural to begin the other clause with *then*. Austin gives us a plausible positive account of the uses of these non-conditional *ifs* and shows how they may be used to express, or to assert, hesitation, doubt, or stipulation. For example, the *if* of 'I shall marry him if I choose', provided the sentence is one in which the *shall* may be stressed, 'qualifies the *content* of the undertaking given, or of the intention announced, it does *not* qualify the giving of the undertaking'.

This account does not hold of all non-conditional *ifs*, however. There are some which are simply vulgarisms; e.g. 'That's poisonous if you drink it' and 'I hope you have a good time in Paris if I don't see you again'. And there is another type of non-conditional *if* which Austin does not mention—those *ifs*, namely, that may be replaced by *even ifs*. 'If it rains I will go', when the statement is intended in such a way that 'even' may be inserted at the beginning, or 'just the same' at the end, cannot be contraposed to 'If I do not go it will not have rained'. Here, too, 'then' is inappropriate. (The non-conditional 'even if *p, q*' seems to be equivalent to '*q* whether or not *p*' and to '*q* and it is false that if *p* then not-*q*.')

Austin's first question—'When we say "I can", "He could", etc., is there an *if* in the offing?'—arises in connexion with the treatment of the problem of free will (Austin says 'the problem, so-called, of Free Will') in G. E. Moore's *Ethics*. Moore had answered the question affirmatively in trying to show that the thesis of determinism is compatible with saying that people can, or could, do things that they do not do. Moore said:

> There are certainly good reasons for thinking that we *very often* mean by 'could' merely 'would, *if* so and so had chosen'. And if so, then we have a sense of the word 'could' in which the fact that we often *could* have done what we did not do, is perfectly compatible with the principle that everything has a cause: for to say that, *if* I had performed a certain act of will, I should have done something which I did not do, in no way contradicts this principle.

Austin intimates that, in the course of this discussion, Moore made a 'first-water, ground-floor mistake', but it is not clear to me just what the mistake is that Moore is supposed to have made.

It *would* be a mistake to say that the *ifs* in 'I can if I choose' and 'He could have if he had chosen' are conditional *ifs*, for, as Austin points out, these sentences cannot be contraposed and their *ifs* ordinarily perform quite a different function. In the first chapter of his *Ethics* Moore did repeatedly use such expressions as 'can if I choose' and 'could have if he had chosen', but in chapter six, in which the discussion of free-will occurs (and from which the above quotation is taken) he does not use these expressions. He says there that 'could' means 'would, if so and so had chosen', and he says 'I could have' means 'if I had performed a certain act of will, I should have'; he does not suggest there that 'can' and 'could' are accompanied by implicit *if*-clauses, much less that they are accompanied by *if*-clauses containing conditional *ifs*.

Moore's point, in showing that the thesis of free will might be reconciled with that of determinism, was to indicate that certain sentences in which 'can' or 'could' occur may be replaced by certain *if-then* sentences in which 'can' or 'could' do not occur. It was unfortunate that he used the particular verb 'choose' in his *if*-clauses, for, as Austin notes, there are objections applying to 'choose' which do not apply to other verbs which Moore might have used instead. (Note that Moore does use another verb in his example at the end of the passage quoted.) If Austin is right, *if*-clauses containing 'choose' or one of its variants as the principal verb are almost always non-conditional, in the sense just described. Was Moore's mistake simply that of interpreting 'choose' in a way in which it is not ordinarily interpreted? This would be a mistake, but not a 'first-water, ground-floor mistake'.[1]

What Austin took to be Moore's basic mistake may have been that of supposing that 'can' may be expressed in terms of 'will if', or 'would if', and that the indicative 'could have' may be expressed in terms of 'would have if'. This may well be a mistake, but Austin's objections to it can be met, I think. He considers two ways of rendering 'can' in terms of 'will if', etc., and he shows that one of these is unsatisfactory, but I do not think that he shows the other to be unsatisfactory.

The first of these is the account of 'could have' in P. H. Nowell-Smith's *Ethics*. Nowell-Smith considers the sentence (*C*) 'Smith could have read *Emma* last night' and says that what it means could also be expressed by (*W*): 'Smith would have read *Emma* last night, if there had been a copy, if he had not been struck blind, etc. etc., and if he had wanted to read it more than he wanted to read anything else.' (This statement, which has the form 'if *p*, if *r*, and if *s*, then *q*', may also be put as 'if *p* and *r* and *s*, then *q*'.) Austin offers several objections, the most telling of which seems to me to be the following: To establish *W* we need evidence, not merely as to Smith's abilities and opportunities, but also as to his character, motives, and the like; to establish *C* we do not need such evidence. But Austin also says this of *W*: So far from *W* being what we mean by saying Smith could have read the book, 'it actually implies that he could *not* have read it, for more than adequate reasons: it implies that he was blind at the time, and so on'. Unless I have seriously misunderstood Austin at this point, there would seem to be *two* mistakes underlying this remark. It is a mistake, first, to suppose that subjunctive conditionals, such as *W*, are

---

[1] 'Then you agree, I said, that the pleasant is the good and the painful evil. And here I would beg my friend Prodicus not to introduce his distinction of names, whether he is disposed to say pleasurable, delightful, joyful. However, by whatever name he prefers to call them, I will ask you, most excellent Prodicus, to answer in my sense of the words.

'Prodicus laughed and assented, as did the others.' *Protagoras*, p. 358.

necessarily contrary-to-fact—to suppose that they assert, imply, or presuppose that their antecedents are false. A man may assert W, for example, in the course of trying to decide whether its antecedent is true. ('Did he read *Emma* last night? I don't have the whole picture yet. But if there had been a copy . . . etc.') Or he may know that the antecedent is true and use the subjunctive in order to be non-committal. ('I'm not saying, one way or the other. But this much is true: if there had been a copy . . . etc.') And the second mistake is that of supposing that, from the fact that the antecedent of 'if p and r and s, then q' is false, it follows that p is false and r is false and s is false.

There is still another possible way of expressing 'can' in terms of 'will if', or 'would if', and expressing 'could have' in terms of 'would have if'. Austin concedes that there is some plausibility in the 'suggestion that "I can do X" means "I shall succeed in doing X, if I try" and "I would have done X" means "I should have succeeded in doing X if I had tried" '—plausibility, he says, 'but no more', and he rejects the suggestion.

Among the objections to saying that 'He can' means the same as 'He will if he tries' are the following, all indicating possible cases in which 'He can' is true and 'He will if he tries' is not true. (i) A man who can do X may try to do X and because of an unexpected diversion or intrusion abandon the enterprise before he finishes; he gives up the puzzle because of a call to dinner. (Here we may say 'He can but he wants his dinner' but not 'He could if he did not want his dinner'.) (ii) The man may try half-heartedly—i.e. he may not try as hard as he *can* try—and thus not complete the task. (iii) I can close my eyes, but it makes no sense to speak of me, now, *trying* to close my eyes. (iv) Austin suggests (this seems to be his principal objection to the formula) that 'He can' is consistent with failure and 'He will if he tries' is not. He says of the case where he misses a very short putt: 'I may try and miss, and yet not be convinced that I could not have done it; indeed further experiments may confirm my belief that I could have done it that time although I did not.' And finally (v) there may be things a man can do only if he does *not* try to do them. The golfer landed the ball at a certain place p; hence landing it at p was something which, at that time, he could do ('does' implies 'can'); but had he tried to land the ball precisely at the place p where he did land it, then, in all probability, he would have failed.

These are valid objections to saying that 'He can' means the same as 'He will if he tries.' But we may replace 'He will if he tries' by a longer formula and then, I believe, they no longer apply. Suppose we say: 'He can do X' means that there is something such that if he tried to do *it* then he would do X—i.e. that there is something Y such that if he tried to do Y then he would do X.

Then (i) we may say, of the man who could do the puzzle but gave it up in order to have his dinner, that there was something— e.g. doing the puzzle without having dinner—which was such that, had he tried to do *that*, he would have done the puzzle. (ii) Or if doing the puzzle required only a little more effort than he cared to put into it, then there was something—putting more effort into the puzzle—which was such that had he tried to do it he would have done the puzzle. (iii) Perhaps it makes no sense to say of me, now, that I may try to close my eyes; but there are other things I can be said to try to do—I can try to look the way I do when I'm asleep—which are such that if I do try to do them I will close my eyes. (iv) If Austin's golfer really could have holed it that time, then there was something such that, had he tried to do it along with the other things he did do, then the absent condition (e.g. applying more pressure with the thumb) would have been supplied, and he would have holed the ball. And (v) we may say of the man who landed the ball at p and who would not have done it had he tried to do it, that there were things such that had he tried to do *them* he would have landed the ball at p; they were just the things he did try to do. (We cannot say, however, that landing it at p is something that he can do 'at will', or something he 'knows how to do', for landing it at p is not itself something he can do if he tries.)

But there is still another possible difficulty: the statements 'He does X if and only if he tries to do Y' and 'He *cannot* try to do Y' are inconsistent with 'He can do X', but they are not inconsistent with our *analysans*—they are not inconsistent with 'There is a Y such that if he tries to do Y he will do X'. (There are, of course, many acts which one cannot even *try* to perform.) This is the serious difficulty, I think. If it is a genuine one, then it applies not only to the present formula, but also to those which Austin mentions and, in all probability, to any attempt to define 'can' in terms of 'will if'. For any such attempt will presumably introduce a verb of which 'he' may be made the subject; it will then be grammatically permissible to insert 'can not' between the subject 'he' and the verb; and then it will be possible to describe a situation in which the *analysans* is true and 'He can' is false. To overlook this possibility *is* a 'first-water, ground-floor mistake'.

All of which confirms Austin's profound remark: 'In philosophy it is *can* in particular that we seem so often to uncover, just when we had thought some problem settled, grinning residually up at us like the frog at the bottom of the beer mug.'

9. 'A Plea for Excuses' (1956) and 'Pretending' (1958) are concerned almost exclusively with the grammar of certain philosophically important expressions—with that of 'excuse' and a variety of related terms, and with that of 'pretend'. There is no technical vocabulary, beyond a few initials, for the reader to keep track of, and Austin is not trying to show that other philosophers are muddled and naïve. The result is that the two papers are 'linguistic phenomenology' (Austin's term) at its best.

I have only one criticism that may be worth noting: in the first of the two papers, Austin tells us that there are two types of defence we may offer if we are accused of doing something bad: 'In the one defence, briefly, we accept responsibility but deny that it was bad: in the other, we admit that it was bad but do not accept full, or even any, responsibility. . . . The first is a *justification*, the second an *excuse*.' I suggest that there is still another type of defence, also properly called an 'excuse'.

There is a class of actions—we might say they are cases of 'non-obligatory well-doing'—which philosophers and theologians have described as being acts of 'supererogation'; these acts include, not only the great deeds of saints and heroes, but those small favours and little deeds of kindness which are good things to do but which (we like to think) are things we really do not *have* to do. If it is plausible to suppose that there *are* cases of 'non-obligatory well-doing', then, I believe, it is equally plausible to suppose that there are also cases of 'permissive ill-doing'. These latter—which are *not* to be identified with the omission of 'non-obligatory well-doing'— would include trifling discourtesies, some of the 'venial' misdeeds which (we like to think) our position entitles us to, many of those things that are just this side of actually cheating, and in general all of those acts that may be excused by saying: 'After all, I was within my rights.' With this type of defence we accept responsibility *and* admit that the act was bad.

AUSTIN'S PHILOSOPHY OF ACTION[1]

L. W. Forguson

THE concept of action, though it has been an object of philosophical scrutiny since the infancy of philosophy, has come in for a growing amount of discussion in recent years, particularly among English-speaking philosophers. The importance of achieving an adequate understanding of this concept can scarcely be denied, standing as it does at the crossroads of such notorious problem areas as ethics, the free-will controversy, the philosophy of law and the philosophy of mind. For it has become evident that, in these and other areas of interest to philosophers, one can hardly expect eventually to talk sense about the central issues without first clearing the way by an elucidation of what is and what is not an action.

It is usually claimed, for instance, that a man's behaviour is to be excused, or in other ways exempt from full, or any, moral censure, just in so far as we think that it does not, or at least does not wholly, constitute an action of his. But the general efficacy of this claim, as implemented in particular cases, depends upon having arrived at an understanding of what constitutes certain behaviour as the performance of an action.

Nearly all of Austin's later work, from 1955 until his death in 1960, involved an examination of various aspects of the concept of action. The cluster of views presented in these writings, if

---

[1] This paper was first published, under the title 'La Philosophie De L'Action de J. L. Austin', in the January–March, 1967 issue of *Archives de Philosophie*. It was intended for an audience of French-speaking philosophers having little or no acquaintance with Austin's writings. Therefore, the paper is primarily expository and contains virtually no criticism of Austin's views. The English version is printed here with only minor stylistic changes, in the hope that it may be of some use in promoting a wider understanding of one of the more constructive aspects of Austin's philosophy.

considered together, taking special care not to *impute* views, will show that his contribution to the philosophy of action was of great originality and importance.

I

It would be claiming too much to claim that Austin set forth, or even held at all, anything like a general *theory* of action, in the sense of a systematic and comprehensive view of the 'nature' of human action. Indeed, Austin thought that the construction of general theories, or rather the unrestrained zeal for such activity, has been responsible for a great deal of darkness and confusion. But this needs explanation, and perhaps some qualification.

It was Austin's belief that, in pursuing the perfectly legitimate aim of providing solutions to fundamental philosophical problems, philosophers have usually resorted to generalization and definition much too early in the game, with the consequence that the theories in which these occur have been greatly oversimplified, failing utterly to account in any way adequately for the facts needing explanation. Austin would not have claimed that the search for general truths is misguided in principle. But he did insist that generalizations, if they are to hope to be true, much less illuminating, must be built upon solid and carefully prepared ground. A patient survey of the facts to be explained, and a clear delimitation of exactly what issues are at stake must precede any adequate generalization.

Austin thought that what has generally been said about human action has suffered from this sort of oversimplification. What is needed is an entirely fresh start, a new 'latter day version of conduct', based upon a thorough examination of all the available data, and leading to cautious classification and finally to definition. But all these stages are necessary; we must unearth the facts, and we must proceed slowly and cautiously from there, being careful all the while not to give way, in a moment of speculative exuberance, to premature classification and hasty generalization: a structuring that is really stricturing. Austin never thought that he had got much beyond the initial stages of the inquiry. It will, however, be worthwhile to see how well he set the stage for further inquiry, and how much of lasting importance he did accomplish in aiding our understanding of human conduct. In what follows, I shall largely limit my attention to two papers in which Austin discussed this topic most directly and most extensively: 'A Plea for Excuses',[1] and 'Three Ways of Spilling Ink'.[2]

Austin contended, as we have seen, that traditional discussions of the notion of action have been unsatisfactory. Let us now consider in some detail what Austin found most objectionable in these discussions.

Until fairly recent times, philosophers have not been very directly concerned with the concept of action in its own right, but have generally talked about action almost in passing, while attending to other issues, such as problems in ethics. Nevertheless, while there are perhaps few explicit traditional doctrines concerning the nature of action, there is to be found a rather loose and certainly implicit group of assumptions or presuppositions which, according to Austin, show that philosophers have tended to draw unfounded conclusions from their own use of certain expressions, chief among which are expressions like 'doing an action' itself. Unlike the use of 'action' in ordinary speech,

> 'doing an action', as used in philosophy, is a highly abstract expression—it is a stand-in used in the place of any (or almost any?) verb with a personal subject, in the same way that 'thing' is a stand-in for any (or when we remember, almost any) noun-substantive, and 'quality' a stand-in for the adjective. ('A Plea.')

Austin is not here condemning the *use* of these expressions by philosophers, for there is no doubt that they have perfectly legitimate uses, not only in philosophical prose but in everyday speech. Conversation would, indeed, be awkward and certainly rather boring were these convenient 'substitute' expressions not to exist. But it must be remembered that they are *merely,* expressions of convenience, having no special significance apart from their roles as 'stand-ins'. We should not, for example, be misled by the pervasiveness in speech of such expressions as 'thing' and 'quality' into taking them to be 'names' for every fundamental features of 'reality'. Yet it is notorious that questions such as 'What is a thing?' and

---

[1] This paper will be referred to hereafter as 'A Plea'.

[2] A draft of this paper, which was read to the American Society of Political and Legal Philosophy in Chicago, in December, 1958, was found among Austin's papers after his death. It has been edited by the present author, and was published in the October, 1966 issue of *The Philosophical Review*. It will be referred to hereafter as 'Three Ways'.

'Is a thing anything apart from the sum of its qualities?' have been asked, and have been answered in the form of oversimplified ontologies that divide 'reality' into two mutually exclusive categories.

Just as philosophers have often tended to place too much weight on the significance of such expressions as 'thing' and 'quality' in metaphysics, Austin thought that there has been a tendency to view the expression 'doing an action', which is quite useful as a stand-in for certain verbs, as a 'self-explanatory ground level description, one that brings adequately into the open the essential features of everything that comes, by simple inspection, under it'. ('A Plea'). That is, 'doing an action' comes to be taken as a primitive expression, not capable of further analysis, which illuminates the *nature* of conduct, and to which all other descriptions of conduct can be, in some way, reduced. This leads to an oversimplified view of human behaviour in which,

> we come easily to think of our behaviour over any time, and of life as a whole, as consisting in doing now action *A*, next action *B*, then action *C*, and so on, just as elsewhere we come to think of the world as consisting of this, that and the other substance or material thing, each with its properties. ('A Plea.')

Consequently, there is a tendency to think that,

> All 'actions' are, as actions (meaning what?), equal, composing a quarrel with striking a match, winning a war with sneezing. ('A Plea.')

Once this view is made explicit, however, its difficulties are seen to be manifest. First of all, it is far from clear precisely what the verbs are, and on what occasions of their use, for which 'doing an action' may be substituted. It is not difficult to think of cases in which we use verbs with personal subjects for which this expression quite clearly cannot be substituted. 'I fell down the stairs', for instance is one such case. These are perhaps easy to recognize; but is it equally easy to see *why* they are to be excluded?

More difficult are the many borderline cases: cases in which it is no simple matter to determine whether or not the verb, as used on a particular occasion, is a 'verb of action'. For example, is to believe something to do an action, or to sneeze, or to decide to do something? The existence of cases like these shows that many other considerations need to be introduced in order to pick out verbs of action from other, grammatically similar verbs. It is certainly not enough merely to ask whether there is an occurrence of a verb with a personal subject.

Now one way of making a decision in these border line cases, and of providing a general account of what 'doing an action' is, gives rise to another of the difficulties adumbrated above. For one might wish to say, (and Austin thought that this is in the background in much of what philosophers have said on this score), that doing an action, whatever else we may wish to say about it, must be, in the ultimate analysis, the making of bodily movements. In much the same way in which philosophers have, in metaphysics, tended to assimilate the furniture of the world to the model of a few obvious instances, usually actual furniture such as tables and chairs, here, in their discussions of conduct, the tendency has been to take rather simple and obvious instances of actions—instances, moreover, that fit this general account in terms of bodily movements—and to set these up as models of the performance of an action, to which all action is simply assimilated.

Although it would be a mistake to minimize unduly the role of bodily movements in at least a large class of actions, a simple and wholesale assimilation of actions to bodily movements is equally mistaken.[1] As Austin says, 'even the simplest named actions are not so simple—certainly are not the mere makings of physical movements.' ('A Plea.') Thus we need to ask what more comes in: what more is included in the doing of an action, besides bodily movements. We shall return to this question later. But before it can be taken up, we must turn to a consideration of Austin's views on the proper method of unearthing the facts in pursuit of a 'latter day version of conduct'.

II

According to Austin, the main source of facts is what we *say*: what might be called, for lack of a better epithet, 'the language of conduct'. We should begin our investigation by a study of the many resources we have, the many words we have for talking about human conduct. We are, after all, active beings, and our own and others' actions are a matter of continuous and often pressing interest

---

[1] For instance, some acts, some of our conduct, involve no bodily movements at all. I can *allow* you to enter, I can *fail* to prevent him from taking your wallet, I can *wait* for someone, without moving a muscle.

to us. Consequently, we may expect to find a rich stock of expressions used in everyday discourse from which to draw. Again, whatever version of conduct we finally arrive at will have to take account of what we actually do say, even if—especially if—we wish to criticize ordinary ways of talking. In order to have grounds for criticizing what we say, we must have a clear understanding of what we do say, and why we say it. This much is plain common sense.

But, it might be objected, why begin here? Why think that words have any significance for an inquiry into conduct? After all, we're interested in what we *do*, not in what we say. Austin's justification of this method of procedure constitutes what has been called his 'evolutionary view' of language. It is perhaps best brought out in the following passages:

> *In the very long run*, the forms of speech which survive will be the *fittest* (most efficient) forms of speech. ('Three Ways.')

And again:

> Our common stock of words embodies all the distinctions men have found worth drawing, and the connections they have found worth marking, in the lifetimes of many generations: these surely are likely to be more numerous, more sound, since they have stood up to the long test of the survival of the fittest, and more subtle, at least in all ordinary and reasonably practical matters, than any that you and I are likely to think up in our arm-chairs of an afternoon—the most favored alternative method. ('A Plea.')

Now this view, which points to the enormous resources of any natural language, has a great deal to recommend it. (Indeed, Austin thought that it was perhaps so obvious as to be a truism.) If an expression has survived, there is every reason to believe, until we are given some reason to believe to the contrary, that it has a use, that it marks some real distinction. What we actually say, then, will be of the utmost importance for any inquiry into what we *do*. An attention to language is indispensible to any study of conduct because, according to Austin, a language reflects the accumulated thoughts and experiences of its users.

This is not to say that Austin wished to rest content with a study of 'ordinary language'. On the contrary, he realized that ordinary language sometimes cannot cope with extraordinary situations, and it is always open to purges, changes and adjustments in the light of discoveries from sources, such as science, outside the scope of everyday experience. Ordinary language may not be 'in order as it is', but this is something that must be discovered (and the disorders pointed out in detail), and not merely assumed at the outset, perhaps from a superior, 'scientific' point of view. All this is only to say that a study of our actual language of conduct is not going to constitute the 'last word'. But, and this is a point on which Austin insisted, it is going to constitute the 'first word': we must first determine what we do say, and why, before we can hope to pass upon what we should say. Austin once remarked that the method here recommended—using a study of ordinary language as a tool to get at the facts without preconceptions—might well be called 'linguistic phenomenology', though, he added characteristically, 'that would be rather a mouthful.'

Austin thought that there are two main ways in which a study of what we say will be helpful in uncovering the facts about action. First, initial intuitions lead us to suspect that contexts, circumstances, or situations are highly relevant for determining what actions people are said to perform. It is always an event in a context that is singled out as an action. Thus, one fruitful method of approach would be to examine cases or situations and see if agreement can be reached about how these are to be described. First on the list would be actual cases, as reported or described by the participants themselves or by observers. Another source would be fictional cases: there is much to be learned by reading the descriptions of conduct in novels, for instance. Finally, we can *imagine* cases, 'if we imagine them thoroughly and comprehensively and in detail', being careful not to import theoretical biases into our accounts of them. These, if we can agree about what to say about them, will give us data—Austin even called it 'experimental data' —which we can then go on to explain.

Following this method, we may profit by going even further afield, outside the confines of 'ordinary language', and draw upon specialized fields where a keen interest is taken in action. Austin suggested making use of the law and psychology in this connexion. In both of these areas we will find a wealth of descriptions of cases which are highly extraordinary, yet highly relevant to the study of human action.

The second way in which a study of what we say will help unearth the facts about conduct is closely associated with the first, yet requires a special standpoint and special methods of its own. This is a detailed study of the language of conduct itself. Here, it is necessary to attend to the different grammatical kinds of such words and the rules (or regularities) of their use. Austin also thought that it would be important to attend to the etymology of these expressions, in order to see what lessons can be learned from their histories that will illuminate their present uses. A use of this method should, Austin was confident, give us a means for delineating classes or 'family groups' of words and hence of family groups of actions, which will allow us to begin to introduce some classification into the study of action.

Although verbs comprise the largest grammatical class of words employed in the language of conduct, there is not really too much that can be learned from an examination of verbs alone, and Austin did not devote much attention to them. He was, however, very much interested in the expressions which are used to modify 'verbs of action'. Austin's interest in modifying expressions grew out of his conviction that we can best come to understand what is involved in normal cases of 'doing an action' by means of a study of allegedly abnormal cases. For it is often only when something goes wrong that we begin to pay attention to the conditions under which it goes right. We don't worry about how the clock works until it begins to malfunction: Thus,

> The abnormal will throw light upon the normal, will help us to penetrate the blinding veil of ease and obviousness that hides the mechanisms of the normal successful act. ('A Plea.')

When we begin to study modifying expressions and their roles with respect to verbs of action, we see fairly quickly that they tend to fall into 'family groups'. Austin was particularly interested in two such groups, which are complementary, and which are important for our understanding of human conduct. These are, first, expressions used to modify the verb in an attempt to *excuse* conduct, such as 'accidentally', 'inadvertently', 'unintentionally', etc., and those which are used in an attempt to rule out excuses, or in general to assign responsibility, such as 'intentionally', 'deliberately', 'on purpose'. Austin thought that further distinctions within these families would also point to family groups of actions, the verbs for which are modified by these expressions, and would also illuminate distinguishable features or components in the normal

—or abnormal—performance of an action: what he called 'the complicated internal machinery of action'. Consequently, we may be in a better position to explain and classify verbs of action themselves if we first study the kinds of words, and their special features, that modify these verbs.

It must be realized, first of all, that there are, in actual practice, definite restrictions on our use of modifying expressions. There is, Austin said, a temptation to think that for any verb of action, there is, on any occasion of its use, at least one modifying expression or its 'opposite' which is applicable without anomaly: either he picked it up intentionally or unintentionally. However, if we attend to what we actually say in our descriptions of conduct, we will find that

> the natural economy of language dictates that for the *standard* case covered by any normal verb . . . no modifying expression is required or even permissible. Only if we do the action named in some *special* way or circumstances, different from those in which such an act is naturally done . . . is a modifying expression called for, or even in order. ('A Plea.')

Once it is realized that the use of modifying expressions is restricted in normal discourse, the next step is to determine the 'limits of application' of such expressions. The results of such an investigation will, Austin thought, enable us to illuminate the peculiar characteristics of the group of action verbs to which a given expression is applicable. For instance, Austin found that expressions which, on first glance, would seem to be 'opposites' are not really opposites at all, but are applicable to different sorts of actions, despite the fact that, in philosophy and in the law, they are often used dichotomistically. Austin uses as an example 'voluntarily' and 'involuntarily'.

> I can perhaps 'break a cup' voluntarily, *if* that is done, say, as an act of self-impoverishment: and I can break another involuntarily, *if*, say, I make an involuntary movement which breaks it. Here, plainly, the two acts described each as 'breaking a cup' are really very different. ('A Plea.')

Austin pointed out that the opposite of 'voluntary' would most properly be 'under constraint' or 'duress', that of 'involuntary' would be 'deliberately' or 'on purpose'.

Not only are the opposites of many modifying expressions not what they would appear to be at first glance, but many modifying expressions have no 'opposites' at all, for there is no use for them. We have 'wilfully' but not 'willessly', 'inadvertently' but not 'advertently'.

> In passing the butter I do not knock over the cream jug, though I do (inadvertently) knock over the teacup—yet I do not by-pass the cream jug *advertently*: for at this level, below supervision in detail, *anything* we do is, if you like, inadvertent, though we only call it so, and indeed only call it something we have done, if there is something untoward about it. ('A Plea.')

The 'natural economy' of language also indicates that we should at least begin with the assumption that words that are often said to be synonymous have distinct jobs to perform. This is nowhere more evident than in the case of expressions which modify action verbs, and Austin gave three of these allegedly synonymous expressions special attention in 'Three Ways of Spilling Ink'. We often ask whether someone did something intentionally, or deliberately, or on purpose. And there is a temptation to treat these as really amounting to the same question. However, a consideration of some situations in which we might imagine these questions asked shows that they are different questions entirely, and that using one of these expressions rather than another to modify a verb gives us quite different notions of the 'actions' performed. The following example used by Austin will help bring out these differences.

> The notice says 'do not feed the penguins'. I, however, feed them peanuts. Now peanuts happen to be, and these prove, fatal to these birds. Did I feed them peanuts intentionally? Beyond a doubt. I am no casual peanut shedder. But deliberately? Well, that seems perhaps to raise the question, 'Had I read the notice?' Why does it? Or 'on purpose?' That seems to insinuate that I knew what fatal results would ensue. ('Three Ways.')

Doing things deliberately, on purpose, and intentionally are, therefore, not at all the same thing. What also needs mentioning is that these expressions may on occasion be used in combination. They are, though distinct, not always to be dissociated.

> Do children pull the wings off flies 'on purpose?' Yet see them at it, and it is patent that they do it intentionally and also deliberately. ('Three Ways.')

One group of modifiers needing special attention are prepositions. Austin was convinced that it is not purely accidental that some expressions qualifying verbs of action are governed by 'in', others by 'after', 'with', 'by', etc. If we look closely, we can usually find a reason for the difference. A case in point is 'deliberation'. We can use either 'with deliberation' or 'after deliberation'. In both cases, the adjectival form is 'deliberately'. This might lead us to think that it makes no difference which preposition is used. But it does. 'After deliberation' indicates that one has deliberated about what one has done; one has weighed up the positive and negative aspects and then has decided to do it anyway. 'With deliberation', however, indicates a certain way or 'style' of performing the action itself. Many adverbs have this secondary, style-indicating sense.

The foregoing has been a sample only of the kinds of words the uses of which can be studied with profit. Austin was aware that much more remains to be done: many other words, and even parts of words, are in need of scrutiny before we can hope to generalize about human conduct. But the above gives some indication of the worth of this sort of study, and of the care with which Austin pursued it.

III

Let us now go on to consider some of the results that may be obtained from the employment of Austin's directions for the study of conduct. In applying these considerations, there is one question which seems to be pre-eminent: what distinguishes an action from other aspects of behaviour? Austin's answer is that there is no *one* distinguishing factor, but many, which are important in different ways. By using the methods outlined above, we can be led to see that what is called simply 'doing an action' is actually a very complicated affair. Not only are there many different factors relevant to determining what, on a given occasion, counts as 'the action' performed by an agent, but what Austin calls the 'internal machinery of action' is also quite complex, and can be divided into several 'departments', each with its proper function, and each with its characteristic ways of malfunctioning. We have, of course, to begin with, the agent's bodily movements. But, as was seen earlier, an action is not to be simply identified with the bodily movements involved in its performance. So we have to ask what more comes in, besides bodily movements, in determining what action, if any, is performed.

Austin asked, then, what determines whether a stretch of behaviour shall count as an action, or as one action rather than another? What grounds do we use, what do we take into account, in addition to the bodily movements made, in choosing one act 'name' or one description of 'what is done' rather than another? Quite obviously, a great many factors are relevant in this connexion, more than can be taken up within the scope of this paper. However, Austin singled out several of the contributing factors for special comment, and made some suggestions which can be mentioned and developed.

First of all, there is the matter of *conventions* to be considered. For a large class of actions at least, conventions are what determine whether certain behaviour is described as one action rather than another, or rather than as no action at all. This may perhaps be brought out most distinctly by a consideration of the following example. Consider someone kicking a ball into a certain spot on a field. Then consider someone kicking a goal, as in a soccer match. Now there is nothing physical involved in kicking a goal over and above that which is involved in kicking the ball. But in certain circumstances, for example, the playing of a certain game, certain conventions—here, the rules of the game—come into play, which *constitute* these bodily movements, together with certain of their results, as the performance of the act of kicking a goal. In the appropriate circumstances, that is, to kick a ball into a certain spot just *is* to kick a goal. In answer to the question, 'What did he do?' we may answer either (*a*) 'He kicked the ball into that spot', or (*b*) 'He kicked a goal', or even (*c*) 'He scored a point'.

What does this show us about 'doing an action'? It shows us that a great many actions, if not all, are as much socially constituted as they are physically constituted. Conventions are social phenomena, patterns of social organization. Not only games, but such 'ordinary' actions as waving good-bye, greeting someone, buying merchandise, and a great deal more are socially defined practices. Much of what we consider as actions simply could not be performed, that is, would not be the actions they are, though certain movements might be made, apart from the social framework, which is a framework of conventions, in terms of which they are constituted as actions. Waving good-bye and moving one's arm in a certain way may be the same thing physically, but there is a vast conceptual difference here, which can be accounted for only in terms of conventions.

Intentions play an equally significant role in our identification and description of human action. It was pointed out before that for most verbs of action, on normal occasions of their use, it does not make sense to use a modifying expression in connexion with the verb. Thus, it is in normal circumstances inappropriate to *say* 'He did it intentionally', instead of merely saying that he did it. This is not, however, because we do not for the most part do what we do intentionally. On the contrary, adding 'intentionally' is usually out of place because intentions are so intimately connected with our normal actions that the use of this modifier would in normal circumstances be *redundant*. Most verbs of action contain, as part of their 'meaning', the notion of some intention to be carried out. And this is one reason why viewing human conduct of the model of bodily movements is grossly oversimplified. A description of what someone does which relied purely upon 'behaviouristic' terms simply could not make use of the greater part of our common stock of action verbs.

Austin described the role of intentions in the following way:

> As I go through life, doing, as we suppose, one thing after another, I in general always have an idea . . . or picture, or notion, or conception of what I'm up to, what I'm engaged in, what I'm about or in general 'what I'm doing'. . . . I must be supposed to have *as it were* a plan, an operation-order or something of the kind on which I'm acting, which I am seeking to put into effect, carry out in action: only of course nothing necessarily, or usually even faintly, so full-blooded as a plan proper. ('Three Ways.')

This idea of what I'm doing Austin characterized as being like 'a miner's cap on our forehead which illuminates always just so far as we go along'. But this illumination is restricted in several ways. It does not extend indefinitely into the future: I do not have my whole future life structured by intentions that I can be said to 'have' *now*. And quite a bit of what I 'do'—many, perhaps most, of my bodily movements—is 'below the level of any intention . . . that I may have formed'. I intend, let us suppose, to go to the store. But I do not *intend* to do everything I do *in* going to the store.

Much of it is too minor and too much 'second nature' to be intended. Of course, it would be equally wrong to say that I do these things unintentionally. Intentions simply do not extend to this level of 'what I do'.

Austin thought that this account of the role of intentions has very important consequences for our description and assessment of conduct. For intentions have what he calls a 'bracketing effect' which enables us to 'structure' human behaviour to a large extent. It is partially in terms of intentions that we take some stretch of a man's behaviour as constituting *a single action*. That is, our view of the intentions involved will influence our choice of words for describing 'what he did'. We may, for instance, take X, Y, Z as three separate actions, described by three separate names (he did this, that, and finally the other), or, if we think that there is a single intention, and there are no special considerations that would lead us to make finer distinctions, we may take X, Y, Z to be one action, described by one name. We may say 'He picked up his pipe, selected a pipe cleaner, blew through the bit, etc.' or, simply, 'He cleaned his pipe'.

Caution is required, however, in describing the actions of others in terms of intentions. For this 'bracketing' will always be somewhat arbitrary unless we take into account, even if we later have grounds for disregarding it, the way the agent himself structured his behaviour in his own mind. His account of what he is (or was) doing—his avowal of intentions—will always be relevant, and may in certain circumstances be decisive. He may, for instance, in terms of what his intentions were, insist that we describe his action as (what he takes to be) a whole, and not in terms used to describe (what he takes to be) only a 'part' of the 'whole' action. Considerations like this will come into play especially when there is a question of assessing his conduct. Thus, along with conventions, but in a different way, intentions help to determine our descriptions of actions.

Not only are there many factors that have bearing on what is identified, in a particular situation, as 'one' or 'the' action, but, from a slightly different point of view, the study of actual situations makes it clear that 'we can generally split up what might be named as one action in several distinct ways'. Austin distinguished three such ways. We can 'split up' an action into 'phases', or 'stretches' or 'stages'.

Often, what is described as one action, usually something that goes on over a fairly long period of time, and perhaps even intermittently, can be broken up into 'phases', each of which can without anomaly be described as a separate action. We can say that someone wrote a book, or that he wrote first this sentence, and then that, and then the other, etc.

When we turn to 'stretches', however, the principle of individuation is drawn from a distinction between an action and certain of its consequences, results, or effects, which may also be ascribed to the agent as *his* actions. If I turn the key and, as a result, the car starts, I can be said to have 'started the car'. That's what I did, start the car. Yet I also, of course, turned the key, and that is also something that I did. Such things as intentions ('a man also intends the normal foreseen consequences of his intentional actions'), and the interests of the speaker in describing 'what is done' are influential in determining whether any of the consequences, etc. are included in the description of 'his action', as are moral considerations and also the law. Of course, there are limits here: certainly not everything which is a result, etc. of something I do is itself something that I *do*.

When we ask 'What is an action?' we may be asking, as above, how an action is to be identified or described: what name to call it. But we may also be asking 'What is involved in the "doing" of an action?' And here we would be referring to what Austin called 'the complicated internal machinery of action.' Austin tended to make use of either a military or a business model when discussing this aspect of action. The distinctions that can be made within the 'complete' performance of an action are talked of as if they corresponded to the various departments of organization in an army or a corporation. No doubt this tends to be somewhat of an oversimplification. Yet distinctions are there to be made, and Austin's models are helpful, especially if it is kept in mind that it is not the models, but what they help to clarify, that is important. Austin thought, in particular, that we could better understand the 'breakdowns' to which all actions are susceptible by seeing that different sorts of 'breakdowns' or abnormalities of action are the result of the malfunctioning of different 'stages' of the doing of an action.

There is the initial stage of the 'receipt of intelligence'. Action takes place in an environment, against a background of events and actions of other people. We generally act in response to some information (true or false) that we have got about this environment. Breakdowns often have their source here, as a result of faulty intelligence.

Having received some information, one must always put some interpretation on it, see it for what it is, or in short 'appreciate the situation'. We act as we do because we *construe* our information in a certain way. But things can go wrong here:

> We can know the facts and yet look at them mistakenly or perversely, or not fully realize or appreciate something, or even be under a total misconception. ('A Plea.')

Usually, when I act, I will do so in terms of certain principles which I think are applicable to the situation. These may be either standards of right and wrong conduct or much more mundane principles. In any case, it is evident that merely having certain information and having 'appreciated' it can't lead directly to action or even to the decision to act. There must be what Austin called an 'invocation of principles'.

Closely associated with the invocation of principles is 'deliberation'. I need not always deliberate before I act, but whenever I weigh the 'pros and cons' of the situation—and Austin was careful to say that these need not be *moral* pros and cons—this stage in the machinery of action comes into play.

Making our way to the top floors of the corporation, there is a stage where the decision must be taken whether to do it or not. And decision, of course, is influenced by the results of the other stages. The soundness of the decision will reflect the workings of the lower orders of the machinery.

Having decided, however, we realize that there is more than one way to accomplish something, more than one way of doing something in the light of the considerations thus far. Thus, there is usually to be gone through some consideration of 'ways and means', which is a planning of how and when to actually carry the action through. There must be some thought, no matter how minimal or even habitual, given to the practical matter of avoiding difficulties and choosing the appropriate means and time for execution.

Finally, we move into action. Actually *doing* the thing—the most 'outward' stage of the machinery—Austin called the 'executive stage'. Most of the verbs that 'name' actions are used in connexion with this stage, and of course, many of the possible 'breakdowns' occur here as well. In the executive stage, we must exercise sufficient control over the necessary bodily movements, and we must take sufficient care to avoid possible impingements and dangers, realizing that the action is performed against a background of circumstances, including the actions of other agents, so that we successfully complete the execution.

Now Austin did not think that looking at these features to be distinguished in the normal performance of an action on the model of stages or departments should be pushed very far. He certainly did not think that they function as independently as they must seem in being presented and discussed separately. Yet any adequate account of conduct must take these features into account. And Austin did think that this model might provide a means for introducing some classification into the language of conduct. For we may classify the expressions we use in terms of the different stages of the machinery to which they apply. For purposes of the moral assessment of conduct, too, it is evident that we may praise or blame separately the workings of different parts of the machinery.

Such, then, are some of the more important results obtained, in Austin's hands, from a study of the facts: a study of what we say. Although it is clear that most of these results are tentative and not worked out in detail, and although there is much more 'field work' to be done, it is equally clear that Austin has made a fundamental contribution to the philosophy of action.

IV

Before ending, and as a means for showing that the mansion of action has many rooms, it will be instructive to consider, along with the foregoing, Austin's treatment of a very important special class of actions: speech-acts.

It is fairly obvious, once it has been pointed out and handed to us on a platter, that to say something is normally also to do something. A man's words are his deeds, we say: by talking, one acts. What we say, then, is included as part of our conduct.

From an early interest in the notion of promising, Austin developed a doctrine of 'performative utterances': utterances which, though grammatically indicative, do not *state* anything, true or false, but actually perform acts. To say 'I promise to do so-and-so' is not to say or report *that* one promises: it *is* to promise. However, in his attempt to find a criterion which would distinguish performatives from all other sorts of utterance, Austin came to see that, in the relevant respects in which, say, an utterance of 'I promise . . .' performs an act, so do *all* utterances perform acts All utterances have their performative function. Thus, what is needed, Austin thought, is an entirely new examination of saying-as-doing: of speech-acts. The fullest treatment of this subject is found in the posthumously published *How To Do Things With Words*.[1]

For Austin, there are several distinguishable senses in which to say something is to do something. First, there is the act *of* saying something itself; the 'locutionary act'. Within this class there are several subsidiary senses in which saying something is always, 'in the full normal sense' doing something. Saying something always involves the act of producing certain noises, (or marks on paper, which are surrogates for noises), which comprise the 'phonetic act'. These noises are produced as belonging to a certain vocabulary and as conforming to a certain grammar. This is the 'phatic act'. Finally, the 'rhetic act' is an act of using the words thus produced with a certain meaning.

To know what locutionary act was performed on a certain occasion, however, is usually not to know enough. I may know that someone has performed the locutionary act of saying 'Pass the salt', and yet not know whether this was meant as (or constituted, in the circumstances) an order or merely a request. In short, I may know what was said but not know the *force* of the utterance: what it was meant to be taken *as*. Thus, to perform a locutionary act is also to perform an 'illocutionary act'. An illocutionary act is an act performed *in* saying something. For instance, to report an utterance as 'He warned me that the train was coming' rather than merely as 'He said that the train was coming', is to indicate that the utterance had the force of a warning: it was an illocutionary act of warning me that the train was coming. It is obvious that many of our 'names' for utterances single out illocutionary acts: 'promise', 'argue', 'concede', 'conjecture', 'commend', etc.

Very often, our illocutionary acts have effects, consequences or results on the thoughts and actions of others. For instance, as a result of *arguing* that the government is spending too much money

[1] Edited by J. O. Urmson, Oxford, 1962.

on space exploration (illocutionary act), I may *convince* you of this. And this is also something I am said to have 'done'. Such acts, which are the results, etc. of what one says, and yet are not themselves something one *says*, Austin called 'perlocutionary acts'. They are acts performed not so much *in* saying something as *by* saying something. Often, these results are *intended* by the speaker: I argue with the intention (or at least the hope) of convincing you. Yet sometimes they are not intended at all. But, if the circumstances are appropriate, the agent is said to have 'done' the act. As a result of arguing as above, I may alarm you. And this, alarming you, is also an act of mine.

Although one can be said to have performed a certain perlocutionary act as a consequence of having performed a certain illocutionary act, the illocutionary act is not in any sense a consequence of the locutionary act, nor is the locutionary act a consequence of its subsidiary acts. I don't 'say something' as a consequence of uttering certain noises. Rather, uttering them in the appropriate way *is* to say something. Similarly, to perform a certain locutionary act in the appropriate circumstances *is* to perform a certain illocutionary act.

The considerations and distinction that were made concerning other sorts of action are also relevant to the case of speech-acts. For example, speech-acts can be broken up into stages (the receipt of intelligence, etc.), and phases. We can say 'He argued that the government is overspending', or 'First he contended that . . ., and then he concluded that . . .' The distinction between illocutionary and perlocutionary acts, and the fact that we sometimes describe *the* act by use of the perlocutionary name or expression, is a matter of stretches: including or excluding certain of the consequences, etc. of what he said in the description of what he 'did'. Here, also, it can be seen that conventions and intentions are relevant for distinguishing between kinds of speech-act, and in determining how we describe *the* speech-act performed.

Conventions are of course of prime importance for any analysis of language and speech, since a language is a set of conventions. That words should mean what they do and may be combined in the way they are is all a matter of conventions. But conventions are also important for a discussion of speech as action. Many ceremonial illocutionary acts are conventional acts in a very explicit and formal sense. Greeting, promising, marrying, paying homage, are all ceremonies of life, and have appropriate verbal formulae for their performance. Many of these acts can be performed non-verbally as well, but when this is possible, there are explicit conventions to be followed. However, conventions also enter at less 'formal' levels, influencing our choice of illocutionary act names, and influencing also our choice of whether to describe 'what was done' in illocutionary or perlocutionary terms.

Intentions are very important factors in our ascriptions of illocutionary acts, for we usually decide what illocutionary act has been performed by our idea of the intentions of the speaker. (Did he intend it as a request or as a command?) And it is interesting to note that it usually does not make sense to say that a person performed an illocutionary act unintentionally, which may indicate that intentions are part of the constitutive conditions for illocutionary acts. I cannot unintentionally argue that the government is corrupt, for the intention is part of what makes it my argument.

Bodily movements, in particular movements of the tongue, lips, etc., are of course necessary for the performance of any (oral) speech-act, though it would obviously be a mistake to say that *this* is what saying something 'really is'. However, other bodily movements are more directly relevant in this respect. For instance, gestures, particularly facial gestures, are influential in our understanding of someone's speech-act in any full sense.

Again, in the study of speech-acts, as in the study of other acts, we must take into account the importance of the context of the utterance. We speak in, and in response to, our environment, and thus we cannot attend to the utterance alone, but must take the total speech-situation into account.

An examination of all these factors, as well as a consideration of actual cases and of the rules of use of the expressions we have for assigning, describing, or otherwise talking about speech-acts, will also enable us to begin to classify kinds of speech-acts, in terms of different sorts of illocutionary force. Austin thought that he had only scratched the surface here, and his classifications were only tentative; however, he distinguished five 'family groups' of illocutionary acts which may very briefly be characterized according to their uses in approach.

First, there is a class of speech-acts in which one gives verdicts or estimates or appraisals about some matter that calls for official or expert judgment. Austin called these 'verdictives', some examples of which are diagnosing, assessing, or valuing some article as to its worth. The second group is comprised of illocutionary acts used in the exercise of power, influence or rights. These, Austin called 'exercitives'; some instances are warning, voting, choosing, appointing, ordering. Austin called 'commissives' those acts, such as promising, consenting, guaranteeing, in which one commits oneself, in saying something, to a certain course of behaviour. In the fourth place are 'behibatives', which have to do with etiquette or social behaviour, such as apologizing, thanking, greeting, or even protesting or challenging. Finally, Austin outlined a group of illocutionary acts, called 'expositives', which make clear how our utterances are to be taken, or explain our position on something we have said or are about to say. Examples of expositives are affirming, denying, reporting, informing, and conceding.

For all these family groups and for any others that may be distinguished, we can bring in the results of our other considerations, especially those relating to modifying expressions, in order to see what further classifications may be made within these groups. In particular, like other actions, it will be illuminating to classify them in terms of the characteristic flaws of performance, or in general, the breakdowns, to which each is subject. Speech-acts are not only subject to the breakdowns peculiar to language, such as being vague, ambiguous, or meaningless, they are also subject to 'the ills that all acts are heir to'. Here, then, it will be necessary, in carrying the investigation farther, to determine which speech-acts are subject to which sorts of characteristic flaws. This will in turn give us a basis for fitting speech-acts into our general picture of conduct.

There is much that remains to be done: many facts to be unearthed and classified and explained. Yet Austin did not think it an impossible task. He thought that, with patience and imagination, a 'latter day version of conduct' could be achieved. Although Austin did not finish the task, his work forms an unescapable prolegomena to any future theory of conduct. The great misfortune for philosophy is that Austin did not live to carry the inquiry further. For, without his acuteness and imagination, it will be a much slower and more difficult task.

A PLEA FOR LINGUISTICS

C. G. New

I

ONE type of 'linguistic' philosophy is primarily an attempt to discriminate the uses of related expressions in what is vaguely called 'ordinary language'—that is, educated, non-technical English. The most authoritative and detailed exposition of the aims and methods of this kind of analysis is contained in J. L. Austin's celebrated paper 'A Plea for Excuses'. The aims have aroused a good deal of more or less inconclusive controversy, but not much has been said about the methods. Yet it is the methods that are most obviously controversial. In fact they are open to objections that are fatal to this type of investigation as Austin conceived it. These objections are revealed by a consideration of the relationship between philosophy and linguistics. A clear distinction must be drawn between the methods of descriptive linguistics and those of philosophical analysis. Neglecting this distinction has led some philosophers to talk about philosophy as though it were linguistics and about linguistics as though it were philosophy; which they are not. Not that philosophy and linguistics have no concern with each other: in some respects at least they clearly have. Only they should not be confused.

In the following sections I shall recapitulate some of Austin's aims and then examine in detail the methods he advocates for achieving them. It will become clear that the methods are in principle unreliable; and this conclusion will be reinforced by examining some of the results that Austin reached by means of them.

In 'A Plea for Excuses', Austin restricted himself to the topic of actions and, in particular, excuses. I shall restrict my criticism in the same way. But it is clear that his explanatory and methodological remarks are meant to be applicable to other topics (aesthetics, for example) also.[1]

II

Why study ordinary usage? Austin's answer can be summarized under three points.[2]

(i) To understand what we mean, we must examine the words we use. Language sets traps, especially for philosophers, and it is only by rigorously examining what we all ordinarily do with language that we can forearm ourselves against these traps. Forgetting, in the grip of some theory, the ordinary usage of some expression, we may easily slide into a misuse of it that leads us hopelessly astray.

(ii) Moreover, our ordinary words are themselves inadequate and arbitrary. Examining how they work will help us to realize this and to 're-look at the world without blinkers'. Some actions for instance, like heaving a brick through your neighbour's window, involve physical movements. The etymology of the word 'action', combined with our familiarity with relatively simple cases of actions which do involve physical movements, tends to suggest that all actions in the last analysis come down to making physical movements. By examining how the word 'action' is actually used in a variety of cases, we come to see that and how this tendency is misleading.

(iii) The study of ordinary usage has a positive value also. For 'our common stock of words embodies all the distinctions men have found worth drawing, and the connexions they have found worth marking in the lifetimes of many generations'. We should understand these at least before we go any further. Noticing and understanding these distinctions is not merely looking at words. In examining how we use the words we do, we are also examining the 'realities we use the words to talk about'. Thus by examining the ordinary usage of the words with which we describe actions, we shall both rid ourselves of possible misconceptions and bring to light distinctions in the kinds of things and situations we use the words to talk about.

These three points constitute, very briefly, Austin's justification

---

[1] References are to J. L. Austin, *Philosophical Papers* (O.U.P., 1961).
[2] See especially pp. 129–30.

of this type of 'linguistic' philosophy. The brevity of my summary can only be excused by the plea that I do not want to discuss here the justifiability of Austin's aims, but only to point out what they are. It is important to notice that there are really two aims. Points (i) and (ii) declare that ordinary language must be investigated so that we shall avoid distorting it or being misled by it. Point (iii) declares that understanding ordinary language will give us a sharper awareness of distinctions in the phenomena we use the words to talk about. These two aims appear complementary; as Austin formulates them they seem to be no more than two sides of the same penny. But they can come apart, and I shall argue that the methods Austin advocates in fact force them apart, so that distinctions which are all his own are foisted onto expressions in ordinary language although they may be quite inconsistent with the actual usage of these expressions. And so far as this happens, or is likely to happen, it is clear that the first of these aims—the avoidance of misconception and error by charting actual usage—is not being fulfilled. Austin recognized of course that ordinary language is not the last word: it can in principle be supplemented and improved on everywhere. But his main contention is that it *is* the first word. We are not entitled to supplement or improve on it until we understand it. I shall argue that since Austin's method of investigating actual usage is defective, this is just what is bound to happen to anyone that adopts it. Improving after understanding ordinary usage is permissible: altering by misunderstanding it is not.

III

How then is ordinary language to be investigated? Austin's method can be summarized under a further two points.[1]

(i) The field of ordinary language that the philosopher investigates must be germane to some philosophical problem. This defines the scope of the inquiry. There is no philosophical interest in the study of expressions like 'grin', 'smile', 'laugh', 'chuckle', 'cackle' and 'guffaw', for instance. For these expressions have no connexion with anything that has ever been called a problem of philosophy. But there *is* a philosophical interest in studying the uses of expressions like 'deliberate', 'intentional', 'accidental', 'by mistake' and 'involuntary'. For these ordinarily mark distinctions

[1] See especially pp. 130–7.

in the doing of actions which may be significant in the philosophical discussion of freedom and responsibility. Similarly, the investigation of the uses of expressions like 'elegant', 'graceful', 'pretty', 'ugly', 'dumpy', 'coarse' could conceivably yield results of some importance for aesthetics.

(ii) Having thus chosen our field, we are to go through the dictionary, listing all the words that seem relevant. When the list is complete, we can set to work discriminating the uses of these expressions and the distinctions that they mark in the phenomena. This is to be done by imagining appropriate situations and asking ourselves how they should be described—that is, by asking ourselves what precise discriminations these expressions ordinarily mark. Our imagination can be supplemented by the examination of actual legal reports, in so far, that is, as we are investigating the topic of excuses and the doing of actions. For legal reports obviously have a great deal to do with pleas and excuses. Here, however, we have to guard against the possibility that an ordinary expression may be used in an extraordinary way, under the pressure of the need to reach a decision and to work from precedents.

The first step then is to examine the actual uses of the groups of words by means of which we describe and classify the doing of actions. Austin's method can be illustrated by an example. Among the expressions listed from the dictionary as relevant to the notions of 'action' and 'excuse' will be such expressions as 'voluntarily', 'deliberately', 'intentionally', 'purposely', 'wilfully'. To make clear to ourselves what distinctions these related expressions serve to mark, we try to imagine situations with a 'suitable background of story' which it would be appropriate to describe in each of these ways. We try to imagine a situation for example in which it would be right to say 'X did Y *deliberately*' but wrong to say 'X did Y *intentionally (voluntarily*, etc.)'. In this case we are examining the effect of making different substitutions for 'Mly' in the sentence frame 'X did Y Mly'. But we shall also make structural changes in the sentence whilst retaining the same words. What is the difference between saying 'X did Y *deliberately*' and 'X *deliberately* did Y'? In this case we are examining the effect of changing the frame 'X did Y Mly' to the frame 'X Mly did Y', substituting for the variable 'Mly' each of the various modifiers under consideration.[1]

[1] Compare Austin's syntactic variations on the theme 'He clumsily trod on the snail', p. 147.

The main attraction of this method as an approach to philosophy has seemed to many to be that it relies on a disciplined and systematic study of facts. Here, it seems, is an opportunity for 'field work' in philosophy. In examining ordinary usage, we are dealing with hard facts. 'Here at last we should be able to unfreeze, to loosen up and get going on agreeing about discoveries, however small.' Hence Austin finds this 'an attractive subject methodologically'. But, paradoxically, it is just here that a radical objection arises.

The facts that are the subject of this field work are facts of 'ordinary language'—that is, of certain educated, non-technical English usages. It is by making clear to ourselves what distinctions are made in actual usage that we are to get going on agreeing about discoveries. Now facts of this kind must be studied empirically if they are to be studied at all. But the method Austin formulates is not empirical; it is self-consciously intuitive and frequently prescriptive. As an elucidation of actual usages, it must therefore be unreliable. Yet that is what Austin claims it is: 'It will go hard with us if we cannot arrive at the meanings of large numbers of expressions.'[1]

It is fairly easy to see how this objection arises and to appreciate its force. 'Ordinary language' (an ominously vague phrase) is for philosophical purposes that range of the English language whose lexis is the main subject of English dictionaries and whose grammar is the main subject of English grammars. How then are we to find out the meanings of expressions in ordinary language? Take the words 'deliberately', 'intentionally', 'purposely' from the example given above. We want to find out what precise distinction these expressions ordinarily mark. Often, of course, we use them synonymously; we all know that. But are there cases where each of them may describe some feature of a situation which the others do not? The only way to answer this question is to inspect ordinary language and find out. The obvious first step is to consult the dictionary. Some dictionaries are more informative than others and the unabridged *Oxford English Dictionary* (*O.E.D.*) is the most informative of all. Therefore the first step will be to consult the *O.E.D.*

Before thumbing through the pages in search of 'deliberately' however, we should look at the editors' preface. Describing how the project developed, the editors write:

> It was resolved to begin at the beginning and extract anew typical quotations for the use of words. . . . The materials continued to accumulate till upwards of two million quotations had been amassed (p. iv).

In the scrutiny of 'upwards of two million quotations', it is not likely that many words will have slipped past unnoticed, nor that many uses of words will have done so either. The editors' declaration of aims reassures us further:

> The aim of this dictionary is to furnish an adequate account of the meaning, origin and history of English words now in general use or known to have been in use at any time during the last seven hundred years (p. vi).

Passing to the expressions whose use we want to determine, we now look up 'deliberately', 'intentionally' and 'purposely', which involves looking up of course the adjectives of which these expressions are the adverbs. Each expression has various uses listed, each use being documented with at least one example. The glosses suggest that in some uses these expressions may be nearly synonymous. Our interest is not in semantic overlaps, however, but in the distinctive uses of each word. A closer inspection of the glosses and the passages quoted makes some differences clear. The full gloss on 'deliberately' for example (which presupposes the gloss on 'deliberate') is:

> In a deliberate manner. 1. With careful consideration, not hastily or rashly; of set purpose. 2. Without haste, leisurely, slowly.

Seven quotations illustrate these uses.

This is pretty valuable information; but we may feel it is not enough. There are three points we might legitimately raise. First, it is possible that there are uses of 'deliberately' that the *O.E.D.* has missed. This could have come about either through change of meaning over the course of time or through the *O.E.D.*'s reliance on written rather than spoken language. There is a temptation to think of written language as speech on paper; but in fact ordinary usage in speech is often considerably different from ordinary usage in written language.

Second, the uses that the *O.E.D.* does note may not be *accurately* noted. Take the use of 'deliberately' which the dictionary glosses 'with careful consideration'. Now we can consider things in two ways: we can consider *whether* to do x or not; and we can consider *how* to do x. Possibly 'deliberately' is used normally to indicate the first of these ways of considering, but not the second. If this is so (*if*), the *O.E.D.*'s gloss is not as accurate as it might be.

Third, the *O.E.D.* sometimes notes usages accurately, but does not explain them clearly. Thus we have the two main uses of 'deliberately' noted as: '1. With careful consideration. 2. Without haste.' But it is not pointed out that whether the word is used in sense 1 or sense 2 depends on the linguistic context in which it appears. Compare these two sentences:

1. He *deliberately* trod on my toe.
2. He trod *deliberately* on my toe.

In the syntactic structure of sentence 1 'deliberately' has sense 1: in the structure of sentence 2, it has sense 2. The introduction of further words of a certain kind will complicate matters however. Consider now

1(*a*). He *very deliberately* trod on my toe.
2(*a*). He trod *quite deliberately* on my toe.

'Deliberately' in 1(*a*) seems now to be being used in sense 2, whilst in 2(*a*) it appears to have sense 1. It would be possible to complicate matters still further by considering how the sense of 'deliberately' also depends on the type of verb with which it is collocated. But it is enough here only to point out that the *O.E.D.* does not investigate the role of these factors in the meanings of words.

In these three ways then it is possible in principle to add to or revise the *O.E.D.*'s rich and detailed information about ordinary language. The question is how to do so. There is only one method that is reliable. First, we must have at our disposal a body of techniques that will enable us to sort out, systematize and generally handle the complicated linguistic material we are working with. Second, with the help of these techniques, we must survey texts of actual language (spoken and written) and examine the expressions we want to investigate in the context of these texts. What we are interested in is 'the ordinary meanings' of our 'ordinary expressions'. Consequently the test of our analyses and descriptions will always be whether people actually do use these expressions in the way we say they do.

This, very generally, is the method that any linguist, whether lexicographer or grammarian, must adopt. The one danger to be avoided above all is that of relying exclusively on linguistic intuitions—especially when they are self-conscious. The compilers of the *O.E.D.* did not let their intuitions decide what words mean. They looked at more than two million quotations.

Now compare the method Austin adopts in 'A Plea for Excuses'. We are to consult the dictionary, certainly; but only in order to *list* expressions. Hence 'quite a concise' dictionary will do. This suggests that the unique documentation of ordinary usage contained in the unabridged *O.E.D.* is just not relevant. But to use a dictionary just for listing words when we want to find out what they mean is about as good as using a map for listing place names when we want to find out where the places are.

The second stage, in Austin's exposition, is to imagine situations in describing which one might use some of these expressions and to ask ourselves which expression would in fact be appropriate and why. The shortcomings of this method as an inquiry into ordinary language must be obvious. It is not empirical, but self-consciously intuitive; and consequently it is likely to fall into exactly those traps of language which it is intended to expose. So far from charting the exact distinctions marked by our ordinary expressions, the most this method will establish linguistically is how a group of philosophers *think* they would describe certain (often highly imaginative) situations. This is a pretty far cry from the impartial examination of ordinary language. For all we know, these conclusions may go beyond, distort or conflict with ordinary usage (in fact they sometimes do: see section IV). But if so, this cannot be a reliable method of investigating the distinctions and connexions embodied in 'our common stock of words'. What we think we do with words is not necessarily what we actually do with them.

It is important to make clear the scope of this objection, for it may seem to be exposed to an obvious rejoinder. A counter-objection to what I have been saying might take this form: Surely it is a fact that as speakers of language we operate intuitively. Why then should it be objected to Austin that he relies on intuition? We should need to make an empirical study of words in texts only if we were not already familiar with them. But this is clearly not true of the expressions ('deliberately', 'intentionally', 'purposely', etc.) whose distinctive uses Austin is exploring. For Austin's aim is only to make explicit what is already contained in our ready, intuitive use of the familiar expressions of ordinary language.

This objection is plausible but mistaken. It rests on the false assumption that all our ordinary, intuitive usages are in principle accessible to further deliberate processes of intuition—in other words, that we can always self-consciously introspect our unself-conscious intuitions.

There are of course in any language certain grammatical and lexical (as well as other) usages which any competent speaker of the language will recognize immediately. Anyone who thinks the sentence 'Dog bites man' is synonymous with the sentence 'Man bites dog' shows that he has not mastered English grammar. Now it is true that it would normally be superfluous to consult a grammar on this point. Our intuitive recognition of the semantic difference between these two sentences would not need to be checked against the facts of actual usage. But that should not obscure the fact that it is *only* because ordinary grammatical usage is as it is that these two sentences are not synonymous. Our intuitive denial of synonymity would simply be wrong if ordinary usage did not deny it too. Consequently, anyone who questioned our denial could only be refuted by an appeal to the facts of actual usage.

In the same way, but at the lexical level, anyone who could see no semantic difference between 'deliberately' and 'accidentally'— anyone who used these two words as synonyms—simply would not know what these two expressions meant in English. Again, it would normally be superfluous to consult a dictionary or check actual usage on this point. Nevertheless it is the dictionary, or, ultimately, actual 'standard' usage that we should have to appeal to if our denial that the two expressions are synonymous were to be questioned.

Usages of this kind we might call 'requirements' of a language. Anyone who claims to speak English is required amongst other things to be able to distinguish the semantic function of certain (not all) syntactic patterns and to distinguish semantic contrasts of the 'accidentally'—'deliberately' type over a tolerably wide area (certainly not all) of the lexicon of English.

On the other hand, there are grammatical and lexical usages which we should hesitate to call 'requirements' of English in this sense. Someone who claims to speak English is not required to be able to specify immediately a semantic distinction between the two sentences 'The man deliberately bit the dog' and 'The man bit the dog deliberately'. Nor is he required to be able to specify immediately a semantic distinction between the expressions 'accidentally' and 'unintentionally'. Yet these distinctions do exist and can be discriminated, even in ordinary language. We might call such usages 'options' of the language.

Now for discriminating usages which are 'requirements' of a language, it may be enough *for practical purposes* to trust our intuition. But for discriminating 'options', we need to be much more careful. And the more finely we want to distinguish usages, the more careful we need to be. Intuition may suggest; but only evidence will confirm. It is all right to imagine situations and construct intuitively-based examples; it is not all right to rely exclusively on such examples unsupported by any appeal to the independent evidence of actual texts.

Consequently, the objection I have been bringing against Austin's method is not necessarily an objection to the validity or interest of the distinctions he makes. It is an objection to the method of establishing such distinctions as *part of the meanings* of our ordinary expressions. In some cases his conclusions are in fact correct, and in others they are wrong: but in all cases they rest on *unsupported* intuition and introspection. It is clear that a method permitting such vagaries is in principle unreliable.

IV

Finding out what an expression means in a language, whether or not we are speakers of the language, is ultimately an empirical, not an intuitive, matter. Its meaning is (roughly) the way in which it is actually used by speakers (and writers) of the language in various contexts of situation. Different groups vary in their usage, and so do different individuals: so do the same individuals at different times and in different contexts. 'Ordinary usage' is therefore usage above a certain minimum of generality that excludes 'private'—such as family and strictly idiolectal—uses. How an expression is actually used is a study which belongs to descriptive linguistics, the disciplines and techniques of which

are directed to assist us in making statements of meaning. Every scientific worker must work out his field in accordance with the resources of his disciplines and techniques and develop them in the handling of his chosen material. The linguist studies the speaking person in the social process.[1]

In this section I want to illustrate the necessity of these disciplines and techniques for the kind of linguistic analysis that Austin undertakes in 'A Plea for Excuses'. I will mention three points where the lack of them has led Austin to torture the ordinary usages he claims to be describing.

1. *Standards of the unacceptable.* One move that Austin makes is to consider excuses that he thinks are 'unacceptable'. Linguistically, this move consists in contrasting several sentences in which an adverb (say) is collocated with different verbal phrases.[2] Sometimes these collocations produce sentences that he thinks we would reject, and he then tries to explain why we should do so. An example of this is his treatment of the adverb 'inadvertently': 'We may plead that we trod on the snail inadvertently: but not on a baby—you ought to look where you are putting your great feet.'[3]

Now consider the following exponents of the sentence frame 'I x inadvertently'.

A1. I trod on the snail inadvertently.
A2. I broke my promise inadvertently.
B1. I trod on the baby inadvertently.
B2. I he inadvertently.

Of these exponents, A1 and A2 give no trouble: A1 describes a 'physical' action, A2 describes an action that is not 'physical'. B2 infringes a grammatical rule for sentence formation in English and so is not a sentence at all. B1 does not infringe any obvious grammatical rule of English. What then (if anything) is wrong with it? Austin's suggestion is that to say B1, as an excuse for treading on the baby is to offer an excuse that is unacceptable. The argument is that 'inadvertently' picks out an act that is done when, in the course of performing some other act, I failed to proceed with such meticulous care and attention as would have ensured the non-occurrence of the unfortunate event in question. Hence,

---

[1] J. R. Firth, *Papers in Linguistics*, 1934–51 (O.U.P., 1957), p. 190.
[2] On the notion of collocation, see J. R. Firth, op. cit., and A. McIntosh, 'Patterns and Ranges', *Language*, xxxvii 3 (part (i)), 1961.
[3] p. 142.

Austin concludes, to plead that I trod on the baby inadvertently is to suggest that treading on the baby is the sort of thing that would naturally happen unless I exercised *meticulous* care and attention over the details of what I was doing. And to suggest this is to imply that I have odd views as to what requires *meticulous* care and attention in order to be avoided in the course of doing something else.

Now the distinction Austin draws here may be an interesting one in its own right, but it is not an accurate account of ordinary usage. So far as the evidence of ordinary usage goes, it is not necessary that I should have failed to exercise 'meticulous supervision' of detail before I can be truly said to have done something inadvertently. I can do something inadvertently without exercising any conscious supervision over what I am doing at all, as when I press the wrong door bell inadvertently—I simply wasn't paying attention to what I was doing. Or I can do something inadvertently simply by not realizing what side-effects I am producing *even although* I am exercising meticulous supervision over the details of what I am doing. In the course of a very careful summing up in a capital murder trial, the judge says 'I may inadvertently have misled you in one thing I said yesterday about the law'. This is not a misuse of English; but it is clear that what may have happened is that although the judge exercised meticulous supervision over what he was doing, something nevertheless may have gone wrong.

What then is wrong with B1 ? I am not sure whether we all do or ought to find anything wrong with it at all. For we know nothing about the context in which it is presupposed to have been uttered. This indeed is one of the dangers of constructing examples on a solely intuitive basis: we are likely to draw conclusions about the meanings of expressions that are really due to an implied context of utterance. Suppose however that we do all find this sentence, isolated as it is, one that we are intuitively inclined to doubt or reject. What factors should we have to consider in explaining this ? There are three at least; I will only indicate them.

(*a*) *Normal situation*. People tread on snails and break promises more often than they tread on babies. This conditions our linguistic expectations. Consequently, if we are asked to complete the sentence frame 'I trod on the X', 'baby' is less likely to be produced than 'step', 'edge', 'pin', or even 'snail'—unless of course some particular context is supplied. Hence the sentence 'I trod on the baby' may also have the queerness which is at first thought to belong uniquely to 'I trod on the baby *inadvertently*'. Compare 'I trod on the H-bomb'.

(*b*) *Contextual association*. Possibly 'inadvertently' (except in its legal use, which resists change) is coming to be used more in certain types of context than in others. For many people it may thus develop contextual associations which would make it seem out of place, or even in bad taste, to use 'inadvertently' to describe the circumstances in which they had trodden on the baby. If 'inadvertently' is usually associated with slips like pressing the wrong door bell or taking the wrong umbrella, it may well sound positively frivolous to use it in baby-treading contexts too.

(*c*) '*Not realizing*.' When I press the wrong bell inadvertently I do not realize what I am doing until it is too late. Walking down the public footpath, I may very well not realize I am about to tread on a snail, and so I may tread on it inadvertently. But how could I *help* realizing I was about to tread on a baby? This indicates another reason why B1 may seem queer: we may be supplying the same sort of context as for A1. If so, what is 'unacceptable' about B1 is not that it suggests I would have had to exercise 'meticulous supervision' of detail to avoid treading on the baby, but that we do not see how anyone could have failed to *realize* that that was what he was about to do. (You don't have to be meticulous to see there is a baby there.) A few changes in the context presupposed and the queerness may diminish (suppose the lights had just fused?).

2. '*Deliberately*' *and* '*Intentionally*'. Is there a clear distinction between types of situation which can be picked out by the use of 'deliberately', contrasted with 'intentionally'? Austin says there is. He explains the distinction in these terms: 'We walk along the cliff, and I feel a sudden impulse to push you over, which I promptly do: I acted on impulse, yet I certainly intended to push you over, and may have even devised a little ruse to achieve it: yet even then I did not act deliberately for I did not (stop to) ask myself whether to do it or not.' The suggestion is then that 'when you act deliberately you act after weighing it up (*not* after thinking out ways and means)'.[1] On the other hand 'intentionally' covers both these cases.

[1] pp. 143, 150.

Now no evidence is brought in favour of this contention about ordinary language except the wholly unsatisfactory evidence of etymology (on which see below). Going just by intuition, I myself would reject Austin's account of ordinary usage: and working the dictionary and noting actual (unself-conscious) usages of educated speakers, we find that the facts conflict with Austin's account. There are certainly cases of deliberate actions in which the agent considered whether or not to do it. But there are also cases, equally sanctioned by ordinary usage, where he had thought out ways and means: 'He laid his plans deliberately'; 'He arranged his arguments deliberately'; 'He aimed his blows deliberately'. In these sentences 'deliberately' may pick out the fact that he gave careful thought to *how* to do what he did, not to *whether* or not to do it. Lastly, there are a vast number of cases in which (as we should expect) weighing up *whether* to do X involves thinking out *how* it would be done. In these cases, 'He did X deliberately' refers to the fact that he did consider 'it' carefully, but simply does not specify what kind of consideration he gave it. How 'deliberately' is to be construed in a particular sentence therefore will depend on the lexis of the sentence, the syntax and grammar and the wider linguistic and (perhaps) extra-linguistic context. These are the factors we should have to consider if we had to translate 'He did it deliberately' into a language in whose lexicon there were separate words corresponding to the two senses of 'deliberately' in English. It may seem a pity, at any rate to some philosophers, that English does not mark this distinction clearly by means of separate words in its lexicon too. But the fact is, it does not. And would it be much better off if it did?

All this does not mean of course that there is no distinction between doing X deliberately and doing X intentionally. A glance at the unabridged *O.E.D.* will reveal quite a few differences. What I have said above is only an indication of how we should establish what ordinary usage is. And how we should not.

3. *Clouds of etymology.* One of the reasons why Austin thought the correct use of 'deliberately' was 'after weighing it up' is etymological. One point of method which he is convinced is an 'indispensable aid' is to investigate a word's etymology: 'In spite of all changes in and extensions of and additions to its meanings, and indeed rather pervading and governing these, there will still persist the old idea. In an *accident* something befalls: by *mistake*

you take the wrong one: in *error* you stray: when you act *deliberately* you act after weighing it up (*not* after thinking out ways and means).'[1] This is a very revealing mistake.

The etymology of a word may be important and interesting. But it is in principle impossible to establish the contemporary use of a word by appealing to its etymology. What uses a word once had may have affected many of the uses it has now: they cannot *tell* us what uses it has now. Past actions in the life of John Smith may have affected what John Smith is doing today. But they cannot *tell* us what John Smith is doing today. What John Smith did five years ago may make what he is doing today intelligible: but you do not establish what John Smith is doing today by asking what it would be intelligible for him to be doing, considering what he did five years ago. What uses a word had five hundred years ago may make the uses it has today intelligible: but you do not establish what uses it has today by asking what uses it would be intelligible for it to have, considering the uses it had five hundred years ago. It is clear surely that if you are trying to distinguish the uses of words by reference to their etymologies, you are not describing their *present* uses. If you do happen to get their present uses right in this way, it is not because of the 'words' etymology, but because its etymology happens in this case to correspond with its present use.

Austin's own examples illustrate the pitfalls of this method in practice. Take them in turn from the passage quoted above.

(i) *Accident*. The most general and widest use of this word, according to the *O.E.D.*, is 'anything that happens'. Austin prefers what he wrongly believes to be the etymology of 'accident'— 'something that befalls'. His etymology is wrong because 'befalls' is not an accurate translation of the Latin components of 'accident', 'ad' +'cadere'. The prefix 'be-' in English means (originally) 'about' or 'around' (hence 'bestir'); the nearest equivalent to Latin 'ad' is 'to' or 'towards'. So, on his own principles, Austin should have preferred 'fall to' to 'befall'.

This is a minor point. But now what about the word 'fall'? Studying its etymology, we come across Old English 'fallan', cognate with German 'fallen'. These may be derived from Latin 'fallere', to deceive. Are we to understand then that in the meaning of the word 'fall' there may be contained some idea of deception?

[1] p. 149.

What are we going to find when we look further into the etymology of Latin 'fallere'? Is there any limit to how far back we should trace the history of a word in pursuit of its present meaning? These facts of language plainly refute the notion that 'the old idea' persists through all changes of a word's meaning.

(ii) *'Mistake' and 'error'*. The first recorded use of 'error' in English is to describe the action of going astray; the first use of 'mistake' is a reference to taking something wrongly (*not*, as Austin puts it, 'taking the wrong one'). This shows that at that time 'mistake' and 'error' were distinguished in use in accordance with their etymology. It does not show that in contemporary ordinary usage this same distinction persists. In fact the evidence is against it. In this case, it is enough (and particularly revealing) to compare Austin's *actual* usage with the etymological uses he *prescribes*. He claims that 'by *mistake* you take the wrong one: in *error* you stray'. Earlier in the same paper occurs the sentence 'But by the way, and more negatively, a number of traditional cruces or *mistakes* in this field can be resolved or removed.'[1] Surely what he has in mind here is a case of 'going astray', not 'taking the wrong one'? Or is there after all no difference? Certainly we cannot say that the sentence quoted is faulty by any standard of ordinary usage.

(iii) *'Deliberately'*. I have pointed out already that a survey of actual usage does not show that to do something deliberately is necessarily to do it after considering *whether* to do it, but necessarily not to do it after considering *how* to do it. Austin makes it clear that etymology has influenced him in his attempt to make a distinction here. It is interesting to see how etymology has misled him. 'Deliberately' derives from Latin 'de'+'libra', a balance. Hence Austin glosses 'deliberately' as 'after weighing it up (*not* after thinking out ways and means)'. Now if we read its etymology into the present meaning of a word in this way, it is only too likely that we shall arrive at a conclusion like Austin's. But the trouble is, it conflicts with the facts of actual usage which it is his declared aim to elucidate. The sentence 'He always planned deliberately how to achieve ends he had adopted on impulse' is a sentence in which 'deliberately' is used in the sense which Austin claims ordinary usage forbids: but no one not in the grip of an etymology would reject it. Ordinary usage makes no ruling here.

[1] p. 128 (my italics).

These examples should make clear how unreliable it must be to argue from a word's past to its present. Etymology is the study of the history of words, not (as etymology's etymology may suggest) the study of their 'true' meanings.

V

I hope I have now demonstrated the radical defects in Austin's method of elucidating the precise meanings of our ordinary expressions. The exact distinctions and connexions marked in the lexical and grammatical features of ordinary language cannot be explained by means of a purely intuitive approach, especially one that disregards the techniques available in general linguistics for the handling of the linguistic material to be explained. How disabling, lastly, is this faulty method? How damaging a criticism is this of the whole enterprise outlined in 'A Plea for Excuses'?

To answer this question, we must look again at Austin's justification of this type of analysis. In section II, I pointed out that the aims were really twofold: negatively, 'the traps that language sets us' are to be revealed and understood: positively, we are to be made aware of all the distinctions and connexions embodied in ordinary usage, which are likely to be 'more sound and more subtle than any that you or I are likely to think up in our arm-chair of an afternoon'.[1] These are the aims. But what Austin actually does with ordinary language is rather different. He notices a distinction between doing X after weighing it up and doing X after thinking out ways and means; and he reads this distinction into the expression 'deliberately'—in accordance with its etymology, but in defiance of its use. He imagines a situation in which someone might be said to have done Y *inadvertently*; and prescribes this as the *only* legitimate usage without regard to the full range of linguistic factors involved. He distinguishes between 'error' and 'mistake', although his own usage shows this distinction is far from ordinary. The distinctions he draws are, or may be, valid. But they are not necessarily distinctions of ordinary language. The dictionary, and the etymologies of words, have thus become a sort of heuristic device for finding distinctions in a given area of discourse, whether or not the distinctions correspond to, go beyond or distort actual usage.

[1] p. 130.

But does it matter? Surely what matters is whether the distinctions are real and important, not whether they are marked by grammatical and lexical features of English? The answer to this depends on the importance of Austin's primary aim. This is to understand the distinctions that we *do* mark with our ordinary expressions. Ordinary language is 'the first word'. Unless we understand that, we are only too likely to fall into its traps. What I have argued here is that since his method of investigating ordinary language is unreliable, he is only too likely to fail to understand the distinctions that ordinary language does in fact mark; and I have indicated some (only) places where he actually does fail. The answer to the question 'Does it matter?' then is this: If it is important to map the exact distinctions marked in ordinary language, then the fact that they are being inaccurately mapped is important too. If we use inaccurate maps, we are just as likely to get lost as before.

IFS AND CANS*

P. H. Nowell-Smith

IF someone were to ask what idea is expressed by the verb 'can' in all its moods and tenses, he might be told that it expressed power, potency or potentiality, capacity, capability or ability, contingency or possibility—all or some of these. But this answer, though true enough, is unenlightening, and unenlightening just because it is so obviously true. If there are puzzles about 'can' there will be puzzles about these. Human actions, the things people actually do, are, we feel, ground-floor members of the world; their abilities are not. Philosophers have often felt that particular statements, expressed by sentences in the indicative mood with names of entities as subjects, are somehow paramount. We use the indicative mood to say flatly that something is or was or will be the case. Hypothetical and universal statements, by contrast, are suspect. This feeling has led some philosophers (for example some logicians who have been incautious about the relation between the logical constants of a language and those of a calculus) sadly astray. It is certainly wrong to say flatly that 'all mules are sterile' means the same as 'if anything is a mule, it is sterile' or 'nothing is both a mule and non-sterile'; but the idea that it is not sufficiently categorical to get in on the ground floor but requires to show its connexions with true-blue categoricals about this and that mule before it can be

* This is Professor Nowell-Smith's reply to Austin's British Academy Lecture: 'Ifs and Cans'. In addition to the following paper by Professor Thalberg the reader may wish to consult the following works (listed in the bibliography) that concern 'Ifs and Cans': Aune (1), (2), (3) and (4), Ayers, Baier, Behre, Bradley, Chisholm (3), Dore (1) and (2), Dray, Ewing, Gallop, Goldberg and Heidelberger, Henschen-Dahlquist, Honoré, Hunter, Lehrer (1), (2) and (3), Locke, O'Connor, Ofstad (1) and (2), Osborn, Raab, Ranken, Scarrow, Stroup, Taylor, Thalberg (1), (4) and (5), Tietz, Watling, and Whitely.

admitted is not wholly erroneous. Likewise statements about the next mule are not wholly irreproachable, and the drive to analyse universal statements into hypotheticals and then treat these hypotheticals as truth-functional sets of particular categoricals is not wholly to be resisted.

There is a notorious connexion between universal statements and statements made with 'can' which leads us to suspect that the latter, though in one sense categorical enough, are not wholly, flatly and irreducibly categorical. One of the many features which these two types of statement have in common is that, while they must always be backed in the end by statements as to what is or was the case, they always assert more than this. We can see Tom and Dick playing bridge, but we cannot see the class of all bridge-players, and in much the same way, though we can see someone playing bridge and perhaps see him manifesting his ability to play bridge, we cannot see his ability. Abilities are somehow parasitic on performances, if only because an ability to do something is an ability to *do* that thing.

This is one reason why philosophers have so often tried to analyse can-statements in terms of if-statements, a type of analysis which it is the main purpose of Austin's paper to defeat. Their attempts have often been complicated and confused by two factors. (i) They have, as Austin plainly shows, confused analysis with supplementation, the idea that 'X can do Y' must be *analysed* into some statement in which the word 'can' does not occur (for example 'X will do Y, if the tries'), with the idea that 'X can do Y' is always *incomplete* as it stands, that it always means something of the form 'X can do Y, if . . .', a form in which the word 'can' is still present. (ii) The topic is usually raised in the context of free-will and responsibility; and here it is usually 'could have' that requires analysis. On the face of it, it is much more plausible to maintain that 'could have' requires analysis in terms of or supplementation by an if-clause than that the whole verb 'can' in all its moods and tenses does so. Hence philosophers (including myself) have confused considerations which might lead one to give an hypothetical analysis of 'could have' with those that make for an hypothetical analysis of 'can'.

On the first point, both in *Ethics* and in this paper I am concerned to argue that 'can' requires analysis in terms of 'if', not that it requires supplementation. Moore was quite wrong when he said that 'I could have walked a mile in twenty minutes' means 'I *could* have walked a mile in twenty minutes, if I had chosen'. To avoid the second error I shall start here with 'can' and move to 'could have' later.

There are two points in Austin's paper which may be accepted. from the start. (i) There are at least three senses of 'can', which Austin calls the 'ability', the 'opportunity' and the 'all-in' senses. (ii) The form 'could have' is often, not a subjunctive, but the past indicative of 'can' in any of these three senses. It means, not 'would have been able, if . . .' but categorically '*was* able'. In the first part of this paper I shall discuss the relations between the three senses of 'can'. Austin's view here is that there is 'an all-in, paradigm use, around which cluster and from which divagate, little by little and along different paths, a whole series of other uses',[1] among them 'ability' and 'opportunity'. In the second part of the paper I shall argue that, in all three senses, the whole verb 'can' requires to be analysed in terms of 'does . . ., if . . .'.

I

My first thesis, then, is that the all-in 'can' (to be *fully* able) is a conjunction of ability and opportunity. These are umbrella-like words covering a host of things such as 'having the strength, skill, know-how etc.' and 'being in a position to, having the means or equipment to etc.' So my first thesis is still highly schematic in character. A full treatment would have to go into these differences and I suspect that it might emerge that ability and opportunity are not as clearly distinct *genera* as we usually take them to be.

That the all-in 'can' is a conjunction of ability and opportunity emerges, I think, from what Austin himself says about the case in which 'he could have done X' really is a conditional, requiring, to give its full sense explicitly, to be completed by an if-clause, typically 'if he had had the ability' or 'if he had had the opportunity'.[2] 'He could have smashed that lob, if he had been any good at the smash' is a conditional; yet, according to Austin, 'it nevertheless manages to assert, by means of its main clause, something categorical enough, that he *did* have a certain opportunity'. We must ask here which of the three senses of 'can' is being used in

---

[1] *Philosophical Papers,* p. 178.
[2] op. cit., p. 177.

the main clause. It cannot be the 'can' of ability; for if it were, the whole sentence would read 'He would have had the ability, if he had had the ability', and it is clearly not this tautology that we mean to assert. Nor can it be the 'can' of opportunity; for in that case the whole sentence would read 'he would have had the opportunity, if he had had the ability'. But according to Austin we assert categorically that he *did* have the opportunity, not that he *would* have had it if he had had the ability; the opportunity was there whether or not he had the ability to make use of it. It must, then, if the statement is genuinely conditional, be the past subjunctive of the all-in 'can' that we are using here. For clarity we may re-write the sentence as 'he would have been fully able, if he had had the ability'. Now this certainly does imply, even though it does not state, something that is 'categorical enough'. For it implies that he actually had everything other than ability which is necessary for being fully able, that he had, among things, an opportunity to smash that lob.

These categorical implications of 'he could have done X, if he had had the ability' and of 'he could have done X if he had had the opportunity' lead Austin to suggest that they are not conditional sentences at all. He has already introduced us to an 'unorthodox' type of if-sentence, exemplified by 'there are biscuits on the sideboard if you want them', which does not express a conditional and for which the ordinary logical rules for conditionals do not hold.[1] Perhaps, then, these sentences *just* assert respectively opportunity and ability, their if-clauses being of the unorthodox type. To reinforce this suggestion Austin tells us that 'he can' in the ability sense may be expressed by 'he can in the full sense if he has the opportunity' and that when 'he can' is used in this way no one would take it to be a subjunctive or conditional. If therefore, the 'could have' in 'he could have smashed that lob, if he had had the ability' is the past indicative tense of 'can', that statement also will not be a conditional. This is true, but irrelevant. For it is not clear that 'could have' in the two hypothetical-seeming examples under discussion *must* be taken to be the past indicative of a restricted

[1] op. cit., pp. 158–60. The main features of these unorthodox cases are that they do not entail their contrapositives but do entail their own main clauses. From 'there are biscuits on the sideboard if you want them', we cannot infer 'if there are no biscuits, you do not want them', but we can infer 'there are biscuits on the sideboard'.

sense of 'can'. Why should it not be, what it certainly seems to be, the past subjunctive of the all-in 'can'? And, if this is what it is the statements will be genuine subjunctive conditionals equivalent to 'he would have been fully able, if he had had the ability' and 'he would have been fully able, if he had had the opportunity'.

The question, then, is this: when we use these sentences are we *just* making categorical assertions of opportunity or ability—the if-clauses adding something indeed, but not imposing a condition —or are we making an hypothetical assertion, from which a categorical can indeed be deduced, but which cannot be identified with that categorical? It may be that these two come to the same thing for all practical purposes, just as 'q' and 'p v q: -p' come to the same thing; but it is important to see whether or not they do. Suppose that there were another restricted sense of 'can' which we will call 't' and that it seems likely that 'he can (all-in)' means 'he has the ability and the opportunity and t'. There will now be a great difference between 'he would have been fully able, if he had had the opportunity' and the simple categorical 'he had had the ability'. The categorical will still follow from the hypothetical; but the converse inference will not hold. From 'he had the ability' we cannot infer 'he would have been fully able if he had had the opportunity' since, if t were absent, the premise would be true and the conclusion false.

If Austin is prepared to identify 'he can do X, if he has the ability' with 'he has the opportunity to do X', which at one point in his argument he actually does, it must be because he thinks (in my view rightly) that there is no further relevant sense, t. But if this and the corresponding identification of 'he can do X, if he has the opportunity' with 'he has the ability to do X' are correct, not only will the restricted categoricals follow from the relevant hypotheticals; we can also conclude that the all-in 'can' is a conjunction of ability and opportunity.[1]

---

[1] If 'he has the ability' is equivalent to 'he is fully able, if he has the opportunity' and 'he has the opportunity' is equivalent to 'he is fully able, if he has the ability', it follows truth-functionally that 'he is fully able' is equivalent to 'he has ability and he has opportunity'. Mr. P. T. Geach has pointed out to me that this conclusion can be reached without relying on the rules for the 'if' of material implication, which is certainly an unreliable procedure in an area in which 'ifs' are as slippery as they are here. We need rely only on the principle 's ⊃ t.v ⊃ w: ⊃ :s.t ⊃ y.w' which is valid for a greater variety of 'ifs', including the counter-factual 'if'.

Nevertheless, though ability and opportunity do add up to make the all-in 'can', it would be wrong to say that the all-in 'can' is a *mere* conjunction of ability and opportunity; for these two are themselves conceptually related. Let us consider first what it is to have an opportunity. To say that someone has, here and now, an opportunity for doing X is not to say how things are in the world, though, to be sure, if you know about the activity X, you can deduce much about how things are. It is rather to say that the stage is *so* set that anyone who has, in general, the ability to do X is fully able to do it here and now. For example, to say that he was in a position to smash that lob is not to describe, even in outline, the relative positions of man, ball and net and the posture of the man. It says rather that man, ball and net were *so* placed in relation to each other and that the man's limbs were *so* disposed that if he has, in general, the ability to smash lobs, he could have smashed that one. But surely, it might be objected, the ability of the player makes no difference to the question whether there was an opportunity or not. Can I not conclude from the relevant statements about the positions of the objects concerned that there certainly was an opportunity to smash a lob, whether or not the player had the ability to smash it? Certainly, if I know about tennis, I can. But to describe the situation as an *opportunity* is to do more than merely to describe it; it is to say that the conditions for exercising a certain ability obtained. The description of the spatial relations remains true whether or not the player has any ability; but to see these relations as constituting an opportunity is to see them *as* conditions for the exercise of an ability. An opportunity is essentially an opportunity *for* someone who has an ability (which is why we can know exactly how we are placed without seeing in our situation an opportunity). If this is right, the concept of opportunity presupposes that of ability in the sense that, if there were no abilities, if everything in the world remained exactly as it is, nothing would constitute an opportunity.

In a somewhat different way the concept of ability includes that of opportunity. For an ability to do something is always the ability to do that thing in certain conditions without which the ability could not (logically) exist. Thus, if there are four men in a room where there are no cards, it may be that they can all play bridge in the sense that they have learnt and not forgotten. They cannot play bridge here and now; but this does not mean that their ability has deserted them, to return again when some cards arrive. It is rather that the ability they have is the ability to play-bridge-if-there-are-cards, not the remarkable ability to play-bridge-if-there-are-no-cards. The presence of cards, three other players, etc., may be collectively described as constituting an opportunity to play bridge; so that when we say of someone that he has the ability to play bridge we are saying that he has it *when* these conditions are fulfilled. It does *not* follow that when we assert ability we also assert or imply that the conditions *are fulfilled* here and now; the conditions are included in the description of the ability; for the ability is to do the thing in these conditions. It is the fact that an ability is always an ability to do-X-given-an-opportunity that makes it inevitable that, if we have any such concept as 'can' at all, we should have the triple concept of ability, opportunity and both together.

If this account of the relations between the three senses is correct in outline, Austin's picture of the 'all-in' use as the 'paradigm use, around which cluster and from which divagate, little by little and along different paths, a whole series of other uses' is radically misleading. In the first place it is not the all-in, but the ability sense that is fundamental.[1] But I would not put too much emphasis on this point; it is not so much a question of getting one fundamental sense clear at the start and then seeing how other senses cluster round it, as of getting all three senses clear together by seeing how they fit in with each other. It is the word 'paradigm' that, as so often, gives a false impression; for it suggests that the all-in use provides a pattern or model to which the other uses, to a greater or lesser extent, conform. But, whatever the relations between the all-in and the other uses, it is not paradigmatic of them. The unravelling of a complex concept consists in showing how the elements that make it up (for example the different words which have the same stem, the different senses of a word, the different constructions into which it can enter) are related to each other. In particular we want to know which relations are logically necessary,

[1] As the etymological connection with 'know' would lead us to expect. Austin finds the same three senses in the case of 'know'; but while there is an ability-sense of 'know' we cannot use 'know' to assert opportunity without ability. A man cannot be said to know Chinese merely on the strength of his living in China and hence having many opportunities to speak it; nor, to take Austin's example, could he be said to know what the thing in my hand is if he has an opportunity to identify it but lacks the ability.

which elements could not exist without some other. There is no doubt a good explanation for the fact that we use 'foot' both for a measure of length and for a part of the body; but, not only could we have different words for these two concepts, we could have either concept without the other. With 'can' the position is different; for we could not have either of the concepts of ability or opportunity unless we had both. Here we have to do, not with two related concepts, but with one complex concept. In a situation such as this it may be useful to exhibit one or more elements in the complex as fundamental, as giving the key to the others; but it is seldom or never the case that these key elements are paradigmatic of the others. To put the relation in this way is to suggest that, though they cannot be understood without it, it could be understood without them.

II

So far I have been concerned with the different senses of 'can'. There is no doubt whatever that Austin is right in saying both that this verb is used to make categorical statements and that 'could have', being sometimes its past indicative tense, is also used to make categorical statements. In so far as the idea that 'can' requires analysis in terms of 'if' stems from the idea that 'could have' is subjunctive it is wholly mistaken. But I shall argue in this section that the central 'can' of ability is radically hypothetical, in all its moods and tenses, not in the sense that it must always be escorted by a spoken or unspoken 'if', but in the sense that it can be analysed in terms of 'if'.

I shall be concerned, in this section, solely with that use of 'can' which is relevant in connexion with the freedom of the will, to the ascription of responsibility and to moral condemnation. In such cases we are always concerned, not with the question whether anyone can, in general, do or avoid something, but with the question whether he could or could not have done or avoided doing some particular thing that, as a matter of fact, he failed to do or did. This feature gives 'could have' a counter-factual air which tempts us to treat it as a past subjunctive, a temptation into which I certainly fell in *Ethics* with, as Austin shows, disastrous results. When we say, in preparation for an accusation of some kind 'he could have avoided doing that', we are not saying anything conditional or subjunctive. We are saying categorically that he was both able and in a position to avoid doing what he did, and this is shown by the fact that if it can be shown that, as a matter fact, he lacked either the ability or the opportunity, the accusation fails. Nevertheless it does not follow from the fact that 'could have' is a past indicative and used to make categorical assertions that these assertions may not require analysis in hypothetical terms; for it may be that the whole verb 'can' is susceptible of, or indeed requires analysis in terms of 'does . . ., if . . .'. Abilities are a sort of dispositional, and the idea of a dispositional does not seem to me, as it does to Austin, too obscure to be helpful. 'That chair is unstable' is categorical enough, compared with 'that chair would be unstable if one of its legs were an inch shorter than it is'; but it does seem to mean something like 'that chair would actually fall over, if p'. To be sure, when we call a chair unstable, we do not say precisely what it would do in precisely what conditions; we cannot spell out the analysis. But this only shows that the concept of instability in ordinary speech is inherently imprecise. Dispositional statements are used to connect an ill-defined, but not limitless set of occurrences with an ill-defined, but not limitless set of conditions.

Of all attempts to analyse 'can' in terms of what actually does or would happen, if something, Austin allows the greatest plausibility to 'he succeeds, if he tries'. This will certainly not do in all cases, since there are things that we can do without trying and in such cases 'trying' and 'success' are not in point. Neither this nor any other single analysis of all 'can'-statements is correct, but, I suggest, some analysis of this kind will always be found to work. I shall, however, limit my discussion to an example which Austin gives in connexion with 'I shall succeed in doing X, if I try' as an analysis of 'I can do X'. The example is that of a golfer who misses a short putt, fails, and kicks himself because, things being exactly as they were, he could have holed it. 'It is not', he says, 'that I should have holed it if conditions had been different: that might of course be so, but I am talking about conditions as they precisely were, and asserting that I could have holed it. There's the rub. Nor does 'I can hole it this time' mean that I shall hole it this time if I try or if anything else: for I may try and miss, and yet not be convinced that I couldn't have done it; indeed further experiments may confirm my belief that I could have done it that time although I didn't. But if I tried my hardest, say, and missed, surely there *must* have been *something* that caused me to fail, that made me unable to succeed? So that I *could not* have holed it. Well, a modern belief in science, in there being an explanation of everything, may make us assent to this argument. But such a belief is not in line with the traditional beliefs enshrined in the word *can*: according to them, a human ability or power or capacity is inherently liable not to produce success, on occasion, and that for no reason (or are bad luck and bad form sometimes reasons?).'[1] Since this brings us to the edge of the determinist controversy, I propose to examine this example in some detail.

1. Austin notes that the facts alleged conflict with determinism but are in line with the traditional beliefs enshrined in the word 'can'. 'Determinism' he regards as the name for 'nothing clear'; but it can be made clear enough for our purposes. For Austin, an ability is something that is inherently liable not to produce success, on occasion, and that for *no* reason; so we may, with sufficient clarity, say that a determinist is one who maintains that if an ability fails to produce success on some occasion there *must* have been a reason. Such a determinist has several lines of reply.

(*a*) He might say that Austin's indeterminist belief is not, in fact, enshrined in our use of 'can'; ordinary language is quite non-committal on this point. Common sense, he will say, has a healthy habit of not coming down on one side or the other in a theoretical controversy which is not in practice decidable. If there *was* a reason for the failure of the ability on that occasion, we do not know it and have no hope of discovering it; so we shrug it off with the phrase 'it was just one of those things'. But it would be quite wrong to suppose that the use of this phrase implies a belief either that 'those things' have causes or that they do not; on this point traditional belief is silent.

(*b*) He might argue that if our ordinary use of 'can' really does enshrine an indeterminist belief, so much the worse for it. You might as well argue that the heliocentric hypothesis is false on the grounds that it conflicts with the traditional beliefs enshrined in the phrase 'terra firma'. To be sure, he must now give up the claim that he is only analysing 'can' as it is traditionally used. But this would not trouble him much. Our actual use of 'can', he will now say, enshrines a false belief, and the sooner we get rid of it the better.

[1] op. cit., pp. 119–20 n.

2. To accept the possibility of Austin's example and the interpretation he puts on it is to reject the thesis that 'he can' in this sort of case means 'he *always* does, if . . .'; but it invites, and I shall try to show that it requires, the thesis that 'he can' means 'he *usually* does, if . . .'. This would be a crucial, indeed a fatal change, if the issue were between determinism and indeterminism; but it is not; the issue is the possibility of an hypothetical analysis of 'can'. Let us agree for the moment that an ability is inherently liable not to produce success, on occasion, and that for no reason. It is also inherently liable to produce *success*, at least on most occasions. If you miss an occasional three-foot putt your ability to hole three-foot putts may not be in doubt; but if you miss too many, you lack the ability. 'He can', then, implies 'he usually succeeds, if he tries'; and equally, though one success might be a fluke, 'he usually succeeds, if he tries' implies 'he can'. One might object that 'he usually succeeds, if he tries' is a much more guarded remark than 'he can', expressing some doubt as to whether he can or not. But since 100 per cent success is not, on Austin's view, required for the assertion of 'he can', something less than 100 per cent success must be sufficient if the assertion is ever to be made at all. There is, therefore, at least a material equivalence between 'he can' and 'he usually succeeds, if he tries' in this sort of case.

3. But, if there is a material equivalence, can we go further and assert a connexion of meaning? It would certainly be odd to suggest that abilities are *causally* connected with successes.

It may well be that all human abilities are causally dependent on the possession of suitable muscles, nerves, brain cells and the like, and we learn from experience what equipment of this sort is required for each ability; but we do not learn from experience that if a man has a certain ability he will usually succeed when he tries or that he will not usually succeed if he lacks the ability. Austin talks of an ability as *producing* success or failure, as if it were a tool or a part of the body with which we do something and without which we cannot (contingently) do it. The metaphor of 'producing' can hardly be seriously intended; but the point is crucial. We can identify a niblick and then go on to say that it is used for getting out of bunkers; but we cannot identify the ability to get out of bunkers and then establish a contingent, but almost universal correlation between having this ability and actually getting out of bunkers. We do not, in short, learn by experience that people succeed in doing something if and only if they have the ability to do it.

Consider a contrasting case. I am looking out of the window and see that it is raining hard; I turn away for a moment and when I look back it is still raining. It would be ludicrous to suggest that it was not raining while my back was turned; for we know that rain is not that sort of thing. But, though ludicrous, the suggestion is not unintelligible, not logically absurd. Rain before and rain after is very good evidence; but it is not conclusive evidence. This is quite different from Austin's case, since in his case a run of successes before and after the one failure *conclusively* establishes the truth of the statement that he had the ability even on the occasion on which he failed. Why does Austin's golfer only say that further experiments may *confirm* his belief that he could have holed that putt? They prove it up to the hilt, since, given that n is large enough, a run of n-1 successes *entails* the presence of an ability throughout the run. We are not arguing, as we are in the rain case, on the inductive grounds that rain is known to be the sort of thing that does not stop and start when people turn round. Abilities are by definition a sort of things that cannot suddenly stop and start, because they continue through periods of time in spite of failures; so the relation of evidence to conclusion in Austin's case is, like that of the evidence in the rain case to the conclusion 'the weather was foul the whole time I was in the room', one of entailment.

But, it might be asked, might he not have retained his ability to hole putts of that sort throughout half an hour except at the one crucial moment? Not only did he fail, as we know; perhaps also he lacked the ability just then and there? It is important to see that this suggestion is ruled out by Austin's account, not as false, but as unintelligible. Statements of ability are statements to the effect that someone is usually, or would usually be successful in a series of attempts; and what could be meant by saying 'he was usually successful just then and there'? An ability endures through a period and can only be said to exist *at* a time in the sense that everything that endures may be said to exist at every time during its span of endurance. We may, then, say that he had the ability just then and there only in the sense that the time referred to by 'then and there' was within this span; and the evidence for his having had the ability just then and there in *this* sense is conclusive.

If Austin's indeterminism (abilities are liable not to produce success, on occasion, and that for no reason) is allowed, why should we not also allow this alternative account of the matter? Abilities, we say, are inherently liable to *desert* us, on occasion, and that for no reason. I lose my ability when I am drunk or tired or in a panic, and sometimes I *just* lose it for no reason at all. If both kinds of indeterminism were allowed, we should have to say that it was an open question which was the correct story to tell on some particular occasion; for the stories are critically different. It might be that he *could* have done it—this being one of the rare occasions on which his ability did not produce success; or it might be that he could *not* have done it—this being one of the rare occasions on which his ability deserted him. But it is clear that we cannot allow this choice of 'explanations'; for since, *ex hypothesi*, there is *no* difference between the two cases, we should never have any reason for preferring one to the other.

I conclude, then, that so far from being a reason for rejecting the possibility of an hypothetical analysis of 'can', Austin's account of the case of the golfer actually confirms it. For, unless the idea of an ability *producing* success is taken more seriously than he intended—and I have given reasons for saying that it cannot—there is a logical equivalence, in this type of case, between 'he can' and 'he succeeds if he tries'. It is true that, if we accept Austin's account, we must rewrite the analysis as 'he usually succeeds, if he tries'; but this, while an important change, leaves the hypothetical analysis intact. One caution is necessary here. Philosophers who have offered analyses of this kind have often written as if they supposed that there was a *causal* connexion between the consequent 'he does, or will, or succeeds' and the antecedent 'if he wants to, or chooses, or tries'. This is certainly incorrect.[1] There is a large number of verbs, including all those mentioned above and many others, which belong to the general area of *intentional action*. Many of the connexions between them are, like that between ability and success, certainly not causal but, unlike that between ability and success, not logical either. What their status is I do not know; to find out would be to get to the heart of the matter.

[1] On this point see Richard Taylor: '*I can*' in the *Philosophical Review*, January 1960, pp. 82–6.

III

Austin was not, in his paper, directly concerned with questions of freedom and responsibility; but this is an area in which questions of the form 'could he have done it?' typically come up for an answer, and he touches on it when he says that the golfer kicks himself for missing the putt. There are cases in which everything else is beyond reasonable doubt and the question whether or not an ascription of responsibility or some accusation is called for turns solely on the question 'could he have done it?' or 'could he have avoided doing it?' No solution to the second-order philosophical question 'what do statements made with "can" and "could have" mean in these contexts?' can be considered satisfactory unless it succeeds in showing why the first-order questions should be considered relevant to ascriptions and accusations. The fact that they so obviously *are* relevant has sometimes blinded philosophers to the difficulty of seeing why this should be so and hence into giving theories of 'can' which will not explain it. This is the rock on which many theories founder. They give us senses of 'can' and 'could have' which may well be correct for other uses of these protean words, but which are such that they cannot explain why 'could have' questions are thought relevant to ascriptions and accusations. This is typically the case with theories of an intuitionist or introspectionist type, according to which both the meaning of 'I can' and the truth (on at least some occasions) of statements in the form 'I can' are held to be transparent.

Austin's theory would be immune from this criticism if it were not for the fact that the golfer reproaches himself for his failure. But it is not clear why he should do this, rather than cursing his luck. Certainly it was *he*, and not one of his team-mates, who missed the putt and, perhaps, thereby lost the match; and certainly he might lament the fact that his prowess was not greater than in fact it was. But, by the terms of the case, having tried as hard as he could and failed, he has nothing for which to reproach himself. We must distinguish (as philosophers are prone not to do) between the question 'Is determinism true?' and the question 'What, if any, is the bearing of departures, if any, from strict determinism on the freedom of the will, in that sense of freedom which is thought to be a necessary condition of responsibility?'. If we accept the terms of Austin's case, we must give a negative answer to the first question; but if we have no criterion for distinguishing cases in which an ability inexplicably fails to produce success (he could have done it, but did not) from cases in which the ability inexplicably lapses (he could not have done it), the indeterminism which we must accept will have no bearing whatever on freedom. The type of theory that I was criticizing in *Ethics* would say that, given the terms of Austin's case, it remained an open question whether or not the golfer could have holed the putt and hence whether or not he could be blamed for the consequent loss of the match. On Austin's view, as we have seen, the first question is no longer open, the evidence being sufficient to entail that he could have holed it; but we are obliged to construe 'he could have holed it' in such a way as to make the man as blameless for the loss of the match as he would have been if he had been unable to hole it. He is, of course, responsible for losing the match in the trivial sense already noticed, that it was he who missed the vital putt; but he would have been equally responsible in this sense if he had missed it through lack of ability. Even if Austin is right in giving an indeterminist account of abilities, he fails to show how and why ascriptions of responsibility may turn on the answers that we give to 'could have' questions.

In Austin's example as it stands no question of moral responsibility or moral appraisal comes up. How could it be made to come up? The player might have been bribed by the other side and have missed the putt on purpose, while pretending to try his hardest. Or, knowing that it was a critical shot in an important match, he may have been culpably negligent in its execution. (Negligence of this sort, thoughtlessness, lack of consideration, failure to see something in a situation that is morally relevant—all these, though different, belong in the same bag, and it is a bag which moral philosophers have not examined as carefully as they should; for nine tenths of our moral shortcomings will be found in it.) But, to make moral assessment relevant at all, *something* of this kind must be introduced into the situation. I suggest that when, in preparation for a judicial or moral appraisal, we ask 'could he have helped it?' what we want to know is the answer to such questions as 'why did he do it?', 'why did he not succeed?', 'what prevented him?', 'but for what factor in the situation would he have done it?'. Some answers, notably lack of ability and lack of opportunity, exculpate, if not wholly at least to some degree;

these are the answers that we summarize in the blanket phrase 'he could not help it'; other answers, notably 'he was bribed' and 'he just didn't care' have the opposite effect. The problem of the freedom of the will, in so far as this is not only a metaphysical problem but relevant to moral philosophy, is that of discerning some general feature that distinguishes the exculpatory from the non-exculpatory answers. To say that some things are in our power to do or not do and others not, though perhaps true, is wholly unenlightening. It merely restates the problem; and theories about what it is in our power to do cannot be acceptable unless they succeed in explaining why the question whether something is or is not in our power should be considered relevant to our moral status.

AUSTIN ON ABILITIES[1]

Irving Thalberg

I want to evaluate and develop further the view of human powers which runs through J. L. Austin's masterful essay, 'Ifs and Cans'. I am particularly intrigued by the connexions and contrasts he discerns between having an ability and performing the kind of action one has the ability to perform. I'll start with two of Austin's remarks on this topic which appear to clash. They are: (i) 'It follows merely from the premiss that [a person has done something], that he has the ability to do it, according to ordinary English' (p. 175); and (ii) 'There are . . . good reasons for not speaking of "I can lift my finger" as being directly verified when I proceed to lift it, and likewise for not speaking of "He could have done it" as being directly verified by the discovery that he did do it' (p. 172; see pp. 170 and 173, n.). Austin's proposals sound inconsistent because, whenever the premiss, 'I raised my finger', entails the conclusion, 'I had the ability to raise my finger', as (i) provides, then the discovery that I raised my finger should directly verify, or suffice to prove the truth of, the same ability statement, which goes against (ii).

After I sketch in some indispensable background for discussion of these issues, I will demonstrate the compatibility of Austin's remarks (i) and (ii). Then I will show the bearing of both suggestions upon Austin's more disputed thesis (iii) that statements specifying what a person *can* do are not hypothetical or conditional assertions, in particular his thesis that 'So-and-so can do X' never

[1] This essay incorporates a few passages from my 1962 paper, 'Abilities and Ifs' (*Analysis* XXII). I thank the editor of *Analysis* for permitting me to draw upon that article. My parenthetical references to Austin's 'Ifs and Cans' specify page numbers in Austin's *Philosophical Papers*, edited by J. O. Urmson and G. J. Warnock (Oxford, 1961).

means 'So-and-so will do X if he tries'. I will look into Austin's famous counter-example against this standard hypothetical interpretation of a golfer's ability to sink an easy putt; and I will offer a new account of the moral he draws from it—namely (iv), that our abilities are 'inherently liable not to produce success, on occasion', even when we try our best and nothing causes us to fail (p. 166, n.). This moral is naturally tied up with Austin's concluding remark (v) that the assumption of Determinists, that our successes and failures always have causes, 'appears not consistent with what we ordinarily say and presumably think' about our powers (p. 179). I attempt to show that Austin's confusions regarding (iv) will explain why he need not have maintained (v). Finally, I will say something positive about the logical and pragmatic relations between ascriptions of ability and conditional statements. My verdict will be that ability statements resist translation into conditional form; nevertheless they have hypothetical overtones: they always entail one or another type of conditional statement. Still I salvage part of Austin's theory in connexion with (iii), that conditionals like 'So-and-so will do X if he tries' never state causal hypotheses.

1. *Stage setting: various senses of 'can' and 'being prevented'.* My discussion of ability will be limited in several respects. I will not investigate what it means, in general, to assert that something can happen or that a person can perform some task. As Wittgenstein noticed in the *Brown Book*, 'can' is not univocal. All that seems to be constant, from situation to situation where we say that a person can do something, is that we exclude one or another impediment. Wittgenstein's dictum goes:

> When we ask a doctor 'Can the patient walk?', we shall sometimes be ready to substitute for this 'Is his leg healed?'—'Can he speak?' under circumstances means 'Is his throat all right?' under others (e.g., if he is a small child) it means 'Has he learned to speak?' . . . We use the phrase 'He can walk, as far as the state of his leg is concerned', especially when we wish to oppose this condition for his walking to some other condition, say the state of his spine.[1]

Austin himself, in 'Plea for Excuses', set out a similar theory of what we mean when we say that a person is acting freely, which

[1] *The Blue and Brown Books* (New York, 1958), p. 114. See also Wittgenstein's *Philosophical Investigations* (New York, 1953), Part I, § 182-3.

presumably entails that he *can* act differently. Austin's account of this kindred notion begins:

> While it has been the tradition to present 'freedom' as the 'positive' term requiring elucidation, there is little doubt that to say that we acted 'freely' (in the philosopher's use, which is only faintly related to the everyday use) is to say only that we acted *not* un-freely, in one or another of the many heterogeneous ways of so acting (under duress, or what not) . . . 'Free' is only used to rule out the suggestion of some or all of its recognized antitheses.[1]

The uses of 'can', as well as 'acting freely', that interest a philosopher, occur mainly within contexts of judicial, moral and similar forms of evaluation. Typically, the 'can' of ability crops up when someone has not done what he ought to have done. My doubles partner in a tennis match does not return a serve. Your neighbour does not alert the police when he hears a prowler force open the door of your apartment. At that very moment, an off-duty patrolman wanders by, but does not arrest or shoot the intruder. More dramatically, there is a child drowning in the river, and the only bystander at the scene does not rescue the child. Before we censure these people, we should ask whether they *could* have acted as we think they ought. Against this evaluative backdrop, what meanings has the verb 'can'? We already noticed that it rules out one or another impediment. On the positive side, however, we might be asking the very general question: 'Was it within the power of these agents to do what they ought?' This is not equivalent to asking whether they had any specific powers, such as powers of concentration, of endurance, or persuasion. Specific powers of that type are abilities. The general question of whether it is within someone's power to act in a certain manner stands in for at least five more definite questions. One is: 'Did the agent have the ability to act?' The others are:

'Was he in a position to act?' ('Can' of opportunity.)

'Was he aware of relevant features of the situation? For example, did the bystander notice that the child was in danger?' ('Can' of knowledge or awareness.)

'Did he have the necessary equipment to act? For instance, was a telephone available to your neighbour? Was the off-duty patrolman carrying his revolver?' ('Can 'of means.)

[1] *Philosophical Papers*, p. 128.

'Was he entitled to act? Is an off-duty policeman authorized to detain or shoot suspected lawbreakers?' ('Can' of right or authority.)

When a person is to blame for not doing what he ought to have done, presumably it is true, in *all* of these senses of 'can', that he could have performed the action. To say that it was within his power, from every standpoint, is to say that he could have acted, in what Austin calls the 'all in' sense of 'can'. Often we inquire only about someone's ability, opportunity, knowledge, means or rights, because we assume it to have been within his power, from other standpoints, to act.

Now I want to connect these senses of 'can' with the various impediments I mentioned above. It seems to me that in 'Ifs and Cans', Austin does not sufficiently emphasize how each sense of 'can', beginning with his 'all in' sense, serves to 'rule out' one or another obstacle to action. Clearly one thing we always mean, when we ask whether the people in my illustrations could have done better, is: 'Were they prevented?' I will try now to elucidate this notion of being prevented. It has as many senses as 'can'. What qualifies as an obstacle will depend upon at least three factors: (*a*) which sense of 'can' we are using, (*b*) how important the action was that the agent did not perform, (*c*) what consequences he might have faced if he had performed it. If we are using the 'all in' sense of 'can', then every type of impediment is ruled out whenever a person could have done something. The more restricted senses of 'can' exclude hindrances of their own level. With respect to factors (*b*) and (*c*), it is noteworthy that many circumstances which may have influenced the agent, perhaps causing him to fall short of his duty, will not count as obstacles which prevented him from doing what he ought. Causes are not hindrances if the action was urgent or the consequences of action were negligible. Imagine that my tennis partner declares: 'I couldn't return the serve because I was overcome by muscle cramps'. Plainly the cramps interfered with his ability. On the other hand, if he complains, 'There was a puddle on the court between me and the place where the serve landed, so that I would have got my new sneakers wet if I had gone after the ball', we would deny that he was disabled. Did the puddle deprive him of the opportunity to return the serve? That depends upon the importance of the match. If it was purely recreational, all right; but if it was a grudge meeting, or a championship, then the water was no impediment, even if it caused my partner to let the serve go.

The difference between mere causes and impediments is striking when we turn to the bystander who does not haul a drowning child from the river. Suppose that he tells us: 'I was wearing a brand new suit; it would have been ruined if I had plunged into the water; and by the time I stripped, the child had disappeared'. We would deny that the danger of ruining his clothes deprived him of the opportunity to help the child. The task was too serious, and the consequences for his clothing were too trivial. But now suppose that the child did not fall in; it let a toy sailboat drift out into the current. Then evidently we would rank the danger to the man's suit as a circumstance that prevented him from going into the water.

The hindrances I have catalogued so far are causes, but some obstacles are not. The legal status of being off duty appears not to have brought it about, in a causal sense, that the patrolman had lost his power of arresting wrongdoers. Heavy drinking might disable him temporarily or permanently, but going off duty does not seem to operate on him as alcohol might. The disparity emerges clearly if we recall that any event which causes another might conceivably fail to produce its regular upshot, although other conditions remain as before. Thus it is not self-contradictory to suppose that the policeman should consume a gallon of gin and yet suffer no loss of ability. But is it conceivable that, without any change in our laws and customs, the patrolman should go off duty and, contrary to all our previous experience in these matters, retain his authority to arrest people? If that sounds absurd, then this kind of impediment upon one's rights is not a cause. Incidentally, I am not denying that there are causes which prevent policemen from making arrests. For instance, a policeman might trip while chasing a culprit, with the result that the culprit escapes arrest. In that case, however, tripping did not limit or cancel out the patrolman's authority; it prevented him from exercising the authority he had.

My distinction between impediments and causes goes beyond saying that not all obstacles function as causes. What I wish to underscore is that not all circumstances which cause a person's failure to accomplish some task rank as circumstances which prevented him, so that he could not have accomplished the task. This distinction will help us reject Austin's indeterministic theory of abilities (iv) and his conclusion (v) that Determinism conflicts with the commonsense view of abilities, which Austin believes to be indeterministic.

Before we stray into that familiar arena of debate, however, we should explore Austin's other doctrines regarding abilities, for they are original and challenging. Just as I have had to neglect many connexions between the concepts of ability, opportunity, awareness, means, rights, and hindrances,[1] I must overlook many nuances in our concept of ability. Thus I will blur distinctions between specific ability terms: aptitude, talent, flair, fitness, capacity, competence, knack, skill, proficiency, even dexterity and strength. My only concern will be the relation between all species of ability and action.

2. *Ability and being able.* Recall Austin's remark (i), 'It follows merely from the premiss that he does it, that he has the ability to do it, according to ordinary English'. If this principle of 'ordinary English' were correct, it would support Austin's thesis (iii) that ascriptions of ability are not hypothetical, but categorical assertions. Take as a premiss this report of Brown's performance at the shooting gallery: 'He hit three bulls-eyes in a row'. This assertion is categorical enough; so if it entails the proposition, 'Brown had the ability to hit three bulls-eyes in a row', at least some ascriptions of ability are categorical. But is this inference valid? I admit that we are entitled to conclude, 'Brown *was able* to hit three bulls-eyes in a row'. I deny, however, that this conclusion is equivalent to asserting that Brown has a certain degree of ability at target practice.

The non-equivalence becomes noticeable if we expand our account of Brown's display of marksmanship: 'Before he hit three bulls-eyes, he fired 600 rounds, without coming close to the bulls-eye; and his subsequent tries were equally wild'. This amplified record of Brown's performance in no way compels us to retract our assertion that he *was able* to hit three bulls-eyes in a row. He was able to do it, but without any regularity. Therefore he does not have this sort of ability at target shooting.

This story reveals the ambiguity of expressions from the 'being

---

[1] For elaboration of these conceptual ties, see P. H. Nowell-Smith, 'Ifs and Cans', reprinted above. There is also a suggestive footnote in Austin's 'Ifs and Cans', p. 171, regarding the interdependency of 'being prevented' and 'being rendered unable'.

able' family. A similar story would uncover the same ambiguity of 'being unable', 'not being able' and 'could not', which would prove that it never follows from the fact that a champion *once* could not (was not able to) hit a bulls-eye that he lacked ability on that occasion. 'Was able' sometimes means 'had the ability', and sometimes means 'did'. Here is an illustration with 'will be able'. It may be irrational, but it is not self-contradictory to declare: 'Regardless of his meagre skill, I have faith that Brown will be able to hit three bulls-eyes tomorrow'. This concept of 'being able', which does not entail ability, is quite familiar. Everyday examples would be: 'The village sorcerer was able (Heaven knows how!) to cure my lumbago'; 'The dude managed to ride a ferocious broncho'; 'Somehow or other, the castaway survived for ten days without food or drink'; 'The ill-prepared rebels brought off a *coup d' état*'; 'The inexperienced kidnapper contrived to elude an F.B.I. dragnet'. On the negative side, a skilled portrait painter might exclaim: 'I just cannot get the shadows right today!' For simplicity, call the 'being able' and 'being unable' in these examples the 'being able' and 'being unable' of managing and not managing, respectively. These expressions carry the hint that the subject had a lucky break or a bad break, but that is immaterial. What matters for us is that our distinction will explain why Austin allows (i) that in 'ordinary English', 'He did it' entails 'He had the ability to do it', and nevertheless maintains (ii) that there are 'good reasons' for blocking these inferences. Perhaps what Austin had in mind is the fact that colloquial discourse seldom discriminates between the 'ability' and the 'managing' senses of 'being able', and thus sanctions invalid arguments of the form: 'Brown hit three bulls-eyes in a row; so he was able to do it; therefore he had the ability to do it'. Exegetical considerations aside, the distinction is crucial to an understanding of ability. Before we go on to that, however, I anticipate one criticism.

3. *Objection: the person who manages to do something must have a momentary ability.* A philosopher might agree that Brown, as well as the sorcerer, the novice rider, the castaway, the rebels and the inexperienced kidnapper do not have enduring abilities; but he might insist that they necessarily had some kind of short run ability at the moment they succeeded. On this view, my 'managing' sense of 'being able' collapses into the 'being able' of ability—an ability which only lasts a moment. Now what sort of ability is this? Is

anything to be said for this notion of an ability that 'just comes and goes',[1] except that it again permits inferences from action to ability?

Now standard proficiencies and skills come and go in the sense that they develop, wane and disappear as time passes. But they do not 'just come and go'. In particular, when a man is suddenly disabled, it is never the case that his ability just deserts him. Various identifiable circumstances deprive him of his powers: fatigue, vehement emotion, illness, heart attack, injury. There was no hint of any disabling circumstance like this in our story of Brown's target practice. Nothing is said which explains how his ability might have 'gone' after he shot three bulls-eyes. The sudden ripening of his skill, at precisely the instant he hit the first bulls-eye, is also unexplained.

A more positive reason for denying that Brown was endowed with a momentary ability is that one of the things we always mean when we attribute an ability to a man is that you can rely on him, in normal situations of opportunity, knowledge, equipment, and right, to perform a certain kind of task. We want fairly consistent success from a person with ability. A wine-taster whose powers of discrimination 'just come and go', a typist with 'momentary proficiency', or a wrestler who possessed strength for two minutes during the middle of a bout, would be totally useless to us. Since these pragmatic requirements are woven into our notion of an ability, this notion will not stretch to allow for momentary abilities, on which we cannot rely.[2] Having thus dismissed the objection against my 'managing' sense of 'being able', I want to explore further the relation between ability and performance.

4. *Criteria for competence.* How frequently must people succeed, and how many catastrophic miscarriages are tolerated by our standards for ascribing ability to them? The answers will vary with the task that we say a person has the ability to execute. A racetrack tout who predicts one-tenth of the season's Daily Double winners would rank as a skilled prognosticator by anyone's standards. A surgeon who loses one-third of his patients when he does appendectomies would be declared incompetent, unless there

---

[1] Stuart Hampshire, in *Freedom of the Individual* (New York, 1965), seems to countenance momentary abilities. See pp. 16, 20, 24. Hampshire also constantly and explicitly assumes a principle equivalent to Austin's thesis (i).

[2] Nowell-Smith offers additional arguments in his 'Ifs and Cans', loc. cit.

were peculiar conditions, such as unavailability of a scalpel and sterilizing equipment, which explained these failures.

Often we decide that someone has an ability without waiting to count up his successful and faulty performances. All we require is success at analogous tasks in testing situations. Thus a young lieutenant might be judged fit to lead a platoon in battle, merely on the strength of his handling of problems during manoeuvres.

How about rudimentary performances such as lifting one's fingers? Isn't it ludicrous to imagine tests, and ratios of success to failure as criteria for ascribing to someone this kind of ability? Of course it would be ridiculous, *when* we know that a person is in normal condition; because normalcy includes the power to move one's limbs! But if we intend to establish whether someone is normal, tests are in order. A person whose hands are crippled with arthritis visits Lourdes. He dips his hands in the holy water of the grotto, and his fingers begin to move. Has he regained the ability to lift his fingers? Surely we need more than one display to be convinced.

5. *Success, failure and effort.* Here is another crucial element in our notion of ability. When we speak of a person's successes and failures, in testing situations and in settings where he has the opportunity, the necessary information, the equipment and the right to do something, we make assumptions about his will. That is, we take it for granted that he wants to execute the task, that he prefers doing it rather than alternative tasks, that he intends to do it, or that he is attempting to do it. The very concept of success incorporates assumptions of this kind regarding his conative attitude. Let me explain. A man might unintentionally put a radio together—while distractedly juggling the components. But it would be self-contradictory to report that he *succeeded* in assembling the radio if he did not intend to. Therefore success entails intention. The same holds for unsuccessful actions. The statement, 'John did not succeed in assembling the radio, but he made no attempt to, and had no intention of putting it together' is also self-contradictory.

Now 'He failed to assemble it, but he neither tried nor intended to' is not absurd. That is because the verb 'fail' is ambiguous. In one sense, to fail to assemble the radio is simply to omit the whole undertaking; and omitting to assemble it does not entail trying or intending to assemble it. In fact, to fail by omitting is not to try at all. The cases I imagined in section 1, beginning with the doubles partner who does not return a serve, were instances of omission-failure. They do not concern us now. The sense of 'fail' which is germane now is equivalent to 'does not succeed'. The story of Brown at the shooting gallery, in section 2, exemplifies this kind of failure. So will every case in which we test people and observe their displays of ability.

We have seen that one successful attempt to do something does not prove ability, and that one unsuccessful attempt never proves inability. Therefore it seems fair to depict the relation between action and ability as follows. If a man usually succeeds, under allowably difficult circumstances, he has the ability; if he usually fails, then he lacks it. To say that he has the ability to perform a particular act, here and now, in suitable conditions of opportunity, and so on, is to say, *inter alia*, 'He will *probably* succeed'. And the evidence you need to refute the forecast of probable success is just the same as you need to refute the original ascription of ability: regular failure in optimum conditions similar to the present ones.

This part of our analysis, together with the account of impediments and causes in section 2, equips us to grapple with a celebrated Austinian footnote, in which he defends the views I numbered (iii), (iv) and (v). Austin is beleaguering hypothetical analyses of 'He can' as meaning 'He will if he tries.' We are to imagine Austin on the golf course. Conditions are ideal. Austin faces a short putt. He attempts to knock the ball into the cup, but fails. He remains convinced that he had the ability, then and there, to hole it. If he is correct, the hypothetical analyses is refuted, since 'He will if he tries' is falsified, while 'He can' seems to have been true. Austin writes:

> Indeed, further experiments may confirm my belief that I could have done it that time although I did not.
> But if I tried my hardest, say, and missed, surely there *must* have been *something* that caused me to fail, that made me unable to succeed? So that I *could not* have holed it. Well, a modern belief in science, in there being an explanation of everything, may make us assent to this argument. But such a belief is not in line with the traditional beliefs enshrined in the word *can*: according to *them*, a human ability or power or capacity is inherently liable not to produce success, on occasion, and that for no reason (or are bad luck and bad form reasons?) (p. 166).

Numerous commentators on this passage have missed Austin's

confusion between two species of cause, which our analysis has repeatedly distinguished: (*a*) causes 'that made me unable to succeed', so that 'I could not have holed' the ball; and (*b*) other causes for my failure. Causes of family (*a*) are impediments, which either incapacitate a golfer, spoil his opportunity, interfere with his awareness, rob him of the means he requires, or invalidate his right to play on that golf course. What would constitute a non-hindering cause of type (*b*)? Slight nervous tension, which makes him swing less accurately than usual; an imperceptible ridge in front of the cup, which deflects the golf ball. Austin's error is to reason that, since the golfer might fail without being hindered by any cause from group (*a*), on those same occasions there is no cause at all, not even a cause of type (*b*), for his failure. This *non sequitur* plainly reinforces Austin's beliefs (iv) and (v) that Determinism clashes with the assumptions we encapsulate in our everyday uses of the terms 'ability' and 'can'. For if it is true that a man with an ability might try and fail, but nothing causes his failure, then this action (his failure) is uncaused, and Determinism is false. On the other side, if Determinism were correct, and failures like this are always caused, then it is not true that the golfer could have sunk the putt he missed. It is needless to add that his whole line of reasoning is drawn from an assimilation of all causes to hindrances.

6. *Chisholm's reply.* In his perceptive discussion of 'Ifs and Cans', Professor Chisholm objects to Austin's short putt example:

> If Austin's golfer really could have holed it that time, then there was something such that, had he tried to do it along with the other things he did do, then the absent condition (e.g., applying more pressure with the thumb) would have been supplied, and he would have holed the ball.[1]

Chisholm provisionally reinstates, as the general analysis of 'He can X', an hypothetical proposition: 'There is something Y such that if he tried to do Y then he would do X'. One point is unclear in Chisholm's treatment of the putting example: what action Y is the golfer supposed to *try* to perform, with a view toward sinking the putt (X*ing*)? If the golfer has normal control over his thumb, and nothing interferes with him, does it make sense to say, 'He is trying to apply more pressure with his thumb'? Chisholm surely does not

[1] From Chisholm's essay, 'Austin's *Philosophical Papers*', [p. 125 above].

mean that the golfer will sink the putt if he tries, in the sense of exerting himself, and presses as strenuously as he can with his thumb upon the golf-club. Trying in this sense would certainly wreck his shot. Successful putting demands a relaxed grip. Perhaps what Chisholm means is that the golfer should try harder to sink the putt, and that his 'trying harder' would *consist* in pressing more firmly with his thumb. If so, Y is the same as X in this case, and Chisholm is merely re-asserting 'He will X if he tries'.

Chisholm's objection does not confuse hindering causes of type (*a*) with other causes of type (*b*) which account for a wild putt. But Chisholm does appear to think that a skilled golfer can overcome every cause of type (*b*) by means of a sufficiently careful attempt to sink putts. Evidently we would not say that the golfer who leaves out the extra thumb pressure only made a half-hearted attempt. A conscientious or 'full-fledged' attempt to exercise your putting skill consists in guarding against the most frequent, noticeable and bothersome causes of inaccurate putting which figure in group (*b*): extreme nervousness, gripping the golf-club very tightly, gross irregularities of the terrain. But even if Chisholm does not think that extra thumb pressure is comprised in a proper attempt to hole the ball, he supposes that precautions of this kind will always enable you to succeed in your attempt. I doubt this. Aren't there minor causes of inaccurate putting that a skilled golfer cannot detect in advance? If so, they would not count as hindering causes of type (*a*), due to their rarity and comparative innocuousness; still they would make him miss occasional shots, and he could do nothing to neutralize them. Contrary to Chisholm, then, it is untrue that if a man with ability tries and fails, additional effort on his part would have resulted in success.

Chisholm's reply to Austin's golfing story is offered in defence of the analysis of 'He can do X' which Austin is challenging, namely that 'He can do X' means 'He will do X if he tries (to do Y)'. Although Chisholm denies that Austin's story refutes that hypothetical interpretation of 'can', he has independent reasons for discarding such hypothetical accounts. Chisholm's statement of these reasons in his discussion of 'Ifs and Cans' is laconic:

> The statements 'He does X if and only if he tries to do Y' and 'He *cannot try* to do Y' are inconsistent with 'He can do X', but they are not inconsistent with our *analysans*—they are not inconsistent with 'There is a Y such that if he tries to do Y he will do X'. (There

are, of course, many acts which one cannot even *try* to perform.)
. . . If this difficulty is genuine, then it applies not only to the
present formula, but also . . . to any attempt to define 'can' in
terms of 'will if'. For any such attempt will presumably introduce
a verb of which 'he' may be made the subject; it will then be grammatically permissible to insert 'can not' between the subject 'he'
and the verb; and then it will be possible to describe a situation in
which the *analysans* is true and 'He can' is false.

In a subsequent essay, 'He Could Have Done Otherwise',
Chisholm spells out this objection of his against 'He will do X if
he tries (to do Y)' and similar hypothetical interpretations:

> In saying 'You could have arranged things this morning so that
> you would be in Boston now', are we saying: . . . 'There are
> certain things such that, if this morning you had undertaken
> (chosen, willed, tried, set out) to bring it about that those things
> would occur, then you would be in Boston now . . .'?
>
> Consider . . . those things which are such that, if this morning
> our agent had undertaken (chosen, willed, tried, set out) to bring
> them about, then he would be in Boston now. And let us suppose
> (i) that he *could not* have undertaken . . . to bring any of those
> things about and (ii) that he would be in Boston now only if he *had*
> . . . These suppositions are consistent with saying that he *would* be
> in Boston now *if* he had undertaken those things, but they are not
> consistent with saying that he could then have arranged things so
> that he would be in Boston now.[1]

From the rest of his essay, it is evident that Chisholm believes that
any cause of his protagonist's not taking measures to be in Boston
now prevented him from taking those measures, so that he could
not take them. Chisholm writes: 'If our agent had it within his
power . . ., then . . . at 10 o'clock this morning there was no
sufficient causal condition for his not then undertaking those
things' (p 413; see his definition (D1) on p. 414; and pp. 415–17).
In other words, Chisholm's reply to Austin was free of the confusion
we found in Austin's golfing anecdote between (*a*) causes which

---

[1] *Journal of Philosophy* LXIV (1967), p. 411. My objection against this
pattern of reasoning has been stated forcefully in general terms by Wilfrid
Sellars, 'Fatalism and Determinism', in *Freedom and Determinism*, edited by
K. Lehrer (New York, 1966). Lehrer's contribution to the volume, 'An
Empirical Disproof of Determinism?' usefully distinguishes between 'It is
causally impossible for Smith to move' and 'Smith cannot move' (p. 193).

disable or otherwise hinder one and (*b*) other causes of one's failure. But Chisholm is guilty of the same mixup, and assimilates causes of group (*b*) to those of group (*a*), when he offers his own refutation of the view that 'He can' means 'He will if'. A sign that he has made this assimilation is that he nowhere describes a case of someone being rendered *powerless* to elect some course of action, in contrast to simply being caused not to elect the course of action.

Since this muddle is so pervasive in discussion of human powers, I will illustrate it again in Chisholm's reasoning. Imagine that Chisholm's would-be traveller was standing alongside a train at 10 o'clock this morning, and knew that the train would arrive in Boston by this time. He had a ticket. He had a right to visit Boston, in contrast, say, to visiting Havana. What caused him not to board the train? If a negligent conductor dropped an immense suitcase on him, and knocked him unconscious, then he was indeed prevented from taking the appropriate measures to be in Boston now. It would be true, under those causal conditions, that he could not have taken the measures. But this is more a case of being powerless to *go* to Boston than of being powerless to choose or try.

Instead of a hindering cause, consider this: the prospective traveller recognizes a long-lost college chum and decides to go over and talk with him, since there will be a later train to Boston. Did the appearance of the friend cause the traveller not to take measures which would have put him in Boston by now? Decidedly. Was he disabled or impeded in any way from boarding the train, as he was when the suitcase felled him? Heavens no. Although there was a sufficient causal condition for his not taking measures to be in Boston now, it would be erroneous to conclude, with Chisholm, that the traveller was powerless to take these measures. He simply did not. He could have stepped on to the train, and so he could have got to Boston by now.

Actually there are causes which hinder a man from choosing, or even from contemplating, a particular line of action. If the would-be traveller had been hypnotized, and left with the post-hypnotic suggestion that he must change his mind at the last moment about going to Boston, then I concede that he could not have taken all the necessary measures to be in Boston by now. The man could not have stuck to his decision that he would leave for Boston at

10 a.m. Therefore the hypothetical analysis of 'can' as 'will if'
breaks down.[1] However, we might repair the hypothetical account
by making *ad hoc* exceptions for people who are labouring under
hypnotic suggestions, pathological urges and the like. All we
say is: ' "He can do X" means "He will do X if he undertakes
(chooses, tries, etc.) to Y, *and* his failure to undertake Y is not due
to hypnosis, uncontrollable impulse, brain-washing and similar
volitional impediments." ' The hypothetical analysis, so modified,
does not explain why these states of the agent deprive him of
his power to act; but neither will the categorical view that the
statement, 'He can do X', simply records the present condition
of the agent. A defender of the categorical interpretation must
also take it as a brute fact that hypnotized people lack certain
powers.

Before I return to Austin's theory, I think it is worth noticing
that Chisholm seems to believe that a person's desires are hindering
causes, just like post-hypnotic suggestions and pathological urges.
Although Chisholm does not say anything which directly implies
that the traveller's desire to converse with a long-lost friend has
rendered him unable to *choose* or *undertake* to begin his journey to
Boston, Chisholm appears to believe that such volitional factors
prevent a traveller from going to Boston. His belief comes out in
yet another essay, 'Freedom and Action'. There Chisholm focuses
upon a parallel case: a killer has desires and beliefs which cause
him to shoot someone. Chisholm begins by saying that there is no
important difference between this man and a hypnotized killer.
Chisholm declares:

> If what we say he did was really something that was brought
> about by a second man, one who forced his hand upon the trigger,
> say, or who, by means of hypnosis, compelled him to perform the
> act, then, since the act was caused by the *second* man, it was nothing
> that was within the power of the *first* man to prevent. And precisely
> the same thing is true, I think, if instead of referring to a second
> man who compelled the first one, we speak instead of the *desires* and
> *beliefs* which the first man happens to have had . . . Since *they*

[1] Bruce Aune ('Hypotheticals and "Can": Another Look', *Analysis* XXVII
[1967]) demonstrates that inferences of the form, 'The hypnotized man cannot choose (or try) to get to Boston; therefore he cannot get to Boston',
are *deductively* invalid. Still I think that premises like this are rational grounds
of some kind for denying that the hypnotized man can travel to Boston.

caused [his action], *he* was unable to do anything other than just what he did do.[1]

Later on Chisholm considers again a hypothetical interpretation of 'The killer could have acted differently'. He argues:

> What the murderer saw, let us suppose, along with his beliefs and desires, *caused* him to fire the shot; yet he was such that *if*, just then, he had chosen or decided *not* to fire the shot, then he would not have fired it . . .
>
> . . . Suppose, after all, that our murderer could not have *chosen*, or could not have *decided*, to do otherwise . . . Then he could not have done anything other than just what it was that he did do. (pp. 15–16)

Why suppose 'that our murderer could not have chosen . . . to do otherwise'? Presumably because his desires and beliefs caused him to make the choice he did make, and hence, according to Chisholm, prevented him from electing a different course of action. At any rate, no other causes of his actual choice are mentioned by Chisholm, and therefore nothing else seems to be a candidate for a hindering cause. Now if Chisholm does hold that ordinary desires and beliefs, which do not result from hypnosis, brain-washing or cerebral lesions, prevent a man from choosing otherwise, and thereby render him powerless to act otherwise, this is a mistake. What entitles Chisholm to assume that desires whose origin is not abnormal will prevent a man from choosing or acting differently? He must demonstrate their similarity to circumstances which disable or otherwise hinder a person.

There is a hint in 'Ifs and Cans' that Austin commits the same error. Austin denies that 'I can' means 'I shall if I choose'; he also denies that 'the meaning of "I shall if I choose" is that my choosing to do the thing is sufficient to cause me inevitably to do it' (p. 159). What is Austin's point? A swimmer who is caught in a riptide drifts inevitably out to sea. Even if he desires and struggles to reach the shore, he cannot avoid drifting seaward. The current stops him from returning to the beach. But when a swimmer is not in the grips of a current, but instead goes out because he wants to,

---

[1] Included in *Freedom and Determinism*, edited by K. Lehrer (New York, 1966). Aune (see note above) criticizes Chisholm's reasoning here in somewhat different terms, Aune attacks a similar argument in Lehrer's own contribution, pp. 195–6.

it sounds extremely incongruous to say, 'Even if he desired or struggled to go back, he would inevitably move out to sea'.

This error of assimilating all causes to hindering causes has received more than enough attention. I hope that it is clear how Austin's indeterministic theses (iv) and (v) depend upon this confusion. In the remaining section of this paper, I want to scrutinize a kindred, but less pernicious assumption, which appears both in 'Ifs and Cans' and in Chisholm's commentary: the assumption that every conditional statement of the form, 'He will if he chooses (tries, etc.)' must record a causal relationship.

7. *Non-conditional 'if's, causal 'if's and non-causal but conditional 'if's.* Among the five remarks by Austin on ability that I began with, I have said very little about (iii), his thesis that statements specifying what a person can do are irreducibly categorical. I want to investigate Austin's denial that such assertions may be translated into hypothetical form. As before, I will focus on ascriptions of ability. My modifications of Austin's thesis will read: an ability statement is not equivalent to one or more conditionals, but it must entail one or more; however, such conditionals do not specify causal relationships. Austin, and Chisholm as well, seems to overlook the possibility that a conditional assertion might not describe a cause-effect sequence. Austin therefore appears to believe that his disproof of the view that 'He will if he tries' is a *causal* conditional also proves that a statement of this form is not a conditional of any sort. Moreover, Austin seems to assume that just because 'can' statements are not analysable into hypothetical form, they are logically unrelated to statements of that form. Actually these are minor errors in such a ground-breaking paper as 'Ifs and Cans'. But we will not have a satisfactory account of human power, and how causality bears upon it, until we correct them.

My study of the connexion between having an ability to do something and doing it, in sections 1 through 5, was that having an ability does not guarantee succees, even under ideal circumstances. Furthermore, you might not succeed even though you are unhindered by disabilities and similar interferences. That is, a man's failure does not prove that he could not do it. However, one's failures may still have causes, of the non-hindering variety. For these reasons, I suggested that when you ascribe an ability to someone, in a situation that is free of impediments, you imply that if he sets out to do what he has the ability to do, he will *probably* succeed. The degree of likelihood to which you commit yourself will vary, as I noted in Section 4, with the type of action that concerns you.

How do these conclusions affect Austin's thesis (iii)? His doctrine, that ability statements are categorical, is not a grammatical remark. He gives many compound sentences which contain an 'if' clause as examples of sentences which are used to make categorical assertions. His paradigm is: 'There are biscuits on the sideboard if you want them'. He allows that this is connected with a statement in which the 'can' of right will appear: 'There are biscuits on the sideboard which you can (or may) take if you want them'; but he says that this is equally non-conditional. I think that one might also use Austin's paradigm to ascribe an ability. That is, one might mean: 'You will find biscuits on the sideboard if you want (or bother trying) to find them'. Anyway, besides his paradigm of a non-conditional 'if', Austin gives the following ability statements as non-conditionals:

I could have walked a mile this morning in twenty minutes, if I had chosen;
I am capable of doing it (if I choose);
I could have ruined you this morning (if I had chosen);
I could have won if I had chosen to lob.

With what is Austin comparing these 'if's? He gives a causal paradigm which does not contain a 'can': 'I pant if I run'. The only causal ability statement he gives is: 'I can squeeze through if I am thin enough', of which he reports that it includes 'an ordinary causal "if" ' (p. 158). He mentions a number of other conditionals having to do with ability:

He could shoot you if you were within range;
I could do it if I had a thingummy;
I could have ruined you this morning, if I had had one more vote;
I could, or should, have won if he had chosen to lob (or to let me win).

Austin never says whether the 'if'-clause in these examples specifies a cause, but it is significant that he fails to mention the possibility that it does not, and that the statement should still be conditional.

The distinctive features which set apart all such conditional 'if'-statements from their non-conditional counterparts are these. You may deduce a contrapositive from conditional 'if'-statements, and not from the others. Non-conditional 'if'-statements allow you to infer, or detach, the main clause; but this is forbidden with conditional 'if'-statements. Austin explains:

> From 'If I run, I pant', we *can* infer 'If I do not pant, I do not run' (or, as we should rather say, 'If I am not panting, I am not running'), whereas we can *not* infer either 'I pant, whether I run or not' or 'I pant' (at least in the sense of 'I am panting') . . . These possibilities and impossibilities of inference are typical of the *if* of causal condition: but they are precisely reversed in the case of 'I can if I choose' or 'I could have if I had chosen'. For from these we should not draw the curious inferences that 'If I cannot, I do not choose to' or that 'If I could not have, I had not chosen to' (or 'did not choose to') . . . But on the contrary, from 'I can if I choose' we certainly should infer that 'I can, whether I choose to or not' and indeed that 'I can' period: and from 'I could have if I had chosen' we should similarly infer that 'I could have whether I chose to or not' and that anyway 'I could have' period. So that, whatever this *if* means, it is evidently not the *if* of causal condition. (pp. 157–8).

The inference pattern Austin sketches is distinctive. However, his final sentence suggests that Austin believes the pattern to mark off only two kinds of 'if'-statement: causal conditionals and non-conditionals. What about non-causal conditionals? It seems doubtful to me whether there is 'an ordinary causal "if" ' in 'I can squeeze through if I am thin enough'. How does being thin enough bring it about that I have the ability? And it is even more questionable whether being thin brings it about, in any causal sense, that I have the opportunity, the knowledge, the means or the right to squeeze through. Austin's other conditionals sound just as uncausal as the squeezing one, by a similar test.

I am particularly interested to see whether Austin has established that statements of the form, 'He will probably do X if he chooses (tries, etc.) to do Y' are non-conditional. I agree that they are not causal. You do not cause yourself to sink a putt by trying or choosing; you only cause the ball to tumble into the cup by striking it in a certain manner.

Now suppose it is probable that if Green attempts to beat

Thomas at ping-pong, Green will defeat Thomas. There are no hindrances around to bother Green. Isn't it equally probable, in this case, that if Green does not win, his attempt was faulty? At any event, the statement, 'It is probable that if Green tries to beat Thomas at ping-pong, he will', does not conform to the inference pattern of non-conditional 'if'-statements; for it hardly entails that Green will defeat Thomas whether he tries to or not, and that Green will probably defeat him *tout court*. So this 'if' is at least different from non-conditional 'if's.

How is this sort of conditional linked with ascribing skill to Green? In the following way, I think: if you attribute to Green the ability to defeat Thomas, you must be prepared to accept some hypotheses of this form, although with considerable choice among antecedent clauses. Also you must be prepared to reject the sub-contraries of these conditional statements. It would be very odd for an admirer of Green to declare: 'He has the ability to smear Thomas, but I have no idea whether he will win, even if he puts his heart into the game'. That is: if you believe Green has this ability, you must believe that there is some condition, perhaps even Green's relaxing and not caring, which is more likely to presage a victory by Green than a loss. The likelihood of his triumph does not, of course, exclude the possibility that it is Thomas' lucky day, and that he will manage to turn the tables on his more skilled opponent.

This view of the entailment relation between an ability statement and non-causal, but conditional, probability statements deserves more scrutiny than I will give it here. I believe that the entailment in question is partly pragmatic: when you ascribe an ability to someone you thereby commit yourself to accepting some hypotheses and not others about the conditions under which the agent will do what you say he has the ability to do. Why have philosophical adherents of this hypothetical account so often favoured 'if'-clauses which specify quasi-psychological conditions of the agent, such as trying and choosing? I think that this unexamined assumption is justified by the fact that our concept of an ability is the concept of a power which is under the control of its possessor. By contrast, the corrosive power of nitric acid is not within the acid's control.

The principal error about the agent's control has been a further assumption that the only way a person ever controls an event is by causing it to occur, to continue, to stop or not to occur. If we carry over this latter assumption to the case of doing what you have the ability to do, we get the absurd result that you bring it about that you sink a putt by first desiring or trying to sink it. With regard to Green's victory, the causal assumption suggests to us that Green's method of defeating Thomas consisted in his wanting or attempting to defeat him. But the questions, 'How did Green triumph?' and 'What caused his victory?', are not answered if you say, 'He wanted and tried to win'.

If the connexion between quasi-psychological states of the agent, such as desire or endeavour, and his doing what he has the ability to do, is not a causal connexion, what is it? Perhaps it is better to keep silent, rather than propose something to replace the demonstrably incoherent causal view. My own hesitant conjecture about the relation is this. The 'if' we find in 'Green will defeat Thomas if he tries (to defeat him, to keep him running from side to side)' introduces a supposition. In other words, when you ascribe skill at ping-pong to Green, you are committed to predicting a certain kind of performance by Green, under some range of conditions. These conditions must be conditions of Green: for example, his desiring or making an effort to win. You have considerable latitude in specifying these relevant conditions, and for that reason your statement that Green has the ability to defeat Thomas is not synonymous with any particular if-then statement. Nevertheless, your ability statement, together with the supposition that the condition obtains, which you have selected as relevant to Green's victory, gives you reason to say that Green will win. On this conjectural interpretation, 'Green has the ability to beat Thomas at ping-pong' entails some statement of the form 'If Green . . ., then he will probably win', and this in turn means: 'Suppose that Green . . .; then probably he will win'.[1] Your evidence for all these assertions is the frequency of Green's success, under a wide range of similar circumstances in the recent past.

[1] I believe that my speculative proposal to interpret 'if . . .' as 'suppose . . .' is close to Austin's notion of asserting or implying 'that certain *conditions* . . . *were satisfied*', which Austin finds 'totally different' from asserting '*something conditional*' (p. 173). Austin returns to the point later, and compares this distinction to a similar one in probability theory, between 'asserting on evidence h that p is probable' and 'asserting that on evidence h p is probable'; Austin says that 'only the former . . . asserts that p is (really) probable' (p. 176).

Austin presents a clever argument to dissolve this epistemic bond, through common evidence, between ability statements and the sort of conditional I connect with them. His argument is directed against the analysis in Professor Nowell-Smith's *Ethics*. Should we, as Nowell-Smith proposes, conclude from the evidence of a man's success in reading a certain book, not only that he *could* have read it yesterday, but also that he *would* have, if his conative attitude had been suitable? Austin contends that considerations of the man's attitude and probable actions are out of place. He explains:

> Whether or not we should describe our conclusion here as 'categorical' it seems that it should still be a conclusion of the form 'he *could* have done so and so', and not in the least a conclusion concerning what he would have done. We are interested, remember, in someone's abilities: we want to know whether he could have read [the novel] *Emma* yesterday: we ascertain that he did read it the day before yesterday, and that he does read it today: we conclude that he could have read it yesterday. But it does not appear that this says anything about what he *would* have done yesterday or in what circumstances: certainly, we are now convinced, he *could* have read it yesterday, but *would* he have, considering that he had read it only the day before? (p. 173.)

Far from severing the tie between ability, attitude and performance, Austin's reasoning actually strengthens it. Austin's closing rhetorical question implies that the reader of *Emma* is the sort of person who cannot bring himself to wade through the same novel two days in a row. Then we have excellent grounds to deny, both that he would, *and* that he *could*, have read *Emma* yesterday. Of course he had the ability to read classics of English literature, but his uncontrollable aversion toward reading the same book again hindered him from reading *Emma* yesterday. It worked analogously to a post-hypnotic suggestion. He lacked the ability to read that novel then and there, because of his temporary loathing for it. He could have read a similar novel yesterday. And today, after his respite from *Emma*, he has recovered his ability to read it. All this reinforces the connexion between 'could' and the 'would' of probable action, as well as the 'would' of volition. If both of these 'would's were logically independent of our ascription of reading ability to the fellow, why does Austin bother 'considering that he had read [*Emma*] only the day before'?

I conclude, in appraisal of Austin's much debated thesis (iii) that he is right to deny that ability statements are synonymous with conditionals, especially causal conditionals, but misguided in denying that ability statements are connected in any way with any sort of conditionals. His remarks (i) and (ii) proved mutually consistent, and undercut the indeterministic view of ability and action we found in (iv). By (i) and (ii), we see that ability does not guarantee success, even in perfect conditions, and failure does not prove inability. However, it hardly follows (iv) that the failures of a skilled person, in optimum conditions, are uncaused. Nor will it follow, from the contrary assumption that a man's failures have causes, that these causes prevented him from exercising his ability, or that they disabled him. Again, if we do admit that his failure to do what he had the ability to do, or for that matter his success, had one or more causes, we are not thereby admitting that his desires and efforts were among these causal factors. And even if a person's conative attitudes do operate as causes of his behaviour, it would be fallacious to conclude that they prevent him from acting differently. Only some desires and decisions, such as those resulting from hypnosis, render one powerless to do anything else. As for other circumstances that might qualify as causes of one's behaviour, some do and some do not hinder one. To assume that a man's failure to do what he has the ability to do was caused is quite different from conceding that, after all, he could not have done it. And of course these conclusions invalidate Austin's remark (v), that the ordinary concept of ability is inimical to a deterministic outlook on human conduct. Whether or not peoples' actions, including their doing and not doing what we say they can do, is causally determined, is totally independent from questions about what we mean by 'can' and 'ability'.

ASSERTIONS AND ABERRATIONS

John R. Searle

IN his paper 'A Plea for Excuses' Professor J. L. Austin makes the following point. The expressions which we use to qualify descriptions of actions, expressions such as intentionally, voluntarily, on purpose, deliberately, etc., are not used to qualify an action unless the action is in some sense aberrant or untoward. It is linguistically improper, says Austin, to assert *or deny* of an action that it is intentional, deliberate, voluntary, done on purpose, etc., unless the action is aberrant. (A corollary of this point is that to state that an action is voluntary or involuntary, etc., is to imply that it is in some sense untoward or aberrant.) Austin says:

> The natural economy of language dictates that for the standard case covered by any normal verb no modifying expression is required or even permissible. Only if we do the action named in some special way or circumstances, different from those in which such an act is naturally done (and, of course, both the normal and the abnormal differ according to what verb in particular is in question) is a modifying expression called for or even in order.

He summarizes his thesis in the slogan 'no modification without aberration'.

In a paper defending Austin, called 'Must we mean what we say?'* Professor Stanley Cavell adds to Austin's thesis the qualification that the aberration can be 'real or imagined'.

This thesis has long puzzled me: On the face of it, it is a somewhat surprising thesis, for Austin is saying that, for example, it is neither true nor false that I came to write this article of my own free will, for unless there is some aberration, the concept of free will just does not apply to such cases. How does one state the thesis exactly? Austin's statement in the article seems to me to depart

* *Inquiry* vol. I (1958), 172–212.

from his usual standards of exactness. And is the thesis true? If it is true, what kind of *impropriety* is involved in modifying without aberration? What is the force of Cavell's saying that the aberration can be real or imagined? Should it not arouse our suspicions to be told that a presupposition of an utterance need not be 'real' but can be merely imagined? If the thesis is true, what consequences does it have? How important is it?

I am puzzled by all this and more, and this paper is the result of my attempt to resolve this puzzlement. To answer the last question: the thesis certainly sounds very important, for note that it runs counter to a whole tradition of discussing these concepts in philosophy. For example, in discussions of free will from Aristotle to the present certain sorts of examples such as raising one's arm or walking across the room have been presented as paradigm cases of acting freely or voluntarily. What Austin is saying is that far from being paradigm cases, such actions are neither done freely nor not done freely, neither done voluntarily nor not done voluntarily, for unless certain conditions are satisfied these concepts simply do not apply to raising one's arm or walking across the room. It seems that if what Austin says is true these discussions cannot even get started.

Let us try to state the thesis again. There is a class of expressions (mostly adverbs) used to describe or qualify descriptions of actions. It is incorrect to use any of these expressions or their negations to describe or qualify a description of an action unless the action satisfies certain conditions, which conditions Austin denotes by the notion of an aberration. It is also suggested, though not by Austin, that these aberrations can be either real or imagined.

Now we have our thesis. Is it true? Well, if one considers the actual use of these words there seems to be a good deal in it. Consider the following sentence: 'He went to the Philosophical Society meeting of his own free will.' When would one naturally utter such a sentence? In describing a normal man under ordinary conditions attending such a society meeting? I think not. To imagine a case where we would actually utter the sentence would involve imagining rather special or aberrant conditions.

Or again consider the sentence: 'He tied his shoes on purpose.' It is not easy to imagine a situation where this would be in order. But try: 'He stepped on the dog on purpose.' Here it is easy to imagine a situation where this would be appropriate, and the reason seems to be that stepping on dogs is aberrant in some way that tying shoes is not.

So far, then, we have a thesis, and it seems to be true. What I now propose to do is to make five points about the thesis which will enable us to see it in an entirely different light from what I think Austin originally intended.

(1) It exemplifies a common pattern of analysis in contemporary philosophy. Similar points have been made by several philosophers. An obvious example which springs to mind is Ryle's discussion of the word 'voluntary' in the *Concept of Mind*. Ryle says that in their ordinary employment the adjectives 'voluntary' and 'involuntary' are used as adjectives applying only to actions which ought not to be done. He says: 'In this ordinary use, then, it is absurd to ask whether satisfactory, correct or admirable performances are voluntary or involuntary.'

Furthermore, this pattern of analysis is not confined to words we have been considering. Similar points have been made about certain other expressions.

In an article entitled 'Remembering' B. S. Benjamin says that if 'remember' is used in its usual sense there is 'an absurd inappropriateness' in speaking of Englishmen speaking English as remembering words in the English language, or to speak of oneself after signing a cheque as having remembered one's own name. One could, says Benjamin, 'generate' a sense of remember which would apply to such cases, but in the usual sense it is inappropriate to bring up the concept of remembering at all in such cases. The reason for this inappropriateness is that 'we reserve the use of these expressions for occasions when there is some possibility that one may not remember whatever happens to be in question'.

Some of the things Wittgenstein said about the verb 'know' suggest a similar view. Wittgenstein objects to saying 'I know I am in pain' or 'I know what I am thinking', and also in an unpublished work on scepticism he seems to object to some of Moore's uses of the verb 'know'. Moore imagines himself confronting a tree in broad daylight at point-blank range and announcing, 'I know that that is a tree'. Wittgenstein finds this utterance in these conditions odd: 'I am sitting with a philosopher in a garden; he says again and again "I know that that is a tree" pointing to a tree near us. Someone else arrives and hears this, and I tell him: "This fellow isn't mad: we are just philosophizing." '

These views all seem to have a family resemblance. Ryle says it is neither true nor false that I bought my car voluntarily because the concept has no application to cases where there is nothing wrong with the action. Benjamin says that it is neither true nor false that I remember my own name, because the concept of remembering has no application to such cases. Wittgenstein says or seems to be saying it is neither true nor false that I know I am in pain or that Moore knows the object in front of him is a tree, and Austin says it is neither true nor false that I went to the society meeting of my own free will because unless there is some aberration, neither the concept of free will nor for that matter any other action-modifying concept at all is applicable to my coming here tonight.

In each case the author claims that a certain concept or range of concepts is inapplicable to certain states of affairs because the states of affairs fail to satisfy certain conditions which the author says are presuppositions of the applicability of the concepts. And in terms of the history of philosophy we see a pattern emerging. The traditional philosopher says such and such is a paradigm case of voluntary action, free will, knowledge, memory, etc. The linguistic philosopher replies: In the cases you are imagining it does not even make sense to use the expressions 'voluntary', 'free will', 'remember' or 'know' because each of these requires certain special conditions for its applicability, which conditions are lacking in your example. It might seem we could get a list of such words—let us call them for short A-words, and the conditions of their applicability A-conditions—a list which Ryle, Austin, Wittgenstein and Benjamin among others have begun. This leads me to my second point.

(2) The sorts of conditions exemplified by the slogan 'no modification without aberration' are not confined to the words which have interested philosophers but seem to pervade language in general and apply to all sorts of words. Consider the following examples:

(a) The President is *sober* today.
(b) The man at the next table is *not lighting his cigarette with a* $20 *bill*.
(c) Jones *is breathing*. (Or perhaps: Jones is still breathing.)

Now what I am suggesting is that these sentences are like the previous examples in that their utterance is only appropriate under certain aberrant or fishy conditions. Imagine circumstances in which they might be uttered.

(*a*) The first where it is a known fact that the President is an habitual drunkard.

(*b*) The second in a Texas oilmen's club, where it is a rule that cigarettes are lit with $20 bills, not $10 bills or $5 bills, much less matches, which are reserved for igniting cash.

(*c*) The third where Jones has just been pulled out of the water and is presumed drowned.

In such cases the utterance of such sentences would be in order. But they would not be appropriate in standard, non-aberrant situations, e.g.:

(*a*) when a normally sober company President is addressing the Board of Directors;

(*b*) when a man in an ordinary restaurant is lighting his cigarette with a match;

(*c*) when Jones is quietly listening to a public lecture.

And the inappropriateness or impropriety of uttering these sentences in non-aberrant, non-fishy conditions seems quite similar to the impropriety of uttering the philosophers' examples in non-aberrant, non-fishy conditions. As yet I am making no attempt to *characterize* this impropriety, but only calling attention to its *generality*. If we are to compile a list of A-words, it will not be confined to such philosophical favourites as 'intentional', 'voluntary', 'know', 'remember', etc.

(3) The third point I wish to make is that contrary to our initial supposition, the opposite or negation of an A-word is not an A-word. Thus, going through our examples:

I did not buy my car voluntarily, I was forced to.
I did not come of my own free will, I was dragged here.
I don't remember my own name.
He doesn't know whether the object in front of him is a tree.

and similarly:

The President is drunk today.
The man at the next table is lighting his cigarette with a $20 bill.
Jones has just stopped breathing.

An utterance of each of these in any of the situations, aberrant or non-aberrant, which we have considered, will be true or false. And indeed, as we shall see later on, in normal circumstances they would all be false, for their falsity is one of the things that makes the circumstances normal.

Thus, at this point there seems to be a serious as$\overset{m}{\text{s}}$ymetry between A-words and their opposites or negations. That is, to justify fully an utterance containing an A-word we need, first, evidence of an aberration or of one of the other special conditions, and, secondly, evidence for the truth of the utterance. But for the opposite or negative we need only evidence of the truth of the utterance. This, I should note, is my first flat disagreement with Austin's account. He says that both require an aberration. I will state later how the ambiguity in the notion of aberration led him to this view. But at this stage of the argument I want just to note that for every sentence which requires an A-condition, there is a negation or opposite sentence which does not require an A-condition. At any rate, we have found this to be true of the examples considered, and I suggest that it is true generally.

At this point we shall want to focus our attention on the vague and so far unexplained notion of an aberration. This notion is clearly the crux of the thesis 'no modification without aberration'. What is meant by the word 'aberration' as it occurs in the statement of the thesis?

(4) An aberration or A-condition for a sentence is in general a reason for supposing that the assertion made in uttering the opposite or negation of that sentence is or might have been true, or at least might have been supposed by someone to be true. An A-condition for a remark is just a reason for supposing the remark might have been false or might have been supposed by someone to be false.

Austin's account is misleading, for the slogan 'no modification without aberration' suggests that any aberration will justify modification. But, clearly, not just any old aberration will do. If, for example, I buy my car while strumming a guitar with my bare toes, though this is an aberrant way of buying a car, it gives no grip to the remark 'he bought his car voluntarily'. In order that this remark should be in order, there must be some reason for supposing, or for supposing someone might have supposed, that I might have bought it under compulsion or otherwise *not* have bought it voluntarily. And in all of the cases we have been considering, the aberrations which would render the remarks in order are reasons for supposing that the negations of the remarks might have been true. The 'aberrations' which would render our examples inappropriate are reasons for supposing I might have forgotten my own name; Moore might not have known that that was a tree; I might not have bought my car voluntarily; I might not have gone to the meeting of my own free will; the President might have been drunk; the man might have been lighting his cigarette with a $20 bill; and Jones might have stopped breathing.

We are now in a position to see that the thesis 'no modification without aberration' seems really to mean something like 'no modification without some reason for supposing the negation of the modification might have been true'.

(5) We cannot get a list of A-words, for whether or not a given word requires any aberration will depend on the rest of the sentence and on the surrounding context. Thus, e.g., 'he bought his car voluntarily' requires an A-condition; but 'he went into the Army voluntarily' just means he volunteered rather than was drafted. And an utterance of it requires no A-condition, it is just true or false (that is assuming that he did enter the Army). The reason for this, as we shall see, is that the standard way of buying a car is to do it voluntarily, but there is in that sense no standard way of going into the Army.

The point I am making now is: there is no such thing as a list of A-words. For any sentence in which a word requires an A-condition we can find another sentence in which the same word does not. The thesis 'no modification without aberration' at this stage, then, seems not to be a thesis about words but about sentences, and, as we shall see, it is only about sentences given a background of assumptions about people's habits and expectations.

So far, then, my investigations of the thesis 'no modification without aberration' have yielded five tentative conclusions:

(1) It expresses a common pattern of argument in contemporary philosophy.

(2) It is a general thesis applying to all sorts of subject matter.

(3) For any sentence to which it applies it never applies to its negation.

(4) An A-condition for a sentence is in general a reason for supposing that the statement made in the utterance of the negation of that sentence might have been true (or might have been supposed by someone to be true).

(5) It is not a thesis about words but about sentences, and, indeed, only about sentences in certain contexts.

Now I wish to offer what seems to me to be the obvious explanation of all these five points.

There are standard or normal situations. (People normally, e.g., buy their cars voluntarily, go to meetings of the Philosophical Society of their own free will, know when they are confronting a tree, remember their own names, are sober, do not light their cigarettes with $20 bills and breathe.) It does not in general make sense simply to assert of a standard or normal situation that it is standard or normal unless there is some reason for supposing that it might have been non-standard or abnormal, or that our audience might have so supposed, or might have been supposed to so suppose. For to remark that it is standard is to imply or suggest that its being standard is (in some way) remarkable, and to imply or suggest that is often or in general to imply or suggest that there is some reason for supposing that it might not have been standard. If a speaker describing a situation knows of no reason why anyone might suppose the situation non-standard or aberrant, or of any other reason why its standard character is worth remarking on, then his assertion that it is standard is out of order.

Austin's point, then, is not, properly speaking, about words or even sentences. It is a point about what it is to make an assertion. To make an assertion is to commit oneself to something's being the case as opposed to that thing's not being the case. But if the possibility of its not being the case is not even under consideration, or if its being the case is one of the assumptions of the discourse, then the remark that it is the case is just pointless.

Austin's slogan 'no modification without aberration' ought to be rewritten 'no remark without remarkableness' or, to steal and redefine a term from Dewey, 'no assertion without assertibility'.

As this explanation may not be clear I shall try to restate it. In general to remark that p, is to suggest that p is in some way remarkable or noteworthy. One of the characteristic ways in which p will be remarkable or noteworthy is for there to be at least the possibility of *not p* in the offing. All of the examples we were inclined to call A-sentences, were sentences which in standard situations could not be uttered to record something remarkable or noteworthy, because their not being remarkable is what makes those sentences standard. They could not, therefore, be appropriately uttered in such standard situations but could only be uttered in 'aberrant' situations, and the aberration was in general some reason for supposing that the negation of the proposed remark might have been true. This explanation accounts for all the five facts we noted.

(1) and (2) The point being about assertions in general is not confined to a certain class of words or a certain subject matter or to assertions about a certain subject matter.

(3) Since the opposite of a standard condition is non-standard, no A-condition is required for the utterance of the negation of an A-sentence. A-sentences mark standard situations; their negations do not.

(4) An A-condition is in general a reason for supposing the negation of the A-sentence to be true, because in general only where there is some reason for supposing a standard situation might have been non-standard is there any point to asserting that it is standard.

(5) Obviously, no set of *words* (except words like 'standard') can invariably mark standard conditions. For what is standard will depend on a variety of facts about people's culture and habits as well as about their language. It is possible to imagine a culture where it is non-standard to buy cars voluntarily. In such a culture our discussion of this example would have to be reversed.

We are also now in a position to see the point of Cavell's saying that the aberration can be real or imagined. An assertion will have a point both in cases where there is a good reason for supposing it might have been false and in cases where there is no good reason, but where people merely believe there is a good reason. Thus, to someone who thinks I was dragged to the meeting there is a point in saying, 'Searle came here of his own free will', whether his reasons for thinking I was dragged are good reasons or bad reasons.

I am suggesting that Austin and others have seen this matter in the wrong light. I now want to explain how that came about. Consider, e.g., the concept of intention.

Many verbs of human action have the notion of intention built into them as it were. To *do* X is just to do X intentionally. So as Austin saw, it is out of place to add the adverb 'intentionally' unless the situation is very odd. He also saw that to deny that X was done intentionally is to *assert* that the situation was very odd, odd just because it is odd to do something not intentionally. What he did not see is that the oddness necessary to assert 'X was done intentionally' is simply a reason for supposing it might have been true that 'X was not done intentionally'. Seeing the oddness in both cases and not seeing their relation, he concluded that only in odd cases *could one properly assert or deny that X was done intentionally.* But what I have been claiming is that the oddness or aberration which is a *condition of utterance*, for 'X was done intentionally' is *evidence*, etc., *for the truth* of 'X was not done intentionally'. And it is a condition of utterance for the one precisely because it is evidence for the truth of the other. Since, in general, unless there is some reason for supposing it was not done (or might not have been done, etc.) intentionally, there is no point in asserting that it was done intentionally.

What exactly is the nature of the dispute here? Both sides agree on the existence of certain data, data of the form: It would be odd or impermissible to say such and such except under certain conditions. But there is a disagreement about the explanation of the data. I say the data are to be explained in terms of what, in general, is involved in making an assertion. The view I am attacking says the data are to be explained in terms of the applicability of certain concepts. So far the claims I can make for my account are greater simplicity, generality and perhaps plausibility. But now it seems to me I am in a position to present actual counter examples to try to refute the view in a more knock-down fashion. It is argued that the conditions of applicability of certain concepts render certain statements in certain conditions neither true nor false. But now recall, as I mentioned earlier, that the negations of those statements are not neither true nor false but in standard conditions simply false. Recalling our examples:

I didn't go to the meeting of my own free will, I was dragged there.

I didn't buy my car voluntarily, I was forced to.

I don't remember my own name.

I don't know whether the thing in front of me is a tree.
He is not sober.
He is now lighting his cigarette with a $20 bill.
He has stopped breathing.

In the present standard or normal conditions there is nothing non-sensical about such utterances, they are all just false. Furthermore, if we get away from the very simple examples we have so far been considering, we shall see that these concepts are explicable without any of the conditions we have had in mind. Take the following examples:

The system of voluntary military recruitment is a total failure in California.
The knowledge of and ability to remember such simple things as one's name and phone number is one of the foundation stones of modern organized society.
It is more pleasant to do things of one's own free will than to be forced to do them.

These statements contain such words as 'knowledge', 'remember', 'free will' and 'voluntary', and their utterance is appropriate without any of the special conditions of the sort the philosophers I have considered said were necessary conditions of their applicability.

Now I wish to make some clarification of what I have been saying so far. First, I am not saying there are no conditions of applicability at all for such terms as 'voluntary', 'intentional', 'of one's own free will', etc., that any of these can be sensibly applied to any action; rather I am saying that the sorts of conditions expressed in Austin's slogan 'no modification without aberration' are not conditions of application of these concepts, but rather are conditions for making assertions in general.

The word 'voluntary' in particular seems to me to be an excluder, like 'real' or 'normal'. A statement of the form: 'act A was done voluntarily' has a certain indeterminacy of sense until we know what is being excluded—compulsion, duress, force or what not; in the same way as the statement 'this chain is a real chain' has a certain indeterminacy of sense until we know what is being excluded: toy, papier maché or what not.

Nor, of course, am I attempting to rescue the traditional view that all voluntary and intentional acts are preceded by mental acts of volition and intention.

Furthermore, I am not saying that the possibility of something not being the case or not having been known or supposed to be the case is a necessary condition for making any assertion whatever. There are all sorts of conditions which will make a remark worth remarking and this is only one, though a rather important one, and one which has often been confused by philosophers with features of the analysis of particular concepts.

Now I wish to consider some possible objections which could be made to what I have been saying. The point of considering these objections will be both to forestall them and to clarify my argument.

First: Someone might object to my saying that there are true propositions which it is improper to assert except in certain conditions. Surely, someone might claim, this is paradoxical, for how can it ever be improper to tell the truth. I seem to be saying that it is true that Moore knew that the object in Trinity garden was a tree, that I remember my own name, that I went to the meeting of my own free will, etc., but that it is somehow logically improper to assert these true propositions except under certain special conditions which might call their truth in question. This seems paradoxical.

That this should seem paradoxical is a consequence of a failure to distinguish between propositions which form, as it were, the content of assertions (and other speech acts) and the speech acts themselves. I distinguish between the propositions that p and the act which I perform when I *assert* that p. That there is a distinction is shown by the fact that the same proposition can be a common content of such different speech acts as questioning whether p, commanding that p, warning that p, expressing doubt as to whether p, etc., as well as asserting that p.

And once we recognize the distinction between propositions and speech acts it should no longer surprise us, or at least no longer surprise us *a priori*, that the conditions for the truth of the propositions are not the same as the conditions for the performance of the speech act of asserting that proposition. And just as I can only make a promise or issue a warning under certain conditions, so I can only make assertions under certain conditions. Just as I can only properly make a promise if there is some reason for supposing that the thing promised will benefit the promisee, and just as I can only issue a warning if there is some reason for supposing the thing warned about might harm the person warned, so I can only make an assertion if there is some reason for supposing the state of affairs asserted to obtain is worthy of note or in some respect remarkable. And in each case I am not saying that the proposition which forms the content of the speech act entails that the condition obtains—but that the speaker in performing the speech act implies that it obtains.

And if you still doubt that a speaker in making an assertion can imply more than is entailed by the proposition asserted, consider the following example from real life. When Dr. Pusey was made President of Harvard, Senator McCarthy announced to the Press that in his opinion Dr. Pusey was not a Communist. And I take it that Dr. Pusey was not complimented by this assertion, because it suggests that what is, in fact, obvious is not obvious and is somehow noteworthy, that considering everything about Dr. Pusey, and perhaps about Harvard as well, it is a notable fact that he is not a Communist.

I shall now consider a second objection, a modification of the first. Supposing everything I have said is true, still isn't it somehow only a psychological thesis about what people expect in conversation? Isn't it at best part of the pragmatics rather than the syntax or semantics of language? In response to this I should say first that I have never found this distinction, between pragmatics on the one hand and syntax and semantics on the other, very useful, as it seems to presuppose a particular theory in the philosophy of language, and thus beg several crucial questions at the outset. But in any case I should deny that I was making a contingent psychological point. The point I am making is about what it is to make an assertion, and therefore is a part of an analysis of the concept of asserting. But I am fully aware that this is only the beginning of an answer to these objections, and that a development of these points would require at least another paper, a paper about the concept of assertion.

There is also a methodological moral to be drawn from this discussion. It is characteristic of contemporary philosophers that they construe such traditional philosophical questions as what is a voluntary action, what is knowledge, what is truth, etc., as questions about the use of the words 'voluntary', 'true', 'know', etc. They make this identification in most cases because they hold a theory about meaning to the effect that the meaning of a word is its use. The trouble with this theory is that the notion of use is so vague as to engender confusion, and here is how, in the present case, I think that confusion has come about: A philosopher wishes to analyse the notion of, e.g., voluntariness. He asks:

(1) What does 'voluntary' mean? And since he holds the view that meaning is use he takes this question as equivalent to—
(2) How is 'voluntary' used?
But then, by restricting his study of examples to rather simple categorical indicative sentences, that question is tacitly taken as equivalent to—
(3) How is 'voluntary' used in these simple categorical indicatives? Which question is then tacitly taken to mean—
(4) Under what conditions would we utter these sentences? Which is in effect equivalent to—
(5) Under what conditions would we call an act voluntary?

But this amounts to confusing the question 'What is it for an act to be voluntary?' with the question 'Under what conditions is it correct to call an act voluntary?' And this is only an instance of the general methodological error of supposing that the conditions in which it is correct to assert that p are identical with the conditions in which it is the case that p. But there is no reason at all to suppose that these are identical, since assertion is only one kind of speech act among many, with its own special conditions for its performance.

Without any coherent general theory of syntax and semantics on which to base particular linguistic analyses, the philosopher who looks to the so-called use of expressions has no way of distinguishing features of utterances which are due to particular words from features which are due to other factors, such as the syntactical character of the sentence or the type of speech act being performed.

MENTIONING
THE UNMENTIONABLE[1]

Alan R. White

THERE are two theses in recent philosophical literature which I am going to call Austin's Thesis and Searle's Thesis. In fact neither thesis is peculiar to or originated with the philosopher named. Ryle, Wittgenstein and others have held a version of Austin's Thesis about certain concepts, while Malcolm, Grice, Ryle and others have held Searle's Thesis about other concepts. In a recent article ('Assertion and Aberration') Mr. J. R. Searle suggested in regard to a battery of concepts that Austin's Thesis is either a confused species of Searle's Thesis or an incorrect thesis which ought to be replaced by Searle's Thesis. I shall try to show that Searle has completely misunderstood what Austin and other analysts were doing and that Austin's Thesis is neither incorrect nor at all similar to Searle's Thesis. It is in fact a thesis with a long and honourable history. Austin's Thesis and Searle's Thesis are two quite distinct interpretations of 'mentioning the unmentionable'. Searle's is a pragmatic objection to mentioning what is *not worth* mentioning; Austin's is a logical objection to mentioning what *cannot be* mentioned. Whereas Austin's motto might be 'Whereof one cannot speak, thereof one must be silent', Searle's could be 'If you have nothing worth saying, then keep it to yourself'. I shall not discuss the merits of Searle's Thesis, nor the moral he wrongly draws from his discussion.

Austin said ('A Plea for Excuses', *Proceedings of the Aristotelian Society* 57 (1957) p. 16): 'Only if we do the action named (*sc.* eat, kick, sit, yawn, etc.) in some *special* way or circumstances, different

[1] I am indebted to my colleagues B. Falk, R. D. L. Montague, R. G. Swinburne and C. J. F. Williams and to Mr. G. J. Warnock for criticisms of an earlier draft.

from those in which such an act is naturally done . . . is a modifying expression (*sc.* voluntarily, unintentionally, automatically, etc.) CALLED FOR, or even IN ORDER.'

Ryle said (*The Concept of Mind* (1949) pp. 69–74): 'In the ordinary use, to say that a sneeze was involuntary is to say that the agent could not help doing it, and to say that a laugh was voluntary is to say that the agent could have helped doing it.' 'In this ordinary use, then, it is ABSURD to discuss whether satisfactory, correct or admirable performances are voluntary or involuntary.'

Wittgenstein said (*Philosophical Investigations*, Sections 246, 408): 'It CAN'T be said of me at all (except perhaps as a joke) that I *know* I am in pain'; 'I CANNOT be said to learn of my sensations. I *have* them'; 'it MAKES SENSE to say about other people that they doubt whether I am in pain; but not to say it about myself.' ' "I don't know whether I am in pain or not" is NOT a SIGNIFICANT proposition.' (The capital letters are mine.)

It is important to emphasize that Austin, Ryle and Wittgenstein all hold that to use an expression in a certain way in certain circumstances is *without significance*, that is, the concept expressed by the expression is not applicable in these circumstances. This is quite explicit in the quotations from Ryle and Wittgenstein. Austin, indeed, uses various phrases to make his point, e.g., 'not called for', 'not in order', 'not required', 'not permissible', 'it will not do to say', 'not naturally be said', 'not be in place'. But he does explicitly say that 'it will not be found that it makes good sense', and, again, that in certain circumstances it is not true to say either 'I did A Mly' or 'I did A not Mly'. For instance, he says, I often yawn without yawning either involuntarily or not involuntarily; I often sit without sitting either automatically or not automatically.

In Searle's account it is not altogether clear whether he wishes to argue (i) that Austin and the others did indeed hold Austin's Thesis, but that, since it is a mistaken thesis, they *ought* to have held Searle's Thesis, or (ii) that the thesis which Austin and the others held is *really* not what they thought it was but is, indeed, the one held by Searle.

Searle's Thesis is that there are certain conditions for the utterance of a sentence, that is, for the making of an assertion; that these conditions are that there should be some reason for supposing that what is asserted is in some way remarkable, and, more particularly, that there should be some reason for supposing that what is asserted 'might have been false or might have been supposed by someone to be false'. If these conditions are not present, then the assertion is 'pointless' or 'out of order'. As Searle himself says, Austin tried to explain the impermissibility of saying something 'in terms of the applicability of certain concepts', while Searle tries to explain what he thinks to be the same impermissibility 'in terms of what, in general, is involved in making an assertion'.

The evidence for supposing that Searle thought Austin's Thesis was a somewhat confused species of his own Thesis is as follows:

(i) in describing Austin's Thesis Searle speaks of what is 'linguistically improper', what one would 'naturally utter', what would be 'in order' or 'appropriate', 'the presuppositions of an utterance'; and in describing his own Thesis he speaks of what is 'odd' or 'impermissible', of what it 'doesn't make sense to assert', of whether an utterance 'has a point', is 'appropriate' or 'is out of order'.

(ii) in describing the relations of Austin's Thesis to his own he says that Austin's Thesis will appear 'in an entirely different light from what I think Austin originally intended', that it 'seems really to mean' what Searle's own Thesis means, that Austin's point is 'properly speaking' Searle's point and that Austin has 'seen the matter in the wrong light'.

(iii) Searle thinks Austin's Thesis can be 'generalized' to all language, so that, e.g., the 'inappropriateness or impropriety' of uttering 'The President is *sober* today' in certain conditions (e.g. when said of a normally sober president) is 'quite similar' to the impropriety alleged by Austin's Thesis.

(iv) Searle thinks that he and Austin would agree on the data of the problem, namely that 'it would be odd or impermissible to say such and such except under certain conditions'.

On the other hand, the evidence for supposing that Searle thought that Austin's Thesis is mistaken and should be replaced by his own quite different Thesis is as follows:

(i) Searle sometimes describes Austin's Thesis in ways which could not be used of his own, e.g. that according to Austin's Thesis the concepts in question 'do not apply' in certain circumstances, that in these circumstances an alleged statement containing them would be 'neither true nor false', that an action might be done neither Mly nor non-Mly.

(ii) Searle claims to find various objectionable consequences of Austin's Thesis, but not of his own.

(iii) He thinks that Austin's Thesis, which purports to be about the significance of a word, 'ought to be rewritten' so that it is about the 'conditions of utterance' of a sentence. Searle's Thesis purports to be a different and correct explanation of the same data which Austin's Thesis fails to explain. Searle produces examples which he thinks enable him 'to refute the view in a more knock-down fashion'.

Whatever Searle thinks are the exact relations between Austin's Thesis and his own, I shall now try to show that (*a*) Austin's Thesis is quite different from Searle's and (*b*) that Austin's Thesis is correct.

(*a*) Austin's Thesis is that it would *not make sense* to use certain words when certain circumstances do not obtain and, therefore, that by using them we would not then say anything which was *either true or false*. For instance, if I remark to my secretary in the normal course of the day's work that I have a committee this afternoon, then it does not make sense to say, and it is neither true not false, that I made this remark tactfully or tactlessly, carefully or carelessly. If I blow out a match after lighting my cigarette, I need not have done this either considerately or inconsiderately. Searle's Thesis, on the other hand, is that it would not be appropriate to make an assertion, however true, if there was no reason to suppose that it was false or that someone might have thought that it was false.

(*b*) The correctness of Austin's Thesis follows from the nature of a concept. A particular concept is what it is because it has certain relations to other concepts and it has these relations because it is what it is. Thus, in *no* circumstances would it make sense to say, nor would it be true or false, that someone *knew* the date of the Battle of Waterloo, *found* a half-crown, or *became ill*, carefully or carelessly, inadvertently or intentionally. The concepts of care, intention, etc., can *never* go with the concepts of knowledge, discovery, and becoming ill. Consequently the very *sentence* 'He knew carefully the date of the Battle of Waterloo' is meaningless. On the other hand, in *certain* circumstances, but not in all, it would not make sense to say that someone had sobered up or recovered his breath or stopped beating his wife; namely, if he had not previously been drunk or out of breath or beating his wife. Whatever the circumstances, a man is either drunk or sober, beating or not beating his wife, breathing or not breathing. But it need be neither true nor false that he has sobered up, recovered his breath or stopped beating his wife. It depends on certain prior circumstances. It is part of the notion of having sobered up, as contrasted with being sober, of having recovered one's breath, as contrasted with breathing, of having stopped beating, as contrasted with beating, that certain prior circumstances should obtain in order to make them applicable. It would not be true to say of a man who had not been drunk and was not now drunk that he had not sobered up, but it would equally not be true to say that he had sobered up. This is not, however, to say that the *sentence* 'He has now sobered up' is meaningless, although the sentence 'He has now sobered up, though he was not drunk before' may be meaningless. Similarly, there are circumstances in which concepts like *care, tact, consideration, inadvertence, intention,* are not applicable to actions to which they are sometimes applicable. For instance, if my action cannot affect anyone's feelings, it makes no sense to say that after lighting my cigarette I inconsiderately (or considerately) blew out the match; whereas this would make sense if I could see that my wife was waiting for a light. When I remark to my secretary that I am going to a committee meeting it ordinarily makes no sense to say that my remark was either tactful or tactless. But if I made this remark just after reprimanding her for forgetting to notify me of committee meetings, my remark might reasonably be called 'tactless'; whereas if I make this remark in the knowledge that she had told a visitor I would be engaged, it might reasonably be called 'tactful'. To ask whether somebody did something automatically or not is to enquire about the relation of his action to some stimulus. If there was no previous stimulus, that is, if the action was not a reaction, the question of whether the action was automatic or not would not make sense. If I look up from my book when there is a noise at the door, it is logically pertinent to ask whether I looked up automatically or not. But if I look up when nothing has happened, there can be no question of whether I looked up automatically or non-automatically.

Similarly, Ryle's thesis that it is absurd to ask whether satisfactory, correct or admirable performances are voluntary or involuntary rests on his view—which I do not wish to defend—

that 'voluntary' and 'involuntary' mean 'could have helped' and 'could not have helped'. Granted this, his thesis is that the notion of being unable to help doing something is logically connected to those of having the skill to avoid it, of trying and making efforts to prevent oneself doing it, and of succeeding or failing in these efforts. One can have the skill and try to be successful, but not have the skill and try to fail, except where 'try to fail' means try to be successful in doing what others count as a failure. 'You couldn't fail if you tried' and 'No one could help getting it right' are deliberate paradoxes. Hence, no question can arise of being able or unable to help oneself doing what one is skilled in and trying to do or what one succeeds in doing. The reasons that Ryle gives for his thesis are of the same kind as those he gives elsewhere for supposing, e.g., that many of the qualifications of tasks, e.g., carefully, assiduously, methodically, intermittently, cannot apply to achievements, or that what is true of dispositions is not necessarily true of processes.

Wittgenstein's thesis about self-knowledge arises from his contention that the concept of *knowledge* is related logically to the notions of *learning, doubting, being mistaken, having evidence, etc.* Where these notions do not apply—as he thought to be the case with one's own sensations—then the notion of *knowledge* also does not apply. Whether Wittgenstein was right or wrong—and I think that what he says is correct about the notion of *discovery*, though not about *knowledge*—his thesis is about the conditions which make a concept applicable, not about the conditions in which it would be appropriate to assert something true. The reasons that Austin, Ryle and Wittgenstein have for their views are essentially of the same kind as those which Aristotle had for asserting that we can wish, but cannot choose, to be happy (*Nicomachean Ethics*, III. 2).

Searle has confused the reasons for not mentioning that which is not worth mentioning and the reasons for not mentioning that which cannot be mentioned. Several reasons may be suggested for his misunderstanding of Austin's Thesis and his mistaken assimilation of that Thesis to his own:

(i) Searle's use of phrases like 'inappropriate', 'to the point', etc., which are applicable to both theses, though for quite different reasons, makes him lose sight of the differences.

(ii) Searle has overlooked the difference between saying (*a*) an applicability condition for a remark is just a reason for supposing the remark *might* (empirically) have been false and saying (*b*) an applicability condition for a remark is just a reason for supposing the remark *could* (logically) have been false. (*a*) is Searle's Thesis, while Austin's Thesis is (*b*).

(iii) Searle's attempted 'generalization' of Austin's Thesis leads him to introduce examples of his own to which, as he later sees, Austin's Thesis does not apply. But instead of asking why Austin's Thesis does not apply to them and wondering therefore whether he has misunderstood Austin, he uses the examples to try to refute Austin's Thesis. Searle has in fact not seen the difference between, e.g., 'The President is sober today' (his example) and 'The President has sobered up today', between 'Jones is breathing' (his example) and 'Jones has recovered his breath'. His Thesis, namely that it would be odd to assert any of these, however true, unless there was some reason to suppose that they were false or that someone doubted them, covers all the examples; but Austin's Thesis was designed to distinguish the examples and to refer only to the second member of each pair. The oddness of saying 'He has stopped beating his wife', if he has never beaten her, is due to the nature of the concept of 'stopped'; the oddness of saying 'He has stopped beating his wife', if there is no reason to suppose that this is false or that anyone doubts it, is not due to the nature of this concept. It may, as Searle asserts, have been *inappropriate* for Senator McCarthy to announce that Dr. Pusey *was not* a communist, since there was no reason to suppose he was or that anyone had suggested that he was. But it would have been downright *illogical* of the Senator to say that Dr. Pusey *was no longer* (had ceased to be) a communist, if he had never been a communist. 'Dr. Pusey is not a communist' may have been perfectly true, whatever the circumstances; but 'Dr. Pusey is no longer (has ceased to be) a communist' could not have been either true or false, unless Dr. Pusey had once been a communist.

AUSTIN ON TRUTH

Jon Wheatley

I INTRODUCTION

AUSTIN, it seems to me, was basically right about truth even if, as he himself said, his theory is somewhat truistic. But though the theory is truistic it is not, I think, really clear: indeed, something must explain the enormous controversy which developed round his original paper if the theory is both right and truistic. In addition, he did very little about the fact that his thesis offered an account of truth for only one very limited sort of statement. In what follows, therefore, I shall first outline the conflict which developed round Austin's original paper; I shall then offer an explication of his thesis modified so as to be clearer and avoid some criticisms; and finally I shall briefly discuss the relationship between the truth conditions for statements for which Austin's account was designed and other types of statement.

II THE CONFLICT

I shall not discuss each thrust and counter-thrust of the conflict which surrounded Austin's original paper in detail. However, to have the background clear, I offer the following outline:

Outline of the Conflict

1

Thesis: Strawson in 'Truth' (1)[1] claims that ' "is true" *never* has a

---

[1] Full references are given in the Bibliography at the end of the paper. A number of different papers are called 'Truth'. These I number chronologically as 'Truth' (1), 'Truth' (2), etc., and they are always referred to in this way in the body of the text. Whenever a page number is cited, it always refers to that printing of the paper which appears last in the bibliographical listing.

statement making role', is a 'performatory[1] word' and, in general, is used in 'confirming, underwriting, admitting, agreeing with, what someone else has said'.[2]

Thesis denigrated: Austin in 'Truth' (2) agrees that Strawson has noticed a use of 'is true' but (more or less) claims that it does not explain what it is for a statement to be true however much it explains what it is we do when we say it is true. In addition, he offers a

New Thesis: A statement is true when it fits (corresponds to) the facts: this he offers as a correspondence theory of truth which is conventional in nature.

2

Counter-thesis and Shift: Strawson's paper 'Truth' (3), though officially a reply to Austin's paper, is in many ways *oblique* to it. Thus though Strawson says many interesting things about statements, facts, etc., he never discusses the formal statement which Austin gave of his thesis. Instead he argues that there are no facts in the world (or suitable substitutes, like situations) to which correspondence might take place. This is oblique to Austin's original account just because, though Austin did want to maintain that there are facts in the world, it is far from obvious that his thesis on truth requires him to.

Shift thesis denied: Austin, in 'Unfair to Facts', offers straight arguments against Strawson's shift thesis above, i.e., for facts in the world.

Further Submissions

New thesis supported: Warnock in 'A Problem about Truth' argues for the compatibility of the performatory aspects of Strawson's original thesis and Austin's theory and adds that if anything the situation favours Austin.

New support for new thesis denied: Strawson, in 'A Problem about Truth—A Reply to Mr Warnock', argues very obscurely that, granting much of what Warnock says, none of it seriously supports Austin's thesis.

[1] 'Performatory' was the preferred term at the time Strawson wrote this paper. It is synonymous with the now more widely known 'performative'.

[2] This paper was itself part of a conflict about the Semantic Theory of truth. All participants in the Austin conflict were agreed that this theory is false.

New thesis defended: Warnock in 'Truth and Correspondence' argues somewhat sketchily against some of Strawson's original criticisms.

3

New thesis reconsidered and denied: Strawson in 'Truth: A Reconsideration of Austin's Views' considers the formal statement of Austin's position (which he did not do in 'Truth' (3)) and rejects it.

A good deal of this conflict is in fact somewhat perverse and large parts (including some by Austin) are irrelevant to the main issue. I do not propose to substantiate this charge in detail but the following anomaly is worth noticing. Austin remarked at the beginning of the controversy that the theory of truth, as he saw it, is a series of truisms; he conceived his task as making plain and elaborating these truisms. Strawson, in the final paper of the controversy, and after putting some fairly remarkable interpretations onto what Austin wrote, says that it is a truism that such and such a thesis is correct (p. 300). This thesis, on inspection, turns out to be very close to what Austin originally wrote, but clearly requires elaboration and explication. It never appears to have occurred to Strawson, what seems to be palpably the case, that Austin was trying to carefully elaborate that truism. It is for these sorts of reasons that I do not follow the controversy through in detail. Instead, I consider Austin's central thesis (truism), for it is certainly correct that to get exactly clear about it is important and difficult.

III THE THEORY

Austin held what he himself referred to, if somewhat in passing, as a correspondence theory of truth, where the correspondence involved is entirely conventional. He is usually taken to have offered something like this: to say that a statement is true is to assert that a suitable correspondence holds between the subject term of the statement and some element in the world and the predicate term and a situation (fact) in the world. The correspondence is, and has to be, conventional because it depends solely on the conventions involved in speaking meaningfully within our language.

Such is, I think, the common view of Austin's position and the view Strawson was attacking, or appeared to be attacking, in his first paper in reply. However, it is important to realize, as Strawson did when he wrote his final paper, that this view is not explicitly Austin's.

Austin starts by saying that to communicate at all we must have a language (words) and something to communicate about (the world). Then, there must then be 'two sets of conventions: *Descriptive* conventions correlating the words (=sentences) with the *types* of situation, thing, event, etc., to be found in the world. *Demonstrative* conventions correlating the words (=statements) with the *historic* situations, etc., to be found in the world' (p. 22).

We then get the definition proper: 'A statement is said to be true when the historic state of affairs to which it is correlated by the demonstrative conventions (the one to which it "refers") is of a type with which the sentence used in making it is correlated by the descriptive conventions.'

The difference between the common view, given above, and Austin's statement, is this: on the common view, the statement is divided into subject and predicate or, in Strawson's formulation, into parts, a referring part and a describing part, while in Austin's formulation it is not explicitly so divided. In discussing Strawson's first interpretation (the common interpretation), I shall use his notion of a describing part (a D-part) and a referring part (an R-part) of statements to avoid some of the luggage involved in the subject-predicate way of talking.

IV STRAWSON'S FIRST REFUTATION

We must notice that Strawson does not just have doubts about Austin's theory, he thinks it plainly false: he wrote, 'the correspondence theory requires, not purification, but elimination'.

To put it somewhat crudely, Strawson has this picture of Austin's theory: a statement has two parts, an R-part and a D-part.[1] From other areas of his own work ('On Referring'), we know that Strawson holds that it is a precondition of a statement being true *or* false that the R-part must refer to or correspond to something. He then interprets Austin as saying that the D-part of the statement must correspond to something, and indeed something else,

---

[1] 'Parts of statements' here, as Strawson points out, should not be equated with parts of sentences. In some ways, 'feature' would be a better word, though I use 'part' for the sake of historical consistency.

for the statement to be true; that is, there must be a different thing, event, situation, state of affairs, feature or fact in the world which makes it true. Thus on this interpretation there must be two correspondencies to different things which hold between 'words and world' for the statement to be true. Strawson's refutation consists in arguing in a great deal of subtle detail that the second thing, that to which the D-part of the statement corresponds, could not be a thing in the world; that therefore there is no possibility of a truth condition being such a correspondence.

This can do with exemplification. Someone, let us suppose, truly asserts:

> The cat has mange.

The R-part of the statement corresponds to the cat. But what does the D-part correspond to? The condition of the cat, as having mange? The fact of the cat's mange? The situation of the cat's being mangy? None of these, Strawson claims. There is only *one* thing in the world, namely the (mangy) cat, and therefore one part of the statement (the D-part) has nothing in the world to which it can correspond.

The point of Strawson's is an interesting one though I confess to not knowing quite how to assess it because of the ambiguity of 'in the world'. However, as Strawson did not notice, the point just does not matter for Austin's theory of truth. That is, Austin personally did want to hold that there are, in some sense, facts in the world but quite clearly there is nothing in his formal statement on truth which precludes both the D-part and the R-part of a statement corresponding in different ways to the same thing, event, etc., in the world, which only requires there to be things, events, etc., in the world. I shall elaborate this way of looking at Austin's theory in a later section.

V STRAWSON'S SECOND REFUTATION

In 'Truth: A Reconsideration of Austin's Views', Strawson tells us that the subject of his inquiry is somewhat different from what it was in his first paper. Originally, he claims, he was arguing against Austin's thesis 'as an analysis of the meaning of "is true" '. Here, however, he will ask whether Austin's thesis 'embodies a clear statement of the truth at all'. He concludes that it does not (p. 290). However, one must keep in mind that the obvious and crucial difference between the two papers is that he interprets Austin differently in each: in the first, statements are divided into parts, in the second, they are not. This, in effect, means that he is considering an entirely different thesis.

In this paper, Strawson starts by refining the Austinian definition of truth in the light of some hints from Austin (footnote 10, p. 22) and some statements in Warnock's second paper (footnote 4, p. 67). He reaches this formulation: 'A historical statement is true when the particular historical situation with which the words used in making it are, as then used, correlated by semantical conventions is of the general type with which those words are standardly correlated by semantical conventions' (p. 295).

Strawson then offers a refutation of this position. Its basis is this: Statements are no longer divided into parts but he is prepared to allow, what he did not allow in his first paper, that in a particular case both the demonstrative and descriptive conventions can have, so to speak, an earthly terminus in the same thing. But because of this last point, he claims, knowing what the statement is about, which is a matter of the statements identity, is automatically to know that it is true. And this, he says, is absurd.

What one must say here is that if one plays the game according to Strawson's rules, then Strawson will win. But, as I illustrated, the rules do change to suit whatever objection Strawson is offering at any given moment. It never seems to occur to him that Austin's thesis (like his own in 'On Referring') requires that statements can be divided into parts and that, if a statement is true, these parts correspond in different ways to the same thing, event, etc., in the world. Yet these positions, taken in conjunction, easily avoid both his objections; in addition, they constitute the most plausible interpretation (elaboration) of Austin's position. To it I shall now turn.

VI THE WAY THROUGH THE DIFFICULTIES

What has caused much of the trouble with Austin's thesis is, I think, that in talking of descriptive and demonstrative conventions, Austin put these conventions, and the correspondencies they give rise to, far too fully on a par. In fact, they are both very different. I shall work this out in more detail.

In the original paper, Austin wrote that there must be 'two sets of conventions: *Descriptive* conventions correlating the words

(=sentences) with the *types* of situations, things, events, etc., to be found in the world. *Demonstrative* conventions correlating the words (=statements) with the *historic* situations to be found in the world.' The mistake is to say that there are two *sets* of conventions when in fact there are two *types* of conventions;[1] to mark the difference more strongly, I would prefer to say that there are desscriptive *conventions* and demonstrative *mechanisms*. This requires further working out.

If we ignore proper names,[2] any word which appears in the subject of a sentence can also appear in the predicate (though perhaps in a different case, e.g., 'I' may become 'me'). Some of the words (most notably nouns and adjectives) are correlated via conventions with certain *types* of things, situations, events, qualities and so on: e.g., 'cat' is correlated via (semantic) conventions of English with a type of furry animal, 'red' with a certain class of colors, and so on. These are aspects of English; they concern the meanings of words in English. This is a somewhat simple-minded account, though adequate for our present purposes, of Austin's 'descriptive conventions'.

On the other hand, there are certain, mainly grammatical and structural, mechanisms by which we can pick out linguistically some *historical* situation, event, happening, etc., from other situations of the same type. Most of the time, this picking out is not done entirely linguistically; it is accomplished as well by the location of the speaker, the circumstances in which he has uttered or written, the nature of the situation, etc., being picked out, and so on. Thus an actual utterance of 'The cat has mange' in a living situation, if the utterance is to come off at all, picks out a unique cat. However, it only does this because of the circumstances in which it is uttered. This form of picking out is equally a convention-bound activity; it involves grammatical and structural conventions of English as well as conventions to do with the use of English in general. However it is in general only because the semantic conventions considered in the last paragraph obtain (as

---

[1] Warnock comes close to remarking this problem, though in a peculiarly oblique way, in his second paper. See footnote 4, p. 67.

[2] The only reason we have to ignore proper names is because of false but fashionable philosophical theories about names. If one takes the view of names offered in 'Names', *Analysis* (Supplement), 1965, pp. 73–85, then they could be included in this account without difficulty.

preconditions) that these demonstrative mechanisms can work at all (the one exception, of course, is the use of 'this' and 'that' as demonstrative pronouns). Thus the demonstrative conventions (mechanisms) and the descriptive conventions operate at different levels; and they certainly have very different functions. I prefer to call the demonstrative conventions *mechanisms* partly to mark this difference and partly because they are ways we operate with words rather than conventions which we must follow whenever we use words for communication.

Let us return to the example. There is a cat; it has mange. Someone asserts:

The cat has mange.

There are descriptive (semantic) conventions correlating the sort of animal we have in front of us with 'cat'; there are demonstrative mechanisms by which it is indicated that just this cat is concerned; there are descriptive (semantic) conventions correlating the type of condition of the cat with 'has mange' or 'mange'. The statement is true when the descriptive (semantic) correspondence obtains for the object picked out. There are not, as Strawson correctly points out in his first paper, two things in the world but just one: the (mangy) cat. The two correlations of which Austin speaks are both to the cat; they are not even to different aspects of the cat though they are different sorts of correlations. Equally, we do not have to pick out some cat as being 'the mangy cat referred to' before we can assess the statement for truth-value; this would be, as Strawson says in his final paper, absurd.

We are now in a position to reformulate Austin's position in such a way as to avoid the difficulties that Strawson raised. However, before doing so, there are one or two smaller points worth remarking.

Austin speaks of a statement being true (roughly) when both the demonstrative mechanisms and the descriptive conventions are working as they should. I shall maintain that this is correct but it hides a complication which is worth noticing. As I mentioned earlier, Strawson, in a different paper ('On Referring'), maintained that, in the terminology used so far, the R-part of the statement must correspond suitably as a *pre*condition of the statement's being *either* true *or* false. Thus though the appropriate correspondence for the R-part is of course a necessary condition for the statement's truth, it is also a precondition for the statement's having a truth value at all. Austin accepted this point.[1]

VII THE AUSTINIAN THEORY

In this section I give modification of Austin's theory. I use Austin's words as often as I can but do not put them in quotation marks: if I had, the passage would be impossible to read.

As preconditions of informative utterances there must be at least the following conventions and mechanisms:

> *Descriptive* conventions (semantically) correlating words or phrases such that their correct application involves class membership, i.e., conventions which correlate words or phrases with *types* of situation, thing, event, etc., to be found in the world.
>
> *Demonstrative* mechanisms by which historic situations, events, objects, happenings, etc., to be found in the world can be picked out by (a sub-portion of) a statement (in conventional terminology, the subject of the statement); these mechanisms need not be wholly linguistic.

A statement is correctly said to be true when there are two specific relationships (correspondences) between the statement and the world, or a piece of the world, or an event in the world, etc.: the first relationship being demonstrative and the second descriptive (there may, with more complicated statements, be more than one demonstrative correspondence involved and there usually is more than one descriptive correspondence involved). These relationships are conventional in the sense, and only in the sense, that they depend on our language, though in different ways for the different types of relationship. Then the truth conditions for straightforward statements are as follows:

(*a*) It is a precondition of a statement having a truth-value at all that the first relationship holds.

(*b*) To say that a statement is true presupposes that the (*a*) condition holds and is to say (i.e., the utterance means) that the second relationship holds, i.e., the descriptive phrase in the predicate covers what the demonstrative phrase picks out.

I am not sure how much this formulation differs from Austin's position except in relatively unimportant, verbal ways. By inten-

---

[1] See *How To Do Things With Words*, pp. 47–52.

tion at least, the serious difference comes only in the demonstrative mechanisms. It amounts to this: where Austin speaks of 'demonstrative conventions correlating the words (=statements) with historic situations . . .', I speak of 'demonstrative mechanisms by which historic situations . . . can be picked out by (a sub-portion of) a statement'. Putting it this way has the advantage that it avoids, in different ways, all the criticisms so far discussed. It also has a further merit. The position now is surely just correct, even if it applies only to what Austin called 'straightforward' statements which is certainly a limited class.

There are several further points which are worth noticing quickly here because difficulties have arisen about them. First, to say that a statement is true is not, on the presentation of Austin's theory given above, to talk about the *terms* of the relationship (correspondence), i.e., it is not to talk *about* the descriptive and demonstrative conventions whose existence are preconditions of making any statement at all, but to assert that the correspondence holds. What caused the difficulties about this point was that Austin said the following: suppose the relationship between words and world he has discussed 'does genuinely occur, why should the phrase "is true" not be our way of describing it?' This is, of course, quite wrong, though how he came to say it is obvious enough (it stems from his idiosyncratic use of 'describe'). However, what Austin meant is clear: In writing the paper 'Truth' (2), Austin was at least attempting to describe the relationship between words and world which results in a statement being true, but the phrase 'is true' does not describe that relationship. However, when we say 'S is true', according to Austin, what the utterance means is that the relationship (correspondence) he gave holds in this particular case. I sometimes suspect that missing this point was the cause of many of the oddities in Strawson's 'Truth' (3).

There are two further connected differences which are worth mentioning before going on. It was decidedly deceptive of Austin to speak of his theory as a correspondence theory at all; he was not maintaining a theory which was particularly like other theories called correspondence theories and not maintaining a theory which was any more like a correspondence theory than, say, the Semantic Theory. Equally, to speak of the correspondences (relationships) involved in his theory as purely conventional, the conventions such that they could be changed at will, was highly deceptive. A convention, like that of always addressing a colleague as 'Mr' at a meeting of the Faculty Board, can be changed at will and nothing much hangs by it except what is correct form. A language is not like that. It is a huge, interlocking structure where to alter one portion (say, the mechanisms for demonstrative reference) may change the whole. It depends for its success as a medium of communication (that is, for its existence as a language) on large numbers of people being conversant with it and any changes which occur in it. It is conventional in the sense that there are no necessities (logical or empirical) to force it into being just one way. But to say, blandly, that a relationship is conventional because it depends on language is to invite misunderstanding.

VIII THE SCOPE OF AUSTIN'S THEORY

Austin quite deliberately gave a limited analysis of the notion of truth. We should first notice, therefore, that this would seem to be highly desirable. If we try to formulate a theory of truth which covers all possible uses of 'is true' in English we can only say that it is a highly general assessment phrase. (To say, as Austin said in 'Performative Utterances', that ' "true" and "false" are just general labels for a whole dimension of different appraisals which have something or other to do with the relation between what we say and the facts' (p. 237) is still, I suspect, too confining[1]). Some such general theory of truth is doubtless correct, in fact truistic, but well worth offering (indeed, Strawson did offer such a theory in 'Truth' (1)). But there are other philosophical problems to do with truth. One might ask, 'Granting that "is true" has such a very general use, can we not ask how it is correctly used (or what it means) when applied seriously to simple, factual statements ("straightforward" statements, in Austin's terminology)?' In so far as he said anything about it, this is the question to which Austin was addressing himself in 'Truth' (2). But he could have said a great deal more, and should have done so to counter the predictable criticism from Strawson that his account covered far too confined a class of statements ('Truth' (3), p. 51).

Up to this point, I have offered some amendments to Austin's original account. What is called for now, however, is to write a good deal onto it. This would be a presumptuous task and one I

---

[1] See also *How To Do Things With Words*, pp. 147 and ff.

do not propose to undertake. However, I do wish to indicate the sort of thing Austin could have said without attempting to work it out in detail.

As I pointed out above, to give some single account of how 'is true' is used on all occasions, though interesting, necessarily involves giving some highly unspecific account which misses much of what is involved in most actual uses of the phrase. One can, however, start at the other end. One can choose the most uncomplicated sort of statement imaginable and give a highly precise account of what 'is true' means when applied correctly to that sort of statement. Supposing this endeavor to be successful, i.e., supposing an account has been given which covers at least some simple statements, one can then turn round and see how, with additional mechanisms, one can give an account of the meaning of 'is true' for more complicated sorts of statements. Whether or not the original account is of real interest will depend to a large extent upon whether or not this further attempt is successful. But in the case of Austin's account it seems likely that it will be at least partially successful.

Let us postulate, what is in any case true I think, that Austin's account works for some statements (it does not matter how few). Call those statements Austinian statements. We must ask whether it is the case that the truth of Austinian statements governs the truth of any non-Austinian statements. Take Strawson's example:

The cat is not on the mat.

It is not, as Strawson points out, an Austinian statement. But it is entailed by several sets of Austinian statements (which it does not itself entail). For instance, it is entailed by the two statements (offered in appropriate times and places):

The cat is up a tree,
The mat is on the ground,

both of which are Austinian statements. Similarly, the statement

The cat is on the mat again

is not an Austinian statement, but it is entailed by several possible sets of Austinian statements. Of course, this does not solve the problems associated with the truth conditions for all the old philosophical worry-statements. For instance, it does not solve the problems associated with the truth conditions of

All cats have long whiskers.

But then, why should it? We are surely over the days when we expect one simple theory to solve all the problems over a huge field. Furthermore, the sorts of questions which have concerned philosophers about, e.g., universal, existential, hypothetical statements have always come down, roughly, to: what, if any, is the connection between these sorts of statements and simpler statements; and the 'simpler statements' have usually been what at least look like Austinian statements. If Austin really has been successful in giving an account of the truth conditions for the statements which are the touchstone in such inquiries, the account was well worth giving. And its worth is independent of whether or not all statements have truth values which are functions of the truth values of Austinian statements. Equally, drastically incorrect accounts of the truth conditions for such statements have been given, e.g., the Semantic Theory, so Austin's account cannot be entirely obvious.

Strawson, it would seem, is well aware of much of this. But he makes the wrong use of it. That is, he apparently objects to any extension of Austin's theory to cover more complicated sorts of statements on the grounds that it destroys the simplicity of the original formulation ('Truth' (3), p. 51). But Strawson is well aware, as his own writing shows, that philosophical accuracy and simplicity do not necessarily go together. The objection is surely not a serious one.

Such an outline defense as I have offered above does not clear Austin's account of the accusation that it is trivial, uninteresting, truistic. But then this is the sort of accusation which used to annoy Austin so much when he was alive; and, I would have thought, rightly. Certainly it led him to write, 'I am not sure that importance is important. Truth is' ('Pretending', p. 219). But the charge that Austin's theory is truistic is, in any case, uninteresting. Once we really know what is going on in any given area, the philosophical truths in that area will all be truistic; this does not make them, or the general clarification of which they are a sign, any less important. It is now a truism that the meaning of a word is not an object, that the structure of the world is not necessarily the structure of any logical calculus, that not every word is a name, and so on. If

Austin's position on truth falls into that category, we should be well pleased, for it would then be, I suspect, the only positive, philosophically significant truism that we have.

BIBLIOGRAPHY

The following abbreviations have been used: *P.P.* for Austin, *Philosophical Papers*, Oxford, 1961; *T.* for *Truth* (ed. G. Pitcher), Prentice-Hall, 1964; *P.A.S.* for *Proceedings of the Aristotelian Society* and *P.A.S.S.* for the *Supplementary Proceedings* of that Society. Page references in the text are always to the last printing cited.

AUSTIN, J. L. 'Truth' (2), *P.A.S.S.*, 1950; *P.P.*; *T.*
—. 'Pretending', *P.A.S.*, 1957-8; *P.P.*
—. 'Unfair to Facts', *P.P.*
—. 'Performative Utterances', *P.P.*
—. *Sense and Sensibilia*, Oxford, 1962.
—. *How To Do Things With Words*, Oxford, 1962.

STRAWSON, P. F. 'Truth' (1), *Analysis*, 1949.
—. 'Truth' (3), *P.A.S.S.*, 1950; *T.*
—. 'On Referring', *Mind*, 1950; *Essays in Conceptual Analysis* (ed. A. N. Flew), Macmillan, London, 1956.
—. 'A Problem about Truth—A Reply to Mr Warnock', *T.*
—. 'Truth: A Reconsideration of Austin's Views', *Philosophical Review*, 1965.

WARNOCK, G. J. 'Truth and Correspondence', *Knowledge and Experience* (ed. C. D. Rollins), Pittsburgh, 1962.
—. 'A Problem about Truth', *T.*

Part III

Sense and Sensibilia

A CRITICAL STUDY OF
SENSE AND SENSIBILIA

R. J. Hirst

MANY philosophers outside Oxford have been puzzled by Austin's remarkable influence over his colleagues, an influence picturesquely described in Mr. G. J. Warnock's words as reported in the *New Yorker* of December 9th, 1961: 'Like Wittgenstein, Austin was a genius, but Wittgenstein fitted the popular picture of a genius. Austin, unfortunately, did not. Nevertheless, he did succeed in haunting most of the philosophers in England, and to his colleagues it seemed that his terrifying intelligence was never at rest. Many of them used to wake up in the night with a vision of the stringy, wiry Austin standing over their pillow like a bird of prey. Their daylight hours were no better. They would write some philosophical sentences and then read them over as Austin might, in an expressionless, frigid voice, and their blood would run cold.'* The lectures here published hardly have the range and depth of genius, rather they are like a brilliant light concentrated on a narrow patch of the philosophical field, but they do enable one to see how Austin was able to cow many of his Oxford contemporaries. Partly this was achieved by his acuteness in spotting hidden assumptions in his opponents' positions, assumptions which had only to be stated in his direct uncompromising manner to appear ridiculous; partly it was his picking on departures from ordinary usage and making them seem to be errors about it, such elementary errors that anyone committing them appeared unfitted for philosophy or academic life; and partly it was the lively, vigorous style of his castigations, for while he was kinder to his pupils he could be merciless with those who had pretensions to philosophical expertise.

* See Ved Mehta in the bibliography.

The spoken word is generally the less inhibited, and Austin's style comes through well in this reconstruction, even though Warnock only claims authenticity for '*many* points of phraseology' (as opposed to 'all points of substance'); expressions like 'glibly trotted out', 'already half way to perdition', 'this degree of insouciant latitude' or 'not even faintly sensible', certainly give a freshness. Less happily there is some hinting as disingenuousness in his philosophical opponents, e.g. 'concealed motives' (p. 5), 'all along . . . really completely convinced of the arguments he purports to "evaluate" with so much detachment' (p. 61), 'strong *suggestio falsi*' (pp. 10, 12), 'trades on confusion' (p. 22), 'quiet undermining' (p. 9), 'quietly slipping in here that dichotomy' (p. 136), 'little better than a frame up' (p. 138)—harmless perhaps, but Gellner's book was refused a review in *Mind* for no worse. Anyhow, it is useful to have this Austinian phraseology, since so far as public life was concerned the style of controversy was very much the man, and without it those who never knew him might wonder how he could be said to haunt and terrify. So on these grounds, as well as for the more obvious and important one of preserving for us the usually acute and sometimes devastating arguments, we should be very grateful to Mr. Warnock for the careful and laborious research which must have underlain this reconstruction. And this industry is crowned by remarkable self-abnegation, in that without a word of protest or even a footnote in answer, Warnock ends with a chapter in which part of his own book on Berkeley receives the full Austin treatment—'this comparison is really quite disastrous', 'extraordinary perverse', 'picture . . . upside-down as well as distorted', the charges ring out.

For almost all the book, however, the target is part of Ayer's *Foundations of Empirical Knowledge*, though there are side-swipes at Price's *Perception*. As is admitted, the latter was first published in 1932, and the former in 1940, its views being later abandoned or modified. But one cannot shrug off *Sense and Sensibilia* as an out-of-date book review posthumously published out of pupillary piety or as a historical curiosity. It claims a far-reaching validity, seeking to save us from some particularly seductive fallacies of the *philosophia perennis*.

First and foremost Austin wishes to demolish the 'scholastic' doctrine that we never perceive or anyhow never *directly* perceive or sense material objects, but only sense-data; his position being not only that the arguments for this are invalid, but that its anti-thesis is also false—the simple dichotomy of material objects and sense-data is completely bogus. To show this there is a long and detailed examination of the Argument from Illusion. Secondly, there is associated with this an attack on that 'venerable bug-bear', the pursuit of the incorrigible. Austin claims to show that senten-ces cannot be divided up into two groups, incorrigible sense-datum ones which provide the evidence for all others and always corri-gible material-object ones which are in need of verification and never conclusively obtain it. Thus 'this looks red' is always open to retraction, while 'this is a pig' may be absolutely certain. Indeed, the general doctrine of knowledge as a structure based on in-corrigible data is radically misconceived. Thirdly, Austin admits that this operation 'leaves us, in a sense, just where we began', but the words 'in a sense' are an important qualification for they introduce his own evaluation of his methods: besides the good work done in reducing falsity and nonsense, he claims the positive achievements of acquiring a technique for dissolving some kinds of philosophical worry and of learning something about the meanings of some English words, e.g. 'real', 'seems', 'looks', 'appears', 'vague', etc. (p. 5).

Whether of course we allow that falsity is reduced or the tech-nique is useful and appropriate can only depend on how far we accept his first two claims, but before considering them we may at least chalk up the gains of the lexicographical exercises. They form a useful prolegomenon (but only that) to epistemological discus-sion, and the treatment of 'real' is particularly valuable. The Austinian doctrine that there is no general sense of 'real' because 'the negative use wears the trousers' (p. 70), i.e. 'real' takes its meaning from what it is contrasted with (e.g. fake, decoy, dyed, synthetic), should dispel confusion and help in dealing with a problem—what do we mean by 'real'?—which worries physicists, for example, as well as philosophers. All the same, it is possible to find some fault. 'Real'='existent' gets rather scanty recognition, while none at all is accorded to 'unreal', which surely has no trousers to wear. And the technique does carry one to the verge of the ridiculous, e.g. the soul-searing problem of why false teeth are called false and artificial limbs artificial, rather than the other way round (p. 72). More important, Austin twice refers to all this as 'a discussion of the Nature of Reality', a description which was presumably meant as a joke or tongue-in-cheek, but seems in this reconstruction at least to be taken seriously. No doubt as Austin shows there is no one single quite general account of the use of the word 'real' (in ordinary speech), but how absurd to suppose that that was what metaphysics was trying to provide!

Since the whole book is packed with arguments, illustrations, polemics and asides, all of them stimulating, I can discuss only the more important or provocative points in its two main themes. In the first theme, the attack on the argument from illusions and its attendant dichotomy, these seem to be:

(1) There is no one kind of thing that we perceive, but many different kinds; it is nonsense to suggest that the plain man thinks that we always perceive material things, which, though not defined by Ayer, appear to be 'moderate-sized specimens of dry goods'. We perceive people, voices, rivers, flames, rainbows, vapours, even cream and glass, which do not come under that or any one heading (pp. 7–8, 80 n). Austin is being captious here. The items on his list would be covered by a less perversely limited interpretation of 'material thing', for anything can be called a thing and most of Austin's list are obviously material (or physical); so indeed are voices *qua* sounds, i.e. vibrations in air, or people *qua* organisms, while shadows and rainbows may be regarded as coloured patterns on the surface of material things (including raindrops) and even light is a physical or material entity. Anyhow, the term is in common philosophical use, and the differentiae of a material thing were stated very carefully by Price (*Perception*, pp. 35, 145–6), which Austin never considers. Not all of Price's differentiae (e.g. spatial completeness) apply to all cases of objects of perceptions, and externality seems missed out, but 'publicity' applies to them all and the others to almost all. Even though Price's list is not perfect, what we perceive does differ from mental images, hallucinations, or bodily sensations, and so we need some general term for it in philosophical discussion, which is not the plain man's concern.

(2) To say that we never directly perceive ordinary objects offends against the normal use of 'directly'. The philosophers glibly trot out their peculiar use of the word without explaining it (pp. 14–19). Austin's comments here are unfair. Price states clearly in *Perception* (p. 3) what he means by 'directly', viz.: 'consciousness of [the object] is not reached by inference nor by any other intel-

lectual process . . ., nor by any passage from sign to significate'. The doctrine that we are directly or immediately aware of colours, sounds, or other data, while perception of material objects involves inferences or assumptions, was surely well known, and in fact is attacked in Austin's later discussion of Berkeley (pp. 133–9). His line is that while we *may* make such inferences from sound to object in hearing, it is quite false and deceitful to suggest that this is universal in perception: seeing occurs without inferences or assumptions, and the immediately perceived visual field may as well be said to consist of books, shelves and similar objects as of colour patches. Berkeley, Price and presumably Warnock, had however maintained that even the seeing of material objects involves inference or 'taking-for-granted', and Austin's reason for flatly denying this is not clear. Seemingly it is that perception of such objects may be perfectly certain, more certain than that of colours, etc.—his second main theme, in fact. But inferences may be perfectly certain and it is the *possibility* (not universality) of error in seeing and other perception which is the main ground of the doctrine he attacks. Another ground for rejecting the immediacy of perceiving and for supposing that it involves many complex mental processes lies in the psychological evidence, e.g. the dependence of perception on our degree of attention, on our learning and past experience (for recognition, identification, etc.), on the use of 'cues' (for depth, distance and solidity), on figure/ground and object constancy adjustments. I don't myself think these factors justify one's distinguishing an immediate sensing of sense-data as opposed to mediate perception of objects, but for the opposite reason to Austin; not because perceiving is direct, but because awareness of colour patches, etc., is not direct either. But in any case Austin's treatment is rather cavalier, and it is a pity he had not apparently read Blanshard, for example, or reflected on the full psychological evidence. (He does mention a very small selection of this evidence in accepting the notion of 'seeing as' (p. 100), but does not develop the point.)

(3) Usual discussions of the whole question are tendentious and question-begging. *Inter alia:* (*a*) they wrongly suggest we think there is only one way of being deceived by the senses (pp. 12–14); (*b*) they trade on the confusing of illusion with delusion (pp. 20–5) and blandly assume a dichotomy of veridical and delusive experiences (p. 48); (*c*) they wrongly define and analyse 'illusion'

(pp. 26–8); (*d*) they slip in the unclear notion of a 'perception' without explanation (pp. 11, 30, 47, 53).

There is something in all this, though Austin's charges are exaggerated. On (*a*) he does not make it clear who makes this odd suggestion; it is not in the passage from Ayer he is discussing, and most writers clearly distinguish illusion and hallucination, though Ayer is admittedly not exact about 'delusive' and 'illusory' (point (*b*)). The major point behind (*b*) is valid enough, that philosophers have often classed cases of the relativity of perception as illusions, but it is not of vital importance, for the question of how it is that this relativity occurs still survives and is one the Sense-datum Theory tries to answer. (*c*) is directed against Price. Austin points out that his provisional definition of illusion does not fit all the cases (I wonder whose definition does—Austin does not attempt one), and quite properly objects to Price's account of 'illusions' in which if X looks A something exists possessing character A. But he might have done better to take Price's analysis at its first appearance in *Perception* and examine it more fully. Based on what I call the Immediacy Assumption, it seems to me far more important in the genesis of the Sense-datum Theory than linguistic mistakes. Point (*d*) also is unfair: 'perception' is a perfectly good English word so I do not see why it should need special treatment in these introductory contexts. It clearly just means a 'perceiving' or 'perceptual experience' in the passages cited from Ayer (*F.E.K.*, pp. 1–9) who there treats perceptions as experiences *of* an object, and not as 'entities of which we are aware'. Hence Austin's criticism, p. 47, is quite beside the point. (Cf. also p. 11.)

(4) Ayer's distinction of two senses of 'perceive' is wrong—his second sense ('I see X' does not imply 'X exists') does not ordinarily occur—and is based on a misunderstanding of the different ways we can describe the object of our perception. Hence his claim that sense-data are introduced to avoid this ambiguity is false (pp. 84–103). Austin's discussion of these pages contains many good points; my chief reservation concerns p. 103, where it is suggested that as the ambiguity alleged in 'perceive' by Ayer and Price does not exist, their official grounds for introducing sense-datum terminology are invalid, but that this does not matter, since the real motive is not the avoidance of ambiguities but the production of incorrigible statements. This seems unfair, especially to Price, for (*a*) the ambiguity exists in *philosophical* currency and hence needs to

be guarded against, (*b*) how Price guards against it is by inventing the term 'perceptual consciousness', not 'sensing' (Austin never seems very clear about the difference between sensing and perceiving: careful writers would not now say we *perceive* sense-data), (*c*) like Russell, for example, Price is perfectly open about the relation between sensing and incorrigibility—he has none of this double-think Austin 'sees' everywhere.

(5) There is nothing in illusions to show that during them we do not perceive physical objects (pp. 29–31), nor does the plain man think this (p. 14). This seems in general valid and Austin's refutation of Ayer's discussion of reflection and refraction is quite cogent. Unfortunately, however, he does not discuss the trickier illusion of double vision—not even the plain man supposes that the 'second' bottle is a physical object, so what is it?

(6) By grotesquely exaggerating the frequency of illusion and hallucination, and by neglect of special circumstances, the philosophers falsely suggest that perceiving is dubious (pp. 10–12, 52, 54, cf. pp. 114, 138). I should not have said the exaggeration was *grotesque*—there is exaggeration, but it is understandable, as the philosophers are drawing attention to something not normally realized. Austin claims that philosophers are trying to represent perceiving as dubious and chancy, but I don't think they really mean that there is anything uncertain in practice about well-tested perception; the uncertainty is theoretical, i.e. as there is *some* possibility, however slight, of error, perceiving has not the absolute certainty applicable to a proven mathematical or analytical truth. No doubt they overestimate the difference, but Austin goes too far the other way in apparently suggesting that there is no less uncertainty about mathematical propositions (cf. p. 117 n—but the 'firm establishment' is only possible because they are analytic or demonstrable in a way an empirical proposition can never be).

(7) Finally, the most important of Austin's points, which attacks the centre of the 'philosophical' view. He argues (*a*) the fact that people fail to distinguish hallucinations and genuine perceptions does not mean that they are not distinguishable; (*b*) if they are sometimes indistinguishable this is rare, occurring in special circumstances only, and they do not thereby have to be identical, i.e. even if hallucinations are awareness of sense-data, normal perceptions need not be (pp. 48–54). This certainly shows that the argument from hallucinations is not a *proof* of the existence

of sense-data or other objects of immediate awareness in perception. But the argument may well be regarded as postulating sense-data in order to explain the facts of illusion and hallucination. So considered (i.e. as propounding a hypothesis, not a proof), it is not refuted by Austin, and the test is then: does he provide a better explanation of the facts? It is certainly arguable that Austin underestimates the convincingness and indistinguishability of hallucinations or even of dreams—he has obviously never had any realistic ones. The data given in J. R. Smythies' *Analysis of Perception* Ch. IV, or even Lord Brain's *Nature of Experience* Ch. I, particularly the cases where hallucinatory objects are fully integrated with a perceived background, e.g. cast shadows, certainly provide a difficult problem for a common-sense theory. The comparative rarity of such cases is irrelevant: that hallucinations occur as they do is enough to present a theoretical problem—as Austin himself says elsewhere 'it is the differences that matter'. He has no explanation of hallucination to offer and so his expostulations against sense-data lose much of their force.

Austin's second theme, the attack on the alleged distinction between incorrigible sense-datum sentences and corrigible material-object ones, has already been mentioned. Its main points are: (i) truth depends on the circumstances in which the sentence is uttered, so one cannot in abstraction from such circumstances pick out any group of non-analytic sentences and say they are incorrigible or testable or are such as to provide evidence for another group of sentences. Indeed, questions of evidence only arise when one cannot see the object. (Pp. 111, 115–16). (ii) Some sense-datum statements are in given circumstances incorrigible, but equally so are some material-object sentences, e.g. 'this is a pig'. Confidence in a sentence is a matter of the circumstances, not its form (p. 114, cf. pp. 42–3 where he says that descriptions of looks may always be retracted). (iii) One must reject other views of Ayer's, e.g. that material-object statements as such need to be verified, and that they cannot be conclusively verified because they entail an infinite set of sense-datum statements (pp. 117–20). (iv) He sums up, 'there *could* be no *general* answer to the questions what is evidence for what, what is certain, what is doubtful. . . . If the Theory of Knowledge consists of finding grounds for such an answer, there is no such thing' (p. 124).

Of these points, (iii) seems cogent and I shall say no more about it, but I have grave doubts as to much of the rest. Take the alleged incorrigibility of 'that is a pig'. I agree that there are circumstances in which we should say that this was certain, but the point is that we can only claim certainty for it as the result of a series of tests and observations. One glance would hardly rule out misidentifications, illusions or hallucinations, and Austin himself lists several tests, 'if I watch it . . .' (p. 114). We can therefore say: (*a*) these observations plus other facts, e.g. it is a farm and not a zoo, amount to evidence for 'that is a pig'—any material-object statement needs evidence if it is challenged as illusory or hallucinatory, even if we seem to see the object concerned. (*b*) Sense-datum statements, e.g. 'this is brown' meaning in fact 'this looks brown to me now', are not open to challenge on the same grounds: indeed *pace* Austin pp. 43 or 112 I don't believe they are open to challenge or retraction if they are sincere statements of personal experience of the moment and, in more complicated cases, if the speaker uses the words correctly. (*c*) A series of different kinds of observations is in no way relevant to the support of such a statement while it is essential to that of a material-object one: 'this looks brown to me now' is complete and final in one observation. (*d*) The kind of observation which would establish the material-object statement against challenge may be expressed by 'it's got four legs and a curly tail', 'it looks like a pig', 'it smells like a pig', etc., i.e. statements about the properties that the object has (or, on further challenge, appears to have) or about how it looks, smells, etc. Some of these seem statements of ostensible perceptions and I doubt whether they can be reduced to incorrigible sense-datum statements of the simple quality type discussed so far. If they can be so reduced, Ayer is substantially right; even if they cannot, Austin is still wrong. While truth admittedly depends on circumstances, the point is that if one assumes that certain circumstances (e.g. sincerity and absence of verbal slips) hold good in all cases, one can discover important distinctions between the two types of statements, viz. (i) material-object statements are open to theoretical challenge in a way that statements like 'this looks brown to me now' are not: (ii) material-object statements if challenged need evidence which is ultimately based on statements of looks or appearances of some kind.

Some such general answer seems possible, and Austin's denial of this seems to depend on equating 'general' with 'universal and unconditional'. By similarly overemphasizing obvious or trivial qualifications one could make nonsense of general laws in the sciences, and Austin is here failing to see the wood for the trees, missing *general* distinctions in the reliability of different types of statements and in the evidence appropriate to them. Consequently his attack on the Theory of Knowledge is misconceived, quite apart from the fact that the subject covers many topics which he does not discuss, e.g. *a priori* knowledge, memory, introspection, universals, and truth.

Denials of general answers or principles of classification seem in fact to be one of the more dubious parts of Austin's technique for dissolving the philosophical worry (cp. also pp. 8, 13, 39, 76). Despite such denials he manages to give a fairly full classification of the uses of 'look' and 'real' and list their main features. All he seems to be saying, therefore, is that previous philosophers have oversimplified their classifications and dichotomies, which is fair enough; but that does not mean that there is no general answer, merely that there is no simple one. The trouble with Austin's position is that it is sterile and stultifying, and it may easily give the impression that the variety of cases is such that nothing useful can be achieved in the way of general classification.

Another point of his technique is his affection for ordinary language—any attempt to alter it is frowned upon as 'tampering' (p. 63)—and this also seems obscurantist. Science and knowledge have advanced not only by classification and generalization but also by new concepts and terms or by new senses of ordinary words like 'mass', 'force', 'wave', 'cell', or 'energy'. The growth of knowledge and the increase in the complexity of both problems and explanations render inadequate the distinctions embodied in ordinary expressions, so that philosophical departure from what the plain man in his innocence would say becomes sheer necessity, not a blunder. Of course, Austin is careful to leave loopholes and does not say that one must never amend ordinary language, but his whole tone is unduly hostile to altering it. On the other hand his main successes in this book have been gained, I think, by using traditional techniques—unearthing hidden assumptions or question-begging terms in his opponents' arguments (e.g. pp. 50 ff.), or pointing out facts they have overlooked or misinterpreted (e.g. pp. 20–31).

Finally, I must emphasize one serious danger in this book:

students, and even Oxford dons to judge from their reviews in the press, may easily get the impression that Austin has completely disposed of the philosophical case for distinguishing sense-data or immediate objects of awareness from physical objects. True, the Argument from Illusion will never be the same again—it must now at best be an explanatory hypothesis rather than an argument—but that was only part of the case and not the strongest part. Austin never discusses the arguments based on the causal processes, particularly on the subjective conditioning by our nervous system and sense organs of what we perceive, even though these arguments are found in Price (*Perception*, pp. 37 ff.), Ayer (*F.E.K.*, pp. 9–11), Broad, Russell, Descartes, Locke and even Hume. They are the most difficult nut for the common-sense view to crack (as I have tried to show elsewhere), because they cannot satisfactorily be accounted for without some Generative Theory, i.e. without supposing sense-data or contents which are brought into being by cerebral processes and so must be distinct from external objects. Even the facts of relativity and illusion cannot properly be discussed in isolation from them. As soon as we ask how it is that relativity, refraction, reflection, double vision, realistic hallucinations, etc., occur, we are forced into consideration of these processes. Ryle did try to deal with them in his *Dilemmas*, though briefly and unsuccessfully; Austin does not venture to tackle them at all.

It seems to me one of the tragedies of recent English philosophy that undoubtedly brilliant and influential leaders like Austin and Wittgenstein have been so blind in their philosophizing to the importance of scientific findings. 'Philosophy begins in wonder', said Aristotle, but these latter-day exponents have conspicuously failed to wonder how it is that hallucinations and illusions occur or even how perception itself takes place. As a result there is a brittle superficiality in their cleverest performances in this field. No doubt they would have said that such questions should be left to the scientist, but this unadventurous approach obviously will not do; for the answer which any scientist or psychologist gives is the very one which they regarded as philosophically beyond the pale, namely some form of the Representative Theory.

AUSTIN'S ARGUMENT FROM ILLUSION

Roderick Firth

I T is unlikely that the philosophical genius of the late John Austin will ever be adequately appreciated by those who have merely read his words in print; and even to listen to his lectures, brilliant as they sometimes were, was to feel only reverberations of the extraordinary analytical power that has made him one of the most influential philosophers of his generation. It was during periods of creative philosophical discussion that Austin's genius was most fully displayed, for he was above all else master of a philosophical art that he taught to others by example—an art that is perhaps best described as the topography of concepts. This art is not of course the whole of philosophy. But without it philosophy is impossible, and it is doubtful that any philosopher who has had the privilege of watching John Austin in action has failed to become for that reason a better philosopher.

In the lectures to which he gave the title *Sense and Sensibilia*, Austin applies his art to a set of concepts that have played a crucial role in the history of Western epistemology, especially since the time of Descartes. According to Descartes and many philosophers who have followed him (including Ayer, whose book *The Foundations of Empirical Knowledge* Austin selects as 'chief stalking horse') the primary task of a theory of empirical knowledge is to clarify certain epistemic terms (for example, 'evidence', 'rational', and 'knowledge' itself) by showing how our empirical knowledge can be justified (or 'reconstructed' if we use Descartes' metaphor) on a perceptual basis. To say simply that empirical knowledge has a perceptual basis, or that it must ultimately be justified by perception, can of course mean many different things. It might mean, for example, that the evidence for our knowledge of the external world must ultimately be formulated in demonstrative statements like 'This is a tomato', 'This is a pig', and 'This meter reads 3.5'— statements which express a judgment (a 'perceptual judgment') about the objects that we perceive. But the traditional 'Cartesian enterprise', as I shall call it, is rooted in a very different conception of the 'perceptual basis' of knowledge. The philosophers whom Austin is criticizing—I shall call them 'Cartesians'—are those who have maintained that the most basic evidential statements are statements about perceptual experience itself (as opposed to the tomatoes and pigs which are the *objects* of perceptual experience) and, more specifically, that they are statements about a particular *constituent* of this kind of experience—a constituent that is perhaps most impartially described as 'sense experience'. There is also, these philosophers have said, a 'judgmental' constituent of perceptual experience—a state of 'accepting' or 'having faith in' some proposition about an object in the external world; but this state, they have held, varies independently of sense experience to some degree so that the two constituents of perceptual experience can easily be discriminated.

Although philosophers in the Cartesian tradition have apparently felt that there is no room for serious doubt about the existence of a sensory constituent of perceptual experience, they have usually made some effort to identify it by showing how it can be distinguished from the judgmental constituent; and for this purpose they have used a method that has become very familiar to us. The objective of this method is to distinguish the two constituents of perceptual experience by drawing attention to pairs of cases in which one constituent is approximately the same but the other quite obviously different; and to provide the most radical contrast we are asked to compare cases of normal perception with corresponding cases of abnormal perception. When Macbeth has his hallucination, runs a typical argument, he is in doubt whether there is really a dagger before him and therefore does not 'accept' a dagger or 'judge' that he is confronted by a real dagger; yet in another respect (the 'sensory' respect) his experience may be indistinguishable from the one he would have if he were seeing, and believed that he were seeing, a real dagger. Although arguments of this kind may take many different forms, the name 'argument from illusion' is sometimes used broadly enough so that it can be applied to any such attempt to identify sense experience by appealing to cases of abnormal perception. (The name is also applied to a very different argument used by Berkeley and others against naïve realism—an argument which assumes that sense experience has already been identified.) In this broad sense of the term, and neglecting a few relevant digressions, most of what Austin says in *Sense and Sensibilia* can be construed as an effort to show that the argument from illusion, in its traditional form, has been seriously impaired by conceptual obscurities and confusions.

If we think of Austin's objective in this relatively limited way, there seems to be no room for doubt that he has achieved it with a high degree of success. In the course of his lectures he has many stimulating and often brilliant things to say about the terms 'illusion', 'delusion', 'material', 'perception', 'looks', 'appears', 'seems', 'sense', and 'real'; and no philosopher who has followed his systematic analysis of these terms and other terms that have played a key role in the argument from illusion, will ever again be able to formulate and use this argument with the carelessness that has been characteristic of the Cartesian tradition. This adds up to a very significant achievement with important historical implications, but admirers of Austin may nevertheless be tempted to conclude that he has accomplished much more than this, and even to suppose that perceptual experience (or, at least, most perceptual experience) does not contain a sensory constituent. To prove this would of course undermine the deepest foundations of the entire Cartesian enterprise, and it is therefore important to see that Austin's arguments, even if they are all valid, are too limited in their scope to accomplish a result as revolutionary as this.

The most obvious limitation of Austin's arguments is the one resulting from his use of the traditional sense-datum terminology. At the outset he formulates in the following way a 'general doctrine' that he intends to discuss during the course of his lectures:

> We never see or otherwise perceive (or 'sense'), or anyhow we never *directly* perceive or sense, material objects (or material things), but only sense-data (or our own ideas, impressions, sensa, sense-perceptions, percepts, etc.) [p. 2].

Throughout the lectures he continues to employ the technical philosophical terminology of 'sense-data', 'direct perception', and so forth in formulating and criticizing the distinction that philosophers have tried to draw by means of the argument from illusion between perceiving (or perceptual experience) and sensing (or sense experience). This sense-datum terminology, as traditionally understood and as Austin himself construes it, entails a particular *analysis* of sense experience—a relational act-object analysis that seems to allow us to ask (as the passage just quoted from Austin indicates) what kinds of *immaterial objects* we can or must experience in order to have a sense experience. Consequently, a philosopher who advocates a nonrelational (for example, an 'adverbial') analysis of sense experience, or one who believes that he can introduce and use the sense-datum terminology in such a way that it is neutral with respect to questions concerning the proper analysis of sense experience, may reasonably conclude that most of Austin's arguments leave him quite unscathed and quite free to attempt a reconstruction of knowledge on a sensory basis. This is a conclusion that must be approached with caution, for one of Austin's arguments, as I shall point out, can be applied to forms of the argument from illusion that do not presuppose an act-object analysis of sense experience. There is an even more general reason, however, why Austin's method of attacking the argument from illusion is not one that can yield any revolutionary conclusions.

To see this we must recognize that the argument from illusion, although not incorrectly called an argument, is in fact a method for the *ostensive definition* of terms that are supposed to denote the sensory constituent of perceptual experience. It is intended to locate and exhibit the sensory constituent by describing some of the circumstances in which it occurs, just as a dictionary may define redness ostensively as 'the colour of arterial blood', and an itch as 'a sensation in the skin that causes a desire to scratch'. The Cartesian does not of course offer the argument from illusion in support of a *scientific theory*, if this implies that the warrant for accepting his analysis of perceptual experience depends on its success in explaining some body of empirical data. He maintains, on the contrary, that the sensory constituent in perception is itself 'the evidence of the senses' on which the warrant for all physical theory, and much of psychological theory, ultimately depends. From this point of view the identification of sense experience is epistemically pre-theoretical. Even the narrow and primitive theory that we formulate when we assert of a physical object 'This is square' or 'This is blue' would be unwarranted, according to the Cartesian, if we could not identify the 'evidence of the senses' that the theory serves to explain.

This has an important consequence. If the argument from illusion is an ostensive definition, not an attempt to defend a scientific theory and not an attempt to analyse the concept of sense experience, it does not have to be airtight in any formal respect in order to accomplish its purpose. The best ostensive definition of a given term for a given person is probably the simplest set of instructions that will actually succeed in teaching him how to use the term; in practice, therefore, we usually introduce qualifications and remove possible ambiguities in our instructions only when we believe that these particular refinements are necessary to prevent misunderstanding. A philosopher who is attempting to provide an ostensive definition of 'sense experience' for a wide and varied audience will naturally want to make his instructions tight enough to take account of all of the most common sources of misunderstanding. But there is of course no hope that he can forestall all *possible* misunderstanding, for every term that he uses in his instructions is itself subject to misinterpretation. From his point of view, therefore, the discovery of a loophole in the instructions does not prove that there is no sensory constituent in perceptual experience, but merely challenges him to modify the instructions by adding suitable qualifications. If the Cartesian philosopher is to be won away from his analysis of perceptual experience, he must be made to feel that the traditional method of identifying sense experience has actually led him to believe in the existence of something (called by him 'sense experience') that in fact does not exist, and one way to do this would be to persuade him that the argument from illusion involves confusions that cannot be eliminated even by adding the most ingenious of qualifications. Austin, however, does not make a serious effort to do this. Most of his arguments are focused on a few statements that philosophers have actually made when talking about the nature of sense experience, and he almost never speculates about ways in which these statements might be reformulated to meet his criticisms. Thus he does not show that the confusions and obscurities that he uncovers are necessary ingredients of *any* formulation of the argument from illusion. Nor can he show that these confusions and obscurities, undesirable as they may be, have always prevented philosophers from teaching other philosophers how to use terms like 'sense experience'. In the following pages I shall say more on this score while commenting very briefly on some of Austin's principal objections to the argument for illusion.

But it is of course obvious that to offer a convincing defence of this argument and the Cartesian enterprise would be a task far transcending the scope of the present discussion.

If we concentrate our attention solely on Austin's criticism of the argument from illusion, neglecting every digression and even the most interesting of his remarks concerning secondary issues, it is still possible to find in *Sense and Sensibilia* several fairly distinct objections to the traditional formulations of this argument. In order to classify and evaluate these objections, it is important to observe that the argument from illusion has commonly been formulated so that it makes explicit reference to the use of some familiar expression in ordinary speech. With respect to a hallucinatory experience like Macbeth's, for example, it has not seemed sufficient to most philosophers to say simply that the sensory constituent of this experience is what it has in common with the perceptual experience of a real dagger. Perhaps some philosophers have thought that the weakness of this relatively simple ostensive definition lies in the fact that the two experiences may share in common, in addition to sense experience characteristic of seeing a real dagger, a *feeling of inclination* to suppose that one *is* seeing a real dagger. In any case, they have usually elaborated such appeals to hallucination by telling us that the sensory constituent is one that we might naturally describe in such and such familiar words. Formulations of the argument from illusion can be classified, therefore, by reference to the 'pointer words', as I shall call them, that are supposed to guide us to the sensory constituent. When the argument from illusion is formulated as Austin considers it (cf., e.g., p. 21) in a terminology that prepares the way for saying that to have a sense experience is to *perceive* a sense-datum (as opposed to 'experiencing', 'sensing', or just 'having' a sense-datum) the pointer words are the perceptual verbs 'perceive', 'see', 'hear', and so forth, and the appeal to Macbeth's hallucination might be supplemented as follows: 'Although Macbeth has not decided, and does not think, that he sees a real dagger, and is in fact not perceiving a real dagger or any other material ("external") object, there is a special but familiar use of "perceive" (or "see") that allows him to say correctly that he is perceiving (seeing) a dagger. In these circumstances he shall be said to see a sense-datum (a dagger sense-datum) and his seeing of the sense-datum is an example of the kind of experience that is to be called "sense experience". ' If we want to avoid the sense-datum terminology and formulate the argument from illusion so that it is neutral with respect to the analysis of sense experience, we can do so in a number of different ways by substituting certain other pointer words for the perceptual verbs. Using the words 'looks as if', for example, instead of 'perceives', the argument might run as follows: 'Macbeth does not think he sees a real dagger and in fact he does not see one for there is no material ("external") thing that serves as the object of his abnormal perceptual experience. But there is an experiential sense of "looks" in which it surely *looks* to Macbeth *as if* he is perceiving something; and the experience that can be described in these terms is an example of the kind of thing that is to be called "sense experience". ' Although I shall speak of these formulations as two 'forms' of the argument from illusion, and shall refer to them respectively as Form A and Form B, they are in fact merely skeletons that would have to be fleshed out by the addition of qualifications and examples if the ostensive definition were to be as effective as possible for a wide audience.

Now there is, I think, only one argument in *Sense and Sensibilia* that can be construed as an important criticism of both Form A and Form B of the argument from illusion, and this criticism would in fact be equally valid against any other form of the argument from illusion. Early in his lectures (pp. 7–8), Austin points out (but afterwards says little more about it) that, unless we are first told how to understand the term 'material', there is a defect in any method that proposes to identify a sense-datum by contrast with a material thing. This is an interesting and important point. Although the standard examples that have usually been given of material (or 'objective' or 'external') things are what Austin describes as 'moderate-sized specimens of dry goods', it is clear that philosophers in the Cartesian tradition have generally wanted to maintain that people, rainbows, shadows, flames, pictures, and even images in a looking glass, are all 'external' or 'objective' things, open to observation by more than one person, and possible objects of *perceptual* experience (as opposed to *sense* experience). But no philosopher has yet provided a satisfactory definition of this class of material or external objects, and without such a definition there are possible sources of confusion in any ostensive definition that refers to the perceiving of external objects or includes terms like 'illusion' and 'hallucination' that can be defined only by employing the concept of external object. In line with my earlier remarks about the nature of ostensive definition, it should be observed that the Cartesian can eliminate any particular sources of confusion that Austin actually points out to him simply by enumerating types of things (shadows, rainbows, voices, mirror images, beams and glows and flashes of light, and so forth) which are not to count as objects of sense experience. In the future, however, it is to be hoped that philosophers interested in reconstructing our knowledge of the external world will try to meet Austin's challenge and will define for us in general terms a class of objects that includes dry goods and all these other 'external' things as well.[1]

The remaining objections to the argument from illusion in *Sense and Sensibilia* are based on Austin's analysis of the ordinary use of the perceptual verbs ('perceive', 'see', 'hear', and the like), and these objections are applicable only to Form A of the argument and to other forms that use these perceptual verbs as pointer words. In presenting the most basic of these objections, which as I construe it runs through Chapters III and V, Austin maintains that in cases of genuine *delusion* (for example, hallucination) 'there *is* something not "part of any material thing" ' (p. 28), something 'conjured up' (pp. 23, 25) which the victim of the delusion can be said to experience. As an example of such a thing Austin mentions the mirage that is a hallucination and not a reflection (p. 32). But there is no reason why we should allow ourselves, Austin argues, to be led from this fact to the conclusion that we also experience something of this kind (something said to be 'immaterial') in normal cases when we see trees, flowers, chairs, tables, and other 'material' things. And even in those abnormal cases that are properly described not as delusions but as *illusions* (for example, the Headless Woman or the church camouflaged as a barn) there is no need to suppose that in seeing a 'material' thing (for example, the church) we are *also* seeing or experiencing something 'immaterial' (for example, an immaterial barn). The way to describe

[1] It is possible, I suspect, to characterize an external object by reference to the role that it can play in the processes by which the sense organs are stimulated. But the task is much more difficult than it might appear at first thought. (Cf. my essay 'The Men Themselves; or, the Role of Causation in our Concept of Seeing' in H.–N. Castaneda, *Intentionality, Minds, and Perception*, Detroit, *1967*).

a case of this kind is simply to say, for example, that we are seeing a church that looks like a barn (p. 30).

Now whatever our final assessment of Austin's argument, I think it does show very clearly that there can be a serious ambiguity in Form A or any other form of the argument from illusion which asserts without cautious qualification that experiencing a hallucination is an *example* of seeing a sense-datum or having a sense experience. Because of this ambiguity it may appear that Austin, despite his objections to the term 'sense-datum', is in effect conceding the existence of a sense-datum in cases of hallucination when the sense-datum can be called, for example, a mirage. It may appear, to put the point in another way, that Austin has correctly followed the instructions for identifying sense experience in cases of hallucination, and that he objects to the traditional Cartesian analysis of perceptual experience only because he fails to find in ordinary perceptual experience a constituent of the kind that he has successfully identified in hallucinations. But to interpret the situation in this way would be to misconstrue the respect in which experiencing a hallucination is supposed to be an example of experiencing a sense-datum; for if it is an essential part of the instructions that we are to compare hallucinations with normal perceptions and seek out a *common* constituent, then experiencing a mirage and seeing a hallucinatory ('conjured up') dagger are obviously not themselves examples of the kind of constituent that we are supposed to find. We do not have a hallucination whenever we see an oasis or a dagger, and consequently we cannot infer that Austin has succeeded in isolating even a single instance of sense experience. According to the Cartesian tradition, the sensory constituent in the case of Macbeth's hallucination is supposed to be something that can in principle exist *whether or not* Macbeth is having a hallucination, and something that Macbeth can recognize before he decides that he is having a hallucination. To say that this constituent *is* a hallucination, or that to experience it *is* to experience a hallucination, must therefore be understood to state a fact that Macbeth himself can know only after his doubt is resolved—a fact, according to most of the Cartesian tradition, about the relationship of this constituent to its causal conditions. And the argument from illusion must be extended to make it perfectly clear that the use of 'see' referred to in Form A is one that would allow Macbeth to say, without inconsistency of any kind,

'I see a dagger but I do not know whether I am seeing a real dagger or having a hallucination'.

By extending the instructions in this way the Cartesian can remove an ambiguity from the argument from illusion. But the fact that there is some use of 'see' that meets this additional requirement, does still not guarantee that the ostensive definition will be successful. A critic might maintain that this additional requirement can be met only by supposing that 'dagger' is in effect the name of a genus of which hallucinatory daggers and 'real' daggers are two species. In that case the statement 'I see a dagger but I do not know whether I am seeing a real dagger or having a hallucination' can be understood to mean simply 'I see a real dagger *or* I am having a dagger hallucination, but I don't know which'. Since this is merely a statement about what the speaker knows or believes, it fails to distinguish a 'sensory' from a 'judgmental' constituent of his experience. Or a critic might grant that Macbeth's experience has something in common with seeing a real dagger, but hold that this common element is just a feeling of inclination to believe that one is seeing a real dagger.

In the face of such resistance the Cartesian will have to supplement his ostensive definition in some other way. He might ask his critic to consider why Macbeth feels that he should choose between this *particular* pair of alternatives (seeing a dagger and having a dagger hallucination) as opposed to other possible pairs of corresponding alternatives such as seeing a horse and having a horse hallucination. Surely, he might urge, you can identify some feature of Macbeth's experience—some qualitative characteristic or set of characteristics—which leads him to think that he is either seeing a dagger or having a dagger hallucination, and which would normally have to be very different to make him wonder whether he were seeing a horse. And surely you can imagine what it would be like for this qualitative feature to vary with some degree of independence from the tendency to think that one is seeing a dagger. It might remain relatively constant, for example, while Macbeth's strong tendency to think that he is seeing a real dagger decreases toward the end of his soliloquy to a very slight tendency indeed. It is only when 'I see a dagger' is used to describe this non-judgmental feature of Macbeth's experience that it is used to describe sense experience.

This kind of appeal to the 'qualitative similarity' of

corresponding pairs of normal and abnormal perceptual experiences is discussed by Austin at some length in Chapter V, but nothing he says there tends to discredit such an appeal when it is used solely as a way of identifying sense experience. The fact that delusory perceptual experiences are relatively rare, and are in most cases 'qualitatively' quite different from normal experiences (pp. 48–9), is of course no objection to an ostensive definition that asks us to consider a case like Macbeth's as we *imagine* it to be. And since Austin says, 'I do not, of course, wish to deny that there may be cases in which "delusive and veridical experiences" really are "qualitatively indistinguishable" ' (p. 52), he clearly does not intend to deny that such cases are imaginable. For the most part he is trying to show that from such qualitative similarity we cannot *infer* that what we see in a hallucination is something of the same kind that we see in normal perception. ('For why on earth should it *not* be the case that, in some few instances, perceiving one sort of thing is exactly like perceiving another?' [p. 52]) But this would all be irrelevant to the argument from illusion if that argument were free from ambiguity in the various respects we have just discussed. For then it would be clear that when 'see' is being used as a pointer word in the argument from illusion, it is not intended to imply the existence of something that has to be *inferred* from the qualitative similarity of a normal and an abnormal perception. It is intended, on the contrary, in the special use illustrated by the statement 'I see a dagger but . . .,' to draw attention to one of the respects (the sensory, as contrasted with the judgmental, respect) in which a normal and an abnormal perception sometimes *are* qualitatively similar. The Cartesian would argue, indeed, that it is impossible for anyone to decide whether or not delusive and veridical experiences are sometimes exactly similar without deciding whether they are sometimes similar in this sensory respect. If the two perceptual experiences are not qualitatively similar in this respect, then they are surely not among the instances, to repeat Austin's words, in which 'perceiving one sort of thing is exactly like perceiving another'.

The rest of Austin's objections to the argument from illusion are directed against certain ways of supplementing the ostensive definition as we have so far construed it. Thus in order to help identify the use of 'see' in which Macbeth might consistently say 'I see a dagger but I do not know whether I am seeing a real dagger or having a hallucination', philosophers in the Cartesian tradition have said, in one way or another, that in this use of 'see' Macbeth's statement does not entail the existence of *something seen*. To this Austin objects that there is no such use of 'see'. He maintains that in the case of ghosts, for example, 'if I say that cousin Josephine saw a ghost . . . there was, in *some* sense, this ghost that Josephine saw' (p. 95); and he would maintain, I suppose, that if Macbeth were to describe his abnormal experience by asserting 'I see a dagger', this statement would be true only if Macbeth sees a hallucinatory dagger.

This raises an interesting question. If the Cartesian maintains that Macbeth can say 'I see a dagger' *merely* as a way of describing his sense experience, does he intend to deny that Macbeth's statement entails the *disjunction*: 'Either I am seeing a real object or I am having a hallucination'? To answer this question it would be necessary to define 'real object' and 'hallucination' with more precision than anyone has yet done it. For the purposes of his ostensive definition, however, it does not seem difficult for the Cartesian to avoid this question by adapting his argument to the Austinian premise. The point that is important to the Cartesian is just that in an appropriate context Macbeth can correctly say 'I see a dagger' although his statement does not entail (1) that there exists a real dagger, nor, alternatively, (2) that there exists a hallucinatory dagger. It is this particular neutrality that is important, for this is the neutrality that is supposed to allow Macbeth to say, without inconsistency: 'I see a dagger but I do not know whether I am seeing a real dagger or having a hallucination.' The Cartesian can grant, at least for the sake of the argument, that to see is always to see *something*. If he wants to defend certain forms of the sense-datum terminology he will no doubt grant this with alacrity. But if there is no use of 'see' that is neutral in the one particular respect demanded by his ostensive definition, then he had better give up Form A of the argument from illusion in favour of some other form.

Philosophers using Form A of the argument from illusion have also tried to distinguish this neutral use of 'see' from some other uses by telling us that in this use of 'see' it is not possible for what is said to be seen to look or seem different from what it is. With respect to this distinction, also, Austin's objections reveal possible sources of confusion. His discussion, for example, of Ayer's case of the man who looks at a star and says that he sees a silvery speck no bigger than a sixpence, shows that the 'speck' is most naturally thought of as something observable from different places, something which will look different to people wearing glasses of different colours, and so forth, and which is therefore not an example that helps to illustrate the Cartesian's special sense of 'see'. I think, however, that Austin himself suggests a way of clarifying the very point that the Cartesian wants to make concerning this special sense of 'see'. Contrasting the speck and the star, Austin asks: 'Can the question whether the speck really *is* no bigger than a sixpence, or whether it just *seems* to be no bigger than a sixpence, be seriously raised? What difference could there be between the supposed alternatives?' (pp. 95–6). The Cartesian can ask a corresponding question with respect to the statement 'I see a dagger but I do not know whether I am seeing a real dagger or having a hallucination'. He might ask: 'Can the question be seriously raised whether the dagger that is said to be seen *is* bloody or whether it just *looks* bloody?' And the fact that there *could* be no difference between these supposed alternatives—the fact that the distinction between 'is' and 'looks' is not applicable—is exactly what I mean, the Cartesian could say, when I maintain that in this special sense of 'see' it is not *possible* for what is said to be seen to look different from what it is.

These brief comments on some of Austin's arguments may help to explain why I have said that *Sense and Sensibilia* does not undermine the Cartesian tradition by proving that there is no sensory constituent in perceptual experience. Nevertheless, Austin has uncovered so many possible sources of confusion in Form A of the argument from illusion that even philosophers who are convinced that they can tighten up the argument to meet Austin's criticism might well decide that this is not the easiest way to produce an effective ostensive definition of 'sense experience'. Form B is one of the most promising alternatives, for it does not presuppose an act-object analysis of sense experience and it is not touched by most of Austin's objections to Form A. But of course difficult questions can be raised about the meaning of the expression 'looks as if', and if Austin had devoted one or two of his lectures to an analysis of this expression, there might not seem to be any important reason for preferring Form B to the more traditional form of the argument from illusion.

'REAL'

Jonathan Bennett

PHILOSOPHERS have often sought criteria for a general distinction between appearance and reality. In chapter VII of *Sense and Sensibilia*, J. L. Austin claims to show that this enterprise is radically misconceived; and, characteristically, he bases his argument on the niceties of the use of 'real' in English. I shall try to show that Austin's account of how 'real' is used is unclear and inaccurate; and that the uses of 'real' which Austin explores are irrelevant to the traditional enquiry into the distinction between appearance and reality.

The second point matters more, but most of my paper will treat of the first. The uses of 'real' which interested Austin may have some philosophical importance, so we might as well get them right. Also, although there are general grounds for denying that those uses are relevant to traditional epistemology, a tighter and more Austinian argument for the same conclusion can be based upon a correct account of the uses of 'real' in question. I should concede that I may have stated my thesis a little too strongly: for all I know, some philosophers may have pursued the traditional enquiry in such a miserably inadequate way that Austin's points about the use of 'real' are, when suitably emended, effective against them.

The fact that Austin did not publish *Sense and Sensibilia* suggests that he was not satisfied with its contents. Nevertheless, his views about the use of 'real' have been published and may be believed: personal considerations cannot be allowed to disarm criticism.

I shall describe four ways of using 'real' in expressions of the form 'a real F', where 'F' stands for a general noun. Note the indefinite article: Austin writes as though nothing turns on the choice between 'a real . . .' and 'the real . . .', but this is not so.

I shall argue that these four ways of using 'real' are distinct, though a single use of 'real' may partake of more than one of them. I believe but cannot prove that my four headings cover practically all idiomatic uses of the form 'a real *F*', other than the metaphorical, slipshod or pretentious. I hope to show through my criticisms of Austin that mine is a good way—I do not say the right way—of classifying uses of 'a real *F*'.

I. THE APPROVING USE

Where *F*s are items to which we look for utility or enjoyment, we speak of an *F* which is insufficiently useful or enjoyable in the relevant way as 'a bad *F*'. In general, those features of an *F* which make it a bad *F* will also serve, if present in high enough degree or great enough quantity, to disqualify a thing from being an *F* at all. This fact is exploited when, in order to spice our denigration of something which we classify as literally 'an *F*', we say that it is 'not a real *F*', 'not really an *F*', 'not what I call an *F*', 'not my idea of an *F*' and the like, often with the words '. . . at all' added. Dramatized denigrations may take the form not of joking denials but rather of joking counter-descriptions, as in 'You call that steak? I call it leather!', which may well be said of something which the speaker would soberly classify as steak. The approving use of 'real' works against the background of this sort of denigration. 'Now this is real coffee!', said as praise, involves an unspoken rider like 'Not that hogwash that passes for coffee in the canteen'. If someone, surveying my study, said admiringly 'That's a *real* desk!', one would naturally assume that he had encountered many desks which he had thought to merit abuse in such terms as 'That's not what I call a desk' or 'That's not a desk, it's a see-saw'. It would be surprising if he said of my telephone 'Now that's a *real* telephone!', for few telephones are so bad as to merit, in the average person's judgement, the kind of denigration in question. Of course the speaker might for special reasons find it difficult to use any telephone whose dial is not of a certain rare sort; and in that case, seeing that my telephone has a dial of that sort, he might well say 'Now that's a *real* telephone!' With the praise, as with the denigration, 'real' and 'really' may occur but they need not. Similar work is done by such expressions as 'Now *that's* what I call a *desk*!' To summarize: in type (1) uses of 'real', good *F*s are called real *F*s because, in the speaker's opinion, many Fs are such bad Fs as to deserve to be characterized in terms which, taken literally, imply that they are not Fs at all.

2. THE STRESSED CLASSIFICATION USE

Someone may say 'This is a real chop suey', using the word 'real' not because he has been served with too many bad chop sueys but because he thinks that much of what passes for chop suey is, literally, not chop suey at all. There may be general ignorance about the stuff which is wrongly taken to be chop suey: if housewives knew what went into those tins, they would realize that it just is not chop suey. Or the trouble may be that many people do not know what a dish has to have in it to be counted as chop suey by the gourmets, or the experts, or the Chinese. This falls within a notable sub-class of type (2) cases, namely those in which someone uses the form 'a real F' because the word for which 'F' stands is, in his opinion, too often not used in its true or proper or best sense: 'Stevenson's second campaign was a real tragedy' may be said by one who uses 'real' because he knows that any mishap will be called a tragedy by many people, and who wishes to stress his preference for restricting 'tragedy' to calamities which have a certain kind of grandeur. Stressed classifications do not always use 'real': grammar may demand 'really'; and there are also more specialized expressions such as 'literally an F', 'an F, and I choose my words with care', 'an F in the good old sense', 'a genuine F', 'strictly an F', 'an authentic F', and the like. To summarize: in type (2) uses of 'real', Fs are called real Fs because, in the speaker's opinion, things which are not in fact Fs are often mistakenly classified as Fs because people do not know the facts about them or because they do not attach to the revelant word its best, or right, or strict, or old, or dictionary, or technical, sense.

(1) and (2) are distinct: I use 'a real F' (1) approvingly because there are many Fs which I am prepared to characterize jokingly as non-Fs; I use it (2) in stressed classifications because I think that non-Fs are often wrongly described as Fs. A restaurant which announces 'Waffles with Real Maple Syrup' is probably (2) stressing a classification, and implying that its competitors pass off as maple syrup something which is not maple syrup at all. On the other hand, the television advertisement in which someone sips

coffee and says 'Man, oh man, that's *real* coffee!' is probably making a (1) approving use of 'real', and implying that rival brands of coffee are, although undeniably coffee, very bad coffee indeed. The law takes note of this distinction.

A rare use of 'real' might hover between (1) approval and (2) stressed classification. Someone may be given to saying of certain things that they are 'not real *F*s' or 'not *F*s at all' or 'not my idea of *F*s', and be unsure how far he intends this literally and how far as joking denigration: 'I suppose this slop is whisky, but there ought to be a law against calling stuff "Whisky" when it has so little kick.' For a clear intersection of the two we should need a case where someone says, for example, 'This is a real chop suey!', using 'real' because of the prevalence of (1) bad chop sueys, and (2) fake chop sueys.

3. THE INTENSIFYING USE

Where being an *F* is in some clear way a matter of degree, admitting of more and less, one may say 'a real *F*' meaning 'very much of an *F*'. Thus one may declare a state of affairs to be 'a real shame', a person to be 'a real swine', or a birthday party to be 'a real shambles'. In the same way 'really' can have the force of 'very', as in 'a really ugly waistcoat'. This type of use, unlike (1) approvals and (2) stressed classifications, need not involve any background of beliefs about or attitudes to other things which are, or are often called, *F*s.

Type (3) uses may, rather boringly, intersect with (1) or (2): the latter depend upon what a thing has to be like to count as an *F*, or as a good *F*, and this is sometimes a matter of degree. An action may be described as 'a real help' with the force of 'very much of a help' or 'a big help' (3), with the added suggestion that would-be helpers all too often describe as 'a help' what is in fact no help at all (2). Cases could also be contrived in which (3) intersects with (1). Mostly, though, the (3) intensifying use of 'real' occurs without any of the associations which define (1) and (2).

On p. 73 Austin presents the (1) approving-use example 'Now this is a *real* carving-knife!', and observes that this may be a way of saying that it is a good carving-knife. In a footnote he calls attention to 'I gave him a real hiding', which would normally be a (3) intensifying use, and notes that one might instead say 'I gave him a good hiding'. In (1) approvals, of course, 'good' is always a fair substitute for 'real'. In (3) intensifications, this is not so: 'a good hiding' is all right, but not 'a good shambles'; so it seems that there is something to be learned here, not about 'real' but about 'good'. One's understanding of the facts, however, is not enlarged by Austin's handling of the two cases. Presumably taking the carving-knife case as one in which 'real' has the force of 'good', and the hiding case as one in which 'good' has the force of 'real', he speaks of the latter as 'the converse' of the former!

4. THE ELLIPSIS-EXCLUDING USE

This is the use of 'real' from which Austin draws most of his examples, and which mainly explains his description of 'real' as 'what we may call a *trouser-word*' (p. 70).

In the type (4) or ellipsis-excluding use of 'real', a statement containing 'a real *F*' has the same truth-conditions if the word 'real' is dropped from it. The criteria for a thing's counting as 'a real dog', where 'real' has a type (4) use, are just those which it must satisfy in order to count as a dog. If something is a real dog then it is not a gasometer, a rose-bush, a stuffed dog, a model dog, a toy dog, a dream dog, a picture of a dog, an ice-cream dog: its being a real dog excludes its being any kind of non-dog and excludes nothing else. It follows that in the type (4) or ellipsis-excluding use of 'real', real *F*s are not *F*s of a certain kind: in this respect (4) ellipsis-exclusion is like (2) stressed classification, and unlike (1) approval and (3) intensification. I have, in effect, already answered the question 'If "real" in its (2) stressed-classification use does not serve to mark off *F*s of a certain kind from *F*s of other kinds, what work does it do?' I shall now answer the analogous question for (4) the ellipsis-excluding use of 'real', and in answering it I shall explain what this use is.

For good reasons, we have phrases of the form 'a . . . dog', with an adjective in the blank, which are properly and literally applied to things which are not dogs; and similarly with many other general nouns beside 'dog'. This fact gives rise to a certain kind of ellipsis, in which 'It is a dog' is properly though elliptically said of an object which is not a dog: of a stuffed dog, when there is no question about its status as a taxidermal product but there is one about what sort of animal it is whose skin has been stuffed to produce the object in question; or of a piece of marble, when there is no question about its being a piece of marble but there is one about what it is supposed to represent. The exchange: 'Is that a dog or a wolf ?'—'It is a dog'—can properly occur where 'it' refers to something which is known not to be a dog. For the exchange may be elliptic for: 'Is that a marble dog or a marble wolf?'—'It is a marble dog.'

Such ellipses do not require that the object be literally describable by a phrase of the form 'a . . . F' with an *adjective* in the blank. One may properly say 'That is a dog' of a picture of a dog, if it is known to be a picture and there is a question only about what it depicts. Similarly with a statue of a dog. We might insist upon the adjectival form and speak of 'a pictorial dog' and 'a marble (iron, etc.) dog'; but the former is forced, and the latter is not available if the statue is made of a mixture of many materials. Again, my phrase 'a dream dog' is a stilted substitute for the non-adjectival 'a dog in a dream'; but dreams are nevertheless relevant to these ellipses, for one may in reporting a dream properly say 'It was an F' of what was not an F. Speaking to someone familiar with my recurring dream, I can properly say 'Last night it was a dog which chased me, not a wolf'.

I guess that such ellipses are always connected with something's being taken to be an F, made to represent an F, or the like; but I am not sure of this.

When one says something of the form 'It is an F', there may be uncertainty about whether one is (*a*) asserting of something that it is a non-F of a kind which can properly though elliptically be spoken of as 'an F' or (*b*) asserting of something that it is an F. It is the task of 'real', in its (4) ellipsis-excluding use, to prevent such uncertainties from arising. The following example is stylized for the sake of brevity and clarity, but it epitomizes the (4) ellipsis-excluding work of 'real'. Someone seeing my dog lying on the floor says 'Is that a . . .?', and tails off with an interrogative gesture. He can see that it is either a dog or a stuffed dog, and is wondering which. If I say 'It is a dog', I may not answer the question he has in mind: for my words can properly be used (*a*) of a stuffed dog, when its taxidermal status is not in question, or (*b*) of a dog; and the questioner may not know in which way to take what I say. I may, for all he knows, think that he is wondering 'Is it a stuffed dog or a stuffed cat?', in which case my answer falls under (*a*); but I may think that he is wondering 'Is it a dog or a stuffed dog?', in which case my answer may fall under (*b*). Now, the question he *does* have in mind is '. . . a dog or a stuffed dog?'; and if he takes my answer according to (*a*) his question is answered in one way, if according to (*b*) it is answered in the other. The words 'It is a dog' thus do not answer his question. But the answer 'It is a real dog' says that it is a dog, and excludes not only its being a cat but also its being a stuffed dog.

What gives point to a (4) ellipsis-excluding indicative use of 'real' is the likelihood that one's hearers might otherwise take one to be using an 'F' as a proper but elliptic way of referring to a non-F. Speaking to a friend who knows of my nightmares, I may report an encounter with a burglar in the words 'I was badly scared last night by a big ugly brute of a man—a *real* man'. But if in reporting a cocktail-party I say 'There was a big ugly brute of a man there', there will normally be no point in adding '—a *real* man', unless I am using 'real' (1) approvingly or perhaps (3) intensifyingly. If I am speaking of a real F I can of course show that this is so, that no ellipsis is involved, without using the word 'real'; for I can say things about it which it would be absurd to say about the relevant kind of non-F. It occurs to you that when I speak of 'the break-up of their marriage' I may be referring not to a marriage but to a marriage in a book; you are about to ask 'A real marriage or a fictional one?', when I say '. . . and they gave me custody of the children'.

The (4) ellipsis-excluding use is obviously distinct from (3) the intensifying use and, less obviously but just as thoroughly, distinct from the (1) approving and (2) stressed-classification uses. In (4) ellipsis-exclusions there is usually no background of jokingly exaggerated denials or counter-descriptions, or of frequent misapplications of an expression. (Austin blurs the distinction between (4) ellipsis-exclusion and (2) stressed-classification by bracketing 'decoy ducks' with 'paste diamonds' (p. 67). One might indeed use 'a real diamond' because the simple 'a diamond' could be taken as an elliptic reference to a paste diamond; but 'a real diamond' may also be used because of the frequency not of elliptic but of mistaken references to paste diamonds as 'diamonds'.) Here again, however, an individual case may involve both (4) ellipsis-exclusion and either (1) approval or (2) stressed classification. For example, I announce that I have visited some people who own 'a real Corot', using the word 'real' for two reasons: (*a*) I think that the simple 'a Corot' may be taken by my hearers as an ellipsis for 'a reproduction of a Corot', and (*b*) I wish to stress that my classification of the picture as a Corot is made in the full realization that many pictures which pass for Corots are fakes. The former reason makes my use of 'real' a (4) ellipsis-excluding one, while the latter makes it a (2) stressed-classification one. A combination of (4) ellipsis-exclusion and (1) approval in a single use of 'a real *F*' would involve my calling something 'a real Corot' in order to convey (*a*) that it is not a reproduction, and (*b*) that it is a very good Corot, unlike those daubs, those 'so called Corots' as I like to call them, of which Corot unfortunately painted so many. A single use of 'real' is unlikely to get this double message across; though this might be achieved, archly, by 'That's a real Corot; and, my word! *isn't* it a *real* Corot?'

DEFECTS IN AUSTIN'S ACCOUNT

I have made some minor complaints against Austin's treatment of 'real', and could make more; but I shall here pick out six of the larger mistakes in what he says.

(*a*) On p. 67 Austin says: 'That may not be a real duck because it is a decoy, or a toy duck, or a species of goose closely resembling a duck, or because I am having a hallucination.' It is true that a goose, like a sparrow or a lamp-stand, is not a real duck; but Austin is talking about ordinary uses of 'a real duck', and something false about these uses is implied by his inclusion of 'a species of goose . . .' in his list. The other items in the list suggest (4) ellipsis-excluding uses of 'real', but I know of no kind of goose of which one can properly though elliptically say 'It is a duck'. Nor can I connect geese with 'not a real duck' in any of the other three uses of 'real'. Perhaps my classification omits something which Austin noticed, but I doubt this. I have not yet found anyone who thinks it natural to report the discovery that something which looked like a duck was after all a goose in the words 'It is not a real duck'. Many think they might say 'It is not really a duck'. Perhaps Austin assumed that there are no noteworthy differences between 'real' and 'really'. If so, he erred.

We have here a hint that Austin thought that 'real' may come into play wherever a distinction is to be made between an *F* and a non-F which is very like an F. This assumption is false, but one can see how it might be thought true for (2) stressed classifications: non-Fs which people wrongly call Fs, through factual ignorance or linguistic malpractice, may be expected to be rather like Fs. Similarly with (4) ellipsis-exclusions: non-Fs which can properly though elliptically be referred to as Fs do in general resemble Fs, perhaps because these ellipses always concerns non-Fs which in some way represent Fs. Thus, similarities do have something to do with type (2) and (4) uses of 'real'; but it is not true that similarity as such is what brings 'real' into play in these cases.

(b) On p. 69 Austin says: 'The question "Real or not?" does not always come up, can't always be raised. We *do* raise this question only when, to speak rather roughly, suspicion assails us—in some way or other things may not be what they seem . . . .' The qualification 'to speak rather roughly' must not disarm criticism here.

Austin seems to have overlooked the difference between what makes 'Real or not?' appropriate and what makes 'real' appropriate. In fact, the interrogative does not sit happily with (1) approving or (3) intensifying uses, and one presumes that in speaking of 'suspicion' Austin did not have these cases in mind.

What he says is more or less true of uses of 'real' in (2) stressed classification, for these concern prevalent mistakes. You tell me of the chop suey you had for supper, and I ask 'Was it real chop suey?' because I know that the contents of tins labelled 'Chop Suey' are often *not what they seem*. Again, I say 'That jazz is awful', and then I wonder 'Is it real jazz?': *suspicion has assailed me* because I recall being told that most people don't know what jazz is. In these cases, then, the notion of 'suspicion [that] things may not be what they seem' can be introduced without too much strain.

In (4) ellipsis-exclusions, however, from which Austin draws so many of his examples, there is usually nothing remotely like a suspicion that things may not be what they seem. Someone comes in when I am in the middle of boasting about 'the dog I bought yesterday', and asks 'A real dog?' He may not be voicing a suspicion but merely asking for detail. My words do not make it 'seem' to him that I have bought a real dog: he realizes that I may be using 'dog' in either of two ways; and until he knows which way I am using the word he knows only that I have made a satisfactory purchase of a dog, or of a statue of a dog or a painting of

275

a dog or . . . something else for which 'a dog' is a proper ellipsis. His question 'Was it a real dog that you bought?' no more voices a 'suspicion [that] things may not be what they seem' than does any other request for specification, e.g. when I tell someone of my new car and he asks 'Is it a convertible?'

I have taken a case in which a thing is spoken of in its absence; and it may be thought that this is why I have been able to suppress the notion of things not being what they seem. We need the antithesis between real dogs and statues of dogs—it may be said—only because statues of dogs do very often seem like real dogs. Taken in the relevant way, this is false: statues of dogs hardly ever seem like real dogs in such a way as to engender 'suspicions'; and even if they did, and pictures of dogs did seem like real dogs, etc., such resemblances are not *the point* of (4) ellipsis-excluding uses of 'real'. Furthermore, if we must restrict ourselves to what is said about things with which both speaker and hearer are confronted, we are in danger of having to say that all our simple descriptive talk reflects suspicions that things may not be what they seem. When I ask 'Is it red or not?' of something which is under my eyes, must I be voicing such suspicion? There are as good grounds for answering 'Yes' to this as to the analogous question about the case where I ask, of something which is under my eyes, 'Is it a real dog or not?'

Thus, Austin offers as true of all uses of '. . . real . . .?' a thesis which is false of, at a guess, about half of them. It is true of a somewhat higher proportion of uses of '. . . really . . .?', but that is another matter.

(*c*) On pp. 71–2 Austin says that 'real' belongs to, and 'has the same function as', a group of words including 'proper', 'genuine', 'live' and 'natural'. Because 'real' is supposed to be the most general and comprehensive member of this group of words, Austin calls it a 'dimension-word'; but I suggest that the facts about 'real' are seriously obscured by throwing it in with this rag-bag collection in the first place, and that Austin would have discovered this if he had tried to say what the function is which all these words are supposed to have. Austin's examples so far have all been (2) stressed classifications or (4) ellipsis-exclusions; and 'a real F' in those uses does not mark off Fs of a kind from Fs of other kinds, but marks off Fs from things which are not literally Fs at all. Some of the other words which Austin lists as having the same function

276

as 'real'—as belonging to the 'dimension' of 'real'?—do not have this property. A makeshift theatre may be a theatre, and so a proper theatre may be a kind of theatre; a synthetic fibre is a fibre, and so a natural fibre is a kind of fibre. 'A real F' does in some of its uses marks off Fs of a kind from other Fs, notably in type (1); and it is true that Austin here calls attention to the type (1) example 'Now this is a *real* carving-knife!' But he gives the reader no help in finding his bearings, presents none of the necessary contrasts and comparisons. On the contrary: having called 'real' a dimension-word and noted that 'good' is a dimension-word too because it is the most general and comprehensive term of commendation, Austin tells us: 'It is a curious point, of which Idealist philosophers used to make much at one time, that "real" itself, in certain uses, may belong to this family', i.e. to the group of words of which 'good' is the most general. Another aspect of this unfortunate passage has been discussed on pp. 270–1 above.

Some of the antonyms of 'real' in its (4) ellipsis-excluding uses can also mark off Fs of a kind from other Fs: a stuffed elephant is not an elephant, but a stuffed leg of lamb is a leg of lamb; a plastic rose is not a rose, but a plastic plate is a plate. But this does not restore the analogy between 'real'/'stuffed' or 'real'/'plastic' on the one hand and 'natural'/'synthetic' or 'proper'/'makeshift' on the other. The phrase 'synthetic fibre' *both* marks off fibre of a kind from other fibre *and* is antithetical to 'natural fibre'; whereas there is no adjective G such that 'a $G\ F$' *both* marks off an F of a kind from other Fs *and* is antithetical to 'a real F' in its ellipsis-excluding use. We do not deny that a plate is plastic, or a leg of lamb stuffed, by calling them real. This points to further complexities which are masked by Austin's account. For example, consider whether 'real teeth' is antithetical to 'false teeth' from the point of view of (*a*) ordinary people, (*b*) a dental anatomist in his professional capacity.

(*d*) On p. 70 Austin says: 'I don't know *just* how to take the assertion that it's a real duck unless I know *just* what, on that particular occasion, the speaker has it in mind to exclude.' Certainly, unless I know something of what the speaker has it in mind to exclude I do not know whether to take his use of 'a real duck' as type (1), (2), (3) or (4); but this cannot be the sort of point Austin wanted to make, for in that same sentence he says: ' "A real duck" differs from the simple "a duck" only in that it is used to exclude various ways of not being a real duck—but a dummy, a toy, a picture, a decoy, etc.' This is circular, but its general effect is to put (1) approvals and (3) intensifications out of consideration.

Let us see, then, what happens when Austin's 'I don't know just how to take . . . etc.' is applied to (2) stressed classifications and (4) ellipsis-exclusions. If someone says 'It is a real duck', I take him to be saying that the thing is a duck, i.e. merits the label 'duck' used non-elliptically and used in its proper or strict sense. Also, because he has used the word 'real', I take it that he has it in mind to exclude one or more of the special ways in which a thing can be a non-duck and yet commonly though wrongly (2), or properly though elliptically (4), be referred to as 'a duck'. If I do not know just how to take his assertion unless I know just which of these special ways of being a non-duck he 'has it in mind to exclude', then no one knows 'just how to take' anything said by someone else. Perhaps no one does; but Austin implies that he has here a contrast between what is said with 'real' and some things which are said without it.

(*e*) Echoing the remark last discussed, Austin says on p. 76: 'It should be quite clear . . . that there are no criteria to be laid down in general for distinguishing the real from the not real. How this is to be done must depend on *what* it is with respect to which the problem arises in particular cases.' The words 'criteria . . . for distinguishing' show that (1) approvals and (3) intensifications are not in question here; and in respect of (2) stressed classifications and (4) ellipsis-exclusions the quoted statement is false. The criteria for whether something is a real *F*, with a type-(2) or type-(4) use of 'real', are identical with the criteria for whether something is an *F*. The variousness of the circumstances in which there may be a *point* in using 'real' either (2) to stress a classification or (4) to exclude an ellipsis need not be matched by a variousness in the criteria which determine whether a statement using 'real' is *true*. The distinction between the pointfulness of using a word and the truth of what is said with it may sometimes be a delicate one; but here, where it is straightforward enough, Austin writes as though it did not exist.

Austin rightly says that no general criteria can be laid down for distinguishing the real from the not real because there are as many sets of criteria for 'a real *F*' as there are values of *F*, i.e. because 'real' is 'substantive-hungry'. But he insists that this is not his whole point, and that the criteria proliferate even for a single value of F.

(f) On pp. 73-5 Austin deploys his claim that 'real' is an adjuster-word, i.e. one which helps us to cope with borderline cases.

Consider the following sentences:

   (i) 'It is not a real pig, but is like a pig'

   (ii) 'It is not a pig, but is like a pig'.

If we encounter a new kind of animal which we do not want to call a pig but which is very like a pig, the word 'real' is useful, says Austin, because 'if I can say "Not a real pig, but like a pig", I don't have to tamper with the meaning of "pig" itself' (p. 75). In this, however, 'real' is idle: Austin has picked on (i) where (ii) would do just as well. All the work of adjusting, in short, is done here by 'like'. While conceding that 'like' is *the* great adjuster-word', Austin thinks that 'real' may do some of the adjustment even in the presence of 'like'. He adduces no evidence for this, and of his one example it is clearly false.

Austin sees this difficulty, and on p. 76 he asks: 'Why then do we need "real" as an adjuster-word as well as "like"?', and he follows this with another question which he wrongly takes to raise the same issues: 'Why exactly do we want to say, sometimes "It is like a pig", sometimes "It is not a real pig"?' Austin offers no solutions, but the answer to his second question is a straightforward one which has nothing to do with adjuster-words: the cases where it is proper to say 'It is like a pig' have only a tiny overlap with those where it is proper to say 'It is not a real pig', because it is not the task of 'a real F' to mark off Fs from other things which are like Fs. I remarked under (a) above that many uses of 'a real F' have something to do with resemblances between Fs and certain other things; but resemblances as such are not what give point to these uses of 'a real F'; and *close* resemblances—such as there must be in borderline cases requiring 'adjustments'—hardly come into the story at all except in one sub-class of (2) stressed classifications. Thus, it is only because of his earlier confusions about resemblances that Austin takes his second question to be difficult, and to be relevant to the alleged adjusting function of 'real'. He has, indeed, unwittingly given a case in which we should in fact say 'like a . . .' but should not say 'not a real . . .', namely that of the goose which is very like a duck.

I am not convinced that 'real' ever works as an adjuster-word in the way Austin says it does, even in the absence of 'like'. Whether or not we use 'like', our decision to describe the border-line case as 'not a real pig' is a decision about how the creature relates to the borderline, specifically, a decision that it is not a pig. Austin gives 'real' a semblance of utility by presenting a case in which our first reaction to the creature is that 'we don't want positively to say that it *is* a pig, or that it is *not*' and then, a little later, 'we may proceed with the remark "But it isn't a real pig" '. This shows only that it may take time for us to make up our minds. To present 'real' as an adjuster-word one needs a case in which we should deny that the animal is a real pig *while* refusing to deny that it is a pig. I doubt whether such a case could be found.

THE QUESTION OF RELEVANCE

What has all this to do with the old questions about appearance and reality? Almost nothing. The one result which may look relevant is that sets of criteria for 'a real F' are as numerous as the values of F. Even if I was right, in (*e*) of the preceding section, in disallowing Austin's attempt to inflate it, this point might still be thought to show the absurdity of seeking a general distinction between appearance and reality. But do those who pursue this distinction hope for a handful of rules which will tell us how to distinguish Fs from non-Fs for any F?

The epistemological tradition which Austin opposed is concerned above all with the distinction between something's seeming to one (going by what one can see, feel, hear, etc.) to be the case and its really being the case. Descartes' *Meditations*, the great issue between Locke and Berkeley, Hume's section 'Of Scepticism with regard to the Senses', Kant's theory of objectivity concepts, phenomenalism, Wittgenstein's arguments about private languages—this, with all its faults, is the great tradition of modern epistemology, and it has an identifiable and roughly statable theme. If we must tie that theme to an English word, then the word is 'really'.

Now, 'really', unlike 'real', is not substantive-hungry. 'Really' may be satisfied by an article-plus-substantive, or by an adjective, adverb, verb, preposition, phrase or sentence. The great epistemologists have, in effect, been concerned with 'really' as a sentence-qualifier; but they have not sought detailed rules for determining, of anything which seems (going by what one can see, feel, etc.) to be the case, whether it really is the case. They have enquired into what sort of thing we do when we ask and answer questions about what really is the case: what kinds of procedure we use, how these relate to one another, what their logical status is, and what light all this throws on situations where we do not ask, and perhaps should find it ludicrous to ask, whether what seems to be the case really is the case. In short, they have sought high-level generalizations to cover extremely complex data.

It may be that such a general enquiry cannot succeed: that there are no fairly watertight generalizations to be found at this level. No one, however, has begun to show that this is so.

Again, it may be that the odds are against the success of a philosophical enquiry in which linguistic minutiae are neglected. I think that Austin had begun to show this of some of the general enquiries which philosophers undertake. On the other hand, it is mere dogmatism to say that unless the detailed work is done the results are bound to be wrong: a detailed dissection of a class of uses of a word may show only that the whole class is irrelevant to the general enquiry in whose statement the word occurs; and such irrelevance may sometimes be obvious from the outset. It is, for example, moderately obvious that the uses of 'a real F' differ from most uses of 'really' in such ways that someone interested in the latter can fairly safely ignore the niceties of the former. In taking something as obvious one risks being wrong; but the reduction of this risk may be bought at too high a price. Someone who cannily suspends judgement on all the larger issues until he has probed every possibly relevant detail may well fail to discover anything worth knowing. In philosophy, as in science, we need to carry *into* our investigations something in the nature of a hunch, a hypothesis, a general question, if we are to solve problems and not merely amass impeccably random data.

Also, relevance is a dyadic relation: a judgement of relevance requires a grasp of both the related terms. In order to show that philosophers are neglecting data relevant to their concerns, one needs to understand what their concerns are; and such understanding requires some measure of intellectual sympathy with modes of thought whose largeness one may find distasteful.

In the light of this, consider the structure of Austin's discussion.

On p. 65 he embarks on 'a preliminary, no doubt haphazard, survey of some of the complexities in the use of "real" '. He proceeds to two pages on 'the real colour of' and 'the real taste of', in which he displays familiar difficulties which led earlier philosophers to draw the useful distinction between primary and secondary qualities. Austin then moves to a problem about 'the real shape of'. This is of an entirely different kind from the others, as indeed it had to be; but there is no hint from Austin that he has moved across an important distinction between two sorts of qualities. His problem about shape concerns the real shape of a cat: how do we name this shape? how snugly does it fit the cat's outline? does it change as the cat moves? Austin remarks that we can name some shapes which are not the real shape of the cat—e.g. it is not cylindrical—and comments on the desperateness of trying to specify the cat's real shape by elimination. Now, cats do have shapes; and one's readiness to say this is not weakened by Austin's awkward questions. Did he, then, think that when we speak of 'the real shape of the cat' we are committed to a precision and explicitness from which the omission of 'real' would excuse us? Austin does not say, and the bland casualness of his discussion precludes even a guess.

What comes next is more alarming still. Having displayed 'some of the complexities in the use of "real" ' in connexion with 'the real colour, taste, shape of', Austin says (p. 67): 'Contrast this with cases in which we *do* know how to proceed: "Are those real diamonds?", "Is that a real duck?" ' He makes some brief debating points about these, offers to mention 'under four headings some of the salient features of the word "real" ', and launches into the material which I have criticized in my preceding section. He does not acknowledge that the shift has been not just from hard to easy cases but also from 'the real colour of', etc. to phrases of the form 'a real *F*'. Yet each of his four 'salient features' depends upon this shift: what he says about 'a real *F*' is largely false, but as applied to 'the real colour of', etc. it is not even intelligible. In one whose main polemical weapon was the demand for rigour and precision, these facile transitions are astonishing.

Here, incomprehension of what the epistemological tradition is about goes with a massive neglect of required distinctions: no lines are drawn between 'the real' and 'a real', between 'real' and 'really', between '. . . real . . .' and '. . . real . . .?' This conjunction of slipshod analysis with ignorance of what the opposition are up to is probably not a coincidence.

One hopes that Austin gave the death-blow to the sterile subtradition of handling epistemological problems in terms of bent sense-data, different senses of 'see', direct and indirect perception, and so on. The tragedy is that his keen eye for specific mistakes was not attended by an understanding of why, and in the attempted solution of what problems, the mistakes were made. Such an understanding might have saved him from his extraordinary unfairness to Ayer, Price and Warnock; and I think it would have been accompanied, whether as cause or as effect, by a more accurate account of the use of 'real'.

HAS AUSTIN REFUTED
SENSE-DATA?

A. J. Ayer

IN the series of lectures, entitled *Sense and Sensibilia*, which Mr. G. J. Warnock has reconstructed from J. L. Austin's manuscript notes, Austin makes a sharp and witty attack upon the theory of sense-data. The texts which he singles out for criticism are Professor H. H. Price's book on '*Perception*', Mr. Warnock's study of *Berkeley*, and most of all my own *Foundations of Empirical Knowledge*. Though he says that he chose these books for their merits rather than their deficiencies, he sets about my book especially in a rather scornful way. It may even be questioned whether he is always scrupulously fair. I am not, however, now concerned to vindicate the honour of my self of twenty-seven years ago. My reason for taking up the subject is that it is widely believed that the sense-datum theory succumbed to Austin's attack. The purpose of this essay is to see how far this belief is justified.

The best way to achieve this will be to examine Austin's arguments in detail. I make them just seventeen in number and shall go through them very nearly in the order in which they occur in the book. As might be expected, they vary a good deal in their depth, and there is a certain amount of overlap between them.

(1) Austin's first objection to the sense-datum theorist is that the contrast which he tries to draw between perceiving physical objects, like chairs and tables, on the one hand, and sensing sense-data, on the other, is a typical philosopher's over-simplification. The plain man does not speak in such a way as to imply that what he perceives is always something like furniture. He talks of seeing, or, in the appropriate instances, feeling or hearing or smelling, people, people's voices, rivers, mountains, flames, rainbows,

shadows, pictures on cinema screens, pictures in books, vapours, gases. Austin asks ironically whether all these are material things, the suggestion being that it is a mistake to lump them all under one heading.

He has a point here. Sense-datum theorists have tended to confine their examples 'to moderate sized specimens of dry goods', as Austin characteristically calls them, perhaps for the reason that they do constitute the largest single category of things that we take ourselves to perceive. And the result of this has been that in drawing a distinction between material things of this sort and sense-data, they have not sufficiently considered how such things as shadows and photographs fit into their scheme. For instance, they have sometimes fallen into the inconsistency of both treating sense-data as private objects and citing mirror-images as instances of them. Nevertheless, I hope to show that the tendency of sense-datum theorists to rely on a limited set of stock examples has not made any serious difference to the validity of their arguments.

(2) Austin goes on to take exception to my quoting Locke's dictum that 'the certainty of things existing *in rerum natura*, when we have the testimony of our senses for it, is not only as great as our frame can attain to, but as our condition needs'. He says that it contains a strong *suggestio falsi*, which is that there is *any* uncertainty about the existence, say, of a chair when it is a few yards in front of me and I am looking at it in broad daylight. The plain man would say, quite correctly: 'Well, if that is not seeing a real chair, I don't know what is.'

This argument goes much deeper; indeed it touches on the fundamental point at issue. The fact on which Austin is relying is that one would not ordinarily say that the existence of the chair was uncertain unless one had some *special* reason for supposing it to be so, such as that the light was very bad, or that one had something wrong with one's eyes, or that this would be a particularly odd place to find a chair, or whatever. But if one is going to say that the existence of the chair is uncertain even when the conditions under which one takes oneself to be perceiving it are normal in the sense that they give one no reason for suspecting anything to be amiss, then the distinction which we mark in this kind of context by contrasting what is certain with what is uncertain will cease to have any application.

This is true, so far as it goes. But if we consider the reasons which have led sense-datum theorists to speak of uncertainty in this connexion, we shall find that they remain untouched. The most that is proved against them is that they have chosen a misleading way of expressing the point that they were trying to make. As I see it, this point is a purely logical one. It is that in any such situation as that described by Austin the occurrence of the experience which gives rise to the perceptual judgement is logically consistent with the judgement's being false. Even if we have a use for the word 'certain' which makes it proper to say, in these circumstances, that it is certain that the chair exists, its existence is still not logically deducible from that of the experience: the certainty in question is not based on a logical entailment. Of course, if the situation is described as that of someone's looking at a chair, the question is begged: it is then already implied that in supposing that he sees a chair the observer is not mistaken. But the point on which the sense-datum theorist takes his stand is that the situation does not have to be described in this way; indeed, he will argue that to insist on describing it in this way is to hamper any attempt to arrive at a satisfactory analysis of perception. The kind of description which is needed for this purpose is one that will uncover rather than conceal the fact that the observer could be having the experience in question even though the physical object which he takes himself to be perceiving did not exist: that the occurrence of the experience is consistent with his having been hypnotized or otherwise deluded. So, when the sense-datum theorist says, no doubt misleadingly, that even in the most favourable conditions of perception it remains uncertain whether the chair exists, what he must be understood to mean is that the statement that the chair exists does not follow logically from any statement, or indeed from any finite number of statements, which are limited to describing the content of the observer's experience.

Admittedly, this way of speaking also begs the question. It commits us to holding not only that in making even so simple a judgement as that this is a chair one is going beyond the evidence which is yielded by the senses on this occasion, but that it is possible to formulate a statement which does not go beyond the evidence, in the sense that it carries no implication about the status of what is seen. A statement of this kind, which I propose to call an 'Experiential Statement', will simply record the presence, say, of a visual pattern. It will leave it entirely open whether the observer is right in treating this pattern as a manifestation of the kind of physical object which he claims to perceive, or indeed of a physical entity of any sort at all. These are the assumptions that lie at the root of the sense-datum theory, and it is only by showing them to be unwarranted that the theory can be cut off at its source.

(3) In fact, Austin makes very little attempt to do this. The only argument which he brings forward is that we do not normally speak of verifying statements about physical objects through verifying statements of any other kind. Taking as his example the statement 'That is a pig', he roundly denies that there are or have to be 'statements of the form, "It looks . . .", "It sounds . . .", "It smells . . .", of which we could say straight off that "That is a pig" entails them'.[1] 'We learn the word "pig", as we learn the vast majority of words for ordinary things, ostensively—by being told, in the presence of the animal, "*That* is a pig"; and thus, though certainly we learn what sort of thing it is to which the word "pig" can and can't be properly applied, we don't go through any kind of intermediate stage of relating the word "pig" to a lot of *statements* about the way things look, or sound, or smell. The word is just not introduced into our vocabulary in this way. Thus, though of course we come to have certain expectations as to what will and won't be the case when a pig is in the offing, it is wholly artificial to represent these expectations in the guise of *statements entailed by* "That is a pig". And for just this reason it is, at best, wholly artificial to speak as if *verifying* that some animal is a pig consists in checking up on the statements entailed by "That is a pig". If we do think of verification in this way, certainly difficulties abound; we don't know quite where to begin, how to go on, or where to stop. But what this shows is, not that "That is a pig" is very difficult to verify or incapable of being conclusively verified, but that this is an impossible travesty of verification. If the procedure of verification were rightly described in this way, then indeed we couldn't say just what would constitute conclusive verification that some animal was a pig. But this doesn't show that there is actually any difficulty at all, usually, in verifying that an animal is a pig, if we have occasion to do so; it shows only that what verification *is* has been completely misrepresented.'[2]

And there he leaves it. He does not tell us what he thinks that verification is, but presumably he takes it to consist in carrying out

[1] *Sense and Sensibilia*, p. 121.   [2] Ibid.

certain familiar procedures, inspecting the object in question in various ways. His main point is that in a case of this sort, as opposed, say, to the case in which we are testing a scientific theory, the process of verification does not involve our checking the truth of statements which are deduced from the statement which we are verifying. And it is on this ground apparently that he concludes that 'it is not true of sentences about "material things" that *as such* they must be supported by or based on evidence'.[1]

Now it is perfectly true that when it is a question of an object which we have no difficulty in identifying, like the pig in Austin's example, we do not normally go through the process of saying to ourselves: 'It looks so and so, it feels so and so, it has such and such a smell, therefore probably, almost certainly, it is a so and so.' We just take it straight off to be a pig, or whatever. It is true also that in a situation of this kind it would sound odd to ask someone what evidence he had that he saw a pig. We should say this only if we had some reason to distrust his identification. Not that it is always incorrect to speak of having evidence for propositions of this type. If I detected the pig by its footprints, I could be said to be going on evidence: perhaps also if I detected its presence only by its squeak or by its smell. For these are indications that a pig is, or has been, in the neighbourhood. But seeing a pig in perfectly normal conditions is more than merely having an indication of its presence. So Austin elsewhere rebukes Professor Wisdom for speaking of perceiving all the signs of bread when one goes to the larder, sees a loaf in front of one, handles it, tastes it, and so forth. When one sees only a few crumbs, one sees signs of a loaf, but not when one sees the loaf itself. The point here is that seeing signs of *x* is to some extent *contrasted* with seeing *x*. In any normal case in which I am seeing or handling a physical object, it is an abuse of language to say that I thereby obtain evidence of its existence, especially if the implication is that the evidence is not conclusive.

All this may be accepted, as a comment on ordinary usage. As a general rule, when one speaks of having evidence for a proposition *p*, one expects it to be understood that one is not entirely convinced of the truth of *p*, that one does not answer for its being more than probable. If I think that I know that *p*, I am underplaying my hand, and so misleading my audience, if I say no more than that I have good evidence for *p*. It would, however, be rash to lay any weight

[1] Op. cit., p. 123.

upon this in the present context, since my knowing that p is certainly not inconsistent with my having good evidence for it. On the contrary, in very many instances it would not be proper for me to claim to know that p unless I did have such evidence. It is just that I am taken to commit myself more strongly to the truth of p by straightforwardly asserting it than by asserting that there is good evidence for it, and our habit is not to make the weaker claim when we are in a position to make the stronger one. But it does not follow from this that when I know that p I have not got evidence for it, any more than from the fact that when I think I know something, it is misleading for me to say only that I believe it, it follows that if I do know something I do not believe it. Consequently Austin's example fails to prove his point. The fact that when one is looking at a pig, under normal conditions, it is not good usage to speak of having evidence for its existence, in no way entails that seeming to see the pig is not having evidence for its existence. The truth is that it is very strong evidence: and it does not cease to be evidence just because of its strength.

Against this it may be argued that to say that one has evidence for a proposition p is to imply that one's knowledge of p is indirect, in the sense that one is inferring p from some other proposition q which supports p but does not entail it. But surely my belief in the existence of the table in front of me is not the outcome of an inference. I may infer from its appearance that it is not a new table or that it is not an antique, but I do not have to infer that it exists. Since I see it and touch it no inference is needed.

This is the old argument about certainty, in a slightly different guise, and it is to be met with the same answer. Of course, it would be absurd to suggest that the perception of familiar objects normally involves any conscious process of inference. On the rare occasions on which we are unable to identify an object, whether because it is of a kind with which we are not familiar, or because the conditions under which we are perceiving it are unfavourable, we may try to work out what sort of thing it is, but even in this case we do not have to work out that it is, for example, a solid three-dimensional object. There might be situations where even this was in doubt, but the point is that they are exceptional. The rare cases in which our judgements of perception do contain an inference stand in contrast with the normal case in which they do not.

Again the answer is that this is true, but not to the purpose. For those who say that even the most straightforward judgement of perception like 'This is a table' embodies an inference are trying to make exactly the same logical point as are those who say that all such judgements are uncertain. In both instances the contention is that the judgement goes beyond the data on which it is grounded, that it claims more than is contained in the experience which gives rise to it, that it makes assumptions which may be false, consistently with this experience. The question whether these assumptions are made consciously or unconsciously, hesitantly or spontaneously, is irrelevant.

But is this contention valid? Is one entitled to speak of 'the content of an experience' as distinct from the judgement of perception to which it gives rise? Some purists may object to this 'philosophical' use of the word 'experience' altogether, and even if this is allowed to pass, and such expressions as 'visual experience' are admitted as technical terms, it may still be said that my present visual experience just is the experience of seeing a table. How then can this kind of resistance be overcome?

The best way that I can think of overcoming it is to draw attention to the far-reaching implications of even so unambitious a statement as that this is a table. To begin with, it commits us to all the assumptions which are involved in asserting the existence of any physical object of this type. It is required of the object at least that it shall occupy a position in three-dimensional space, that it shall endure throughout a period of time, that it shall be accessible to touch as well as to sight, that it shall be accessible to different observers, and that it should continue to exist even when no one is perceiving it. Not all these assumptions hold of every type of object. Shadows and images, for example, are accessible only to the sense of sight, and there is a sense in which they do not occupy space, although they are spatially located; but in their case also it is required that they be accessible to different observers, and that they be capable of existing unperceived.

Now one way of looking at these assumptions is to regard them as setting the framework in which the results of our observations are to be fitted. For example, in dealing with Berkeley's contention that things cannot exist unperceived, I believe that we should interpret him not as raising a question of empirical fact but rather as denying the legitimacy of a fundamental element in this framework and also as suggesting an alternative to it. I do not here propose to consider whether Berkeley's position is tenable, or what other framework there might be into which our observations could consistently be fitted. I only remark that this is a proper question for philosophical discussion and that it cannot be settled merely by a study of the ways in which we habitually speak.

There is, however, another way in which these common-sense assumptions may be taken. In particular instances, they can be construed empirically as implying that some particular object passes the tests which the general scheme imposes. If this is a material thing of the kind I take it to be it must be tangible as well as visible; in the appropriate circumstances it must be perceived by others besides myself; it must satisfy the causal criteria of persistence; for instance, if the room is left empty and I return in a few minutes' time to find that the supposed table has vanished or been displaced, there must be some way of accounting for this; some explanation which will fit in with our general theories about the ways in which such things can happen.

But do I see that all this is so? There is indeed a sense in which I can be said to see that this thing is tangible, public and persistent. Namely, it looks like a perfectly ordinary table, and ordinary tables do have these properties. But, in making this judgement, I am drawing on my considerable past experience. I have found out that when things look like this, they normally do satisfy these further conditions. But surely this is an inductive inference. One starts with certain visual clues, and on the basis of these clues, one leaps to one's far-reaching conclusions. But the conclusions are not contained in the clues. If I may speak of a visual presentation in an entirely neutral sense, which carries no implication about the status of what is presented, then the existence of this visual presentation leaves it open whether the further conditions, of the object's being tangible and so forth, will be satisfied. In the vast majority of cases they will be satisfied, but sometimes they are not. For instance, I might have been hypnotized to see a table here, when there really was not one, or it might be a trick of the light. But then, it will be said, it would not look like a perfectly ordinary table. I shall deal with this objection later on.

So far I have been speaking only of the inferences which are involved, as I maintain, in taking this thing, which I seem to see in front of me, to be a physical object, as opposed, say, to an image or an hallucination. But when we make a perceptual judgement we do not normally content ourselves with assuming that we are confronted with a physical object of some sort or other. We identify it as a thing of some specific kind, and this brings in a number of further assumptions. For instance, in identifying something which I see as an apple, I assume not only that it is tangible but that it has a certain characteristic texture. I make assumptions about the way it smells and tastes and about the material of which it is made, for example that it is a fleshy fruit and not an object made of wax. I may also be assuming something about its origin, for example that it was grown on a tree, and about its causal properties. I assume further that it has other faces than the one which is turned towards me, that it has an inside, that it is not hollow. But can it seriously be maintained that I see all this? Of course it is perfectly correct for me to say that I see the apple: but this just proves the point that in making a statement of this kind I commit myself to the existence of much more than I do strictly see; some of what I claim to exist is visible in principle but not seen by me on this occasion; and some things, like the taste and texture of the apple in our example, are not an affair of sight at all.

It should be clear from what I have just said that I am not suggesting that the fact that normally neither the whole of the surface nor the interior of a solid object is visible to a given observer at any one time invalidates his claim to see the object. For, as it is ordinarily interpreted, this claim is consistent with his not seeing the whole of the object. Or rather, when we talk of seeing the object as a whole, we do not mean that we see every part of it. There is perhaps some vacillation here in ordinary usage. As Moore puts it: 'In the case of any opaque object, that you are seeing it *entails* that you are seeing some part of its surface: but that you are seeing some part of its surface does not entail that you are seeing it if the part is very small; we should often rightly say "Well, I see a little bit of your arm, but I can hardly say that I am seeing your arm".'[1] Moore goes on to argue that there are two different senses of the word 'see' at work here; so that when I say, truly, that I see the moon, even though part of it is hidden by cloud, or, in the case of the unobscured full moon, even though only one side of it is turned towards me, I am using the word 'see' in a different sense from that in which I use it when I say that I see only one side of the moon, or only a part of its surface. Whether he is right on

[1] G. E. Moore, *Commonplace Book*, p. 330.

this point will depend on the criteria which we use for deciding what is a single sense of a word like 'see'; and this is a question to which I doubt if an investigation of ordinary usage would return any clear answer. Neither, as I shall argue later on, is it of any great importance. Probably, what Moore's example should be taken to show is that we allow ourselves some flexibility, in ordinary usage, in deciding what is seen. It is a somewhat arbitrary question how much of an object we have to see in order to be able to say correctly that we are seeing it rather than just some part of it.

However this may be, the fact that we commonly do not see the whole of any object provides yet another ground for holding that our judgements of perception go beyond the data on which they are based. I have been referring so far only to visual perception, but exactly the same arguments apply *mutatis mutandis* to what we perceive by touch. In the case of the other senses it will hardly be disputed that our judgements are inferential. If I identify an object only by the noise which it makes, or by its taste or smell, then however quick and sure my identification, it embodies an inference from an observed effect to the existence of what may in this instance be an unobserved cause. The part played by inference is more easily overlooked in the cases of sight and touch, largely because we habitually speak of seeing or touching physical objects themselves rather than their visual and tactual effects. This may be taken to prove that the inferences which we make in these cases are not causal. It does not prove that they do not exist. They are involved, as I have shown, first in the assumption that the things which we perceive by sight and touch are public and persistent, secondly in the assumption that they have parts which are not perceived by us on the given occasion, and thirdly in their identification as things of such and such a sort, in so far as this carries implications about their causal properties, their history and the materials of which they are made.

This being so, I do not see how it can reasonably be denied that our ordinary judgements of perception go beyond the evidence on which they are based. Another way of expressing this fact would be to say that they are the conclusions of inductive inferences. But if they are the conclusions of inductive inferences, it ought to be possible to formulate the premises. It ought to be possible to make statements which are tailored to our experiences, in the sense that they offer a qualitative description of what is sensibly presented on a given occasion, without carrying any further implication of any kind whatsoever. I admit that this is not an easy undertaking, but I have yet to come across any arguments which convinced me that it was not feasible. At least I am safe in saying that if there are conclusive arguments against it, Austin does not produce them.

(4) What he does produce is a further argument against those who say that what we take to be the perception of a physical object never yields certainty as to its existence. This argument, which has also been used by Ryle, is that 'talk of deception only makes sense against a general background of non-deception'.[1] On the rare occasions when our senses do deceive us, we are able to discover this because we check the odd cases against the normal ones. It follows that there can be no question of our being generally deceived.

This argument has gained wider currency than it deserves. It is not even effective against the sceptic, since it establishes no more than that we arrive at the conclusion that some perceptual judgements are false because they conflict with others which we take to be true. But this gives us no guarantee, in any particular instance, that the judgement which we take to be true will not itself turn out to be false. Moreover, so far from refuting the contention that perceptual judgements are uncertain, in the technical sense that they go beyond the evidence on which they are based, the argument tacitly admits it. For what characterizes the deviant case is just that the assumptions which are involved in the perceptual judgement are not corroborated by further experience, whereas in the normal case they are.

(5) After some further remarks about deception, in the course of which he makes the valid point that there are many different ways of being deceived, Austin goes on to criticize the use which philosophers have made of expressions like 'directly see'. He belabours the obvious fact that they are not using these expressions in any ordinary sense and then complains that they give no explanation or definition of the way in which they are using them. Although Austin does not mention him, the technical use of expressions like 'directly see' gained currency mainly through the work of Moore, and it is in fact a fair criticism of Moore that he did not lay down any definite rules for their use, perhaps because he did not sufficiently realize that it was technical. It is, however,

[1] *Sense and Sensibilia*, p. 11.

reasonably clear that he intended these expressions to be understood in the same non-committal fashion as the designations of the sensibly 'given' to which they were meant to be correlative. To say of something that it was directly seen was to refer to it as a visual datum, without implying anything about its status. A statement of this kind would, therefore, be a version of what I have been calling an experiential statement, and the force of the word 'directly' is to make the point that these statements provide the evidence on which all our perceptual judgements are based. I do not think that this is an altogether happy usage, but, if I am right in what I have so far been saying, the point itself is valid.

(6) Moore was much concerned with the question whether the objects which we directly see are ever identical with the surfaces of material things. He was inclined to think that they could not be but was never quite certain of this. Austin complains, justifiably, that it is not at all clear what the question means. There may be a way of interpreting it which would leave the answer in doubt, but certainly, as I have construed expressions like 'directly see', it would be contradictory to speak of directly seeing material things, or any parts of them. The reason is that the reference to material things brings in assumptions which the use of these expressions is intended to exclude.

In the *Foundations of Empirical Knowledge* I made the true historical remark that what had led philosophers to deny that they were directly aware of material things was their acceptance of the so-called argument from illusion. This argument, which has played a very large part in the theory of perception, is based on four sets of admitted empirical facts. These are first the existence of hallucinations, mainly exemplified by cases of seeing objects which are not really there, such as Macbeth's dagger and the drunkard's pink rats: secondly cases, like that of mistaking a wax figure for a flesh and blood policeman at Madam Tussaud's, where an object is misidentified: thirdly the variations in the appearance of an object which may be due to perspective, the condition of the light, or the presence of some distorting medium, the stock examples here being the large tower which looks small when seen from a distance, the round coin which looks elliptical when seen from an angle, the straight stick which looks bent when it is immersed in water, and the white wall which looks green when seen through green spectacles; finally, the dependence of the way an object looks or otherwise appears to us on the nature of the physical conditions under which it is perceived and on the physiological and psychological states of the observer.

The main comment which Austin has to make upon these facts is that since they are not all of the same kind it is misleading to lump them all together. He also points out, quite correctly, that in many of the instances in question the word 'illusion' is a misnomer, since they are not cases in which the observer is deceived by the appearances or likely to be so. Except for certain cases of mistaken identification, they are not like the illusions which are created by a conjuror.

These points are unimportant. Let it be granted that the argument from illusion is infelicitously named. The question is whether anything of philosophical interest can be inferred from the facts which it assembles. Admittedly, some of the conclusions which have been drawn from them are very dubious. For instance, they have been taken to prove that strictly speaking we never perceive physical objects at all or at least that we never perceive them as they really are. The facts which have been taken to justify this conclusion are principally those of my fourth class. It is mainly because of the causal conditions of perception that it has been thought necessary to draw a sort of curtain between things as they appear to us and things as they are themselves. What exactly is meant by this distinction and how far it is necessary or even tenable are questions which need to be examined in some detail, and it is rather surprising that Austin makes no attempt at all to measure the force of any such causal arguments. Though it is clear that they cannot legitimately be used in the service of thoroughgoing scepticism, since their premises themselves incorporate a good deal of alleged knowledge about the external world, they do create at least a *prima facie* difficulty for naïve realism.

What the argument from illusion, at least as represented in my first three sets of facts, does clearly establish is the humdrum conclusion that there is not a perfect coincidence between appearance and reality. It shows that if we were always to take appearances as it were at their face value we should sometimes go wrong and, what is important here, that we should go wrong predictively. When we misidentify an object, or misjudge its properties, or misperceive its status, taking it for example to be a physical solid when it is in fact an image, we issue a draft on our further experiences which they fail to honour. But this again implies that our judgements of perception are, in my sense, inferential.

It should be noted that in order to arrive at this conclusion we do not need to rely on the empirical fact that illusions, in this sense, actually occur. That is, it is not necessary for this purpose that we should ever actually be deceived by appearances or even that anything should ever actually appear in any way different from what it is. It is enough that these things be possible; and this possibility is already secured by the fact that our judgements of perception go beyond the data on which they are based. To the extent that they make the venture, they can also come to grief, and this would remain true even if they were never in fact mistaken. At the same time, by directing our attention to cases in which our judgements of perception diverge from the phenomenal description of what is sensibly presented to us, and also to cases in which the assumptions which are involved in them break down, the argument from illusion reinforces the contention that 'illusions', in this special sense, are abstractly possible, by adducing concrete examples of them. The argument, therefore, retains a certain usefulness, in spite of its unhappy title and in spite of the misconstructions which have sometimes been put upon it.

(7) In my exposition of the argument from illusion and elsewhere in the *Foundations of Empirical Knowledge*, I had used the words 'look', 'appear' and 'seem' more or less interchangeably. Austin protests that these words are not synonymous in ordinary usage and goes on to show that each of them is used in subtly different ways. He has some interesting things to say on this topic, but nothing that is relevant to the main argument. All that the sense-datum theorist requires is that the purely phenomenal sense in which he employs words like 'look' and 'appear' shall be legitimate, and once this is granted, it does not greatly matter to him what word is chosen to mark it. Attempts have indeed been made to show that this sense is not legitimate, but they have not been successful. For example, the suggestion that what we must mean by saying that something looks round is that we are inclined to judge that it is round is clearly unacceptable. For why should we be inclined to judge that the thing is round? Surely, in most cases, it is because of the way it looks, in just the phenomenal sense that is in question.

The most substantial point which Austin makes under this

heading is that 'the way things look is, in general, just as much a fact about the world, just as open to public confirmation or challenge, as the way things are. I am not disclosing a fact about *myself*, but about petrol, when I say that petrol looks like water.'[1] This is true, but the fact remains that this most common dispositional sense of words like 'look' rests upon an occurrent sense. We determine how something of a certain kind would look to normal observers under normal conditions on the basis of the way things of that kind do look to particular persons on particular occasions. So once again, inevitably, the phenomenal sense is fundamental.

(8) We next come to a more central issue. Price and I had maintained, in my words, that 'there is no intrinsic difference in kind between those of our perceptions that are veridical in their presentation of material things and those that are delusive'. Having assumed from the start that there are sense-data, Price makes the same point by saying that 'there is no qualitative difference between normal sense-data as such and abnormal sense-data as such'. After recording his objection both to my use of the word 'perceptions' and to Price's assumption about sense-data, Austin queries the truth of our assertions. Could it be seriously suggested, he asks, that dreaming of being presented to the Pope is qualitatively indistinguishable from actually being presented to him? Seeing a bright green after-image against a white wall is not, he maintains, exactly like seeing a bright green patch actually on the wall; seeing a white wall through blue spectacles is not exactly like seeing a blue wall; seeing a stick refracted in water is not exactly like seeing a bent stick; seeing pink rats in *delirium tremens* is not exactly like really seeing pink rats.[2] Finally he accuses Price and myself of assuming that it must be the case that veridical and delusive experiences are not as such qualitatively distinguishable because if they were distinguishable we should not be deluded. And he replies to this that from the fact that we may be taken in by failing to distinguish *A* from *B* it does not follow that *A* and *B* are indistinguishable. It just may be that we are not good at distinguishing things or that we have not looked hard enough.

Much of this is true, but also, I think, beside the point. What Price and I were maintaining was not that it would never be possible to find any qualitative difference between experiences known

<hr />

[1] Op. cit., p. 43.   [2] Op. cit., pp. 48–9.

to be veridical and experiences known to be delusive, in a sense of the word 'delusive' which did not necessarily imply that anyone was actually deluded, but only that appearances were in some way deceptive. It was rather that from a consideration of the experience alone it was not possible to tell to which category it belonged. No doubt, if I have both dreamed of being presented to the Pope and actually been presented to him, these experiences seem very different to me when I compare them in retrospect. But at the time, when I am dreaming of being presented to the Pope is it obvious to me that this is not really happening? Is it always clear from the quality of the dream itself that it is only a dream? Plainly not, otherwise no one would ever suffer from nightmares. And the same applies to the other examples. Perhaps it is always possible to find some qualitative difference between the experience of looking at a blue wall in a good light and that of looking at a white wall through blue spectacles. The point is that if one did not know about this distorting factor, one could not infer just from the character of the experience that the wall was not the colour that it looked. Once one has learned about perspective, refraction and so forth one can, usually though not in fact invariably, discriminate between delusive and veridical experiences. But this is the result of a fairly elaborate process of finding out about the ways in which experiences of different kinds are normally connected. There is nothing in the character of any experience, considered by itself, which licences the inference that it does not present things as they really are. Austin's arguments do not bear against this contention and I am not even sure that he would have disputed it.

(9) Austin goes on to protest that even if it were allowable to speak of sensing sense-data in cases like that of Macbeth's dagger or the straight stick which looks bent when seen in water, there is no warrant for extending this usage to cases of veridical perception. To justify this extension, Price had employed a rhetorical argument which I had accepted with some reservations. The argument appealed to considerations of continuity. If, for example, one is walking towards a distant object, it is implausible, we said, to maintain that one begins by sensing a series of sense-data, and then suddenly at the point where the object looks to be the size and shape that it really is one starts directly seeing a physical object instead. Austin says that he can see no force at all in this argument. I should have thought that, for his purposes, he might have done

better to allow it some force, but turn it the other way. It could be maintained that since it is implausible to say that one is not seeing the same kind of thing all along, then from the start one is seeing a physical object and not a series of sense-data. But in any case, whatever its force, this argument is not needed by the sense-datum theorist. For if he can make good his initial step, that in any case in which anything of whatever kind is perceived, something is directly apprehended, or, as I prefer to put it, that every statement which claims perception of a physical object is founded on an experiential statement, and if he chooses to use the term 'sense-data' to refer to the 'objects', which figure in experiential statements, he will already have established the conclusion that every case of perception, whether veridical or delusive, involves the sensing of sense-data. The proof that physical objects do not figure in experiential statements has already been given with reference to Moore's question whether they can ever be directly seen. It can be formulated succinctly by saying that whereas statements which refer to physical objects are always in some measure proleptic, experiential statements are not.

(10) The next argument is directed against me personally rather than against sense-datum theorists in general. My excuse for mentioning it is that it brings up a point of philosophical importance. I had maintained in the *Foundations of Empirical Knowledge* that what was at issue in the case of rival theories of perception, such as straightforward naïve realism on the one hand and, on the other, Whitehead's and Alexander's theory that things had properties from a point of view, was a choice between different forms of language. And I argued that if one found the naïve realist's way of talking unsatisfactory, one was not forced to adopt the sense-datum terminology. There might be other possibilities, such as choosing to deny the assumption that the real shape, say, of a penny remained the same when one changed the point of view from which one looked at it. Austin found this ridiculous. 'If we allow ourselves this degree of *insouciant* latitude, surely we shall be able to deal—in a *way* of course—with absolutely anything.'[1] But this misses the point. It overlooks the fact that I was not operating within our ordinary conceptual scheme but considering a revision of it. Of course I could not, consistently with our present criteria, maintain that the penny changed its shape when it was observed

[1] Op. cit., p. 58.

from a different angle. I was not suggesting that people who were operating with these criteria might in fact be mistaken in supposing that the shape of things like pennies remained unaltered unless they underwent some physical change. I was suggesting that we might change our criteria, that we might employ a different method of determining what the shapes of such things really were. It might indeed be that the proposal which I mentioned was not viable, but this could only be decided when it had been worked out in some detail. It could not just be laughed off. I do not reproach Austin for failing to see this, since I did not put the point at issue very clearly. Probably at that time, I was not entirely clear about it myself.

The only point of substance which Austin makes in this section is that I was taking it for granted that we were presented with a 'sensible manifold' which it was open to us to characterize in different ways, to organize in accordance with different conceptual schemes. And of course I did make this assumption, surely rightly. I am, however, willing to admit that even so it does not necessarily follow that there are no limits to the forms that this organization can take. It may, for example, be essential that some objects of perception be taken as public, for the reason that a language in which the rules of identity were such that no object perceived by one person could be identified with any object perceived by another would be incoherent. If this were so, as I now think it well may be, one form of phenomenalism could be shown to be untenable. This is, however, a conclusion which can only be reached by trying out such a language and seeing where it breaks down. Merely to point out that we do not ordinarily speak in such a way is nothing to the purpose.

(11) Having reproached me for my cavalier use of the word 'really', Austin proceeds to give an account of the ways in which the word 'real' is actually used. That this account is in some measure defective has been shown by Mr. Jonathan Bennett in an excellent article on the same topic, which appeared in the October 1966 issue of *Mind*.* Nevertheless Austin does achieve what seems to be his main purpose of showing how multifarious are the uses to which the word 'real' is put. We talk of real ducks as opposed to decoy ducks, real pearls as opposed to cultured pearls, a real sword as opposed to a toy one, and so forth. The fact remains, however,

* Reprinted in this volume.

that we do also contrast what is real with what is only apparent, as in the example 'the penny looks elliptical from this angle but it is really round' and that we do contrast what is real with what is illusory as in the example of the drunkard's seeing pink rats which are not really there. The sense-datum theorist concentrates on these distinctions because they are the ones that are relevant to his argument. The fact that he does not deal with distinctions which are not relevant is not a reproach to him.

(12) Having in view the cases, like that of the penny, in which we contrast the perceptible property, the shape or size or colour, which an object really has, with that which it may only appear to have, I had suggested that our procedure was to identify the object's real properties with those that it normally appeared to have under conditions which afforded the best basis for prediction; for instance, if we see something in a good light we can better predict how it will look in a bad light than *vice versa*. Austin points out that there are many cases in which this distinction is not clearly applicable. For example, we should be hard put to say what was the real colour of the sun or the real shape of a cat. This is true, but it does not prove that my explanation of the distinction was incorrect, in the cases where it does apply. I agree that it does not cover the case where we say of a woman 'That's not the real colour of her hair', on the ground that she has dyed it. I was not concerned with the distinction, also sometimes marked by the word 'real', between the natural and the artificial. Could Austin really (i.e. genuinely) have believed that I was?

(13) The next point is more serious. As I have already indicated, Moore set the fashion of distinguishing between different senses of words like 'see'. The sense in which I see the table was supposed by him to be distinct from that in which I see part of the surface of the table and from the sense in which I see, that is directly see, a sense-datum of the table. He also thought it probable, though not certain, that these two last senses were distinct from one another. To some extent following him, I had suggested that there were at least two senses in which such words were ordinarily used, one in which to say that something was seen implied that it existed but did not imply that it had the qualities which it appeared to have, and one in which to say that something was seen did not admit of its lacking the qualities that it appeared to have, but did not imply that it existed. And I suggested that the sense in which Moore

wished to say that we 'saw' sense-data was a fusion of these two. Austin denies that there is any such sense of 'see' as the second of my alleged senses, the one which does not admit of the object's failing to have the qualities it appears to have, but also does not imply that it exists. But surely, and most surprisingly, he is just wrong here on a question of linguistic fact. Indeed, he himself supplies an example of this usage, when he speaks of the drunkard's seeing pink rats. When we say this, we do not imply that the pink rats exist, but equally we do not admit the possibility that the drunkard's pink rats were really green, though he was so drunk that they looked pink to him. It is his hallucination and what he says about it goes. Of course he may misdescribe the colour of the illusory rats, but that is a different question. A mistake of this sort is not of the same order as the mistake which he would be making if he saw what really were grey rats but because of his drunkenness saw them as pink: the criteria are different. Admittedly, my second sense of 'see' is uncommon, but that is because the occasions for employing it are so.

Since he holds that what Moore and others have mistaken for different senses of the word 'see' are at best differences in the nature of the objects seen, Austin goes on to reject an example which I had given of the use of 'see' in different senses. The example was that of someone's saying, in the same perceptual situation, both that he saw a large star and that he saw a silvery speck no bigger than a sixpence. In this instance, Austin denies even that there are different objects. One and the same object, he says, both is a large star and a small speck, just as one and the same object which I saw this morning both is a man shaved in Oxford and a man born in Jerusalem.[1] But here he has been led astray by a false analogy. If one is using the word 'see' in the sense which implies that what is seen exists, it is impossible that one should see an object which is both larger than the earth and no larger than a sixpence, because no such object can exist. Of course one may say with perfect propriety 'that small speck is a large star' but when one says this one is not implying that there *is* an object which is both a small speck and a large star; one is implying that something which from this distance *looks* very small *is* very large. So when one talks in this context of seeing a small speck, the word 'see' does not carry the implication that some small object exists, whereas when one talks

[1] Op. cit., p. 98.

of seeing a large star, the word does carry the implication that some large object exists. In this respect, therefore, the uses of the word are different. Whether it is proper to characterize this fact by speaking of there being different 'senses' of the word 'see' is immaterial.

The fact is that when we talk of seeing an object, like a star, we are inclined both to attribute it the properties which we believe that it really has, even though we do not see it *as* having them, and to represent ourselves as seeing whatever properties are phenomenally apparent to us. If these apparent properties are incompatible with those that we think the object really has, we bring in 'phenomenal' objects, like specks and dots and figures, to carry them. This is clearly a step in the direction of the sense-datum terminology, though not one that takes us all the way, since the size of the speck is a matter of how it would look to the generality of observers under normal conditions and not just a matter of how it looks to me on this occasion. For instance, if I suffered from double vision and seemed to see two specks, I should be undergoing an illusion. It is, however, quite natural for me to say, in a case of this kind, not that I seem to see but simply that I see two specks: and then we are admitting sense-data, if it is allowed that what I say is true.

One moral to be drawn from this example is that in dealing with locutions of this kind we must not be too quick to assume that the 'is' is the 'is' of identity. This comes out clearly in such instances as that of pointing to a photograph and saying 'That is my Uncle James' or pointing to a map and saying 'Those are the Pyrenees'. The case of the speck's being a star is more complicated because here there are not two objects, or at least not in the same sense as in the case of the photograph or map. To treat the speck as a representation of the star would be to insinuate a theory of perception rather than to analyse ordinary usage. For common sense, there is only the one object, the star. The puzzle then arises that the properties ascribed to it under one appellation are incompatible with those ascribed to it under another. This looks like an infringement of the law of identity, until it is realized that in talking of the speck we are not referring to an object which is identical with the star, but only to the way the star appears to us. If we go on to treat such appearances as objects in their own right, which we are not bound but may be entitled to do, we cannot consistently identify them with the things of which they are appearances.

(14) I come now to the question of incorrigibility. This is an important question for the theory of knowledge because the admission of incorrigible propositions puts a stop to what otherwise threatens to become an infinite regress. If one holds that to know a proposition p to be true normally involves accepting it on the basis of some other true proposition q which strongly supports p, then it seems to be required that one should also know q to be true; and this leads to an infinite regress unless we come at some stage to propositions which are as it were knowable in their own right, propositions which do not require support from other propositions. If there were propositions with regard to which it made no sense to say that the person who accepted them might, in the circumstances in question, be factually mistaken about their truth, they would fill the bill. The obvious candidates are propositions in which a person refers to his present thoughts and feelings or to the way things currently appear to him. Austin maintains that not even these propositions satisfy the required condition. In particular, he argues that it is possible to be mistaken about the way things appear to one, and this not merely in a verbal sense.

On this point I am not sure whether he is right or wrong. There is no doubt that it is possible to misdescribe the way things appear to one, but it is not clear to me whether there are any cases in which a mistake of this kind ought to count as factual rather than verbal. Since I am on the whole inclined to think that there are, I do not wish to commit myself to the view that my experiential statements are incorrigible. On the other hand, I do wish to maintain the slightly weaker principle that the subject is the final authority with regard to their truth. The criterion for saying that his description was mistaken will be his own decision to revise it.

Even if this weaker principle could be shown to be untenable, it would not be fatal to my main contention that the truth of statements claiming the perception of physical objects is founded on the truth of experiential statements. It would, however, be a weakness in my general position if I were unable to give a satisfactory account of the criteria by which the truth of experiential statements themselves is to be determined.

(15) As I have already indicated, the support which experiential statements give to statements which imply the existence of physical objects never, in my view, amounts to logical entailment. This is sometimes said to have the consequence that statements which

imply the existence of physical objects are not conclusively verifiable. Austin objects to this way of speaking, I think justifiably. Though it may be defended on the ground that it is no more than a picturesque way of making a valid logical point about the relation of different classes of statements, the idea which it gives of conclusive verification as an end which is pursued but never attained is anyhow misleading. The position which I now hold is that statements about physical objects are at a theoretical level with respect to experiential statements. Like all theoretical statements, they are constantly subject to revision, but in any particular instance we always have some latitude in deciding what revisions we shall make.

(16) It may have been noticed that while I have spoken of perceptual statements as being necessarily founded on experiential statements, I have not spoken of their entailing them. The reason for this is that since there are no sharp boundaries to the range of experiences on which a given perceptual statement may be founded, it is impossible to say exactly what disjunction of experiential statement it entails. In the *Foundations of Empirical Knowledge* I made the same point by saying that one's references to material things were imprecise, or vague, in their application to phenomena. Austin takes exception to my speaking of vagueness and imprecision in this way. No doubt I could have expressed myself better, but I think that it was reasonably clear, in the context, what I was intending to say and I also think that what I was intending to say was true.

(17) Finally, Austin reproaches Warnock for being too indulgent to Berkeley. His grievance is that Warnock concedes to Berkeley what is essentially the position that I have been defending. Warnock allows that, in the case of physical objects, statements about the way things are are founded on statements about the way they seem, and takes issue with Berkeley, as I now think correctly, only in denying that statements about physical objects are reducible to experiential statements. The arguments which Austin brings against him are with one addition a selection of those that I have already reviewed. The additional argument is that 'statements of "immediate perception", so far from being that from which we *advance* to more ordinary statements, are actually arrived at, and are so arrived at in his own account, by *retreating from* more ordinary statements, by progressive hedging. (There's a tiger—there *seems*

to be a tiger—it seems *to me* that there's a tiger—it seems to me *now* that there's a tiger—it seems to me now *as if there were* a tiger.) It seems extraordinarily perverse to represent as that on which ordinary statements are based a form of words which, *starting from* and moreover incorporating an ordinary statement, qualifies and hedges it in various ways. You've got to get something on your plate before you can start messing it around.'[1]

This would be an effective argument if the thesis against which it is directed were that we in fact always go through a process of accumulating experiential statements before we venture to make a perceptual statement. I hope, however, that I have made it clear that in maintaining that perceptual statements are based upon experiential statements one is not implying that they are consciously inferred from them. They are based upon them just in the sense that it is necessary for any perceptual statement to be true that some experiential statement be true, but possible for the experiential statement to be true even though the perceptual statement is false. The thesis that experiential statements are primary, in this sense, is not in the least invalidated by the fact that their role is brought to light by what Austin calls the process of retreating from more ordinary statements. It is not invalidated even by the fact that the form of experiential statements is partly determined by that of the conclusions which they are thought to justify. No doubt, with sufficient ingenuity and labour, we could construct a purely sensory vocabulary, which would not draw on the vocabulary which we use to refer to physical objects. The fact would remain that the character of our experiences themselves is affected by our beliefs concerning the physical world, beliefs which are incorporated in the language which we first learn to speak. This is a fact of which too little account has been taken by sense-datum theorists. But while they may fairly be criticized for this, their logical thesis is not affected by it.

After this full and, I hope, fair review of Austin's arguments, I conclude that he has not disposed of the sense-datum theory. In particular, it seems to me that he has entirely failed to establish his conclusions that 'there is no *kind* or *class* of sentences ("propositions") of which it can be said that *as such* . . . they provide the evidence for other sentences' and that 'it is not true of sentences

[1] Op. cit., pp. 141–2.

about "material things" that *as such* they must be supported by or based on evidence'.[1] There may be good reasons for accepting these conclusions but, if there are, Austin has not given them. It is, in my view, a tribute to his wit and to the strength of his personality that he was able to persuade so many philosophers that he had succeeded.

[1] Op. cit., p. 123.

HAS AYER VINDICATED THE
SENSE-DATUM THEORY?

L. W. Forguson

OLD friends are the best friends. They do not desert you when the chips are down. In his reply[1] to J. L. Austin's *Sense and Sensibilia,*[2] A. J. Ayer has shown once again that he is one of the staunchest friends of the sense-datum theory of perception. His new paper is not, however, simply a defence of *The Foundations of Empirical Knowledge,*[3] for nearly three decades have passed since it was first published, and Ayer has, understandably, had some second thoughts about the doctrine as set forth there. Yet he is still prepared to defend the theory itself with all his characteristic vigour.

His main strategy is to concede to Austin that many of the arguments advanced in *FEK* are defective as they stand. They suffer mainly from hasty or misleading formulation, though some minor philosophical (as opposed to terminological) deficiencies are admitted. However, most of Austin's criticisms are dismissed as fundamentally shallow or beside the point. The central doctrines of the theory are said to remain untouched by Austin's efforts at demolition. Indeed, Ayer seems to view these central doctrines as being rather obvious, albeit regrettably recalcitrant to clear and unambiguous formulation. Consequently, his procedure is to examine Austin's chief arguments one by one, to rebut them, and simultaneously to reformulate, in a manner immune to Austin's criticisms, the central assumptions and arguments of the theory.

[1] 'Has Austin Refuted The Sense-Datum Theory?' (reprinted in this volume). Hereafter: *S.*

[2] Reconstructed from the manuscript notes by G. J. Warnock, Oxford University Press, 1962. Hereafter: *S & S.*

[3] MacMillan & Co., 1940. Hereafter: *FEK.*

The present paper is an attempt to assess the success of Ayer's undertaking. For the most part, I shall consider his arguments in the order in which they are presented in *S*, though considerations of space will prevent me from discussing all the points he raises in his paper.

1. Philosophical doctrines seldom succumb to direct refutation. The proponents of the target positions are usually too nimble, managing to find a way to meet the objections in a manner convincing to themselves if not to the objectors. Ayer maintains that Austin has not refuted the sense-datum theory. But was straightforward refutation Austin's primary aim? Did he, that is, set out to mount a frontal attack on the theory so devastating that no reply in kind would be possible? Ayer appears to understand *S & S* in this light. Most of his arguments are designed to show that Austin has failed to establish that no viable version of the theory can be advanced. But, though it is true that much of what Austin says seems intended to be destructive in this way, I think that to view this as the main burden of the book is seriously to misunderstand it. Austin's primary motive was to show, not so much that the sense-datum theory is an unsatisfactory solution to the philosophical problems to which it is addressed, but that it is fundamentally otiose, for the reason that the problems themselves are misconceived. His general view was that the entire framework of the traditional philosophical controversy within which the sense-datum theory is one alternative should be abandoned.

Historically, the sense-datum theory is a response to certain philosophical problems which are alleged to confront ordinary thought and experience. The traditional method of raising these problems is to argue that the unreflective beliefs of the plain man[1] concerning sense perception, its objects and its efficacy as a means of gaining knowledge, give rise to difficulties when subjected to scrutiny. Not only are some of these beliefs mutually inconsistent, it is maintained, but some of them are in conflict with established empirical facts.

There has always been disagreement among philosophers about just how serious these difficulties are,[2] and about what needs to be

---

[1] The beliefs, that is, we all have and act upon outside the philosopher's and the scientist's closets.

[2] Ayer himself had expressed the view in *FEK* that the plain man need not be bothered by some of these alleged difficulties if he is prepared to revise

done in order to overcome them. But the raw material for the philosopher's interest in perception has traditionally been the problems which supposedly beset 'the plain man's view'. The sense-datum theorist's characteristic response to these problems has been to claim that they arise because the plain man fails to realize—or at least fails consistently to talk as if he realizes—that 'we never see or otherwise perceive (or "sense"), or anyhow we never *directly* perceive or sense material objects (or material things) but only sense-data (or our own ideas, impressions, sensa, sense-perceptions, percepts, &c.)' (*S & S*, 2).

Austin's first major objection to the sense-datum theory[1] is that the philosopher's plain man is in fact a straw man. According to Austin, the plain man is usually represented as believing that he always perceives one kind of thing: 'material objects', which are nearly always characterized as 'medium-sized specimens of dry goods' such as tables and stones; that when he is not perceiving material things his senses are deceiving him; that when his senses are not deceiving him, he is perceiving material things; that material things really are just as they appear to be. But Austin argues that these are gross oversimplifications, and in some cases false characterizations entirely, of what the plain man actually believes. Furthermore, what he does believe, as revealed by attending to what he actually says and does in everyday situations, does not engender the philosophical problems which the sense-datum theory is designed to solve. The plain man is not nearly as naïve as he is represented as being by philosophers. In particular, he is not a naïve realist.

Moreover, throughout the book Austin argues that the empirical facts to which the sense-datum theorist appeals in order to raise the problems of perception do not actually conflict with our everyday beliefs, if we take the trouble to describe these facts carefully, and fully, and in detail. It is only by restricting attention to a certain very narrow range of facts, by misdescribing even these, and by setting them against the straw plain man's beliefs, that the sense-datum theory has been able to gain its initial foothold.

[1] This objection is formulated in Sections I and II, but pursued throughout the book.

---

some of his ideas about the constitution and behaviour of such things as pennies and sheets of writing paper.

These are the points Austin is mainly concerned to establish. This is why he says, in the closing passage of *S & S*, that the right policy for dealing with the sense-datum theory is not to try to patch it up and make it work properly, but 'to go right back to a much earlier stage, and to dismantle the whole doctrine before it gets off the ground'.

It may legitimately be questioned whether Austin is successful in establishing these claims or in making them even very plausible. Yet they are scarcely discussed by Ayer in *S*. He does admit that the sense-datum theorist tends to oversimplify the views of the plain man with regard to the kinds of things he would say that he perceives. But he denies that this affects the validity of the sense-datum theorist's arguments. We shall see whether Ayer is right about this. However, if the above characterization of the main direction of Austin's criticisms is correct, it is clear that Ayer must show, in order successfully to rebut Austin's 'refutation' of the theory, not merely that the theory is possible but that it is inevitable. He must show, that is to say, that there are philosophical difficulties inherent in what we ordinarily believe which establish the claims (or make compelling the assumptions) of the sense-datum theory.

2. The fundamental assumptions of the sense-datum theory are necessitated, Ayer maintains, by the realization that no ordinary 'perceptual judgement' is ever certain. Although it may be admitted that in ordinary life it would be absurd, as Austin claimed in *S & S* (page 10), to question the existence of a chair at which one is looking under perfectly normal conditions, unless one had some special reason for doing so, the sense-datum theorist would say that there is an element of uncertainty even in such a context as this. For to talk of uncertainty in such a situation is to make the purely logical point that 'the statement that the chair exists does not follow from any statement, or any finite number of statements, which are limited to describing the content of the observer's experience' [*S*, 286].

To describe the situation as Austin does actually begs the question at issue, Ayer says; for it implies 'that in supposing that he sees a chair the observer is not mistaken' [*S*, 286]. But this description conceals the important fact that the observer could be having the experience in question even though the chair does not exist.

However, the sense-datum theorist also begs the question, Ayer admits; for in talking of uncertainty in this connexion he commits himself to the assumption that

> in making even so simple a judgement as that this is a chair one is going beyond the evidence which is yielded by the senses on this occasion, but that it is possible to formulate a statement which does not go beyond the evidence, in the sense that it carries no implications about the status of what is seen. A statement of this kind, which I propose to call an 'Experiental Statement', will simply record the presence, say, of a visual pattern. It will leave it entirely open whether the observer is right in treating this pattern as a manifestation of the kind of physical object which he claims to perceive, or indeed of a physical entity of any sort at all. [*S*, 286.]

It is, Ayer concludes, only by showing that these fundamental assumptions are unwarranted that the sense-datum theory can be 'cut off at its source'.

Since it would scarcely be denied by the plain man that his 'perceptual judgements' are uncertain in the sense in which this term is used by the sense-datum theorist, why is this sort of uncertainty alleged to constitute a philosophical problem? The traditional answer is that scepticism cannot be avoided unless knowledge-claims are grounded at some point in certainty. And it has been a characteristic claim of sense-datum theorists that statements about 'the contents of the observer's experience' are certain in the required sense. Both the answer and the claim need to be questioned. Of more immediate concern, though, are the two basic assumptions of the sense-datum theory, as set forth above.

The assumptions are supposed to be necessary because ordinary statements reporting perception *conceal* the fact that the observer could be having an experience identical to that which he would be having when he sees a chair even in a case in which no chair is there to be seen.[1] Experiential statements, on the other hand, are neutral in the sense that they carry no implications about 'the status of what is seen'. By this, I take Ayer to mean that an experiential statement carries no implications with respect to the question of whether or not what is seen is itself a chair, for instance,

[1] But what about 'experiential statements?' Do they not conceal the fact that what the observer sees may *be* a chair?

313

or part of one. But this neutrality is only professed. For we are told that our eventual choice is to be whether or not the 'visual pattern', the presence of which is 'recorded' by the experiential statement, is a *manifestation* of a physical entity. We don't even have as an option the question of whether the 'pattern' thus presented is *itself* to be identified as (or with) a chair, or part of one. Thus, it is already clear that sense-data are the only live candidates for 'what is seen'. By making his initial assumptions, the sense-datum theorist has already drawn the veil between the observer and 'the external world'.

Later in the paper [*S*, 295], in his discussion of the sense-datum theorist's use of the expression 'directly see', Ayer admits that the assumptions of the sense-datum theory make it simply analytic to say that what we directly see (i.e., whatever is described in a (visual) experiential statement) is sense-data, and contradictory to say that what we directly see ever has the 'status' of being a physical entity. The hypothesis that we do directly see chairs, etc., has simply been ruled out by linguistic legislation. Far from having to argue that what is seen is never a material thing, it becomes true by definition.

A key expression in Ayer's doctrine is 'the content of the observer's experience'. It is a characteristic feature of the sense-datum theory that the content of an observer's experience cannot be identified as the object that the observer claims to see (e.g., the chair), but must be a feature inherent in 'the experience' itself. But if it can be shown that nothing in experience could, on grounds Ayer himself presents, answer to the sense-datum theorist's conception of an experience-content which could *also* be used to play the central epistemological role Ayer wishes to assign to the sense-datum—namely, an entity, statements about which could serve as the uninferred premises for perceptual inferences—then the second assumption of the sense-datum theory, whatever its other merits might be, would be epistemologically sterile. This I shall attempt to show in later sections.

3. Ayer next attempts to establish the first of the sense-datum theorist's assumptions: that ordinary 'judgements of perception' go beyond the evidence on which they are based. This involves establishing the sister claims that all statements which assert or imply the existence of physical objects stand in need of verification, and that experiental statements, being descriptions of the

evidence on which we base our judgements of perception, provide the only philosophically acceptable verification. Here, Ayer is replying to Austin's charges that verification is not a matter of checking up on statements entailed by, e.g., 'That's a pig', and that it is incorrect to talk of obtaining (or needing) evidence when the object itself is there in plain view.

Austin had maintained that one needs to rely on evidence only when one is not in a position to just see (or otherwise perceive) the thing itself. If one has the pig there before one in plain sight, then one doesn't need evidence for its existence, and it is wrong to speak of such a situation as one in which the observer is only obtaining evidence for the truth of 'That's a pig' (or 'I see a pig'). This is accepted by Ayer 'as a comment on ordinary usage'. He says

> when one speaks of having evidence for a proposition p, one ex-
> pects it to be understood that one is not entirely convinced of the
> truth of p. . . . If I think that I know that p, I am underplaying my
> hand, and so misleading my audience, if I say no more than that I
> have good evidence for p [S, 288].

But Ayer thinks that this carries no philosophical weight, for 'my knowing that p is certainly not inconsistent with my having good evidence for it' [289]. Knowing that p does not entail that I have no evidence for p, any more than knowing that p entails that I don't believe it, since, knowledge being stronger than belief, we usually make the stronger claim rather than the weaker when we feel entitled to do so. Thus,

> the fact that when one is looking at a pig, under normal conditions,
> it is not good usage to speak of having evidence for its existence,
> in no way entails that seeming to see the pig is not having evidence
> for its existence. The truth is that it is very strong evidence: and it
> does not cease to be evidence just because of its strength [289].

This objection misses Austin's point. It is true that seeing something *is* (constitutes) evidence for claiming knowledge of it. If someone sees that x is y, he has evidence for claiming to know that x is y, in the sense that if someone should challenge him (how do you know?) he can reply that he sees that it is so. But Austin's point in *S & S* is that (*a*) talking about evidence when the pig is standing there in plain view misleads us into thinking that we're not in the best possible position (namely, being eye-witnesses) for claiming knowledge, and (*b*) this in turn suggests that if we do need evidence in such a case, it must be something other than seeing the pig itself.[1]

In fact, Ayer takes just this step. For what *he* takes as evidence is not seeing the pig, but *seeming* to see it. Now 'seeming to see a pig' is surely not equivalent to 'looking at a pig, under normal conditions'. Yet it would have to be equivalent for Ayer's point to have any force. If his description of the situation (or experience) as one of 'seeming to see the pig' is allowed to stand, then of course talk of evidence is relevant. But isn't there a suppressed 'only' here, which needs to be inserted before 'seeming' in Ayer's description? One might be prepared to agree, in analogy with the dictum 'knowing that *p* entails believing that *p*', that 'looking at *p* entails seeming to see *p*'.[2] But everything is changed if the 'only' is inserted. For this implies that one does *not* see *p*, which is not even in question under the description 'looking at *p* under normal conditions'. And the analogy with knowledge and belief clearly breaks down if there's a (*sotto voce*) 'only' operative behind the scenes, since 'He knows that *p*' does not entail 'He only believes that *p*'. However, the 'only' does seem to be required here. For his seeming to see the pig is taken by Ayer to be the observer's evidence for the pig's existence, and a description of the situation as one in which the observer sees a pig is ruled out by the sense-datum theorist's assumption that experiential statements cannot refer to material objects (such as pigs) but only to experience-contents. Since looking at a pig, under normal conditions, cannot plausibly be said to be gathering evidence for the truth of 'That (which I see) is a pig', and since Ayer cannot, in terms of his second assumption, allow 'He sees a pig' as a description of the perceptual situation, he must rely on the 'seeming to see' description.

Consequently, his rebuttal of Austin's argument that looking at something, under normal conditions, is not gathering evidence for

---

[1] An analogous point can be made about 'visual clues', an expression Ayer makes use of later. Clues have their place in detective novels and archaeological investigations: cases in which we have to piece together a true account of something from more or less meagre bits of information left at the scene. However, if we're eye-witnesses—if we actually see Smith stabbing Jones—we needn't rely on clues to get our man, though a detective who comes on the scene later might also come to the same conclusion—that Smith did it—with the aid of clues, etc.

[2] But should even this be allowed?

the existence of that at which one is looking is actually just a re-assertion of the sense-datum theorist's first assumption: that all ordinary judgements of perception go beyond the evidence on which they are based. But this is what Ayer set out to *establish*.

4. At this point, Ayer brings forward an imagined objection to his doctrine about evidence and proceeds to overcome it. 'To say that one has evidence for a proposition *p*', the imagined objector says, 'is to imply that one's knowledge of *p* is direct, in the sense that one is inferring *p* from some other proposition *q*' [*S*, 289]. However, my belief in the existence of the table in plain view before me is not an inference. I just see it. Ayer replies that although it is absurd to suppose that perception normally involves any con-scious process of inference, this is quite irrelevant to the point that the sense-datum theorist is making. For the view that all percep-tion embodies inferences 'makes the same logical point' as the view that all judgements of perception are uncertain:

> the judgement goes beyond the data on which it is grounded . . .
> it claims more than is contained in the experience which gives rise
> to it . . . it makes assumptions which may be false, consistently
> with this experience [290].

But Ayer foresees resistance to this view, which would take the form of calling into question his use of expressions such as 'content of an experience', and of insisting that, even if talk of 'visual experi-ences', is allowed to pass, my present visual experience is simply the experience of seeing a table. Ayer ignores these questions about his terminology, and goes on to 'overcome the resistance' by pointing out that even the most unambitious perceptual statement (e.g., 'This is a table') has 'far-reaching implications'. In particular, it commits us to assumptions regarding position in space, endurance through time, accessibility to more than one sense, etc. According to Ayer, though, I can't *see* that these assumptions are true.[1] On the contrary, 'one starts with certain visual clues, and on the basis of these clues one leaps to one's far-reaching conclusions. But the conclusions are not contained in the clues' [291]. And this, he con-cludes, is surely a case of inductive inference.

The ground has now been prepared for the introduction of

[1] Well, I can see that some of them are true, in a 'loose' sense which admits that I've made use of past experiences, and thus indulged in inductive infer-ences.

sense-data in their primary epistemological role: as the 'given' premisses for inductive perceptual inferences. Before witnessing this step and examining the consequences Ayer claims for it, it would be well to take another, harder look at his preparations.

The claim that all 'judgements of perception' are the conclusions of inductive inferences is based, first, on the fact that statements such as 'This is a table' have implications which commit one to a number of 'assumptions' about space and time, accessibility to other observers (and other senses), and about the constitution, history and future behaviour of the object itself. There is little in this to which anyone could object.

It is claimed, secondly, that although it may be said (not too strictly) that I can see that some of these assumptions are true, others refer to the past, or to the future, or are a matter for some sense other than sight. And even in the case of those assumptions I see to be true, my seeing that they are true involves my making use of considerable knowledge (or beliefs)[1] acquired from past experience.

All this, too, may readily be admitted. Indeed, to admit it is simply to admit that, in the full normal sense of the word 'see' (referring not just to the capacity, but to its normal exercise), we have to learn to see just as we have to learn to walk and to talk. And just as walking and talking involve (or are) making use of an acquired skill, so does perceiving facts, identifying persons or things, etc.

Does the recognition of these facts commit us to the conclusion that ordinary perception is (or involves) the making of inductive inferences? On the evidence presented, to say that perception is inferential is simply to say that 'perception is inferential' is a short-hand way of asserting the above facts about perception. And, since not only perception, but such activities as walking and talking also involve making use of knowledge acquired from past experience and involve the making of many assumptions (e.g., about the solidity of the walking surface), and since the exercise of these skills similarly has far-reaching implications (not usually noticed, because not usually noteworthy), we should also admit that walking and talking are inferential, as well as the exercise of all other acquired skills. Perhaps we should speak of walking as practical reasoning from ambulatory data.

[1] For brevity, I shall omit the expression 'or beliefs' hereafter.

Now there may be nothing in this to which Ayer would object. Perhaps he would be sympathetic to an extension of the characterization 'inferential' to the exercise of all learned skills. There is not much to cavil about if he does, except to say that this characterization might lead us to ignore the differences between these basic human activities and what we normally single out as cases in which inductive inferences are made. However, Ayer maintains that it is possible to isolate the *premisses* of these perceptual inferences, and the soundness of this claim needs examination.

In order to do this, it will be necessary to backtrack a bit and consider Ayer's characterization of the facts cited in support of his claim that perception is inferential. First of all, we need to object to Ayer's characterization of what the perceptual inference is. He represents the 'far-reaching conclusions' as being that what I see is solid, exists unperceived, has a certain history, etc. But, though these things are of course implied by my conclusion (if it is correctly so called), in the sense that the truth of my 'perceptual judgement' implies the truth of statements asserting these things, surely the conclusion itself is that what I see is a table, or my mahogany dining-room table. My conclusion is an *identification* of what I see. As for all the other things implied by my so concluding, I don't actually conclude anything about them. Most likely, I don't even think about them, much less leap to any conclusions about them. Ayer has built all of the implications and assumptions into the conclusion itself.

However, if my actual conclusion is simply that this thing I see is a table, what is it about which I am concluding that it is a table? What, that is, are my 'visual clues'? It is clear that for Ayer the answer must be 'the content of my experience itself'. And it follows from the sense-datum theorist's assumptions that this can't be the table or any part of it (or my seeing of any part of it). But at this point we need to ask: why not? Why should we buy this assumption? Why can't it be that what I see, *sans judgement*, and that which I judge or conclude that it is, are one and the same thing: namely, a mahogany table about three yards in front of me? So far, even admitting all the facts Ayer cites, nothing compels us to say that what is seen—even quite strictly seen—is not a table. For, might I not say that my evidence for judging that what I see before me is a table is the fact that it looks like a table looks from this point of view? And couldn't it be that what I am presented with in a visual presentation is a table (or, if one wishes to speak quite 'strictly', part of one)? Couldn't I infer, from such premisses as (1) this looks like my dining-room table, and (2) all other relevant features of the context, including my memories of past experiences, are consistent with its actually being my dining-room table, to the conclusion that what I see *is* my dining-room table? We haven't yet been given any compelling reason, other than merely assuming it, to believe that we have to reach this conclusion *via* the consideration of something else seen at a previous stage or in another way.

Consider next Ayer's use in this argument (and throughout his paper) of the expression 'judgement of perception'. The very *description* of normal perception as the making of judgements already strongly suggests Ayer's favoured *analysis* of perception as arriving at conclusions which must have been preceded, if only very briefly, by an internal argument. It is true that in abnormal situations (e.g., where the light is particularly poor) one might, in order to identify something that one sees, go through a procedure which might very well be called considering evidence or premisses, as a result of which one judges or concludes that what one sees is such-and-such. But does it follow from this that *all* perceptual recognition or identification is likewise judging or concluding upon the consideration of evidence or premisses?

If so, then difficulties arise for the sense-datum theorist's programme. For, according to Ayer, experiential statements, which are said to constitute the premisses for our ordinary judgements of perception, are not themselves judgements of perception, but rather qualitative descriptions of the contents of our experiences. They 'simply record the presence, say, of a visual pattern'. Presumably, in order to be able to formulate experiential statements, the observer has to be able to recognize, identify, attend to his visual patterns.[1] Yet, if the observer-cum-sense-datum-theorist is able to recognize a sense-datum as a particular visual pattern, does not this mean that he is, in so doing, drawing on his considerable past experience? This would seem to be a consequence of the theory. But then the recognition of visual patterns is also the conclusion of an inductive inference, requiring further premisses,

---

[1] He may not be conscious of doing this in actual practice, any more than we are normally conscious of the inferences we allegedly make in recognizing chairs and pigs. But surely, the plausibility of the theory depends upon its being possible for sense-data to be recognized, identified, scrutinized.

which for their own part must be capable of recognition, and so on without assignable limit. Thus, if perception is inferential, the ability to identify sense-data is also inference-dependent. Consequently, the introduction of sense-data cannot satisfy the epistemological requirement of providing uninferred premisses for perceptual inferences.

All this talk of 'visual clues', 'visual presentations', and the like does point—though in a highly misleading way—to an undeniable fact about visual perception: the fact, namely, that one cannot make use of knowledge acquired from past experience in a present perceptual situation unless it is a genuine perceptual situation. That is, one cannot visually perceive (see) anything at all unless one becomes visually aware: unless one has what philosophers call 'a visual experience', or 'a visual sensation'. It is also true that the facts Ayer cites on pages 285–286 with regard to 'certainty' show that seeing and identifying a table is not *the same thing* as merely having a visual experience. But it does not follow from this that having a visual experience, which is a necessary feature in seeing anything, is the same thing as, or even very much like, being given clues or premisses from which one draws conclusions.[1] Nor does it follow from this, or from any of the facts Ayer cites, that when one is correctly described as seeing a chair—and Ayer does not wish to deny that very often we are correctly so described—one's visual experience is *of* anything other than that chair, or part of it. One can admit (1) that normal perception involves having experiences (or sensations), (2) that it involves the exercise of acquired knowledge, (3) that it involves committing oneself to the truth of (unexpressed or at least not consciously expressed) statements concerning the past or future or any number of other things, without being forced to say, or even very strongly tempted to assume, that any intermediate entity is always perceived (or sensed) in perceiving a table. On the contrary, we have seen that difficulties arise if one *does* take the sense-datum route.

I do not wish to suggest, by the foregoing remarks, that the question of how we make use of acquired knowledge in present perceptual situations is not an important and interesting question. However, I believe that it is a question which philosophers, *qua* philosophers, are not competent to discuss very intelligently. For

[1] For an excellent discussion of this issue, see Gilbert Ryle's 'Sensations', in *Contemporary British Philosophy III*, ed. H. D. Lewis, Allen & Unwin, 1956.

its answer requires a comprehensive theory of perceptual mechanisms (or processes), which is a matter requiring scientific investigation. It is not settleable by argument from the facts presented by Ayer.

5. At this point Ayer enlists the help of Moore to provide additional grounds for his position. He does not, he says, wish to claim that the fact that 'neither the whole of the surface or the interior of a solid object is visible to a given observer at any one time invalidates his claim to see the object'. For this claim is 'perfectly consistent with his not seeing the whole of the object' [*S*, 292]. But what does Ayer make of this fact? He quotes Moore, with approval, as saying

> in the case of any opaque object, that you are seeing it *entails* that you are seeing some part of its surface: but that you are seeing some part of its surface does not entail that you are seeing it if the part is very small; we should often rightly say 'Well, I see a little part of your arm', but I can hardly say that I am seeing your arm.[1]

Ayer takes this to show that 'it is a somewhat arbitrary question how much of an object we have to see in order to be able to say correctly that we are seeing it rather than just some part of it.' He then concludes: 'the fact that we commonly do not see the whole of any object provides yet another ground for holding that our judgements of perception go beyond the data on which they are based' [293].

This argument is reminiscent of an argument Moore used in 1918 to prove the existence of sense-data.[2] There he argued that the word 'this', in 'this is an inkstand' (as said in a perceptual situation), cannot refer to *the inkstand*, for I am not judging that what I see is itself a whole inkstand. What does 'this' refer to? A sense-datum. This argument trades upon confusing 'seeing a whole *x*' with 'seeing the whole of *x*'. For one does not, in order to see (what is in fact) a whole inkstand, have to see the whole of it. The present argument is involved in a similar confusion.

Seeing a sufficiently large, or sufficiently significant part of something is, depending upon the context, a *criterion* of seeing it. That's what counts as seeing that thing. And if I do see such a part

---

[1] *The Commonplace Book,* ed. C. Lewy, Allen & Unwin, 1962, p. 330.
[2] 'Some Judgements of Perception', *Proceedings of the Aristotelian Society,* 1918.

of such a thing, I may say that I see it, *sans phrase*. Someone might challenge me, saying that I didn't see enough of it, or didn't see the right part of it, and thus object to my saying that I see it, *sans phrase*. But he can hardly challenge my right to say that I see it (*sans phrase*) on the grounds that I didn't see the whole of it.

But what if all I've seen is a tiny, insignificant part of it? Here, seeing what I've seen doesn't count as seeing it, *simpliciter*, and I would not be justified in saying, without appropriate qualifications, that I've seen it. I can't say that I've seen it, *sans phrase*. But, of course, seeing part of something, even the tiniest, most insignificant part, is still seeing the object of which it is a part (though to avoid misleading others, I must add qualifications), in the sense that what I see is part of *that* thing and not, for instance, part of something else. When Ayer claims that the fact that we do not usually see the whole of any object shows that 'our judgements of perception go beyond the data on which they are based', he mistakes criteria for seeing *x* for evidence (data) from which we infer that we see *x*, and he confuses (with Moore) what we would be justified in saying with qualifications in certain cases for something we would be justified in saying *sans phrase* about something else. The practice of treating parts of things as things in their own right can be useful enough. But if one is not careful the practice can have sinister consequences. Since it would be mad to suppose that in order to see a table one has to see the whole of it, and since it is admitted in the passage under consideration that one does see part of it, and finally, since seeing relevant parts of things is a criterion of—that is, constitutes—seeing those things, our judgements in such cases don't go beyond the data at all. Rather they are either identifications of the data as parts of the things in question ('I see part of his arm'), or identifications of the objects of which seeing such parts constitutes seeing the objects themselves ('I see his arm').

6. Summing up the points he believes to have been established thus far, Ayer says

> I don't see how it can reasonably be denied that our ordinary judgements of perception go beyond the evidence on which they are based. Another way of expressing this fact would be to say that they are the conclusions of inductive inferences. But if they are the conclusions of inductive inferences, it ought to be possible to formulate the premisses. It ought to be possible to make statements

which are tailored to our experiences, in the sense that they offer a qualitative description of what is sensibly presented on a given occasion, without carrying any further implication of any kind whatever [293–94].

Ayer means, presumably, that the qualitative description should neither covertly nor overtly presuppose or imply that a physical object is there which fits the description. Nor should it presuppose or imply that it is *not* there. Well, what about 'I see what looks exactly like a table, in fact my mahogany dining-room table'? This would seem to be neutral enough; for it may turn out that it just is my table, and again it may turn out that it is not. It might be another table, or there may be nothing there at all, due to some optical trick, or to my being hypnotized.

However, such a description does not seem to be what Ayer has in mind. It isn't tailored to our experiences closely enough, evidently, in not being purely 'qualitative'. However, difficulties lie at the root of this notion of 'qualitative descriptions'.[1] The difficulties arise when we ask what constitutes a single sense-datum. That is, what is included, and what is excluded, in the qualitative description of a single 'sensible presentation'? If Ayer should answer, as he did in *FEK*, that the data are whatever in a given case they appear to be or are taken to be, then all the difficulties about judgements and inferences arise again at this level, as we have seen. For if we *take* the data to be anything at all, if our data appear in any way at all which admits of our recognizing and describing them, even qualitatively, then we have a case, it would seem, of having to make inferences and judgements in order to arrive at our qualitative descriptions. Qualitative descriptions are as inference-ridden as ordinary descriptions of what we see. If 'this is a table' is the conclusion of an inductive inference, so is 'this looks red to me' or 'I am sensibly presented with something red'.

7. Against Austin's claim that 'talk of deception only makes sense against a general background of non-deception', Ayer argues, quite correctly, that this sort of argument will not work against those, like the sceptic, who claim that perceptual judgements are never certain. For the sceptic would reply that Austin's argument establishes only that we take some perceptual judgements to be

[1] As Austin argued in *S & S*, 53–4, when he raised questions about Ayer's talk, in *FEK*, of 'our perceptions'.

false because they conflict with others that we take to be true. But this, Ayer continues, 'gives us no guarantee, in any particular instance, that the judgement we take to be true will not itself turn out to be false' [294].

Although Austin's argument cannot show that perception ever yields certainty (in the sense in which the sense-datum theorist uses this term), it does have a certain force. He cannot, by its use, establish that ordinary perceptual statements are ever incorrigibly *true*, but he can establish the very important point that claims to perceive can be incorrigibly *justified*. He cannot establish that perceptual statements are ever incorrigibly true because, no matter how many precautions one may take in making a perception-claim, it may nevertheless turn out to be false; and the falsity may not *in any sense* be the 'fault' or responsibility of the observer. No amount of precautions (considerations of evidence, tests, or whatever), can ever completely rule out the possibility that one's claim be false. However, one can have reasonable or unreasonable, good or bad *grounds* for making the claims one makes. And one's grounds —including the precautions one takes, the tests one performs, the evidence one considers, when relevant—are one's own responsibility.[1] Now a philosophically interesting question in this connexion is: what constitutes adequate justification for perception-claims?[2] And related to this is the question: can one be incorrigibly so justified? What Austin's argument does show is that the answer to this latter question should be in the affirmative.[3] For we can, on perfectly good grounds, pick out cases in which we have not been 'deceived', and it is against these that doubtful cases are compared. Furthermore, in learning to tell the difference between cases of deception and non-deception, we also learn how we can fall into errors and how we can avoid them. And in so learning we learn also about the kinds of circumstances in which errors, tendencies to carelessness and so forth are in the offing and thus constitute

[1] An excellent discussion of this issue is contained in the chapter entitled 'The Ethics of Belief' in Roderick Chisholm's *Perceiving*, Cornell, 1956.

[2] It is interesting because it is concerned with human capacities and frailties.

[3] This is argued at greater length, and more explicitly, in 'Other Minds', *Philosophical Papers*, ed. J. O. Urmson and G. J. Warnock, Oxford, 1961. For a new development on the same theme, see John Pollock's 'Criteria and Our Knowledge of the External World', *Philosophical Review*, January 1967.

relevant precautionary considerations. These considerations provide us with our criteria for justification. If in a particular case one does take all of the relevant precautions—one doesn't have to try to eat the putative telephone—one is certain, in the sense of being certainly, incorrigibly justified in making the 'judgement' one makes. And this is, as Austin says (though he misses the significance of it), unretractable, no matter what happens subsequently. Even in such a case one's claim may nevertheless be, though incorrigibly justified, in fact false. Thus the sceptic is not refuted by these considerations. However, it is only by accepting the impossible-to-fulfil requirement that (logical) certainty be attained that one finds oneself in a philosophical bind by the recognition that it is unattainable.

8. Much of *S & S* is devoted to a sustained attack on the argument from illusion, the assumptions and interpretations of facts which underlie its use in philosophy, and the conclusions which have been drawn from it.[1] The argument is based upon four sets of empirical facts, which Ayer characterizes on page 295 of *S*:

> The existence of hallucinations, mainly exemplified by cases of seeing objects which are not really there.
>
> Cases, like mistaking a wax figure for a flesh and blood policeman at Madame Tussaud's, where an object is misidentified.
>
> Variations in the appearance of an object which may be due to perspective, the conditions of the light, or the presence of some distorting medium.
>
> The dependence of the way an object looks or otherwise appears to us on the nature of the physical conditions under which it is perceived and on the physiological and psychological state of the observer.

Do these facts pose philosophical problems?

Hallucinations do occur; but is it entirely 'neutral' to characterize hallucinations as 'seeing objects which are not really there'? This description implies that something, at least, really is seen, but is not, unfortunately, 'really there'. However, this is not the only way to characterize hallucinations. One could also say that the man undergoing an hallucination *seems* to see, or falsely believes that he

---

[1] It is rather odd that Ayer should say that Austin's 'main comment' on this argument is merely that it is misleading to lump illusions and hallucinations together.

sees, some object, but that no such object is there to be seen. This characterization has difficulties of its own; for an explanation is wanted of what it is for someone to believe that he is seeing something when he is not. However, this characterization does have the merit of showing that one is not forced, by recognizing the existence of hallucinations, to say that something really is seen which is not really there.

Cases of misidentifying what one perceives do not give any grounds for concluding, or even for suspecting, that what one perceives in such cases is not a material thing.[1] A wax figure is a material thing. So is a policeman. And if I mistake a wax figure for a policeman, what I see is a wax figure. As Austin argued, cases of this sort are not even cases of illusion, nor of hallucination, nor of one's senses deceiving one.

What about the set of facts pertaining to 'the variations in the appearance of an object'? This characterization is innocent enough, if by 'variations in the appearance of an object' is meant merely that the way something looks, feels, etc. varies under specifiable conditions. As was pointed out by Reid and others, and repeated by Austin, we would be very much put out if these variations did *not* occur in the contexts in which they do occur. Their occurrence doesn't normally even tend to deceive us. However, these facts are often given another interpretation, in which they are taken as facts about entities called 'appearances'. Under this interpretation, if some object x appears red (or elliptical) under conditions y, then some other entity (an appearance-of-x) really is red (or elliptical). And this, together with the claim (or assumption) that all we ever get to perceive, strictly speaking, are appearances ('manifestations of some physical entity') and never the objects themselves,[2] is taken to prove that all we ever 'directly perceive' are sense-data. However, this interpretation can easily be avoided. It doesn't follow from the fact that x looks blue that something else is blue. 'Looks blue' is as 'primitive' as 'is blue'. We do not always mean to say that something that looks blue looks as if it is blue, nor that we even tend to believe that it is blue. The fact that the penny looks elliptical when seen at an angle doesn't mean that we believe

[1] Austin produced examples to show this: the headless woman, the church disguised as a barn.

[2] Because, presumably, we never see or feel things without their looking or feeling some way or other to us.

(or even tend to believe) that it, or anything else that we see in the situation, really is elliptical.[1] To say, as some do, that its looking elliptical shows that something is elliptical in my visual field is merely to adopt another way, which can easily prove misleading, of saying the same thing.

As for the fourth set of facts, we are aware, as plain men, at least *that* there are physiological, physical and psychological factors operative in perception, even if we cannot explain or even say *what* they are or how they operate. But this need not force us to admit that we directly perceive sense-data. In fact, as we have seen, in the role philosophers wish to give to sense-data, our awareness of sense-data would not be, could not be, innocent of these influences. And, as Ayer rightly points out, these facts cannot be used in arguments in support of scepticism.

Ayer is also right in claiming that these facts 'do create at least a *prima facie* difficulty for naïve realism' [296]. But does he wish to suggest that Austin was defending naïve realism in *S & S*? Austin explicitly denies (*S & S*, 3–4) that he is defending naïve or any other brand of philosophic realism, if these are taken to be theories that we do 'directly perceive material objects'. As I mentioned earlier, Austin's purpose with regard to both the sense-datum theory and philosophic realism was entirely negative. He didn't wish to argue for any philosophical theory of perception, for the reason that, in his view, the problems these theories attempt to solve either aren't problems at all or, at least, aren't philosophical problems but scientific problems.

Ayer himself admits that nothing very startling follows from the facts adduced by the proponents of the argument from illusion. The argument cannot, for instance, establish the conclusion that there is 'a sort of curtain' drawn 'between things as they appear to us and things in themselves'. What it does establish, however, 'is the humdrum conclusion that there is not a perfect coincidence between appearance and reality' [296].[2] Since we *began* by admitting

[1] Not that the penny is 'really round' in any more primary *physical* sense than it is elliptical. The 'real shape' of physical objects is largely a matter of convention, though these conventions are not, as Ayer suggested in *FEK*, based entirely or in every case upon predictive value.

[2] Of course, it has not been established that there is not a perfect coincidence between two kinds of entities: appearances and realities. It has merely been established that circular things, for instance, don't look circular from every angle.

—what the four sets of facts are facts about—that there is not a perfect coincidence between appearance and reality, the conclusion certainly is humdrum.

Ayer does, however, attempt to squeeze some juice out of this rather withered fruit. He claims that even this humdrum conclusion shows once again that 'our judgements of perception are, in my sense, inferential'. For the argument from illusion shows that 'if we were always to take appearances as it were at their face value we should sometimes go wrong and . . . that we should go wrong predictively' [296]. Now if we did always 'take appearances at their face value', we should not merely sometimes go wrong, we should nearly always go wrong, as is shown by the third set of facts alone. However, this would actually strengthen Ayer's claim that perception is, in his sense, inferential. But, as was pointed out before, admitting that our 'judgements of perception' are inferential hasn't the slightest tendency to force the admission that what we see, even quite strictly so (unless one adopts Ayer's linguistic legislation), are sense-data and not physical objects, except, perhaps, in those cases where we are having hallucinations or in a hypnotic trance. And an alternative characterization has been given of cases such as these which suggests that this need not be admitted even here. All we need admit is that since we always see things from some point of view, and since there are always conditions which influence our perception of anything, we are not provided, at the time of making a perception-claim, with all the information that would be needed to entail its truth. But admitting that what we ('directly') perceive only provides us with partial information does not necessitate the admission that it does provide us with full information about something else: information, moreover, which is itself inference-free.

9. If the argument from illusion had been a successful argument, it would have proved that *sometimes* we perceive (or sense) sense-data. But the sense-datum theorist wishes to prove that all perception is a matter of inferring on the basis of sense-data. A favourite argument used by sense-datum theorists to bridge the gap between some and all involves claiming that 'there is no intrinsic difference in kind between those of our perceptions that are veridical in their presentation of material things and those that are delusive' [S, 298]. Austin made several attacks on this claim, attempting to show that the 'perceptions' generally cited are not indistinguishable at all.

Ayer admits that much of what Austin says is true but beside the point:

> What Price and I were maintaining was not that it would never be possible to find any qualitative difference between experiences known to be veridical and experiences known to be delusive, in a sense of 'delusive' which did not necessarily imply that anyone was actually deluded, but only that appearances were in some way deceptive. It was rather that from a consideration of the experience alone it was not possible to tell to which category it belonged [298].

If, by 'appearances are deceptive', Ayer means that sometimes, on the basis of the way things appear, and not being sufficiently on guard, we tend to make perceptual mistakes (tend, for instance, to misidentify what we see), then he is correct. But the qualitative identity argument is a rather cumbersome instrument to prove such a point, which really doesn't need proof. For we all recognize that appearances can be deceptive in this sense. Does the argument, however, *prove* even this? It could only do so if it could establish that there really *is* no 'difference in kind' in our experiences ('our perceptions') in the cases usually cited in the literature of this controversy. And Austin argued that there are such differences in these cases, unless one simply excludes from consideration all respects in which these 'experiences' differ. 'Inevitably,' he says, 'if you rule out the respects in which *A* and *B* differ, you may expect to be left with respects in which they are alike' (*S & S*, 53). The point here, once again, is that there is no non-question-begging way of saying *what*, in a given case, the 'perception' is.[1]

Ayer has two slightly different objections to Austin's argument about 'qualitative difference'. In the first, he concedes that perhaps we can always find a qualitative difference, but such differences are often discovered only in retrospect and elude us at the time we are having the experience. Although we can distinguish dreams from waking experiences in retrospect, while we are dreaming we are often convinced of the dream's reality. 'Otherwise, no one would ever suffer from nightmares' [299].

I am not sure what to say about the dream problem, which has played such a prominent role in these disputes since Descartes. I tend to think, however, that dreams are so little understood and our method of reporting them is so makeshift, that not too much

---

[1] This would hold also for 'visual presentation' and 'content of an experience': expressions Ayer uses in *S*.

philosophic weight should be placed on them, either by those who use dreams to stress differences or by those who base 'indistinguishability' claims on them. Is it not perhaps misleading, for instance, to say that we entertain any beliefs when dreaming? It is true that when we awake from a dream, we often say that we were convinced of its reality. But is our being convinced while dreaming really the same thing, *qua* conviction, as our being convinced when awake that it was only a dream? On the other hand, when we are, as we say, 'taken in' by dreams, particularly nightmares, it is often not because of any 'qualitative similarity' at all. Dreams are usually thoroughly, even grotesquely 'unreal', and unlike normal (or even abnormal) waking experiences. Being frightened by a nightmare is very often more like being frightened by a horror film, where there is no question of really believing that what is on the screen is really happening, much less that we are participants in the horror that is unfolding before us.

Ayer's second objection is that, even though there might always be found some qualitative difference between 'delusive' and 'veridical' experiences, our ability to tell the difference in practice depends upon our ability to make use of past experience. Hence, it is still the case that there's nothing about the experience itself which enables us to tell whether it is 'delusive' or not. But this does not advance the sense-datum theorist's position. For past experience is employed just as much in identifying the characteristics of the present experience itself as it is in identifying what one sees as a real, external object. The one activity is as 'inferential' as the other. Thus, the characteristics of the present experience are not, in the required sense, 'sensibly given'. In Ayer's use of the term, perception is inferential throughout, and there could not be an epistemologically potent half-way house occupied by sense-data. The fact that perception is complex and constructive rather than simple and passive does not itself establish that what we perceive, even immediately, is not what we ordinarily say we perceive.

10. Ayer has now given up the 'continuous series' argument he had used in *FEK* to prove that we always sense or perceive sense-data. But this argument, he says, is not really needed by the sense-datum theorist.

> For if he can make good his initial step, that in any case in which anything of whatever kind is perceived, something is directly apprehended, or, as I prefer to put it, that every statement which claims

perception of a physical object is founded upon an experiential statement, and if he chooses to use the term 'sense-data' to refer to the 'objects' which figure in experiential statements, he will already have established the conclusion that every case of perception, whether veridical or delusive, involves the sensing of sense-data. The proof that physical objects do not figure in experiential statements . . . can be formulated succinctly by saying that whereas statements which refer to physical objects are always in some measure proleptic, experiential statements are not [300].

I have already argued that the sense-datum theorist can only make good his initial step by assuming its truth.[1] For it has not been shown, except by assuming it, that what is directly apprehended is not often a physical object or a part thereof; and it has not been shown, except by linguistic legislation, that physical objects cannot figure in experiential statements. And it has been argued, making use of the facts Ayer cites to support his claim that perception is inferential, that if statements which refer to physical objects are proleptic, so are experiential, statements.

11. In *FEK*, Ayer had maintained that the sense-datum theory is not really a two-entity doctrine at all. It is a recommendation to use a special technical terminology for talking about sense perception and its role in the foundations of empirical knowledge. Austin charged that this 'two-languages' view is both incorrect and disingenuous. Ayer's real view, said Austin, is that *in fact* we perceive only sense-data. Since Ayer maintains that the only empirical facts are facts about 'sensible appearances', he holds the traditional 'sensible manifold' doctrine. In his reply, Ayer says that though his presentation of the 'two-languages' doctrine may have been confused, Austin's criticisms of it miss the point. He also admits that he did take for granted the 'sensible manifold' doctrine, but maintains that he was correct in so doing.

Ayer's main point, in advancing the 'two-languages' doctrine, was that disputes between rival theories of perception are not factual but linguistic. The empirical facts are not in dispute. Rather, the dispute is about the correct 'conceptual scheme' in terms of which to order or characterize these facts. Thus, the sense-datum theory is just one way of talking about, of ordering, the empirical

[1] Ayer admits, of course, that the sense-datum theorist's way of talking begs the question. To admit it, however, does not make the question any less begged.

facts and our everyday conceptual scheme is another way of talking about the same facts. The only real choice between them is one of convenience or perspicuity. Since the empirical facts are facts about the sensible appearances, if we limit ourselves in the beginning to a mere description of sensible appearances, we can go on to consider how best to order these descriptions in terms of the requirements of a satisfactory conceptual scheme. In any case, Ayer cautions, the original programme was one of considering a revision of our present conceptual scheme. He was not simply advocating a programme of talking any way one wishes, as Austin charged.

This programme contains two important assumptions which need to be brought to light and examined. The first assumption is that our present conceptual scheme is that which philosophers have traditionally presented as 'the plain man's view'. It is important to focus attention on this assumption because it forms the chief reason for thinking that a revised conceptual scheme is necessary or even desirable (or more convenient). But, as I argued earlier, it was one of Austin's central claims in S & S that what philosophers, including Ayer in *FEK*, have taken the plain man's view to be isn't the plain man's view at all.[1] Furthermore, Austin attempted to show, by example and by argument, that our present conceptual scheme is not in fact 'inconvenient'. It accounts for the empirical facts, orders them, perfectly satisfactorily.

The second major assumption upon which Ayer's proposal depends is the assumption that the empirical facts can be identified and described quite independently of *any* conceptual scheme. This is the whole rationale of all the claims to neutrality made in *FEK* and throughout Ayer's recent paper. It is also the basis for the claim that one cannot be factually mistaken, but only verbally confused, about the sensible appearances. However, if what I have argued earlier is correct, then it is no more possible for the sensible manifold to be described neutrally (independent of any interpretation imposed by any conceptual scheme) than it is for ordinary perception-claims to be independent of interpretation in terms of a conceptual scheme. There could not be a description which simply sets out, *sans* interpretation of any kind, what we sense.

[1] There is no easy way of characterizing systematically what the plain man's view actually is. But we all know in practice what it is, for we are all plain men in everyday, non-professional life. And, knowing this, we know also that 'the plain man's view' is not the plain man's view.

This is not to claim that we are not presented with a sensible manifold which we order in terms of some conceptual scheme or other. Nor is it to deny that our conceptual scheme (including our social practices and conventions, our interests, and above all our language) is functional to a high degree in perception. I have denied only that we can isolate and describe purely neutrally the 'empirical facts' about sensible appearances. Any attempt to say *what* 'the facts' are will influence the rest of the discussion about *how* we are to characterize or arrange these facts in a conceptual scheme. There is a sensible manifold. But any description of it, since it is a description, is already infected by carry-over from whatever conceptual scheme one happens to be using. This not only influences any attempt to describe the facts: it influences perception itself, as has been pointed out by anthropologists and linguists such as Sapir and Whorf, by Wittgenstein, and by Austin himself, when he says (*S & S*, 100–101) that not only may different observers see different things on a single occasion, they may see the same thing differently.

Ayer's doctrine is, however, based upon a truth which is swept aside in Austin's attack on it: namely, the conceptual scheme we do have is not a matter of natural necessity. It might have been otherwise; and there may be room for change. However, if we are asked to exchange it for another, there should be ample reason for thinking that it is deficient in a way that the proffered substitute is not. I can agree with Ayer that philosophical disputes about perception are largely, if not wholly, linguistic, not factual. But these disputes, I would maintain (as, I think, would Austin), centre around the assessment of attacks upon the satisfactoriness of the conceptual scheme we already have. And if any progress is to be made in these disputes, then a task of high priority is to describe, and classify, as accurately as we can, that conceptual scheme itself. This, I take it, would be one of the functions of what Austin elsewhere calls 'linguistic phenomenology'.[1] In this task, too, absolute neutrality could not be achieved. We could not, as Austin thought, 'relook at the world without blinkers'.[2] But a good many of the blinkers could, I think, be removed. At the very least, we might as a result be in a better position to take up the question of whether our present conceptual scheme needs radical revision.

[1] 'A Plea for Excuses', *Philosophical Papers*, 130.
[2] Ibid.

12. In *FEK*, Ayer had distinguished two 'familiar' senses of the word 'see':

> one in which to say that something was seen implied that it existed but did not imply that it had the qualities it appeared to have, and one in which to say that something was seen did not admit of its lacking the qualities that it appeared to have, but did not imply that it existed [*S*, 302].

Austin denied that this second alleged sense of 'see' exists at all. If one does claim that something is seen, then one does imply that it exists, in *some* sense; for otherwise the phrase 'but it has the qualities it appears to have' is incoherent. *What* is said to really have these qualities?

Ayer now claims that Austin is wrong here on a question of 'linguistic fact'. For Austin himself talks of the drunkard seeing pink rats, which does not imply that these rats exist, but does imply that they are pink and not, say, green. But in fact it is Ayer who is mistaken here, not about linguistic facts, but about what his earlier doctrine was. For in *FEK* he had said that in the second sense of 'see',[1] we do not imply that what is seen exists *in any sense at all*. What Ayer probably meant to say then, and does mean to say now, is that one does not imply that what is seen exists as an external object. But if I claim that I see pink rats, then I imply in so saying that they exist in some sense; and Austin is prepared to admit that hallucinations and mirages do exist. They simply do not (on one explanation of their occurrence, at least), exist as external objects.[2] But there is no compelling reason to say that they are sense-data, in the full, philosophical, theory-laden sense of that expression. With respect to the colour of the drunkard's pink rats, Austin argued, in the same connexion, that the question of whether they are really pink or only appear to be pink makes no sense. The choice we are asked to make is not a genuine choice.

Austin's own explanation of the facts Ayer cited is that there are either different objects involved, or different ways of talking about the same object, or perhaps different ways of seeing the same object (seeing it *as* an *x*, seeing it double), none of which give rise

[1] Actually, in *FEK* he said this about his second sense of 'perceive' (p. 21). But the case of 'see' is exactly parallel.

[2] But it is only by forcing the 'material object' *vs.* 'sense-datum' dichotomy on us in the first place that this admission has any tendency to raise problems.

to any good reason for adopting a sense-datum terminology. In any case, Austin's main object of attack, with regard to the doctrine about two senses of 'see', was not its use to prove that we sometimes see things that don't exist, but its use to show that we always, in every case of seeing, see (in some sense) two things. Thus Austin rejects Ayer's interpretation of examples such as the one in which a man says, in one and the same perceptual context, both that he sees a large star and that he sees a silvery speck no larger than a sixpence.

> Most of us know that stars are very, very big, and that they are a very, very long way away; we know what they *look* like to the naked and earthbound eye, and we know a bit at any rate about what they *are* like. Thus, I can't see any reason at all why we should be tempted to think that 'seeing an enormous star' is incompatible with 'seeing a silvery speck'. Wouldn't we be quite prepared to say, and be quite correct in saying, that the silvery speck is a star? (*S & S*, 92).

The only object seen is a star which looks *from here* like a silvery speck.

Ayer does not find this convincing. He takes Austin to be saying that 'one and the same object . . . both is a large star and a small speck, just as one and the same object which I saw this morning both is a man shaved in Oxford and a man born in Jerusalem' [*S*, 303]. But this is a false analogy, says Ayer, for

> if one is using the word 'see' in the sense which implies that what is seen exists, it is impossible that one should see an object which is both larger than the earth and no larger than a sixpence, because no such object can exist. Of course, one may say with perfect propriety 'That small speck is a large star' but when one says this one is not implying that there *is* an object which is both a small speck and a large star; one is implying that something which from this distance *looks* very small *is* very large [303].

In reply to this, it should be pointed out that Ayer's characterization of the meaning (or force) of 'that small speck is a large star' is the *same* as that which Austin gives in the passage quoted above. Hence, whether Austin is forcing a false analogy on us or not, it can't be true that Austin has made the elementary logical blunder with which Ayer attempts to saddle him. Rather, Austin is claiming, as is Ayer, that what 'that small speck is a large star' *means* is that the thing which looks small from here is actually very large. The 'properties' Austin ascribes to what he sees (viz., the star) would only be incompatible if he were saying that one and the same thing is both larger than the earth and no larger than a sixpence *in the same respect*. And this is not what Austin, or anyone else who talks this way, is claiming. As Austin argues, (*S & S*, 95–6), the question of whether *the speck* is or is not really larger than a sixpence is a completely mad question: it demonstrates that the questioner doesn't understand the function, in this context, of the expression 'that speck'.

Ayer then goes on to use the fact, about which he and Austin are in agreement, that the expression 'that small speck . . .' refers to the way the star looks from here, to support another move into the sense-datum terminology:

> When we talk of seeing an object, like a star, we are inclined both to attribute it the properties which we believe that it really has, even though we do not see it *as* having them, and to represent ourselves as seeing whatever properties are phenomenally apparent to us. If these apparent properties are incompatible with those that we think the object really has, we bring in 'phenomenal' objects, like specks and dots and figures, to carry them. This is clearly a step in the direction of the sense-datum terminology [304].

But this step should be resisted. I do not mean to say that we should not bring in 'phenomenal' objects, but that Ayer's account of the taking of the step need not appear to be so philosophically potent. For representing ourselves as seeing whatever properties are phenomenally apparent to us is simply a linguistically convenient way of dealing with the fact that from here, in the case of the star, for instance, what we see looks very small indeed.[1] But, far from these apparent properties being incompatible with those that we think the object really has, its looking small from here, over a distance of several light years, is just what we should expect of a very large object like a star. As Austin says, (*S & S*, 93), it isn't as if the star, even from here, looks *to be* no larger than a sixpence, in the sense that we tend to judge that it is no larger than a sixpence.

[1] It is more convenient because it requires less vocal energy in normal contexts to bring in 'phenomenal objects': to say 'That white dot is my house' rather than 'What looks from here rather like a white dot is actually my house'.

This being so, Ayer's next move:

> If I suffered from double vision and seemed to see two specks, I should be undergoing an illusion. It is . . . quite natural for me to say . . . not that I seem to see but simply that I see two specks: and then we are admitting 'sense-data'.

doesn't seem so serious. For, in cases such as this, as Austin admitted, there are independent grounds for saying that sense-data exist: grounds which do not exist in the case of seeing the star under normal conditions. And even here, we need not bring in sense-data. We can say, as Austin suggests, that I 'see the star double', and then go on to explain the 'speck' terminology, as well as our use of 'seeing . . . double', in an entirely innocent way, along lines suggested above.

Ayer draws an interesting, and in the circumstances a surprising, moral from the discussion of the speck and the star. The moral is that 'we should not be too quick to assume that the "is" is the "is" of identity' when dealing with locutions like 'that silvery speck is a star'. Evidently, Ayer thinks that Austin has made this mistake in his discussion of such examples in *S & S*. But in fact, Austin seems to have accused Ayer of just this mistake:

> Ayer has jumped to the conclusion that 'perceive' must have different 'senses'—for if not, how could *different* answers to the question [what does *S* perceive?] all be *correct*? But the proper explanation of the linguistic facts is not this at all; it is simply that what we 'perceive' can be described, identified, classified, characterized, named in many different ways. If I am asked 'What did you kick?' I might answer 'I kicked a piece of wood', or I might say 'I kicked Jones' front door'; both of these answers might well be correct. . . What I kicked . . . could be described as a piece of painted wood, *or* identified as Jones' front door; the piece of wood in question *was* Jones' front door. Similarly, I may say ' I see a silvery speck' or 'I see a huge star'; what I see . . . can be described as a silvery speck, or identified as a very large star; for the speck in question *is* a very large star (*S & S*, 98).

That Austin has not assumed that the 'is' in question is the 'is' of identity is further shown by Austin's remark in a footnote to the passage just quoted:

> It doesn't follow, of course, that we could properly say, 'That very

large star is a speck'. I might say, 'That white dot on the horizon is my house', but this would not license the conclusion that I live in a white dot!

Ayer's failure to see that Austin does not assume that the 'is' is the 'is' of identity may be attributed to his own failure to see the significance of Austin's remarks about identification and description, which in turn may arise from Ayer's tendency to treat the way something looks from some position as a thing of a different sort (an appearance) that I see, with properties of its own.

13. The traditional philosophical motive for advancing a sense-datum theory is to provide foundations for our knowledge of the world. It has been widely held that the foundations must be both indubitable (for otherwise the knowledge-claims based upon them will not be secure) and factual (for our knowledge of the world is not analytic). Sense-data allegedly fill this double epistemological requirement. For sense-datum statements are obviously advanced as factual statements and, with the exception of verbal errors, it has been held that no factual mistake can be expressed by the utterance of such a statement. Austin strongly criticized the view that sense-datum statements are, as a class, incorrigible. He attempted to establish two main points in this connexion: (1) we can make factual mistakes about the way things appear to us, and (2) although some perception-claims are 'in fact incorrigible', these include 'material object' claims as well as claims about the way things appear. I argued in an earlier section that Austin confuses 'being incorrigibly justified' with 'being in fact incorrigible'. Some perception-claims are *unretractable* but, for some perhaps bizarre reason, untrue. Nevertheless, if Austin's first point is correct, then it would seem that one of the fundamental reasons for holding the sense-datum theory has been removed.

Ayer now says that he is 'inclined to think' that experiential statements can embody factual errors. He still wishes to maintain the 'slightly weaker' principle that 'the subject is the final authority' of the truth of experiential statements. But the falsity of even this weaker principle would not, he thinks, destroy the claim that 'the truth of statements claiming perception of physical objects is founded on the truth of experiential statements' [305]. It has already been argued that Ayer's notion of 'experiential statements' is defective. No statement can simply record, in a completely neutral way, that is sensibly given. If, however, Ayer had meant by this claim merely that the truth of statements claiming perception of physical objects is founded upon the truth of statements about experiences the claimant has, or has had, in the sense that statements of the latter sort are used as justification for our claims to perceive physical objects when such justification is in order, then the claim could be accepted. But, as Austin points out (*S & S*, 116), experiential statements of *this* sort will often in practice be other 'physical object' statements. They need not be, and often are not, the sort of 'qualitative descriptions' Ayer has in mind.

14. In his attack on Ayer's 'linguistic' version of the sense-datum theory, Austin attempted to establish the following claims:

> 1. There is no *kind* or *class* of sentences ('propositions') of which it can be said that *as such* (*a*) they are incorrigible; (*b*) they provide the evidence for other sentences; and (*c*) they must be checked in order that other sentences may be verified.

> 2. It is not true of sentences about 'material things' that *as such* (*a*) they must be supported or based on evidence; (*b*) they stand in need of verification; and (*c*) they cannot be conclusively verified (*S & S*, 123).

In the conclusion to his paper, Ayer denies that Austin has established 1.*b* and 2.*a*.[1]

However, Ayer has not in his paper argued against either of these theses. What he has done is to argue against theses which would result from the substitution of 'statement' for 'sentence' (or 'proposition') in Austin's claims. But these are claims Austin specifically *contrasts* with the theses about sentences or propositions. In fact, one of the main burdens of *S & S* is to argue that what we have to deal with in the assessment of perception-claims is always a sentence issued in a specific context: namely, a statement. These, however, must always be assessed on their own merits in individual cases. Some statements provide the evidence for other statements; others do not. Some statements about 'material things' must be supported by or based upon evidence; others do not need evidential support. It all depends upon the circumstances in which the individual statement is made. Austin is not always consistent in his own terminology in this sections of *S & S*. But it is clear what his criticisms of Ayer are and also what his own view is. To

[1] Although he accepts the force of 1(*a*), Ayer would also, presumably, wish to deny the other claims as well.

confuse the distinction between sentences and statements is to confuse the issue under dispute.

My main contentions may be summarized as follows: (1) Ayer has not adequately taken into account Austin's primary objections to the sense-datum theory; (2) the fundamental assumptions and claims of the theory, as presented by Ayer, can be resisted without compromise to our everyday beliefs and without denying the facts to which Ayer appeals; (3) the facts Ayer cites in support of the claim that perception is inferential actually militate against the central epistemological aims of the sense-datum theory. For these reasons, I conclude that Ayer has not vindicated the sense-datum theory.[1]

[1] Part of this paper was completed during the tenure of a generous fellowship from the National Endowment for the Humanities.

REJOINDER TO
PROFESSOR FORGUSON

A. J. Ayer

I will make a few brief comments on what appear to me to be the main points that Professor Forguson has raised.

1. Professor Forguson thinks that Austin was mainly concerned to show that 'the plain man's view' did not give rise to any philosophical problems, or at any rate not to any problems that would call for the introduction of sense-data. If this was Austin's intention, one might have expected him to say what these problems had been taken to be, and why he thought that they were not genuine. In fact, he does not attempt to do this, except indirectly by arguing that propositions about material things do not as such stand in need of justification. He proceeds rather as if he thought that he had only to discredit sense-datum theory for the problems which had called it forth to vanish with it. Since this conclusion would have been open to question even if Austin had succeeded in disposing of sense-datum theory, Professor Forguson is quite mistaken in saying that in order to rebut Austin's arguments I should have to show that the introduction of sense-data was 'inevitable'. It is enough if I have been able to show that it is legitimate.

As for the suggestion that the plain man of the sense-datum theorists is a straw plain man, I shall be surprised if Professor Forguson can point to any sense-datum theorist who has represented the plain man as believing that 'he always perceives one kind of thing'. If solid three-dimensional objects like tables and stones are commonly taken as examples, it is because they figure most prominently in what Moore called the common-sense view of the world. Neither is it in general true of sense-datum theorists that they have held the common-sense view of the world to be false. It is only when the common belief that we see and touch physical objects passes into the philosophical theory of naïve realism that their arguments come into play. If, as Professor Forguson thinks, the plain man is not a naïve realist, sense-datum theorists have no quarrel with him.

2. Professor Forguson admits that perceptual judgements are uncertain, 'in the sense in which this term is used by the sense-datum theorist'. He objects only in that he does not see why this sort of uncertainty should be held to constitute a philosophical problem. The answer is that it constitutes a problem only in the sense that it invites further analysis. If perceptual judgements go beyond their evidence, in the way I tried to indicate, then, as I said, it ought to be possible to formulate experiential statements which record the evidence without going beyond it. Professor Forguson argues that the effect of introducing such experiential statements is to draw a veil between the observer and the external world, but here he is mistaken. No doubt he has been misled by the sense-datum theorist's use of such expressions as 'directly see'. But, as I explained, all that can properly be meant by saying that material things are not directly seen is that no reference to them can occur in experiential statements: and the reason why no reference to them can occur in experiential statements is that such references have implications which experiential statements by definition do not carry. But from the fact that material things are not directly seen, in this special sense, it does not follow that they are not seen at all. Professor Forguson foists this conclusion on me, but without any warrant.

3. I explained in my essay that I was using the word 'evidence' in such a way that one proposition p was evidence for another proposition q, just in case p supported q, without entailing it. Consequently, I should not speak of seeing a pig as being evidence for the pig's existence, because the expression 'seeing a pig' would normally be understood as entailing that the pig existed. It was in order to avoid any suggestion of this entailment, that I spoke not of seeing a pig but of seeming to see one. Professor Forguson thinks that what I meant by 'seeming to see' in this usage, was 'only seeming to see', where the addition of the word 'only' carries the implication that one does not see what one seems to see. In fact, I did not mean this and I cannot find that Professor Forguson has any ground for supposing that I did.

4. When I said that perceptual judgements were the conclusions

of inductive inferences, I was not thinking only of the fact that in order to identify a physical object one has to draw upon one's past experience. As Professor Forguson correctly remarks, this is also true of the identification of sense-qualia. The point which I was concerned to make was rather that if a perceptual judgement, which incorporates the identification of some physical object, is to be true, a number of conditions must be satisfied which are not deductively established by the content of the sense-experience on which the judgement is immediately based. Since the only rational ground that one can have for assuming that these conditions are satisfied in the present instance is that one has found that experiences of the given kind have regularly fitted into the appropriate wider patterns, I think it proper to speak here of there being an inductive inference, even though no conscious process of inference may actually occur. There is not the same ground for speaking of inductive inference in the case where one simply records the presence of a sense-quale, because in this case there is no corresponding range of conditions which need to be satisfied for the statement to be true. To put it succinctly, the identification of a physical object is predictive in the way that the identification of a quale is not.

As for Professor Forguson's example of his seeing his mahogany dining room table, I am not at all inclined to follow Prichard in speaking of our mistaking colours for bodies. If I am obliged to give an answer to the rather strange question: 'What is it about which I am concluding that it is a table?', I am quite content to say that what Professor Forguson identifies as his table is either the table itself or some other physical object which he mistakes for it. In the case where he is undergoing a total hallucination, I should hesitate between saying that the question had no answer in these terms and cooking up an answer to it by saying that what he then mistakes for his dining room table is a figment of his imagination. In short, I do not wish to say that qualia are objects with regard to which it is ever significant, in concrete instances, to raise the question whether or not they are identical with the physical objects which they are taken to present. This does not, however, in the least debar me from holding that one's belief that one sees a physical object of such and such a sort is in all cases based on the presentation of some sense-quale, and that it is only the presentation of other qualia that enables one to determine whether the belief is true or false.

344

5. I have no thought of denying either that it is correct to speak of seeing an object when one does not see the whole of it or that seeing even an insignificant part of something is still seeing the object of which it is a part in the sense which Professor Forguson intends. On the other hand I am sure that he is entirely mistaken in saying that in a case where one sees only a part of a thing, and judges that the other parts of it are also present, one is making a judgement which does not go beyond the data at all. The proof that it does go beyond the data, even if the data are here taken as including the existence of the part in question, is that it is logically consistent with them that the other parts should not be there. Of course, if the part which one sees is described from the outset as a part of such and such an object, then the possibility that the other parts of the object are not present has already been excluded. But all that this shows is that one already goes beyond the data in giving such a description. If one confined oneself, as one evidently could, to giving a purely qualitative description of the part, it would become clear that in characterizing it as a part of something of which the other parts were not manifest, one would be drawing a conclusion which the data did not entail.

6. It is not true that 'qualitative descriptions are as inference-ridden as ordinary descriptions of what we see'. If I say 'this looks red to me' or 'I am sensibly presented with something red', in a sense in which it is understood that my use of the word 'this' or 'something' does not imply the presence of a physical object, the truth of my statement depends uniquely on the character of the visual datum to which I am referring. If I say 'this is a table' I am extrapolating beyond any present visual datum. It is because of this extrapolation, which does not occur in the other case, that statements at the level of 'this is a table' can be held to be inference-ridden in a way that descriptions of qualia are not.

7. I am not sure what is meant by saying that claims to perceive can be incorrigibly justified, if this is to be consistent, as Professor Forguson wishes it to be, with their turning out to be false. Perhaps what he has in mind is that once one has carried out the standard tests there is nothing more that one can reasonably do. It would be pointless to keep on examining the telephone, on the off-chance that one had previously misidentified it. With this I should agree, but I should not wish to say that in cases where I had made certain, in this sense, that it was a telephone this conclusion

345

was 'unretractable'. Suppose, what is surely conceivable, that the telephone had been removed but that I had been hypnotized into continuing to 'see' it. When I realized that this was the case, why should I be debarred from saying that my judgement that there was a telephone there had been mistaken?

8. On the subject of the argument from illusion, I do not think that Professor Forguson and I are in any serious disagreement. I have said that the argument, when properly stated, supplies a motive for adopting the sense-datum terminology, but I have never maintained that it left us with no alternative.

9. It is not clear to me whether Professor Forguson wishes to maintain that there is always something in the intrinsic character of delusive experiences which distinguishes them as such from veridical experiences. If he does maintain this, the empirical evidence goes against him; one set of counter-examples would be the perceptual illusions which physiologists can produce by directly stimulating the relevant areas of the brain. If he does not maintain it, he concedes my point.

10. I admit that it is through 'linguistic legislation' that physical objects are debarred from figuring in experiential statements, in the sense that this is a consequence of the way in which experiential statements have been defined. The question at issue is whether the use which I made of this concept is legitimate. It is not true that I simply assume its legitimacy. I give arguments in favour of it, as Professor Forguson himself must recognize, since he tries to rebut them.

11. Whether one conceptual scheme is more convenient than another is a relative question. We need to ask: convenient for what? I have never said that the plain man's way of talking about perceptual situations was inadequate to the facts: the shoe pinches at times but it can be made to fit. What I have argued is that the sense-datum terminology is in some ways more perspicuous, and that it is therefore convenient for the purposes of philosophical analysis.

Again, I have never said that experiential statements record what we sense without interpretation of any kind. I concede that any form of description involves some interpretation. I hoped that I had made it clear that what I meant by the neutrality of experiential statements was that they did not imply either the truth or falsity of the special assumptions which our perceptual statements ordinarily carry.

12. I am rather surprised to find Professor Forguson saying that the drunkard's pink rats must exist in some sense. Of course, when the drunkard himself claims to see pink rats, he may be implying that they exist, though even he need not be if he knows that he is undergoing an hallucination: but it clearly does not follow from this that when we say of the drunkard that he is seeing pink rats, we commit ourselves to assuming their existence in any sense at all. To say that the drunkard sees illusory pink rats would not ordinarily be construed, in the way that Professor Forguson takes it, as saying that he sees entities of a special, non-existent, type but rather as saying that the things which he sees, in one usage of the term, or only thinks he sees, in another, do not in fact exist. Professor Forguson has been misled here by his assumption that if we ascribe qualities to anything we must be implying that the thing in question exists in some sense in order to have these qualities. But this assumption, though plausible, is mistaken. If I say that my friend hopes to have a handsome son, my statement is not rendered incoherent by the fact that the son which he hopes for may never in any sense exist. I am certainly not saying that he hopes for a son who does not exist as an external object. In the case of the drunkard, one can indeed take the decision to say that there is something which he sees. But, as I pointed out in my essay, this is to take a crucial step towards the adoption of a sense-datum terminology.

I continue, therefore, to believe that Austin was mistaken here on a question of linguistic fact. I also still think that he was confused about the speck and the star. If he meant the analogy with the man who was shaved in Oxford and born in Jerusalem to be taken seriously, he was committing himself to the self-contradictory proposition that one and the same object both is a large star and a small speck. If he did not mean it to be taken seriously, and really meant to say no more than that referring to the speck was a way of referring to what the star looked like when seen from a distance, then the point of his saying that 'what I see can be described as a silvery speck or identified as a very large star' is elusive, to put it mildly. To the extent that he represents the speck as an object of sight he is in fact allying himself with the sense-datum theorist.

13. I am still puzzled about incorrigibility, but have nothing useful to add to what I said in my essay. Professor Forguson is quite right in saying that one perceptual statement, in my sense of

the term, may be used to justify another. This is, however, in no way inconsistent with my thesis that the justification of any perceptual statement can always be taken to the point where it consists in the truth of an experiential statement.

14. Professor Forguson says that I have not argued against Austin's theses that 'there is no kind or class of sentences ("propositions") of which it can be said that as such they provide the evidence for other sentences' and that 'it is not true of sentences about material things that they must be supported or based on evidence', because I have spoken of statements where Austin spoke of sentences or propositions. I do not think that there is anything in this. It is clear that Austin was using the word 'sentence' to refer not simply to types of series of marks but rather to types of signs to which a meaning had been attached in accordance with some standard linguistic rule; and this is just how I was using the word 'statement'. I certainly did not intend to imply that it was only in a limited set of contexts that perceptual judgements were founded on descriptions of sense-qualia. I explicitly claimed that this was true in all cases. Consequently I am sure that I was arguing against Austin's theses, and I believe that I fulfilled my aim of showing that he failed to establish them. Professor Forguson does not share this belief, but I do not find that he has given me sufficient reason to think that it is false.

Part IV

How to Do Things with Words

CRITICAL REVIEW OF
HOW TO DO THINGS WITH WORDS

Walter Cerf

I INTRODUCTION

DURING his lifetime Austin fathered one book, a translation of Frege's *Foundations of Arithmetic*. In 1961, one year after Austin's death, Urmson and Warnock collected his *Philosophical Papers* (*PhP*). In their foreword to *PhP*, Urmson and Warnock expressed the hope that Austin's Harvard lectures on the concept of performatives be published later. Urmson fulfilled this hope in 1962 with the publication of *How To Do Things With Words* (*HTD*), the book presently under discussion. Earlier the same year Warnock had edited *Sense and Sensibilia* (*S & S*).

Austin had discovered performatives in the late thirties and had been dealing with them for many years in his Oxford lecture courses and occasionally in his papers. In fact, performatives became Austin's hallmark as the ghost in the machine had become Ryle's and language games Wittgenstein's. It is not easy to undo the effects of hallmarks. Kant said of his distinction between synthetic and analytic judgements that it deserved to be called classical, and the future submitted to his dictum. Austin, on the contrary, had become quite critical of his distinction between performatives and constatives in a 1956 B.B.C. broadcast published in *PhP*. Yet the distinction continued to be treated in philosophical literature as if it deserved to be called classical. In *HTD*, Austin presents his doctrine of speech acts. This doctrine is the *Aufhebung* of his old distinction between performatives and constatives. The old distinction is being absorbed by a new one: that between the force and meaning of an utterance. The doctrine of speech acts classifies the forces of an utterance. (To utter something is, in terms proposed in *HTD*, to perform a speech act.) With respect to what

351

Austin *had* been doing, the doctrine of speech acts represents the culmination of his attempts to rejuvenate and clarify the use of 'uses of language' (*HTD*, p. 100). On the other hand, with respect to what Austin might have had in mind for the future, the doctrine of speech acts would appear to lead to 'a general doctrine about action' (*HTD*, p. 106) and in another direction to a new science of language (*PhP*, p. 180). Thus the doctrine of speech acts has a pivotal role—or, rather, would have had such a role if Austin had been allowed to continue his work.

I propose to focus my discussion on the doctrine of speech acts: that is, on lectures VIII–XII. From Urmson's introduction to *HTD* it is not clear when Austin began to develop the concept of speech acts. I would surmise that at the very latest this must have been in his Oxford lectures in Words and Deeds, 1952–54, more than ten years ago. Yet this tremor in linguistic philosophy has so far found few registrants. I shall also try to sketch a few lines of communication between aspects of Austin's thought and certain preoccupations of phenomenologists and existentialists. For, though Austin's is but a wave in the turbulences engendered by Wittgenstein, the wave has a quite distinctive colour. It is not all English silver sea. It is tinted by foreign bodies of a continental sort. It is tinted by a descriptive attitude made popular by phenomenology and by a holism in conflict with traditional English atomism and in harmony with existentialism from Heidegger to Merleau-Ponty. However tenuous these lines of communication between English and continental philosophies turn out to be, they are preferable, I presume, to none at all. My first task, however, is to give a rough outline of the whole territory covered in *HTD*.

II LINNAEUS OF SPEECH ACTS

Lectures I and VII of *HTD* draw, and then begin to erase, the distinction between constatives and performatives, between utterances used to state something and utterances used to do something. The former are true or false whereas the latter, though they might in some sense imply (p. 45) statements that are true or false, are primarily felicitous or infelicitous. In dealing with the various kinds of infelicities that can befall performatives, Austin has constant recourse to the situation or circumstances in which they are uttered. There is something about performatives that makes them situation-bound in a way and to a degree absent in constatives, as traditionally conceived. 'As traditionally conceived' is an important reservation. For, as soon as Austin has established the apparently clear-cut distinction between constatives and performatives, he proceeds to show that the distinction breaks down. It breaks down because statement as traditionally conceived turns out to be a typical philosophical simplification ('It's not things, it's philosophers that are simple'. *PhP*, p. 23; *HTD*, p. 38). A careful examination of criteria supposedly distinctive of performatives leads Austin to the conclusion that none of these criteria will quite do. On the one hand, a great many performatives require to be assessed in a general dimension of correspondence with facts. On the other hand, statements turn out to have dimensions similar to those of felicity and infelicity (*HTD*, pp. 55, 91). Statements are 'speech acts no less than all those other speech acts that we have been mentioning and talking about as performative'. They 'are not so very different, after all, from pieces of advice, warnings, verdicts and so on' (*PhP*, pp. 237-8; *HTD*, pp. 147 f.). Constatives and performatives are similarly tied to the whole situation in which they are uttered (*HTD*, p. 142). In brief, the presumed island of performatives and constatives turns out to be part of a continent, the continent of speech acts. The exploration of this continent becomes the core enterprise of *HTD*. Austin is returning 'to fundamentals', to the 'many senses . . . in which to say something *is* to do something' (p. 94). The Columbus of the performatives turns into the Cortez of the realm of speech acts. Let us look more closely at the way he administers it.

Austin divides the land of speech acts into three provinces. The first province is that of the *locutionary* acts (*HTD*, pp. 94 f.). The capital of the whole realm is situated in this province. Roughly, a locutionary act is any act *of* saying something in the full normal sense of 'saying'. To this full, normal sense of 'saying' (*HTD*, pp. 92, 5 f.) belong, first, the uttering of noises ('performing phonetic acts', 'uttering phones'); second, the uttering of noises as belonging to a certain vocabulary and conforming to a certain grammar ('performing phatic acts', 'uttering phemes'); and third, the uttering of phemes as having a certain sense and reference ('performing rhetic acts', 'uttering rhemes'). The other two provinces of the realm of speech acts are those of the *illocutionary* and *perlocutionary* speech acts (*HTD*, pp. 99, 101). An *illocutionary* act is an act we perform *in* saying something, and a *per*locutionary act is an act we perform *by* saying something.

After having made these preliminary distinctions Austin, as is his wont, develops scruples about them. The borderline between illocutionary and perlocutionary acts is particularly disturbing (cf. pp. 109 f.). Austin takes the 'in' and 'by' to be symptoms of a difference of two general kinds of acts, but runs into difficulties in trying to distinguish them clearly (*HTD*, pp. 122 f.; cf. p. 104). *In* saying, 'The bull is ferocious' I am warning you. I am 'performing the illocutionary act' of warning you. I intend my utterance 'to have the force' of warning you. *By* saying, 'The bull is ferocious' I am persuading you or I mean (hope, am trying) to persuade you, not to enter the arena. I am performing or mean to perform a perlocutionary act of persuasion. I intend my utterance to have, Austin *might* have said, the force of persuading you. This, however, is not what he does say. He disallows that 'he performed a perlocutionary act' and 'his utterance had a perlocutionary force' are mutually substitutable. In fact, I do not remember him ever using 'perlocutionary force'. Austin reserves the term 'force' rather arbitrarily, it would seem, for illocutionary acts; and he is at his tortuous worst—but also at his subtle best—in lecture IX where he tries to clarify the distinction between illocutionary and perlocutionary acts by way of their having or not having consequences, effects, responses, sequels, or objects. It will be noted that perlocutionary acts are allowed nearly to fade away in the last part of the book. He does not classify them and this is surely the strongest proof of his loss of interest in them. His interest is mainly with the illocutionary acts, that is, with what he dubs the 'forces' of an utterance. The old distinction between constatives and performatives becomes a distinction within the class of illocutionary acts. To state, describe, and report are no less illocutionary acts than to warn, promise, and order. 'I am merely stating a fact; the bull is ferocious' and 'I am warning you; the bull is ferocious' make both explicit in different situations what I am doing in saying, 'the bull is ferocious'. Though the meaning (sense and reference) of my saying, 'The bull is ferocious' might be the same, the *forces* of my utterances are different. The distinction between the illocutionary forces and the meaning of an utterance is one important distinction he leaves untouched in *HTD*. It is quite likely, though, that this distinction, too, might have turned out to be unsatisfactory to him.

There are indications of doubts concerning the theory according to which 'meaning' is equivalent to 'sense' and 'reference' (*HTD*, p. 148). And the very use of the metaphorical term 'force' as well as the already mentioned difficulties of distinguishing clearly the illocutionary force of an utterance from its perlocutionary consequences make one suspect that there remained much to be elucidated about 'the performance of a speech act'.

Austin divides the illocutionary acts into five subclasses meant to replace his old distinction between constatives and performatives. There are the illocutionary acts of giving a verdict (verdictives like 'acquit' or 'assess'), of exercising powers (exercitives like 'appoint' and 'name'), of commitments (commissives like 'promise' and 'bet'), of social behaviour (behabitives—'a shocker this' (p. 150)—like 'apologize' and 'commend') and finally 'acts of exposition involving the expounding of views', etc. (p. 160) (expositives like 'state' and 'reply').

Altogether, Austin shows himself to be quite a Linnaeus in the field of speech acts. He classifies speech acts into locutionary, illocutionary and perlocutionary acts; he classifies locutionary acts into uttering phones, phemes and rhemes; and he classifies illocutionary acts into uttering verdictives, exercitives, commissives, behabitives and expositives. Some of Austin's critics, admitting his superb gifts of linguistic discrimination, regret that they were used by him to change philosophy into a sort of botany of utterances (cf. *Philosophical Books*, vol. IV, No. 2, p. 31). I disagree. His efforts at classification, to be sure, do push the 'logical' analysis of language one step further from philosophy and toward grammar. It may well be the case, however, that the new science of language Austin occasionally envisages must start with loosening up and replacing traditional grammatical categories. And Austin is not alone in taking a new grammatical look at language and developing what he rather tentatively calls 'linguistic phenomenology' (*PhP*, p. 130). There is not only the school of Zellig Harris with which I suppose he must, or would, have felt rather kindred in intent; there is also the Heidegger of *The Introduction to Metaphysics* (pp. 52–74) who moves in the same direction, though he would have appeared to Austin barbaric—both in his revolutionary ferocity and in his total lack of analytic talents. Anyhow, Austin's botanizing rarely loses sight of the grand problems of traditional and contemporary philosophy. When he feels that his public is tiring of his distinctions and subtleties—'Why not cut the cackle?' (*HTD*, p. 122)—he is able to remind them of the philosophical problems to which he believes his minutiae to be relevant—though he might add, as if pleased by his role of philosophical *enfant terrible* that he is not sure importance is important (*PhP*, p. 219). As a composer of linguistic minuets and *Kleine Nachtmusiken*, Austin will probably delight generations of civilized listeners (if not dancers). The doctrine of speech acts, however, is not a *Kleine Nachtmusik*; its scope demands the grander design of a symphonic structure. His doctrine, to be sure, abounds in subtle effects; yet it is precisely its over-all structure that is weak; and I confess to, and apologize for, being less interested in the wealth of his linguistic observations than in the doctrine's over-all structure. I will be told that this is like removing the salt in order to judge the taste of the sea. Granted; but no one thirsty will care. The weaknesses in the over-all structure of the theory of speech acts are as follows. There is, in the first place, a strange lack of incisiveness about the business of classification itself. Secondly, the very genus 'speech act' or rather, 'performance of speech act', appears to be an unfortunate choice. Finally, Austin's preoccupation with the classification of speech acts and forces is quite likely a flight from what he himself recognizes as his main subjects: 'the total speech act in the total speech situation' (*HTD*, p. 147). I shall discuss these points in that order.

III CLASSIFICATION

What is Austin doing when he classifies speech acts? To begin with, what is the nature of Austin's classification of locutionary acts into phonetic, phatic and rhetic acts?

'We had made three rough distinctions between the phonetic act, the phatic act, and the rhetic act' (p. 95) and similar passages suggest in their context that phonetic, phatic and rhetic acts are meant to be subclasses within the class of locutionary acts. However, phonetic, phatic and rhetic acts are also shown to form an obvious hierarchy of dependences. One cannot utter words without making noises, but one can make noises without thereby uttering words. Words can be uttered that have no meaning, while meanings cannot be conveyed in speech without words being uttered. The suspicion arises that the phonetic act, the phatic act and the rhetic act are not subclasses, but parts of the locutionary act—as blossom, stem, leaf and root are parts and not classes of flowers. And this is what we find Austin to imply when he says (p. 107) that 'the locutionary act embraces doing many things at once to be complete'. Phonetic, phatic and rhetic acts belong together, not like species of a genus, but like parts of a composite. They all have to flow together if a locutionary act is to come off.

Yet the new model of the relation of phonetic, phatic and rhetic acts has shortcomings of its own. It is true that the hierarchy of dependences between them seems to indicate that a phonetic act could exist in isolation from the other two acts, and the phatic act in isolation from the rhetic. But when thus taken in isolation, are they locutionary acts? Austin has told us (*HTD*, p. 94) that a locutionary act is any act of saying something in the full, normal sense. And in this full, normal sense, the monkey's making noises—being only a phonetic and not also a phatic and rhetic act—is not a locutionary act (p. 96). It would seem, then, that phonetic, phatic and rhetic acts must be understood to be, not separable parts, but mere moments or aspects, of the locutionary act. And so Austin says (p. 146) that '. . . the phatic act, the rhetic act, etc., are mere abstractions'. I do not know if Austin's hiding the phonetic act under the 'etc.' is a symptom of some unconscious sort of behaviouristic commitment that made it difficult for him to lower the minimal observable core of the whole locutionary act to a mere abstraction (cf. *HTD*, pp. 110 f.) (The use of 'abstraction' is an excusable slide into empiricist folklore). In any case, phonetic, phatic and rhetic acts are no longer constitutive parts, but abstract moments or aspects of the locutionary act. And in saying that without these aspects being present the locutionary act is not genuine (p. 146) Austin must be understood to assert, I think, that these aspects define his use of the term 'locutionary act'. But if phonetic, phatic and rhetic acts are mere aspects of the locutionary act, why call them acts? Surely, the red of the rose will be a flower only to one who does not know how to use 'flower'.

Austin's classification of speech acts into locutionary, illocutionary and perlocutionary acts suffers similar vicissitudes. In fact, they are more pronounced here. He begins with what appears to be a division of the genus speech act into three species (pp. 99, 101, 103, 107, 109). But we are also given the occasional impression that the three acts are really the basic constitutive parts that must unite to bring off the speech act (Chapter VIII, IX). In the end, however, we are told that locutionary and illocutionary acts are 'aspects' (pp. 144/5) of the speech act and it is only through abstracting from one that the other comes into focus. (It would follow, by the way, that phonetic, phatic and rhetic acts are mere aspects of an aspect.) 'The locutionary as much as the illocutionary is an abstraction only: every genuine speech act is both' (p. 146). That is to say, I suppose, that the term 'speech act' is to be applied only to such uses of language as are both locutionary and illocutionary (perlocutionary acts being lost in the shuffle). This leads to some awkwardness. Suppose I am reading aloud to my wife. Having phonetic, phatic and rhetic aspects, my reading aloud would be a locutionary act; but if it were true that my reading aloud to her had no illocutionary aspect, it would not be a speech act at all. Or take the 'Ouch!' a patient utters in the dentist's chair. 'Ouch!' is not saying something—in the full, normal sense of 'saying something'. It has, however, illocutionary forces that can be made explicit: the patient is showing his pain and warning the dentist. Should we not say that 'Ouch!' is a speech act? We cannot, if we accept Austin's definition. This sort of argument, however, is of little weight. Austin's definition of 'speech act' deviates from whatever ordinary use the term might seem to have; but these deviations are surely defensible if 'speech act', though it sounds ordinary enough, is meant by Austin to be a technical term. My criticism is concerned, to repeat, with a certain weakness in the over-all structure of Austin's doctrine of speech acts. He presents his doctrine as a classification of speech acts. Yet this supposed classification changes its character repeatedly and, it would seem, without Austin being aware of the changes. His doctrine begins with what appears to be a division of the class of speech acts into subclasses. This division of the class of speech acts changes into a dissection of the composite speech act into its constituent parts. And this dissection, in turn, changes into the isolation of characteristics or aspects definitory of 'speech act'. I find these hidden metamorphoses surprising. One expects a sharpshooter to know the mechanism of his rifle.

Yet, quite apart from the changes it undergoes, the classificatory business itself is surprising in view of the purpose it is meant to serve. Austin summarizes in the form of 'morals' the few 'hopeful fireworks' he was able to explode in his book. The first and most important of these morals is the following: 'The total speech act in

CRITICAL REVIEW OF *How to Do Things with Words*

the total speech situation is the *only actual* phenomenon which, in the last resort, we are engaged in elucidating' (*HTD*, p. 147). As this moral is formulated in the very last lecture, we might suspect Austin of wanting to show that he has come only at the end of his lectures to see their true target. Hence, he must not be accused of having missed it. This is surely to misunderstand him. His aim was from the beginning that of elucidating the total speech act in the total speech situation (*HTD*, pp. 8, 16, 52, etc.). And the classification of speech acts into locutionary, illocutionary and perlocutionary acts; the classification of locutionary acts into phonetic, phatic and rhetic acts; and the classification of illocutionary acts into verdictive, exercitive, commissive, behabitive and expositive acts—in one word, this whole classificatory doctrine of speech acts—is meant to elucidate the total speech act in the total speech situation. There seems something surprisingly disproportionate between the doctrine and the purpose it is supposed to serve, between the business of classification and the 'moral' Austin has in mind. In order to see more clearly this disproportionateness, we will proceed to the very thing the classification of which Austin undertakes: the speech act. We have looked at what Austin does when he classifies speech acts; but we have said nothing yet about the genus speech act itself. Indeed, we have used the term 'speech act' as if it expressed a legitimate concept. An examination of this concept or rather of the concept of performing a speech act is our next subject.

IV 'PERFORMING A SPEECH ACT'

'He said, "Dangerous bull"' is one thing. 'He performed a certain locutionary act having phonetic, phatic and rhetic aspects, and in performing this locutionary act he performed the illocutionary act of warning me' is quite another. The second purports to be Austin's elucidation of the first—Austin prefers 'elucidation' to 'analysis', perhaps because it is less commissive—using his classification of speech acts as a basic conceptual framework. In this section I shall argue that the generic concept of performing an act obfuscates rather than elucidates how we do things with words.

It must be observed, first of all, that, as an ordinary phrase of everyday discourse, 'performing an act' is of a rather limited use. In fact, the only context in which 'performing an act' sounds quite ordinary is the somewhat extraordinary world of the circus and variety shows. In a less dramatic way, someone is said to be performing an act when he is doing things as if he were on the stage. It is certainly not in this sense that Austin intends our saying something to be the performance of an act. Nor does Austin wish to imply that saying something is performing an act in the related, but no longer quite ordinary, sense of taking up a role, either in the sociological sense of more or less explicit assignments given by a group to its members, or psychologically, as in Sartre, where anything—being a waiter, being sad—that a man *knows* himself to be is declared to be *eo ipso* something he plays at or performs as a rôle. Nor is 'performing a speech act' similar to 'performing an act of courage', which might be heard in ordinary English, natural languages being, after all, rather hospitable to words and phrases that have been invented or given a peculiar use in metaphysics, science, psychology or any other discourse that happens to be respected. 'He performed an act of courage' does not say what it was he did, but praises whatever it was he did as something courageous. 'He performed a speech act' says what it was he did— he spoke—and does not praise (or blame) what he did as something speechy. Besides, 'performing an *act* of courage' would usually— though not necessarily—be understood to imply that someone was engaged in an *action*, in a sense of the term 'action' in which speaking is rarely taken to be an action. I will have to say a few things below about the relations between 'action' and 'act' and between 'performing an action' and 'performing an act'. At present I merely wish to stress that Austin uses 'performing an act' in none of the ways in which 'performing an act' is accepted in common English usage. In substituting 'performing a speech act' for 'saying something' he is not substituting one ordinary English phrase for another.

What, then, is he doing? Is he doing the sort of thing that so delighted Mr. Jourdain, *bourgeois gentilhomme*? Mr. Jourdain is saying that the bull is dangerous? Not at all. In performing a locutionary act he is performing an illocutionary act. Mr. Jourdain is taking walks for his health? Really not. By performing ambulatory acts he is performing salutary acts. Mr. Jourdain would be delighted. He mistakes new words for new insights. If one is not Mr. Jourdain, however, he may well doubt that he was offered anything 'elucidatory' about either the total speech act in the total speech situation or the total walking act in the total walking situation—if these are the sort of things that need elucidation. He has merely learned a peculiar linguistic game or, possibly, some useful classification.

It would appear preposterous to suspect Austin of playing such a game with us. He must have had good reason for wanting us to see people saying something as people performing speech acts. I am unable to find a statement of his reasons. The choice of 'performing an act' as basic term or highest genus in his doctrine of speech acts remains without explicit justification.

I am inclined to think that Austin saw no need for such justification, because he was not aware that he had been making a choice. He must have been led from 'talking', 'saying something', and 'speaking' to 'performing a speech act' by a chain of substitutions that appeared harmless. To say something or to speak is to issue an utterance. To issue an utterance is to do something. To do something is to perform an action. To perform an action is to perform an act. To say something is, then, to perform an act of speaking, that is, a speech act. Very smoothly one is led from an ordinary word—'speaking', 'talking', 'saying something'—to a quite nonordinary use of the phrase, 'performing a speech act'. And there can really be no doubt that this is a non-ordinary use. You are asking, 'What is John doing?' Imagine someone answering, 'He is performing speech acts'. Is John putting on a show? Is he doing tricks? Is he playing a rôle? Is he on the stage? Nonsense, he is just talking.

I propose to scrutinize for a moment the above chain of substitutions. All its links are questionable, some more, some less. First of all, 'to say something' and 'to speak' stand for concepts which are not the same, however close their relation. Asked to report what John did, I may say, 'He spoke' and I may not say, 'He spoke something'. On the other hand, I may not say, 'He said'; but I may say, 'He said something'. Yet there is quite a difference between 'He spoke' and 'He said something'. 'He spoke' is indeed an answer to the question, 'What did he do?'; 'He said something' really is not—somewhat as 'He listened' and 'He looked' do report what he did, while, 'He heard something' and 'He saw something' do not, or do it quite differently, indirectly stressing the result rather than the effort. If, then, 'to say something' and 'to speak' are different concepts, there would seem to be some *prima facie* reason to suspect an elucidation of 'saying something' that substitutes 'performing a *speech* act' for 'saying something'.

Equally questionable is the link that leads from 'saying something' to 'issuing an utterance'. The latter surely introduces a concept quite different from both 'saying something' and 'speaking'. It introduces the idea of something inner becoming outer, in the metaphysical sense of something mental becoming physical. 'Utterance' thus perpetuates a metaphysical aspect of the very term 'expression' that it was obviously meant to replace. 'Expression' Austin calls 'an odious word' (p. 75). 'To utter' is not exactly lovable either, and 'to issue an utterance' even less so. The latter has, however, one advantage. Issuing an utterance appears very much like doing something, in the strong sense of performing an action, while expressing does not, or much less so. However, one might well ask whether it is logic or accident that permitted the linguistic version of the law of conspicuous consumption to turn the simple word 'to utter' into the complex phrase 'to issue an utterance' while not permitting it to turn the simple 'to express' into the complex 'to issue an expression'. The latter would have appeared just as much a sort of doing something as issuing an utterance does. This 'issue' business can become a bit of a hoax, anyhow. It is not a hoax at all if someone is said to issue an order or to issue a proclamation, instead of simply being said to order X or to proclaim Y, for the more complete phrase separates the ordering and proclaiming from what is ordered or proclaimed. 'He issued an order' does not demand completion by adding what the order was, while, 'He ordered' does of course need this completion. Also, it introduces overtones of physical doings—water issuing from the ground or pus from the pimple—at the same time that it succeeds in stressing typical human aspects as are those of initiative and authority. One can only marvel at the ingenuity of a linguistic device which permits so many flies to be killed with one stroke. 'Issuing an utterance', however, sails under false flags. In the first place, the separation of the uttering from what is uttered is in need of no extra device, as this is precisely one of the functions of the ordinary distinction between 'to speak' and 'to say'. Secondly, the emphasis of initiative and authority, so useful in the change of 'to order' and 'to proclaim' into 'to issue an order' and 'to issue a proclamation', seems ordinarily to be quite out of place with respect to 'to utter'; the situations in which saying something or uttering something demand a particular show of initiative and authority are far and few between. In sum, 'issuing an utterance' alters considerably what is ordinarily meant by 'saying something'. Austin has turned saying something into the sort of doing something that must be called performing, or engaging in, an action. 'Performing an action' is, indeed, the link in the chain of secret substitutions that leads to 'performing an act' as the terminal concept whose division into classes is the core of Austin's doctrine of speech acts.

Why must we be led beyond 'performing an action' to 'performing an act'? Because of two related difficulties that 'performing an action' does raise, and 'performing an act' does not. The first difficulty is that, usually, saying something just is not the sort of thing at all that is meant by 'engaging in (or performing) an action' at the sense in which issuing an order and issuing a proclamation may be said to be performances of action. Secondly, if saying something is doing something in the relatively strong sense of performing an action—engaging in a speech action—then saying, 'The wall is yellow', (locutionary); talking English, or warning you, *in* saying that the wall is yellow (illocutionary); answering your question, or misleading you *by* saying that the wall is yellow (perlocutionary); all of these would be equally performances of actions. And yet there seems to be no doubt that some of them are more like actions than others and that some of them are not like actions at all.

'Performing an act' makes these difficulties disappear. Though saying something cannot normally be classified as the performance of an action in any ordinary sense of the phrase without offending the rules of linguistic propriety, it can apparently be called the performance of an act without being challenged. Secondly, though 'action' and 'performing an action' do not apply equally well to locutionary, illocutionary and perlocutionary spheres, the concepts of act and performance of act do seem so to apply and thus permit a homogeneous specification of the genus 'saying something' (='performing speech acts') into locutionary, illocutionary and perlocutionary acts. Hence, 'performing a speech act' rather than 'performing a speech action' becomes the terminal link of the chain. For much that could not possibly qualify as an action can still be said to be an act.

All of this may explain Austin's preference for 'act' and 'performing an act' over 'action' and 'performing an action'. Yet there remains a mystery. How could Austin fail to see the differences between the concepts of act and action? Passages in which 'act' and 'action' (and the corresponding 'performances') are handled as mutually substitutable are too numerous to be explained away. (cf. pp. 6, 8, 11, 13 f., 20 f., 45 f., 62 f., 65, 69 f., 70, 80, 94 f., 109 f.) The following observations might throw some light on this puzzle. 'Taking action', 'engaging in action', and 'performing an action' are of course perfectly familiar phrases within our everyday discourse. So is 'performing an act'. Within everyday discourse, 'performing an act' means, as noted above, any sort of behaviour that is the taking over of a rôle or the putting on of a show. Acts performed in this sense—the act, say, of the trapeze artist—have a strong action character, and sounding very much alike, the ordinary 'act' thus sneaks in the place of 'action' without raising suspicions. Once in place, it is in fact employed by Austin in an entirely different way, completely unacceptable in ordinary discourse. Yet this new way remains undetected because it is a way *philosophers* are in fact quite familiar with—familiar, though, not in everyday discourse, but in the learned discourse of metaphysics, epistemology and philosophical psychology. In these discourses, almost any verb whose grammatical subject is man may be traditionally and familiarly translated into 'performing an act of X'. 'Performing an act', as it is familiarly used in everyday discourse— the performance of a trapeze act—and 'performing an act' as it is familiarly used in some learned discourses, slide into each other and the second succeeds in replacing the first without notice and challenge. 'To perform an action', in the familiar everyday sense, has become 'to perform an act' of traditional metaphysics, epistemology and psychology; and, to summarize the whole chain, 'saying something' has become 'performing a speech act'.[1]

It may be objected that I have assumed without argument that the actual meaning of Austin's generic 'performing an act' is the one familiar from traditional metaphysics. However, as Austin does not try to give meaning to 'performing an act' he must have thought that we are familiar with it; and the only 'performing an act' that we are familiar with, apart from the context of the circus and variety show, is its use in philosophy and psychology. This, then, must be the meaning of Austin's 'performing an act'. There is perhaps a more convincing, though rather circuitous, way of

[1] 'Act' and 'action' also get Stuart Hampshire into trouble. Cf, for instance, *Thought and Action*, p. 116.

arguing my case. I begin by pointing out a basic difference between the use of 'performing an action' and the Austinian 'performing an act'. 'Performing an action' permits comparative application, 'performing an act' does not. What I mean by comparative application is this. In comparison with gossiping, the issuance of orders and proclamations is the performance of actions while gossiping is not. Yet it is also quite feasible to say that all John did was just issue orders and proclamations instead of taking action. On the other hand, any of these verbs can be expressed as 'performing the act of X' with no idea of comparative degrees involved. Even 'daydreaming' can be translated into 'performing the act of daydreaming'. It is as much or as little of an act as issuing orders. It would surely be impossible to talk of performing the *action* of daydreaming, daydreaming being exactly the sort of thing against which the concept of action, but not the concept of act, must be held in order to be understood.

Does this mean that act and performing an act are higher concepts, and action and performing an action the lower, more specific classes? One might think so. Austin himself, however, tells us that the doctrine of *speech acts* should lead to a general doctrine about *action* (*HTD*, p. 106). This might entail that the class of acts is identical with the class of actions, which would corroborate what has been said regarding Austin's failure to distinguish between 'action' and 'act'. At the same time, however, it would contradict what he is in fact doing, namely reserving 'performing an action' for a smaller sphere of human doings than 'performing an act'. The decisive point lies somewhere else. We must come to realize that if there is any class relation between act and action (or between performing an act and performing an action), that relation is a very peculiar one. It is not the relation of genus to species in a homogeneous hierarchy of classes, like the relation of the class of flowers to the class of roses. It is rather like the relation that the concept of causality has to the falling of stones, the growing of flowers, the movements of animals and the works of men; or like the relation that substance has to souls and siblings, stones and stars. It is not at all like an empirical genus for empirical classification, but rather like a metaphysical genus for an *a priori* ordering. That is to say, 'act' and 'performing an act' carry a theoretical weight that is not empirical, but metaphysical, however attenuated this weight is. There is no other meaning to 'performing an act' than that left to it by the metaphysical weight it once carried. This metaphysical weight is in part Aristotelian. The concept of act belongs to the group of concepts that are dialectically related to the concept of the potential. (In one sense, the actual is not the potential, in another sense it is.) The other part of the metaphysical weight is Cartesian. The concept of act is narrowed down to the *cogito*, over and against material action. Daydreaming, gossiping, issuing orders are performances of acts in the large sense that they report what someone is doing 'actually'; and in the narrower sense that there is the logical possibility with respect to any of these to say, 'I am X-ing', that is, '*cogito*'. Why can 'sleeping' not be translated into 'performing the act of sleeping?' Because my faculties (as a rational being) are merely faculties when I am sleeping, and because it is logically impossible that 'I am sleeping' can take the place of '*cogito*'; that is to say, it is logically impossible that I mean what I say if I should be heard saying, 'I am sleeping' while I am sleeping. There are corresponding explanations for the impossibility of translating 'being silent', 'being in a mood', etc., into 'performing an act of . . .'. Another indirect indication of the metaphysical weight carried by 'performing an act' is the otherwise inexplicable linguistic fact that physicists talk about the actions, but never about the acts, which particles perform. 'Performing an act' has become so intimately connected with the Cartesian *cogito* that it is altogether perverse to use it with respect to merely physical doings.[1] And though, to be sure, both 'performing an action' and 'performing an act' are complex forms derived from the same verb 'to act', the two forms have gone their different ways. 'Performing an act', except in the language of show and stage, became and remained part of a learned and esoteric discourse; and whenever ordinary verbs indicating human doings are translated into performing of acts, Aristotle and particularly Descartes are ringing their metaphysical bells, though the bells are so far away from us now that our mere wishing not to hear them makes them inaudible.

It must be conceded, then, that Austin is playing the sort of game with us that delighted Mr. Jourdain precisely because he does not see that it is a game. There is a difference, however, be-

---

[1] The physicist's concept of action is of course quite different from the use of 'action' that permits gossiping, issuing commands, preparing for battle, etc. to be dubbed 'performance of actions'.

tween Molière's and Austin's games. Molière has Mr. Jourdain take delight in learning that, when writing letters, he is 'composing prose'. The theoretical weight of this phrase is harmless. The distinction between prose and poetry makes empirical sense. But what empirical sense is there in classifying saying something as the performance of a speech act? 'Performing an act' looks as if it could do no wrong, like a high level civil servant: dignifiedly technical, impartially neutral, abstractly colourless. It looks so because we no longer look at it. The currency it has gained in traditional philosophy has made its metaphysical pigmentation too familiar to be noted. Without that pigmentation 'performing an act' would be totally vacuous and, hence, the cause of no delight whatever to Mr. Jourdain. Nor would it be of any use to Austin; for the generic function it has in Austin's doctrine of speech acts is predicated on its having, apparently, a semantic function. It would even be useless to Austin as a device to avoid behaviouristic language and to mark himself off from logical behaviourism—which might have been what recommended 'performing an act' to Austin in the first place.[1]

The sum of it all is that a concept such as performing an act cannot be expected to contribute anything to an elucidation of how we do things with words. In fact, to elucidate how we do things with words by way of classifying all these doings as performances of acts seems to be little better than to elucidate how we do things with our hands by classifying all manual doing as cause-effects relations.

In this section I have, first, tried to make explicit the several steps that mediate more or less secretly between 'saying something' and Austin's purported elucidation of it, namely 'performing speech acts of various kinds'. We discussed these mediating steps in some detail, paying particular attention to the step leading from 'performing an action' to 'performing an act'. We found that the concept to be elucidated was altered by each step. We then focused our attention on the concept of performing an act, obviously the genus to the performing of speech acts of which Austin aims to

[1] With unfailing instinct philosophers are permitting the 'performing an act' language to grow into a new specimen of exuberant gobbledygook. In *Knowledge and Experience* (University of Pittsburgh Press, 1962, Calvin Rollins, ed.), one of the contributors writes (p. 47): ' "Good" is used to *perform the speech act of uttering a word* (my italics) "answering to certain interests".'

give a doctrine. The phrase 'performing an act' is used by Austin, not in the sense familiar from everyday discourse, but in a sense familiar from metaphysics. This sense is a blend of Aristotle and Descartes; from Aristotle comes the actuality versus potentiality part, from Descartes, the *cogito* versus extension part. This traditional weight is still present today. Only such verbs can be translated into 'performance of act' as (*a*) refer to actual doings and (*b*) require a doer who can be said to have a mind. The concept of performing an act is exhausted by these two rules, and these rules are present day witnesses of the traditional metaphysical weight of 'performing an act'.

In the next section I shall discuss Austin's aim of elucidating the total speech act in the total speech situation (*HTD*, p. 147) and his failure to achieve this aim.

V ELUCIDATING THE TOTAL SPEECH ACT

Austin's avowed aim is the elucidation of the total speech act in the total speech situation. The elucidation offered by Austin has the form of classification: classes are divided into sub-classes. The genus to which speaking belongs is that of performing an act. My critique of the doctrine of speech acts has so far been limited to Austin's concepts of classification and performing an act. I should perhaps repeat here a warning given before: I am deliberately neglecting the lovely goods one can buy in Austin's store. I am trying to show why the enterprise is not profitable. In this last section I am prepared to go to what I take to be the root of the trouble: Austin's own failure to go to the roots. His elucidation of the total speech act in the total speech situation is not radical enough in two closely connected respects. First, Austin appears not to be aware of the obscurity in his concept of elucidation; he does not proceed to question it. In philosophy, however, an elucidation that does not aim at being lucid about itself will not throw much light on anything. Second, in trying to make us see the total speech act in the total speech situation Austin seems to ignore a loose system of concepts that forms a horizon of sorts for his investigations. He does not proceed to question these basic concepts that are affecting, or affected by, his new look at language. In this section I propose to discuss these two interconnected aspects of Austin's lack of radicalness.

I shall begin with a few remarks on the term 'total' so strongly emphasized in Austin's formulation of his task as that of elucidating the *total* speech act in the *total* speech situation. Quite obviously, Austin uses 'total' to express a holistic conception. The situation as a whole must be seen in order for the speech act, as part of the situation, to be understood properly. (*Cf. PhP*, pp. 32, 57, 87 f., 138, 198, 240, etc.; *S & S*, p. 118; *HTD*, pp. 16, 52, 100, 137, etc.) One is inclined to say, on the basis of these passages, that Austin is thoroughly holistic and refreshingly untouched by the atomism which in one form or another has been a less than enviable heirloom of traditional empiricism. Yet if one remembers Dewey stressing the situations in which people employ their reason; if one remembers Morris' investigations of the syntactic, semantic and pragmatic dimensions of language, and Waismann and others pushing the context, he begins to wonder, not only if Austin's holism is unique enough within more recent empiricism to be meritorious, but where exactly the difference lies, *qua* holism, between Austin's total speech situation and the other holistic preoccupations. In fact, one begins to wonder if the emphasis on total situation is more than a token nod in the direction of contemporary ideas, whether of gestaltism in psychology or of wordliness and similar concepts in Heidegger and Merleau-Ponty. To be sure, in connection with 'speech situation', 'total' has indeed a holistic ring; but when used with 'speech act', it does not. By 'the total speech act' Austin does not appear to mean the concept of a whole that is a unity—organic, internal—of its parts, over and against a whole that is a mere sum. Rather he appears to have in mind a concept that hovers indecisively between 'all', 'essential', and 'concrete'. The total speech act is meant to be the speech act considered in all its aspects, or at least in all its essential aspects, and not in just one or some; and it is thus taken to be the concrete speech act over and against some abstraction.

Yet this total speech act is surely too much for any philosopher to bite off. There are aspects of the speech act that are interesting to the sociologist, others to the psychologist, others again to the communications technician, and so on. Are philosophers supposed to be interested in all of these, synthesizing them into an overall theory? This is nineteenth century old hat, and nothing that Austin aimed at doing. Yet, as he does speak as philosopher, one must ask oneself in what sense the total speech act in the total speech situation is an object of an elucidation that may be called philosophical.

In 'A Plea for Excuses' (*PhP*, p. 130) Austin suggests that 'linguistic phenomenology', though 'it is rather a mouthful', might be a better name for his way of doing philosophy than 'linguistic' or 'analytic' philosophy or 'the analysis of language'. He says (*PhP*, p. 130, my italics) 'words are not (except in their own little corner) facts or things: we need therefore to prise them off the world, to hold them apart from and against it, so that we can realize their inadequacies and arbitrariness, and can *relook at the world without blinkers*'. 'When we examine what we should say when, what words we should use in what situations we are looking again not *merely* at words (or "meanings" whatever they may be) but also at the realities we use the words to talk about: we are using a sharpened awareness of words to sharpen our perception of, though not as the final arbiter of, the phenomena.' (*PhP*, p. 130. Austin's italics.)

These are rather commonsensical ideas on the relation of man, language and world and correspondingly on phenomenology; and they are themselves full of blinkers. Yet they throw an interesting light on the concept of elucidation. Taken as linguistic phenomenology, elucidation must be understood to be aiming at removing conceptual blinkers that keep us from relooking at events and things in the world. However, the conceptual blinkers to be removed in the elucidation of the total speech act in the total speech situation are not words and meanings. They are second-level affairs, theories about language; and what Austin wishes us to relook at in *HTD* are not the facts and things, but the words as used by men in situations. Linguistic phenomenology turns into something considerably more complicated than the above quotes conceive of it. What Austin does in *HTD* is quite different from prising words off the world and holding them apart and against it. He is not pulling words out of the little corner they occupy in the world of facts and things, whatever this may mean. Rather, he is trying to remove traditional views on language in order to relook and see afresh how men use language in situations, that is, in the world. To elucidate the total speech act in the total speech situation is more than, and different from, anything that goes by the name of logical or linguistic analysis. Elucidation is a relooking, a looking without blinkers, a seeing things freshly. And the things to be so viewed are not the things and facts that make up the universe, but the whole complex nexus of man doing things in the world by way of using words.

Austin's preference for the term 'elucidation' shows, and is probably intended to show, his feeling of the distinctiveness of what he is doing. 'Analysis' with its logico-linguistic commitments does not quite do. Unfortunately, 'elucidation' is better than 'analysis' only because it is different from it; by itself it is much too vague, casting no light whatsoever on the sort of light-casting Austin is aiming at. 'Relooking' and 'looking without blinkers' are mere metaphors, and perhaps misleading ones at that, carrying with them, as they do, the belief that conceiving things is to be understood in analogy with looking at them and seeing them. To 'relook' at how we do things with words; to 'relook' at man as relating himself to his world through language; to 'relook' at this complex nexus is to examine—and to examine for what must first be established as good reasons—the concepts traditionally directing man's understanding of himself, his world and their interrelations, among which interrelations understanding is itself most eminent. While Austin seemed to feel that his elucidation was a step away from linguistic analysis, he surely was in no way aware of having moved, ever so modestly, toward an existential analysis of sorts. His elucidation, when elucidated, might turn out to be quite different from the stupid stare which looking without blinkers is condemned to be. It might be rather close to the concepts of *Verstehen* and interpretation: concepts which the existentialists (and before them, German historians and philosophers of history) succeeded in having all sober-minded philosophers arrayed against, but which it might be time now to domesticate rather than slaughter.

Austin's lack of radicalness in elucidating elucidation is inseparable from his lack of radicalness in exploring basic concepts involved in looking at language without blinkers. We can discover some of these basic concepts if we take seriously a question asked before somewhat frivolously: why does the total speech act in the total speech situation need elucidation, and not rather the total walking act in the total walking situation, or any other total act in a total situation? One might answer that a so-called linguistic phenomenology is necessarily interested in the use of language rather than of legs. This is surely no answer. For why is linguistic phenomenology immediately acceptable while a phenomenology elucidating the total walking act in the total walking situation would be as immediately judged to be unacceptable? In the end, the only satisfactory answer is a series of trivialities so trivial that an unusual degree of philosophical foolhardiness is required to assert that they should never be forgotten. Language is, and walking is not, typically, uniquely and essentially human. The philosophical interest in language and its uses takes it for granted that language is man's language, that 'how to do things with words' is how human beings do things with words, and that our being human lies in doing things with words: man is the animal that has language. The concept of man is part of a loose, and loosely hierarchical, system of basic distinctions through which men, or in any case the Greeks, brought order to their experiences. To have the concept of man is to understand also the term 'animal'. And to be able to use these terms is to be involved in the system of which they are parts. Ordinary experience distinguishes in principle a crow's warning signals from the noise a stone makes when it hits the ground, and from a crow's warning signals it distinguishes in principle man's stating that the cat is on the mat. This ability of stating what is, was, and will be the case is the typical and in some sense basic example of what is meant by 'rational animal', by 'animal having logos'. Logoi are sounds which have been given relations to each other under rules and can have a relation of references to all and everything, though the sphere of reference that is often taken to be humanly basic is that of the things and facts in the world, among them the speakers and, in a sort of gigantic category mistake, the world itself and its relatives—that is to say, universe and nature on the one hand, and the many worlds of man on the other. Furthermore, these ordinary concepts of man, animal, etc., *qua* concepts, commit one to a conception of concepts according to which their primary function is that of detecting and imposing classes. In sum, the conceptual horizon surrounding the idea of linguistic phenomenology is a self-conception of man which is part of a loose system of concepts marking basic distinctions within the world and involving a conception of concepts as classes. A very Greek horizon indeed. Austin's relooking at how we do things with words presupposes in a non-technical sense these concepts that are sediments of old Greek looks at man and his world. They form part of his retina of concepts. They are his blind spots, or his blinkers, taken for granted and remaining unquestioned.

Yet there is one aspect of the doctrine of speech acts that goes counter to the Greek look. Austin reminds us of how many things men can do with words: they can state facts and describe what they see; they can warn people and frighten them, persuade and dissuade them; they can promise things and hide things, deflect attention and attract love—all of these and many more by and in 'performing speech acts'. Yet quite obviously some of these things animals can do, too, and can so do with the sounds they emit. Animals warn, frighten, fight, court and do a great many other things by way of sounds. There are, however, some things that only man can do by way of sounds: for example, stating or describing or promising. It will be remembered that in his doctrine of speech acts Austin brings together under the same class (of illocutionary acts) uniquely human uses such as stating, describing and promising, and uses which are not uniquely human but are shared by men and animals alike as, for instance, warning. To be sure, warning as the crow warns and warning as the teacher warns are very different sorts of warning. The point of the difference, however, is that the teacher's sort of warning is in a very complex sense dependent upon the human ability to state what is, was, and will be the case. No animal needs *logoi* in order to warn. Only animals that have *logoi* can warn by way of making statements. The Greeks selected the making of statements as the typical and basic use of language. In doing so they stuck to their cosmological conception of man's position in the universe. Austin's doctrine of speech acts might be said to affect this traditional conception of man; for it lowers the stating use of words to the warning use of words. Both stating and warning are performances of illocutionary acts. Does not Austin leave himself open to the accusation of having contributed to a humanistic delinquency of sorts? Does not his doctrine of speech acts contribute, however slightly and unwillingly, to weakening the hold of the Greek decision on rationality as the distinctive mark of humanity? Silly questions, perhaps; yet meant to enliven a feeling for the import on philosophical doctrines of concepts directing man's understanding of himself, his world and his position in the world. Austin did not care to see that his doctrine of speech acts, to the extent that it is philosophical, was both affected by, and affecting, man's self-conception. He believed that his doctrine of speech acts needed a theory of action as its foundation. However, this theory of action, as philosophical theory, would itself remain conceptually blind and without foundation if it did not lead to an examination of man's concept of himself and of the nature of that concept. Such two-pronged examination, however, is the very core of existential analysis when divested of its dreadful preoccupation with 'Being'.

I shall now, in these last pages, look at Austin and the road beyond Austin in a deliberately continental perspective. The development, some thirty years ago, that led from phenomenology to existentialism, permits some prediction as to the course Anglo-American philosophy might choose after digesting Austin's linguistic phenomenology.

VI BEYOND LINGUISTIC PHENOMENOLOGY

Austin's linguistic phenomenology is, to some degree, the counterpart 'in the formal mode' of mundane phenomenology—if I may so call a broad stream of continental phenomenology which was primarily concerned not, like Austin's, with words and their uses, but with the world or rather, the things and facts in this world as we experience them. What makes the elucidation of the total speech act in the total speech situation phenomenological is the programme of removing blinkers and relooking at things, which was Husserl's battle cry of more than half a century ago. Unfortunately, Husserl spent more time elucidating the programme itself than executing it; and, misled by blinkers he was not aware of, he ended up with the blueprint for a philosophy as scientific foundation of all sciences which belongs among the most abstruse fancies ever entertained by philosophers. In Husserl's early *Philosophy as Rigorous Science* (1911) the first question that he believed the prerogative of philosophy to ask and answer turned out to be that old blinker thing, 'How can experience as consciousness give or contact an object?' (Edmund Husserl, *Phenomenology and the Crisis of Philosophy*, p. 87, Harper Torchbooks.) It would be a caricature, but a revealing one, to describe the later stages of his phenomenology as detailed programme for answering this 'problem'. He answered it by claiming that acts of the transcendental subject constitute the whole sphere of objects, including myself, the essences, God, the actual world, and possible worlds as well as the existence or non-existence of all of these. Husserl assigned to phenomenology the study of these constitutive acts and their interconnections; and he believed that this study should and could be as rigorous a science as, say, geometry. He conceived geometry to be *a priori* and synthetic; and he proposed phenomenology to be synthetic and *a priori*, dealing, not with this or that act, but with their essences. These essences he claimed to be visible in intuitions which it was in principle possible to formulate in apodictic statements. Analogous to what Husserl conceived to be the foundational function of geometry with respect to natural science, phenomenology, as eidetic science of the constitutive acts of the transcendental ego, was to be the very foundation of all science, natural or not so natural—as in some older and equally ambitious thought the science of God or, in Hegel, logic, was the proper foundation of all human knowledge and of all possible worlds.

Husserl had believed his programme of a transcendental phenomenology to be the blueprint that would enable generations and generations of philosophers to engage in building the absolute foundations of all knowledge. Even during Husserl's life, however, history, with its usual ruthlessness, had thrown this blueprint into the garbage pail. Phenomenology attracted the younger German generation, not with this esoteric blueprint, but with its slogan of relooking at the world and our experiences in a fresh and blinkerless way. This appealed to people rightly sick of anaemic epistemological discussions and wrongly in rebellion against discipline, logical or otherwise. They went ahead lustily describing things as they experienced them trusting the Lord and their genius that the way they saw things was indeed blinkerless and fresh enough to justify describing to others what they saw, without raising many problems as to the adequateness of either experience or description or, for that matter, as to the adequateness of the whole analogy of conception and vision. Had not the master himself declared that the 'I see it' is the ultimate foundation of all knowledge claims and included as prime example the acts of eidetic intuition?[1] As long as one was blinkerless in one's vision and honest in one's description, how could one possibly go wrong? Clearly, there is an enormous difference within mundane phenomenology between the esoteric, radically idealistic, methodically self-conscious work of its founder and the popular phenomenology of many of his followers who were commonsensically realistic in epistemology, satisfied with blinkerlessness of vision and honesty of description as method,

[1] Cf. Edmund Husserl *Ideas*, Collier Books, pp. 75–6; 83.

and, as to their subject, preferred this world to all possible worlds. When Austin called himself a linguistic phenomenologist, he must have had in mind, not the transcendental constitutive phenomenology of Husserl, but the popular descriptive phenomenology of Husserl's followers. However, this descriptive phenomenology, as developed in Germany, was unable to grow into a major philosophical enterprise. Its inherent weaknesses—lack of methodological and logical rigor, subjectivism, unsystematic activity—were so glaring as to eclipse its revolutionary fervour. However, there was a germ within Husserl's phenomenology that did prove itself able to grow. This was Husserl's formulation of a philosophical task which he held to be of greatest importance and yet hardly conceived by anyone: the analysis—or rather, the unprejudiced (i.e. blinkerless) description—of the natural world attitude of man. He himself had sketched such a description in the *Ideas*[1] and elaborated aspects of it in his lectures. It was the energetic and revolutionary work by Heidegger on this task that launched existentialism. Ignoring romanticisms and medievalisms of the worst kind in Heidegger's work we come directly to its useful core: the discovery, first of all, of the blinkers that had kept Husserl's sketch of the natural world attitude from being the unprejudiced description he himself had demanded, and the revision, secondly, of the whole idea of blinkerless looking. The blinkers Heidegger discovered in Husserl were in the main the nexus of traditional concepts supposedly grasping man's being in the world: man as subject or consciousness relating himself through acts to objects the totality of which is the world.

Here is one point of resemblance between Austin and Husserl himself. Husserl's transcendental doctrine stands and falls with the concept of acts performed by consciousness; Austin made 'performance of act' the concept serving as genus in the doctrine of speech acts. The point of this resemblance, however, is not any similarity between Austin's and Husserl's doctrines, but the ironical fact that both of these hopefully blinkerless thinkers were victimized by blinkers and, what is more, by the same metaphysical blinkers, those aristotelian-cartesian concepts carried by the *cogito* as an act through which subject or consciousness or mind relates itself to an object and to the world understood as the totality of— basically material—objects. But this, after all, is a resemblance that

[1] Ibidem, pp. 91–100.

CRITICAL REVIEW OF *How to Do Things with Words*

unites not just Austin and Husserl but almost all pre-existentialist thinkers. Most of them continue to use terms which, though quite meaningless, preserve a semblance of meaning by virtue of a meta-physico-epistemological load that has become so familiar as to be no longer felt to be a load, or to be judged harmless or appear unavoidable: man is a subject or consciousness relating itself through acts to objects.

Although Heidegger considers *Sein und Zeit* merely a stage in reopening the question of Being, it is in the first 100 pages or so of *Sein und Zeit*, that one can find the critique of this traditional conception of man, which is the real meat of existentialism. Much less fortunate are Heidegger's reflections on his method which, as hermeneutics, is meant to replace phenomenology's naïve trust in relooking without blinkers. Romantically anti-science and anti-reason, Heidegger shies away from logic and argument as from the devil himself.

The gist, then, of the development leading from mundane phenomenology to existentialism is to force philosophy to conceive of itself as focusing on man's self-conception; that is to say, to bring to the fore and question, in response to some deeply felt malaise, the traditional concepts man has of himself, the world, and his position in it.

One could summarize this core of existentialism by characterizing 'philosophy itself as a search for "a definition of man"'. This passage, however, is not taken from Heidegger or any other continental existentialist. It is taken from Stuart Hampshire's *Thought and Action* (p. 232), a work meant to be a contribution to what Hampshire calls the philosophy of mind or, occasionally, descriptive anthropology (ibidem, pp. 233 f.). 'Philosophy of mind' or 'descriptive anthropology' are, however, only other names for the core enterprise of *Sein und Zeit* and, in general, of existentialism. And in saying of philosophy as linguistic analysis that it is 'unwillingly lured into a kind of descriptive anthropology', Hampshire is in fact saying that he is taking contemporary empiricism beyond the elucidation of the total speech act in the total speech situation, and even beyond a theory of action toward an existential analysis of sorts. From this perspective it will no longer sound preposterous to say that Austin was moving unknowingly from logico-linguistic analysis in the direction of existential analysis. Nor will it take courage to predict that there will be some post-Austinian liaison between analysis and existentialism; for Hampshire's *Thought and Action* is evidence of a relation with existentialism that is certainly pre-marital if it is not downright matrimonial. Whether Hampshire has seen the situation clearly and whether he has handled it adroitly and decisively are questions, however, that one cannot help asking as soon as one notes Hampshire's reliance, quite Austinian, on classification. It is true that *Thought and Action* is not only an essay *in* classification (of human powers) but also *on* classification. Yet it is also true that what Hampshire has to say on classification is mainly a retelling of the empiricist folkmyth for which concepts are class concepts, and class concepts the result of abstractive comparisons directed by practical interests, etc. To relook at man becomes, in Hampshire, to reclassify human powers; and, classification being what it is, one may surmise that if Hampshire does succeed in relooking at man, this will probably be at odds with, and at the expense of, his theory of concepts as classes. Or *vice versa*: if his theory of concepts should succeed in presenting a new conception of concepts, it will very likely be at odds with, and at the expense of, his conception of philosophy of mind as classification (of human powers). There is another Austinian heritage in Hampshire that might cause doubt as to the effectiveness of Hampshire's turn toward existentialism. This is the increasing difficulty in distinguishing the logico-linguistic way of doing philosophy from the mundane way. In the passages on linguistic phenomenology quoted above, Austin talked about prising the words off the world and about the task of relooking at the words, and this was to be done, it must be noted, for the sake of relooking at the things and facts themselves. There were, then, two phenomenologies: linguistic phenomenology and mundane phenomenology, phenomenology in the (informally) formal mode and phenomenology in the material mode, with the former being developed for the sake of the latter. In Austin's *HTD*, however, this distinction becomes fuzzy. Looking at the total speech act in the total speech situation is quite different from looking at language in the way the Wittgensteinians used to. Language has become part of a whole nexus of transactions between man and world. To relook at this whole dimension may be called phenomenology; but it may hardly be called phenomenology in the formal mode, not even in the most informally formal mode. Reaching Hampshire, we notice an even greater difficulty of distinguishing between formal and material modes of doing philosophy. One should expect a representative of contemporary empiricism to existentialize, if at all, in the formal mode. Yet though Hampshire does 'classify', or rather analyse, how men talk about themselves and what, for instance, the 'necessary conditions' are of using personal pronouns, all this sort of thing becomes a very secondary business indeed in comparison with what he states to be the primary business of the philosophy of mind, *viz.* classification of human powers. If one had hoped that continental existentialism would find its *logico*-linguistic counterpart and discipline within the Anglo-American tradition, one has so far waited in vain; but then, that very hope might have been quite illconceived and Strawson's kind of metaphysics be a sounder development than Hampshire's kind of existentialism.

In sum, then, Austin's task of showing how we do things with words gains but little from being conceived as elucidation of the total speech act in the total speech situation, particularly if this elucidation becomes a classificatory doctrine dividing the genus speech act into its species. However, in wanting to elucidate the total speech act in the total speech situation, Austin happens to start on a road that turns out to be somewhat similar to the road leading from Husserl to Heidegger. From Austin's linguistic phenomenology the road leads Hampshire into surprising proximity with positions usually taken to be characteristic of existentialism. I have no hope that this perspective will reconcile those who, rightly seeing Austin's unique merit in the wealth and philosophical impact of his linguistic observations, would abstain from judging his doctrine of speech acts.

INTENTION AND CONVENTION
IN SPEECH ACTS

P. F. Strawson

I

IN this paper I want to discuss some questions regarding J. L. Austin's notions of the illocutionary force of an utterance and of the illocutionary act which a speaker performs in making an utterance.[1]

There are two preliminary matters I must mention, if only to get them out of the way. Austin contrasts what he calls the 'normal' or 'serious' use of speech with what he calls 'etiolated' or 'parasitical' uses. His doctrine of illocutionary force relates essentially to the normal or serious use of speech and not, or not directly, to etiolated or parasitical uses; and so it will be with my comments on his doctrine. I am not suggesting that the distinction between the normal or serious use of speech and the secondary uses which he calls etiolated or parasitical is so clear as to call for no further examination; but I shall take it that there is such a distinction to be drawn and I shall not here further examine it.

My second preliminary remark concerns another distinction, or pair of distinctions, which Austin draws. Austin distinguishes the illocutionary force of an utterance from what he calls its 'meaning' and distinguishes between the illocutionary and the locutionary acts performed in issuing the utterance. Doubts may be felt about the second term of each of these distinctions. It may be felt that Austin has not made clear just what abstractions from the total speech act he intends to make by means of his notions of meaning and of locutionary act. Although this is a question on which I

[1] All references, unless otherwise indicated, are to *How To Do Things with Words* (Oxford, 1962).

have views, it is not what the present paper is about. Whatever doubts may be entertained about Austin's notions of meaning and of locutionary act, it is enough for present purposes to be able to say, as I think we clearly can, the following about their relation to the notion of illocutionary force. The meaning of a (serious) utterance, as conceived by Austin, always embodies some limitation on its possible force, and sometimes—as, for example, in some cases where an explicit performative formula, like 'I apologize', is used—the meaning of an utterance may exhaust its force; that is, there may be no more to the force than there is to the meaning; but very often the meaning, though it limits, does not exhaust, the force. Similarly, there may sometimes be no more to say about the illocutionary force of an utterance than we already know if we know what locutionary act has been performed; but very often there is more to know about the illocutionary force of an utterance than we know in knowing what locutionary act has been performed.

So much for these two preliminaries. Now I shall proceed to assemble from the text some indications as to what Austin means by the force of an utterance and as to what he means by an illocutionary act. These two notions are not so closely related that to know the force of an utterance is the same thing as to know what illocutionary act was actually performed in issuing it. For if an utterance with the illocutionary force of say, a warning is not understood in this way (that is, as a warning) by the audience to which it is addressed, then (it is held) the illocutionary act of warning cannot be said to have been actually performed. 'The performance of an illocutionary act involves the securing of uptake'; that is, it involves 'bringing about the understanding of the meaning and of the force of the locution' (pp. 115–6).[1] Perhaps we may express the relation by saying that to know the force of an utterance is the same thing as to know what illocutionary act, *if any*, was actually performed in issuing it. Austin gives many examples and lists of words which help us to form at least a fair intuitive notion of what is meant by 'illocutionary force' and 'illocutionary act'. Besides these, he gives us certain general clues to these ideas, which may be grouped, as follows, under four heads:

1. Given that we know (in Austin's sense) the meaning of an utterance, there may still be a further question as to *how what was*

---

[1] I refer later to the need for qualification of this doctrine.

said was meant by the speaker, or as to *how the words spoken were used*, or as to *how the utterance was to be taken* or *ought to have been taken* (pp. 98–9). In order to know the illocutionary force of the utterance, we must know the answer to this further question.

2. A locutionary act is an act *of* saying something; an illocutionary act is an act we perform *in* saying something. It is what we *do, in* saying what we *say*. Austin does not regard this characterization as by any means a satisfactory test for identifying kinds of illocutionary acts since, so regarded, it would admit many kinds of acts which he wishes to exclude from the class (p. 99 and Lecture X).

3. It is a sufficient, though not, I think, a necessary, condition of a verb's being the name of a *kind* of illocutionary act that it can figure, in the first person present indicative, as what Austin calls an explicit performative. (This latter notion I shall assume to be familiar and perspicuous.)

4. The illocutionary act is 'a conventional act; an act done as conforming to a convention' (p. 105). As such, it is to be sharply contrasted with the producing of certain effects, intended or otherwise, by means of an utterance. This producing of effects, though it too can often be ascribed *as an act* to the speaker (his *perlocutionary* act), is in no way a conventional act (pp. 120–1). Austin reverts many times to the 'conventional' nature of the illocutionary act (pp. 103, 105, 108, 115, 120, 121, 127) and speaks also of 'conventions of illocutionary force' (p. 114). Indeed, he remarks (pp. 120–1) that though acts which can properly be called by the same names as illocutionary acts—for example, acts of warning—can be brought off nonverbally, without the use of words, yet, in order to be properly called by these names, such acts must be *conventional* nonverbal acts.

II

I shall assume that we are clear enough about the intended application of Austin's notions of illocutionary force and illocutionary act to be able to criticize, by reference to cases, his general doctrines regarding those notions. It is the general doctrine I listed last above—the doctrine that an utterance's having such and such a force is a matter of convention—that I shall take as the starting point of inquiry. Usually this doctrine is affirmed in a quite unqualified way. But just once there occurs an interestingly qualified statement of it. Austin says, of the use of language with a certain illocutionary force, that 'it may . . . be said to be *conventional* in the sense that at least it could be made explicit by the performative formula' (p. 103). The remark has a certain authority in that it is the first explicit statement of the conventional nature of the illocutionary act. I shall refer to it later.

Meanwhile let us consider the doctrine in its unqualified form. Why does Austin say that the illocutionary act is a conventional act, an act done as conforming to a convention? I must first mention, and neutralize, two possible sources of confusion. (It may seem an excess of precaution to do so. I apologize to those who find it so.) First, we may agree (or not dispute) that any speech act is, as such, at least in part a conventional act. The performance of any *speech* act involves at least the observance or exploitation of some *linguistic* conventions, and every illocutionary act is a speech act. But it is absolutely clear that this is not the point that Austin is making in declaring the illocutionary act to be a conventional act. We must refer, Austin would say, to linguistic conventions to determine what *locutionary* act has been performed in the making of an utterance, to determine what the *meaning* of the utterance is. The doctrine now before us is the further doctrine that where force is *not* exhausted by meaning, the fact that an utterance has the further unexhausted force it has is also a matter of convention; or, where it is exhausted by meaning, the fact *that* it is, is a matter of convention. It is not just as being a speech act that an illocutionary act—for example, of warning—is conventional. A nonverbal act of warning is, Austin maintains, conventionally such in just the same way as an illocutionary—that is, verbal—act of warning is conventionally such.

Second, we must dismiss as irrelevant the fact that it can properly be said to be a matter of convention that an act of, for example, warning is correctly called by this name. For if this were held to be a ground for saying that illocutionary acts were conventional acts, then any describable act whatever would, as correctly described, be a conventional act.

The contention that illocutionary force is a matter of convention is easily seen to be correct in a great number of cases. For very many kinds of human transaction involving speech are governed and in part constituted by what we easily recognize as established conventions of procedure additional to the conventions governing the *meanings* of our utterances. Thus the fact that the word 'guilty' is pronounced by the foreman of the jury in court at the proper moment constitutes his utterance as the act of bringing in a verdict; and that this is so is certainly a matter of the conventional procedures of the law. Similarly, it is a matter of convention that if the appropriate umpire pronounces a batsman 'out', he thereby performs the act of *giving the man out*, which no player or spectator shouting 'Out!' can do. Austin gives other examples, and there are doubtless many more which could be given, where there clearly exist statable conventions, relating to the circumstances of utterance, such that an utterance with a certain meaning, pronounced by the appropriate person in the appropriate circumstances, has the force it has *as* conforming to those conventions. Examples of illocutionary acts of which this is true can be found not only in the sphere of social institutions which have a legal point (like the marriage ceremony and the law courts themselves) or of activities governed by a definite set of rules (like cricket and games generally) but in many other relations of human life. The act of *introducing*, performed by uttering the words 'This is Mr. Smith', may be said to be an act performed as conforming to a convention. The act of surrendering, performed by saying '*Kamerad!*' and throwing up your arms when confronted with a bayonet, may be said to be (to have become) an act performed as conforming to an accepted convention, a conventional act.

But it seems equally clear that, although the circumstances of utterance are always relevant to the determination of the illocutionary force of an utterance, there are many cases in which it is not as conforming to an accepted *convention* of any kind (other than those linguistic conventions which help to fix the meaning of the utterance) that an illocutionary act is performed. It seems clear, that is, that there are many cases in which the illocutionary force of an utterance, though not exhausted by its meaning, is not owed to any *conventions* other than those which help to give it its meaning. Surely there may be cases in which to utter the words 'The ice over there is very thin' to a skater is to issue a warning (is to say something with the *force* of a warning) without its being the case that there is any statable convention at all (other than those which bear on the nature of the *locutionary* act) such that the speaker's act can be said to be an act done as conforming to that convention.

Here is another example. We can readily imagine circumstances in which an utterance of the words 'Don't go' would be correctly described not as a request or an order, but as an entreaty. I do not want to deny that there may be conventional postures or procedures for entreating: one can, for example, kneel down, raise one's arms and *say*, 'I entreat you'. But I do want to deny that an act of entreaty can be performed only as conforming to some such conventions. What makes X's words to Y an *entreaty* not to go is something—complex enough, no doubt—relating to X's situation, attitude to Y, manner, and current intention. There are questions here which we must discuss later. But to suppose that there is always and necessarily a convention conformed to would be like supposing that there could be no love affairs which did not proceed on lines laid down in the *Roman de la Rose* or that every dispute between men must follow the pattern specified in Touchstone's speech about the countercheck quarrelsome and the lie direct.

Another example. In the course of a philosophical discussion (or, for that matter, a debate on policy) one speaker *raises an objection* to what the previous speaker has just said. X says (or proposes) that p and Y *objects* that q. Y's utterance has the force of an objection to X's assertion (or proposal) that p. But where is the *convention* that constitutes it an objection? That Y's utterance has the force of an objection may lie partly in the character of the dispute and of X's contention (or proposal) and it certainly lies partly, in Y's *view* of these things, in the bearing which he takes the proposition that q to have on the doctrine (or proposal) that p. But although there may be, there does not have to be, any convention involved other than those linguistic conventions which help to fix the meanings of the utterances.

I do not think it necessary to give further examples. It seems perfectly clear that, if at least we take the expressions 'convention' and 'conventional' in the most natural way, the doctrine of the conventional nature of the illocutionary act does not hold generally. Some illocutionary acts are conventional; others are not (except in so far as they are locutionary acts). Why then does Austin repeatedly affirm the contrary? It is unlikely that he has made the simple mistake of generalizing from some cases to all. It is much more likely that he is moved by some further, and fundamental, feature of illocutionary acts, which it must be our business to discover. Even though we may decide that the description 'conventional' is not appropriately used, we may presume it worth our while to look for the reason for using it. Here we may recall that oddly qualified remark that the performance of an illocutionary act, or the use of a sentence with a certain illocutionary force, 'may be said to be conventional in the sense that at least it *could* be made explicit by the performative formula' (p. 103). On this we may first, and with justice, be inclined to comment that there is no such *sense* of 'being conventional', that if this is a *sense* of anything to the purpose, it is a sense of 'being *capable* of being conventional'. But although this is a proper comment on the remark, we should not simply dismiss the remark with this comment. Whatever it is that leads Austin to call illocutionary acts in general 'conventional' must be closely connected with whatever it is about such acts as warning, entreating, apologizing, advising, that accounts for the fact that *they* at least *could* be made explicit by the use of the corresponding first-person performative form. So we must ask what it is about them that accounts for this fact. Obviously it will not do to answer simply that they are acts which can be performed by the use of words. So are many (perlocutionary) acts, like convincing, dissuading, alarming, and amusing, for which, as Austin points out, there is no corresponding first-person *performative* formula. So we need some further explanation.

III

I think a concept we may find helpful at this point is one introduced by H. P. Grice in his valuable article on *Meaning* (*Philosophical Review*, LXVII, 1957), namely, the concept of someone's *non-naturally meaning something by utterance*. The concept does not apply only to speech acts—that is, to cases where that by which someone non-naturally means something is a *linguistic* utterance. It is of more general application. But it will be convenient to refer to that by which someone, *S*, non-naturally means something as *S*'s *utterance*. The explanation of the introduced concept is given in terms of the concept of intention. *S* non-naturally means something by an utterance *x* if *S* intends (i_1) to produce by uttering *x* a certain response (*r*) in an audience *A* and intends (i_2) that *A* shall recognize *S*'s intention (i_1) and intends (i_3) that this recognition on the part of *A* of *S*'s intention (i_1) shall function as *A*'s reason, or a part of his

386

reason, for his response *r*. (The word 'response', though more convenient in some ways than Grice's 'effect', is not ideal. It is intended to cover cognitive and affective states or attitudes as well as actions.) It is, evidently, an important feature of this definition that the securing of the response *r* is intended to be mediated by the securing of another (and always cognitive) effect in *A*; namely, recognition of *S*'s intention to secure response *r*.

Grice's analysis of his concept is fairly complex. But I think a little reflection shows that it is not quite complex enough for his purpose. Grice's analysis is undoubtedly offered as an analysis of a situation in which one person is trying, in a sense of the word 'communicate' fundamental to any theory of meaning, to communicate with another. But it is possible to imagine a situation in which Grice's three conditions would be satisfied by a person *S* and yet, in this important sense of 'communicate', it would not be the case that *S* could be said to be trying to communicate by means of his production of *x* with the person *A* in whom he was trying to produce the response *r*. I proceed to describe such a situation.

S intends by a certain action to induce in *A* the belief that *p*; so he satisfies condition (i_1). He arranges convincing-looking 'evidence' that *p*, in a place where *A* is bound to see it. He does this, knowing that *A* is watching him at work, but *knowing also that* A *does not know that* S *knows that* A *is watching him at work.* He realizes that *A* will not take the *arranged* 'evidence' as genuine or natural evidence that *p*, but realizes, and indeed intends, that *A* will take his arranging of it as grounds for thinking that he, *S*, intends to induce in *A* the belief that *p*. That is, he intends *A* to recognize his (i_1) intention. So *S* satisfies condition (i_2). He knows that *A* has general grounds for thinking that *S* would not wish to make him, *A*, think that *p* unless it were known to *S* to be the case that *p*; and hence that *A*'s recognition of his (*S*'s) intention to induce in *A* the belief that *p* will in fact seem to *A* a sufficient reason for believing that *p*. And he intends that *A*'s recognition of his intention (i_1) should function in just this way. So he satisfies condition (i_3).

S, then, satisfies all Grice's conditions. But this is clearly not a case of attempted *communication* in the sense which (I think it is fair to assume) Grice is seeking to elucidate. *A* will indeed take *S* to be trying to bring it about that *A* is aware of some fact; but he will not take S as trying, in the colloquial sense, to 'let him know' something (or to 'tell' him something). But unless S at least brings it about that A takes him (S) to be trying to let him (A) know something, he has not succeeded in communicating with A; and if, as in our example, he has not even *tried* to bring this about, then he has not even *tried* to communicate with A. It seems a minimum further condition of his trying to do this that he should not only intend A to recognize his intention to get A to think that p, but that he should also *intend A to recognize his intention to get* A *to recognize his intention* to get A to think that p.

We might approximate more closely to the communication situation if we changed the example by supposing it not only clear to both A and S that A was watching S at work, but also clear to them both that it *was* clear to them both. I shall content myself, however, with drawing from the actually considered example the conclusion that we must add to Grice's conditions the further condition that S should have the further intention (i_4) that A should recognize his intention (i_2). It is possible that further argument could be produced to show that even adding this condition is not *sufficient* to constitute the case as one of attempted communication. But I shall rest content for the moment with the fact that this addition at least is necessary.

Now we might have expected in Grice's paper an account of what it is for A to *understand* something by an utterance x, an account complementary to the account of what it is for S to *mean* something by an utterance x. Grice in fact gives no such account, and I shall suggest a way of at least partially supplying this lack. I say 'at least partially' because the uncertainty as to the sufficiency of even the modified conditions for S's non-naturally *meaning* something by an utterance x is reflected in a corresponding uncertainty in the sufficiency of conditions for A's understanding. But again we may be content for the moment with necessary conditions. I suggest, then, that for A (in the appropriate sense of 'understand') to understand *something* by utterance x, it is necessary (and perhaps sufficient) that there should be *some* complex intention of the (i_2) form, described above, which A takes S to have, and that for A to understand the utterance correctly, it is necessary that A should take S to have *the* complex intention of the (i_2) form which S does have. In other words, if A is to understand the utterance correctly, S's (i_4) intention and hence his (i_2) intention must be fulfilled. Of course it does not follow from the fulfillment of these intentions that his (i_1) intention is fulfilled; nor, consequently, that his (i_3) intention is fulfilled.

It is at this point, it seems, that we may hope to find a possible point of connexion with Austin's terminology of 'securing uptake'. If we do find such a point of connexion, we also find a possible starting point for an at least partial analysis of the notions of illocutionary force and of the illocutionary act. For to secure uptake is to secure understanding of (meaning and) illocutionary force; and securing understanding of illocutionary force is said by Austin to be an essential element in bringing off the illocutionary act. It is true that this doctrine of Austin's may be objected to.[1] For surely a man may, for example, actually have made such and such a bequest, or gift, even if no one ever reads his will or instrument of gift. We may be tempted to say instead that at least *the aim, if not the achievement*, of securing uptake is an essential element in the performance of the illocutionary act. To this, too, there is an objection. Might not a man really have made a gift, in due form, and take some satisfaction in the thought, even if he had no expectations of the fact ever being known? But this objection at most forces on us an amendment to which we are in any case obliged:[2] namely, that the aim, if not the achievement, of securing uptake is essentially *a standard, if not an invariable*, element in the performance of the illocutionary act. So the analysis of the aim of securing uptake remains an essential element in the analysis of the notion of the illocutionary act.

IV

Let us, then, make a tentative identification—to be subsequently qualified and revised—of Austin's notion of uptake with that at least partially analysed notion of understanding (on the part of an audience) which I introduced just now as complementary to Grice's concept of somebody nonnaturally meaning something by an utterance. Since the notion of audience understanding is introduced by way of fuller (though partial) analysis than any which Austin gives of the notion of uptake, the identification is equivalent to a tentative (and partial) analysis of the notion of uptake and hence of the

[1] I owe the objections which follow to Professor Hart.

[2] For an illocutionary act *may* be performed *altogether* unintentionally. See the example about redoubling at bridge, p. 397 below.

notions of illocutionary act and illocutionary force. If the identification were correct, then it would follow that to say something with a certain illocutionary force is at least (in the standard case) to have a certain complex intention of the (i_4) form described in setting out and modifying Grice's doctrine.

Next we test the adequacy and explanatory power of this partial analysis by seeing how far it helps to explain other features of Austin's doctrine regarding illocutionary acts. There are two points at which we shall apply this test. One is the point at which Austin maintains that the production of an utterance with a certain illocutionary force is a conventional act in that unconventional sense of 'conventional' which he glosses in terms of general suitability for being made explicit with the help of an explicitly performative formula. The other is the point at which Austin considers the possibility of a general characterization of the illocutionary act as what we *do, in* saying what we say. He remarks on the unsatisfactoriness of this characterization in that it would admit as illocutionary acts what are not such; and we may see whether the suggested analysis helps to explain the exclusion from the class of illocutionary acts of those acts falling under this characterization which Austin wishes to exclude. These points are closely connected with each other.

First, then, we take the point about the general suitability of an illocutionary act for performance with the help of the explicitly performative formula for that act. The explanation of this feature of illocutionary acts has two phases; it consists of, first, a general, and then a special, point about intention. The first point may be roughly expressed by saying that in general a man can speak of his intention in performing an action with a kind of authority which he cannot command in predicting its outcome. What he intends in doing something is up to him in a way in which the results of his doing it are not, or not only, up to him. But we are concerned not with just any intention to produce any kind of effect by acting, but with a very special kind of case. We are concerned with the case in which there is not simply an intention to produce a certain response in an audience, but an intention to produce that response by means of recognition on the part of the audience of the intention to produce that response, this recognition to serve as part of the reason that the audience has for its response, and the intention that this recognition should occur being itself intended to be recognized. The speaker, then, not only has the general authority on the subject of his intention that any agent has; he also has a motive, inseparable from the nature of his act, for making that intention clear. For he will not have secured understanding of the illocutionary force of his utterance, he will not have performed the act of communication he sets out to perform, unless his complex intention is grasped. Now clearly, for the enterprise to be possible at all, there must exist, or he must find, means of making the intention clear. If there exists any conventional linguistic means of doing so, the speaker has both a right to use, and a motive for using, those means. One such means, available sometimes, which comes very close to the employment of the explicit performative form, would be to attach, or subjoin, to the substance of the message what looks like a force-elucidating *comment* on it, which may or may not have the form of a self-ascription. Thus we have phrases like 'This is only a suggestion' or 'I'm only making a suggestion'; or again 'That was a warning' or 'I'm warning you'. For using such phrases, I repeat, the speaker has the *authority* that anyone has to speak on the subject of his intentions and the *motive* that I have tried to show is inseparable from an act of communication.

From such phrases as these—which have, *in appearance*, the character of comments on utterances other than themselves—to the explicit performative formula the step is only a short one. My reason for *qualifying* the remark that such phrases have the character of comments on utterances other than themselves is this. We are considering the case in which the subjoined quasi-comment is addressed to the same audience as the utterance on which it is a quasi-comment. Since it is *part* of the speaker's audience-directed intention to make clear the character of his utterance as, for example, a warning, and since the subjoined quasi-comment directly subserves this intention, it is better to view the case, appearances notwithstanding, *not* as a case in which we have two utterances, one commenting on the other, but as a case of a single unitary speech act. Crudely, the addition of the quasi-comment 'That was a warning' is *part* of the total act of warning. The effect of the short step to the explicitly performative formula is simply to bring appearances into line with reality. When that short step is taken, we no longer have, even in appearance, two utterances, one a comment on the other, but a single utterance in which the first-person performative verb *manifestly* has that peculiar logical character of which Austin rightly made so much, and which we may express in the present context by saying that the verb serves not exactly to *ascribe* an intention to the speaker but rather, in Austin's phrase, to *make explicit* the type of communication intention with which the speaker speaks, the type of force which the utterance has.

The above might be said to be a deduction of the general possibility and utility of the explicitly performative formula for the cases of illocutionary acts not essentially conventional. It may be objected that the deduction fails to show that the intentions rendered explicit by the use of performative formulae *in general* must be of just the complex form described, and hence fails to justify the claim that just this kind of intention lies at the core of all illocutionary acts. And indeed we shall see that this claim would be mistaken. But before discussing why, we shall make a further application of the analysis at the second testing point I mentioned. That is, we shall see what power it has to explain why some of the things we may be *doing, in* saying what we say, are not illocutionary acts and could not be rendered explicit by the use of the performative formula.

Among the things mentioned by Austin which we might be doing in saying things, but which are not illocutionary acts, I shall consider the two examples of (1) showing off and (2) insinuating. Now when we show off, we are certainly trying to produce an effect on the audience: we talk, indeed, for effect; we try to impress, to evoke the response of admiration. But it is no part of the intention to secure the effect *by means of* the recognition of the intention to secure it. It is no part of our total intention to secure recognition of the intention to produce the effect at all. On the contrary: recognition of the intention might militate against securing the effect and promote an opposite effect, for example, disgust.

This leads on to a further general point not explicitly considered by Austin, but satisfactorily explained by the analysis under consideration. In saying to an audience what we do say, we very often intend not only to produce the primary response *r* by means of audience recognition of the intention to produce that response, but to produce further effects by means of the production of the primary response *r*. Thus my further purpose in informing you that *p* (that is, aiming to produce in you the primary cognitive response of knowledge or belief that p) may be to bring it about thereby that you adopt a certain line of conduct or a certain attitude. In saying what I say, then, part of what I am *doing* is trying to influence your attitudes or conduct in a certain way. Does this part of what I am doing in saying what I say contribute to determining the character of the illocutionary act I perform? And if not, why not? If we take the first question strictly as introduced and posed, the answer to it is 'No'. The reason for the answer follows from the analysis. We have no complex intention (i_4) that there should be recognition of an intention (i_2) that there should be recognition of an intention (i_1) that the further effect should be produced; for it is no part of our intention that the further effect should be produced by way of recognition of our intention that it should be; the production in the audience of belief that p is intended to be itself the means whereby his attitude or conduct is to be influenced. We secure uptake, perform the act of communication that we set out to perform, if the audience understands us as *informing* him that p. Although it is true that, in saying what we say, we are in fact *trying* to produce the further effect—this is part of what we are doing, whether we succeed in producing the effect or not—yet this does not enter into the characterization of the illocutionary act. With this case we have to contrast the case in which, instead of aiming at a primary response and a further effect, the latter to be secured through the former alone, we aim at a complex primary response. Thus in the case where I do not simply inform, but warn, you that p, among the intentions I intend you to recognize (and intend you to recognize as intended to be recognized) are not only the intention to secure your belief that p, but the intention to secure that you are on your guard against p-perils. The difference (one of the differences) between showing off and warning is that your recognition of my intention to put you on your guard may well contribute to putting you on your guard, whereas your recognition of my intention to impress you is not likely to contribute to my impressing you (or not in the way I intended).[1]

---

[1] Perhaps trying to impress might sometimes have an illocutionary character. For I might try to impress you with my *effrontery*, intending you to recognize this intention and intending your recognition of it to function as part of your reason for being impressed, and so forth. But then I am not *merely* trying to impress you; I am *inviting* you to be impressed. I owe this point to Mr. B. F. McGuinness.

Insinuating fails, for a different reason, to be a type of illocutionary act. An essential feature of the intentions which make up the illocutionary complex is their overtness. They have, one might say, essential avowability. This is, in one respect, a logically embarrassing feature. We have noticed already how we had to meet the threat of a counterexample to Grice's analysis of the communicative act in terms of three types of intention—(i_1), (i_2), and (i_3)—by the addition of a further intention (i_4) that an intention (i_2) should be recognized. We have no proof, however, that the resulting enlarged set of conditions is a complete analysis. Ingenuity might show it was not; and the way seems open to a regressive series of intentions that intentions should be recognized. While I do not think there is anything necessarily objectionable in this, it does suggest that the complete and rounded-off set of conditions aimed at in a conventional analysis is not easily and certainly attainable in these terms. That is why I speak of the feature in question as logically embarrassing. At the same time it enables us easily to dispose of insinuating as a candidate for the status of a type of illocutionary act. The whole point of insinuating is that the audience is to *suspect*, but not more than suspect, the intention, for example, to induce or disclose a certain belief. The intention one has in insinuating is essentially nonavowable.

Now let us take stock a little. We tentatively laid it down as a necessary condition of securing understanding of the illocutionary force of an utterance that the speaker should succeed in bringing it about that the audience took him, in issuing his utterance, to have a complex intention of a certain kind, namely the intention that the audience should recognize (and recognize as intended to be recognized) his intention to induce a certain response in the audience. The suggestion has, as we have just seen, certain explanatory merits. Nevertheless we cannot claim general application for it as even a partial analysis of the notions of illocutionary force and illocutionary act. Let us look at some reasons why not.

v

I remarked earlier that the words 'Don't go' may have the force, *inter alia*, either of a request or of an entreaty. In either case the primary intention of the utterance (if we presume the words to be uttered with the *sense* 'Don't go *away*') is that of inducing the person addressed to stay where he is. His staying where he is is the primary response aimed at. But the only other intentions mentioned in our scheme of partial analysis relate directly or indirectly to recognition of the primary intention. So how, in terms of that scheme, are we to account for the variation in illocutionary force between requests and entreaties?

This question does not appear to raise a major difficulty for the scheme. The scheme, it seems, merely requires supplementing and enriching. *Entreaty*, for example, is a matter of trying to secure the primary response not merely through audience recognition of the intention to secure it, but through audience recognition of a complex attitude of which this primary intention forms an integral part. A wish that someone should stay may be held in different ways: passionately or lightly, confidently or desperately; and it may, for different reasons, be part of a speaker's intention to secure recognition of *how* he holds it. The most obvious reason, in the case of entreaty, is the belief, or hope, that such a revelation is more likely to secure the fulfillment of the primary intention.

But one may not only request and entreat; one may *order* someone to stay where he is. The words 'Don't go' may have the illocutionary force of an order. Can we so simply accommodate in our scheme *this* variation in illocutionary force? Well, we can accommodate it; though not so simply. We can say that a man who issues an order typically intends his utterance to secure a certain response, that he intends this intention to be recognized, and its recognition to be a reason for the response, that he intends the utterance to be recognized as issued in a certain social context such that certain social rules or conventions apply to the issuing of utterances in this context and such that certain consequences may follow in the event of the primary response not being secured, that he intends *this* intention too to be recognized, and finally that he intends the recognition of these last features to function as an element in the reasons for the response on the part of the audience.

Evidently, in this case, unlike the case of entreaty, the scheme has to be extended to make room for explicit reference to social convention. It can, with some strain, be so extended. But as we move further into the region of institutionalized procedures, the strain becomes too much for the scheme to bear. On the one hand, one of its basic features—namely, the reference to an intention to secure a definite response in an audience (over and above the securing of uptake)—has to be dropped. On the other, the reference to social conventions of procedure assumes a very much greater importance. Consider an umpire giving a batsman out, a jury bringing in a verdict of guilty, a judge pronouncing sentence, a player redoubling at bridge, a priest or a civil officer pronouncing a couple man and wife. Can we say that the umpire's primary intention is to secure a certain response (say, retiring to the pavilion) from a certain audience (say, the batsman), the jurymen's to secure a certain response (say, the pronouncing of sentence) from a certain audience (say, the judge), and then build the rest of our account around this, as we did, with some strain, in the case of the order? Not with plausibility. It is not even possible, in other than a formal sense, to isolate, among all the participants in the procedure (trial, marriage, game) to which the utterance belongs, a particular audience to whom the utterance can be said to be addressed.

Does this mean that the approach I suggested to the elucidation of the notion of illocutionary force is entirely mistaken? I do not think so. Rather, we must distinguish types of case; and then see what, if anything, is common to the types we have distinguished. What we initially take from Grice—with modifications—is an at least partially analytical account of an act of communication, an act which might indeed be performed nonverbally and yet exhibit all the essential characteristics of a (nonverbal) equivalent of an illocutionary act. We gain more than this. For the account enables us to understand how such an act may be linguistically conventionalized right up to the point at which illocutionary force is exhausted by meaning (in Austin's sense); and in this understanding the notion of wholly overt or essentially avowable intention plays an essential part. Evidently, in these cases, the illocutionary act itself is not *essentially* a conventional act, an act done as conforming to a convention; it may be that the act is conventional, done as conforming to a convention, only in so far as *the means used to perform it* are conventional. To speak only of those conventional means which are also *linguistic* means, the extent to which the act is one done as conforming to conventions may depend solely on the extent to which conventional linguistic meaning exhausts illocutionary force.

At the other end of the scale—the end, we may say, from which Austin began—we have illocutionary acts which *are* essentially conventional. The examples I mentioned just now will serve—marrying, redoubling, giving out, pronouncing sentence, bringing in a verdict. Such acts could have no existence outside the rule- or convention-governed practices and procedures of which they essentially form parts. Let us take the standard case in which the participants in these procedures know the rules and their roles, and are trying to play the game and not wreck it. Then they are presented with occasions on which they have to, or may, perform an illocutionary act which forms part of, or furthers, the practice or procedure as a whole; and sometimes they have to make a decision within a restricted range of alternatives (for example, to pass or redouble, to pronounce sentence of imprisonment for some period not exceeding a certain limit). Between the case of such acts as these and the case of the illocutionary act not essentially conventional, there is an important likeness and an important difference. The likeness resides in the fact that, in the case of an utterance belonging to a convention-governed practice or procedure, the speaker's utterance is standardly *intended* to further, or affect the course of, the practice in question in some one of the alternative ways open, and intended to be recognized as so intended. I do not mean that such an act could *never* be performed *unintentionally*. A player might let slip the word 'redouble' without *meaning* to redouble; but if the circumstances are appropriate and the play strict, then he *has* redoubled (or he may be *held* to have redoubled). But a player who continually did this sort of thing would not be asked to play again, except by sharpers. Forms can take charge, in the absence of appropriate intention; but when they do, the case is *essentially* deviant or nonstandard. There is present in the standard case, that is to say, the same element of wholly overt and avowable intention as in the case of the act not essentially conventional.

The difference is a more complicated affair. We have, in these cases, an act which is conventional in two connected ways. First, if things go in accordance with the rules of the procedure in question, the act of furthering the practice in the way intended is an act required or permitted by those rules, an act done as falling under the rules. Second, the act is identified as the act it is just because it is performed by the utterance of a form of words conventional for the performance of that act. Hence the speaker's utterance is not only *intended* to further, or affect the course of, the practice in question in a certain conventional way; in the absence of any breach of the conventional conditions for furthering the procedure in this way, it cannot fail to do so.

And here we have the contrast between the two types of case. In the case of an illocutionary act of a kind not essentially conventional, the act of communication is performed if *uptake* is secured, if the utterance is taken to be issued with the complex overt intention with which it is issued. But even though the act of communication is performed, the wholly overt intention which lies at the core of the intention complex may, *without any breach of rules or conventions*, be frustrated. The audience response (belief, action, or attitude) may simply not be forthcoming. It is different with the utterance which forms part of a wholly convention-governed procedure. Granted that uptake is secured, then any frustration of the wholly overt intention of the utterance (the intention to further the procedure in a certain way) must be attributable to a breach of rule or convention. The speaker who abides by the conventions can avowably have the intention to further the procedure in the way to which his current linguistic act is conventionally appropriated *only* if he takes it that the conventional conditions for so furthering it are satisfied and hence takes it *that his utterance will not only reveal his intentions but give them effect*. There is nothing parallel to this in the case of the illocutionary act of a kind not essentially conventional. In both cases, we may say, speakers assume the responsibility for making their intentions overt. In one case (the case of the convention-constituted procedure) the speaker who uses the explicitly performative form also explicitly assumes the responsibility for making his overt intention effective. But in the other case the speaker cannot, in the speech act itself, explicitly assume any such responsibility. For there are no conditions which can conventionally guarantee the effectiveness of his overt intention. Whether it is effective or not is something that rests with his audience. In the one case, therefore, the explicitly performative form *may* be the name of the very act which is performed if and only if the speaker's overt intention is effective; but in the other case it cannot be the name of this act. But of course—and I shall recur to this thought—the sharp contrast I have here drawn between two extreme types of case must not blind us to the existence of intermediate types.

Acts belonging to convention-constituted procedures of the kind I have just referred to form an important part of human communication. But they do not form the whole nor, we may think, the most fundamental part. It would be a mistake to take them as the model for understanding the notion of illocutionary force in general, as Austin perhaps shows some tendency to do when he both insists that the illocutionary act is essentially a conventional act and connects this claim with the possibility of making the act explicit by the use of the performative formula. It would equally be a mistake, as we have seen, to generalize the account of illocutionary force derived from Grice's analysis; for this would involve holding, falsely, that the complex overt intention manifested in any illocutionary act always includes the intention to secure a certain definite response or reaction in an audience over and above that which is necessarily secured if the illocutionary force of the utterance is understood. Nevertheless, we can perhaps extract from our consideration of two contrasting types of case something which is common to them both and to all the other types which lie between them. For the illocutionary force of an utterance is essentially something that is intended to be understood. And the understanding of the force of an utterance in all cases involves recognizing what may be called broadly an audience-directed intention and recognizing it as wholly overt, as intended to be recognized. It is perhaps this fact which lies at the base of the general possibility of the explicit performative formula; though, as we have seen, extra factors come importantly into play in the case of convention-constituted procedures.

Once this common element in all illocutionary acts is clear, we can readily acknowledge that the types of audience-directed intention involved may be very various and, also, that different types may be exemplified by one and the same utterance.

I have set in sharp contrast those cases in which the overt intention is simply to forward a definite and convention-governed practice (for example, a game) in a definite way provided for by the conventions or rules of the practice and those cases in which the overt intention includes that of securing a definite response (cognitive or practical) in an audience over and above that which is necessarily secured if uptake is secured. But there is something misleading about the sharpness of this contrast; and it would certainly be wrong to suppose that all cases fall clearly and neatly into one or another of these two classes. A speaker whose job it is to do so may offer information, instructions, or even advice, and yet be overtly indifferent as to whether or not his information is accepted as such, his instructions followed, or his advice taken. His wholly overt intention may amount to no more than that of making available—in a 'take it or leave it' spirit—to his audience the information or instructions or opinion in question; though again, in some cases, he may be seen as the mouthpiece, merely, of another agency to which may be attributed at least general intentions of the kind that can scarcely be attributed, in the particular case, to him. We should not find such complications discouraging; for we can scarcely expect a general account of linguistic communication to yield more than schematic outlines, which may almost be lost to view when every qualification is added which fidelity to the facts requires.

AUSTIN ON PERFORMATIVES

Max Black

THE late John Austin's William James Lectures[1] might well have borne the subtitle 'In Pursuit of a Vanishing Distinction'. Although the chase is remorseless, glimpses of the quarry become increasingly equivocal and the hunter is left empty-handed at last. It is hard to know what has gone awry. Has the wrong game been pursued—and in the wrong direction?

There seems deceptively little mystery about the starting point. It is by now a commonplace that in uttering a sentence a speaker need not always be saying something true or false, but may be doing something other than or more than that.[2] The point has been well remembered since Austin's provocative paper on 'Other Minds'.[3] Austin's original example of 'I promise [such-and-such]', spoken in a situation in which uttering the words counts as the making of a promise, is a good illustration. It would require a perverse attachment to what Austin used to call the 'descriptive fallacy'[4] to insist that the promise-maker is primarily making a

[1] J. L. Austin, *How to do things with Words*, edited by J. O. Urmson. Oxford University Press, 1962, pp. vii, 166.

[2] It is worth recalling Wittgenstein's remark about 'the muliplicity of the tools in language': 'But how many kinds of sentence are there? Say assertion, question and command?—There are *countless* kinds: countless kinds of use of what we call "symbols", "words", "sentences".' (*Philosophical Investigations*, Section 23.) The long list of examples of linguistic activities given in the same section should be consulted.

[3] Originally part of a symposium in *Aristotelian Society Proceedings*, supp. vol. xx (1946), reprinted in J. L. Austin, *Philosophical Papers* (Oxford, 1961).

[4] 'To suppose that "I know" is a descriptive phrase, is only one example of the *descriptive fallacy*, so common in philosophy. Even if some language is now purely descriptive, language was not in origin so, and much of it is still not so' (*Other Minds*, p. 174). See also the brief reference to the fallacy at p. 3 of the lectures, where the label 'descriptive' is now criticized and rejected.

truth-claim: one might as well argue that a chessplayer who moves a bishop is primarily *saying that* he is moving the piece. (Still less plausible would it be to contend that the player is saying anything else.) The analogy with promising is still closer when the move is 'announced' at blindfold chess: in both cases, words are used in order to do something other than making an assertion. There is a manifest contrast between the first-person promise and the corresponding third-person remark *about* the episode ('Austin promised [such-and-such]'). The latter might be attacked for failure to correspond with the facts, but not the former: we cannot retort to 'I promise [such-and-such]' with the objection 'It isn't so!'

In connexion with a number of similar sentences, such as 'I name this ship [such-and-such]', 'I give and bequeath [such-and-such]', 'I bet you [such-and-such]', Austin says: 'None of the utterances[1] cited is either true or false: I assert this as obvious and do not argue it' (p. 6). He adds that the point needs no argument, because it is just as obvious as that 'Damn!' is neither true nor false. But something's being obvious has never prevented philosophers from denying it or offering arguments to the contrary. For instance, E. J. Lemmon has recently said[2] that 'I promise [such-and-such]' is 'verifiable by its use'[3] and is satisfied to call it a 'proposition' that is 'true'. From his comparison with 'I am speaking now',[4] he seems to be thinking of a promise as if it were a self-referential statement, i.e., as if it were a remark about itself that would be both necessarily and trivially true. But it is hardly plausible to suppose that a promise-maker is telling his hearer that he is uttering the very words that he is uttering—for what would be the point of *that*? This way of looking at the speech episode looks wilfully perverse: candid consideration of what happens in such episodes should establish beyond any controversy that the point of the promise, its whole *raison d'être*, is not to inform the hearer about itself, or about anything else, but to serve primarily as a way of binding the speaker to a subsequent performance (on

---

[1] By 'utterance' Austin usually means a sentence or, occasionally, an expression, together with the circumstances of some specified use of the words (cf. p. 5 for examples, so p. 6 and especially f.n. 2 on that page). Statements, i.e. sentences used to make a truth-claim, are a subclass of 'utterances'.

[2] E. J. Lemmon, 'On Sentences Verifiable by their Use', *Analysis*, vol. 22, no. 4 (March 1962), pp. 86–9.

[3] Lemmon, op. cit., p. 89.

[4] Lemmon, op. cit., p. 88.

pain of the familiar penalties of being thought fickle, irresponsible, dishonourable, etc.). Of course, the promise serves also to 'inform the hearer' (Austin's phrase), as moving a pawn informs the opponent that it has been moved, but it would be impossible for that to happen unless there was something to be informed about, viz. that the speaker was promising: promising is constituted by, not described by, utterance of the promise-formula. Perhaps all of this is too obvious, after all, to need further belabouring.

Let us follow Austin in calling 'I promise [such-and-such]' a *performative utterance* or a *performative* for short.[1] Though one might think it easy to say what we mean by that label, this proves to be exasperatingly difficult: a great part of Austin's exposition is in effect devoted to this task of definition.

Austin says: 'The name ["performative"] is derived, of course, from "perform", the usual verb with the noun "action"; it indicates that the issuing of the utterance is the performance of an action—it is not usually thought of as just saying something' (pp. 6–7).[2] Here it seems to me of the first importance to bear clearly in mind that 'saying something' has to be construed as 'saying something *true or false*', if Austin's explanation is not to be altogether useless. For a man who makes a promise is certainly 'usually thought of as saying something', viz. the very words that he pronounces ('I promise [such-and-such]'): the point is that what he is saying is not rightly taken to have a *truth-value*. Similarly, 'action', as it occurs in Austin's explanation, must be understood to mean at least 'doing something *other than saying something true or false*', for it is certainly not wrong to think of a man who makes an assertion as doing something, viz. asserting; the point is that he is not doing something other than making a truth-claim. (The trouble is that we normally use 'saying' and 'doing' so loosely, and in such overlapping ways, that any explanation in terms of those words is apt to be unsatisfactory.)

Austin's explanation of 'performative', cited above, suggests the following provisional definition of the notion:

(A) An utterance is said to be *performative*_A, when used in specified circumstances, if and only if its being so used counts as a case of the speaker's doing something other than, or something more than,

---

[1] The label is introduced at p. 6.

[2] This is the closest that Austin comes to giving a formal definition. Cf. conditions A. and B. on p. 5, where almost exactly the same language is used.

saying something true or false. An utterance that is not performative is called *constative*.[1]

A few explanations may be helpful:

'utterance': I follow Austin in using this word to stand for the sentence or other expression used by the speaker. (Sometimes, however, Austin also uses the word to stand for the entire speech-act in question.)

*'performative*ₐ*'*: The suffix is attached to distinguish the sense from another to be discussed immediately.

'in specified circumstances': We are considering a classification of sentences or other expressions *as used in given settings*. Thus one and the same sentence may have to count as performative in one use and constative in another. Application of the definition will require not only specification of the circumstance of use, but in difficult cases an analysis of what is really going on in such a type of speech episode.

'counts as': It is not enough that the utterance should *in fact* be a case of something other than or more than making a truth-claim; there must be a convention or rule making it wrong not to recognize that this is so. (A man who says 'The bull is loose' may *in fact* be warning this hearer, but this does not make his utterance performative.)

'something other than, or more than, saying something true or false': Not in the way in which to walk jerkily is to do something more than just walk: the speaker must be doing something more than making a truth-claim or more than making one in a special way that is indicated by the utterance.

Some such definition as the above might seem to answer to our initial insight about the difference between 'constatives' and 'performatives', between a form of words used to make a truth-claim only and one that conventionally counts as being used to do something other than or more than this. Unfortunately, Austin, like other writers on the same topic, confuses the investigation by relying in effect upon another conception of the meaning of 'performative' that seems to me less important and interesting. That he does so is shown by his reasons for classifying 'I state' as a performative (e.g. at p. 90). (The example is of the first importance for him, because it seems to show that the intended contrast between 'saying' and 'doing' breaks down when its implications are followed

[1] 'Constative' is Austin's useful label for an utterance having truth-value (cf. p. 3).

through. The recalcitrance of 'I state' and 'I maintain' is one of Austin's main reasons for rejecting the original distinction between constatives and performatives as ultimately unsatisfactory.) The reason for classifying 'I state' as performatory is the undeniable fact that a man who says 'I state [such-and-such]' counts as stating, just as a man who says 'I promise [such-and-such]', in appropriate circumstances, counts as promising.

The criterion Austin uses in connexion with 'I state' suggests another definition of 'performative' that might be formulated as follows:

(B) An utterance of the form 'I X [such-and-such]' is said to be performative$_B$, when used in specified circumstances, if and only if its so being used counts as a case of the speaker's thereby X-ing.

Here, both occurrences of 'X' have to be imagined replaced by some English verb in its 'first person singular present indicative active' form (p. 64).

That 'performative$_A$' and 'performative$_B$' are distinct notions is at once shown by the case of 'I say'. For anybody who says 'I say' of course counts as saying something, but does not count as doing something other than or more than saying something true or false. Since it would obviously be desirable to have separate words for the two notions, I would prefer to reserve 'performative' for 'performative$_A$', using something like 'self-labelling utterance' for the other. For what often seems to be happening in the cases of performatives$_B$ is that the utterance includes some formal marker or indicator of the character of that utterance (cf. Austin's good discussion of how the character of the performative is 'made explicit', pp. 69–70). Now this seems to be a special feature of English, not universally present in all languages, and in any case something that ought not to be confused with the more interesting contrast embodied in definition (A). To identify the notion of 'performative' with that of 'performative$_B$' blurs the intended contrast between making a truth-claim and doing something else, or something more, by means of an utterance and focuses our attention too narrowly on a specific verbal form ('I X [such-and-such]'). Austin convincingly shows that there are many other types of utterances (e.g., the umpire's 'Out!', the formula 'You have been warned') that do not come out of the same mould. If his formidable ingenuity in trying to link such cases with a formula of the type 'I X' fails in the end, as it does, I see no prospect of anybody else doing better. (The fact that he pays such close attention to utterances that do not conform to the pattern of definition (B) shows that Austin is not satisfied with sense (B).)

I am therefore inclined to think that some such notion as that of 'performative$_A$' will serve the purposes of Austin and all the philosophers who have had high hopes of the notion, and that many if not all of the difficulties that Austin encountered will be overcome by this choice.

It might be objected that definition (A) is too broad, e.g., because it applies to the utterances 'Hallo' and 'I detest you'. (Austin would certainly wish to exclude the latter: cf. his remark 'To be a performative utterance, even in cases connected with feelings and attitudes . . . is not *merely* to be a conventional expression of feeling or attitude, [p. 81]. Cf. also his remarks on p. 121 about excluding from consideration 'expressive uses of language'.) To this the retort might be that to say 'Hallo' is undoubtedly to do something other than make a truth-claim, viz. to *greet* the hearer, and that to say 'I detest you' is to perform the action (?) of conventionally expressing detestation. Anybody who feels uncomfortable about using 'action' in such cases should be invited to say how greeting and expressing detestation fail to qualify. Were this to be done, definition (A) could easily be modified accordingly, by imposing corresponding restrictions upon what is to be understood by 'doing something' in the formulation of that definition given above. (The original definition might then survive as locating the class of *non-constatives*, of which performatives in the narrower sense would then be a subclass.) Whether this can be done, and whether it is worth doing, I do not know. At any rate, definition (A) in its present form is no worse than the outcome of Austin's discussion: that he wants to use 'action' in some narrowed sense is plain, but what that sense may be never becomes sufficiently clear.

Austin often refers to the action performed by uttering a genuine performative as 'conventional' or 'ritual' or 'ceremonial',[1] but he does not explain how he is using these terms, so central to the understanding of his investigation. One might try to characterize such prime cases of 'conventional' acts as bowing (p. 69), shaking hands, cocking a snook, challenging a man to a duel (p. 27), 'pick-

[1] See, for instance, pp. 19, 20, 25, 31, 36, 69, 80, 84, 102, 103, 104, 106, 108, 120, 121, 127.

ing sides' in a game (p. 28), etc., in the following way: (i) There is a set and prescribed way in which the act in question is supposed to be performed (within a certain range of permissible variation): you may not use a pseudonym for signing a cheque, nor may you omit the words 'I swear' when preparing to testify on oath. To put the point in another way: there are valid and invalid ways of doing the act in question. (Cf. the opening of Austin's condition [A. 1] on p. 14: 'There must exist an accepted conventional procedure . . .') (ii) Provided the act in question is performed in the standard form and in the correct circumstances by a duly qualified person (where the restriction is relevant), the act counts as valid: even if the officiating clergyman deplores the marriage he is solemnizing and performs only under protest, he does marry the couple he 'pronounces' to be man and wife. (iii) The mere doing of the act in accordance with the standard conditions normally makes the actor liable for certain social consequences: a man swearing to tell the truth may be sued for perjury, a man who bets on a horse can be made to pay whether he was in earnest or not. (Cf. the reference in Austin's condition [A. 1] on p. 14 to an accepted conventional procedure *having a conventional effect* [italics added].) More generally: there are a set of understandings, agreements, rules or regulations, in virtue of which the performer of the act (in the correct way) *counts* as satisfying certain demands, acquiring certain rights or privileges, becoming subject to determinable claims, etc. (iv) The act in question is taken to have a certain non-natural meaning or significance, which can usually be rendered specific by an available description (betting, marrying, pronouncing a benediction, signing a cheque, etc.). But this may be just another way of making point (iii) over again. To summarize, let us say that a conventional act is one that is (i) rule-governed, (ii) self-validating, (iii) claim-generating (an inadequate label) and (iv) conventionally significant. It is worth noting that some of these criteria can vary independently, so that we do not have a set of necessary and sufficient conditions. (There would be something pedantic about saying that the utterance of 'Hallo' confers privileges or generates liabilities; yet surely this is a case of what we would want to call a 'conventional' act?)

The trouble in trying to apply some such notion as I have sketched to verbal performances is that *any* correct use of words may plausibly be held to be 'conventional' in the relevant sense:

speaking is already a conventional act. Austin's practice suggests that part of the time he is really thinking of a subclass of 'conventional' acts that have a close analogy to ritual or 'ceremonial' acts in rather narrow senses of those words (he often has the analogy of legal 'acts' in mind). But the analogy can easily be pressed too far: after all there are many ways of promising without using a set formula. At any rate, if the notion of *conventional* act can be sufficiently clarified, definition (A) can easily be amended by inserting the corresponding qualification.

A more serious weakness of definition (A), in my judgement, is the prevalence of 'mixed cases' of utterances that serve, in specified circumstances, both to make a truth-claim and to do something more. When I say 'I warn you that the bull is loose', I may plausibly be said to be doing something other than making a truth-claim (cf. the alternative form 'The bull is loose—that's a warning!' where the second sentence seems to perform a distinct function). But it is plausible also to say that I am at least 'implying' or 'contextually implying'[1] a truth-claim to the effect that the bull is loose. So, as Austin argues, considerations of truth and falsity seem to be relevant to cases such as these. (Even in the paradigm case of 'I promise that I shall be there' it begins to look as if there is at least an implied assertion, 'I shall be there'.) One might then be led to think of the 'performative'-'constative' contrast as dealing with *aspects* of utterances, rather than with mutually exclusive *classes* of utterances.

Considerations of this sort plainly played a large part in Austin's decision 'to make a fresh start on the problem' (p. 91) by introducing the doctrine of 'illocutionary forces'.[2] He proposes to reconsider the senses 'in which to say something is to do something, or in saying something we do something, or even *by* saying something we do something' (p. 108). This is a hopeful programme: one must agree that most of the troubles in handling the original performative-constative distinction arise from the fact that ' "doing something" is a very vague expression' (p. 91) and any clarification of this obscure expression may be expected to render the distinction more useful.

Austin proposes a threefold distinction between 'locutionary',

[1] Cf. Austin's interesting discussion of 'implies' at pp. 50–2.
[2] 'I shall refer to the doctrine of the different types of function of language here in question as the doctrine of "illocutionary forces" ' (p. 99).

'illocutionary' and 'perlocutionary' acts. We perform a *locutionary act* when we utter 'a certain sentence with a certain sense and reference, which again is roughly equivalent to "meaning" in the traditional sense' (p. 108). To perform a locutionary act is to say something 'in the full normal sense . . . which includes the utterance of certain noises, the utterance of certain words in a certain construction, and the utterance of them with a certain "meaning" in the favourite philosophical sense of that word, i.e., with a certain sense and with a certain reference' (p. 94). We normally report the performance of a locutionary act [or, strictly, that aspect of it, viz. meaning and referring, which constitutes what Austin calls the 'rhetic act'] by using indirect speech, e.g., by saying 'He said that the cat was on the mat', 'He said he would go', 'He said I was to go' (p. 96). (We use quotation marks normally only when the sense or reference of the original words is unclear—cf. p. 96, last paragraph.)

An *illocutionary act* is something we do *in* performing a locutionary act—e.g., informing, ordering, warning, undertaking, etc. (p. 108). In reporting the locutionary act we say what the speaker *meant*; in reporting the illocutionary act (he urged, protested, advised me to do such and such—cf. p. 102 for examples) we convey the 'force' of the original utterance, the 'way it is (conventionally) to be taken'. (Clearly the 'illocutionary act' is what we are supposed to be performing when we produce a performative.)

Finally, a *perlocutionary act* is something we may do *by* producing an illocutionary act (e.g., persuading, getting somebody to do something, checking somebody, annoying him, etc.—see pp. 101–2 for these examples).

(I shall not discuss Austin's subdivision of the locutionary act into 'phonetic', 'phatic' and 'rhetic' acts [pp. 92–3]. It seems to me somewhat crude and perversely idiosyncratic in its choice of labels; whatever its intrinsic interest, it has little bearing upon Austin's main problem.)

Austin says that his interest 'is essentially to fasten on the second, illocutionary act and contrast it with the other two' (p. 103) and thinks that 'It is the distinction between illocutions and perlocutions which seems likeliest to give trouble' (p. 109). For all the subtleties in the uses of 'in' and 'by' which Austin proceeds to uncover, it seems to me that this distinction is not the likeliest to give trouble. The performance of the 'illocutionary act' has to be *conventional* in the sense of being assured by the words that were in fact used: 'Illocutionary acts are conventional acts: perlocutionary acts are *not* conventional' (p. 120). 'A judge should be able to decide, *by hearing what was said*, what locutionary and illocutionary acts were performed, but not what perlocutionary acts were achieved' (p. 121). Suitably elaborated, this test seems to me sufficient in practice to distinguish an illocutionary act, such as threatening, from the associated perlocutionary act of intimidating with which it might sometimes be confused. (Austin's careful discussion is illuminating, however, and should be compared with what he said about related topics in his paper 'A Plea for Excuses', reprinted in the *Philosophical Papers*.)

The serious troubles, that threaten to render Austin's scheme of classification nugatory, arise in trying to distinguish the locutionary act from the illocutionary one. Austin is himself unhappy about his use of 'sense' and 'reference' in the definition of the locutionary act ('I have taken the old "sense and reference" ["distinction" omitted?] on the strength of current views' [p. 148]) and admits that the distinction between locutionary and illocutionary acts has been no more than 'adumbrated' (p. 148) by him.

I find it difficult to conceive what a locutionary act (supposedly identified by giving sense and reference alone) would be like. In order to report what a speaker said 'in the full sense of "say"' (p. 92), it seems necessary to report how the speaker meant his words 'to be taken' (whether as a statement, an order, a question, etc.), i.e., to include in the report an indication of the 'illocutionary force', in Austin's terminology, of the original utterance. Reference to the examples of such reports of allegedly locutionary acts given by Austin (e.g., at pp. 101–2) will show that indication of the illocutionary force is indeed included in each case. Indeed, how could it be otherwise? A speaker cannot make a complete utterance merely by meaning and referring—he must assert, question, order, or do whatever else he is doing. The only proper unit for investigation seems to be what Austin has called an illocutionary act and the supposed locutionary act is at best a dubious abstraction. Austin says that 'To perform a locutionary act is in general, we may say, also and *eo ipso* to perform an *illocutionary* act' (p. 98). I am urging that in order to perform a locutionary act one *must* perform an illocutionary one (and Austin seems to agree at p. 133). But then we seem to be back to the old difficulty of being unable to make the performative-constative distinction or anything that will replace it. That Austin was troubled by the outcome is clear from a note he made as late as 1958 (p. 103, f.n.) in which he says that the distinctions he is trying to introduce are not clear and adds: 'in all senses relevant . . . won't all utterances be performative?' (ib.). I think the answer is Yes—at least if we agree with Austin's analysis.

In the end, one remains doubtful whether Austin's investigations have brought some interesting and profitable problems to light—or whether he has allowed himself to be diverted by an interest in what may be no more than a specific peculiarity of linguistic idiom (the use of the 'first person singular present indicative'). I do not know which of these views is the sounder. I am inclined to think at present that the outcome of Austin's patient work illustrates the limitations of trying to 'screw out of ordinary language' (p. 122) all that one can without trying to elaborate a plausible theoretical framework. In practice, this leads to somewhat uncritical reliance upon such questionable distinctions as that between 'sense' and 'reference'. Appeal to ordinary language is very useful when the logical grammar of particular words and families of words is under investigation; it is likely to be less profitable when what is at stake is a general view of how language works.

IN PURSUIT OF PERFORMATIVES

L. W. Forguson

IT sometimes happens that a philosopher will develop a view on some topic and then later come to reject it. J. L. Austin was perhaps unique in that he not only rejected a philosophical view of which he himself was the author, he patiently developed the view and then showed it to be ultimately unsatisfactory within the compass of the same work. And he did this not once but three times, in material intended for publication.[1] I am thinking, of course, of his notion of performative utterances: the view that there is a class of utterance, the members of which would on standard grammatical grounds be classed as statements, yet whose proper business is not to state anything but to perform some act. For example, to say 'I promise to be there' *is* to promise to be there, and not (or at least not merely) to state that one promises nor even to state that one will be there.

It has recently been suggested, however, by Professors Chisholm[2] and Black,[3] that Austin bungled the job with performatives: that he 'despaired'[4] of the notion too readily. Consequently, Chisholm and Black each puts forth an amended definition of performatives which is intended to avoid the difficulties Austin encountered and which led him to abandon the doctrine alto-

[1] See 'Performative Utterances', in Austin's *Philosophical Papers*, ed. J. O. Urmson and G. J. Warnock (Oxford, 1961), 220–39; *How To Do Things With Words*, ed. J. O. Urmson (Oxford, 1962); and 'Performative-Constatif', tr. G. J. Warnock from 'Performatif-Constatif', in *La Philosophie Analytique* (Paris, 1962), 271–304, and reprinted in *Philosophy and Ordinary Language*, ed. Charles E. Caton (Urbana, 1963), 22–54.

[2] Roderick Chisholm, 'J. L. Austin's Philosophical Papers' [reprinted above].

[3] Max Black, 'Austin on Performatives' [see above].

[4] Chisholm, op. cit. [109].

gether in favour of a more thoroughgoing analysis of 'the forces of utterances'.[1]

In this paper I wish to suggest that neither Chisholm's nor Black's amendment in any way avoids the difficulties Austin foresaw, and that both of these attempts to amend Austin's analysis are based upon a fundamental misunderstanding of his reasons for abandoning it.

First of all, what did lead Austin to 'despair' of performatives? The main reason seems to be that he could not find a satisfactory answer to his own question: 'How can we be sure, how can we tell, whether any utterance is to be classed as a performative or not?'[2] That is to say, what criterion can be found which will enable us to distinguish all and only those utterances which are genuinely performative?

The most promising criterion—the grammatical criterion that any genuine performative either is or can be 'reduced' to an *explicit* performative: an utterance in which the performative verb occurs in the first person singular present indicative active—breaks down because, in addition to such obvious performatives as 'I promise . . .' and 'I bet you . . .', the straightforward assertive 'I state that . . .' also neatly fills the bill. But the whole point in talking about performatives in the first place was to distinguish them as a class of utterance from (among other things) straightforward assertive statements.

Even if the extra requirement is made that in performatives 'the little word "hereby" either actually occurs or might naturally be inserted',[3] the prospects are no more pleasing. For the utterance 'I hereby state that the cat is on the mat' is, if a bit pompous, still good sense.

Chisholm, however, thinks that Austin has put the question the wrong way round, and suggests that instead of asking, as Austin does, what are 'those characteristics of *utterances* which would make them merely performative [we should instead] try to describe those characteristics of *performances* which would make them merely utterable'.[4] Accordingly, he goes on to give the following

---

[1] Mentioned briefly in 'Performative Utterances', and 'Performative-Constative', and carried out in more detail in *How To Do Things With Words*.
[2] 'Performative Utterances', op. cit., 228.
[3] 'Performative Utterances', op. cit., 230.
[4] Chisholm, op. cit., [109].

definition of *strict* performatives:

> There are acts (e.g. requesting) which have the following charac-
> teristics: when the circumstances are right, then to perform the act
> it is enough to make a certain utterance (e.g. 'I request . . .') con-
> taining an expression which the speaker commonly uses to desig-
> nate such an act. . . . Let us say, of anyone who performs an act in
> this way, that his utterance is a performative utterance—in the *strict*
> sense of this term.[1]

There are utterances, though (Chisholm mentions those containing the expressions 'I want . . .', and 'I know . . .'), which
are plainly not performative in this strict sense, but can be seen to
be performative in another, *extended* sense which Chisholm characterizes as follows:

> The utterance of an expression (e.g. 'I want . . .') is performative
> in an extended sense of the term, if it is made in order to accom-
> plish that act in virtue of which the utterance of some other ex-
> pression (e.g. 'I request . . .') can be performative in the strict sense
> defined.[2]

Thus, 'I want you to leave me alone' is performative in the extended sense, according to Chisholm, since it is one way of accomplishing an act (requesting you to leave me alone) which could have
been accomplished by saying instead, 'I request that you leave me
alone'. And, 'I know that he put the arsenic in the soup' is
performative in the extended sense, for I could just as well have
said, and accomplished the same act in saying, 'I guarantee that he
put the arsenic in the soup'.

It is difficult to see what Chisholm hopes to accomplish by distinguishing between strict and extended performatives, however.
For considering performative utterances as a special class of act
avoids none of the problems involved in considering them as a
special class of utterance. For instance, Chisholm's class of strict
performatives appears to be no more than what Austin meant by
'explicit' performative utterances, and is open to the same main
objection. For the verb 'to state' is a word commonly used by
speakers of English to designate an act: the act of uttering or
making or otherwise issuing statements. And it is enough to
perform this act (if the circumstances are right) that one make an
utterance (namely, a statement) which includes the prefix 'I state

[1] Chisholm, op. cit., [109].   [2] Ibid., [110].

that . . .' (or even 'I hereby state that . . .'). Thus, 'I state that the cat is on the mat' is a performative utterance in the strict sense of the term as defined by Chisholm. But Austin despaired of performatives for the very reason that statement making could not justifiably be kept out of the club. Its credentials are impeccable both as a performable utterance and as an utterable performance.

Furthermore, Chisholm's definition of strict performatives does manage to exclude certain utterances which Austin considered to be paradigm examples of performative utterances. Consider, for instance, the utterance 'I will', as uttered in a marriage ceremony. The utterance of this expression by the appropriate person at the appropriate juncture of the marriage ceremony *is* to marry, and not (or at least not just) to state that one will (or predict that one will, or state one's intention to) take the person standing next to one as one's lawful wedded spouse. Or, putting it Chisholm's way, in order to perform the act of marrying it is enough (again, if the circumstances are right) to make the utterance 'I will'. However, the expression 'I will' does not contain a word commonly used by the speaker to *designate* the act of marrying. Marrying is marrying and not another thing (except perhaps being wed). So, according to Chisholm's definition, 'I will' is not a performative in the strict sense of the term.

Unfortunately, it is not even a performative in the *extended* sense of the term, as defined by Chisholm. For to utter the expression 'I will' in a marriage ceremony is to accomplish an act (the act of marrying) which could not be accomplished by means of some other expression, the uttering of which in the appropriate circumstances would be performative of marrying in the strict sense of the term. There simply is no expression in English, other than 'I will' (in particular, there is no expression 'I marry . . .'), the utterance of which in the right circumstances will successfully get one married. And even if there were some other expression that one could utter and thereby marry, it need not be the case that all performatives function in this way. It is not difficult to imagine an expression ('I hereby X . . .') the utterance of which alone can perform some act (the act of Y-ing), which is never itself used to designate that act; and every word which can be used to designate that act is never used in the actual performance of it.

Chisholm's notion of utterances performative in an extended sense of the term has, if anything, less explanatory interest than his class of strict performative utterances. An utterance is supposed to be performative, it will be remembered, in an extended sense of the term 'if it is made in order to accomplish that act in virtue of which the utterance of some other expression can be performative in the strict sense defined'. But practically any utterance whatever can be used, *if the circumstances are right*, to accomplish an act which could also be accomplished by means of a strict performative formula.

Consider 'requesting' again. Depending upon the circumstances of the particular situation, there are a great number of things one can say, the saying of which in those circumstances accomplishes an act which otherwise could be accomplished by an utterance containing the expression 'I request . . .'. If an acquaintance of mine overstays his welcome at my house, I could request him to leave by means of the strict performative 'I (hereby) request that you go home'. But there are any number of other things I could say, the saying of which could accomplish the same act. I could, for example, say any of the following:

'Oh, why don't you go home?'

'Please go home now.'

'Don't let me keep you from another engagement.'

'It's getting rather late, don't you think?'

'I'm afraid I must get up early tomorrow.'

'Where has the time gone?'

and so on. In fact, it is difficult to think of any utterances which *fail* to be performative in the extended sense.

Of course, Chisholm may mean to designate not just any utterance which in fact accomplishes an act which can be accomplished by an utterance using a strict performative formula, but any *standard* or *accepted* way of accomplishing such an act. However, any act which can be accomplished by means of an utterance containing the prefix 'I order . . .' (or 'I command . . .' or 'I hereby direct you . . .') can also be accomplished by the use of a straightforward imperative. Worse yet, since 'I state that . . .' is performative in the strict sense, the utterance of any indicative statement turns out to be performative in the extended sense. For instance, since 'I state that it is raining' is a strict performative, 'It is raining' is a performative in the extended sense.

Although it would be rather extreme to do so, one might finally fall back on the restriction that in order to be performative, even in the extended sense, the utterance must contain an occurrence of the verb in the first person singular present indicative active (e.g. 'I want. . .'). But again, since 'I state (or confess, or maintain) that I feel sick' is performative in the strict sense, 'I feel sick' is by the same token performative in the extended sense of the term.

Plainly, unless 'I state that. . .' and kindred expressions can be effectively excluded from the class, the explanatory and classificatory power of the notion of performative utterances is practically nil. But, as Austin realized, there seems to be no non-arbitrary way to exclude these expressions.

Professor Black also offers two distinct definitions of 'performative'. But his distinction is drawn along different lines and thus avoids some of the problems that beset Chisholm with respect to expressions such as 'I state that . . .'. These two definitions are formulated by Black as follows:

> An utterance is said to be performative_A, when used in specified circumstances, if and only if its being so used counts as a case of the speaker's doing something other than, or something more than, saying something true or false.[1]
> An utterance of the form 'I X[such-and-such]' is said to be performative_B. when used in specified circumstances, if and only if its so being used counts as a case of the speaker's thereby X-ing.[2]

It is, says Black, Austin's failure to distinguish these two senses in which an utterance can be performative that leads Austin into difficulties in the case of 'I state . . .', 'I maintain . . .', and the like. For, although to say 'I state that such-and-such' *is* to state that such-and-such, it is not to do anything 'other than, or more than, saying something true or false', according to Black. Plainly, though, to say 'I warn you that there is a bull in the field' is to do something (namely, warn you) other than, or more than, saying something true or false. Consequently, Black is

> inclined to think that some such notion as that of 'performative_A' will serve the purposes of Austin and all the philosophers who have had high hopes of the notion, and that many if not all of the difficulties that Austin encountered will be overcome by this choice.[3]

I am, on the contrary, inclined to think that few if any of the difficulties Austin encountered will be overcome by this choice, as

[1] Black, op. cit., [403].   [2] Ibid., [405].   [3] Ibid., [406].

I shall attempt to show. It is the function of every utterance, even those which are either true or false, to do something *more* than merely say something true or false. If this were not the case, there would be very little point in ever issuing any utterances. But the 'performative-constative' distinction, being a distinction between two separate *classes* of utterance, obscures this feature of utterances entirely. And it is above all for this reason that Austin gave up the distinction and turn to a consideration of the *forces* of utterances.

Consider, for example, such a simple indicative as 'There's a bull in the field'. To say this is to say something true, if there is a bull in the field, and false otherwise. But think of the very many different things one may be doing, more than merely saying something true or false, in uttering this statement on a particular occasion. To mention just a few:

(1) You are about to go into the field, and I know (but have reason to think that you do not) that there is a vicious bull there. So I warn you.

(2) It's your bull, but you haven't kept your fences mended and the bull is in my field, eating my tomato crop. I express to you my anger.

(3) I'm about to go into my field, but just as I'm going through the gate I see a strange and thoroughly evil-looking bull. I'm certainly surprised, and a bit terrified, at finding it there.

(4) You've lost your bull, and ask if I've seen one about. I have, and inform you where it is.

Thus, I can express anger, surprise, terror; I can warn you, accuse you of laxity, inform you, and any number of other things, all in saying merely 'There's a bull in the field'. And it is extremely unlikely that one would ever say anything of this sort in the normal course of affairs and not be doing thereby something more than saying something true or false.

Usually, what someone is doing in saying something can be determined by attending to such things as the circumstances in which the utterance is made and the intonation with which it is made, etc. It is not usually necessary to make the force of the utterance explicit as part of the utterance itself. This can be done, however, by means of some introductory modifying expression, along the following lines:

I warn you that there's a bull in the field.
I confess that there's a bull in the field.
I am angry to learn that there's a bull in the field.
I am terrified to discover that there's a bull in the field.
I am surprised to find that there's a bull in the field.

In adding these modifying expressions, though, one is doing no more than making verbally explicit the *force* of 'There's a bull in the field' as uttered in a particular context, much as a novelist might attempt to do by other means (e.g. 'He was about to go through the gate when he suddenly stopped dead in his tracks. "There's a bull in the field!" he croaked, trembling.').

Black's notion of 'performative_A' and Chisholm's 'strict' and 'extended' notions of performative utterances still draw a basic distinction between one class of utterance (performatives) and all other utterances. The important point that Austin saw and Chisholm and Black seem to have missed is that there really *is* no good reason to distinguish between performative and other *sorts* of utterances at all. All utterances have their 'performative' rôle to play in discourse: simple assertions as well as promises and requests. It won't do to try to salvage the distinction between two different classes of utterance because there aren't in the relevant sense two classes at all.[1] What is really needed is a new dimension of classification altogether. And it was precisely this discovery which led Austin to consider again 'from the ground up'[2] the many senses in which saying something can be doing something, the many different ways in which things are done with words.[3]

---

[1] It should be mentioned that Black does come to this conclusion himself [op. cit., 411], but apparently fails to see both that Austin realized it, and that it was Austin's main reason for abandoning the performative-constative distinction.

[2] *How To Do Things With Words*, 94.

[3] I should like to thank Mr. G. J. Warnock for helpful criticism of an earlier draft of this paper.

DO ILLOCUTIONARY FORCES EXIST?

L. Jonathan Cohen

I

IF the late Professor J. L. Austin had survived to publish the substance of his William James Lectures himself, he would no doubt have made many alterations in them. With his brilliant sharpness of intellect he would probably have eliminated more flaws than most of his critics will ever see. But, tragic as it is, we have only a posthumously published version of those lectures, and it is to this version, carefully put together by J. O. Urmson under the title *How To Do Things With Words* (Oxford, 1962), that criticism must perforce be directed. I wish to argue that the concept of illocutionary force developed therein is empty.

According to Austin every act of speaking, except perhaps (132) a mere exclamation like 'damn' or 'ouch', is both a locutionary and an illocutionary act. *Qua* locutionary it is, as it were, three acts in one (92 ff.): the (phonetic) act of uttering certain noises; the (phatic) act of uttering certain vocables or words belonging to and as belonging to a certain vocabulary, in a certain grammatical construction, with a certain intonation, etc.; and the (rhetic) act of using those vocables with a certain more or less definite sense and reference. Austin takes 'sense and reference' here on the strength of current views, as he puts it (148), and all he says about them directly is that together they are equivalent to 'meaning'. But he does remark also that phatic acts may be reported by direct quotation, as in 'He said "The cat is on the mat" ', while rhetic acts are reported in indirect discourse. The product of a phatic act is a unit of language, and its typical fault is to be meaningless, while the product of a rhetic act is a unit of speech, and its typical fault is to be vague or void or obscure, etc. Austin claims that to perform such a three-in-one locutionary act is in general also, and *eo ipso*, to perform an illocutionary act. In order to determine what illocutionary act is so performed, says Austin, we must determine in what way we are using the locution. E.g., are we asking or answering a question? Are we giving some information or assurance or a warning? Are we announcing a verdict or an intention? Are we pronouncing sentence? Are we making an appointment or an appeal or a criticism? Or are we making an identification or giving a description? Austin gives the name of 'illocutionary forces' to those different types of function that language has in the performance of an illocutionary act. It is as essential, he suggests, to distinguish force from meaning, as it is to distinguish sense from reference within meaning. (In three passages, pp. 115 n., 124, and 129, Austin treats the rheme as the total speech-act, but the inconsistency between these passages and pp. 92–7 is unimportant for the purposes of this article.)

Moreover, in addition to the performance of the locutionary act *of* saying something, and the performance of an illocutionary act *in* saying something, we may at the same time perform a perlocutionary act *by* saying something. Austin calls an act of speaking perlocutionary so far as it produces certain intended or unintended effects upon the feelings, thoughts, or actions of the audience, of the speaker, or of other persons. E.g., while 'He urged me to shoot her' would describe an illocutionary act, 'He persuaded me to shoot her' would describe a perlocutionary one. Austin claims that, just as expressions like 'meaning' and 'use of sentence' can blur the distinction between locutionary and illocutionary acts, so too to speak of the 'use' of language can blur the distinction between the illocutionary and the perlocutionary act. Speaking of the 'use of language for arguing or warning' looks just like speaking of the 'use of language for persuading, rousing, alarming'. Yet the former may, for rough contrast, be said to be *conventional*, he claims, in the sense that at least it could be made explicit by a performative formula, while the latter could not. Thus we can say, performatively, 'I argue that' or 'I warn you that', but we cannot say 'I convince you that' or 'I alarm you that'. Austin points out, too, that the expression 'the use of language' can cover other matters even more diverse than what he calls illocutionary and perlocutionary acts. We may speak of the use of language *in* poetry or *for* joking, and we can also use language to make insinuations or to express our feelings, as in swearing (121).

Austin thinks that the distinction between illocutions and per-locutions is the one likeliest to give trouble (109), and seeks at some length (120 ff.) to clarify the extent to which the use of the prepositions 'in' and 'by' in sentences of the form 'In/by saying X I was doing Y' may afford a criterion for making this distinction. But since I shall be primarily concerned with the locutionary-illocutionary distinction it will suffice here to mention how Austin emphasizes that the illocutionary act is in no way the consequence of the locutionary act, nor does it consist in the production of consequences. Rather, to perform an illocutionary act is necessarily to perform a locutionary act—to congratulate is necessarily to say certain words (113). What we do import, he says (114), by the use of the nomenclature of illocution is a reference, not to the conse-quences (at least in any ordinary sense) of the locution, but to the conventions of illocutionary force as bearing on the special cir-cumstances of the utterance. Any, or almost any perlocutionary act is liable to be brought off, in sufficiently special circumstances, by the issuing, with or without calculation, of any utterance whatso-ever. But the range of illocutionary acts that may be brought off by a given utterance is restricted by the conventions of illocutionary force. Austin does insist, however, that the performance of an illocutionary act involves 'the securing of uptake' (115 ff., 139). A man cannot be said to have warned an audience, Austin claims, unless it hears what he says and takes what he says in a certain sense. Also an illocutionary act may take effect in certain ways other than the bringing about of changes in the natural course of events. Thus naming a ship 'Queen Elizabeth' has the effect of putting out of order any later references to it by another name. And certain illocutionary acts, such as questions, may characteris-tically invite responses. But any normal production of conse-quences in speech is a perlocutionary act.

Though the term 'perlocutionary' is Austin's own invention, the existence of what Austin calls perlocutionary acts is commonly accepted and, indeed, undeniable. In different circumstances utter-ances with the same meaning can have such vastly different effects on their hearers that it is obviously wrong to identify any part of the meaning of an utterance with its actual effect on its hearers. Obviously the same piece of information about a rise in fat stock prices may cheer farmers quite as much as it distresses butchers. Indeed, we only need a special term 'perlocutionary' to cover this aspect of people's utterances if Austin is right in thinking that, besides having a meaning and an effect, an utterance may also have what he calls an illocutionary force. The line between meaning and effect is in general clear enough. But, as Austin's own work shows, great difficulties arise, and the need for technical terminology is felt, as soon as room is sought for an utterance to have a 'force' as well as a meaning and an effect. I want to argue that this technical terminology is unnecessary, because no utterance can have any such force. I shall approach the problem indirectly, by first examining Austin's concept of meaning.

II

Austin's own account of 'meaning' here is unfortunately rather unhelpful since, though he equates meaning with sense and reference, he does not tell us which of the many current views about 'sense' and 'reference' he shares. Certainly he cannot just have meant by 'meaning' that in virtue of which an utterance is true or false. So many of the utterances with which he deals are not of a kind that can be either true or false. They are questions, commands, curses, resignations, namings, etc., instead. Moreover, even Strawson's distinction (*Introduction to Logical Theory*, 1952, p. 145) between the referring role expressions may have in statements, and the ascriptive, descriptive or classificatory role, will not quite suit Austin's purposes. Strawson's distinction is between the reference and the sense of words or phrases, while Austin's desire to contrast the meaning of an utterance with its illocutionary force suggests that by 'sense' and 'reference' he mainly means the sense and reference of a whole utterance, not of its component words or phrases. Indeed, if Austin had meant to cite the sense and reference of an utterance's component words or phrases he could hardly have considered these two factors sufficient to determine the meaning of a whole utterance for his purposes. He would have had to cite sense, reference *and word-order* instead, for he could hardly have wanted to ascribe the same meaning to 'George hit John' and 'John hit George'. Frege, of course, did extend his distinction to whole statements. But Frege's theory has three considerable disadvantages for Austin's purposes. According to Frege (*Translations from the Philosophical Writings*, ed. P. Geach and M. Black, 1952, p. 68) when a subordinate clause with 'that' occurs after such words as 'command', 'ask', etc., the reference of the clause is to a command, request, etc. So that when—to use Austin's term—the illocutionary force of 'Retreat!' is made explicit in 'I command that you retreat', this illocutionary force ceases to exist as such, contrary to what Austin suggests (131), and disappears into the reference. Moreover, even with regard to statements Austin would be led into the paradoxical position of holding that a statement's illocutionary force can never be made explicit without changing its meaning. According to Frege 'My age is 40' would have a different sense and reference from 'I state that my age is 40'. Worse still, if Austin uses 'meaning' as equivalent to Frege's 'sense and reference', then one cannot know the meaning of a statement on Austin's view unless one knows its truth-value, since Frege took the normal reference of a statement to be its truth-value. This hardly jibes with Austin's claim that the utterance of vocables with a more or less definite sense and reference is normally reported in indirect discourse. When we report 'He said that the cat was on the mat' we do not commit ourselves as to the truth or falsity of the remark reported.

Indeed in some respects it seems doubtful whether Austin can have had any clear idea of meaning at all here. Two of his tenets on the subject are very difficult to reconcile. On the one hand he tells us that, except perhaps for exclamations, every utterance is both a locutionary and an illocutionary act (98, 113, 132). Presumably therefore every utterance, on his view, has both meaning and illocutionary force. On the other hand Austin suggests (131) that when we have an explicit performative we also have an illocutionary act. When we say 'I warn you that' or 'I order you to' as an explicit performative, we perform the illocutionary act of warning or ordering, respectively. But what locutionary act do we then perform? What is the meaning of our utterance, as distinct from its illocutionary force?

It is tempting at first to suppose that in Austin's view the meaning of our utterance is found solely in the clause that follows the performative prefix. The meaning would then lie in the clause 'your haystack is on fire', when the whole utterance was 'I warn you that your haystack is on fire', or in the clause 'go to London' when the whole utterance was 'I order you to go to London'. It would then be plausible to claim that these utterances have precisely the same meaning and illocutionary force as their respective subordinate clauses might have had if uttered alone and without the benefit of performative prefix. Their only difference from the latter kind of utterance would be in having their illocutionary force rendered explicit. But unfortunately there are at least three objections to interpreting Austin's theory in this way.

First, it is not at all clear why one should not suppose the expression 'I warn you that' to refer both to the speaker and to the addressee of the utterance; and if the personal pronouns 'I' and 'you' enable it to have this reference one might also suspect the verb 'warn' to give it a sense. Secondly, it is difficult to see how the addition of such a performative prefix can make no difference to the locutionary act performed, since this act is in part defined in terms of the (phonetic) act of uttering certain noises and the (phatic) act of uttering units of a certain vocabulary in conformity to a certain grammar. Thus viewed the locutionary act of uttering 'I warn you that your haystack is on fire' must be of a different kind from that of uttering just 'Your haystack is on fire'. Perhaps Austin would have claimed here that though the phonetic and phatic acts are different the rhetic act is the same. But an accurate interpreter, assigned the job of rendering the explicit meanings into French, would certainly give different versions for the two utterances.

Neither of these two objections is conclusive. Austin might have wanted to maintain the view, paradoxical though it may be, that personal pronouns do not have a referring role in performative prefixes and that in his use of 'meaning' a necessary difference in accurate translations does not entail difference of meaning. But there is a more serious objection. If every illocutionary act is also a locutionary one, then the performative utterance of 'I protest' (said as the chairman refuses to let you speak) or of 'I apologize' (said as you accidentally tread on someone's toes) or of 'I withdraw', 'I congratulate you', 'I thank you', 'I bless you', 'I take your side', 'I nominate you', or of any other such self-sufficient expression, must have a meaning as well as an illocutionary force. But if these potentially performative expressions can have a meaning when uttered alone one can hardly suppose that they lose this meaning when subordinate clauses are added, as in 'I protest that I have not been allowed to speak' or 'I thank you for helping me'. One is thus forced to the conclusion that on Austin's view the meaning of an utterance like 'I warn you that your haystack is on fire' is not to be found solely in its subordinate clause.

In what way then does the illocutionary force of such an utterance differ from that part of its meaning which belongs to it in virtue of its performative prefix? When you say 'I protest', you are not describing your protest nor reporting it. You are just protesting. If your utterance is to be assigned a meaning of any kind, this meaning must be of a performative kind. The meaning lies solely in the making of the protest. This emerges quite clearly if we judge the meaning by an accurate interpreter's translation. But it also emerges even if we accept Austin's own thesis that the meaning of a locutionary act is reported in indirect discourse. For we can report your utterance not only by 'You protested', but also by 'You said you protested', as Austin remarks elsewhere ('Truth', *Proc. Ar. Soc.* Supp. Vol. xxiv, 1950, p. 125). It is thus clear that wherever explicitly performative expressions are used, the illocutionary force, if such a thing exists at all, cannot be distinguished from the meaning.

But even where explicitly performative expressions do not occur the term 'illocutionary force' turns out to be just as otiose. After all, if the utterance 'Your haystack is on fire' gives a warning that is rendered explicit by 'I warn you that your haystack is on fire', and if the warning is part of the meaning of the latter utterance, it is hardly unreasonable to suppose that the warning is also part of the former utterance's meaning, though inexplicitly so. If one says 'He caught a large one' and is asked to be more explicit, one might say 'James landed a trout more than ten pounds in weight', and certainly then it is meaning—sense and reference, if you like— that has been made explicit. What reason is there for supposing that it is illocutionary force, rather than meaning, that has been rendered explicit in 'I warn you that your haystack is on fire'?

It is no use arguing that meaning is said to be rendered explicit only when the sense or reference of individual expressions within the utterance is vague, ambiguous or otherwise uncertain. It may instead be the whole grammatical structure of an utterance that prevents its meaning from being fully explicit. For example, the meaning of 'He asks, whether it is raining or snowing' might be made explicit either by 'He asks his question irrespective of whether it is raining or snowing' or by 'His question is whether it is raining or snowing'. Similarly it is pretty clear that if you address the English sentence 'Is it raining?' to your friend, as he looks out of the window, your meaning would be made even more explicit if

426

you added, a moment later, 'I ask whether it is raining'. Asking a question, with or without benefit of performative, is on Austin's view (98) a typical illocutionary act. Yet even in your first utterance ('Is it raining?'), let alone in your second ('I ask whether it is raining'), it is impossible to distinguish illocutionary force from meaning. What on earth could be the meaning of your locutionary act other than to ask whether it is raining?

Austin thinks it plausible (71 ff.), as indeed it is, that explicit performatives are a later development in the history of language. In primitive languages, he suggests, it would not yet be clear, nor possible to distinguish, which we were in fact doing of various things that (in accordance with later distinctions) we might be doing. E.g. 'Bull' or 'Thunder' in a primitive language of one-word utterances could be a warning, or information, or prediction, etc. Clarification of such utterances is as much a creative act, in the development of language, as a discovery or prediction. Austin gives a long list of other linguistic devices which may also help clarification here, though the explicit performative is the most successful device: verb-mood ('Shut it—I should' resembles the performative 'I advise you to shut it'), tone of voice, cadence, emphasis (cf. the difference between uttering the sounds 'It's going to charge' as a warning or as a report), adverbs and adverbial phrases (e.g. adding 'without fail' to 'I shall' in making a promise), connecting particles ('therefore' resembles 'I conclude that'), and so on. Austin seems to hold that all such devices clarify illocutionary force, not meaning. But on this view there can be no difference of meaning at all between such utterances as 'It must have rained, because the streets are wet' and 'It must have rained, therefore the streets are wet'. Yet most ordinary speakers of English, let alone linguists and interpreters, would be very surprised indeed to hear that such a pair of utterances have the same meaning. Indeed there is no reason to suppose that particles like 'therefore' must have different functions in the utterance of categorical sentences from those they have in the utterance of conditional ones. But in a conditional sentence like the second part of 'The streets are wet: if therefore it has rained the rivers will rise' we cannot substitute a performative occurrence of 'I conclude that' for 'therefore'. We must suppose that this particle has a meaning, function or use in such utterances, and whatever meaning it has there it can just as well have also in 'It must have rained, therefore the streets are wet'.

It is not that we use 'therefore' with the force of 'I conclude that', as Austin asserts (75), but rather we use 'I conclude that' with the meaning of 'therefore'. An analogous point may be made against exclusively performative accounts of 'is true' (cf. Jonathan Cohen, 'Mr. Strawson's Analysis of Truth', *Analysis* x, 1950, pp. 136 ff., and more generally P. T. Geach, 'Ascriptivism', *Philosophical Review* lxix, 1960, pp. 221 ff., and J. R. Searle, 'Meaning and Speech Acts', *Phil. Rev.* lxxi, 1962, pp. 423 ff.: W. D. Ross made a similar point against Carnap's 'command' theory of moral judgement in *Foundations of Ethics*, 1939, pp. 33–4).

Austin seeks to distinguish (73) between the clarification of meaning and the clarification of illocutionary force. Precision is the objective of the former, explicitness of the latter. Measurement was the most successful device ever invented, he says, for developing precision, just as performatives are the most successful device for developing explicitness. But this particular distinction between precision and explicitness must stand or fall with the distinction between meaning and illocutionary force. It cannot reinforce that distinction because it has no independent support. Admittedly we speak of replacing vague quantitative descriptions by precise measurements. But we also speak of replacing implicit references to a particular person, say, by explicit ones. E.g. 'Wearers of green dinner-jackets ought to apologize to the committee' may be rendered explicit by 'George ought to apologize to the committee'. Moreover, just as explicitness is sometimes needed with regard to the sense or reference of particular terms, so too precision is sometimes sought with regard to the meaning of a whole utterance. Logical or causal connexions are more precisely expressed by conditional, disjunctive, or conjunctive sentences than by the vaguer device of paratactic construction.

Austin's theory of illocutions fares no better if we consider the use of the prepositions 'in' and 'by' in sentences of the form 'In/by saying *x* I was doing *y*' as a criterion for distinguishing between illocutionary force and perlocutionary effect. So far as the use of these prepositions does afford such a criterion it also affords one for distinguishing between meaning and effect. When you remark 'In saying that I was praising his memory, not his intelligence', you are obviously clarifying meaning. So why not also when you remark 'In saying that I was praising, not blaming, him'? Austin suggests that where the use is not illocutionary 'in saying' is replaceable by 'in speaking of', or 'in using the expression', or 'by the word'. But these additional tests will not serve his purpose. For we can describe what Austin would call illocutionary force by remarking 'In speaking of that (viz. his achievement as a political radical) I was praising, not blaming him'. We can also describe illocutionary force by remarking 'In using the word "radical" to describe him I was praising, not blaming, him' or 'In using the word "warn" (viz. in "I warn you") I was threatening, not pre-monishing'. Moreover, there are cases where we cannot describe what Austin would call meaning by such a phrase as 'in using the word', e.g. 'In saying that (viz. "He showed remarkable knowledge of the text") I was praising his memory, not his intelligence'. Thus the availability of the 'In/by saying x I was doing y' criterion as a way of marking off perlocutionary effect from something else is no reason for supposing that that something else must be illocutionary force rather than meaning.

Austin also claims that we can warn or intend to warn, command or intend to command, sympathize or intend to sympathize, and perform many other illocutionary acts, though not all, without the use of language at all (118). But few would be unwilling to concede that within particular communities many gestures and postures come to be as meaningful as linguistic utterances.

In short, what Austin calls the illocutionary force of an utterance is that aspect of its meaning which is either conveyed by its explicitly performative prefix, if it has one, or might have been so conveyed by the use of such an expression. Any attempt to prise off this aspect of meaning, and regard it not as meaning but as something else, leads to paradox and confusion. It blurs the continuity and similarity between questions about meaning at different levels, and puts unnecessary conceptual obstacles in the path of those who wish to study the various ways in which as a culture becomes richer and more sophisticated its languages become able to express more and more subtly diverse shades of meaning.

III

What could have led Austin to put forward so erroneous a theory? Perhaps several different factors combine to make the theory seem plausible, though probably not all of them influenced Austin himself.

First, there are many strings of English words that can have vastly different meanings according to the intonation with which they are uttered. E.g. 'it is raining' may be uttered as a question, with a rising intonation, or as a statement, with a falling one. If English sentences are grammatically ordered strings of English words, and if it makes sense to discuss the meanings of English sentences, as grammarians, lexicographers and logicians often do, then it looks as though any individual utterance of 'it is raining' may be ascribed both a meaning, derived immediately from the meaning of the English sentence 'it is raining', and also an illocutionary force, depending on such variable factors as the intonation with which the sentence has been uttered. But on a stricter phonetic analysis here we have not just one sentence of spoken English, but at least two (cf. L. Bloomfield, *Language*, 1958, pp. 170 ff., or B. Bloch and L. Trager, *Outline of Linguistic Analysis*, 1942, p. 52). The difference between a rising and a falling intonation has as much of a right to affect the classification of individual utterances into English sentences as has the difference of sound between 'raining' and 'hailing'. There are pitch phonemes as well as vowel and consonant ones. So that attention to the meaning of the sentence-type cannot justify a distinction between the meaning and the illocutionary force of such utterances.

Secondly, what is, from any familiar grammatical point of view, exactly the same sentence may be uttered with a wide range of meanings. For instance, 'You are very kind' may be said as praise, as thanks or as a piece of character assessment, and 'Go to London tomorrow!' may be said as a command, an order, a request, a recommendation or a piece of advice. So far as it is possible to determine the precise nature of the utterance, without having it rendered explicit by a performative expression, we determine this by reference to what else is said both before and after the utterance, both by the speaker and by other parties to the conversation, and also by reference to the non-linguistic circumstances of the utterance, such as whether or not someone has just performed a service for the speaker or whether or not the speaker has any authority, status or contractual power *vis-à-vis* his audience. Here again it seems as though the individual utterance has not only a meaning, derived immediately from the general meaning of the sentence-type—the highest common factor, as it were, of all the sentence-type's possible uses—but also an illocutionary force, dependent upon its own, rather more special, circumstances. But it is no peculiarity of what Austin marks off as illocutionary forces that they are often determined only by reference to such contextual considerations. Exactly the same is also often true of what Austin himself would undoubtedly have regarded as meanings. The meaning of 'He hit her' is, according to Austin, the sense and reference of such an utterance. But the reference of personal pronouns depends on their context of utterance. 'They're all gold' means something different when said by someone looking at the clouds in a sunset from what it means when said by someone looking at a tray of cutlery. In one case the colour is being described, in another the material. 'He's lost his case' means one thing when said on a railway platform, another in the antechamber of a law-court, though phonetically it is the same sentence in both cases. If we do not suppose in these cases that the context-dependent element in the commonly accepted meaning of the utterance is not *stricto sensu* meaning at all, then we should treat any utterance of 'Go to London tomorrow!' analogously. That some such utterances command rather than advise, or recommend rather than request, is a feature of their respective meanings and not something that should be distinguished from their meaning under a label like 'illocutionary force'.

Thirdly, English sentences of certain patterns are so commonly uttered with one particular kind of meaning that when they are uttered with another meaning—either in a technical usage confined to some particular kind of profession or social institution, like a law-court, or in a usage that anyone can employ—this may appear as an addition rather than as an alternative to their common meaning. For example, the sentence 'I wish you good afternoon' has a pattern commonly found in utterances that announce wishes. But it might well be uttered in dismissal of its audience and not as a wish at all. In such a case one may be tempted wrongly to suppose that the utterance has the sentence-pattern's common role as a basic meaning, and the dismissal as an additional feature, its illocutionary force, dependent partly on this basic meaning and partly on contextual circumstances. No doubt there are often also cases in which the common meaning is present alongside the special one—where, for example, the utterance is both a wish and a dismissal. In those cases the meaning is a genuinely compound one. But if this is not so—if the utterance is not a wish at all but only a dismissal—there is no need to suppose that it retains any of the sentence's original, common meaning. When one remarks of a sunset 'They're all gold', one is not describing the material of which the clouds are composed as well as the colour they have momentarily taken on. To object to such a remark 'You're wrong: they're minute droplets of moisture' would be just a bad joke, a pun of a peculiarly feeble kind. Nor would it be any better a joke for the man who is dismissed with 'I wish you good afternoon' to reply 'You're a hypocrite: you don't wish me that at all'. And, if he cannot sensibly reply thus, then how can we distinguish the illocutionary force of the dismissal from its meaning?

A fourth factor that contributes to making Austin's theory seem plausible is that people often do not succeed in producing utterances that are as clear and definite in meaning as they are intended to be. A man may say 'Go to London tomorrow!' and intend it as a request, though in the context there is nothing to determine whether it is a request, an order, a recommendation or a piece of advice. If the man is called upon to clarify himself, he might say 'I request you to go to London tomorrow' or, more likely, just 'It's a request', rather than 'I intended it as a request', at least if he still wishes to make the request. It then seems plausible to suggest that the force of the original utterance is distinguishable from its meaning, on the ground that what was understood at once was the meaning and what was in doubt until it had been clarified was the force. But it would in general be better practice to say explicitly how much of the intended meaning was understood at once and how much was not. It is just this that even on Austin's view we should have to say in a case like 'He hit her', where the utterance has exactly the meaning its speaker intends except for the fact that it is not yet clear whether 'he' refers here to her husband or to her lover. And similarly if we know that an utterance was intended as either a recommendation or a piece of advice, but definitely not as an order or a request, Austin's meaning-force distinction will not help us so much. Nor would it help a man who did not know the meaning of 'admonish' when a judicial authority said 'We hereby admonish you'. For if that utterance really had a force as well as meaning then at least one could not know the meaning without knowing the force. Nor again is it of much use to be able to say about an utterance in a foreign language that one understood its force but not its meaning. What one would normally want to say in such a situation is that one knew it was a question though ignorant of what was asked, or that one knew it was an order though ignorant of what was ordered—as one might say that one knew it reported an assault on her though ignorant who was said to have committed it. Certainly Austin himself distinguishes (109) between the illocutionary act intended and the illocutionary act performed. But my point is that this is no more than a special case of the distinction between meaning intended and meaning expressed.

Fifthly, there is the difference between attempted namings, vetoes, excommunications, contracts, conclusions, etc., and successful ones. Unsuccessful attempts go a little bit further than unachieved intentions. If the director's wife says 'I name this ship *Queen Philippa*' and then fails to press hard enough on the button releasing the champagne bottle, she may be described as having tried unsuccessfully to name the ship. Yet her utterance was clearly meaningful. So there seems to be a difference worth noting between the meaning her utterance actually had and the illocutionary force it only just failed to have. Similarly, if a circle-squaring kind of mathematician tries to deduce a contradiction in number theory, there seems to be a difference between the meaning of his final utterance 'I conclude that two is not equal to two' and the illocutionary force—the force of being a genuine conclusion—that this utterance fails to have.

Here Austin's own doctrine of infelicities, as he calls them, is relevant. The performances of the director's wife and the circle-squaring mathematician are unhappy. This naming ceremony had a flaw in it, and this mathematician's proof was invalid. But need we say more of most other naming ceremonies or mathematical proofs than that they go off without a hitch or are valid? Perhaps difficulty is sometimes caused here by the existence of two senses for all illocutionary verbs like 'conclude', 'name', etc. We can say either 'He concluded that . . ., though he was not entitled to' or 'He tried to conclude that . . ., though he did not succeed,' and either 'She named the ship . . ., but the ceremony was invalid' or 'She tried to name the ship . . ., but bungled the ceremony'. There is, as it were, both a happy-or-unhappy sense of these verbs and also a happy one. In the former we either leave it open whether the attempt was successful or imply that it was not: in the latter we imply that it was. Sometimes Austin seems to suggest that in the explicitly performative use of these verbs their sense is always the happy-or-unhappy one. For sometimes (15) he seems to suggest that with regard to any explicitly performative utterance it is always an open question whether or not it is unhappy, and this cannot be an open question in the happy sense. In its happy sense the verb's utterance is either happy, or is not genuinely performative at all because circumstances conspire to prevent its use from being the performance that in another mood, tense, or person it would describe. At other times (8, 105, 125) Austin seem to suggest that if circumstances are inappropriate for the utterance of such words as 'I bet ten bob on the favourite', then no act of betting should be deemed to have been performed. If this is how all explicitly performative utterances are to be regarded, then Austin seems to be suggesting here that the performative use of a verb is always in what I have called its happy sense, because if the verb were used in its happy-or-unhappy sense there would in fact be a performative utterance even where the circumstances were inappropriate. But so long as the happy-or-unhappy sense is also available for performative use it is impossible to defend Austin's concept of illocutionary force by saying that it is what distinguishes genuine betting, naming, concluding, etc., utterances from faulty ones, since the latter too can have such a force.

Austin held (115 ff.) that illocutionary acts consist in the production of consequences just in so far as all illocutionary acts must secure uptake and performances like namings may have an effect on how it is in order to call somebody or something. This is in any case a rather untidy exception to Austin's general principle that only perlocutionary acts consist in the production of consequences. Moreover, once the happy-or-unhappy sense of Austin's illocutionary verbs has been firmly distinguished from their happy sense the need for him to suppose a consequential element in illocutionary acts disappears altogether, since the supposed consequential element is present only in those illocutionary acts that are happy in the appropriate respects. Only if a naming-utterance is ceremonially valid does it have the effect of putting out of order any later references to the ship by another name. Only if the farmer hears and understands me when I say 'I warn you that your haystack is on fire'—only then has my attempt at warning come off. In the happy-or-unhappy sense of 'warn' I can say, without contradicting myself, 'I warned him by shouting in his ear though he was too deaf to hear', but in the happy sense I can only say 'I tried to warn him by shouting in his ear though I failed because he was too deaf'. For a speaker's utterance to be a warning in the happy-or-unhappy sense what is required is that it should be *of a kind that he could reasonably expect* to secure uptake. I cannot warn a man fifty yards away by whispering. But a warning, in this sense, does not actually have to *achieve* uptake. Thus it is quite possible to preserve the general principle that the meaning of an utterance does not include any of its effects even if we regard naming, warning, concluding, etc., as aspects of meaning, provided that we concern ourselves here only with the happy-or-unhappy senses of these verbs or with the corresponding 'try', 'seek', 'attempt', 'endeavour', etc. expressions, as with 'I am trying to warn you'. These are the only usages in which these verbs may occur in an exclusively performative phrase. When used in their happy senses they must normally be supposed instead, if in the first person present indicative active, both to perform an act of the appropriate happy-or-unhappy variety and also to imply the occurrence of circumstances, consequential or otherwise, that render this performance a happy one.

A sixth factor that may perhaps sometimes play a part in making Austin's theory seem plausible is that it is often necessary to distinguish between what is said and the act of saying it. For instance, suppose a civil servant says to a journalist 'The alpha rockets are useless'. What the civil servant says may be fully justifiable on the evidence of the rockets' tests. But his saying it to the journalist may nevertheless be quite unjustifiable because it is a breach of security that can serve no useful purpose. Suppose further that the journalist is somewhat puzzled about the utterance. He may then be unclear either about what the civil servant said or about his saying it, and just as in the former case he requires clarification about meaning, so in the latter he seems to require clarification about something—call it 'force'?—that stands to the civil servant's speech-act in roughly the same relation as meaning stands to what the civil servant said. If what the civil servant said may be true or false in virtue of its meaning, the act of saying it must surely have something else, its force, in virtue of which it can be justified or unjustified, valid or invalid, happy or unhappy.

But we have to be careful about what can count as force here. If by the question of force is meant nothing but whether the utterance is a report, or warning, or prediction, or criticism, etc., then we do not need a special term 'force'. All that is at stake is how to describe the speech-act as a whole in virtue of the meaning of what was said. Determine the meaning fully, paying due regard to contextual circumstances that affect meaning, and you already have all the information you need in order to make this description, and it is in virtue of this description that the act is either happy or unhappy. Of course there are also many other aspects of the civil servant's speech-act about which the journalist might also be puzzled. Was it legal or illegal? moral or immoral? serious or facetious? What was its motive? its immediate effect? its probable long-term consequences? The variety of questions that can be asked here testifies to the importance of distinguishing what is said from the act of saying it. But this distinction cannot itself support Austin's distinction between meaning and force. Indeed Austin himself, by speaking of locutionary acts (that have meaning) as well as of illocutionary ones (that have force), makes it quite clear that this is not how he himself would seek to defend his theory.

Seventhly, people often say things like 'In warning them of danger he was committing himself to their cause'. In such a case the original utterance, which warned of the danger, might merely have been 'There is a plot to kill you', and it seems rather paradoxical to suggest that 'I commit myself to your cause' could have been part of the meaning of this utterance in any everyday sense of 'meaning'. Accordingly it might seem plausible to hold that, if 'he was committing himself to their cause' does not give the meaning of the original utterance, it must give its force. So too, for example, the force of a man's utterance might be supposed to be given when we remark 'In stating that he knew his speed he was admitting his guilt'.

But the trouble here is that, at least on Austin's theory, we have already given the forces of these utterances when we say 'In *warning* them . . .' or 'In *stating* that . . .'. We are in effect referring to the utterances by means of what Austin would call their forces. Are we to suppose, therefore, a second-order force, as it were? But if so we shall need to suppose third-, fourth-, fifth-order forces, and so on, for we might also be in a position to say 'In committing himself to their cause he was condemning his own past actions', 'In condemning his own past actions he was repudiating his previous beliefs', 'In repudiating his previous beliefs he was making the obvious deductions from what had happened', and so on indefinitely. And, quite apart from the complexity of having to accept all these illocutionary meta-forces, meta-meta-forces, meta-

meta-meta-forces, etc., as well as Austin's original illocutionary force, there is the trouble that these higher-order forces cannot be made explicit in the same way as the lowest-order one normally can be. The element of warning in the above mentioned-utterance 'There is a plot to kill you' may be made explicit by prefixing the performative 'I warn you that' to the same sentence. But the element of commitment is only made explicit by prefixing 'I commit myself' to quite a different expression. Similarly the element of statement in the above-mentioned utterance, 'I know my speed was 90 m.p.h.', may be made explicit by prefixing 'I hereby state that' to this very sentence. But the element of admission is only made explicit by prefixing 'I admit that' to the sentence 'I am guilty of driving dangerously.' Certainly there are some kinds of first-order force that cannot be made explicit quite so easily. In the case of naming, defining, analysing, calling, etc., the appropriate performative verb has to be prefixed to an expression of somewhat altered grammatical construction. Instead of saying 'This ship is to be *Queen Philippa*' one might say 'I name this ship *Queen Philippa*'. But though the grammatical construction is altered here the key words remain the same, which is not the case with what I have provisionally called higher-order forces. Indeed not only do the key words differ in these cases, but a wholly different kind of speech-act may be involved—even a speech-act that requires a different mood of the verb, as with 'In advising them to desert he was raising the question of how to escape from the camp'. Furthermore, it is obvious that in sufficiently suitable circumstances almost any two speech-acts whatever can be related together in this way. The relationship is thus more like that present in what Austin called perlocutionary acts, since he insisted that the range of illocutionary acts that may be brought off by a given utterance is conventionally restricted. But the speech-acts described in these statements are not perlocutionary either, because their production of effects is not at stake.

It is clear then, though Austin does not discuss the problem, that these are not illocutionary forces in his sense at all and that their common occurrence lends no support to his theory. Instead, they are most appropriately described as the implications of speech-acts, where a speech-act is said to imply that p if and only if the speech-act gives its audience sufficient reason to take it that p but it is not part of the utterance's meaning that p. Thus in warning certain people that there is a plot to kill them a man might be said to imply his commitment to their cause. If the words 'by implication' are inserted before 'committing' in the statement 'In warning them of the danger he was committing himself to their cause', the effect is to clarify the meaning of the statement, not to alter it. Indeed, once we recognize the existence of such implications, which cannot be illocutionary forces, we see that no small part of the evidence for Austin's theory disappears. Austinians are naturally reluctant to suppose that, when a man asks a question in saying 'I would like to know the time', the question is part of his utterance's meaning. It now appears that perhaps they are *sometimes* right, but not because the questioning is to be classified instead under the heading of 'illocutionary force', as they would have it. They are right because the question was merely implied. The man's utterance genuinely described what he wanted to know though his speech-act implied that he was asking the time.

There may well be many other factors that contribute to the plausibility of Austin's theory. I shall mention here only one other, making eight in all. The word 'performative' does not occur in that portion of Austin's paper 'Other Minds' (*Proc. Ar. Soc.* Supp. Vol. xx, 1946, pp. 169–75) in which he first published a discussion of performative usage. But he does discuss phrases and expressions there rather than utterances, and his later application of the term 'performative' to whole utterances (explicit in the first chapter of *How to do things with Words*) is an unfortunate deviation that may play some part in making the theory of illocutionary forces seem plausible. For as soon as one sees that the whole of the communication achieved by saying 'I promise to go' may also, in appropriate contexts, be achieved by saying 'I shall go', it is reasonable to suppose that if the former utterance is to be called performative in virtue of the promise it makes, so too must the latter be. The only difference will be that the former is explicitly performative and the latter inexplicitly so. By parity of reasoning, if a witness's utterance 'I state that he hit her' is performative, then his statement 'He hit her' is also performative, though again inexplicitly so. But if even statements like 'He hit her' are performative, then all normal utterances are, and the descriptive value of the term has been eroded by a typically philosophical inflation. If all events turn out to be mental (or all material), a new and difficult issue arises as to what can then be meant by the term 'mental' (or 'material'), since within its domain of predictability no contrast is available between the mental and the non-mental (or between the material and non-material). Similarly 'performative' can now no longer serve as a classificatory term, such that some but not all members of its domain may be correctly labelled with it. No wonder then that the need is felt to introduce a new term—a term with a different domain. Inflation often leads to the introduction of a new currency. If all utterances turn out to be performative, then instead of distinguishing some utterances from others it looks as though we have to distinguish one aspect of every utterance from another. We have to regard all utterances as dual, as it were. Every speech-act is said to be really two acts, not just one, and new terms are introduced, 'locutionary' and 'illocutionary', with these symbiotic acts as their domain. Finally, to round out the dualism, meaning is associated with locutionary acts, force with illocutionary ones. But all this philosophical inflation, and consequential coining of new technical terms, can be avoided if we keep 'performative' as a term applicable to verbs, verb-uses, particles, adverbs, phrases or meanings rather than to sentences or whole utterances. We can then make all the further distinctions we need between, say, what is explicitly performative (e.g. 'I promise'), semi-explicitly performative (e.g. 'Without fail'), inexplicitly performative (e.g. 'I shall') or not performative at all (e.g. 'that I shall go'). There is no need now for the locutionary-illocutionary distinction.

IV

What reply could be made to these criticisms of Austin's theory? The most likely reply I foresee would run something like this:

'You have pointed out one or two minor inconsistencies or omissions in Austin's exposition, but in all important respects you really agree with him. Admittedly the thesis that every utterance has distinct locutionary and illocutionary aspects may need to be modified in the case of explicitly performative verb-usage, and perhaps in one or two other cases as well. Admittedly the thesis that illocutionary acts involve the securing of uptake rests on a confusion between two different senses of certain verbs. But you yourself state the core of Austin's theory when you say that the illocutionary force of an utterance is that aspect of its meaning which is either conveyed by its explicitly performative prefix, if it has one, or might have been so conveyed by the use of such an expression. The only difference is that Austin made his point clearer by using the word "meaning" in a narrower sense, so that force stood out as something co-ordinate with meaning rather than as one special form or aspect of it'.

But this is a vital difference. It is, for instance, directly responsible for such paradoxical features of Austin's theory as that even explicitly performative utterances have distinct locutionary and illocutionary aspects. It may tend to obscure, as we have seen, the continuity and similarity between certain kinds of context-dependence in linguistic usage, and it may also tend to obscure the fact that performativeness is just as much tied as reference is to particular parts of speech, particular kinds of idiom, and particular features of grammar. Moreover, Austin's co-ordination of force with meaning wrongly suggests that the dissimilarity between reference and sense is somehow less than that between force, or performative function, and sense, whereas in at least one important respect the latter dissimilarity is less than the former. For consider. We gather what things or people an utterance refers to, in a given context, primarily by attending to its demonstratives, proper names, personal pronouns, definite descriptions, etc. We gather what force the utterance has by attending, in the same context, primarily to its connecting particles, adverbs, verb-mood, explicitly performative verb-use, word-order, etc. But whereas the reference of many sentences, like 'He met her there yesterday', changes on almost every occasion of its utterance, the range of forces a sentence may have is much more stable. A sentence keeps on having one or other of the same range of forces again and again, whereas many of its references never recur, especially if it includes some such word as 'now' or 'yesterday'. And in this respect 'force' is much more like 'sense' than 'reference' is, if we accept any of the familiar definitions of 'sense' that make it a contributory element within the whole meaning of an utterance rather than just identical with that meaning. The sense of a word like 'gold' or of a sentence like 'He lost his case' normally varies only within a certain limited range. There is thus a better case for grouping sense and force together as meaning, so as to distinguish this meaning from reference, than there is for Austin's grouping of sense and reference together as meaning so as to distinguish the latter from force. Not only would the less variable be distinguished in this way from the more variable, but also we should not then be surprised to find that in some cases, such as explicit performatives, there is no clear difference at all between sense and force.

In short, the merit of Austin's book lies in the insight it affords into the wealth and variety of performative meaning. His introduction of the concept of illocutionary force achieves nothing but to obscure the nature of this insight. We need the term 'performative' but not the term 'illocutionary', and we must use 'performative' as an adjective applicable to verbs, verb-uses, particles, adverbs, phrases or meanings, but not to whole utterances or to sentences *qua* sentences. 'Performative' is thus co-ordinate with 'predicative', 'referential', etc., not with 'statement-making' or 'constative'.

'What then', it may be asked, 'is to become of the campaign against the descriptivist fallacy or against the fact-value dichotomy? Austin's theory of illocutionary force was at least in part designed to emphasize how very few of our utterances are really either statements, on the one hand, or evaluations, on the other. Thus he discusses at length the many other ways in which utterances can be appraised for felicity or infelicity besides the consideration of truth-values that may be appropriate in a narrow range of cases, and he urges philosophers who are interested in the word "good" to form a complete list of those illocutionary acts of which commending, grading, etc., are isolated specimens. The case for Austin's theory of illocutionary force seems much stronger when that theory is viewed in the light of the support it affords to the campaign against descriptivist, or fact-value, oversimplification.'

Certainly nothing I have said so far can lend support to the view that statements are commoner than they in fact are. Any genuine difference of illocutionary force that Austin claimed to exist between some utterances and others—any difference that can be rendered explicit by the use of different performative verbs—reappears on my account of speech-acts as a difference of meaning. Nevertheless I suspect that Austin may have been unduly hard on the way in which many philosophers have used the term 'statement', and it is a pity that he does not consider this term in any detail. It is worth while distinguishing (very briefly for present purposes: the problem is really a very much larger one, of course) at least three senses of the word:

(1) In one sense to describe a man as having stated something is to describe him both as having said it and as being somehow committed to it. He can state a problem, a request, an evaluation,

a recommendation, etc., as well as a fact. But stating is more than just saying. There is nothing odd about an utterance like 'What I *say* now is . . ., though I don't want to be held to that view of the situation'. But there is something a little odd about 'What I *state* now is . . ., though I don't want to be held to that view of the situation'. In this sense motorists make statements to the police after road accidents, and in times of crisis politicians issue statements to the press. Such statements are to be contrasted with conjectures, asides, insinuations, hints, suggestions, etc.; and the verb 'to state' is to be contrasted with the corresponding verbs. A wise man therefore considers very carefully the terms in which he is going to make a statement, though not everyone who makes a statement is wise. Moreover, since there is this personal commitment of the speaker involved in the making of statements, two motorists' statements may agree in every particular and yet be regarded as quite different statements. Or the same politician may make one statement on Tuesday and another, in identical terms, on Friday. Statements in this sense are differentiated by their time or place of utterance and by their authorship, as well as by their content, since we may be interested to know who is or was committed to what, and when.

(2) The word 'statement' is also commonly used as a technical term in logic. Roughly, a statement in this sense is defined by the axioms of the propositional calculus, when the connectives of that calculus are given their usual interpretation as logical constants. Statements are those substitution-instances for variables of the calculus that make its theorems come out true under such an interpretation. Of course there are notorious difficulties about this definition. Must a statement be either true or false? Does every utterance of sentences like 'The king of France is bald', or 'All Cretans are liars', make a statement? How are statements related to sentences? and so on. I have discussed some of these problems elsewhere (*The Diversity of Meaning*, 1966 ed., 161 ff. and 249 ff.), but they are unimportant here. What is important for present purposes is that in this sense the word 'statement' does not denote a kind of speech-act at all, but is a technical term of logical analysis. It is to be contrasted with 'predicate', 'term', 'operator', 'connective', etc., rather than with 'conjecture', 'aside', 'insinuation', 'hint', 'suggestion', etc. There is very little work that the verb 'to state' can do in any closely related sense, and scarcely any at all in the

first person present indicative active. Nor can one ask for *the* time, place or authorship of a statement in this sense, because such statements are differentiated by their wording and meaning only, and not by their circumstances of utterance. They are just logical counters—the kind of thing that can occur now as the conclusion of one man's argument, now as the premiss of another. They can also occur just as well in an idle surmise as in a piece of sworn testimony. Hence the people who utter them may or may not thereby commit themselves to their truth. It all depends on the mode of utterance.

(3) Philosophers have also often found it convenient to use the word 'statement' in a sense parasitical on (2). They have often called any speech-act a statement if its content can be regarded for logical purposes as a statement in sense (2). In this sense most conjectures, asides, suggestions, insinuations and hints are just as much statements as are many statements in sense (1), but there are also many statements in sense (1) that are not statements in sense (3). The contrast is now with questions, commands, exclamations, etc. Moreover, in virtue of its utility in the simplification and systematization of logical theory, the 'true-or-false' dichotomy is commonly extended to cover all or most statements in sense (3) too, and becomes their paramount mode of appraisal, rather than 'accurate-or-inaccurate', 'correct-or-incorrect', 'right-or-wrong', etc. Perhaps sometimes philosophers have been a little careless in failing to distinguish sense (3) from sense (1). But it is difficult to see how sense (3) can be in any way objectionable. It has a useful generality which can make it a convenient tool of philosophical theorizing, whereas sense (1) is of no more philosophical interest than thousands of other names for special kinds of speech-act. Certainly there is no merit at all in the charge that philosophers who have used sense (3) have committed a malapropism. It is too easy to find mistakes in what philosophers have said about statements if it is assumed that the word 'statement' has only one legitimate sense, as Austin sometimes seems to assume (e.g. 141).

Moreover, the statement-evaluation dichotomy, whatever it may be, is as erroneous on my view as on Austin's. In sense (1) of 'statement' stating is only one among very many kinds of speech-act that may be concerned with values. In sense (3), on the other hand, stating is a general kind of speech-act of which evaluating is a species—just one species among very many others—since we can perfectly well treat 'It is wicked to kill for pleasure' or 'He has a good chance of winning' as substitution-instances for the variables of the propositional calculus. Indeed there is a case for saying that Austin's recommendation about the word 'good' is itself a hangover from the fact-value dichotomy. He seems to suggest that there is a particular group of illocutionary acts among those he mentions, in the performance of which alone the word 'good' occurs. But I have hardly been able to find any speech-act mentioned by Austin that cannot rely strongly on the word 'good' for its performance on certain occasions. We can use it equally well in what he calls verdictives, like the umpire's ruling 'That was a good service'; exercitives, like the dismissal 'Good riddance to you'; commissives, like the promise 'In all good faith I say that I shall'; behabitives, like the thanks 'It was good of you'; and expositives like the concession 'It is a good point of theirs that . . .'. This fact, and the arguments of Geach and Searle already mentioned, tend to suggest that we shall get more light about 'good' from studying what Austin would call the sense of utterances in which it occurs than from studying their force. 'Good' is a predicative, not a performative, word, even in fundamental value-judgements, in so far as it can be a substitution-instance for any predicate variable of quantification theory, whereas an explicitly performative expression cannot. This problem, too, is a very large one, of course. But my account of speech-acts does not anticipate its solution. My account leaves moral philosophers quite free to discuss the kind of contribution which 'good' makes to the meanings of utterances in which it occurs: how far is its rôle performative, how far predicative? Campaigns against descriptivism, muddle-headed though they often are, have nothing to lose by rejecting Austin's theory of illocutionary force.[1]

---

[1] The remark in the last paragraph that the statement-evaluation dichotomy is erroneous was not intended to imply that the is-ought distinction is erroneous, *pace* Professor A. Flew in 'On Not Deriving "Ought" From "Is" ', *Analysis* XXV (1964), p. 25. What I meant to suggest was that there is no philosophically important class which is exhaustively divisible into statements, on the one hand, and evaluations on the other, and I gave a few reasons for this. The is-ought distinction does seem to me to be very important indeed. But it is essentially a distinction between different modal operators, or types of operator, just as the distinction between 'good' and, say, 'yellow' is a distinction between different predicates, or types of predicate. Nothing is gained by trying to advocate these very important distinctions through the medium of a quite erroneous dichotomy between statements and evaluations. (Added 30 March 1968.)

MEANING AND ILLOCUTIONARY FORCE

Mats Furberg

AUSTIN'S concept of the illocutionary force of utterances is empty, and the phenomenon it is designed to cater for had better be treated as an aspect of the meaning of utterances. This is the tenet of L. Jonathan Cohen's able and challenging paper 'Do Illocutionary Forces Exist?'.

I shall sketch an unorthodox reinterpretation of Austin's doctrine of illocutionary force[1] and try to show that it withstands Cohen's type of criticism.

I. AUSTIN ON ILLOCUTIONARY FORCE

1. *An outline of Austin's doctrine.* According to *How to do Things with Words* (henceforward abbreviated *Words*) every act of speaking, except perhaps mere exclamations like 'Damn!' and 'Ouch!', is both a locutionary and an illocutionary act (98, 113, 132).

The locutionary act consists of three acts: (*a*) the *phonetic* act of uttering certain noises; (*b*) the *phatic* act of uttering certain vocables or words belonging to, and as belonging to, a certain vocabulary, in a certain grammatical construction, with a certain intonation, etc.; and (*c*) the *rhetic* act of using these vocables with a certain more or less definite 'sense' and 'reference'. 'Sense' and 'reference' together are equivalent to 'meaning' (92–3) and are, without specification, taken 'on the strength of current views' (148).

To perform a locutionary act is 'in general . . . and *eo ipso*' to

---

[1] It is developed and defended in the Postscript of the second, revised and enlarged edition of my book *Locutionary and Illocutionary Acts* [*LIA*], Toronto, 1969.

perform an illocutionary act.[1] Such questions as whether a locution (i.e., an utterance with a certain meaning) is, in a given situation, a piece of information or an assurance or a warning are questions about what illocutionary act is performed. An illocutionary act is 'the performance of an act *in* saying something as opposed to the performance of an act *of* saying something'. Austin speaks of 'the doctrine of the different types of function of language here in question as the doctrine of "illocutionary forces" '. He maintains that it is as essential to distinguish the illocutionary force from the meaning of an utterance as it is to distinguish sense from reference within meaning. (Lecture VIII.)

Illocutionary acts are characterized by two closely connected features: (i) They are conventional—done as conforming to a convention. (ii) They are up to the speaker, in the sense that their successful performance does not demand any response from the audience other than a mere understanding of their convention-governed force (103 and Lecture IX, esp. 115–16). In both these respects they resemble locutionary acts and differ from perlocutionary ones.

2. '*Acts*'. There are many obscurities in Austin's account and in my summary of it. Start with the word 'act'.

Austin often speaks as if inquiries into the locutionary and the illocutionary dimension of an utterance are inquiries into different aspects of a speech *episode*. But his practice betrays that he is not really much concerned about speech acts at all; he is concerned about dimensions of results of such acts or episodes. His inquiries into, say, stating and promising are inquiries into, and not merely studies shedding light on, the nature of statements and of promises. And statements and promises are not speech episodes, although the acts of stating and promising are such episodes. A statement can be true or false; but what has truth-value is not, in contradistinction to a speech episode, something clockable and datable,

---

[1] Why does not Austin say simply that every locutionary act is *eo ipso* an illocutionary act?

Consider a given sentence, e.g. 'The cat is on the mat'. Is there merely a high correlation between issuing instances of that sentence as locutionary acts and issuing them as illocutionary acts? Certainly not. If his theory is to be coherent, Austin's qualified claim must be taken as the claim that, with the possible exception of certain *types* of utterance (viz. types of merely expletive utterance), every performance of a locutionary act is also, and necessarily, a performance of an illocutionary act.

446

with a certain duration, etc. These things are true of the act of stating but not of the statement itself. And there is a parallel distinction between the act of promising and the promise.

I suggest that the statement or the promise is a result of an act of stating or promising, and that Austin's inquiries into the locutionary and the illocutionary dimension are inquiries into such a semantic result. But then a study of the locutionary or of the illocutionary dimension is not a study of any act at all. The result of the act of making a statement, viz. the statement, is no more an act than is the result of an act of scribbling, viz. a scribble.[1] The terminology of 'act' is very misleading.

3. *Conventionality in locutionary and illocutionary acts.* The meaning of an utterance, the utterance's locutionary dimension, is governed by the conventions used in the rhetic 'act'. In a language which has passed its initial stage these conventions govern the meaning of the utterance, independent of what the *current* speaker intends to say and what the *current* addressee takes him to mean. As an utterance in English and not in some kind of code language disguised as English, 'I like doing philosophy' means that the speaker likes doing philosophy. Its meaning is not affected if someone happens to use the words when he intends to say that he likes doing philology; nor is it affected if a certain addressee takes the words in the latter way.

In a budding language there is an intimate connexion, but not identity, between what a given speaker S intends with his string of noises N and what N means. But when the components and the structure of N have become incorporated in an established language, an abyss may yawn between what N means and what a certain speaker intends with N. If syntactic structure and its effect on and contribution to meaning are left aside, the meaning of N in an established language has to be elucidated by unearthing standardly accepted rules governing the use of the components (now words) of N. These rules would not be standardly accepted unless the majority of language-users observe them; but they may be violated by the current speaker and the current addressee.

If a speaker is versed in the established language in which N occurs, he knows the conventions governing N. If he uses them perfectly conscious of what he is doing, then N does have the

[1] Cf. W. Cerf's review of *Words* [in this volume], esp. Section IV; and Tore Nordenstam: 'On Austin's theory of speech acts'. *Mind* LXXV (1966).

meaning he intends—whether his current addressees grasp it or not. So the performance of the locutionary act—the production of an utterance as an utterance with a locutionary dimension to it—is up to the speaker.

A distinction, parallel to that between (*a*) meaning, and (*b*) what the current speaker means and/or what the current addressee thinks is meant, has to be made in the case of the illocutionary dimension. Austin falters here. In *Words*. 98–9 he treats the questions

(1) Does the speaker intend to advise?

(2) Has the utterance the force of a piece of advice?

(3) Ought the utterance to be taken as a piece of advice?

as three ways of posing the very same problem, viz. Does the speaker perform the illocutionary act of advising?

To my mind the questions are partly different: (1) is about the *current* speaker's intention in issuing the utterance, whereas (2) and (3) ask the *institutional* question whether the utterance constitutes a piece of advice. They ask it, however, from different points of view, (2) concentrating on speakers and (3) on addressees.

Pace P. F. Strawson's contention in 'Intention and Convention in Speech Acts' [in this volume] it is fairly clear that Austin would not define 'illocutionary force' partly in terms of the *current* speaker's intention in issuing the utterance. An utterance may occasionally have a certain force whatever the speaker intends (e.g. *Words*. 33), and is liable to have a construction as to its force put upon it by judges (*Words*. 115n, 121). And Austin's stress on the conventionality of the illocutionary dimension minimizes the importance of the current addressee as well as of the current speaker. Illocutionary force becomes next of kin to meaning. In an established language it would be disastrous to define these relatives in terms of the current speaker's intentions and/or the current audience's uptake of these intentions.

If both locutionary and illocutionary 'acts' are up to a speaker who knows the conventions of the language employed, in what way(s) are they then diverse? Austin's answer seems to be that the locutionary dimension is topic-directed and the illocutionary dimension audience-directed. Let an utterance be of the pattern 'S is P'. Its locutionary dimension is the one in which something is singled out and something is predicated of the thing thus distinguished. Its illocutionary dimension is the one which the locution is allocated to a certain discourse and/or modifies the commitments normally made within that discourse. The locutionary dimension is concerned with S and P; the illocutionary dimension with guiding the audience as to how what is said about S and P is to be taken.

An investigation of the locutionary dimension of an utterance studies the semantic result of the employment of the utterance's classificatory and referential conventions in its syntactic structure. It is more concerned with language than with speech. An investigation of the illocutionary dimension of the utterance, on the other hand, elicits the conventions which entitle the audience to take the locution in a certain way. Although these conventions may bid us to flag a certain force with a certain verbal expression, they mainly tie the surroundings of the *token*-utterance, the ways in which this *token*-utterance is issued, etc., to a certain uptake normal to all token-utterances of that type in that surrounding and issued with that intonation-contour, etc. The conventions of illocutionary force bear on 'the special circumstances of the *occasion* of the issuing of the utterance' (*Words* 114, my italics). The illocutionary dimension is therefore more concerned with speech than with language.

4. *A digression: different types of direction.* The words 'topic-directed' and 'audience-directed' were suggested by Strawson's 'Intention and Convention in Speech Acts' and are not Austin's. They are somewhat misleading. The locutionary act is topic-directed in the sense that it gives (creates) the topic of the utterance. The illocutionary act is audience-directed not in the sense that it gives (creates) the audience but in the sense that it is directed *to* the audience.

The ramifications of direction cannot be studied here. A few obscure hints must do.

4.1. *On topic-direction.* The locutionary dimension of an utterance is not identical with the descriptive content of the utterance. Cf. *LIA*, Ch. 3: III; and consider the following argument:

'This gift is generous' has an emotive tinge absent in 'This gift is ample'. Someone using 'generous' without meaning to indicate a positive 'attitude' (not necessarily his own), thereby betrays that he does not master the sense of the word. The locutionary dimension is, among other things, concerned with sense. Hence, when a word has emotive sense (i.e., is governed by a linguistic rule tying it to a certain attitude) and this *ipso facto* gives the utterance an emotive tinge, then this tinge ought to be regarded as part of the

449

utterance's meaning, part of its locutionary dimension. So an identification of locutionary dimension with descriptive content will not do, unless the notion of descriptive content is extended.

How does this square with the idea of topic-direction? What is the topic of 'The gift is generous'? The utterance says that the gift exceeds the limits within which most givers (with a certain income) keep. It also says that there is a positive attitude towards this immoderation. It does not say who holds the attitude; if this is indicated, it is indicated by the context, not by the content, of what is said. The topic is, I suggest, an aspect of what is said, concerned with a connexion of the abundance of the gift and the owner-unspecified attitude towards the abundance. The topic of the neutral 'This gift is ample' is simpler, concerned only with the abundance of the gift.[1]

4.2. *On audience-direction.* For want of better words I call two distinguishable, though perhaps unseparable, types of audience-direction 'impersonal' and 'personal'.

4.21. *Impersonal audience-direction.* Two tacit assumptions underlie all serious speech: that there are reasons for what is said and that what is said is relevant to the addressee. (Cf. *LIA*, Ch. 3.) Within this general framework, a speaker who says 'The roof will be repaired tomorrow' may want to convey either (*a*) that his present words (to the best of his knowledge) correspond to the world of tomorrow, or (*b*) that the world of tomorrow will (as a result of his future actions) correspond to his present words. In both types of case, he has bound himself to the truth of 'The roof will be repaired tomorrow'; but in different ways. He hints in (*a*) at his possessing some observational information that the roof will be repaired tomorrow; in (*b*) at his powers to bring it about that the roof will be repaired tomorrow and at his decision to use that power. The utterance exemplifies a piece of 'theoretical' discourse in (*a*) and of 'practical' discourse in (*b*).

It may be important to announce whether the utterance is 'theoretical' or 'practical'. There are gestures, intonation, &c., that from the very beginning express decision or observational confidence. These signs and, by degrees, also phrases describing decision and confidence will eventually be intentionally employed as

---

[1] Problems about 'emotive sense' and owner-unspecified attitudes are discussed in Jan Andersson-Mats Furberg: 'Roll och emotiv mening' (forthcoming).

signals that the utterance is 'practical' or 'theoretical'. Since the point of this signalling is not merely to let the receivers know how the utterance is to be taken but, by the principles of serious speech, to entitle them to rely on it in the way appropriate to the discourse, such (discourse-marking) signals have acquired a conventionalized audience-guiding function.

An audience is also often interested in knowing how good the grounds of an utterance are; and at least when the speaker is unwilling to stand staunchly by his words, it is important to him to indicate to what degree his grounds support his utterance—otherwise he will be blamed if his hearers get into trouble because they rely too heavily on him. One's sureness of grounds for what one says is usually connected with a willingness to stand by one's words, and one's doubt of the grounds with an unwillingness to stand by one's words. Small wonder, then, that signs of certainty and hesitancy and, by and by, also phrases describing certainty and hesitancy come to be used to signal one's commitment to what one says.

The devices then gradually cease to convey much about the speaker's state of mind and become more firmly tied to the sufficiency or insufficiency of backing for what he says. Their invariable duty is to mark how good the grounds of the utterance are; and their point is to do so in order to guide the audience as to how far it, in accordance with the principles of serious speech, is entitled to trust what is said. They have become degree-showing devices.

Degree-showing, and some discourse-marking devices, are *impersonal* audience-guiding devices: their guiding function is an effect of an interaction between the principles of serious speech and the speaker's commitment to his words. The guidance is in this sense derivative and does not turn to anyone in particular. It has no addressee in the way promising and advising have.

4.22. *Personal audience-direction.* Promising and advising exemplify personal audience-direction. When I promise something, a personal commitment is made. It is true that I also, and essentially, bind myself to the content of my promise—e.g. to give you dinner tomorrow. But my commitment to you is not a commitment only by commitment to this content. Otherwise my resolution to give you dinner tomorrow, expressed to someone other than the promisee, would be a promise to give you dinner tomorrow. In promising, the addressee must be the promisee and not someone else, let alone just anyone who hears me. To my promisee I shoulder special obligations and let him understand that I do so.

I suspect, but do not pause to argue, that the personal commitments built into many illocutionary devices have contributed to Austin's and Strawson's tendency to connect illocutionary devices with the current speaker and the current addressee.

5. *Performatoriness and illocutionarity.* At the end of *Words*, Austin's notion of the performative seems to be submerged, without remainder, in his notion of illocutionary 'act'. To my mind he thereby spoilt two useful concepts. Illocutionary force is one thing, performatoriness quite another. Illocutionary force is integral to any utterance as *linguistic* utterance; performatoriness has no necessary connexion with language at all.

If we take seriously Austin's general characterization of a classic explicit performative, and if we stipulate that such a performative be an apparently descriptive utterance in the first person singular present indicative active (an utterance which is a constituent of a ceremonial procedure and whose point is not to *describe* but to *effect* the action it appears to describe), then a lot of Austin's examples of classic explicit performatives will not fill the bill—e.g. the forms of words employed for advising, warning (in the sense of admonishing, not in the perlocutionary sense of cautioning), and—notably enough—promising. These alleged performatives are misclassified: they are, in fact, fairly clear examples of explicit illocutionary 'acts'.

But there remain utterances which meet Austin's general demands on classic explicit performatives. Among them are the ceremonial formulae employed in the institutional procedures of acquitting, convicting, appointing, demoting, excommunicating, baptizing, and naming. I call them *archetypal* performatives.

The difficulties Austin runs into in the last chapters of *Words* are, I think, due to his conflation of explicit illocutionary 'acts' with archetypal performatives. His discussion of stating (*Words.* 132–8) hovers uneasily between the act of stating and the result of that act, a statement (i.e., something with a locutionary and an illocutionary dimension to it). In saying 'I state (that p)', given certain surroundings etc., I certainly state; but not at all in a way reminiscent of that in which I acquit you in saying 'I acquit you'. My arguments for this view are to be found in *LIA*, Postscript, Pt. II. My main contentions—which cannot be defended here—are these:

(1) The explicit illocutionary 'acts' which Austin thinks of as classic explicit performatives are all in a certain sense ancillary. They demand supplementation. This supplementation is a piece of discourse which may be explicit or implicit; and the invariable duty of the illocutionary 'acts' is to indicate how this piece of discourse is to be taken. I cannot promise you (period) or warn you (period) or advise you (period). My act must have a content; otherwise nothing would be promised, warned, or advised. The supplementation is, contextually, a *sine qua non* in promising, warning, and advising. But an archetypal performative is self-sufficient: I can acquit you (period) or demote you (period) or excommunicate you (period). These acts stand on their own feet.

(2) Allegedly classic explicit performatives which are in fact explicit illocutionary 'acts' are of at least two kinds, viz. 'theoretical' and 'practical' (see Sect. 4.21 above). 'I forecast that we'll go tomorrow' is 'theoretical'; 'I promise we'll go tomorrow' is 'practical.' Illocutionary 'acts' of both kinds involve the shouldering of certain obligations, different to different discourses and degrees of commitment. A person who, in the right circumstances, has used a prognostic formula seems to have created a forecast in about the same way as a man who, in the right circumstances, has used a promisory formula has made a promise. But if *all* speech were performatory, the notion of performative would be eroded beyond recognition. We are not, however, as tempted to regard forecasting as a doing as we are to regard promising as a doing. There are at least two reasons for this disanalogy: First, in using a promisory illocutionary formula I have not merely made a promise but I am also committing myself so to act that the world will conform to my words. Secondly, in promising I have not merely bound myself to the topic (as in forecasting) but also made a personal commitment to the addressee.

If we resist the temptation to regard utterances of type (*b*) as performatives, then a worthwhile distinction emerges. It has two features:

(i) In contrast to utterances of type (*b*), archetypal performatives involve no obligation for the future. Their speaker as it were presses a button in a social machine, and after that the machine works without his interference—or if it fails, it is not necessarily his business to put it aright. The person invested with the right, or duty, to employ archetypal performatives is very often not identical with the man appointed to see to it that certain consequences ensure. The oddness of demoting you but refraining from preventing you from keeping your former rank is not explicable by saying, e.g., that a commitment to prevent the victim from keeping his former rank is built into the activity of demoting, in the way a commitment to keep one's word is built into the activity of promising. The explanation has to recur to a general principle of rationality saying that usually there is no point in doing something and then wrecking it; i.e., the explanation falls back on a principle which is not concerned with demoting in particular.

(ii) An illocutionary 'act' is, *qua* illocutionary, addressee-directed. Suppose I want to promise Jones something, warn him of something, or advise him to do something. I have not put my wish into effect if I address someone else and tell him that I promise, warn, or advise Jones. Even if I can rely on my addressee to let Jones know what I say, and even if I can rest assured that Jones takes me as having committed myself in certain ways, I have not promised, or warned, or advised *Jones*—except when the addressee is his deputy. An archetypal performative, on the other hand, is despite its grammatical appearance, directed to society at large. It is almost a chance that the man or thing referred to by the grammatical subject of such a classic and explicit performative has to be present: the form of words in which (say) a naming is done or a sentence is pronounced might as well have been 'The ship is hereby named . . .' or 'John Doe is hereby sentenced . . .'. Contrast the addressee's role when a ship is named or an infant baptized to his role when a promise is made or advice is given!

(3) Archetypal performatives are alinguistic. When one of them is uttered in accordance with the demands of a certain ceremony, it is effective only if certain *vocables* are used. Vocables with the same or nearly the same sense will not do. Again, there are wholly non-verbal equivalents of the total ceremony in which they take part—e.g. accolades. Warnings, promises, etc., are, on the other hand, essentially linguistic. The words in the phrase which makes the force explicit may be replaced with synonyms. Although there are non-verbal equivalents of the illocutionary *phrases*, there is no non-verbal equivalent of the whole speech act: there must always be an essentially linguistic supplementation, to the correct uptake of which the verbal or non-verbal illocutionary devices are ancil-

laries. The illocutionary 'acts' masquerading as performatives certainly fall within the range of what is traditionally thought of as the theory of meaning (cf. *Words*. 148). But archetypal performatives do so only incidentally: they are primarily regarded as sound-patterns, not as anything with meaning or with some kin of meaning.

(4) Some archetypal performatives, and all archetypal performatives of Austin's 'classic' type, may be regarded as noises with a locutionary and an illocutionary dimension to them. But these dimensions do not effect the performatory duty of the noises. As performatives they are primarily sound-patterns whose sense or senselessness does not matter. Hence, they are neither phemes nor rhemes, so they do not satisfy Austin's definitions of the locutionary 'act'. Therefore they cannot be illocutionary 'acts' either, since an illocutionary 'act' is, by definition, something making it clear how a locution is to be taken (cf. *Words*. 98–9). If there is no locutionary dimension to the utterance, how can an illocutionary 'act' be performed?

II. COHEN'S CRITICISMS SCRUTINIZED

1. *Meaning versus sense and reference.* When Austin says that he takes 'sense' and 'reference' 'on the strength of current views' (*Words*. 148), he does not specify what views he has in mind. His wish to contrast the meaning of an utterance to its illocutionary force suggests, says Cohen [op. cit., p. 423], that 'he mainly means the sense and reference of a whole utterance, not of its component words or phrases'.

The best-known current view of the reference of a whole utterance is Frege's. Cohen gives three reasons why it will not do for Austin's purposes. Although I doubt both Cohen's exegesis of Frege and the validity of his inferences from this exegesis, there is no need to penetrate that thorny thicket of problems. For, I shall argue, it is far from certain that Austin held sense and reference to be sense and reference of whole utterances. He says that the rhetic 'act' is the one we report in indirect speech. 'If the sense or reference is *not* being taken as clear, then the whole or part is to be in quotation marks. Thus I might say :"He said I was to go to the 'minister', but he did not say which minister" ' (*Words*. 96). In this example the unclear reference is the reference of the word 'minister', not the reference of the whole of 'He said I was to go to the "minister" ' or of 'You are to go to the minister'. I doubt that Austin would have liked to speak of the reference of whole utterances.

Words. 93 does, however, suggest (but no more than suggest) that what has 'a certain more or less definite "sense" and a more or less definite "reference" (which together are equivalent to "meaning")' sometimes may be the *whole* string of words in an utterance, not separate parts of that string. And Cohen points out that unless Austin used 'sense' for the sense of a whole utterance, he could not explain what he calls the 'meaning' of an utterance as he did, in terms of merely 'sense' and 'reference'. He must also have added word-order, 'for he could hardly have wanted to ascribe the same meaning to "George hit John" and "John hit George" ' [Cohen, op. cit., p. 423].

An interpretation of Austin's 'sense' and 'reference' as the sense and reference of a whole utterance goes, however, counter to *Words.* 97. At that place, 'sense' and 'reference' are paraphrased with 'naming' and 'referring' (as if sense and reference are things done and not results of things done!), and naming and referring are said to be ancillary acts to the rhetic act. So Austin seems to hold that both sense and reference are sense and reference of the words or phrases making up the utterance and not sense and reference of the whole utterance. If, now, he thinks they exhaust the meaning of the utterance, he has forgotten the importance of word-order. An utterance is not to him a jumble of words, since *qua* pheme it conforms to and is uttered as conforming to a certain grammar; but he cannot merely by means of sense and reference account for the difference between 'George hit John' and 'John hit George'.

Cohen says that 'in some respects it seems doubtful whether Austin can have had any clear idea of meaning at all here' [op. cit., p. 424]. I agree and disagree. Austin had not, I think, evolved a general theory of meaning. In *Words* the notion of locutionary 'act' is a mere foil for that of illocutionary 'act'—he devotes almost all his energy to an elucidation of the latter and takes the former more or less for granted. But his idea of the locutionary dimension may go back to his studies of speech situations S_0 and S_1 in 'How to Talk'. The views of sense and reference defended there are, I submit, the 'current views' he has in mind. What has sense is then a word (and, I believe, a phrase) of a type with his T-words; what has reference is also a word (and a phrase) but of a type with his I-words. Also *Words* centres round sentences of what he in the early paper calls form S and form SN, though they now are prefaced with what he labels 'performatory' phrases. The syntax of the utterances he is concerned with does not allow of such differences as those between George hitting John and John hitting George. I suspect that, enticed by the deceptive simplicity of his chosen subject/predicate sentences, he forgets or neglects the problem of word-order. His idea of the meaning, the locutionary dimension, of an utterance is therefore incomplete in an essential respect.

But, whatever Austin *says*, he does not treat meaning as equivalent to sense and reference. What is studied in his inquiries into the locutionary dimension is primarily an aspect of the result of utterances in speech situations like S_0 and S_1. (There is also need of a new type of situation, and a new form of words, in order to speak of future states of affairs. This speech situation, S_f, gives rise to difficulties adumbrated in *LIA*, Ch. 3, §7.) His concern is the aspect in which this result makes ('semantic') sense. As Gilbert Ryle has remarked in 'Ordinary language' (*Ph.R.* LXII, 1953, p. 180), what makes sense is a sentence or a clause, not a word or a phrase. Words and phrases have sense but hardly make sense; what makes sense is certain *ordered* concatenations of them, sentential concatenations which above the sense and reference of the words that are their constituents have a certain structure. The meaning of an utterance is what makes sense and is therefore not exhausted by, though certainly to a large extent constituted of, the sense and reference of the words of the utterance. So in practice Austin seems to presuppose a grammatical structure as necessary to the meaning of an utterance. Though not on a level with sense and reference, word-order is, also on his view, essential to meaning.

The unit of which the locutionary dimension is an aspect is not a word or a phrase but a *sentence-in-use*. It is built up of words, obeying certain linguistic rules and construed according to a certain grammar. Seen in this light, the sentence is a pheme, a unit of *language* (cf. *Words.* 98). But sentences of forms like S and SN are used for saying something about the world; and when their referring type of words is used to refer, they are, to a certain extent, units of *speech*. (Cf. *Words*. 98 on rhemes.) When the referring expression has no referent, the utterance is void. When the meaning of the T-word does not fit the referent, there take place diverse kinds of failure as to preciseness, fit, roughness, generality, etc.

2. *Performatives and meaning.* Cohen argues that the illocutionary force of an utterance is 'that aspect of its meaning which is either conveyed by its explicitly performative prefix, if it has one, or might have been so conveyed by the use of such an expression' [op. cit., p. 429].

A considerable part of his backing drops out, if archetypal performatives are distinguishable from illocutionary 'acts' in the ways suggested in Pt. I of this paper.

(1) Cohen holds that if the utterance 'I protest', said as the chairman refuses to let you speak, 'is to be assigned a meaning of any kind, this meaning must be of a performative kind. The meaning lies solely in the making of the protest.' This is supposed to show that 'wherever explicitly performative expressions are used, the illocutionary force, if such a thing exists at all, cannot be distinguished from the meaning'. [p. 426.]

A protest is in my opinion sometimes regarded as something clockable; it is an act of a certain duration. In that case the words 'I protest' constitute a 'self-sufficient' utterance and are the lodging of the protest. The protest is the protesting, not what is protested. A protest in the former sense must have an occasion but not necessarily a content. *If* such a protest were a linguistic utterance and *if* what makes it a protest were its illocutionary force, then, if no utterance with an illocutionary force can lack a locutionary dimension (which is its meaning), the utterance's illocutionary force could not, I suppose, be distinguished from its meaning.

In this episodic interpretation 'I protest' is not or not primarily a linguistic utterance. It has not, or only incidentally, meaning and illocutionary force. It is essentially a noisy counterpart to cocking a snook or hurling a tomato. The voicing of the noises is only by courtesy a linguistic act at all. It does not bring about a protest with any content.

The case now described is, however, a deviation. At an orderly meeting, making a protest is not or not merely giving vent to one's disapproval. It is part of a formal, institutionalized procedure. Its addressee is the meeting as a whole rather than the chairman, and conventionally it sets a social machinery into action. In this respect it resembles an archetypal performative. But if treated as a 'self-sufficient' utterance on the analogy of archetypal performatives, 'I protest' is—on the strength of this very analogy—a series of noises. There is neither meaning nor illocutionary force to it, except incidentally. Hence, considerations of the 'self-sufficient', 'performatory' 'I protest' cannot show that illocutionary force may be indistinguishable from meaning.[1]

(2) Although the normal use of 'I protest' at a meeting resembles archetypal performatives in certain respects, it differs from them in others. It standardly demands a supplementation. But then it is no longer a 'self-sufficient' utterance, but has become a shorthand notation for an utterance of the form 'I protest that p'. This is, I believe, fatal to the point of Cohen's argument that if (a) 'I protest' has a meaning as well as an illocutionary force, then this meaning will remain even when a subordinate clause is added, as in (b) 'I protest that I have not been allowed to speak' (loc. cit.).

Cohen assumes that (a) is 'self-sufficient' and a 'performative'. But is the same true of (b)?

In (b) the issuing of the words 'I protest' is not 'self-sufficient' but merely a parenthetic insertion, giving the audience to understand the discourse-implications of the locution the words are conjoined with. To protest that p is to tell the audience how p is to be taken: 'I protest that' is designed to accompany a locution in order to help the audience to a correct uptake of it. Protesting that p is a speech episode, just as stating that p; but the result of (b), the protest that p, is no more a speech episode than is the statement that p. In this non-episodic sense of 'protest' the content of a saying is ear-marked so that the audience knows how to take it. The point of the procedure lies in the mark and the locution marked, not in the marking.

Here a gulf is fixed between (a) in Cohen's interpretation and (b). To protest (period) is not to tell anyone how a supplementary locution is to be taken. Your protest is 'self-sufficient', though it must have an occasion. It is a doing which happens to be disguised as a saying. That a protest also normally expresses disapproval explains why the same noise occurs in both the performatory and in the illocutionary formula; but it does nothing to make

[1] I am grateful to Dick A. R. Haglund and Thomas Wetterström for their criticisms of a previous version of this counterargument.

(*a*) essentially linguistic, as is (*b*). It does not make (*a*) something that has and must have a locutionary and an illocutionary dimension.[1]

(3) 'I wish you good afternoon' may be both a wish and a dismissal. Then 'the meaning is a genuinely compound one. But if . . . the utterance is not a wish at all but only a dismissal . . . there is no need to suppose that it retains any of the sentence's original, common meaning.' It would be a feeble joke 'for the man who is dismissed with "I wish you good afternoon" to reply "You're a hypocrite: you don't wish me that at all". And, if he cannot sensibly reply thus, then how can we distinguish the illocutionary force of the dismissal from its meaning?' [Cohen, op. cit., p. 432.]

Cohen seems tempted to say (i) that in its performatory employment 'I wish you good afternoon' has a meaning, and (ii) that this meaning is the meaning of a dismissal. To my mind both contentions are odd.

Start with (ii). There are, in general, good reasons for distinguishing between the meaning of an utterance and the function(s) of an utterance with that meaning. We ought to fight shy of saying that 'This is good' has the meaning of an expression of approval, or has the meaning of an attempt at evoking an approval, or has the meaning of a prescription. For 'This is good' has, in different contexts, an expressive, an evocative, or a prescriptive job *because of* its invariable meaning. Conflations of meaning with function lead to the paradoxes that 'This is good' has at least three distinct and only loosely related meanings, viz. the expressive, the evocative, and the prescriptive one; and that the question 'Why does "This is good" work sometimes expressively, sometimes evocatively, and sometimes prescriptively?' is not sensible, since its answer must be circular: ' "This is good" is expressive (when it is expressive) because its meaning is the expressive one; evocative (when evocative) because its meaning is evocative; etc.'. And for the same reason we ought to fight shy of saying that if 'I wish you good afternoon' is used as a dismissal, its meaning has to be defined in terms of this function. Is not this way of dismissing a person spiteful and arrogant? And is not this due to the fact that the words retain their old meaning which sharply contrasts to the

[1] I try to make this difficult point a bit clearer and more convincing in *LIA*, Postscript, Pt. II. Cf. also W. Cerf, op. cit., p. 271.

situation where the addressee is treated like a dog? Are not the words chosen, and taken as thus chosen, because of this humiliating contrast?

Now for (i). Were it meant in the way just suggested, I would have accepted it. But Cohen says that the dismissal is not a dismissal in virtue of the 'original, common meaning' of 'I wish you good afternoon': it does not retain *any* of this meaning. What, then, is its new meaning, free from the spite suggested by the old one? If there is a spiteless dismissal in this form of words, is it not the *issuing* of certain ceremonial noises, not their *meaning*? Of course they have come to be used as a dismissal because they, in virtue of their 'original, common meaning' are used when our ways part; but the origin of a formula does not necessarily say much about its present duty. And the new meaning assumed by Cohen is characterized simply as not to any extent the same as the common one.

What Cohen really argues is, I think, that the purely performative 'I wish you good afternoon' has no meaning, although it has a function. If there be a purely performatory employment of this form of words, I agree and applaud. But his argument lends no support to his claim that illocutionary force is sometimes indistinguishable from meaning.

(4) Now and then Austin uses phrases of the form 'I (verb) you (that)' as names of members of his class of performatives and illocutionary 'acts'. Cohen seems to mistake this confusing shorthand notation for a warrant to treat an illocutionary device as a *performative*. 'When we say "I warn you that" or "I order you to" as an explicit performative, we perform the illocutionary act of warning or ordering, respectively. But what locutionary act do we then perform? What is the meaning of our utterance, as distinct from its illocutionary force?' [p. 424.]

Cohen cannot mean that when nothing but the phrase 'I warn you that' or 'I order you to' is said, the saying of it constitutes a warning or an order. The phrases are ancillary *parts* or ancillary *clauses* of an utterance. I hold them to be illocutionary devices, employed to guide the audience to a correct uptake of their supplementary locution. Since Austin maintains that both the locutionary and the illocutionary dimension are aspects of whole utterances, it is perfectly wild to ask what locutionary or illocutionary act is performed by the issuing of an illocutionary device without any explicit or implicit supplementary locution.

3. *Meaning, illocutionary force, and audience-direction.* My last criticism of Cohen is, perhaps, unfair. He sees or suspects that there is something odd about asking for the meaning and/or the illocutionary force of what he labels 'performative prefixes'. He considers the possibility that the meaning of 'I warn you that your haystack is on fire' lies in the clause 'your haystack is on fire'. There are, he thinks, three objections to this interpretation of Austin's theory: (i) The expression 'I warn you that' seems to refer to the speaker and to the addressee, 'and if the personal pronouns "I" and "you" enable it to have this reference one might also suspect the verb "warn" to give it a sense'. (ii) 'I warn you that your haystack is on fire' and 'Your haystack is on fire' must be different locutions, for the locutionary 'act' is in part defined in terms of the phonetic and the phatic 'acts'. (iii) If 'the utterance "Your haystack is on fire" gives a warning that is rendered explicit by "I warn you that your haystack is on fire", and if the warning is part of the meaning of the latter utterance, it is hardly unreasonable to suppose that the warning is also part of the former utterance's meaning, though inexplicitly so.' [pp. 425–6.]

These three objections reflect, I think, a lack of discrimination —a failure to keep the topic-directed part of communication distinct from the audience-directed one. I have tried to deal with the ideas behind (i) and (ii) in Sect. 3 of the Postscript of *LIA*. I have nothing to add, except the observation that (on the view defended there) an accurate translator renders into a foreign language not merely an utterance's meaning but also its explicitness or implicitness as to force. Hence, he gives another French version for 'I warn you that your haystack is on fire' than for 'Your haystack is on fire'.

Cohen's objection (iii) must, however, be discussed.

In what way is the warning 'part of the meaning' of 'Your haystack is on fire'? Cohen answers: 'If one says "He caught a large one" and is asked to be more explicit, one might say "James landed a trout more than ten pounds in weight", and certainly then it is meaning—sense and reference, if you like—that has been made explicit. What reason is there for supposing that it is illocutionary force, rather than meaning, that has been rendered explicit in "I warn you that your haystack is on fire"?' [p. 426.]

This is a misleading parallel. If I do not know whom 'he' refers to and what activity the referee is engaged in, then I do not under-

462

stand what 'He caught a large one' is about—what its topic is. But if I understand English and know whom 'you' refers to, I am *not* at a loss as to what 'Your haystack is on fire' is about. In the situations envisaged, there is a topic-directed respect in which the latter utterance is as intelligible as the former is unintelligible. That both of them are equally unclear in an audience-directed respect, leaving it obscure whether they are warnings, reports, etc., does not make them any more alike in the topic-directed respect.

Cohen argues that 'the whole grammatical structure of an utterance' may prevent its meaning from being fully explicit. 'He asks, whether it is raining or snowing' may mean either 'He asks his question irrespective of whether it is raining or snowing' or 'His question is whether it is raining or snowing'. And if you say 'Is it raining?' 'your meaning would be made even more explicit if you added, a moment later, "I ask whether it is raining". . . . Yet even in your first utterance ("Is it raining?"), let alone in your second ("I ask whether it is raining"), it is impossible to distinguish illocutionary force from meaning. What on earth could be the meaning of your locutionary act other than to ask whether it is raining?' [pp. 426–7].

I fail to follow the argument. 'He asks, whether it is raining or snowing' is indeed ambiguous. But this ambiguity is, on Austin's view, an ambiguity of meaning, not of illocutionary force. If there is a question as to how the locution is to be taken—as (say) an assertion, a suggestion, or a guess—it remains unanswered even when Cohen's explicandum is replaced with one of his explicants. And this ambiguity of meaning sheds no light whatsoever on the force or (possibly) force-ambiguity of 'Is it raining?' and 'I ask whether it is raining'. An utterance like 'It is raining' is, in its topic-directed aspect, concerned with saying something about the weather at the time and place of the act of speaking. This is its topic. The intonation-contour, or an inverted word-order, or the addition of the illocutionary prefix 'I ask whether' may show that the locution is to be taken as a question. 'Is it raining?' and 'I ask whether it is raining' are indeed unmistakable in this respect. (Do the linguists quoted on p. 430 in Cohen's paper demand more?) But in what sense is the topic-directed respect indistinguishable from the audience-directed respect, the interrogative force indistinguishable from the question asked? In what sense is the meaning the question? Cohen's rhetorical question 'What on earth could be the meaning of your locutionary act other than to ask whether it is raining?' is to my mind a feeble pun on the ambiguity of 'meaning', taking the word as simultaneously synonymous to 'content' and 'point'.

Having shown, convincingly, that Austin misclassifies some words, e.g. 'therefore', as illocutionary devices and why he does so, Cohen points out that the distinction between clarification of meaning (which aims at precision) and clarification of illocutionary force (which aims at explicitness) rests on the distinction between meaning and illocutionary force. This is true enough; but it seems improbable that Austin intended the former distinction (drawn in *Words.* 73) to reinforce the latter.

Cohen adds that we speak of replacing an implicit reference to someone with an explicit one and that, therefore, explicitness cannot be a necessarily distinguishing mark of illocutionary force. I agree but suggest that the precision/explicitness distinction be abandoned in favour of the vague and intuitive but very Austinian one between clarification of topic and clarification of audience-guidance. The fact that George might be implicitly referred to in 'Wearers of green dinner-jackets ought to apologize to the committee' will then cease to be a counter-example, as it is for Cohen, to Austin's idea of a difference between meaning and illocutionary force.

The distinction between topic-direction and audience-direction is, I think, enough to open to grave doubts most of the remainder of Cohen's main arguments. One of them runs as follows:

'When you remark "In saying that I was praising his memory, not his intelligence", you are obviously clarifying meaning. So why not also when you remark "In saying that I was praising, not blaming, him"?' [Op. cit., p. 428]—Cohen does not say how the utterance thus commented upon runs. Suppose it is 'Your account is very scrupulous'. Then the first comment clarifies that the account is (say) meticulous, not necessarily perspicuous. It elucidates which of a number of related senses 'scrupulous' has here. The comment 'In saying that I was praising, not blaming, him' does, however, *not* specify anything about the account and the thoroughness with which it is done; it says something about how the audience ought to take the comment that the account is scrupulous (if you like, in the sense of 'meticulous'). Of course both comments elucidate what is conveyed. But is it difficult to see that they elucidate two different aspects which deserve to be treated separately?

Another of Cohen's arguments is this: The fact that 'Go to London tomorrow!' is sometimes a command, sometimes a piece of advice etc. and that this is determined by contextual considerations is not peculiar to what Austin calls illocutionary forces. ' "They're all gold" means something different when said by someone looking at the clouds in a sunset from what it means when said by someone looking at a tray of cutlery. In one case the colour is being described, in another the material. . . . If we do not suppose in these cases that the context-dependent element in the commonly accepted meaning of the utterance is not *stricto sensu* meaning at all, then we should treat any utterance of "Go to London tomorrow!" analogously. That some such utterances command rather than advise, or recommend rather than request, is a feature of their respective meanings and not something that should be distinguished from their meaning under a label like "illocutionary force".' [Op. cit., p. 431.]

I gladly concede that the Austinian locutionary dimension of an utterance may be made precise by the context. But this does not show, as Cohen believes, that the contextual factors elucidating the force of an utterance enter the meaning of that utterance. 'I command you to go to London tomorrow' and 'I advise you to go to London tomorrow' do not specify or elucidate the topic of 'Go to London tomorrow' (as 'Joan and John Smith, sail to London tomorrow!' would). They are, in contradistinction to the utterance about the gold, audience-directed, not topic-directed. Place the audience-guiding dimension within the notion of meaning, if it pleases you; but then you have to distinguish, within meaning, what-is-conveyed-in-the-topic from what-is-conveyed-about-how-what-is-conveyed-in-the-topic-is-to-be-taken. And this is what Austin insists on.

4. *The illocutionary and the perlocutionary dimension.* Cohen distinguishes between a happy and a happy-or-unhappy sense of illocutionary verbs. (Like Austin he treats performatory verbs under the same heading; but I shall disregard this conflation.) He quotes Austin's view that illocutionary acts consist in the production of consequences in so far as all illocutionary acts must secure uptake (*Words.* 115 f.) and comments that this is an untidy exception to Austin's general principle that only perlocutionary acts consist

in the production of consequences. 'Moreover, once the happy-
or-unhappy sense of Austin's illocutionary verbs has been firmly
distinguished from their happy sense the need for him to suppose
a consequential element in illocutionary acts disappears altogether,
since the supposed consequential element is present only in those
illocutionary acts that are happy in the appropriate respects. . . .
Only if the farmer hears and understands me when I say "I warn
you that your haystack is on fire"—only then has my attempt at
warning come off. In the happy-or-unhappy sense of "warn" I can
say, without contradicting myself, "I warned him by shouting in
his ear though he was too deaf to hear", but in the happy sense I
can only say "I tried to warn him by shouting in his ear though I
failed because he was too deaf". For a speaker's utterance to be a
warning in the happy-or-unhappy sense what is required is that it
should be *of a kind that he could reasonably expect* to secure uptake. I
cannot warn a man fifty yards away by whispering. But a warning,
in this sense, does not actually have to *achieve* uptake.' [Op. cit., pp.
434–5.]

In Pt. I of this paper, the illocutionary as well as the locutionary
dimension of an utterance was characterized in terms partly of
its *standard* uptake. This consequential reaction, a rule-governed
reaction of the normal audience (though not necessarily of the current addressee) is built into the notions of locutionary and illocutionary 'acts'. I tried to show that Austin probably held this view.
If my suggestion is correct, an illocutionary verb has, *qua* illocutionary, *only* a happy sense. A performative can be unhappy, but
not an illocution. When I say 'I warn you that your haystack is on
fire', I have warned you that your haystack is on fire, whether you
heed it or not—although I have not *cautioned* you unless you, my
current addressee, respond in a certain way. ('Warn' has often a
perlocutionary, cautioning sense and is therefore not a purely
illocutionary verb.) That it would be futile to say anything to you
if you are deaf or too far away or ignorant of my language is true;
but this sort of unhappiness adheres to all linguistic communication and can be left aside here.

My interpretation has a corollary. Since illocutionary force is
tied to standardly accepted rules, not all implications of the act of
saying something and its results will count as illocutionary forces.
By warning you that there is a plot to kill you I may have committed
myself to your cause; but this commitment is not built into my

warning: I may without 'logical oddity' warn you and side against you. The standard intention, as well as the standard uptake of the intention, in uttering 'I warn you...' is to admonish the addressee to be on his guard, not to convey that the speaker sides with him. Now Cohen observes that such implications are not illocutionary forces; but he thinks that this throws doubts on the doctrine of illocutionary force. For he holds that when a man asks a question in saying 'I would like to know the time', a question is in the same way implied and that there is no interrogative force to the utterance [op. cit., p. 438].

I would reply that Cohen could as well say that when he dismisses a person by saying 'I wish you good afternoon' he does, albeit falsely, describe his wish and only imply that the addressee is about to depart. As I argued earlier, this would be more plausible than the line Cohen in fact takes with the dismissal. But I would add that when we say or hear 'I would like to know the time', accompanied with a querying look, we do not think, even for a moment, of a description of a wish to know the time; we intend the utterance as a question and take it as so intended, except in very special circumstances. To someone's *confession* that he wants to know something, e.g. whether there is an after-life, we sometimes correctly react in quite other ways than by telling him the true answer. We take it, and he expects us to take it, as a description of how it is with him, not as a veiled question. But such reactions do not come naturally to us when we hear 'I would like to know the time' in normal circumstances.

I do not contend that in Austin's writings there is a hard line to be drawn between meaning and illocutionary force, between the locutionary and the illocutionary dimension of an utterance. But I do contend that the arguments now scrutinized have not shown that there is nothing to Austin's doctrine of illocutionary force— though it remains vague, and intuitive, and in pressing need of more elucidation. And above all I contend that in the discussion of Cohen's objections there have emerged reasons for holding that there are two distinguishable aspects of what an utterance conveys in a rule-governed and well-established manner.[1]

[1] I am indebted to Jan Andersson for his constructive, incisive and incessant criticisms of a number of versions of this paper.

NOTE BY L. JONATHAN COHEN

Furberg has proposed what he begins by calling an 'unorthodox reinterpretation of Austin's doctrine of illocutionary force'. He does not say whom he considers the orthodox interpreters, or where their interpretation is to be found. But it soon emerges that what he is really offering is an interesting reformulation of Austin's views in which some central features are discarded or changed, though others are retained. In particular, on Furberg's theory there are no illocutionary acts, as in Austin's book, but only illocutionary results of speech-acts (I, 3), and what Furberg calls 'performatoriness'—i.e. ceremonial force—has no necessary connexion with the wholly linguistic phenomenon of illocutionariness (I, 5).

I suspect that these may well be steps in the right direction. But they seem to me to produce a theory so different from Austin's own that it is hardly legitimate to use them as a basis for defending Austin against my own criticisms of him, which is what Furberg seems to be doing in II, 2. Similarly, *pace* Furberg (II, 3) again, my thesis that the audience-guiding dimension, as Furberg calls it, should be placed within the dimension of meaning, and not co-ordinated with it, still seems to me, for the reasons I gave, very different from the thesis that Austin was proposing.

Nor did I claim that 'there is nothing to Austin's doctrine of illocutionary force', only that the concept of illocutionary force, as Austin himself defines it, is empty. Indeed, I agree entirely with Furberg that Austin's doctrine 'remains vague, intuitive, and in pressing need of more elucidation'.

BIBLIOGRAPHY

I. WRITINGS BY AUSTIN

Philosophical Papers, edited by J. O. Urmson and G. J. Warnock. London: Oxford University Press, 1961. Includes the following papers:

'Are There *A Priori* Concepts?' Contribution to a symposium with W. G. Maclagan and D. M. Mackinnon, published in the *Proceedings of the Aristotelian Society* XII (1939), 83–105.

'The Meaning of a Word.' Read to the Moral Sciences Club in Cambridge and to the Jowett Society in Oxford in 1940; published here for the first time.

'Other Minds.' Contribution to a symposium with John Wisdom, published in the *Proceedings of the Aristotelian Society*, Supp. Vol. XX (1946), 148–87.

'Truth.' Contribution to a symposium with P. F. Strawson and D. R. Cousin; published in the *Proceedings of the Aristotelian Society*, Supp. Vol. XXIV (1950), 111–28.

'Unfair to Facts.' Read to the Philosophical Society in Oxford in 1954 and is a sequel to the symposium on Truth; published here for the first time.

'A Plea for Excuses.' His Presidential Address to the Aristotelian Society in 1956 and published in the *Proceedings*, LVII (1956–57), 1–30.

'Ifs and Cans.' First published in the *Proceedings of the British Academy*, XLII (1956), 109–32.

'How to Talk—Some Simple Ways.' *Proceedings of the Aristotelian Society*, LIII (1953–54), 227–46.

'Pretending.' Contribution to a symposium with G. E. M. Anscombe, published in the *Proceedings of the Aristotelian Society*, Supp. Vol. XXXII (1958), 261–78.

'Performative Utterances.' An unscripted talk delivered in the Third Programme of the B.B.C. in 1956; published here for the first time.

Sense and Sensibilia. Reconstructed from the Manuscript notes by G. J. Warnock. London: Oxford University Press, 1962.

How to Do Things with Words. The William James Lectures delivered in Harvard University in 1955, edited by J. O. Urmson. London: Oxford University Press, 1962.

'Critical Notice of J. Lukasiewiez' *Aristotle's Syllogistic: From the Standpoint of Modern Formal Logic*. *Mind* 61 (1952), 395–404.

'Report on *Analysis* Problem No. 1. What sort of "if" is the "if" in "I can if I choose"?' *Analysis* 12 (1952), 125–6.

'Report on *Analysis* Problem No. 12. "All swans are white or black." Does this refer to possible swans on canals on Mars?' *Analysis* 18 (1958), 97–9.

'Performative-Constative' and contributions to discussion, in C. Caton (ed.): *Philosophy and Ordinary Language* (Urbana: University of Illinois Press, 1963), 22–54. First appeared in *Cahiers de Royaumont, Philosophie* No. IV, *La Philosophie Analytique*: Les Editions de Minuit, 1962.

'Three Ways of Spilling Ink.' A lecture given before the American Society of Political and Legal Philosophy in Dec. 1958. Edited and reconstructed by L. W. Forguson. *The Philosophical Review* 75 (1966), 427–40. Austin's outline for the lecture appeared in Carl Friedrich (ed.): *Authority* (*Nomos* III, 1961), 305–8.

'*Agathon* and *Eudaimonia* in the *Ethics* of Aristotle', in J. M. E. Moravcsik (ed.): *Aristotle: A Collection of Critical Essays* (New York: Doubleday, 1967), 261–96.

'Les Excuses.' French version of 'A Plea for Excuses', translated with an introduction by Robert Franck, published in *Revue de Metaphysique et de Morale* 72 (1967), 414–45.

II. WRITINGS ON AUSTIN

ACTON, H. B. 'Review of *Philosophical Papers* and *Sense and Sensibilia*'. *Listener* 67 (February 22, 1962), 353.

ALDRICH, V. C. 'Do Linguistic Acts Make Me Tired?' *Philosophical Studies* 15 (1964), 40–4.

—. 'Telling, Acknowledging and Asserting.' *Analysis* 27 (December, 1966), 53–8.

ALSTON, W. O. 'Linguistic Acts.' *American Philosophical Quarterly* 1 (1964), 138–46.

AMBROSE, A. 'Austin's *Philosophical Papers.*' *Philosophy* 38 (1963), 201–16.

ANSCOMBE, G. E. M. 'Pretending.' *Proceedings of the Aristotelian Society,* Supplementary Volume 32 (1958), 279–94.

ARBINI, RONALD. 'How to be Unfair to First-Person Statement-Introducing Utterances.' *Foundations of Language* 3 (1967), 234–56.

ARDAL, P. S. 'And That's a Promise.' *Philosophical Quarterly* 18 (1968), 225–37.

ARMSTRONG, J. H. SCOBELL. 'Knowledge and Belief.' *Analysis* 13 (1953), 114–15.

ATWELL, JOHN E. 'Austin on Incorrigibility.' *Philosophy and Phenomenological Research* 27 (1966), 261–6.

AUNE, BRUCE. 'Abilities, Modalities, and Free-will.' *Philosophy and Phenomenological Research* 23 (1962), 397–413.

—. 'Hypotheticals and "Can": Another Look.' *Analysis* 27 (1967), 191–5.

—. 'Can.' *Encyclopedia of Philosophy* (New York: Random House, 1967), Vol. 1, 18–20.

—. 'If.' In the *Encyclopedia of Philosophy,* Vol. 4, 127–9.

—. 'Statements and Propositions.' *Noûs* 1 (1967), 215–29.

AYER, A. J. 'Has Austin Refuted Sense-data?' *Synthese* 17 (1967), 117–40. Reprinted in this volume.

AYERS, M. R. 'Austin on "Could" and "Could Have".' *Philosophical Quarterly* 16 (1966), 113–20.

BAIER, KURT. 'Could and Would.' *Analysis* Supplement 23 (1963), 20–9.

BARNES, W. H. F. 'Knowing.' *Philosophical Review* 72 (1963), 3–16.

BEDAU, HUGO A. 'J. L. Austin's Philosophical Writings.' *Mind* 74 (1965), 252.

BEGIASHVILI, A. F. 'A Critical Analysis of Contemporary Linguistic Philosophy in England.' *Voprosy Filosofii* 17, No. 10 (1963), 111–22.

BEHRE, F. 'J. L. Austin's If.' *English Studies* 46 (1965), 85–92.

BENNETT, JONATHAN. 'Real.' *Mind* 75 (1966), 501–15. A revised version reprinted in this volume.

BENVENISTE, ÉMILE. 'La philosophie analytique et le language.' *Les Études Philosophiques* 18 (1963), 3–11.

BLACK, MAX. 'Austin on Performatives.' *Philosophy* 38 (1963), 217–26. Reprinted in this volume.

BLOCK, IRVING. 'Austin and the Cartesians' (abstract). *Journal of Philosophy* 65 (1968), 7–8.

BRADLEY, R. D. ' "Ifs", "Cans", and Determinism.' *Australasian Journal of Philosophy* 40 (1962), 146–58.

BROWN, NORMAN J. P. 'Review of *Philosophical Papers*.' *Dialogue* 1 (1962), 205–7.

BROWN, ROBERT. 'J. L. Austin's *Philosophical Papers* and *Sense and Sensibilia*.' *Australasian Journal of Philosophy* 40 (1962), 347–65.

—. 'Review of *How to Do Things with Words* and Furberg's *Locutionary and Illocutionary Acts*.' *Australasian Journal of Philosophy* 41 (1963), 417–24.

CANFIELD, JOHN V. 'The Compatibility of Free-Will and Determinism.' *Philosophical Review* 71 (1962), 352–68.

CAVELL, STANLEY. 'Must We Mean What We Say?' *Inquiry* 1 (1958), 172–212.

—. 'Austin at Criticism.' *Philosophical Review* 74 (1965), 204–19. Reprinted in this volume.

CERF, WALTER. 'Critical Notice of *How to Do Things with Words*.' *Mind* 75 (1966), 262–85. Reprinted in this volume.

CHARLESWORTH, MAURICE. 'Metaphysics as a Conceptual Revision.' *Philosophical Quarterly* 16 (1966), 308–18.

CHISHOLM, R. M. 'J. L. Austin's *Philosophical Papers*.' *Mind* 73 (1964), 1–26. Reprinted in this volume.

—. 'Preformative Utterances', in his *Theory of Knowledge* (Prentice-Hall, Inc., 1966), 15–18.

—. 'He Could Have Done Otherwise.' *Journal of Philosophy* 64 (1967), 409–17.

COHEN, L. JONATHAN. 'Do Illocutionary Forces Exist?' *Philosophical Quarterly* 14 (1964), 118–37. Reprinted in this volume.

COPLESTON, F. 'Review of *Sense and Sensibilia*.' *Heythrop Journal* 3 (1962), 389–90.

—. 'Review of *How to Do Things with Words*.' *Heythrop Journal* 4 (1963), 177–8.

CORNFORTH, MAURICE. *Marxism and the Linguistic Philosophy*. London: Lawrence & Wishart; New York: International Publishers, 1965.

COUSIN, D. R. 'Truth.' *Proceedings of the Aristotelian Society*, Supplementary Volume 24 (1950), 157–72.

COVAL, S., and TERRY FORREST. 'Which Word Wears the Trousers?' *Mind* 76 (1967), 73–82.

COX, J. W. ROXBEE. 'Fitting and Matching: A Note on Professor Austin's "How to Talk".' *Analysis* 16 (1955), 6–11.

DANIELSON, SVEN. 'Definitions of "Performatives".' *Theoria* 31 (1965), 20–31.

DANTO, ARTHUR C. 'On Knowing That We Know', in Avrum Stroll (ed.): *Epistemology* (New York: Harper & Row, 1967), 32–53.

—. 'Seven Objections Against Austin's Analysis of "I Know".' *Philosophical Studies* 13 (1962), 84–90.

DAVIS, STEPHEN. ' "I Know" as an Explicit Performative.' *Theoria* 30, Part 3 (1964), 157–65.

—. *Illocutionary Acts and Transformational Grammar.* Ph.D. dissertation. University of Illinois, 1968.

DELEDALLE, G. 'Review of *Philosophical Papers* and *Sense and Sensibilia*.' *Les Études Philosophiques* 20 (1965), 523–4.

DORE, CLEMENT. 'On the Meaning of "Could Have".' *Analysis* 23 (1962), 41–3.

—. 'More on the Meaning of "Could Have".' *Analysis* 24 (1963), 41–3.

—. 'Is Free Will Compatible with Determinism?' *The Philosophical Review* 72 (1963), 500–1.

DOSS, SEALE R. *Words and Facts: An Examination of the Correspondence Theory of Truth.* Ph.D. dissertation. University of California, Berkeley, 1966.

DRAY, WILLIAM. 'Choosing and Doing.' *Dialogue* 1 (1962), 129–52.

DUNCAN-JONES, AUSTIN. 'Performance and Promise.' *Philosophical Quarterly* 14 (1964), 97–117.

DURRANT, R. G. 'Promising.' *Australasian Journal of Philosophy* 41 (1963), 44–56.

EAMES, ELIZABETH. 'Review of *Sense and Sensibilia*.' *Philosophy and Phenomenological Research* 25 (1965), 600.

EVANS, DONALD. *The Logic of Self-Involvement.* London: SCM Press, 1963.

EWING, A. C. 'May Can-Statements Be Analysed Deterministically?' *Proceedings of the Aristotelian Society* 64 (1963–64), 157–76.

FAIRBANKS, MATTHEW. 'Review of *Philosophical Papers*.' *The New Scholasticism* 38 (1964), 125–8.

FINGARETTE, HERBERT. 'Performatives.' *American Philosophical Quarterly* 4 (1967), 39–48.

FIRTH, RODERICK. 'Austin and the Argument From Illusion.'

Philosophical Review 73 (1964), 372–82. A revised version reprinted in this volume.

FODOR, J. A., and J. J. KATZ. 'The Availability of What We Say.' *Philosophical Review* 72 (1963), 57–71.

FORGUSON, L. W. 'In Pursuit of Performatives.' *Philosophy* 41 (1966), 341–7. Reprinted in this volume.

——. 'La Philosophie de L'action de J. L. Austin.' *Archives de Philosophie* (Paris) 30, No. 1 (1967), 36–60. English version reprinted in this volume.

FORREST, TERRY. 'P-Predicates', in A. Stroll (ed.): *Epistemology* (Harper & Row, 1967), 83–106.

FRENCH, STANLEY F. 'Kant's Constative-Regulative Distinction.' *Monist* 51 (1967), 623–39.

FURBERG, MATS. *Locutionary and Illocutionary Acts: A Main Theme in J. L. Austin's Philosophy.* Gothenburg Studies in Philosophy; Stockholm: Alongvist & Wiksell, 1963. Second, revised and enlarged edition: Toronto, Canada, 1969.

GALLOP, DAVID. 'Ayers on "Could" and "Could Have".' *Philosophical Quarterly* 17 (1967), 255–6.

GARNER, RICHARD. 'Austin on Entailment.' *Philosophical Quarterly* 18 (July, 1968), 216–24.

——. 'Utterances and Acts in the Philosophy of J. L. Austin.' *Noûs* 2 (1968), 209–27.

GEACH, P. T. 'Review of Austin's Translation of Frege's *Grundlagen*.' *Philosophical Review* 60 (1951), 535–44.

GELLNER, ERNEST. *Words and Things*: A Critical Account of Linguistic Philosophy. Boston: Beacon Press, 1960.

GENDLIN, EUGENE T. 'What Are the Grounds of Explication?: A Basic Problem in Linguistic Analysis and in Phenomenology.' *Monist* 49 (1965), 137–64.

GOCHET, P. 'Performatif et Force Illocutionaire.' *Logique et Analyse* 8 (1965), 155–72.

GOLDBERG, BRUCE, and H. HEIDELBERGER. 'Mr. Lehrer on the Constitution of Cans.' *Analysis* 21 (1960–61), 96.

GOLDSTEIN, LEON J. 'On Austin's Understanding of Philosophy.' *Philosophy and Phenomenological Research* 25 (1964), 223–32.

GRICE, H. P. 'Meaning.' *Philosophical Review* 66 (1957), 377–88.

HAMPSHIRE, STUART. 'In Memoriam: J. L. Austin.' *Proceedings of the Aristotelian Society* 60 (1959–60), I–XIV. Reprinted in this volume.

—. 'J. L. Austin and Philosophy.' *Journal of Philosophy* 62 (1965), 511–13. Abstract of his contribution to the Symposium on Austin. The original version is included in this volume.

HARDIE, W. F. R. 'Austin on Perception.' *Philosophy* 38 (1963), 253–63.

HARRISON, J. 'Knowing and Promising.' *Mind* 71 (1962), 443–57.

HARROD, SIR ROY. '*Sense and Sensibilia.*' *Philosophy* 38 (1963), 227–41.

HART, H. L. A. 'J. L. Austin, Obituary.' *Oxford Magazine* (1960).

HARTNACK, JUSTUS. 'The Performatory Use of Sentences.' *Theoria* 29 (1963), 137–46.

—. 'Performative Utterances', in the Random House *Encyclopedia of Philosophy*, Vol. 6, 90–2.

HEDENIUS, INGEMAR. 'Performatives.' *Theoria* 29 (1963), 115–36.

HENSCHEN-DAHLQUIST, ANN-MARI. 'Remarks to Austin's Criticism of Moore's Analysis of "Can".' *Theoria* 29, Part 3 (1963), 304–11.

HENSON, RICHARD GOODRICH. *Philosophy and the Ordinary Uses of Words.* Ph.D. dissertation. Yale University, 1957.

—. 'What We Say.' *American Philosophical Quarterly* 2 (1965), 52–62.

HIRST, R. J. 'Critical Study on Austin's *Sense and Sensibilia.*' *Philosophical Quarterly* 13 (1963), 162–70, reprinted in this volume.

—. 'Illusions', in the Random House *Encyclopedia of Philosophy*, Vol. 4, 130–3.

HOLDCROFT, D. 'Meaning and Illocutionary Acts.' *Ratio* 6 (1964), 128–43. Reprinted in G. H. R. Parkinson (ed.): *The Theory of Meaning* (Oxford University Press, 1968).

HONDERICH, TED. 'Truth: Austin, Strawson, Warnock', in *American Philosophical Quarterly* Monograph Series No. 2: Studies in Logical Theory (1968).

HONORÉ, A. M. 'Can and Can't.' *Mind* 73 (1964), 463–79.

HOULGATE, L. D. 'Mistake in Performance.' *Mind* 75 (1966), 257–61.

HUBER, CARLO. 'Die Analytische Philosophie in England und Ihre Wandlungen.' *Theologie und Philosophie* 42 (1967), 208–35.

HUNTER, J. F. M. 'Aune and Others on Ifs and Cans.' *Analysis* 28 (1968), 107–12.

ISAACS, NATHAN. 'What Do Linguistic Philosophers Assume?' *Proceedings of the Aristotelian Society* 60 (1959–60), 211–30.

JARVIS, JUDITH. 'Ethics and *Ethics and the Moral Life.*' *Journal of*

Philosophy 59 (1962), 223–4.

KAAL, HANS. 'Senses of "Perceive" or Senses of "Senses of 'Perceive'?"' *Analysis* 24 (1963), 6–11.

KATZ, J. J., and J. A. FODOR. 'What's Wrong with the Philosophy of Language?' *Inquiry* 5 (1962), 197–237.

KAUFMAN, ARNOLD S. 'Moral Responsibility and the Use of "Could Have".' *Philosophical Quarterly* 12 (1962), 120–8.

KENNICK, W. E. 'Review of Austin's Books.' *Massachusetts Review* 4 (Summer 1963), 793–8.

KING-FARLOW, JOHN. '*Sense and Sensibilia.*' *Analysis* 23 (1962), 37–40.

KNOX, T. M. 'Two Conceptions of Philosophy.' *Philosophy* 36 (1961), 289–308.

KUYKENDALL, ELEANOR HOPE. *John L. Austin's Theory of Knowledge.* Ph.D. dissertation. Columbia University, 1966.

LAZEROWITZ, MORRIS. 'Austin's *Sense and Sensibilia.*' *Philosophy* 38 (1963), 242–52.

LEHRER, KEITH. 'Ifs, Cans, and Causes.' *Analysis* 20 (1959–60), 122–4.

—. 'Cans and Conditionals: A Rejoinder.' *Analysis* 22 (1961), 23–4.

—. ' "Could" and Determinism.' *Analysis* 24 (1964), 159–60.

—. 'An Empirical Disproof of Determinism?' in his *Freedom and Determinism* (ed.), (New York: Random House, 1966), 191–3.

—. 'Cans Without Ifs.' *Analysis* 29 (1968), 29–32.

LEMMON, E. J. 'On Sentences Verifiable by their Use.' *Analysis* 22 (1962), 86–9.

LOCKE, DON. 'Ifs and Cans Revisited.' *Philosophy* 37 (1962), 245–56.

MACKAY, ALFRED F. *Speech Acts.* Ph.D. dissertation. The University of North Carolina, 1966.

—. 'Illocutionary Forces.' (Abstract.) *The Journal of Philosophy* 64 (1967), 740–1.

MACKIE, J. L. 'Are There Any Incorrigible Empirical Statements?' *Australasian Journal of Philosophy* 41 (1963), 12–28.

MALCOLM, NORMAN. 'Understanding Austin.' (Abstract.) *Journal of Philosophy* 62 (1965), 508–9.

MARDIROS, A. M. 'Review of *Sense and Sensibilia.*' *Dialogue* 1 (1962), 203–5.

MARTIN, R. M. 'Facts: What They Are and What They Are Not.' *American Philosophical Quarterly* 4 (1967), 269–80.

MATES, BENSON. 'On the Verification of Statements about

"Ordinary Language".' *Inquiry* 1 (1958), 161–71.

MATHEWS, BILL. 'Austin on Implication and Entailment; A Reply to Mr. Wheatley.' *Philosophical Studies* 15 (1964), 88–9.

MATSON, W. I. 'Review of *Sense and Sensibilia.*' *Northwest Review* 5 (Fall 1962), 126–9.

MAYO, BERNARD. 'A Note on Austin's Performative Theory of Knowledge.' *Philosophical Studies* 14 (1963), 28–31.

—. 'Review of *How to Do Things With Words.*' *Philosophical Books* 3 (1963), 4–6.

MCCREA, W. H. 'Review of Austin's Translation of Frege's *The Foundations of Arithmetic.*' *Philosophy* 26 (1951), 178–80.

MEHTA, VED. 'A Battle Against the Bewitchment of Our Intelligence.' *New Yorker* (Dec. 9, 1961), 59–159. Reprinted in his *The Fly and the Fly Bottle: Encounter with British Intellectuals* (Boston: Little, Brown & Co., 1962). Contains an interesting interview with Warnock about Austin.

NARSKY, I. S. 'Sense and Sensibilia.' *Voprosy Filosofii* 17, No. 5 (1963), 169–74.

NEW, C. G. 'A Plea for Linguistics.' *Mind* 75 (1966), 368–84. Reprinted in this volume.

NORDENSTAM, TORE. 'On Austin's Theory of Speech-Acts.' *Mind* 75 (1966), 141–3.

NOWELL-SMITH, P. H. 'Ifs and Cans.' *Theoria* 26, Part 2 (1960), 85–101. Reprinted in this volume.

—. 'Acts and Locutions', in W. H. Capitan and D. D. Merrill (eds.): *Art, Mind and Religion* (University of Pittsburgh Press, 1967), 11–28.

NUCHELMANS, GABRIEL. 'Austin's Term "Performative".' *Algemeen Nederlands Tijdschrift voor Wijsbegeerte en Psychologie* 54 (1961–2), 154–72.

O'CONNOR, D. J. 'Possibility and Choice.' *Proceedings of the Aristotelian Society*, Supplementary Volume 34 (1960), 1–24.

OFSTAD, HAROLD. 'Recent Work on the Free Will Problem.' *American Philosophical Quarterly* 4 (1967), 179–202. Includes an excellent bibliography.

—. Two long footnotes on 'Ifs and Cans' in his *An Inquiry into the Freedom of Decision* (Oslo-Stockholm-London, 1961), 358–9.

O'HAIR, S. G. 'Performatives and Sentences Verifiable by Their Use.' *Synthese* 17 (1967).

OLSEN, CHRISTOPHER. 'Austin's Worries about "I State That

. . .".' *Mind* 76 (1967), 111–14.

OSBORN, JANE M. 'Austin's Non-Conditional Ifs.' *Journal of Philosophy* 62 (1965), 711–15.

PARRY, GERAINT. 'Performative Utterances and Obligation in Hobbes.' *Philosophical Quarterly* 17 (1967), 246–54.

PASSMORE, JOHN. A Section on Austin in his *A Hundred Years of Philosophy*, 2nd edition (New York: Basic Books Inc., 1966), 459–67.

PEARS, D. F. 'Wittgenstein and Austin', in B. Williams and A. Montefiore (eds.): *British Analytical Philosophy* (London: Routledge & Kegan Paul, 1966), 17–39.

PERTRIDGE, A. C. 'Review of *How to Do Things With Words*.' *English Studies in Africa* 5 (March 1963), 105.

PHILLIPS, R. L. 'Austin and Berkeley on Perception.' *Philosophy* 39 (1964), 161–3.

PITCHER, GEORGE WILLARD. *Illocutionary Acts: An Analysis of Language in Terms of Human Acts*. Ph.D. dissertation. Harvard University, 1957.

POLLOCK, JOHN. 'Criteria and Our Knowledge of the External World.' *Philosophical Review* 76 (1967), 28–60.

PRICE, H. H. 'Appearing and Appearances.' *American Philosophical Quarterly* 1 (1964), 3–19.

PUSTILNIK, JACK. 'Austin's Epistemology and His Critics.' *Philosophy* 39 (1964), 163–5.

—. 'Austin on Some Problems of Perception.' *The Southern Journal of Philosophy* 3 (1965), 18–22.

QUINE, W. V. O. 'J. L. Austin, Comment.' *Journal of Philosophy* 62 (1965), 509–10. Abstract of his contribution to the Symposium on Austin. The original version reprinted in this volume.

QUINTON, A. M. 'Contemporary British Philosophy', in D. J. O'Connor (ed.): *A Critical History of Western Philosophy* (New York: The Free Press of Glencoe, 1965), 531–56.

RAAB, FRANCIS V. 'Free-will and the Ambiguity of "Could".' *Philosophical Review* 64 (1955), 60–77.

RADNITZKY, GERARD A. 'Performatives and Descriptions.' *Inquiry* 5 (1962), 12–45.

RAMSEY, IAN. 'Polanyi and Austin', in Thomas Langford and William Poteat (eds.): *Intellect and Hope: Essays in the Thought of Michael Polanyi* (Duke University Press, 1968), 209–27.

RANKEN, N. L. 'The Unmoved Agent and the Ground of Responsibility.' *Journal of Philosophy* 64 (1967), 403–8.

RANKIN, K. W. *Choice and Chance: A Libertarian Analysis* (Oxford: Blackwell, 1961), 80–1, 94–5, 127–8.

RAPHAEL, D. D. 'Linguistic Performatives and Descriptive Meaning.' *Mind* 65 (1956), 516–21.

REINHARDT, L. R. 'Propositions and Speech Acts.' *Mind* 76 (1967), 166–83.

ROMNEY, GILLIAN. 'Review of *Sense and Sensibilia*.' *Philosophical Books* 3 (July 1962), 2–6.

RYAN, A. 'Austin: Faire des Choses avec des Mots.' *Archives de Philosophie* 30, No. 1 (1967), 20–35.

RYDING, ERIK. 'Austin on "I Know" and "It is True" ', in *Philosophical Essays Dedicated to Gunnar Aspelin*. Lund: GWK Gleerup, 1963.

SAMEK, ROBERT. 'Performative Utterances and the Concept of Contract.' *Australasian Journal of Philosophy* 43 (1965), 196–201.

SAYRE, K. 'Review of *How to Do Things With Words*.' *Philosophical Studies* 41 (1963), 179–87.

SAYWARD, CHARLES, and MICHAEL DURRANT. 'Austin on Whether Every Proposition Has a Contradictory.' *Analysis* 27 (1967), 167–70.

SCARROW, D. S. 'On an analysis of "Could Have".' *Analysis* 23 (1963), 118–20.

SEARLE, J. R. 'Meaning and Speech-Acts.' *Philosophical Review* 71 (1962), 423–32. A revised version with comments by Z. Vendler and P. Benacerraf and a rejoinder by Searle appeared in C. D. Rollins (ed.): *Knowledge and Experience* (University of Pittsburgh Press, 1962), 28–54.

—. 'What is a Speech Act?' in M. Black (ed.): *Philosophy in America* (Ithaca: Cornell University Press, 1965).

—. 'Assertions and Aberrations', in B. Williams and A. Montefiore (eds.): *British Analytical Philosophy* (London: Routledge & Kegan Paul, 1966), 44–54. Reprinted in this volume.

—. 'How to Derive "Ought" from "Is".' *Philosophical Review* 73 (1964), 43–58.

—. 'Review of Furberg's *Locutionary and Illocutionary Acts: A Main Theme in J. L. Austin's Philosophy*.' *Philosophical Review* 75 (1966), 389–91.

—. 'Austin on Locutionary and Illocutionary Acts.' *Philosophical Review* 77 (1968), 405–24.

—. *Speech Acts, An Essay in the Philosophy of Language.* Oxford University Press, 1969.

SESONSKE, ALEXANDER. 'Performatives.' *Journal of Philosophy* 62 (1965), 459–68.

SHAPERE, DUDLEY. 'Philosophy and the Analysis of Language.' *Inquiry* 3 (1960), 29–48.

SHWAYDER, D. S. *The Stratification of Behavior.* London: Routledge & Kegan Paul, 1965.

—. 'Uses of Language and Uses of Words.' *Theoria* 26, Part I (1960), 31–43.

SILBER, JOHN R. 'Human Action and the Language of Volitions.' *Proceedings of the Aristotelian Society* 64 (1963–64), 202–7.

SLATER, JOHN GREER. *A Methodological Study of Ordinary-Language Philosophy.* Ph.D. dissertation. University of Michigan, 1962.

SPARSHATT, F. E. 'Review of *How to Do Things With Words.' University of Toronto Quarterly* 33 (1963), 104–7.

STERN, K. 'Malcolm's Dreaming.' *Analysis* 20 (1959), 44–7. Includes Malcolm's reply.

STRAWSON, P. F. 'Truth.' *Proceedings of the Aristotelian Society.* Supplementary Volume 24 (1950), 129–56.

—. 'A Problem about Truth—A Reply to Mr. Warnock', in G. Pitcher (ed.): *Truth* (Prentice-Hall, Inc., 1964), 68–84.

—. 'Intention and Convention in Speech Acts.' *Philosophical Review* 73 (1964), 439–60. Reprinted in this volume.

—. 'Truth: A Reconsideration of Austin's Views.' *Philosophical Quarterly* 15 (1965), 289–301.

STROUP, TIMOTHY. 'Austin on "Ifs".' *Mind* 77 (1968), 104–8.

TAYLOR, R. 'I Can.' *Philosophical Review* 69 (1960), 78–89.

TENNESSEN, HERMAN. 'Ordinary Language *in Memoriam.' Inquiry* 8 (1965), 225–48.

THALBERG, I. 'Abilities and Ifs.' *Analysis* 22 (1962), 121–6.

—. 'Natural Expressions of Emotion.' *Philosophy and Phenomenological Research* 22 (1962), 382–92.

—. 'Freedom of Action and Freedom of Will.' *Journal of Philosophy* 61 (1964), 405–15.

—. 'Do We Cause Our Own Actions?' *Analysis* 27 (1967), 196–201.

—, and SUZANNE MCCORMICK. 'Trying.' *Dialogue* 6 (1967), 36.

THAU, STEWART. 'Illocutionary Breakdowns' (abstract). *Journal of Philosophy* 65 (1968), 719. Original forthcoming in *Mind.*

TIETZ, JOHN HERMANN. *J. L. Austin's 'Ifs and Cans' and the Incompatibility of Free Will and Determinism*. Ph.D. dissertation. Claremont Graduate School and University Center, 1966.

TILLMAN, FRANK A. 'Facts, Events and True Statements.' *Theoria* 32, Part 2 (1966), 116–29.

—. 'On Being Fair to Facts.' *Philosophical Studies* 19 (1968), 1–5.

TODD, DONALD DAVID. *Austin and Sense-Data*. Ph.D. dissertation. University of British Columbia, 1967.

(UNSIGNED). [by David Pears] 'An Original Philosopher.' *Times* (London) *Literary Supplement* No. 3128 (9 February 1962), 80–3. Reprinted in this volume.

(UNSIGNED). 'Review of *How To Do Things With Words*.' *Times* (London) *Literary Supplement* (21 September 1962), 743.

(UNSIGNED). [by Peter Strawson] 'The Post-Linguistic Thaw: Getting Logical Conclusions Out of the System.' *Times* (London) *Literary Supplement* (9 September 1960), Additional page lx. (Contains a photograph of Austin.)

(UNSIGNED). 'Review of *How To Do Things With Words*.' *Month* 29 (February 1963), 120.

URMSON, J. O. 'J. L. Austin, Obituary.' *Analysis* 21 (1960), 121–2.

—. 'J. L. Austin.' *Journal of Philosophy* 62 (1965), 499–508. His contribution to the Symposium on Austin; reprinted in this volume.

—. 'John Langshaw Austin', in the Random House *Encyclopedia of Philosophy* Vol. I, 211–15. Reprinted in this volume.

URMSON, J. O., and G. J. WARNOCK. 'J. L. Austin.' *Mind* 70 (1961), 256. Reprinted in this volume.

VANDERVEER, GARRETT L. 'Austin on Perception.' *Review of Metaphysics* 17 (1964), 557–67.

—. 'Austin's Analysis of "Real" ' (abstract). *Journal of Philosophy* 65 (1968), 7–8.

VENDLER, ZENO. 'A Review of *Sense and Sensibilia* and *How To Do Things With Words*.' *Foundations of Language* 3 (1967), 303–10.

WACKER, JEANNE. 'Ethics and *Ethics and the Moral Life*.' *Journal of Philosophy* 59 (1962), 106–9.

WARNOCK, G. J. *English Philosophy Since 1900* (London: Oxford University Press, 1958), 147–54.

—. 'A Remarkable Philosopher.' *Listener* 7 (1960), 616–17.

—. 'Truth and Correspondence', in C. D. Rollins (ed.): *Knowledge and Experience* (University of Pittsburgh Press, 1962), 11–20.

—. 'John Langshaw Austin.' *Proceedings of the British Academy* 69 (1963), 345–63. Reprinted in this volume.

—. 'A Problem About Truth', in G. Pitcher (ed.): *Truth* (Prentice-Hall, Inc., 1964), 54–67.

—. 'J. L. Austin.' *Archives de Philosophie* 30, No. 1 (1967), 5–19.

WARNOCK, MARY. *Ethics Since 1900* (London: Oxford University Press, 1960), 148–9.

WATLING, JOHN. 'Ifs and Cans.' *Journal of Symbolic Logic* 23 (1958), 74–5.

WEILER, GERSHON. 'Degrees of Knowledge.' *Philosophical Quarterly* 15 (1965), 317–27.

WEITZ, MORRIS. 'Oxford Philosophy.' *Philosophical Review* 62 (1953), 187–233.

WHEATLEY, JON. 'Austin on Implication and Entailment.' *Philosophical Studies* 15 (1964), 46–8.

—. 'How Austin Does Things with Words.' *Dialogue* 2 (1964), 337–45.

—. 'How to Give a Word Meaning.' *Theoria* 30, Part 2 (1964), 119–36.

WHITE, R. ALAN. 'The Alleged Ambiguity of "See".' *Analysis* 24 (1963), 1–5.

—. 'Review of *How To Do Things With Words*.' *Analysis* 23 Supplement (1963), 58–64.

—. 'Review of Mats Furberg's *Locutionary and Illocutionary Acts*.' *Mind* 74 (1965), 131–5.

—. 'Mentioning the Unmentionable.' *Analysis* 27 (1967), 113–18. Reprinted in this volume.

WHITE, MORTON. 'On What Could Have Happened.' *Philosophical Review* 77 (1968), 73–89.

WHITELY, C. H. 'Can.' *Analysis* 23 (1963), 91–3.

WILLIAMS, BERNARD. 'J. L. Austin's Philosophy.' *Oxford Magazine* (6 December 1962), 115–17.

WILSON, PATRICK. 'Austin on Knowing.' *Inquiry* 3 (1960), 49–60.

WISAN, RICHARD NORMAN. *The World in Words: On the Relation Between Meaning of Terms and the Nature of Things with Special Reference to an Evaluation of English in Ordinary-Language Philosophy*. Ph.D. dissertation. Columbia University, 1957.

WRIGHT, MAXWELL. ' "I Know" and Performative Utterances.' *Australasian Journal of Philosophy* 43 (1965), 35–47.

INDEX OF NAMES

INDEX OF SUBJECTS

485

International Library of Philosophy & Scientific Method

Editor: Ted Honderich

List of titles, page two

International Library of Psychology Philosophy & Scientific Method

Editor: C K Ogden

List of titles, page six

ROUTLEDGE AND KEGAN PAUL LTD
68 Carter Lane London EC4

International Library of Philosophy and Scientific Method
(*Demy 8vo*)

Allen, R. E. (Ed.)
Studies in Plato's Metaphysics
Contributors: J. L. Ackrill, R. E. Allen, R. S. Bluck, H. F. Cherniss, F. M. Cornford, R. C. Cross, P. T. Geach, R. Hackforth, W. F. Hicken, A. C. Lloyd, G. R. Morrow, G. E. L. Owen, G. Ryle, W. G. Runciman, G. Vlastos
464 pp. 1965. (2nd Impression 1967.) 70s.

Armstrong, D. M.
Perception and the Physical World
208 pp. 1961. (3rd Impression 1966.) 25s.

A Materialist Theory of the Mind
376 pp. 1967. (2nd Impression 1969.) 50s.

Bambrough, Renford (Ed.)
New Essays on Plato and Aristotle
Contributors: J. L. Ackrill, G. E. M. Anscombe, Renford Bambrough, R. M. Hare, D. M. MacKinnon, G. E. L. Owen, G. Ryle, G. Vlastos
184 pp. 1965. (2nd Impression 1967.) 28s.

Barry, Brian
Political Argument
382 pp. 1965. (3rd Impression 1968.) 50s.

Bird, Graham
Kant's Theory of Knowledge:
An Outline of One Central Argument in the *Critique of Pure Reason*
220 pp. 1962. (2nd Impression 1965.) 28s.

Brentano, Franz
The True and the Evident
Edited and narrated by Professor R. Chisholm
218 pp. 1965. 40s.

The Origin of Our Knowledge of Right and Wrong
Edited by Oskar Kraus. English edition edited by Roderick M. Chisholm. Translated by Roderick M. Chisholm and Elizabeth H. Schneewind
174 pp. 1969. 40s.

Broad, C. D.
Lectures on Physical Research
Incorporating the Perrott Lectures given in Cambridge University in 1959 and 1960
461 pp. 1962. (2nd Impression 1966.) 56s.

Crombie, I. M.
An Examination of Plato's Doctrine
1. Plato on Man and Society
408 pp. 1962. (3rd Impression 1969.) 42s.
II. Plato on Knowledge and Reality
583 pp. 1963. (2nd Impression 1967.) 63s.

International Library of Philosophy and Scientific Method
(*Demy 8vo*)

Day, John Patrick
Inductive Probability
352 pp. 1961. 40s.

Dretske, Fred I.
Seeing and Knowing
270 pp. 1969. 35s.

Ducasse, C. J.
Truth, Knowledge and Causation
263 pp. 1969. 50s.

Edel, Abraham
Method in Ethical Theory
379 pp. 1963. 32s.

Fann, K. T. (Ed.)
Symposium on J. L. Austin
Contributors: A. J. Ayer, Jonathan Bennett, Max Black, Stanley Cavell, Walter Cerf, Roderick M. Chisholm, L. Jonathan Cohen, Roderick Firth, L. W. Forguson, Mats Furberg, Stuart Hampshire, R. J. Hirst, C. G. New, P. H. Nowell-Smith, David Pears, John Searle, Peter Strawson, Irving Thalberg, J. O. Urmson, G. J. Warnock, Jon Wheatly, Alan White
512 pp. 1969.

Flew, Anthony
Hume's Philosophy of Belief
A Study of his First "Inquiry"
269 pp. 1961. (2nd Impression 1966.) 30s.

Fogelin, Robert J.
Evidence and Meaning
Studies in Analytical Philosophy
200 pp. 1967. 25s.

Gale, Richard
The Language of Time
256 pp. 1968. 40s.

Goldman, Lucien
The Hidden God
A Study of Tragic Vision in the *Pensées* of Pascal and the Tragedies of Racine.
Translated from the French by Philip Thody
424 pp. 1964. 70s.

Hamlyn, D. W.
Sensation and Perception
A History of the Philosophy of Perception
222 pp. 1961. (3rd Impression 1967.) 25s.

International Library of Philosophy and Scientific Method
(*Demy 8vo*)

Kemp, J.
Reason, Action and Morality
216 pp. 1964. 30s.

Körner, Stephan
Experience and Theory
An Essay in the Philosophy of Science
272 pp. 1966. (2nd Impression 1969.) 45s.

Lazerowitz, Morris
Studies in Metaphilosophy
276 pp. 1964. 35s.

Linsky, Leonard
Referring
152 pp. 1968. 35s.

MacIntosh, J. J., and Coval, S. C. (Ed.)
The Business of Reason
280 pp. 1969. 42s.

Merleau-Ponty, M.
Phenomenology of Perception
Translated from the French by Colin Smith
487 pp. 1962. (4th Impression 1967.) 56s.

Perelman, Chaim
The Idea of Justice and the Problem of Argument
Introduction by H. L. A. Hart. Translated from the French by John Petrie
224 pp. 1963. 28s.

Ross, Alf
Directives, Norms and their Logic
192 pp. 1967. 35s.

Schlesinger, G.
Method in the Physical Sciences
148 pp. 1963. 21s.

Sellars, W. F.
Science, Perception and Reality
374 pp. 1963. (2nd Impression 1966.) 50s.

Shwayder, D. S.
The Stratification of Behaviour
A System of Definitions Propounded and Defended
428 pp. 1965. 56s.

Skolimowski, Henryk
Polish Analytical Philosophy
288 pp. 1967. 40s.

International Library of Philosophy and Scientific Method
(*Demy 8vo*)

Smart, J. J. C.
Philosophy and Scientific Realism
168 pp. 1963. (3rd Impression 1967.) 25s.

Smythies, J. R. (Ed.)
Brain and Mind
Contributors: Lord Brain, John Beloff, C. J. Ducasse, Antony Flew, Hartwig
Kuhlenbeck, D. M. MacKay, H. H. Price, Anthony Quinton and J. R. Smythies
288 pp. 1965. 40s.

Science and E.S.P.
Contributors: Gilbert Murray, H. H. Price, Rosalind Heywood, Cyril Burt,
C. D. Broad, Francis Huxley and John Beloff
320 pp. about 40s.

Taylor, Charles
The Explanation of Behaviour
288 pp. 1964. (2nd Impression 1965.) 40s.

Williams, Bernard, and Montefiore, Alan
British Analytical Philosophy
352 pp. 1965. (2nd Impression 1967.) 45s.

Winch, Peter (Ed.)
Studies in the Philosophy of Wittgenstein
Contributors: Hidé Ishiguro, Rush Rhees, D. S. Shwayder, John W. Cook,
L. R. Reinhardt and Anthony Manser
224 pp. 1969.

Wittgenstein, Ludwig
Tractatus Logico-Philosophicus
The German text of the *Logisch-Philosophische Abhandlung* with a new
translation by D. F. Pears and B. F. McGuinness. Introduction by
Bertrand Russell
188 pp. 1961. (3rd Impression 1966.) 21s.

Wright, Georg Henrik Von
Norm and Action
A Logical Enquiry. The Gifford Lectures
232 pp. 1963. (2nd Impression 1964.) 32s.

The Varieties of Goodness
The Gifford Lectures
236 pp. 1963. (3rd Impression 1966.) 28s.

Zinkernagel, Peter
Conditions for Description
Translated from the Danish by Olaf Lindum
272 pp. 1962. 37s. 6d.

International Library of Psychology, Philosophy, and Scientific Method
(*Demy 8vo*)

PHILOSOPHY

Anton, John Peter
Aristotle's Theory of Contrariety
276 pp. 1957. 25s.

Black, Max
The Nature of Mathematics
A Critical Survey
242 pp. 1933. (5th Impression 1965.) 28s.

Bluck, R. S.
Plato's Phaedo
A Translation with Introduction, Notes and Appendices
226 pp. 1955. 21s.

Broad, C. D.
Five Types of Ethical Theory
322 pp. 1930. (9th Impression 1967.) 30s.

The Mind and Its Place in Nature
694 pp. 1925. (7th Impression 1962.) 70s. See also Lean, Martin

Buchler, Justus (Ed.)
The Philosophy of Peirce
Selected Writings
412 pp. 1940. (3rd Impression 1956.) 35s.

Burtt, E. A.
The Metaphysical Foundations of Modern Physical Science
A Historical and Critical Essay
364 pp. 2nd (revised) edition 1932. (5th Impression 1964.) 35s.

Carnap, Rudolf
The Logical Syntax of Language
Translated from the German by Amethe Smeaton
376 pp. 1937. (7th Impression 1967.) 40s.

Chwistek, Leon
The Limits of Science
Outline of Logic and of the Methodology of the Exact Sciences
With Introduction and Appendix by Helen Charlotte Brodie
414 pp. 2nd edition 1949. 32s.

Cornford, F. M.
Plato's Theory of Knowledge
The Theaetetus and Sophist of Plato
Translated with a running commentary
358 pp. 1935. (7th Impression 1967.) 28s.

International Library of Psychology, Philosophy, and Scientific Method
(Demy 8vo)

Cornford, F. M. *(continued)*
Plato's Cosmology
The Timaeus of Plato
Translated with a running commentary
402 pp. Frontispiece. 1937. (5th Impression 1966.) 45s.

Plato and Parmenides
Parmenides' *Way of Truth* and Plato's *Parmenides*
Translated with a running commentary
280 pp. 1939. (5th Impression 1964.) 32s.

Crawshay-Williams, Rupert
Methods and Criteria of Reasoning
An Inquiry into the Structure of Controversy
312 pp. 1957. 32s.

Fritz, Charles A.
Bertrand Russell's Construction of the External World
252 pp. 1952. 30s.

Hulme, T. E.
Speculations
Essays on Humanism and the Philosophy of Art
Edited by Herbert Read. Foreword and Frontispiece by Jacob Epstein
296 pp. 2nd edition 1936. (6th Impression 1965.) 40s.

Lazerowitz, Morris
The Structure of Metaphysics
With a Foreword by John Wisdom
262 pp. 1955. (2nd Impression 1963.) 30s.

Lodge, Rupert C.
Plato's Theory of Art
332 pp. 1953. 25s.

Mannheim, Karl
Ideology and Utopia
An Introduction to the Sociology of Knowledge
With a Preface by Louis Wirth. Translated from the German by Louis Wirth and Edward Shils
360 pp. 1954. (2nd Impression 1966.) 30s.

Moore, G. E.
Philosophical Studies
360 pp. 1922. (6th Impression 1965.) 35s. See also Ramsey, F. P.

International Library of Psychology, Philosophy, and Scientific Method
(*Demy 8vo*)

Ogden, C. K., and Richards, I. A.
The Meaning of Meaning
A Study of the Influence of Language upon Thought and of the Science of Symbolism
With supplementary essays by B. Malinowski and F. G. Crookshank
394 pp. 10th Edition 1949. (6th Impression 1967.) 32s.
See also Bentham, J.

Peirce, Charles, *see* Buchler, J.

Ramsey, Frank Plumpton
The Foundations of Mathematics and other Logical Essays
Edited by R. B. Braithwaite. Preface by G. E. Moore
318 pp. 1931. (4th Impression 1965.) 35s.

Richards, I. A.
Principles of Literary Criticism
312 pp. 2nd Edition. 1926. (17th Impression 1966.) 30s.

Mencius on the Mind. Experiments in Multiple Definition
190 pp. 1932. (2nd Impression 1964.) 28s.

Russell, Bertrand, *see* Fritz, C. A.; Lange, F. A.; Wittgenstein, L.

Smart, Ninian
Reasons and Faiths
An Investigation of Religious Discourse, Christian and Non-Christian
230 pp. 1958. (2nd Impression 1965.) 28s.

Vaihinger, H.
The Philosophy of As If
A System of the Theoretical, Practical and Religious Fictions of Mankind
Translated by C. K. Ogden
428 pp. 2nd edition 1935. (4th Impression 1965.) 45s.

Wittgenstein, Ludwig
Tractatus Logico-Philosophicus
With an Introduction by Bertrand Russell, F.R.S., German text with an English translation en regard
216 pp. 1922. (9th Impression 1962.) 21s.
For the Pears-McGuinness translation—*see page 5*

Wright, Georg Henrik von
Logical Studies
214 pp. 1957. (2nd Impression 1967.) 28s.

International Library of Psychology, Philosophy, and Scientific Method
(*Demy 8vo*)

Zeller, Eduard
Outlines of the History of Greek Philosophy
Revised by Dr. Wilhelm Nestle. Translated from the German by L. R. Palmer
248 pp. 13th (revised) edition 1931. (5th Impression 1963.) 28s.

PSYCHOLOGY

Adler, Alfred
The Practice and Theory of Individual Psychology
Translated by P. Radin
368 pp. 2nd (revised) edition 1929. (8th Impression 1964.) 30s.

Eng, Helga
The Psychology of Children's Drawings
From the First Stroke to the Coloured Drawing
240 pp. 8 colour plates. 139 figures. 2nd edition 1954. (3rd Impression 1966.) 40s.

Koffka, Kurt
The Growth of the Mind
An Introduction to Child-Psychology
Translated from the German by Robert Morris Ogden
456 pp 16 figures. 2nd edition (revised) 1928. (6th Impression 1965.) 45s.

Principles of Gestalt Psychology
740 pp. 112 figures. 39 tables. 1935. (5th Impression 1962.) 60s.

Malinowski, Bronislaw
Crime and Custom in Savage Society
152 pp. 6 plates. 1926. (8th Impression 1966.) 21s.

Sex and Repression in Savage Society
290 pp. 1927. (4th Impression 1953.) 30s.
See also Ogden, C. K.

Murphy, Gardner
An Historical Introduction to Modern Psychology
488 pp. 5th edition (revised) 1949. (6th Impression 1967.) 40s.

Paget, R.
Human Speech
Some Observations, Experiments, and Conclusions as to the Nature, Origin, Purpose and Possible Improvement of Human Speech
374 pp. 5 plates. 1930. (2nd Impression 1963.) 42s.

Petermann, Bruno
The Gestalt Theory and the Problem of Configuration
Translated from the German by Meyer Fortes
364 pp. 20 figures. 1932. (2nd Impression 1950.) 25s.

International Library of Psychology, Philosophy, and Scientific Method
(*Demy 8vo*)

Piaget, Jean
The Language and Thought of the Child
Preface by E. Claparède. Translated from the French by Marjorie Gabain
220 pp. 3rd edition (revised and enlarged) 1959. (3rd Impression 1966.) 30s.

Judgment and Reasoning in the Child
Translated from the French by Marjorie Warden
276 pp. 1928. (5th Impression 1969.) 30s.

The Child's Conception of the World
Translated from the French by Joan and Andrew Tomlinson
408 pp. 1929. (4th Impression 1964.) 40s.

The Child's Conception of Physical Causality
Translated from the French by Marjorie Gabain
(3rd Impression 1965.) 30s.

The Moral Judgment of the Child
Translated from the French by Marjorie Gabain
438 pp. 1932. (4th Impression 1965.) 35s.

The Psychology of Intelligence
Translated from the French by Malcolm Piercy and D. E. Berlyne
198 pp. 1950. (4th Impression 1964.) 18s.

The Child's Conception of Number
Translated from the French by C. Gattegno and F. M. Hodgson
266 pp. 1952. (3rd Impression 1964.) 25s.

The Origin of Intelligence in the Child
Translated from the French by Margaret Cook
448 pp. 1953. (2nd Impression 1966.) 42s.

The Child's Conception of Geometry
In collaboration with Bärbel Inhelder and Alina Szeminska. Translated from the French by E. A. Lunzer
428 pp. 1960. (2nd Impression 1966.) 45s.

Piaget, Jean, and Inhelder, Bärbel
The Child's Conception of Space
Translated from the French by F. J. Langdon and J. L. Lunzer
512 pp. 29 figures. 1956. (3rd Impression 1967.) 42s.

Roback, A. A.
The Psychology of Character
With a Survey of Personality in General
786 pp. 3rd edition (revised and enlarged 1952.) 50s.

Smythies, J. R.
Analysis of Perception
With a Preface by Sir Russell Brain, Bt.
162 pp. 1956. 21s.

International Library of Psychology, Philosophy, and Scientific Method
(*Demy 8vo*)

van der Hoop, J. H.
Character and the Unconscious
A Critical Exposition of the Psychology of Freud and Jung
Translated from the German by Elizabeth Trevelyan
240 pp. 1923. (2nd Impression 1950.) 20s.

Woodger, J. H.
Biological Principles
508 pp. 1929. (Re-issued with a new Introduction 1966.) 60s.

PRINTED BY HEADLEY BROTHERS LTD 109 KINGSWAY LONDON WC2 AND ASHFORD KENT